T0178425

Lecture Notes in Computer Science   11689

More information about this series at http://www.springer.com/series/7410

Nuttapong Attrapadung ·
Takeshi Yagi (Eds.)

Advances in Information and Computer Security

14th International Workshop on Security, IWSEC 2019
Tokyo, Japan, August 28–30, 2019
Proceedings

Springer

Editors
Nuttapong Attrapadung 🆔
National Institute of Advanced Industrial
Science and Technology
Tokyo, Japan

Takeshi Yagi
NTT Security (Japan) KK
Tokyo, Japan

ISSN 0302-9743 ISSN 1611-3349 (electronic)
Lecture Notes in Computer Science
ISBN 978-3-030-26833-6 ISBN 978-3-030-26834-3 (eBook)
https://doi.org/10.1007/978-3-030-26834-3

LNCS Sublibrary: SL4 – Security and Cryptology

This Springer imprint is published by the registered company Springer Nature Switzerland AG
The registered company address is: Gewerbestrasse 11, 6330 Cham, Switzerland

Preface

The 14th International Workshop on Security, IWSEC 2019, was held at the Multi-Purpose Digital Hall, Ookayama Campus, Tokyo Institute of Technology, Tokyo, Japan, during August 28–30, 2019. The workshop was co-organized by ISEC (the Technical Committee on Information Security in Engineering Sciences Society of IEICE) and CSEC (the Special Interest Group on Computer Security of IPSJ).

This year, we categorized topics of interests into two tracks, namely, Cryptography Track (Track A) and Cybersecurity and Privacy Track (Track B); each track is formed by separate Program Committee members. We received 63 submissions, 42 in Track A and 21 in Track B, out of which two papers were withdrawn before the review process. After extensive reviews and shepherding, we accepted 18 regular papers (12 from Track A and six from Track B) and five short papers (three from Track A and two from Track B). Each submission was anonymously reviewed by four reviewers. These proceedings contain revised versions of the accepted papers. Track A consists of the sessions on public-key primitives, symmetric-key primitives, cryptanalysis, and cryptographic protocols. Track B consists of the sessions on malware detection and classification, intrusion detection and prevention, Web and usable security, and forensics.

The Best Paper Awards were given to "An Efficient F4-style Based Algorithm to Solve MQ Problems" by Takuma Ito, Naoyuki Shinohara, and Shigenori Uchiyama, and to "Towards Efficient Detection of Malicious VBA Macros with LSI" by Mamoru Mimura and Taro Ohminami. The Best Student Paper Award was given to "CCA-Secure Leakage-Resilient Identity-Based Key-Encapsulation from Simple (not q-type) Assumptions" by Toi Tomita, Wakaha Ogata, and Kaoru Kurosawa. In addition to the presentations of the accepted papers, the workshop also featured two keynote talks, a poster session, and invited talk sessions from domestic symposiums, namely, SCIS (Symposium on Cryptography and Information Security) and CSS (Computer Security Symposium). We also included a special session organized by AIMaP (Advanced Innovation powered by Mathematics Platform).

A number of people contributed to the success of IWSEC 2019. We would like to thank all authors for submitting their papers to the workshop, and also we are deeply grateful to the members of the Program Committee and to the external reviewers for their in-depth reviews and detailed discussions. We must mention that the selection of the papers was an extremely challenging task.

Last but not least, we would like to thank the General Co-Chairs, Toshihiro Yamauchi and Shiho Moriai, for leading the Organizing Committee, and we would also like to thank the members of the Organizing Committee for ensuring the smooth running of the workshop.

June 2019   Nuttapong Attrapadung
                                                             Takeshi Yagi

IWSEC 2019

14th International Workshop on Security Organization

Tokyo, Japan, August 28–30, 2019

co-organized by

ISEC in ESS of IEICE
(Technical Committee on Information Security in Engineering Sciences Society
of the Institute of Electronics, Information and Communication Engineers)
and
CSEC of IPSJ
(Special Interest Group on Computer Security of Information Processing
Society of Japan)

General Co-chairs

Shiho Moriai	National Institute of Information and Communications Technology, Japan
Toshihiro Yamauchi	Okayama University, Japan

Advisory Committee

Hideki Imai	University of Tokyo, Japan
Kwangjo Kim	Korea Advanced Institute of Science and Technology, the Republic of Korea
Christopher Kruegel	University of California, Santa Barbara, USA
Günter Müller	University of Freiburg, Germany
Yuko Murayama	Tsuda University, Japan
Koji Nakao	National Institute of Information and Communications Technology, Japan
Eiji Okamoto	University of Tsukuba, Japan
C. Pandu Rangan	Indian Institute of Technology Madras, India
Kai Rannenberg	Goethe University Frankfurt, Germany
Ryoichi Sasaki	Tokyo Denki University, Japan

Program Co-chairs

Nuttapong Attrapadung	AIST, Japan
Takeshi Yagi	NTT Security (Japan) KK, Japan

Local Organizing Committee

Kazumaro Aoki	Nippon Telegraph and Telephone Corporation, Japan
Keita Emura	National Institute of Information and Communications Technology, Japan
Shota Fujii	Hitachi, Ltd., Japan
Masahiro Fujita	Mitsubishi Electric Corporation, Japan
Yuichi Hayashi	Nara Institute of Science and Technology, Japan
Shoichi Hirose	The University of Fukui, Japan
Makoto Iguchi	Kii Corporation, Japan
Akira Kanaoka	Toho University, Japan
Ryo Kikuchi	Nippon Telegraph and Telephone Corporation, Japan
Yoshihiro Mizoguchi	Institute of Mathematics for Industry, Kyusyu University, Japan
Ken Naganuma	Hitachi, Ltd., Japan
Satsuya Ohata	AIST, Japan
Kazuma Ohara	NEC Corporation, Japan
Yuji Suga	Internet Initiative Japan Inc., Japan
Nobuyuki Sugio	NTT DOCOMO, Inc., Japan
Atsushi Takayasu	The University of Tokyo, Japan
Keisuke Tanaka	Tokyo Institute of Technology, Japan
Yohei Watanabe	National Institute of Information and Communications Technology, Japan
Sven Wohlgemuth	Hitachi, Ltd., Japan
Dai Yamamoto	Fujitsu Limited, Japan
Masaya Yasuda	Institute of Mathematics for Industry, Kyusyu University, Japan

Program Committee

Track A: Cryptography Track

Kazumaro Aoki	NTT, Japan
Nuttapong Attrapadung	AIST, Japan
Olivier Blazy	University of Limoges, France
Bernardo David	Tokyo Institute of Technology, Japan
Itai Dinur	Ben-Gurion University, Israel
Antonio Faonio	IMDEA Software Institute, Spain
Takahiro Matsuda	AIST, Japan
Florian Mendel	Graz University of Technology, Austria
Kazuhiko Minematsu	NEC, Japan
Kirill Morozov	University of North Texas, USA
Fabrice Mouhartem	ENS Lyon, France and Microsoft Research, India
Thomas Peters	Université catholique de Louvain, Belgium
Yusuke Sakai	AIST, Japan
Jae Hong Seo	Hanyang University, Republic of Korea

Yannick Seurin	Agence Nationale de la Sécurité des Systemes d'Information, France
Willy Susilo	University of Wollongong, Australia
Katsuyuki Takashima	Mitsubishi Electric Corporation, Japan
Atsushi Takayasu	The University of Tokyo, Japan
Qiang Tang	New Jersey Institute of Technology, USA
Mehdi Tibouchi	NTT, Japan
Damien Vergnaud	Sorbonne Université, UPMC, CNRS, France
Yuyu Wang	Tokyo Institute of Technology, Japan
Yohei Watanabe	NICT, Japan
Rui Zhang	Chinese Academy of Sciences, China

Track B: Cybersecurity and Privacy Track

Mitsuaki Akiyama	Nippon Telegraph and Telephone Corporation, Japan
Josep Balasch	KU Leuven, Belgium
Gregory Blanc	Telecom SudParis, France
Yue Chen	Palo Alto Networks, USA
Daiki Chiba	Nippon Telegraph and Telephone Corporation, Japan
Herve Debar	Telecom SudParis, France
Josep Domingo-Ferrer	Universitat Rovira i Virgili, Catalonia
Kimmo Halunen	VTT Technical Research Centre of Finland Ltd., Finland
Yuichi Hayashi	Nara Institute of Science and Technology, Japan
Akira Kanaoka	Toho University, Japan
Yuhei Kawakoya	Nippon Telegraph and Telephone Corporation, Japan
Frederic Majorczyk	DGA-MI/CentraleSupelec, France
Yoshihiro Oyama	University of Tsukuba, Japan
Hajime Shimada	Nagoya University, Japan
Junko Takahashi	Nippon Telegraph and Telephone Corporation, Japan
Yuta Takata	PwC Cyber Services LLC, Japan
Giorgos Vasiliadis	Qatar Computing Research Institute HBKU, Greece
Takeshi Yagi	NTT Security (Japan) KK, Japan
Takumi Yamamoto	Mitsubishi Electric Corporation, Japan

Additional Reviewers

Miguel Ambrona	Michalis Diamantaris	Koki Hamada
Carles Anglés-Tafalla	Maria Eichlseder	Keisuke Hara
Sarah Azouvi	Keita Emura	Junichirou Hayata
Michael Bamiloshin	Daniel Escudero	Ehsan Hesamifard
Pascal Bemmann	Scott Fluhrer	Takato Hirano
Alberto Blanco-Justicia	Daisuke Fujimoto	Atsunori Ichikawa
George Christou	Atsushi Fujioka	Akiko Inoue
Pratish Datta	Kaiwen Guo	Toshiyuki Isshiki

Mitsugu Iwamoto
Maxim Jourenko
Saqib A. Kakvi
Shuichi Katsumata
Craig Kenney
Suhri Kim
Michael Klooss
Takuma Koyama
Stefan Kölbl
Wen-Jie Lu
Sergio Martinez
Michael Meyer

Luca Nizzardo
Yasuyuki Nogami
Koji Nuida
Satsuya Ohata
Toshihiro Ohigashi
Javier Parra-Arnau
Arnab Roy
Jacob Schuldt
Vladimir Soukharev
Xiangyu Su
Koutarou Suzuki
Tadanori Teruya

Masayuki Tezuka
Guanyu Tian
Yacheng Wang
Erich Wenger
Friedrich Wiemer
Keita Xagawa
Takashi Yamakawa
Takanori Yasuda
Yusuke Yoshida
Masaya Yoshikawa

Contents

Public-Key Primitives 1

CCA-Secure Leakage-Resilient Identity-Based Key-Encapsulation
from Simple (Not q-type) Assumptions 3
   Toi Tomita, Wakaha Ogata, and Kaoru Kurosawa

(Short Paper) A Faster Constant-Time Algorithm of CSIDH Keeping
Two Points. 23
   Hiroshi Onuki, Yusuke Aikawa, Tsutomu Yamazaki, and Tsuyoshi Takagi

Cryptanalysis on Public-Key Primitives

An Efficient F_4-style Based Algorithm to Solve MQ Problems 37
   Takuma Ito, Naoyuki Shinohara, and Shigenori Uchiyama

How to Solve Multiple Short-Exponent Discrete Logarithm Problem. 53
   Kaoru Kurosawa, Akinaga Ueda, Hayato Matsuhashi,
   and Yusuke Sakagami

Cryptographic Protocols 1

Secure Multiparty Matrix Multiplication Based
on Strassen-Winograd Algorithm. 67
   Jean-Guillaume Dumas, Pascal Lafourcade, Julio Lopez Fenner,
   David Lucas, Jean-Baptiste Orfila, Clément Pernet, and Maxime Puys

An Anonymous Credential System with Constant-Size Attribute Proofs
for CNF Formulas with Negations. 89
   Ryo Okishima and Toru Nakanishi

Symmetric-Key Primitives

More Results on Shortest Linear Programs 109
   Subhadeep Banik, Yuki Funabiki, and Takanori Isobe

Tweakable TWINE: Building a Tweakable Block Cipher on Generalized
Feistel Structure 129
   Kosei Sakamoto, Kazuhiko Minematsu, Nao Shibata, Maki Shigeri,
   Hiroyasu Kubo, Yuki Funabiki, Andrey Bogdanov, Sumio Morioka,
   and Takanori Isobe

Malware Detection and Classification

Correlating High- and Low-Level Features: Increased Understanding
of Malware Classification.   149
   Sergii Banin and Geir Olav Dyrkolbotn

Towards Efficient Detection of Malicious VBA Macros with LSI   168
   Mamoru Mimura and Taro Ohminami

Intrusion Detection and Prevention

IDS Alert Priority Determination Based on Traffic Behavior.   189
   Shohei Hiruta, Satoshi Ikeda, Shigeyoshi Shima, and Hiroki Takakura

(Short Paper) Effectiveness of Entropy-Based Features
in High- and Low-Intensity DDoS Attacks Detection.   207
   Abigail Koay, Ian Welch, and Winston K. G. Seah

Web and Usable Security

API Usability of Stateful Signature Schemes   221
   Alexander Zeier, Alexander Wiesmaier, and Andreas Heinemann

(Short Paper) Method for Preventing Suspicious Web Access
in Android WebView   241
   Masaya Sato, Yuta Imamura, Rintaro Orito, and Toshihiro Yamauchi

Public-Key Primitives 2

Equivalence Between Non-malleability Against Replayable CCA
and Other RCCA-Security Notions   253
   Junichiro Hayata, Fuyuki Kitagawa, Yusuke Sakai, Goichiro Hanaoka,
   and Kanta Matsuura

Cocks' Identity-Based Encryption in the Standard Model,
via Obfuscation Techniques (Short Paper)   273
   Xin Wang, Shimin Li, and Rui Xue

Cryptanalysis on Symmetric-Key Primitives

Finding Ordinary Cube Variables for Keccak-MAC with Greedy Algorithm . . .   287
   Fukang Liu, Zhenfu Cao, and Gaoli Wang

Preimage Attacks on Reduced Troika with Divide-and-Conquer Methods. . . .   306
   Fukang Liu and Takanori Isobe

Cryptographic Protocols 2

VSS Made Simpler   329
  Yvo Desmedt and Kirill Morozov

Bidirectional Asynchronous Ratcheted Key Agreement
with Linear Complexity   343
  F. Betül Durak and Serge Vaudenay

A New Approach to Constructing Digital Signature Schemes (Short Paper) . . .   363
  Ahto Buldas, Denis Firsov, Risto Laanoja, Henri Lakk, and Ahto Truu

Forensics

GRYPHON: Drone Forensics in Dataflash and Telemetry Logs   377
  Evangelos Mantas and Constantinos Patsakis

Toward the Analysis of Distributed Code Injection
in Post-mortem Forensics   391
  *Yuto Otsuki, Yuhei Kawakoya, Makoto Iwamura, Jun Miyoshi,
  Jacob Faires, and Terrence Lillard*

Author Index   411

Public-Key Primitives 1

CCA-Secure Leakage-Resilient Identity-Based Key-Encapsulation from Simple (Not q-type) Assumptions

Toi Tomita[1,2(✉)], Wakaha Ogata[1], and Kaoru Kurosawa[3]

[1] Tokyo Institute of Technology, Tokyo, Japan
{tomita.t.ae,ogata.w.aa}@m.titech.ac.jp
[2] National Institute of Advanced Industrial Science and Technology, Tokyo, Japan
[3] Ibaraki University, Ibaraki, Japan
kaoru.kurosawa.kk@vc.ibaraki.ac.jp

Abstract. In this paper, we propose a new leakage-resilient identity-based encryption (IBE) scheme that is secure against chosen-ciphertext attacks (CCA) in the bounded memory leakage model. It is the first CCA-secure leakage-resilient IBE scheme which does not depend on q-type assumptions. More precisely, it is secure under the DLIN assumption for symmetric bilinear groups and under the XDLIN assumption for asymmetric bilinear groups, respectively.

Keywords: Identity-based key-encapsulation · Leakage-resilience · CCA-security

1 Introduction

1.1 Background

Most of the encryption schemes known so far have been proven secure by assuming that the secret key is completely hidden. However, in the real world, a partial information of the secret key may leak by side-channel attacks [6,14,20] or a cold-boot attack [15]. In recent years, extensive research effort has been invested in providing encryption schemes which are provably secure even in this setting. Such schemes are said to be leakage-resilient.

Akavia et al. [2] introduced the bounded memory leakage model in which a bounded amount of information of the secret key is leaked to the adversary. Naor and Segev [26] showed how to construct leakage-resilient public-key encryption schemes from hash proof systems (HPS) in this model. (Other constructions were given by [4,18,22].) Qin et al. [28] showed a generic method to construct a CCA-secure leakage-resilient encryption scheme from any tag-based strongly universal$_2$ HPS.

Regarding identity-based encryption (IBE) schemes, CPA-secure leakage-resilient IBE schemes were shown by Akavia et al. [2], Alwen et al. [3] and

© Springer Nature Switzerland AG 2019
N. Attrapadung and T. Yagi (Eds.): IWSEC 2019, LNCS 11689, pp. 3–22, 2019.
https://doi.org/10.1007/978-3-030-26834-3_1

Chow et al. [8]. Furthermore, the scheme of Kurosawa and Phong [21] achieves the leakage rate $1 - o(1)$ under the DLIN assumption, where the leakage rate is defined as

$$\frac{\text{size of leakage}}{\text{size of secret key}}.$$

On the other hand, CCA-secure leakage-resilient IBE schemes were shown by Alwen et al. [3], Sun et al. [30] and Li et al. [24]. Unfortunately, all these CCA-secure leakage-resilient IBE schemes rely on q-type assumptions. Due to the Cheon attack [7], it is better to avoid such assumptions.

1.2   Our Contribution

In this paper, we propose the first CCA-secure leakage-resilient IBE scheme which does not depend on q-type assumptions. More precisely, it is secure under the DLIN assumption for symmetric bilinear groups and under the XDLIN assumption for asymmetric bilinear groups. (See Sect. 2.1 for the types of bilinear groups.)

In fact, we construct a CCA-secure leakage-resilient IB-KEM. A CCA-secure leakage-resilient IBE scheme is obtained by combining our IB-KEM with any CCA-secure symmetric-key encryption scheme (which does not need to be leakage-resilient).

Our IB-KEM scheme is obtained by applying the technique of Qin et al. [28] to the CPA-secure leakage-resilient IBE scheme of Kurosawa and Phong [21]. Hereby, we can achieve the leakage rate $1/10$. Our scheme will be able to generalize to k-linear assumption.

Table 1 shows a comparison of CCA-secure leakage-resilient IBE schemes.

Table 1. Comparison of CCA-secure leakage-resilient IBE schemes

Schemes	Assumption	Leakage rate
Alwen et al. [3]	q-type	1/6
Sun et al. [30]	q-type	1/6
Li et al. [24]	q-type	1/4
Ours (KEM)	XDLIN or DLIN	1/10

1.3   Various Models for Leakage-Resilient

Several researchers consider some variants of leakage models to capture practical issues. We summarize some leakage models below.

Micali and Reyzin [25] considered the "only computation leak information" model to deal with physical observation via side-channel attacks. However, this model could not capture key leakage attacks, such as a cold-boot attack. To capture key leakage attacks, Akavia et al. [2] proposed the bounded memory leakage model, in which an adversary can get partial information on secret keys. Brakerski et al. [5] and Dodis et al. [9] presented a new model called continual memory leakage model, which allows leakage on the private key in many periods of time. In this model, the secret key is updated over time and the total leakage over the lifetime of the system is unbounded. Dodis et al. [10] invented the auxiliary input model, in which the entire secret could be leaked information-theoretically, provided that it is computationally infeasible to compute the secret.

All these leakage models only consider leakage occurring before the challenge ciphertext is given to the adversary. In response to this, Halevi and Lin [16] proposed the after-the-fact leakage model, in which an adversary can obtain leaked information after seeing the challenge ciphertext.

1.4   Organization

The rest of the paper is organized as follows. Section 2 introduces notations, some building blocks, and computational assumptions. Section 3 describes the definition of IB-KEM and the leakage-resilient CCA-security. We present the concrete construction of our CCA-secure leakage-resilient IB-KEM scheme in Sect. 4 and its security proof in Sect. 5. Finally, the conclusion of this paper is given in Sect. 6.

2   Preliminaries

2.1   Notations

We introduce some notations used in this paper. Let $\lambda \in \mathbb{N}$ denote the security parameter. We say that a function $f(\lambda)$ is negligible in λ if it is smaller than all polynomial fractions for a sufficiently large λ. For a finite set $\mathcal{S}$, we use $s \leftarrow_\$ \mathcal{S}$ to denote the process of sampling an element s from $\mathcal{S}$ uniformly at random and let $|\mathcal{S}|$ denote its cardinality.

Let GGen be a probabilistic polynomial time (PPT) algorithm that on input the security parameter 1^λ returns a description $params = (\mathbb{G}_1, \mathbb{G}_2, \mathbb{G}_T, q, g_1, g_2, e)$ of pairing groups, where $\mathbb{G}_1$, $\mathbb{G}_2$, $\mathbb{G}_T$ are cyclic groups of a prime order q, g_1 and g_2 are generators of $\mathbb{G}_1$ and $\mathbb{G}_2$, respectively, and $e : \mathbb{G}_1 \times \mathbb{G}_2 \rightarrow \mathbb{G}_T$ is an efficiently computable (non-degenerated) bilinear map. Define $g_T := e(g_1, g_2)$, which is a generator of $\mathbb{G}_T$.

We refer to [31] for a description of types of bilinear groups. There are three types of bilinear groups according to whether efficient isomorphisms exist or not between $\mathbb{G}_1$ and $\mathbb{G}_2$ [13]. In type 1, both the isomorphism $\psi : \mathbb{G}_2 \rightarrow \mathbb{G}_1$ and its inverse $\psi^{-1} : \mathbb{G}_1 \rightarrow \mathbb{G}_2$ are efficiently computable, i.e., it can be regarded as $\mathbb{G}_1 = \mathbb{G}_2$. In type 2, the isomorphism $\psi : \mathbb{G}_2 \rightarrow \mathbb{G}_1$ is efficiently computable but its inverse is not. In type 3, there are no efficient isomorphisms between $\mathbb{G}_1$ and $\mathbb{G}_2$. Type 1 pairing groups are called symmetric, and type 2 and 3 pairing groups are called asymmetric. We assume type 3 pairing groups in our scheme, but our scheme also works in type 1 and 2 setting under appropriate computational assumptions.

We use implicit representation of group elements as introduced in [12]. For $s \in \{1, 2, T\}$ and $a \in \mathbb{Z}_q$ we define $[a]_s := g_s^a \in \mathbb{G}_s$ as the implicit representation of a in $\mathbb{G}_s$. Similarly, for a matrix

$$\mathbf{A} = \begin{pmatrix} a_{1,1} & \cdots & a_{1,m} \\ \vdots & \ddots & \vdots \\ a_{n,1} & \cdots & a_{n,m} \end{pmatrix} \in \mathbb{Z}_q^{n \times m}$$

we define

$$[\mathbf{A}]_s := \begin{pmatrix} g_s^{a_{1,1}} & \cdots & g_s^{a_{1,m}} \\ \vdots & \ddots & \vdots \\ g_s^{a_{n,1}} & \cdots & g_s^{a_{n,m}} \end{pmatrix} \in \mathbb{G}_s^{n \times m}$$

as the implicit representation of $\mathbf{A}$ in $\mathbb{G}_s$. Note that it is easy to compute $[\mathbf{AB}]_s$ given $([\mathbf{A}]_s, \mathbf{B})$ or $(\mathbf{A}, [\mathbf{B}]_s)$ with appropriate dimensions. We define $[\mathbf{A}]_1 \circ [\mathbf{B}]_2 := e([\mathbf{A}]_1, [\mathbf{B}]_2) = [\mathbf{AB}]_T$ that can be efficiently computed given $[\mathbf{A}]_1$ and $[\mathbf{B}]_2$.

2.2 External Decisional Linear Assumption

We assume the following property.

Definition 1 (External Decisional Linear Assumption: XDLIN [1]). *Let $s \in \{1, 2\}$. We say that the XDLIN assumption holds relative to* GGen *in group* $\mathbb{G}_s$ *if for any PPT adversary* D, *the following is negligible in* λ:

$$\mathsf{Adv}_{\mathsf{GGen}, \mathsf{D}}^{\mathsf{xdlin}}(\lambda) :=$$

$$\left| \Pr[\mathsf{D}(params, [\mathbf{A}]_1, [\mathbf{A}]_2, [\mathbf{A}^T \mathbf{r}]_s) = 1] - \Pr[\mathsf{D}(params, [\mathbf{A}]_1, [\mathbf{A}]_2, [\mathbf{y}]_s) = 1] \right|,$$

where $params \leftarrow \mathsf{GGen}(1^\lambda), a_1, a_2 \leftarrow_{\$} \mathbb{Z}_q, \mathbf{r} \leftarrow_{\$} \mathbb{Z}_q^2, \mathbf{y} \leftarrow_{\$} \mathbb{Z}_q^3,$ *and*

$$\mathbf{A} := \begin{pmatrix} a_1 & 0 & 1 \\ 0 & a_2 & 1 \end{pmatrix}.$$

This assumption is a variant of the standard decisional linear (DLIN) assumption [27] for asymmetric pairing groups. The XDLIN assumption is equivalent to the DLIN assumption in the generic group model.

2.3 Statistical Distance, Min-Entropy and Randomness Extractor

The statistical distance between random variables X, Y over a finite domain $\mathcal{S}$ is defined by

$$\Delta(X, Y) := \frac{1}{2} \sum_{s \in \mathcal{S}} |\Pr[X = s] - \Pr[Y = s]|.$$

The min-entropy of X is defined by

$$H_\infty(X) := -\log_2 \left(\max_x \Pr[X = x] \right).$$

Furthermore, average min-entropy of X conditioned on Y is defined by

$$\tilde{H}_\infty(X \mid Y) := -\log_2 \left(\sum_y 2^{-H_\infty(X|Y=y)} \Pr[Y = y] \right),$$

as defined in [11], which also proved the following lemma.

Lemma 1 ([11, Lemma 2.2]). *Let ℓ be a positive integer. Let X, Y and Z be random variables. If Y has at most 2^ℓ possible values, then*

$$\tilde{H}_\infty(X \mid Y, Z) \geq \tilde{H}_\infty(X, Y \mid Z) - \ell \geq \tilde{H}_\infty(X \mid Z) - \ell.$$

One of main tools in our construction is a randomness extractor [11].

Definition 2 (Randomness Extractor). *Let n be a positive integer, and $\phi > n, \epsilon_{\mathsf{Ext}}$ be positive reals, and $\mathcal{D}, \mathcal{S}$ be finite sets. A function $\mathsf{Ext} : \mathcal{D} \times \mathcal{S} \to \{0,1\}^n$ is called a $(\phi, \epsilon_{\mathsf{Ext}})$-randomness extractor if for all pairs of random variables (X, I) such that X is a random variable over $\mathcal{D}$ satisfying $\tilde{H}_\infty(X \mid I) \geq \phi$,*

$$\Delta \left((\mathsf{Ext}(X, S), S, I), (R, S, I) \right) \leq \epsilon_{\mathsf{Ext}}$$

holds, where S is uniform over $\mathcal{S}$ and R is uniform over $\{0,1\}^n$.

2.4 Hash Functions

Let $\mathsf{H} : \mathcal{D} \to \mathcal{R}$ be a hash function, where $\mathcal{D} = \mathcal{D}(\lambda)$ and $\mathcal{R} = \mathcal{R}(\lambda)$ are sets. We require the following property of hash functions for our scheme.

Definition 3 (Target Collision Resistance). *We say a hash function H is target collision resistant if for any PPT adversary A,*

$$\mathsf{Adv}^{\mathsf{tcr}}_{\mathsf{H},\mathsf{A}}(\lambda) := \Pr[x^* \leftarrow_{\$} \mathcal{D}, x \leftarrow_{\$} \mathsf{A}(x^*) : x \neq x^* \wedge \mathsf{H}(x) = \mathsf{H}(x^*)]$$

is negligible in λ.

2.5 Useful Facts

Here, we introduce useful facts used in our security proof. We use the following lemmas to prove adaptive identity security of our scheme.

Lemma 2 (Programmable hash function [17, Theorem 7]). *Let m, Q be integers. We choose $h = (h_1, \ldots, h_m) \in \mathbb{Z}_q^m$ as follows: (1) set $J = Q^2$, (2) sample $u_{i,j} \leftarrow_{\$} \{-1, 0, 1\}$ for $i = 1, \ldots, m$ and $j = 1, \ldots, J$, (3) set $h_i = \sum_{j=1}^{J} u_{i,j}$. For $h = (h_1, \ldots, h_m)$, we define*

$$\beta_h(x) := 1 + \sum_{i=1}^{m} x[i] h_i \bmod q,$$

where $x = (x[1], \ldots, x[m]) \in \{0,1\}^m$. Then, for any distinct $id_1, \ldots, id_Q, id^* \in \{0,1\}^m$, we have

$$\Pr\left[\bigwedge_{j=1}^{Q}(\beta_h(id_j) \neq 0) \wedge (\beta_h(id^*) = 0)\right] \geq \Theta\frac{1}{\sqrt{mQ}},$$

where the probability is taken over the choice of h.

Lemma 3 ([32, Lemma 5]). *Let* $x_1, \ldots, x_l \in \mathbb{R}$ *be reals such that*

$$\sum_{i=1}^{l}|x_i| \leq \frac{1}{2}.$$

Furthermore, let $\delta_1, \ldots, \delta_l \in \mathbb{R}$ *be reals such that* $0 < \delta_{\text{low}} \leq \delta_i \leq \delta_{\text{up}}$ *for* $i = 1, \ldots, l$. *Then, we have*

$$\left|\sum_{i=1}^{l}\delta_i x_i\right| \geq \delta_{\text{low}}\left|\sum_{i=1}^{l}x_i\right| - \frac{\delta_{\text{up}} - \delta_{\text{low}}}{2}.$$

3 Identity-Based Key-Encapsulation Mechanism

In this section, we introduce the syntax, the correctness property, and the security notion for IB-KEM.

Syntax. An IB-KEM scheme $\Pi = (\mathsf{Setup}, \mathsf{KGen}, \mathsf{Encap}, \mathsf{Decap})$ consists of four PPT algorithms.

- $\mathsf{Setup}(1^\lambda) \to (pp, mk)$. The setup algorithm takes as input the security parameter λ, outputs a public parameter pp and a master key mk. We assume that pp implicitly defines an identity space $\mathcal{ID}$, a session key space $\mathcal{K}$, and a secret key space $\mathcal{SK}$.
- $\mathsf{KGen}(mk, id) \to sk_{id}$. The key generation algorithm takes as input the master key mk and an identity $id \in \mathcal{ID}$, outputs a secret key sk_{id} for the id.
- $\mathsf{Encap}(pp, id) \to (ct, K)$. The encapsulation algorithm takes as input the public parameter pp and an $id \in \mathcal{ID}$, outputs a session key $K \in \mathcal{K}$ together with a ciphertext ct with respect to identity id.
- $\mathsf{Decap}(sk_{id}, ct) \to K$ or $\perp$. The decapsulation algorithm takes as input a secret key sk_{id} and a ciphertext ct, outputs a decapsulated key $K \in \mathcal{K}$ or the rejection symbol $\perp$.

Correctness. We require correctness of decapsulation: that is for all λ, all pairs (pp, mk) generated by $\mathsf{Setup}(1^\lambda)$, all identities $id \in \mathcal{ID}$, and all $(ct, K) \leftarrow \mathsf{Encap}(pp, id)$, $\Pr[\mathsf{Decap}(\mathsf{KGen}(mk, id), ct) = K] = 1$.

Security. In this paper, we consider the IB-KEM variant of CCA-security for leakage-resilient IBE in the bounded memory leakage model [3]. Let Π be an IB-KEM scheme. We consider the IND-ID-lrCCA game between a challenger and an adversary A as follows.

Setup phase: The challenger runs Setup to generate (pp, mk), and sends pp to A.

Query phase 1: The adversary A makes queries of the following types:
  - Key generation query $id \in \mathcal{ID}$. The challenger computes and returns the secret key $sk_{id} \leftarrow \mathsf{KGen}(mk, id)$ to A.
  - Leakage query (id, f), where $f : \mathcal{SK} \rightarrow \{0, 1\}$ is an efficiently computable function. The challenger returns $f(sk_{id})$ to A.
  - Decapsulation query (id, ct). The challenger returns $\mathsf{Decap}(sk_{id}, ct)$ to A.

Challenge phase: A sends the challenge identity $id^* \in \mathcal{ID}$ to the challenger. It must be that he has never queried id^* as a key generation query. The challenger chooses a bit $b \leftarrow_\$ \{0, 1\}$. The challenger runs $\mathsf{Encap}(pp, id^*)$ to generate (ct^*, K_0^*), and chooses a random session key $K_1^* \leftarrow_\$ \mathcal{K}$. Then, he sends (ct^*, K_b^*) to A.

Query phase 2: A makes queries of the following types:
  - Key generation query $id \in \mathcal{ID}$, where it must be that $id \neq id^*$.
  - Decapsulation query (id, ct), where it must be that $(id, ct) \neq (id^*, ct^*)$.

Guess phase: Finally A outputs a guess $b' \in \{0, 1\}$.

Note that, in query phase 1 and 2 the challenger computes sk_{id} the first time that id is queried in a key generation, leakage, or decryption query, and responds to all future queries on the same id with the same sk_{id}.

Definition 4 (IND-ID-lrCCA security). *An IB-KEM scheme Π is ℓ-IND-ID-lrCCA (indistinguishability against adaptive identity leakage-resilient chosen-ciphertext attack) secure if for any PPT adversary A that makes at most ℓ leakage queries, the advantage*

$$\mathsf{Adv}_{\Pi, \mathsf{A}}^{\text{IND-ID-lrCCA}}(\lambda) := \left| \Pr[b' = b] - \frac{1}{2} \right|$$

is negligible in λ.

Remark: Challenge-Dependent Leakage. In the security definition, the adversary is not allowed to obtain the leakage $f(sk_{id})$ after the challenge phase. We note that this restriction is indeed necessary: the adversary can encode the decapsulation algorithm for the challenge ciphertext ct^* and the challenge identity id^*.

4 Construction

In this section, we propose a new CCA-secure leakage-resilient IB-KEM scheme.

Let $params = (\mathbb{G}_1, \mathbb{G}_2, \mathbb{G}_T, q, g_1, g_2, e) \leftarrow \mathsf{GGen}(1^\lambda)$, n be the bit-length of a session key (i.e., $\mathcal{K} = \{0,1\}^n$), m be the bit-length of an identity (i.e., $\mathcal{ID} = \{0,1\}^m$), $\ell < \log_2 q$ be any positive integer, $\mathsf{H} : \mathbb{G}_1^5 \times \mathcal{S} \to \mathbb{Z}_q \setminus \{0\}$ be a target collision resistant hash function, $\mathsf{Ext} : \mathbb{G}_T \times \mathcal{S} \to \{0,1\}^n$ be a $(\log_2 q - \ell, \epsilon_{\mathsf{Ext}})$-randomness extractor. We assume that m is independent of λ, ϵ_{Ext} is negligible in λ.

Our scheme $\Pi = (\mathsf{Setup}, \mathsf{KGen}, \mathsf{Encap}, \mathsf{Decap})$ is described as follows.

$\mathsf{Setup}(1^\lambda)$: Choose $a_1, a_2 \leftarrow_\$ \mathbb{Z}_q \setminus \{0\}$ and $\mathbf{B}_0, \mathbf{B}_1, \ldots, \mathbf{B}_m, \mathbf{D} \leftarrow_\$ \mathbb{Z}_q^{2\times 2}$ uniformly at random and set

$$\mathbf{A} := \begin{pmatrix} a_1 & 0 & 1 \\ 0 & a_2 & 1 \end{pmatrix} \in \mathbb{Z}_q^{2\times 3}.$$

Output $pp = ([\mathbf{A}]_1, [\mathbf{B}_0]_1, [\mathbf{B}_1]_1, \ldots, [\mathbf{B}_m]_1, [\mathbf{D}]_1)$ and $mk = (a_1, a_2, \mathbf{B}_0, \mathbf{B}_1, \ldots, \mathbf{B}_m, \mathbf{D})$.
For an identity $id = (id[1], \ldots, id[m]) \in \{0,1\}^m$, let

$$\mathbf{F}_{id} = \left(\mathbf{A} \,\middle\|\, \mathbf{B}_0 + \sum_{i=1}^m id[i]\mathbf{B}_i \right) \in \mathbb{Z}_q^{2\times 5}.$$

$\mathsf{KGen}(mk, id)$: Compute a random matrix $\mathbf{S}_{id} \in \mathbb{Z}_q^{5\times 2}$ such that

$$\mathbf{F}_{id}\mathbf{S}_{id} = \mathbf{D} \tag{1}$$

as follows. Let

$$\mathbf{F}'_{id} = \left(\begin{matrix} 1 \\ 1 \end{matrix} \,\middle\|\, \mathbf{B}_0 + \sum_{i=1}^m id[i]\mathbf{B}_i \right) \in \mathbb{Z}_q^{2\times 3}.$$

Choose $\mathbf{S}' \leftarrow_\$ \mathbb{Z}_q^{3\times 2}$ at random, compute

$$\mathbf{S}'' = \begin{pmatrix} a_1^{-1} & 0 \\ 0 & a_2^{-1} \end{pmatrix} (\mathbf{D} - \mathbf{F}'_{id}\mathbf{S}') \in \mathbb{Z}_q^{2\times 2},$$

and set

$$\mathbf{S}_{id} = \begin{pmatrix} \mathbf{S}'' \\ \mathbf{S}' \end{pmatrix}.$$

Output $sk_{id} = [\mathbf{S}_{id}]_2$ as a secret key for the id.
$\mathsf{Encap}(pp, id)$: Choose $\mathbf{r} \leftarrow_\$ \mathbb{Z}_q^2$ and $sd \leftarrow_\$ \mathcal{S}$ at random, compute

$$[\mathbf{c}]_1 = [\mathbf{F}_{id}^\top \mathbf{r}]_1 \in \mathbb{G}_1^5,$$
$$\alpha = \mathsf{H}([\mathbf{c}]_1, sd) \in \mathbb{Z}_q,$$
$$[k_a]_T = [\mathbf{r}^\top \mathbf{D} \left(\begin{smallmatrix} 1 \\ \alpha \end{smallmatrix} \right)]_1 \circ [1]_2 \in \mathbb{G}_T,$$
$$[k_s]_T = [\mathbf{r}^\top \mathbf{D} \left(\begin{smallmatrix} 1 \\ 0 \end{smallmatrix} \right)]_1 \circ [1]_2 \in \mathbb{G}_T.$$

Output $ct = ([\mathbf{c}]_1, [k_a]_T, sd)$ and $K = \mathsf{Ext}([k_s]_T, sd)$.

$\mathsf{Decap}(sk_{id}, ct)$: On input $sk_{id} = [\mathbf{S}_{id}]_2$ and $ct = ([\mathbf{c}]_1, [t]_T, sd)$, compute

$$\alpha = \mathsf{H}([\mathbf{c}]_1, sd),$$
$$[k_a]_T = [\mathbf{c}^\top]_1 \circ [\mathbf{S}_{id}(\tfrac{1}{\alpha})]_2,$$
$$[k_s]_T = [\mathbf{c}^\top]_1 \circ [\mathbf{S}_{id}(\tfrac{1}{0})]_2.$$

Output $\mathsf{Ext}([k_s]_T, sd)$ if $[t]_T = [k_a]_T$, otherwise $\bot$.

Correctness. Let $sk_{id} = [\mathbf{S}_{id}]_2$, $ct = ([\mathbf{c}]_1, [t]_T, sd)$, and $\alpha = \mathsf{H}([\mathbf{c}]_1, sd)$. If $\mathbf{c} = \mathbf{F}_{id}^\top \mathbf{r}$ and $t = \mathbf{r}^\top \mathbf{D}(\tfrac{1}{\alpha})$ then

$$k_a = \mathbf{c}^\top \mathbf{S}_{id}(\tfrac{1}{\alpha}) = \mathbf{r}^\top \mathbf{F}_{id} \mathbf{S}_{id}(\tfrac{1}{\alpha}) = \mathbf{r}^\top \mathbf{D}(\tfrac{1}{\alpha}) = t$$

in the Decap procedure, and it is similar to k_s. Therefore, our IB-KEM scheme Π satisfies correctness.

5   Security

In this section, we prove the IND-ID-lrCCA security of our scheme.

Theorem 1. *Under the XDLIN assumption relative to GGen in group $\mathbb{G}_1$, our scheme Π is ℓ-IND-ID-lrCCA secure for any positive integer ℓ satisfying*

$$\ell \leq \log_2 q - n - \eta, \tag{2}$$

where $\eta = \eta(\lambda)$ is a positive integer such that $2^{-\eta}$ is negligible in λ.

In particular, given an efficient adversary A breaking the ℓ-IND-ID-lrCCA secure of Π with advantage $\epsilon_\mathsf{A} := \mathsf{Adv}_{\Pi,\mathsf{A}}^{\text{IND-ID-lrCCA}}(\lambda)$, we can construct an adversary D breaking the XDLIN assumption with advantage $\epsilon_\mathsf{D} := \mathsf{Adv}_{\mathsf{GGen},\mathsf{D}}^{\text{xdlin}}(\lambda)$ such that

$$\epsilon_\mathsf{D} \geq \Theta \frac{1}{\sqrt{m}(Q_\mathsf{KGen} + Q_\mathsf{Dec})} \epsilon_\mathsf{A} - \mathsf{Adv}_\mathsf{H}^{\text{tcr}}(\lambda) - \frac{Q_\mathsf{Dec}}{2^\eta(1 - Q_\mathsf{Dec}/q)} - \frac{3}{q} - \frac{Q_\mathsf{Dec}}{q^5 \cdot |\mathcal{S}|} - \epsilon_\mathsf{Ext},$$

holds for such λ, where $Q_\mathsf{KGen} = \mathsf{poly}(\lambda)$ and $Q_\mathsf{Dec} = \mathsf{poly}(\lambda)$ are the number of key generation queries and decapsulation queries made by A, respectively.

Remark. Our scheme works also on type 1 or 2 bilinear groups.

Proof. Let A be an efficient adversary on the IND-ID-lrCCA security of Π. Namely, $\epsilon_\mathsf{A} \geq 1/\mathsf{poly}(\lambda)$ for infinitely many λ. We will consider a sequence of games, $\mathsf{Game}_0, \ldots, \mathsf{Game}_9$ performed by a challenger and A. At the end of each game, the challenger outputs a bit $\gamma \in \{0, 1\}$, which will be described below.

Let W_i be the event such that $\gamma = 1$ in Game_i.

Game$_0$: This game is the IND-ID-lrCCA game. At the end of the game, the challenger outputs $\gamma = 1$ if $b' = b$, otherwise $\gamma = 0$, where b' is A's guessing bit of b. Thus,

$$\left| \Pr[W_0] - \frac{1}{2} \right| = \epsilon_\mathsf{A}. \tag{3}$$

The challenge is (ct^*, K_b^*) where $ct^* = ([\mathbf{c}^*]_1, [k_a^*]_T, sd^*)$. We denote by $\mathbf{r}^*, \alpha^*, k_s^*$ the corresponding intermediate values. The session key K_b^* is $\mathsf{Ext}([k_s^*]_T, sd^*)$ or random over $\{0,1\}^n$, depending on the bit b.

Game$_1$: This game is the same as Game$_0$ except that the challenger changes the generation of the public parameter pp and the ciphertext ct^* as follows.

- In the setup phase, choose $\mathbf{R}_0, \mathbf{R}_1, \ldots, \mathbf{R}_m, \mathbf{E} \leftarrow_\$ \mathbb{Z}_q^{3 \times 2}$ uniformly at random. Set $J := (Q_\mathsf{KGen} + Q_\mathsf{Dec})^2$, sample $u_{i,j} \leftarrow_\$ \{-1, 0, 1\}$ for $i = 1, \ldots, m$ and $j = 1, \ldots, J$, and set $h_i := \sum_{j=1}^J u_{i,j}$. The public parameter is defined as

$$\mathbf{B}_0 = \mathbf{A}\mathbf{R}_0 + \mathbf{I}_2,$$
$$\mathbf{B}_i = \mathbf{A}\mathbf{R}_i + h_i \mathbf{I}_2 \text{ for } i = 1, \ldots, m,$$
$$\mathbf{D} = \mathbf{A}\mathbf{E}.$$

Output $pp = ([\mathbf{A}]_1, [\mathbf{B}_0]_1, [\mathbf{B}_1]_1, \ldots, [\mathbf{B}_m]_1, [\mathbf{D}]_1)$. The challenger holds $(a_1, a_2, \mathbf{R}_0, \mathbf{R}_1, \ldots, \mathbf{R}_m, \mathbf{E})$ as a master key in this game.

In Game$_1$, the $\mathbf{F}_{id}$ for $id \in \{0,1\}^m$ can be written by

$$\mathbf{F}_{id} = \left(\mathbf{A} \middle\| \mathbf{A}\mathbf{R}_{id} + \beta_h(id)\mathbf{I}_2 \right),$$

where $\mathbf{R}_{id} = \mathbf{R}_0 + \sum_{i=1}^m id[i]\mathbf{R}_i$ and $\beta_h(id) = 1 + \sum_{i=1}^m id[i]h_i$.

- In the challenge phase, the challenger computes $[k_a^*]_T$ and $[k_s^*]_T$ as follows:

$$[k_a^*]_T = \left[\mathbf{c}^{*\top} \right]_1 \circ [\mathbf{S}^* \left(\begin{smallmatrix} 1 \\ \alpha^* \end{smallmatrix} \right)]_2,$$
$$[k_s^*]_T = \left[\mathbf{c}^{*\top} \right]_1 \circ [\mathbf{S}^* \left(\begin{smallmatrix} 1 \\ 0 \end{smallmatrix} \right)]_2,$$

where $[\mathbf{S}^*]_2$ is the secret key for the id^*.

Note that this change does not affect the distributions of the public parameter pp and the challenge (ct^*, K_b^*). Therefore, we have

$$\Pr[W_0] = \Pr[W_1]. \tag{4}$$

Game$_2$: Let id^* be the challenge identity and $id_1, \ldots, id_Q$ be identities that A queries in the key generation query and the decapsulation query, where $Q \leq Q_\mathsf{KGen} + Q_\mathsf{Dec}$. Define the event

$$\mathcal{FORCEDABORT} : \bigvee_{i=1}^Q (\beta_h(id_i) = 0) \vee (\beta_h(id^*) \neq 0),$$

and
$$\eta(\mathbf{id_A}) := \Pr[\neg \mathcal{FORCEDABORT}]$$

for $\mathbf{id_A} = (id_1, \ldots, id_Q, id^*)$, where the probability is taken over the choice of h. By Lemma 2, this probability has a minimum value greater than 0. Let η_{low} be the minimum value of $\eta(\mathbf{id_A})$.

In the guess phase, A outputs its guess $b' \in \{0,1\}$ for b. The challenger checks the event $\mathcal{FORCEDABORT}$ occurs for $\mathbf{id_A}$. If yes, the challenger aborts the game and outputs a fresh random bit $\gamma \in \{0,1\}$. Otherwise, the challenger first estimates the probability $\eta(\mathbf{id_A})$ by sampling $(h_1, \ldots, h_m)$ sufficiently large amount of times. Let $\eta'(\mathbf{id_A})$ be the estimation of $\eta(\mathbf{id_A})$. Depending on the estimate $\eta'(\mathbf{id_A})$ the challenger decides γ as follows:

- Case $\eta'(\mathbf{id_A}) \leq \eta_{\text{low}}$: The challenger outputs $\gamma = [b = b']$.
- Case $\eta'(\mathbf{id_A}) > \eta_{\text{low}}$: With probability $\eta_{\text{low}}/\eta'(\mathbf{id_A})$ the challenger outputs $\gamma = [b = b']$. With probability $1 - \eta_{\text{low}}/\eta'(\mathbf{id_A})$ the challenger aborts the game and outputs a fresh random bit $\gamma \in \{0,1\}$.

Lemma 4 in Appendix will show that

$$\frac{\eta_{\text{low}}}{2} \left| \Pr[W_1] - \frac{1}{2} \right| \leq \left| \Pr[W_2] - \frac{1}{2} \right|.$$

From Lemma 2, we have

$$\left| \Pr[W_1] - \frac{1}{2} \right| \leq \Theta \sqrt{m} (Q_{\mathsf{KGen}} + Q_{\mathsf{Dec}}) \left| \Pr[W_2] - \frac{1}{2} \right|. \tag{5}$$

Game₃: In Game₃, we make the following changes to the experiment. When A queries an identity id to the key generation oracle, the challenger checks whether $\beta_h(id) = 0$. If so, the challenger immediately aborts and returns a fresh random bit γ. When A outputs id^* as a challenge identity, if $\beta_h(id^*) \neq 0$ the challenger immediately aborts and returns a fresh random bit γ.

Clearly, the above changes do not affect A's environment if $\mathcal{FORCED} \mathcal{ABORT}$ dose not occur. Then, we have

$$\Pr[W_2] = \Pr[W_3]. \tag{6}$$

Game₄: This game is the same as Game₃ except that the challenger changes the generation of the secret key $sk_{id} = [\mathbf{S}_{id}]_2$ for id as follows.

- Case $\beta_h(id) \neq 0$: The challenger chooses $\mathbf{W} \leftarrow_{\$} \mathbb{Z}_q^{3 \times 2}$, computes $\mathbf{W}' \in \mathbb{Z}_q^{2 \times 2}$ satisfying

$$\beta_h(id)\mathbf{W}' = -\mathbf{AW} + \mathbf{AE}, \tag{7}$$

and sets

$$\mathbf{S}_{id} = \begin{pmatrix} \mathbf{W} - \mathbf{R}_{id}\mathbf{W}' \\ \mathbf{W}' \end{pmatrix}.$$

This $\mathbf{S}_{id}$ satisfies Eq. (1) because

$$\mathbf{F}_{id}\mathbf{S}_{id} = \left(\mathbf{A}\middle\|\mathbf{A}\mathbf{R}_{id} + \beta_h(id)\mathbf{I}_2\right)\begin{pmatrix}\mathbf{W} - \mathbf{R}_{id}\mathbf{W}' \\ \mathbf{W}'\end{pmatrix}$$
$$= \mathbf{A}\left(\mathbf{W} - \mathbf{R}_{id}\mathbf{W}'\right) + \left(\mathbf{A}\mathbf{R}_{id} + \beta_h(id)\mathbf{I}_2\right)\mathbf{W}'$$
$$= \mathbf{A}\mathbf{W} + \beta_h(id)\mathbf{W}'$$
$$= \mathbf{A}\mathbf{W} - \mathbf{A}\mathbf{W} + \mathbf{A}\mathbf{E}$$
$$= \mathbf{D}.$$

Further, the above $\mathbf{S}_{id}$ has the same distribution as the secret key generated by KGen, because 6 elements are chosen at random and the remaining are determined uniquely by Eq. (7).

- Case $\beta_h(id) = 0$: The challenger computes $\mathbf{S}_{id} \in \mathbb{Z}_q^{5\times 2}$ such that

$$(\mathbf{I}_3\|\mathbf{R}_{id})\,\mathbf{S}_{id} = \mathbf{E} \tag{8}$$

as follows. The challenger computes $\mathbf{S}'' := \mathbf{E} - \mathbf{R}_{id}\mathbf{S}'$ where $\mathbf{S}' \leftarrow_\$ \mathbb{Z}_q^{2\times 2}$, and sets

$$\mathbf{S}_{id} = \begin{pmatrix}\mathbf{S}'' \\ \mathbf{S}'\end{pmatrix}.$$

It is easy to see that $[\mathbf{S}_{id}]_2$ is the correct secret key for id by multiplying $\mathbf{A}$ from the left to both hand sides of Eq. (8).
We show that the above $\mathbf{S}_{id}$ has the same distribution of the original KGen as seen from A. Now, $\mathbf{S}'$ is chosen randomly. Hence, we need to show that 2 elements in $\mathbf{S}''$ e.g. $\mathbf{e}\mathbf{S}''$ are also random where $\mathbf{e} := (0\ 0\ 1)$. It suffices to prove $\mathbf{u} := \mathbf{e}\mathbf{E}$ is random even given $\mathbf{A}$ and $\mathbf{D} = \mathbf{A}\mathbf{E}$, since $\mathbf{e}\mathbf{S}'' = \mathbf{e}\mathbf{E} - \mathbf{e}\mathbf{R}_{id}\mathbf{S}'$. It is easy to see that

$$\begin{pmatrix}\mathbf{D} \\ \mathbf{u}\end{pmatrix} = \underbrace{\begin{pmatrix}\mathbf{A} \\ \mathbf{e}\end{pmatrix}}_{\mathbf{A}'}\mathbf{E}. \tag{9}$$

Because $\mathbf{A}'$ is of full rank, the distribution of $\mathbf{u}$ is random and independent from $\mathbf{D}$ that A knows. Hence, $\mathbf{e}\mathbf{S}''$ is also random as seen from A.
Note that this change dose not affect the distribution of the secret key sk_{id} for id. Therefore, we have

$$\Pr[W_3] = \Pr[W_4]. \tag{10}$$

Game$_5$: This game is the same as Game$_4$ except that $[\mathbf{c}^*]_1$ in the challenge is randomly chosen from $\mathbb{G}_1^5$. Furthermore, the challenger chooses $[\mathbf{c}^*]_1 \leftarrow_\$ \mathbb{G}_1^5$, $sd^* \leftarrow_\$ \mathcal{S}$, and computes $\alpha^* = \mathsf{H}([\mathbf{c}^*]_1, sd^*)$ at the beginning of the game. As we will show in Lemma 6, we have that there exists a PPT adversary D such that

$$|\Pr[W_4] - \Pr[W_5]| \leq \mathsf{Adv}_{\mathsf{GGen},\mathsf{D}}^{\mathrm{xdlin}}(\lambda) + \frac{1}{q}. \tag{11}$$

The decapsulation oracle in this game is depicted in Fig. 1. We define that a ciphertext $[\mathbf{c}]_1$ is *valid for id* if there exists $\mathbf{r} \in \mathbb{Z}_q^2$ such that $[\mathbf{c}]_1 = [\mathbf{F}_{id}^\top \mathbf{r}]_1$. With pp and mk, we can efficiently check whether $[\mathbf{c}]_1 = [(c_1, c_2, c_3, c_4, c_5)^\top]_1$ is valid for id by simply verifying

$$[(c_3, c_4, c_5)]_1 = \left[(c_1, c_2)\begin{pmatrix} a_1^{-1} & 0 \\ 0 & a_2^{-1} \end{pmatrix} \mathbf{F}_{id}'\right]_1.$$

Decapsulation of adversarial query $(id, ct = ([\mathbf{c}]_1, [t]_T, sd))$

---

1 : Generate $sk_{id} = [\mathbf{S}_{id}]_2$

2 : $\alpha \leftarrow \mathsf{H}([\mathbf{c}]_1, sd)$

3 : if $\beta_h(id) \neq 0$ then

4 :   return $K \leftarrow \mathsf{Decap}(sk_{id}, ct)$

5 : if $([\mathbf{c}]_1, sd) \neq ([\mathbf{c}^*]_1, sd^*) \wedge \alpha = \alpha^*$ then

6 :   return $K \leftarrow \mathsf{Decap}(sk_{id}, ct)$

7 : if $([\mathbf{c}]_1, sd) = ([\mathbf{c}^*]_1, sd^*)$ then

8 :   if $[t]_T = [k_a^*]_T$ then return K_0^*

9 :   else return $\perp$

10 : if $[\mathbf{c}]_1$ is invalid for id then

11 : $[k_a]_T \leftarrow [\mathbf{c}^\top]_1 \circ [\mathbf{S}_{id}(1, \alpha)^\top]_2$

12 : $[k_s]_T \leftarrow [\mathbf{c}^\top]_1 \circ [\mathbf{S}_{id}(1, \alpha_0)^\top]_2$

13 :   if $[t]_T = [k_a]_T$ then return $\mathsf{Ext}([k_s]_T, sd)$

14 :   else return $\perp$

15 : return $K \leftarrow \mathsf{Decap}(sk_{id}, ct)$

Fig. 1. Decapsulation oracle in Game$_5$

Game$_6$: In this game, at line 6 in Fig. 1, the challenger returns $\perp$. Then we have

$$\Pr[W_5] = \Pr[W_5 \wedge \mathsf{H} \text{ has collision}] + \Pr[W_5 \wedge \mathsf{H} \text{ has no collision}]$$
$$\leq \Pr[\mathsf{H} \text{ has collision}] + \Pr[W_5 \wedge \mathsf{H} \text{ has no collision}]$$
$$\leq \mathsf{Adv}_{\mathsf{H}}^{\mathsf{tcr}}(\lambda) + \Pr[W_6].$$

Therefore, we obtain

$$|\Pr[W_5] - \Pr[W_6]| \leq \mathsf{Adv}_{\mathsf{H}}^{\mathsf{tcr}}(\lambda). \tag{12}$$

Game$_7$: In this game, at line 13 in Fig. 1, the challenger returns $\perp$. As we will show in Lemma 7, we have

$$|\Pr[W_6] - \Pr[W_7]| \leq \frac{Q_{\mathsf{Dec}}}{2^\eta (1 - Q_{\mathsf{Dec}}/q)} + \frac{1}{q}. \tag{13}$$

Game$_8$: In this game, at line 8 in Fig. 1, the challenger returns $\perp$. $([\mathbf{c}]_1, sd) = ([\mathbf{c}^*]_1, sd^*)$ holds with probability $1/(q^5 \cdot |\mathcal{S}|)$ before the challenge phase, since A knows nothing about $(\mathbf{c}^*, sd^*)$ chosen randomly. On the other hand, after the challenge phase $(id^*, ct^* = ([\mathbf{c}^*]_1, [k_a^*]_T, sd^*))$ was already announced to A, any adversarial decapsulation query $(id^*, ([\mathbf{c}^*]_1, [k_a]_T, sd^*))$ with $[t]_T = [k_a]_T$ is equal to (id^*, ct^*). Hence, such adversarial decapsulation query is forbidden by the restriction of IND-ID-lrCCA game.

Thus we have

$$|\Pr[W_7] - \Pr[W_8]| \leq \frac{Q_{\mathsf{Dec}}}{q^5 \cdot |\mathcal{S}|}. \tag{14}$$

Game$_9$: In this game, K_0^* is chosen at random from $\{0,1\}^n$ instead of using $\mathsf{Ext}([k_s^*]_T, sd^*)$. As we will show in Lemma 8, we have

$$|\Pr[W_8] - \Pr[W_9]| \leq \epsilon_{\mathsf{Ext}} + \frac{1}{q}. \tag{15}$$

In Game$_9$, A does not get any information about bit b because both K_0^* and K_1^* are random. Hence, we have

$$\Pr[W_9] = \frac{1}{2}. \tag{16}$$

From Eqs. (3)–(6) and (10)–(16), we have shown that given an adversary A with advantage ϵ_A, there exists an adversary D with $\epsilon_D = \mathsf{Adv}_{\mathsf{GGen},D}^{\mathsf{xdlin}}(\lambda)$ such that

$$\epsilon_A = \left| \Pr[W_0] - \frac{1}{2} \right|$$

$$\leq \Theta(\sqrt{m}(Q_{\mathsf{KGen}} + Q_{\mathsf{Dec}})) \left| \Pr[W_2] - \frac{1}{2} \right|$$

$$\leq \Theta(\sqrt{m}(Q_{\mathsf{KGen}} + Q_{\mathsf{Dec}})) \sum_{i=4}^{8} |\Pr[W_i] - \Pr[W_{i+1}]|$$

$$= \Theta(\sqrt{m}(Q_{\mathsf{KGen}} + Q_{\mathsf{Dec}})) \left(\epsilon_D + \mathsf{Adv}_H^{\mathsf{tcr}}(\lambda) + \frac{Q_{\mathsf{Dec}}}{2^\eta(1 - Q_{\mathsf{Dec}}/q)} + \frac{3}{q} + \frac{Q_{\mathsf{Dec}}}{q^5 \cdot |\mathcal{S}|} + \epsilon_{\mathsf{Ext}} \right).$$

Therefore, we have

$$\epsilon_D \geq \Theta \frac{1}{\sqrt{m}(Q_{\mathsf{KGen}} + Q_{\mathsf{Dec}})} \epsilon_A - \mathsf{Adv}_H^{\mathsf{tcr}}(\lambda) - \frac{Q_{\mathsf{Dec}}}{2^\eta(1 - Q_{\mathsf{Dec}}/q)} - \frac{3}{q} - \frac{Q_{\mathsf{Dec}}}{q^5 \cdot |\mathcal{S}|} - \epsilon_{\mathsf{Ext}}.$$

The right side of the above inequality is non-negligible, since ϵ_A and $\Theta 1/\sqrt{m}(Q_{\mathsf{KGen}} + Q_{\mathsf{Dec}})$ are non-negligible in λ, other terms are negligible in λ. Hence, this contradicts the XDLIN assumption. This completes the proof of Theorem 1. $\qquad \square$

6   Conclusion

In this paper, we proposed the first CCA-secure leakage-resilient IB-KEM scheme which does not depend on q-type assumptions. More precisely, it is secure under the DLIN assumption for symmetric bilinear groups and under the XDLIN assumption for asymmetric bilinear groups. A CCA-secure leakage-resilient IBE scheme is obtained by combining our IB-KEM with any CCA-secure symmetric-key encryption scheme (which does not need to be leakage-resilient). However, the leakage rate of our scheme is smaller than previous works [3,24,30].

A   Proof of Lemmas

To complete the proof of Theorem 1, we prove Lemmas 4, 6, 7, and 8.

Lemma 4.

$$\frac{\eta_{\text{low}}}{2} \left| \Pr[W_1] - \frac{1}{2} \right| \leq \left| \Pr[W_2] - \frac{1}{2} \right|.$$

We introduce a lemma before proving Lemma 4.

Lemma 5. ([19, Claim 6.7]). *Let $0 < \rho < 1$ be a real. For a sequence of identities* $\mathbf{id} \in (\mathcal{ID})^{Q+1}$, *and* $\mathcal{ABORT}$ *be the event that the challenger aborts with added rules in Game$_2$. For any fixed* $\mathbf{id}$,

$$\eta_{\text{low}} (1 - \rho) \leq \Pr[\neg \mathcal{ABORT}] \leq \eta_{\text{low}} (1 + \rho).$$

Proof (of Lemma 4). For a sequence of identities $\mathbf{id} \in (\mathcal{ID})^{Q+1}$, we define $\mathcal{Q}(\mathbf{id})$ as the event that A uses the last entry in $\mathbf{id}$ as the challenge and makes key generation queries and decapsulation queries for the remaining identities. Then, we have $\sum_{\mathbf{id} \in (\mathcal{ID})^{Q+1}} \Pr[\mathcal{Q}(\mathbf{id})] = 1$. Let $\delta(\mathbf{id}) = \Pr[\neg \mathcal{ABORT}]$, and δ_{low} and δ_{up} be reals such that $\delta_{\text{low}} \leq \delta(\mathbf{id}) \leq \delta_{\text{up}}$. Then, we have

$$\left| \Pr[W_2] - \frac{1}{2} \right|$$

$$= \left| \sum_{\mathbf{id}} \Pr[\mathcal{Q}(\mathbf{id})] \Pr[W_2 \mid \mathcal{Q}(\mathbf{id})] - \frac{1}{2} \right|$$

$$= \left| \sum_{\mathbf{id}} \Pr[\mathcal{Q}(\mathbf{id})] \left(\Pr[W_2 \wedge \neg \mathcal{ABORT} \mid \mathcal{Q}(\mathbf{id})] + \Pr[W_2 \wedge \mathcal{ABORT} \mid \mathcal{Q}(\mathbf{id})] - \frac{1}{2} \right) \right|$$

$$= \left| \sum_{\mathbf{id}} \Pr[\mathcal{Q}(\mathbf{id})] \left(\Pr[W_2 \mid \mathcal{Q}(\mathbf{id})] \delta(\mathbf{id}) + \frac{1}{2}(1 - \delta(\mathbf{id})) - \frac{1}{2} \right) \right|$$

$$= \left| \sum_{\mathbf{id}} \delta(\mathbf{id}) \Pr[\mathcal{Q}(\mathbf{id})] \left(\Pr[W_1 \mid \mathcal{Q}(\mathbf{id})] - \frac{1}{2} \right) \right|$$

$$\geq \delta_{\text{low}} \left| \Pr[W_1] - \frac{1}{2} \right| - \frac{\delta_{\text{up}} - \delta_{\text{low}}}{2}.$$

The last inequality above follows from Lemma 3, since we have

$$\left| \sum_{\mathbf{id}} \Pr[\mathcal{Q}(\mathbf{id})] \left(\Pr[W_1 \mid \mathcal{Q}(\mathbf{id})] - \frac{1}{2} \right) \right| = \left| \Pr[W_1] - \frac{1}{2} \right|$$

and

$$\sum_{id} \left| \Pr[\mathcal{Q}(id)] \left(\Pr[W_1 \mid \mathcal{Q}(id)] - \frac{1}{2} \right) \right| \leq \sum_{id} \Pr[\mathcal{Q}(id)] \cdot \frac{1}{2} = \frac{1}{2}.$$

From Lemma 5, we have $\delta_{up} - \delta_{low} \leq \eta_{low}\rho/2$. Therefore, defining $\rho :=$ $|\Pr[W_1] - 1/2|$, we obtain

$$\left| \Pr[W_2] - \frac{1}{2} \right| \geq \delta_{low} \left| \Pr[W_1] - \frac{1}{2} \right| - \frac{\delta_{up} - \delta_{low}}{2} \geq \frac{\eta_{low}}{2} \left| \Pr[W_1] - \frac{1}{2} \right|.$$

$\square$

Lemma 6. *For any PPT algorithm* A, *there exists a PPT algorithm* D *such that*

$$|\Pr[W_4] - \Pr[W_5]| \leq \mathsf{Adv}_{\mathsf{GGen},D}^{\mathsf{xdlin}}(\lambda) + \frac{1}{q}. \tag{17}$$

Proof. Let $([\mathbf{A}]_1, [\mathbf{A}]_2, [\mathbf{y}]_1) \in \mathbb{G}_1^{2 \times 3} \times \mathbb{G}_2^{2 \times 3} \times \mathbb{G}_1^3$ be an XDLIN instance, where

$$\mathbf{A} = \begin{pmatrix} a_1 & 0 & 1 \\ 0 & a_2 & 1 \end{pmatrix},$$

$$\mathbf{y} = \mathbf{A}^\top \mathbf{r}^* \text{ or random.}$$

Then, we build a PPT algorithm D with input $([\mathbf{A}]_1, [\mathbf{A}]_2, [\mathbf{y}]_1)$ that simulates the IND-ID-lrCCA game with A as follows.

Setup phase: D generates $pp = ([\mathbf{A}]_1, [\mathbf{B}_0]_1, [\mathbf{B}_1]_1, \ldots, [\mathbf{B}_m]_1, [\mathbf{D}]_1)$ as same as the challenger, except that D computes

$$[\mathbf{B}_0]_1 = [\mathbf{A}\mathbf{R}_0 + \mathbf{I}_2]_1,$$
$$[\mathbf{B}_i]_1 = [\mathbf{A}\mathbf{R}_i + h_i\mathbf{I}_2]_1 \text{ for } i = 1, \ldots, m,$$
$$[\mathbf{D}]_1 = [\mathbf{A}\mathbf{E}]_1.$$

Finally D sends pp to A.

Query phase: D answers for each query from A as follows.

- Key Generation query id. Assume that $\beta_h(id) \neq 0$. D chooses $\mathbf{S}' \leftarrow_{\$} \mathbb{Z}_q^{3 \times 2}$ at random, computes $[\mathbf{S}'']_2 \in \mathbb{G}_2^{2 \times 2}$ such that $[\beta_h(id)\mathbf{S}'']_2 = [-\mathbf{A}\mathbf{S}' + \mathbf{A}\mathbf{E}]_2$, sets

$$[\mathbf{S}_{id}]_2 = \left[\begin{pmatrix} \mathbf{S}' - \mathbf{R}_{id}\mathbf{S}'' \\ \mathbf{S}' \end{pmatrix} \right]_2,$$

and returns $sk_{id} = [\mathbf{S}_{id}]_2$ to A.

- Leakage query (id, f) and decapsulation query (id, ct). If $\beta_h(id) \neq 0$, then D can generate sk_{id} as above. Furthermore, even in that case that $\beta_h(id) = 0$ (i.e., $id = id^*$), D can generate sk_{id} by computing $\mathbf{S}_{id}$ such that $(\mathbf{I}_3 \| \mathbf{R}_{id})\mathbf{S}_{id} = \mathbf{E}$. Thus, D can answer $f(sk_{id})$ and $\mathsf{Decap}(sk_{id}, ct)$ for any identity.

Challenge phase: D generates the challenge $(ct^*, K_b^*) = (([\mathbf{c}^*]_1, [k_a]_T, sd), K_b^*)$
as same as the challenger, except that D computes

$$[\mathbf{c}^*]_1 = \left[\begin{pmatrix} \mathbf{y} \\ \mathbf{R}_{id^*}^\top \mathbf{y} \end{pmatrix}\right]_1$$

instead of $[\mathbf{c}^*]_1 = [\mathbf{F}_{id^*}^\top \mathbf{r}]_1$. Then, D returns (ct^*, K_b^*) to A.

Finally, D outputs $\gamma = [b = b']$ where $b' \in \{0,1\}$ is the output of A.

We will show that the distribution of (ct^*, K_b^*) is the same as the challenge
in $Game_4$ if $\mathbf{y} = \mathbf{A}^\top \mathbf{r}^*$, while if $\mathbf{y}$ is a random it is the same as that in $Game_5$
with overwhelming probability. First suppose that $\mathbf{y} = \mathbf{A}^\top \mathbf{r}^*$. In this case,

$$\mathbf{c}^* = \begin{pmatrix} \mathbf{y} \\ \mathbf{R}_{id^*}^\top \mathbf{y} \end{pmatrix} = \begin{pmatrix} \mathbf{A}^\top \mathbf{r}^* \\ \mathbf{R}_{id^*}^\top \mathbf{A}^\top \mathbf{r}^* \end{pmatrix} = (\mathbf{A}\|\mathbf{A}\mathbf{R}_{id^*})^\top \mathbf{r}^* = \mathbf{F}_{id^*}^\top \mathbf{r}^*,$$

showing that (ct^*, K_b^*) is the challenge in $Game_4$. Next suppose that $\mathbf{y}$ is random
in $\mathbb{Z}_q^3$. It suffices to prove that $\mathbf{z} := \mathbf{R}_{id^*}^\top \mathbf{y}$ is also random in $\mathbb{Z}_q^2$ even given $\mathbf{A}$,
$\mathbf{U} := \mathbf{A}\mathbf{R}_{id^*}^\top$, and $\mathbf{y}$. It is easy to see that

$$\begin{pmatrix} \mathbf{U} \\ \mathbf{z}^\top \end{pmatrix} = \underbrace{\begin{pmatrix} \mathbf{A} \\ \mathbf{y}^\top \end{pmatrix}}_{\mathbf{V}} \mathbf{R}_{id^*}.$$

Therefore, $\mathbf{z}$ is random because $\mathbf{V}$ is of full rank with probability $1 - 1/q$. Hence,
$[\mathbf{c}^*]_1$ is random as expected.

Thus, $Game_4$ and $Game_5$ are indistinguishable under the XDLIN assumption,
so that we have Eq. (17).   □

Lemma 7.
$$|\Pr[W_6] - \Pr[W_7]| \leq \frac{Q_{Dec}}{2^\eta(1 - Q_{Dec}/q)} + \frac{1}{q}. \tag{18}$$

Proof. We assume that all decapsulation queries are made after the challenge
phase, but a similar (but slight simpler) argument can be used if A makes queries
before the challenge phase. Suppose that $(id^*, ct = ([\mathbf{c}]_1, [t]_T, sd))$ is the first
decapsulation query such that $id = id^*$ and the condition at line 13 in Fig. 1
is evaluated. Let $\mathbf{D} = (\mathbf{d}_1\|\mathbf{d}_2), \mathbf{S}_{id^*} = (\mathbf{s}_1^*\|\mathbf{s}_2^*)$, where $\mathbf{d}_1, \mathbf{d}_2 \in \mathbb{Z}_q^2, \mathbf{s}_1^*, \mathbf{s}_2^* \in \mathbb{Z}_q^5$.
Then, we have

$$\begin{pmatrix} \mathbf{d}_1 \\ \mathbf{d}_2 \\ k_a^* \\ k_a \end{pmatrix} = \underbrace{\begin{pmatrix} (\mathbf{A}\|\mathbf{A}\mathbf{R}_{id^*}) & 0 \\ 0 & (\mathbf{A}\|\mathbf{A}\mathbf{R}_{id^*}) \\ \mathbf{c}^{*\top} & \alpha^* \mathbf{c}^{*\top} \\ \mathbf{c}^\top & \alpha \mathbf{c}^\top \end{pmatrix}}_{\mathbf{M}} \begin{pmatrix} \mathbf{s}_1^* \\ \mathbf{s}_2^* \end{pmatrix},$$

where k_a is computed at line 11 in Fig. 1. From the supposition, we can assume
that $\alpha \neq \alpha^*$, $\mathbf{c}^*$ is chosen uniformly at random, and $[\mathbf{c}]_1$ is invalid for id^*. Hence,

the matrix $\mathbf{M}$ is of full rank with probability at least $1 - 1/q$, that implies that the distribution of k_a is random and independent from $\mathbf{D}$ and k_a^*. In addition to $\mathbf{D}$ and k_a^*, A knows at most ℓ bit leakage $\{f(sk_{id^*})\}$ and n bit challenge session key K_b^* that is probable to provide information on the value of k_a to A. Let K_a, F, and I denote random variables induced by k_a, $(\{f(sk_{id^*})\}, K_b^*)$, and $(\mathbf{D}, k_a^*)$, respectively. Given k_a, $(\{f(sk_{id^*})\}, K_b^*)$, and $(\mathbf{D}, k_a^*)$ that A knows, we have

$$\tilde{H}_\infty(K_a \mid F, I) \geq \tilde{H}_\infty(K_a \mid I) - (\ell + n) = \log_2 q - \ell - n$$

from Lemma 1 and the above discussion. Thus, for any k_a, we have $\Pr[K_a = k_a] \leq 2^{\ell+n}/q$. Therefore, in the first evaluation of line 11, the condition $t = k_a$ is satisfied with probability at most $2^{\ell+n}/q$. Now assuming $t = k_a$ is not satisfied, the number of possible k_a decreases one. So, in the i-th evaluation of line 11, the probability that $t = k_a$ holds is at most $2^{\ell+n}/(q - i + 1)$, in the case that $t = k_a$ is not satisfied in all previous evaluations. From the above discussion, we have

$$|\Pr[W_6] - \Pr[W_7]| \leq \frac{Q_{\mathsf{Dec}} 2^{\ell+n}}{q - Q_{\mathsf{Dec}}} + \frac{1}{q}.$$

From Eq. (2), we obtain Eq. (18). □

Lemma 8.

$$|\Pr[W_8] - \Pr[W_9]| \leq \epsilon_{\mathsf{Ext}} + \frac{1}{q}. \tag{19}$$

Proof. In Game$_9$, the challenger returns $\perp$ to A at line 13 in Fig. 1. Hence, A does not learn any information on k_s^* via the decapsulation oracle, since A can only get decapsulation results of valid ciphertexts. Now, A knows $\mathbf{D}$, k_a^*, and $\{f(sk_{id^*})\}$ as information about k_s^*. Then, we show that the min-entropy of k_s^* is at least $\log_2 q - \ell$ with probability at least $1 - 1/q$.

First, we have

$$k_s^* = \mathbf{c}^{*\top} \mathbf{s}_1^*,$$

and then

$$\begin{pmatrix} \mathbf{d}_1 \\ \mathbf{d}_2 \\ k_a^* \\ k_s^* \end{pmatrix} = \underbrace{\begin{pmatrix} (\mathbf{A}\|\mathbf{AE}) & \mathbf{0} \\ \mathbf{0} & (\mathbf{A}\|\mathbf{AE}) \\ \mathbf{c}^{*\top} & \alpha^* \mathbf{c}^{*\top} \\ \mathbf{c}^{*\top} & \mathbf{0} \end{pmatrix}}_{\mathbf{N}} \begin{pmatrix} \mathbf{s}_1^* \\ \mathbf{s}_2^* \end{pmatrix}.$$

The matrix $\mathbf{N}$ is of full rank with probability at least $1 - 1/q$, since $\alpha^* \neq 0$ and $[\mathbf{c}^*]_1$ is uniformly at random. Then, the distribution of k_s^* is random and independent from $\mathbf{D}$ and k_a^*. In addition to $\mathbf{D}$ and k_a^*, A knows at most ℓ bit leakage $\{f(sk_{id^*})\}$ that is probable to provide information on the value of k_s^* to A. Let K_a, D, and F denote random variables induced by k_s^*, $(\mathbf{D}, k_a^*)$, and $\{f(sk_{id^*})\}$ respectively. Given k_s^*, $(\mathbf{D}, k_a^*)$, and $\{f(sk_{id^*})\}$ that A knows, we have

$$\tilde{H}_\infty(K_s^* \mid D, F) \geq \tilde{H}_\infty(K_s^* \mid D) - \ell = \log_2 q - \ell$$

from Lemma 1 and the discussion when ignoring $\{f(sk_{id^*})\}$. Hence $\mathsf{Ext}(K_s^*, sd^*)$ is statistically indistinguishable from an n bits random string because Ext is a $(\log_2 q - \ell)$-randomness extractor. Therefore, we have Eq. (19). □

References

1. Abe, M., Chase, M., David, B., Kohlweiss, M., Nishimaki, R., Ohkubo, M.: Constant-size structure-preserving signatures: generic constructions and simple assumptions. In: Wang, X., Sako, K. (eds.) ASIACRYPT 2012. LNCS, vol. 7658, pp. 4–24. Springer, Heidelberg (2012). https://doi.org/10.1007/978-3-642-34961-4_3

2. Akavia, A., Goldwasser, S., Vaikuntanathan, V.: Simultaneous hardcore bits and cryptography against memory attacks. In: Reingold, O. (ed.) TCC 2009. LNCS, vol. 5444, pp. 474–495. Springer, Heidelberg (2009). https://doi.org/10.1007/978-3-642-00457-5_28

3. Alwen, J., Dodis, Y., Naor, M., Segev, G., Walfish, S., Wichs, D.: Public-key encryption in the bounded-retrieval model. In: Gilbert, H. (ed.) EUROCRYPT 2010. LNCS, vol. 6110, pp. 113–134. Springer, Heidelberg (2010). https://doi.org/10.1007/978-3-642-13190-5_6

4. Alwen, J., Dodis, Y., Wichs, D.: Leakage-resilient public-key cryptography in the bounded-retrieval model. In: Halevi, S. (ed.) CRYPTO 2009. LNCS, vol. 5677, pp. 36–54. Springer, Heidelberg (2009). https://doi.org/10.1007/978-3-642-03356-8_3

5. Brakerski, Z., Kalai, Y.T., Katz, J., Vaikuntanathan, V.: Overcoming the hole in the bucket: public-key cryptography resilient to continual memory leakage. In: FOCS, pp. 501–510 (2010)

6. Brier, E., Clavier, C., Olivier, F.: Correlation power analysis with a leakage model. In: Joye, M., Quisquater, J.-J. (eds.) CHES 2004. LNCS, vol. 3156, pp. 16–29. Springer, Heidelberg (2004). https://doi.org/10.1007/978-3-540-28632-5_2

7. Cheon, J.H.: Security analysis of the strong Diffie-Hellman problem. In: Vaudenay, S. (ed.) EUROCRYPT 2006. LNCS, vol. 4004, pp. 1–11. Springer, Heidelberg (2006). https://doi.org/10.1007/11761679_1

8. Chow, S.S., Dodis, Y., Rouselakis, Y., Waters, B.: Practical leakage-resilient identity-based encryption from simple assumptions. In: ACM CCS, pp. 152–161 (2010)

9. Dodis, Y., Haralambiev, K., López-Alt, A., Wichs, D.: Cryptography against continuous memory attacks. In: FOCS, pp. 511–520 (2010)

10. Dodis, Y., Kalai, Y.T., Lovett, S.: On cryptography with auxiliary input. In: STOC, pp. 621–630 (2009)

11. Dodis, Y., Ostrovsky, R., Reyzin, L., Smith, A.: Fuzzy extractors: how to generate strong keys from biometrics and other noisy data. SIAM J. Comput. **38**(1), 97–139 (2008)

12. Escala, A., Herold, G., Kiltz, E., Ràfols, C., Villar, J.: An algebraic framework for Diffie-Hellman assumptions. In: Canetti, R., Garay, J.A. (eds.) CRYPTO 2013. LNCS, vol. 8043, pp. 129–147. Springer, Heidelberg (2013). https://doi.org/10.1007/978-3-642-40084-1_8

13. Galbraith, S.D., Paterson, K.G., Smart, N.P.: Pairings for cryptographers. Discret. Appl. Math. **156**(16), 3113–3121 (2008)

14. Gandolfi, K., Mourtel, C., Olivier, F.: Electromagnetic analysis: concrete results. In: Koç, Ç.K., Naccache, D., Paar, C. (eds.) CHES 2001. LNCS, vol. 2162, pp. 251–261. Springer, Heidelberg (2001). https://doi.org/10.1007/3-540-44709-1_21

15. Halderman, J.A., et al.: Lest we remember: cold boot attacks on encryption keys. In: USENIX, pp. 45–60 (2008)

16. Halevi, S., Lin, H.: After-the-fact leakage in public-key encryption. In: Ishai, Y. (ed.) TCC 2011. LNCS, vol. 6597, pp. 107–124. Springer, Heidelberg (2011). https://doi.org/10.1007/978-3-642-19571-6_8

17. Hofheinz, D., Kiltz, E.: Programmable hash functions and their applications. In: Wagner, D. (ed.) CRYPTO 2008. LNCS, vol. 5157, pp. 21–38. Springer, Heidelberg (2008). https://doi.org/10.1007/978-3-540-85174-5_2

18. Katz, J., Vaikuntanathan, V.: Signature schemes with bounded leakage resilience. In: Matsui, M. (ed.) ASIACRYPT 2009. LNCS, vol. 5912, pp. 703–720. Springer, Heidelberg (2009). https://doi.org/10.1007/978-3-642-10366-7_41

19. Kiltz, E., Galindo, D.: Direct chosen-ciphertext secure identity-based key encapsulation without random oracles. Theor. Comput. Sci. **410**(47–49), 5093–5111 (2009)

20. Kocher, P., Jaffe, J., Jun, B.: Differential power analysis. In: Wiener, M. (ed.) CRYPTO 1999. LNCS, vol. 1666, pp. 388–397. Springer, Heidelberg (1999). https://doi.org/10.1007/3-540-48405-1_25

21. Kurosawa, K., Trieu Phong, L.: Leakage resilient IBE and IPE under the DLIN assumption. In: Jacobson, M., Locasto, M., Mohassel, P., Safavi-Naini, R. (eds.) ACNS 2013. LNCS, vol. 7954, pp. 487–501. Springer, Heidelberg (2013). https://doi.org/10.1007/978-3-642-38980-1_31

22. Lewko, A., Rouselakis, Y., Waters, B.: Achieving leakage resilience through dual system encryption. In: Ishai, Y. (ed.) TCC 2011. LNCS, vol. 6597, pp. 70–88. Springer, Heidelberg (2011). https://doi.org/10.1007/978-3-642-19571-6_6

23. Lewko, A., Waters, B.: New techniques for dual system encryption and fully secure HIBE with short ciphertexts. In: Micciancio, D. (ed.) TCC 2010. LNCS, vol. 5978, pp. 455–479. Springer, Heidelberg (2010). https://doi.org/10.1007/978-3-642-11799-2_27

24. Li, J., Teng, M., Zhang, Y., Yu, Q.: A leakage-resilient CCA-secure identity-based encryption scheme. Comput. J. **59**(7), 1066–1075 (2016)

25. Micali, S., Reyzin, L.: Physically observable cryptography. In: Naor, M. (ed.) TCC 2004. LNCS, vol. 2951, pp. 278–296. Springer, Heidelberg (2004). https://doi.org/10.1007/978-3-540-24638-1_16

26. Naor, M., Segev, G.: Public-key cryptosystems resilient to key leakage. In: Halevi, S. (ed.) CRYPTO 2009. LNCS, vol. 5677, pp. 18–35. Springer, Heidelberg (2009). https://doi.org/10.1007/978-3-642-03356-8_2

27. Okamoto, T., Takashima, K.: Fully secure functional encryption with general relations from the decisional linear assumption. In: Rabin, T. (ed.) CRYPTO 2010. LNCS, vol. 6223, pp. 191–208. Springer, Heidelberg (2010). https://doi.org/10.1007/978-3-642-14623-7_11

28. Qin, B., Chen, K., Liu, S.: Efficient chosen-ciphertext secure public-key encryption scheme with high leakage-resilience. IET Inf. Secur. **9**(1), 32–42 (2015)

29. Shamir, A.: Identity-based cryptosystems and signature schemes. In: Blakley, G.R., Chaum, D. (eds.) CRYPTO 1984. LNCS, vol. 196, pp. 47–53. Springer, Heidelberg (1985). https://doi.org/10.1007/3-540-39568-7_5

30. Sun, S.-F., Gu, D., Liu, S.: Efficient leakage-resilient identity-based encryption with CCA security. In: Cao, Z., Zhang, F. (eds.) Pairing 2013. LNCS, vol. 8365, pp. 149–167. Springer, Cham (2014). https://doi.org/10.1007/978-3-319-04873-4_9

31. Tomida, J., Abe, M., Okamoto, T.: Efficient functional encryption for inner-product values with full-hiding security. In: Bishop, M., Nascimento, A.C.A. (eds.) ISC 2016. LNCS, vol. 9866, pp. 408–425. Springer, Cham (2016). https://doi.org/10.1007/978-3-319-45871-7_24

32. Yamada, S.: Adaptively secure identity-based encryption from lattices with asymptotically shorter public parameters. In: Fischlin, M., Coron, J.-S. (eds.) EUROCRYPT 2016. LNCS, vol. 9666, pp. 32–62. Springer, Heidelberg (2016). https://doi.org/10.1007/978-3-662-49896-5_2

(Short Paper) A Faster Constant-Time Algorithm of CSIDH Keeping Two Points

Hiroshi Onuki[1]([✉]), Yusuke Aikawa[1,2], Tsutomu Yamazaki[3], and Tsuyoshi Takagi[1]

[1] Department of Mathematical Informatics, University of Tokyo, Tokyo, Japan
{onuki,takagi}@mist.i.u-tokyo.ac.jp
[2] Department of Mathematics, Hokkaido University, Sapporo, Japan
yusuke@math.sci.hokudai.ac.jp
[3] Graduate School of Mathematics, Kyushu University, Fukuoka, Japan
yamazaki.tsutomu.890@s.kyushu-u.ac.jp

Abstract. At ASIACRYPT 2018, Castryck, Lange, Martindale, Panny and Renes proposed CSIDH, which is a key-exchange protocol based on isogenies between elliptic curves, and a candidate for post-quantum cryptography. However, the implementation by Castryck et al. is not constant-time. Specifically, a part of the secret key could be recovered by the side-channel attacks. Recently, Meyer, Campos, and Reith proposed a constant-time implementation of CSIDH by introducing dummy isogenies and taking secret exponents only from intervals of non-negative integers. Their non-negative intervals make the calculation cost of their implementation of CSIDH twice that of the worst case of the standard (variable-time) implementation of CSIDH. In this paper, we propose a more efficient constant-time algorithm that takes secret exponents from intervals symmetric with respect to the zero. For using these intervals, we need to keep two torsion points on an elliptic curve and calculation for these points. We implemented our algorithm by extending the implementation in C of Meyer et al. (originally from Castryck et al.). Then our implementation achieved 152.8 million clock cycles, which is about 29.03% faster than that of Meyer et al.

Keywords: CSIDH · Post-quantum cryptography · Isogeny-based cryptography · Constant-time implementation · Supersingular elliptic curve isogenies

1 Introduction

RSA and elliptic curve cryptosystems will no longer be secure once a large-scale quantum computer is built. Due to this, the importance of post-quantum cryptography (PQC) has increased. In 2017, the National Institute of Standards and Technology (NIST) started the process of PQC standardization [18]. Candidates for the NIST PQC standardization include supersingular isogeny key encapsulation (SIKE) [14], which is a scheme based on isogenies between elliptic curves.

© Springer Nature Switzerland AG 2019
N. Attrapadung and T. Yagi (Eds.): IWSEC 2019, LNCS 11689, pp. 23–33, 2019.
https://doi.org/10.1007/978-3-030-26834-3_2

SIKE is a variant of supersingular isogeny Diffie-Hellman (SIDH), which was proposed by Jao and De Feo [12] in 2011. SIDH uses isogenies between supersingular elliptic curves over a finite field. SIDH achieves an efficient key-exchange but needs to send torsion points of an elliptic curve as supplementary information. Attacks using this information are discussed in by Galbraith, Petit, Shani, and Ti [11] and Petit [20].

Isogeny-based cryptography was first proposed by Couveignes [8] in 1997 and independently rediscovered by Rostovtsev and Stolbunov [21,23]. Their proposed scheme is a Diffie-Hellman-style key-exchange based on isogenies between ordinary elliptic curves over a finite field and typically called CRS. CRS does not need to send any point of elliptic curves, therefore the attacks to SIDH, which is based on information of points of elliptic curves, cannot be applied to CRS. However, even after optimizations by De Feo, Kieffer, and Smith [9], CRS is much slower than SIDH. In 2018, Castryck, Lange, Martindale, Panny, and Renes [3] proposed commutative SIDH (CSIDH), which adopts supersingular elliptic curves to the CRS scheme. They used supersingular elliptic curves over a finite prime field $\mathbb{F}_p$ and their endomorphism rings over $\mathbb{F}_p$. Since the number of $\mathbb{F}_p$-rational points on a supersingular elliptic curve E over $\mathbb{F}_p$ is $p+1$, one can choose p such that $\#E(\mathbb{F}_p)$ has many small prime factors. This allows CSIDH to compute isogenies faster than CRS.

However, the computational time in the proof-of-concept implementation by Castryck et al. depends on the associated secret key, so their implementation of CSIDH is not side-channel resistant. Recently, Meyer, Campos, and Reith [15] proposed a constant-time implementation of CSIDH and several speedup techniques for their implementation. They achieved the constant-time implementation by using dummy isogenies and by changing intervals of key elements from $[-m, m]$ to $[0, 2m]$, where $m \in \mathbb{N}$. Consequently, their constant-time implementation needs to calculate each degree isogeny $2m$ times, while the worst case of the variable-time CSIDH needs only m times. Therefore, the computational cost of their constant-time implementation is twice as that of the worst case of the variable-time CSIDH. The constant-time implementation in [15] allows variance of the computational time of their implementation with randomness that does not relate to secret information.

On the other hand, implementations which do not allow such variance are proposed by Bernstein, Lange, Martindale, and Panny [2] and Jalali, Azarderakhsh, Kermani, and Jao [13]. The implementation in [2] is for evaluating the performance of quantum attacks for CSIDH. It must not have branches in order to compute in superposition on quantum computers. The implementation in [13] is for classical computers, but it has no branches. As a result, it is slower than the implementation in [15]. We discuss the differences in these implementations in Sect. 3.2.

In this paper, we propose a new constant-time implementation, which is faster than the constant-time implementation by Meyer et al. [15]. Our implementation is "constant-time" in the same sense as that of [15]. In other words, the computational time and the order of scalar multiplications and isogenies in our implementation do not depend on a secret key. We use the dummy isogenies proposed by [15]. but do not change the key intervals of CSIDH, i.e., we use the interval $[-m, m]$. To achieve a constant-time implementation without changing the key intervals, we need to keep two torsion points of both $E[\pi-1]$ and $E[\pi+1]$ and calculation associated with these points, where π is the Frobenius endomorphism of an elliptic curve E. As a result, our implementation needs almost twice as many scalar multiplications on elliptic curves and twice as many calculations of images of points under isogenies as the worst case of the variable-time CSIDH. However, the number of calculations of the images of curves is the same as in the worst case of the variable-time CSIDH, and scalars in a part of additional scalar multiplications on elliptic curves are smaller. Therefore, our implementation is faster than the implementation in [15]. We implemented our algorithm in C and compared its cycle count and running time with those of the implementation in [15]. Our experiment shows that the cycle count of our implementation is 29.03% less than that of the implementation in [15].

Organization. The rest of this paper is organized as follows. The following section describes CSIDH. Section 3 explains a constant-time implementation in [15]. and briefly introduces constant-time implementations based on another definition. We give the details of our new constant-time implementation of CSIDH in Sect. 4. In Sect. 5, we present experimental results. We conclude our work in Sect. 6.

2   CSIDH

In this section, we overview the protocol of CSIDH and its mathematical backgrounds. For more details, see Castryck et al. [3].

2.1   Protocol of CSIDH

For describing the protocol of CSIDH, we define the following notations. Let p be a prime number, $\mathcal{CL}(\mathbb{Z}[\sqrt{-p}])$ the ideal class group of $\mathbb{Z}[\sqrt{-p}]$ and $\mathcal{ELL}_{\mathbb{F}_p}(\mathbb{Z}[\sqrt{-p}])$ a set of $\mathbb{F}_p$-isomorphism classes of supersingular elliptic curves whose endomorphism ring is isomorphic to $\mathbb{Z}[\sqrt{-p}]$. Then we can define an action

$$\mathcal{CL}(\mathbb{Z}[\sqrt{-p}]) \times \mathcal{ELL}_{\mathbb{F}_p}(\mathbb{Z}[\sqrt{-p}]) \to \mathcal{ELL}_{\mathbb{F}_p}(\mathbb{Z}[\sqrt{-p}]), \ (\mathfrak{a}, E) \mapsto \mathfrak{a} * E.$$

We call this action the class group action. The details of these notations and the action are described in the next subsection. CSIDH is a Diffie-Hellman style key exchange as follows:

Alice and Bob share an elliptic curve $E_0 \in \mathcal{ELL}_{\mathbb{F}_p}(\mathbb{Z}[\sqrt{-p}])$ as a public parameter. Alice chooses an ideal $\mathfrak{a} \in \mathcal{CL}(\mathbb{Z}[\sqrt{-p}])$ as her secret key and sends the curve $\mathfrak{a} * E$ to Bob as her public key. Bob proceeds in the same way by choosing a secret key $\mathfrak{b} \in \mathcal{CL}(\mathbb{Z}[\sqrt{-p}])$. Then, both parties can compute the shared secret $\mathfrak{a}\mathfrak{b} * E = \mathfrak{b}\mathfrak{a} * E$. Note that $\mathcal{CL}(\mathbb{Z}[\sqrt{-p}])$ is commutative.

2.2 Ideal Class Group

Let p be a large prime of the form $4\ell_1 \cdots \ell_n - 1$, where $\ell_1, \ldots, \ell_n$ are small distinct odd primes. Let $E \in \mathcal{ELL}_{\mathbb{F}_p}(\mathbb{Z}[\sqrt{-p}])$ and π be its p-th power Frobenius endomorphism. Since E is supersingular, the primes ℓ_i split in $\mathbb{Z}[\sqrt{-p}]$ as $(\ell_i) = \mathfrak{l}_i \bar{\mathfrak{l}}_i$, where $\mathfrak{l}_i = (\ell_i, \pi - 1)$ and $\bar{\mathfrak{l}}_i = (\ell_i, \pi + 1)$. It can be seen that the actions of $\mathfrak{l}_i$ and $\bar{\mathfrak{l}}_i$ can be computed efficiently. In the ideal class group, $\bar{\mathfrak{l}}_i$ is the inverse of $\mathfrak{l}_i$, so we can compute the action of an ideal of the form $\mathfrak{l}_1^{e_1} \cdots \mathfrak{l}_n^{e_n}$, $e_1, \ldots, e_n \in \mathbb{Z}$ by the composition of the actions of $\mathfrak{l}_i$ and $\bar{\mathfrak{l}}_i$. Castryck et al. [3] showed that under some heuristics, $\mathfrak{l}_1^{e_1} \cdots \mathfrak{l}_n^{e_n}$, $-m \leq e_i \leq m$ represent uniformly "almost" all the ideal classes in $\mathcal{CL}(\mathbb{Z}[\sqrt{-p}])$, where $m \in \mathbb{N}$ such that $(2m+1)^n \geq \#\mathcal{CL}(\mathbb{Z}[\sqrt{-p}])$. We denote the exponents (e_i) by secret exponents.

3 Previous Works for Constant-Time Implementation of CSIDH

In this section, we explain a constant-time implementation proposed by Meyer et al. [15] and briefly describe related works.

3.1 Constant-Time Implementation

As already mentioned by Castryck et al. [3], their proof-of-concept implementation is not side-channel resistant because the computational time for a public key and a shared secret depends on the associated secret key. To solve this problem, Meyer et al. [15] proposed a constant-time implementation of CSIDH. According to [15], "a constant-time implementation" means an implementation whose computational time and order of scalar multiplications of each size and isogenies of each degree do not depend on a secret key. Their constant-time implementation is described in Algorithm 1.

To achieve a constant-time implementation, they used dummy isogenies and changed the intervals of the integer key elements from $[-m, m]$ to $[0, 2m]$. We explain these techniques below. In this algorithm, one samples a point on an elliptic curve by using Elligator [1] for CSIDH, which was proposed by Bernstein, Lange, Martindale, and Panny [2]. Elligator enables us to generate x-coordinates of points with suitable y-coordinate by computing only one Legendre symbol. For the details, see Bernstein et al. [2].

Dummy Isogenies. It seems that one should compute a constant number of isogenies of each degree ℓ_i and only use the ones required by the secret key. The function for dummy isogenies is designed to use the same operations on $\mathbb{F}_p$ as the function for isogenies. For more details, see [15,16].

Changing the Key Intervals. By using dummy isogenies, the number of isogeny computations is fixed. However, this is not sufficient to achieve a constant-time implementation, since the sizes of the scalar multiplications vary in accordance with the signs of secret exponents. To remove this effect, Meyer et al. [15] proposed changing the intervals from $[-m, m]$ to $[0, 2m]$.

Algorithm 1. Constant-time evaluation of the class group action in CSIDH [15]

Input: $A \in \mathbb{F}_p$, $m \in \mathbb{N}$, a list of integers $(e_1, \ldots, e_n)$ s.t. $0 \le e_i \le 2m$ for $i = 1, \ldots, n$, and distinct odd primes $\ell_1, \ldots, \ell_n$ s.t. $p = 4 \prod_i \ell_i - 1$.
Output: $B \in \mathbb{F}_p$ s.t. $E_B = (\mathfrak{l}_1^{e_1} \cdots \mathfrak{l}_n^{e_n}) * E_A$, where $\mathfrak{l}_i = (\ell_i, \pi - 1)$ for $i = 1, \ldots, n$, and π is the p-th power Frobenius endomorphism of E_A.
1: Set $e_i' = 2m - e_i$ for $i = 1, \ldots, n$.
2: **while** some $e_i \ne 0$ or $e_i' \ne 0$:
3:     Set $S = \{i \mid e_i \ne 0 \text{ or } e_i' \ne 0\}$.
4:     Set $k = \prod_{i \in S} \ell_i$.
5:     Generate a point $P \in E_A[\pi - 1]$ by Elligator.
6:     Let $P \leftarrow [(p+1)/k]P$.
7:     **for** $i \in S$:
8:       Set $Q = [k/\ell_i]P$.
9:       **if** $Q \ne \infty$:   /* **branch not involving secret information** */
10:        **if** $e_i \ne 0$:   /* **branch involving secret information** */
11:          Compute an isogeny $\varphi : E_A \to E_B$ with $\ker\varphi = \langle Q \rangle$.
12:          Let $A \leftarrow B$, $P \leftarrow \varphi(P)$, and $e_i \leftarrow e_i - 1$.
13:        **else**
14:          Dummy computation.
15:          Let $A \leftarrow A$, $P \leftarrow [\ell_i]P$, and $e_i' \leftarrow e_i' - 1$.
16:        **end if**
17:       **end if**
18:       Let $k \leftarrow k/\ell_i$.
19:     **end for**
20: **end while**
21: **return** A.

3.2 Constant-Time Implementations Based on Another Definition

As we stated above, Meyer et al. [15] allow variance of the computational time of their implementation with randomness that does not relate to secret information (caused by the branch **if** $Q \ne \infty$ in line 9 in Algorithm 1). On the other hand, constant-time implementations that do not allow this variance are known. Bernstein et al. [2] constructed a constant-time implementation of CSIDH for evaluating the performance of quantum attacks. For calculating the class group actions in superposition on a quantum computer, a completely constant-time implementation is required. Therefore, their constant-time implementation has no branches (such as **if** branch). Jalali, Azarderakhsh, Kermani, and Jao [13] proposed a constant-time implementation for classical computers, which also has no branches. As a result of removing all branches, these implementations are slower than that of [15]. We propose a constant-time implementation based on the definition in [15], i.e., our implementation allows branches which do not depend on secret information.

4   Our Constant-Time Implementation

In this section, we propose a new constant-time implementation that is faster than that of [15].

The constant-time implementation in [15]. requires the cost to be the same as that of calculating the action of the ideal class corresponding to secret exponents $(2m, \dots, 2m)$. This cost is twice the cost corresponding to secret exponents $(m, \dots, m)$, which is the worst case in the variable-time CSIDH. We mitigate the cost for achieving constant-time by using positive and negative secret exponents.

4.1   Basic Idea

To achieve a constant-time implementation without fixing the signs of secret exponents, we compute isogenies corresponding to positive and negative secret exponents in the same round in the while loop in Algorithm 1. This requires keeping two points of both $E[\pi - 1]$ and $E[\pi + 1]$ and computing scalar multiplications and images under isogenies for both points. This means that our new method needs almost twice as many scalar multiplications and twice as many computations of images of points per isogeny calculation (the reason we need "almost" twice as many scalar multiplications is explained later). However, it needs only one computation for an isogenous curve coefficient. Therefore, the cost of our method is less than twice of the worst case of the variable-time CSIDH. Combining this method and dummy isogenies of [15, 16], we achieve a more efficient constant-time implementation.

4.2   Proposed Algorithm

Our constant-time implementation for computing the class group action is described in Algorithm 2.

In Algorithm 2, the points P_0 and P_1 are k-torsion of $E[\pi - 1]$ and $E[\pi + 1]$, respectively. The indicator s is the sign bit of a secret exponent e_i (line 8), i.e., $s = 0$ if $e_i \geq 0$ and $s = 1$ if $e_i < 0$. This can be computed by bit operations. For example, $s = e_i \gg 7$ if e_i is stored as a signed 8-bit integer. The point Q is ℓ_i-torsion of $E[\pi - 1]$ if $e_i \geq 0$ or of $E[\pi + 1]$ is $e_i < 0$ (line 9). Therefore, the algorithm computes the isogeny corresponding to the sign of e_i in line 13–17. Note that we need a scalar multiplication on P_{1-s} by ℓ_i in line 10 because the ℓ_i-torsion parts of P_0 and P_1 should drop in order to update k to k/ℓ_i. The ℓ_i-torsion part of P_s is Q and drops by the isogeny φ, since Q is in the kernel of φ. In contrast, the ℓ_i-torsion part of P_{1-s} does not drop by φ. We also note that we need to calculate this scalar multiplication even when $Q = \infty$, i.e., one fails

---

Algorithm 2. Our constant-time evaluation of the class group action in CSIDH

Input: $A \in \mathbb{F}_p$, $m \in \mathbb{N}$, a list of integers $(e_1, \ldots, e_n)$ s.t. $-m \le e_i \le m$ for $i = 1, \ldots, n$, and distinct odd primes $\ell_1, \ldots, \ell_n$ s.t. $p = 4 \prod_i \ell_i - 1$.

Output: $B \in \mathbb{F}_p$ s.t. $E_B = (\mathfrak{l}_1^{e_1} \cdots \mathfrak{l}_n^{e_n}) * E_A$, where $\mathfrak{l}_i = (\ell_i, \pi - 1)$ for $i = 1, \ldots, n$, and π is the p-th power Frobenius endomorphism of E_A.

1: Set $e_i' = m - |e_i|$ for $i = 1, \ldots, n$.
2: **while** some $e_i \ne 0$ or $e_i' \ne 0$:
3:     Set $S = \{i \mid e_i \ne 0 \text{ or } e_i' \ne 0\}$.
4:     Set $k = \prod_{i \in S} \ell_i$.
5:     Generate points $P_0 \in E_A[\pi - 1]$ and $P_1 \in E_A[\pi + 1]$ by Elligator.
6:     Let $P_0 \leftarrow [(p+1)/k]P_0$ and $P_1 \leftarrow [(p+1)/k]P_1$.
7:     **for** $i \in S$:
8:         Set s the sign bit of e_i.
9:         Set $Q = [k/\ell_i]P_s$.
10:        Let $P_{1-s} \leftarrow [\ell_i]P_{1-s}$.
11:        **if** $Q \ne \infty$:   /* **branch not involving secret information** */
12:            **if** $e_i \ne 0$:   /* **branch involving secret information** */
13:                Compute an isogeny $\varphi : E_A \to E_B$ with $\ker\varphi = \langle Q \rangle$.
14:                Let $A \leftarrow B$, $P_0 \leftarrow \varphi(P_0)$, $P_1 \leftarrow \varphi(P_1)$, and $e_i \leftarrow e_i - 1 + 2s$.
15:            **else**
16:                Dummy computation.
17:                Let $A \leftarrow A$, $P_s \leftarrow [\ell_i]P_s$, and $e_i' \leftarrow e_i' - 1$.
18:            **end if**
19:        **end if**
20:        Let $k \leftarrow k/\ell_i$.
21:    **end for**
22: **end while**
23: **return** A.

---

to obtain a generator of the kernel of an isogeny. The equation $Q = \infty$ means the ℓ_i-torsion part of P_s has already vanished but does not mean the ℓ_i-torsion part of P_{1-s} has vanished. Therefore, for updating k to k/ℓ_i, we need the scalar multiplication on P_{1-s} by ℓ_i. In contract, in the variable-time CSIDH algorithm, one calculates nothing when $Q = \infty$. This is why we said "we need "almost" twice as many scalar multiplications" in the previous subsection. However, the number of these additional scalar multiplications is much smaller than the total number of scalar multiplications. For example, it is about 2% of the total number of scalar multiplications in CSIDH-512, which is the parameter set for CSIDH proposed by Castryck et al. [3].

Remark 1. The same as in the implementation in [15], we use Elligator for CSIDH. It enables us to generate x-coordinates of P_0 and P_1 in line 5 in Algorithm 2 by computing only one Legendre symbol. For the details, see Bernstein et al. [2].

Remark 2. Our dummy isogeny includes a dummy calculation corresponding to evaluations of P_1 under φ not only of P_0 so that the calculation costs of lines 13–14 and lines 16–17 in Algorithm 2 are the same.

4.3   Security Comparison with the Implementation by Meyer et al.

We claim that the security of our implementation against side-channel attacks is equivalent to that of the implementation in [15]. Although Algorithm 2 contains a conditional branch on secret information, one can replace the branch by conditional swaps and implement it without conditional branches and memory accesses which depend on secret information.

Meyer et al. [15] claimed that their implementation is constant-time in the sense that it can prevent the two leakage scenarios they consider [15, §3]: timing leakage and power analysis. Timing leakage is leaking information on a secret key by the computational time. Power analysis measures the power consumption of the algorithm and determines blocks that represent the two main primitives in CSIDH, scalar multiplications, and isogeny computation. Their implementation prevents these leakage scenarios because the computational time and the order of scalar multiplications of each size and isogenies of each degree in their implementation do not depend on a secret key.

Our implementation also prevents the above two leakage scenarios. Its computational time does not depend on information on a secret key because of dummy isogenies. By calculating isogenies whose exponents have different signs in the same loop, the order of scalar multiplications of each size and isogenies of each degree do not depend on information on a secret key. Furthermore, our implementation has two branches, the same as the implementation in [15]. The first is **if** $Q \neq \infty$ in line 11 in Algorithm 2, which does not involve secret information and affects the computational time (the corresponding branch in the implementation in [15] is in line 9 in Algorithm 1). The second is **if** $e_i \neq 0$, line 12 in Algorithm 2, which involves secret information and does not affect the computational time (the corresponding branch in the implementation in [15] is in line 10 in Algorithm 1). This branch can be removed by using conditional swaps and implemented securely. See the code of [15], that is available at https://zenon.cs. hs-rm.de/pqcrypto/constant-csidh-c-implementation. We note that our implementation switches calculation for isogenies associated to positive and negative secret exponents by the indicator s in line 8 in Algorithm 2, which can be computed by bit operations. There are memory accesses which depend on the secret bit s in line 9–10 in Algorithm 2. But one can implement it securely by using a conditional swap to swap the values of P_0 and P_1. As a result, we conclude that our implementation is constant-time as that of [15].

5   Experimental Results

We implemented our algorithm with the speedup techniques proposed by Meyer et al. [15] in C. For the parameters used for the speedup techniques, see our full paper [19]. Our code is based on the code of [15][1]. (originally from

---

[1]   The code by Meyer et al. is available for download at https://zenon.cs.hs-rm.de/ pqcrypto/constant-csidh-c-implementation. The commit ID of the version we used is 7fc2abdd, the latest version on 15 Feb, 2019.

Castryck et al. [3]). Table 1 shows the cycle counts and running times for our implementation and that in [15] For the implementation in [15], we used the code on which our code is based (the code in the footnote 1). We ran both codes on an Intel Xeon Gold 6130 Skylake processor running Ubuntu 16.04.5 LTS. Our implementation has 29.03% fewer clock cycles than the implementation in [15], which is almost the same as the reduction ratio expected by the evaluation of our cost model.

Table 1. Performance comparison, averaged over 10,000 runs.

	Clock cycles $\times 10^6$	Wall clock time
Implementation in [15]	215.3	102.742 ms
Our implementation	**152.8**	**72.913 ms**

6 Conclusion

We improved a constant-time implementation of commutative supersingular isogeny Diffie-Hellman (CSIDH), which is isogeny-based Diffie-Hellman-style key exchange and a candidate for post-quantum cryptography. Our implementation is based on the constant-time implementation in Meyer et al. [15]. Whereas they used only non-negative key intervals, we used key intervals symmetric with respect to zero. To achieve a constant-time implementation using these intervals, we constructed a new algorithm that keeps two torsion points on an elliptic curve. The additional cost for calculation associated with this point is less than the additional cost in [15] to achieve constant-time. Consequently, our implementation is faster than the implementation in [15]. We implemented our algorithm in C and measuring its clock cycles. The reduction ratio measured by clock cycles is 29.03%.

Acknowledgment. This work was supported by JST CREST Grant Number JPMJCR14D6, Japan.

References

1. Bernstein, D.J., Hamburg, M., Krasnova, A., Lange, T.: Elligator: elliptic-curve points indistinguishable from uniform random strings. In: Proceedings of the 2013 ACM Conference on Computer and Communications Security, pp. 967–980 (2013)
2. Bernstein, D.J., Lange, T., Martindale, C., Panny, L.: Quantum circuits for the CSIDH: optimizing quantum evaluation of isogenies. IACR Cryuptography ePrint Archive 2018/1059. https://eprint.iacr.org/2018/1059 (to appear at Eurocrypt 2019)
3. Castryck, W., Lange, T., Martindale, C., Panny, L., Renes, J.: CSIDH: an efficient post-quantum commutative group action. In: Peyrin, T., Galbraith, S. (eds.) ASIACRYPT 2018. LNCS, vol. 11274, pp. 395–427. Springer, Cham (2018). https://doi.org/10.1007/978-3-030-03332-3_15

4. Cohen, H., Lenstra Jr., H.W.: Heuristics on class groups of number fields. Number Theory Noordwijkerhout **1983**, 33–62 (1984)

5. Costello, C., Hisil, H.: A simple and compact algorithm for SIDH with arbitrary degree isogenies. In: Takagi, T., Peyrin, T. (eds.) ASIACRYPT 2017. LNCS, vol. 10625, pp. 303–329. Springer, Cham (2017). https://doi.org/10.1007/978-3-319-70697-9_11

6. Costello, C., Longa, P., Naehrig, M.: Efficient algorithms for supersingular isogeny Diffie-Hellman. In: Robshaw, M., Katz, J. (eds.) CRYPTO 2016. LNCS, vol. 9814, pp. 572–601. Springer, Heidelberg (2016). https://doi.org/10.1007/978-3-662-53018-4_21

7. Costello, C., Smith, B.: Montgomery curves and their arithmetic. J. Crypt. Eng. **8**(3), 227–240 (2018)

8. Couveigne, J.-M.: Hard homogeneous spaces. IACR Cryptology ePrint Archive 2006/291. https://eprint.iacr.org/2006/291

9. De Feo, L., Kieffer, J., Smith, B.: Towards practical key exchange from ordinary isogeny graphs. In: Peyrin, T., Galbraith, S. (eds.) ASIACRYPT 2018. LNCS, vol. 11274, pp. 365–394. Springer, Cham (2018). https://doi.org/10.1007/978-3-030-03332-3_14

10. Delfs, C., Galbraith, S.D.: Computing isogenies between supersingulrar elliptic curves over $\mathbb{F}_p$. Des. Codes Crypt. **78**(2), 425–440 (2016)

11. Galbraith, S.D., Petit, C., Shani, B., Ti, Y.B.: On the security of supersingular isogeny cryptosystems. In: Cheon, J.H., Takagi, T. (eds.) ASIACRYPT 2016. LNCS, vol. 10031, pp. 63–91. Springer, Heidelberg (2016). https://doi.org/10.1007/978-3-662-53887-6_3

12. Jao, D., De Feo, L.: Towards quantum-resistant cryptosystems from supersingular elliptic curve isogenies. In: Yang, B.-Y. (ed.) PQCrypto 2011. LNCS, vol. 7071, pp. 19–34. Springer, Heidelberg (2011). https://doi.org/10.1007/978-3-642-25405-5_2

13. Jalali, A., Azarderakhsh, R., Kermani, M.M., Jao, D.: Towards optimized and constant-time CSIDH on embedded devices. In: Polian, I., Stöttinger, M. (eds.) COSADE 2019. LNCS, vol. 11421, pp. 215–231. Springer, Cham (2019). https://doi.org/10.1007/978-3-030-16350-1_12. https://eprint.iacr.org/2019/297

14. Jao, D., et al.: Supersingular isogeny key encapsulation. Submission to the NIST Post-Quantum Cryptography Standardization project. https://sike.org

15. Meyer, M., Campos, F., Reith, S.: On Lions and Elligators: an efficient constatntime implementation of CSIDH. IACR Cryptology ePrint Archive 2018/1198. https://eprint.iacr.org/2018/1198 (to appear at PQCrypto 2019)

16. Meyer, M., Reith, S.: A faster way to the CSIDH. In: Chakraborty, D., Iwata, T. (eds.) INDOCRYPT 2018. LNCS, vol. 11356, pp. 137–152. Springer, Cham (2018). https://doi.org/10.1007/978-3-030-05378-9_8

17. Montgomery, P.L.: Speeding the Pollard and elliptic curve methods of factorization. Math. Comput. **48**(177), 24–264 (1987)

18. National Institute of Standards and Technology (NIST): NIST Post-Quantum Cryptography Standardization (2016). https://csrc.nist.gov/Projects/Post-Quantum-Cryptography

19. Onuki, H., Aikawa, Y., Yamazaki, T., Takagi, T.: A faster constant-time algorithm of CSIDH keeping two points IACR Cryuptography ePrint Archive 2019/353. https://eprint.iacr.org/2019/353

20. Petit, C.: Faster algorithms for isogeny problems using torsion point images. In: Takagi, T., Peyrin, T. (eds.) ASIACRYPT 2017. LNCS, vol. 10625, pp. 330–353. Springer, Cham (2017). https://doi.org/10.1007/978-3-319-70697-9_12

21. Rostovtsev, A., Stolbunov, A.: Public-key cryptosystem based on isogenies. IACR Cryptology ePrint Archive 2006/145. https://eprint.iacr.org/2006/145
22. Siegel, C.: Über die Classenzahl quadratischer Zahlkörper. Acta Arith. $1(1)$, 83–86 (1935)
23. Stolbunov, A.: Constructing public-key cryptographic schemes based on class group action on a set of isogenous elliptic curves. Adv. Math. Commun. $4(2)$, 215–235 (2010)

Cryptanalysis on Public-Key Primitives

An Efficient F_4-style Based Algorithm to Solve MQ Problems

Takuma Ito[1(✉)], Naoyuki Shinohara[1], and Shigenori Uchiyama[2]

[1] National Institute of Information and Communications Technology, Tokyo, Japan
{tito,shnhr}@nict.go.jp
[2] Tokyo Metropolitan University, Tokyo, Japan
uchiyama-shigenori@tmu.ac.jp

Abstract. The multivariate public key cryptosystem (MPKC) is a potential post-quantum cryptosystem. Its safety depends on the hardness of solving systems of algebraic equations over finite fields. In particular, the multivariate quadratic (MQ) problem is that of solving such a system consisting of quadratic polynomials and is regarded as an important research subject in cryptography. In the Fukuoka MQ challenge project, the hardness of the MQ problem is discussed, and the algorithms used for the MQ problem and the computational results obtained by these algorithms are reported. The algorithms to compute Gröbner basis for the polynomial set given by the MQ problem are for solving the MQ problem. For example, the F_4 algorithm and M4GB algorithm have succeeded in solving several MQ problems provided by the project. In this paper, based on the F_4-style algorithm, we present an efficient algorithm to solve the MQ problems with dense polynomials generated in the Fukuoka MQ challenge project. We experimentally show that our algorithm requires less computational time and memory for these MQ problems than the F_4 algorithm and M4GB algorithm. We succeeded in solving Type II problems using our algorithm when the numbers of variables are 36 and 37.

Keywords: Multivariate public key cryptosystems ·
Multivariate quadratic problem · Gröbner basis · F_4-style algorithm

1 Introduction

In recent years, the research on quantum computers has been actively developed. It is well known that we can solve both the integer factorization problem and the discrete logarithm problem in polynomial time by Shor's algorithm with sufficiently large-scale quantum computers if such computers exist. The hardness of solving these problems is used to justify the safety of the widely used public key cryptosystems, namely, the RSA cryptosystem and elliptic curve cryptography. Cryptosystems that retain their safety against quantum computers and current computers are called post-quantum cryptography (PQC). There is ongoing development and standardization of PQC around the world.

© Springer Nature Switzerland AG 2019
N. Attrapadung and T. Yagi (Eds.): IWSEC 2019, LNCS 11689, pp. 37–52, 2019.
https://doi.org/10.1007/978-3-030-26834-3_3

The multivariate public key cryptosystem (MPKC) is a potential candidates for use in PQC, and many MPKCs have been proposed [5–7]. The safety of MPKC depends on the hardness of solving systems of algebraic equations over finite fields. Since these systems are usually given by multivariate quadratic polynomials, the problem of solving them is called the multivariate quadratic (MQ) problem.

Algorithms to compute the Gröbner basis, such as the F_4 algorithm [2] and M4GB [4], are used to solve MQ problems. The basic algorithm used in the computation is Buchberger's algorithm. Faugère proposed the F_4 algorithm by improving it. Buchberger's algorithm alternates between the selection of one critical pair and the reduction of the S-polynomial corresponding to that critical pair. On the other hand, F_4 performs iterations in which a certain number of critical pairs are selected and reduced at the same time. In this paper, an algorithm based on the above strategy of the F_4 algorithm is called an F_4-style algorithm. Makarim constructed the algorithm called M4GB which tail-reduces polynomials appearing in the computation, to decrease the space required to store polynomials. The F_4 algorithm and M4GB are suitable for solving MQ problems.

Our Contribution: In this paper, we propose an algorithm for a degree reverse lexicographical order, which is based on an F_4-style algorithm to solve MQ problems by introducing the following three techniques:

- For a fixed degree d, we select critical pairs (g_1, g_2) such that $\deg(\mathrm{LCM}(\mathrm{LM}(g_1), \mathrm{LM}(g_2))) = d$ where $\mathrm{LM}(g_i)$ is the leading monomial of g_i, and reduce S-polynomials corresponding to these critical pairs. Then, if we find the first critical pair whose S-polynomial is reduced to 0, we omit the remaining critical pairs for degree d.
- Our algorithm terminates when we obtain n linear polynomials, where n is the number of variables.
- We introduce a new order of selecting critical pairs.

Our proposed algorithm subdivides the set of critical pairs for a fixed degree d into a smaller set $C_1, \ldots, C_N$ and reduces all S-polynomials for each C_i at the same time. Here, for example, we suppose that all S-polynomials generated from $C_1, \ldots, C_{i-1}$ have been reduced to non-zero, and the first zero-reduction appears at C_i. Then, the above-mentioned first technique means that we omit $C_{i+1}, C_{i+2}, \ldots, C_N$ and start the computations for degree $d + 1$. Therefore, our algorithm might not be able to compute Gröbner basis, and its termination is not guaranteed. However, we actually succeeded in solving MQ problems by our algorithm.

We performed computational experiments to solve MQ problems over the finite fields $\mathbb{F}_{31}$ and $\mathbb{F}_{256}$ using our algorithm and M4GB and experimentally showed that our algorithm requires less computational time and memory than M4GB. We also succeeded in solving Type II MQ problems generated by the

Fukuoka MQ challenge project[1] [8] when the number of variables was 36 and 37, by our algorithm.

2 Preliminaries

In this section we explain the symbols and definitions used in this paper, which are based on M4GB [4]. Let $\mathbb{N}$ and $\mathbb{Z}_{\geq 0}$ be respectively the set of all natural numbers and all non-negative integers. $\mathbb{F}_q$ is a finite field with q elements, and $\mathcal{R}$ is a polynomial ring of n variables on $\mathbb{F}_q$, namely, $\mathbb{F}_q[x_1, \ldots, x_n] = \mathbb{F}_q[x]$. Next, we define monomials, terms and coefficients. A monomial x^a is a product $x_1^{a_1} \cdots x_n^{a_n}$ where the $a = (a_1, \ldots, a_n)$ is an element of $(\mathbb{Z}_{\geq 0})^n$. The total degree of an x^a is $a_1 + \cdots + a_n$ and is denoted by $\deg(x^a)$. We define the set $\mathcal{M}$ of all monomials in $\mathcal{R}$ as $\mathcal{M} = \{x_1^{a_1} \cdots x_n^{a_n} \mid a_1, \ldots, a_n \in \mathbb{Z}_{\geq 0}\}$. For $c \in \mathbb{F}_q$ and $u \in \mathcal{M}$, the product cu is called a term, and then the coefficient of u is c. The set of all terms is expressed as $\mathcal{T} = \{cu \mid c \in \mathbb{F}_q, u \in \mathcal{M}\}$. For a polynomial $f = \sum_i c_i u_i \in \mathcal{R}$ where the $c_i \in \mathbb{F}_q \setminus \{0\}$ and $u_i \in \mathcal{M}$, The sets $\mathrm{Term}(f)$ and $\mathrm{Mono}(f)$ are respectively defined by $\mathrm{Term}(f) = \{c_i u_i \mid c_i \neq 0\}$ and $\mathrm{Mono}(f) = \{u_i \mid c_i \neq 0\}$.

From the point of view of computational efficiency, we deal with a degree reverse lexicographical order $\prec$ in this paper. For a polynomial $f \in \mathcal{R}$, $\max_\prec \mathrm{Mono}(f)$ is called the leading monomial of f, and is denoted by $\mathrm{LM}(f)$. And then, the coefficient $\mathrm{LC}(f)$ corresponding to $\mathrm{LM}(f)$ is the leading coefficient of f, and the product $\mathrm{LT}(f) = \mathrm{LC}(f)\mathrm{LM}(f)$ is the leading term of f. When $\mathrm{LC}(f) = 1$, f is said to be monic. These above definitions for a polynomial in $\mathcal{R}$ are naturally extended to the case of a set $S \subset \mathcal{R}$ as follows: $\mathrm{Mono}(S) = \bigcup_{f \in S} \mathrm{Mono}(f)$, $\mathrm{Term}(S) = \bigcup_{f \in S} \mathrm{Term}(f)$, $\mathrm{LM}(S) = \bigcup_{f \in S} \mathrm{LM}(f)$, $\mathrm{LT}(S) = \bigcup_{f \in S} \mathrm{LT}(f)$.

3 Gröbner Basis and F_4-style Algorithm

We explain an F_4-style algorithm and introduce symbols as well as definitions for the explanation, based on M4GB [4].

3.1 Gröbner basis

Let $G = \{g_1, \ldots g_l\}$ be a finite subset of $\mathcal{R}$. We define $\langle G \rangle$ by the ideal generated by $g_1, \ldots, g_l$. Let $I \subset \mathcal{R}$ be an ideal. Then G represents a basis of I if and only if $I = \langle G \rangle$. Furthermore for all $f \in I = \langle G \rangle$, there exists $g \in G$ such that $\mathrm{LM}(g) \mid \mathrm{LM}(f)$, and G is said to be a Gröbner basis of I. For $f, g \in G$, we declare that f is reducible by g if there exists $u \in \mathrm{Mono}(f)$ such that $\mathrm{LM}(g)|u$; otherwise, f is non-reducible by g. If $t \in \mathcal{T}$ is reducible by g, then g is said to be a reductor of t. These definitions for the polynomial f are naturally extended to the case of set $G \subset R$. If $\exists g \in G$ and f is reducible by g, then f is reducible

---

[1] https://www.mqchallenge.org/.

by G. For all $g \in G$, if f is non-reducible by g, then f is non-reducible by G. We say a subset $G \subset \mathcal{R}$ is a row echelon form if every $g_1 \in G$ is monic and $\mathrm{LM}(g_1) \neq \mathrm{LM}(g_2)$ for any $g_2 \in G \backslash \{g_1\}$. Furthermore, for a row echelon form G, if every $g_1 \in G$ satisfies $\mathrm{LM}(g_1) \notin \mathrm{Mono}(g_2)$ for all $g_2 \in G \backslash \{g_1\}$, then G is the reduced row echelon form.

Let ReduceSel be the deterministic function such that $\mathrm{ReduceSel}(G, m) = h \in G$, where $\mathrm{LM}(h) = \max \{\mathrm{LM}(g) \mid g \in G, m \in \mathcal{M}$ is reducible by $g\}$. This function outputs $g \in G$ such that $\mathrm{LM}(g)|m$ if m is reducible by G. For $f \in \mathcal{R}$ and $G \subset \mathcal{R}$, the FullReduce function to full-reduce f by G is defined as follows: $\mathrm{FullReduce}(f, G) =$

$$\begin{cases} 0 & \text{if } f = 0, \\ \mathrm{LT}(f) + \mathrm{FullReduce}(\mathrm{LT}(f) - f, G) & \text{if } \mathrm{LT}(f) \text{ is non-reducible by G}, \\ \mathrm{FullReduce}(f - \frac{\mathrm{LT}(f)}{\mathrm{LT}(h)} h, G) & \text{otherwise, where } h \leftarrow \mathrm{ReduceSel}(G, \mathrm{LM}(f)). \end{cases}$$

The subsequent Monic function transforms a polynomial to monic and is expressed as follows: $f \in \mathcal{R}$ monic: $\mathrm{Monic}(f) =$

$$\begin{cases} 0 & \text{if } f = 0, \\ \frac{f}{\mathrm{LC}(f)} & \text{otherwise.} \end{cases}$$

The computation of the Gröbner basis consists of computing S-polynomials and reducing them using polynomial sets, which we will now introduce. For a critical pair $p = \{f, g\} \subset \mathcal{R}$, we respectively define $\mathrm{LCM}(f, g)$ and $\mathrm{GCD}(f, g)$ as $\mathrm{LCM}(f, g) = \min_\prec \{m \mid m \in \mathcal{M}, \mathrm{LM}(f)|m, \mathrm{LM}(g)|m\}$ and $\mathrm{GCD}(f, g) = \max_\prec \{m \mid m \in \mathcal{M}, m|\mathrm{LM}(f), m|\mathrm{LM}(g)\}$. The S-polynomial, $\mathrm{Spoly}(f, g)$, of a critical pair $\{f, g\}$ is defined as follows: $\mathrm{Spoly}(f, g) = \mathrm{Left}(f, g) - \mathrm{Right}(f, g)$, $\mathrm{Left}(f, g) = \frac{\mathrm{LCM}(f,g)}{\mathrm{LT}(f)} f$, $\mathrm{Right}(f, g) = \frac{\mathrm{LCM}(f,g)}{\mathrm{LT}(g)} g$.

3.2 F_4-style Algorithm

Here we introduce F_4-style algorithms and explain how they are used to compute the Gröbner basis. For details about F_4, refer to [2]. In the F_4 algorithm, we select critical pairs and construct a matrix with rows that correspond to the Left and Right polynomials of the selected critical pairs and reductors needed to reduce these Left and Right polynomials. We then perform Gaussian elimination on the matrix to compute the S-polynomials and reduce them simultaneously. This reduction is efficient and can be parallelized.

To compute a Gröbner basis, the algorithm used for selecting and reducing critical pairs simultaneously is called an F_4-style algorithm, such as Algorithms 1 and 3, in this paper. For example, Algorithm 1 full-reduces the S-polynomials corresponding to the critical pairs selected at line 4. Many variants of the F_4-style algorithm construct matrices for these polynomial reductions; however, to decrease memory usage, our F_4-style algorithm does not use the matrices. There are several selection strategies for selecting critical pairs at line 4 of Algorithm 1. For example, the normal strategy ([1], p. 225) is often used for F_4 and M4GB.

Algorithm 1. simple F_4-style algorithm

Input: $F = \{f_1, \ldots, f_l\} \subset \mathcal{R}$
Output: A Gröbner basis of $\langle F \rangle$.
 1: $G \leftarrow F$
 2: $P \leftarrow \{\{g_i, g_j\} \mid g_i \neq g_j \in G\}$
 3: **while** $P \neq \emptyset$ **do**
 4:     $P' \leftarrow$ a subset of P
 5:     $P \leftarrow P \backslash P'$
 6:     $H \leftarrow \{\text{FullReduce}(\text{Spoly}(p'), G) \mid p' \in P'\}$
 7:     $\tilde{H} \leftarrow \text{ReductionToRowEchelon}(G \cup H)$
 8:     $H^+ \leftarrow \{\tilde{h} \in \tilde{H} \mid \text{LM}(\tilde{h}) \notin \text{LM}(G)\}$
 9:     $G \leftarrow \tilde{H} \backslash H^+$
10:     **for** $h \in H^+ \backslash \{0\}$ **do**
11:        $P \leftarrow P \cup \{(h, g) \mid g \in G\}$
12:        $G \leftarrow G \cup \{h\}$
13:     **end for**
14: **end while**
15: **return** G

The ReductionToRowEchelon function (Algorithm 2) at line 7 is comparable to Gaussian elimination, as it converts $G \subset \mathcal{R}$ to the reduced row echelon form.

The set P of critical pairs in the F_4-style algorithm (Algorithm 1) may contain many useless elements that ultimately reduce to zero. To select useful pairs, the Update function ([1], p.230) or a checklist of reduced pairs ([1], p.226) is used. The former is used for the F_4 and M4GB. The M4GB employs a set with elements that are critical pairs of leading monomials of polynomials instead of the polynomials themselves. In this paper, we use the latter and explain the reason in Subsect. 4.3.

Based on the F_4-style algorithm, we propose Algorithm 5 for solving MQ problems. To explain Algorithm 5, we convert the algorithm ([1], p. 226) into an F_4-style algorithm (Algorithm 3). Algorithm 3 uses critical pairs of leading monomials instead of polynomials. The G in the line 1 is a row echelon form, and thus each element $g \in G$ satisfies $\text{LM}(g) \notin \text{LM}(G \backslash \{g\})$. In other words, such $g \in G$ corresponds one-to-one with the monomial $m = \text{LM}(g)$ and can be expressed as $G[m]$ appearing at line 11. The M at the line 4 is an associative array for recording the processed critical pairs in the computation. The SelectUpdate function (Algorithm 4) computes a subset P' of P, which is a set of critical pairs, by using a checklist M, and then updates P and M.

4 Proposed Method

In this section we propose an efficient algorithm based on the F_4-style algorithm (Algorithm 3), to solve MQ problems. Our proposed method, Algorithm 5, employs the degree reverse lexicographical order and is suitable for a finite set $F \subset \mathcal{R}$ satisfying

$$\langle F \rangle = \langle x_1 - \alpha_1, \ldots, x_n - \alpha_n \rangle, (\alpha_1, \ldots, \alpha_n \in \mathbb{F}_q). \tag{1}$$

Algorithm 2. ReductionToRowEchelon

Input: $\{g_1, \ldots, g_l\} = G \subset \mathcal{R}$
Output: The reduced row echelon form of G
1: **for** $1 \leq i \leq l$ **do**
2:    **if** $g_i = 0$ **then**
3:       **continue**
4:    **end if**
5:    $g_i \leftarrow \text{Monic}(g_i)$
6:    **for** $1 \leq j \leq l$ **do**
7:       **if** $i = j$ **then**
8:          **continue**
9:       **end if**
10:     **if** $\exists cm \in \text{Term}(g_j)(c \in \mathbb{F}_q, m \in \mathcal{M}) s.t. \ m = \text{LM}(g_i)$ **then**
11:         $g_j \leftarrow g_j - cg_i$
12:     **end if**
13:    **end for**
14: **end for**
15: **return** G

Algorithm 3. F_4-style algorithm

Input: $F = \{f_1, \ldots, f_l\} \subset \mathcal{R}$
Output: A Gröbner basis of $\langle F \rangle$.
1: $G \leftarrow$ ReductionToRowEchelon(F)
2: **if** $0 \in G$ **then** $G \leftarrow G \backslash \{0\}$
3: $P \leftarrow \{\{m_1, m_2\} \mid m_1 \neq m_2 \in \text{LM}(G) \text{ with } \text{GCD}(m_1, m_2) \neq 1\}$
4: $M \leftarrow [\ ] \ // \text{ an associative array}$
5: **for all** $\{m_1, m_2\}$ with $m_1, m_2 \in \text{LM}(G)$ with $m_1 \neq m_2$ **do**
6:    **if** $\{m_1, m_2\} \in P$ **then** $M[\{m_1, m_2\}] \leftarrow$ **false**
7:    **else** $M[\{m_1, m_2\}] \leftarrow$ **true**
8: **end for**
9: **while** $P \neq \emptyset$ **do**
10:    $(P, M, P') \leftarrow$ SelectUpdate(G, P, M)
11:    $H \leftarrow \{\text{FullReduce}(\text{Spoly}(G[m'_1], G[m'_2]), G) \mid \{m'_1, m'_2\} \in P'\}$
12:    $\tilde{H} \leftarrow$ ReductionToRowEchelon$(G \cup H)$
13:    $H^+ \leftarrow \{\tilde{h} \in \tilde{H} \mid \text{LM}(\tilde{h}) \notin \text{LM}(G)\}$
14:    $G \leftarrow \tilde{H} \backslash H^+$
15:    **for** $h \in H^+ \backslash \{0\}$ **do**
16:       **for** $m \in \text{LM}(G)$ **do**
17:          **if** $\text{GCD}(m, \text{LM}(h)) = 1$ **then**
18:             $M[\{m, \text{LM}(h)\}] \leftarrow$ **true**
19:          **else**
20:             $P \leftarrow P \cup \{\{m, \text{LM}(h)\}\}$
21:             $M[\{m, \text{LM}(h)\}] \leftarrow$ **false**
22:          **end if**
23:       **end for**
24:       $G \leftarrow G \cup \{h\}$
25:    **end for**
26: **end while**
27: **return** G

Algorithm 4. SelectUpdate

Input: G a row echelon form, P a set of critical pairs, M an associative array
Output: Updated P, M and P' a set of critical pairs
1: $\tilde{P} \leftarrow$ a subset of P
2: $P \leftarrow P \backslash \tilde{P}$
3: $P' \leftarrow \emptyset$
4: **for** $\{m_1, m_2\} \in \tilde{P}$ **do**
5:    $M[\{m_1, m_2\}] \leftarrow$ **true**
6:    **if** there does not exist $m \in \mathrm{LM}(G)$ with
     $m | \mathrm{LCM}(m_1, m_2)$ and
     $M[\{m_1, m\}] = M[\{m, m_2\}] =$ **true then**
7:       $P' \leftarrow P' \cup \{\{m_1, m_2\}\}$
8:    **end if**
9: **end for**
10: **return** P, M, P'

---

such as finite sets treated in Type I, II, III of MQ challenge. There is no guarantee that our algorithm computes the Gröbner basis of $\langle F \rangle$ because the reduction of some critical pairs is ignored in this proposal. However, we can compute the Gröbner basis with high probability and find the solution of the system of algebraic equations given by F.

Remark 1. When to solve the system of algebraic equations, we usually compute the Gröbner basis with respect to the degree reverse lexicographical order, and then we change this Gröbner basis to the Gröbner basis with respect to lexicographical order by FGLM algorithm [3]. However for the system of algebraic equations corresponding to such an ideal (1), we do not have to use FGLM algorithm.

We next explain the new functions. The NewSelectUpdate function at the line 10 takes at most $N_{\mathrm{spoly}} \in \mathbb{N}$ critical pairs using one method (Subsect. 4.3) and updates P and M. The RestrictedReductionToRowEchelon function at the line 11 reduces G with a set of pairs P'. To operate this function, we reduce H instead of $G \cup H$ in line 13. The RemoveUpdate function in line 29 updates P and M if zero polynomials appear. Finally, the IsSolvedMQ function in line 25 is Algorithm 6, which determines whether or not a solution for the system of algebraic equations given by F can be found. If IsSolvedMQ returns false, it does not necessarily indicate that the solution is not found or G is not the Gröbner basis.

Theorem 1. *Let F be a subset of $\mathcal{R}$ and G be a basis of $\langle F \rangle$. We suppose $G_{\min}$ is the subset of G and appears in the computation by IsSolvedMQ(F, G). If IsSolvedMQ(F, G) returns true, then G and especially $G_{\min}$ are the Gröbner basis of $\langle F \rangle$.*

Proof. We prove that $G_{\min}$ is a Gröbner basis of the ideal $\langle F \rangle$, since G is a Gröbner basis of $\langle F \rangle$ if $G_{\min}$ is also a Gröbner basis of $\langle F \rangle$. First, we prove

---

Algorithm 5. F_4-style algorithm to solve MQ problem

Input: $F = \{f_1, \ldots, f_l\} \subset \mathcal{R}, N_{\text{Spoly}} \in \mathbb{N}$ the number of S-polynomials to be reduced simultaneously
Output: A basis of $\langle F \rangle$
1: $G \leftarrow$ ReductionToRowEchelon(F)
2: **if** $0 \in G$ **then** $G \leftarrow G \backslash \{0\}$
3: $P \leftarrow \{\{m_1, m_2\} \mid m_1 \neq m_2 \in \text{LM}(G)$ with $\text{GCD}(m_1, m_2) \neq 1\}$
4: $M \leftarrow [\ ]$ // an associative array
5: **for all** $\{m_1, m_2\}$ with $m_1, m_2 \in \text{LM}(G)$ with $m_1 \neq m_2$ **do**
6:     **if** $\{m_1, m_2\} \in P$ **then** $M[\{m_1, m_2\}] \leftarrow$ **false**
7:     **else** $M[\{m_1, m_2\}] \leftarrow$ **true**
8: **end for**
9: **while** $P \neq \emptyset$ **do**
10:    $(P, M, P') \leftarrow$ NewSelectUpdate$(G, P, M, N_{\text{spoly}})$
11:    $G \leftarrow$ RestrictedReductionToRowEchelon(G, P')
12:    $H \leftarrow \{$FullReduce(Spoly$(G[m_1'], G[m_2']), G) \mid \{m_1', m_2'\} \in P'\}$
13:    $H^+ \leftarrow$ ReductionToRowEchelon(H)
14:    **for** $h \in H^+ \backslash \{0\}$ **do**
15:      **for** $m \in \text{LM}(G)$ **do**
16:        **if** $\text{GCD}(m, \text{LM}(h)) = 1$ **then**
17:          $M[\{m, \text{LM}(h)\}] \leftarrow$ **true**
18:        **else**
19:          $P \leftarrow P \cup \{\{m, \text{LM}(h)\}\}$
20:          $M[\{m, \text{LM}(h)\}] \leftarrow$ **false**
21:        **end if**
22:      **end for**
23:      $G \leftarrow G \cup \{h\}$
24:    **end for**
25:    **if** IsSolvedMQ(G, F) **then**
26:      **return** G
27:    **end if**
28:    **if** $0 \in H^+$ **then**
29:      $P, M \leftarrow$ RemoveUpdate(P, M, P')
30:    **end if**
31: **end while**
32: **return** G

Algorithm 6. IsSolvedMQ

Input: $F, G \in \mathcal{R}, G \subset \langle F \rangle$
Output: Whether $(\alpha_1, \ldots, \alpha_n) \in \mathbb{F}_q^n$ s.t. $^\forall f \in F, f(\alpha_1, \ldots, \alpha_n) = 0$ is found
1: **if** $\{x_1, \ldots x_n\} \subset \text{LM}(G)$ **then**
2:    $G_{\min} \leftarrow$ the subset of G s.t. $\text{LM}(G_{\min}) = \{x_1, \ldots x_n\}$
3:    $H \leftarrow \{$FullReduce$(f, G_{\min}) \mid f \in F\}$
4:    **if** $H = \{0\}$ **then**
5:      **return true**
6:    **end if**
7: **end if**
8: **return false**

$\langle F \rangle = \langle G_{\min} \rangle$. We then obtain $\langle F \rangle \supset \langle G_{\min} \rangle$ by assumption that $\langle F \rangle \supset G$. Any $f \in F$ can be represented as $f = r_1 g_1 + \dots r_n g_n, g_i \in G_{\min}, r_i \in \mathcal{R}$ by the fact that $\mathrm{FullReduce}(f, G_{\min}) = 0$. Then, F is the subset of $\langle G_{\min} \rangle$, and hence $\langle F \rangle$ is equal to $\langle G_{\min} \rangle$.

Next, if for all $g_1, g_2 \in G_{\min}$, $\mathrm{FullReduce}(\mathrm{Spoly}(g_1, g_2), G_{\min}) = 0$, and then G_{mim} is the Gröbner basis by Theorem 5.48 in [1]. For all $g_1 \neq g_2 \in G_{\min}$, $\mathrm{FullReduce}(\mathrm{Spoly}(g_1, g_2), G_{\min}) = 0$ because $\mathrm{GCD}(g_1, g_2) = 1$ with Lemma 5.66 in [1]. Therefore $G_{\min}$ is the Gröbner basis of $\langle F \rangle$.

In calculating the set $\tilde{G}_{\min} \leftarrow \mathrm{ReuctionToRowEchelon}(G_{\min})$, $\tilde{G}_{\min}$ becomes the shape of $\{x_1 - \alpha_1, \dots, x_n - \alpha_n\}$, and hence $(\alpha_1, \dots, \alpha_n)$ is a solution for the system of algebraic equations given by F.

4.1 Decrease Number of Reductions

In this subsection we explain the method for decreasing the number of reductions in the ReductionToRowEchelon function (Algorithm 2). This method is useful at the end of the computation of the Gröbner basis via F_4-style algorithm, at which point the polynomials of low degree are more frequently used for reduction than those of high degree. We thus avoid reducing high-degree polynomials in Algorithm 2, which will be explained.

For G and the selected set of critical pairs, P', let $m = \max\{\mathrm{LCM}(p') \mid p' \in P'\}$ and $G^- = \{g \mid g \in G s.t.\ \mathrm{LM}(g) \succ m\}$. The RestrictedReductionToRowEchelon function (Algorithm 7) can then avoid reducing G^-. As a result, this algorithm only reduces $G \backslash G^-$. To operate this function, we reduce H instead of $G \cup H$ at the line 5 in Algorithm 5.

Algorithm 7. RestrictedReductionToRowEchelon

Input: $G \subset \mathcal{R}$ a row echelon form, P a set of critical pairs
Output: A row echelon form of G
1: $m \leftarrow m = \max \{\mathrm{LCM}(p) \mid p \in P\}$
2: $G^- = \{g \mid g \in G s.t.\ \mathrm{LM}(g) \succ m\}$
3: $G^+ \leftarrow \mathrm{ReductionToRowEchelon}(G \backslash G^-)$
4: $G \leftarrow G^+ \cup G^-$
5: **return** G

4.2 Remove Pairs

In this subsection, we explain how to avoid reduction to zero with high probability. Regardless of whether a checklist of reduced critical pair M ([1], p. 226), or Update function ([1], p. 230) is used, there are useless pairs generating S-polynomials reduced to zero. For example, these pairs can be observed in almost all computations for solving the MQ problem $n = 20$ and $m = 40$ via F_4, F_4-style or M4GB. The number of these useless pairs tends to increase as n becomes larger. For MQ problems, when we select critical pairs under the normal strategy and a pair reduces to zero ($0 \in H^+$ in Algorithm 3), let d be the minimal degree of the LCM of the pair, while G is the basis, and P is the set of pairs at the time. Through experiments, we confirmed that for all $p \in P$ s.t. $\deg(p) = d$, FullReduce(Spoly(p), G) $= 0$, and many such patterns exist. Hence, we can avoid reduction to zero by using this phenomenon. The RemoveUpdate function (Algorithm 8) removes pairs as described above and updates a set of critical pairs, P, and a checklist, M. If we use this algorithm, some useful pairs may be deleted. Therefore, we do not ensure calculation of Gröbner bases but it is very effective for breaking the MQ challenge.

If it is sufficient to reduce only some S-polynomials, then it would be more appropriate to select those with a lower reduction cost. In fact, it has been experimentally demonstrated that the normal strategy is not optimal for MQ problems. Therefore, we propose a more efficient selection strategy in Subsect. 4.3.

Algorithm 8. RemoveUpdate

Input: P a set of critical pairs, M an associative array, P' a set of critical pairs
Output: Updated P, M
1: $d \leftarrow \min \{\deg(\mathrm{LCM}(p')) \mid p' \in P'\}$
2: $P_d \leftarrow \{p \mid p \in P, \deg(\mathrm{LCM}(p)) = d\}$
3: $P \leftarrow P \backslash P_d$
4: **for** $p \in P_d$ **do**
5:     $M[p] \leftarrow$ **true**
6: **end for**
7: **return** P, M

4.3 Selection Pair Strategy

Here we introduce an effective selection strategy that outperforms the normal strategy ([1], p. 225). For all elements of critical pairs of leading monomials $\{m_1, m_2\}$, we use the following as selection-marking indicators: $u_1, u_2 \in \mathcal{M}$ s.t. Spoly$(m_1, m_2) = u_1 m_1 - u_2 m_2$. We take $\{m_1, m_2\}$ for $\{m_1, m_2\}$ and $\{m_1', m_2'\}$ (Spoly$(m_1, m_2) = u_1 m_1 - u_2 m_2$, Spoly$(m_1', m_2') = u_1' m_1' - u_2' m_2'$), if $u_1 \prec u_1' \vee (u_1 = u_1' \wedge u_2 \prec u_2')$. We apply this selection strategy to the set of pairs, P^+, as follows. First, we take all critical pairs for which that degree of LCM is smallest and obtain the set $P_d \subset \mathcal{M}$. Next, let $P^+ = \{\{m_1, m_2\} \mid p \in P_d$ s.t. ReduceSel$(G, \mathrm{LCM}(m_1, m_2)) = G[m_1] \vee$ ReduceSel$(G, \mathrm{LCM}(m_1, m_2)) = G[m_1]\}$. Lastly, for all $\{m_1, m_2\} \in P^+$, we replace $\{m_1, m_2\}$ with $\{m_2, m_1\}$ if ReduceSel$(G, \mathrm{LCM}(m_1, m_2)) = G[m_2]$. The SelectOne function (Algorithm 9) executes this selection strategy algorithm, while the NewSelectUpdate function (Algorithm 10) takes pairs, at most N_{spoly} with SelectOne, and updates P, M.

Remark 2. In Algorithm 9, if $P^+ = \emptyset$, then for all $\{m_1, m_2\} \in P^-$ is an unnecessary pair.

Algorithm 9. SelectOne

Input: $G \subset \mathcal{R}$ a row echelon form, P_d a set of critical pairs
Output: $\{m_1, m_2\} \in P_d$
1: $P^+ \leftarrow \{\{m_1, m_2\} \mid \{m_1, m_2\} \in P_d, \text{ReduceSel}(G, \text{LCM}(m_1, m_2)) = G[m_1] \vee$
   $\text{ReduceSel}(G, \text{LCM}(m_1, m_2)) = G[m_2]\}$
2: $P^- \leftarrow P_d \backslash P^+$
3: **for** $\{m_1, m_2\} \in P^+$ **do**
4:    **if** $\text{ReduceSel}(G, \text{LCM}(m_1, m_2)) = G[m_2]$ **then**
5:       $\{m_1, m_2\} \leftarrow \{m_2, m_1\}$
6:    **end if**
7: **end for**
8: **if** $P^+ \neq \emptyset$ **then**
9:    select $\{m_1, m_2\} \in P^+ (\text{Spoly}(m_1, m_2) = u_1 m_1 - u_2 m_2)$ s.t.
      $\{m_1, m_2\} \neq {}^\forall \{m_1', m_2'\} \in P^+ (\text{Spoly}(m_1', m_2') = u_1' m_1' - u_2' m_2'),$
      $u_1 \prec u_1' \vee (u_1 = u_1' \wedge u_2 \prec u_2')$
10:    **return** $\{m_1, m_2\}$
11: **end if**
12: $p \leftarrow$ one element selected from P^-
13: **return** p

Algorithm 10. NewSelectUpdate

Input: G a row echelon form, P a set of critical pairs, M an associative array, N_{spoly}
   the number of S-polynomials to be reduced simultaneously
Output: Updated P, M and a set of critical pairs P'
1: $d \leftarrow \min \{\deg (\text{LCM}(p)) \mid p \in P\}$
2: $P_d \leftarrow \{p \mid p \in P, \deg (\text{LCM}(p)) = d\}$
3: $P' \leftarrow \emptyset$
4: **while** $|P'| < N_{\text{spoly}}$ and $P_d \neq \emptyset$ **do**
5:    $\{m_1, m_2\} \leftarrow \text{SelectOne}(G, P_d)$
6:    $P_d \leftarrow P_d \backslash \{m_1, m_2\}$
7:    $P \leftarrow P \backslash \{m_1, m_2\}$
8:    $M[\{m_1, m_2\}] \leftarrow$ **true**
9:    **if** there does not exist $m \in \text{LM}(G)$ with
      $m | \text{LCM}(m_1, m_2)$ and
      $M[\{m_1, m\}] = M[\{m, m_2\}] =$ **true then**
10:       $P' \leftarrow P' \cup \{(m_1, m_2)\}$
11:    **end if**
12: **end while**
13: **return** P, M, P'

Proof. We prove that $^\exists m \in \text{LM}(G)$ such that $m \neq m_1, m \neq m_2$, $m | \text{LCM}(m_1, m_2)$ and $M[\{m_1, m\}] = M[\{m, m_2\}] =$ **true**. There exists $g \in G$ such that for all $\{m_1, m_2\} \in P^-$, $\text{LM}(g) | \text{LCM}(m_1, m_2)$, $g \neq G[m_1]$ and $g \neq G[m_2]$. If the above g does not exist, then $\text{ReduceSel}(G, \text{LCM}(m_1, m_2)) = G[m_1]$ or $G[m_2]$. Therefore, we obtain that the pair $\{m_1, m_2\}$ is in P^+. However, this fact contradicts the fact that $P^+ = \emptyset$. The monomials $\text{LCM}(m_1, \text{LM}(g))$ and

LCM(LM(g), m_2) are not higher than LCM(m_1, m_2) since LM(g)| LCM(m_1, m_2). Hence, we find that $M[\{m_1, \text{LM}(g)\}] = M[\{\text{LM}(g), m_2\}] = \text{true}$.

5 Implementation and Experimental Results

5.1 Well Known Techniques for Polynomial-Ring Arithmetic

In this section we explain two common techniques for polynomial-ring arithmetic to reduce memory usage and computation time. Let $G \subset R$ be a finite set appearing in the computation by an F_4-style algorithm, ultimately resulting in a Gröbner basis. When reducing a polynomial f by $G = \{g_1, \ldots, g_\ell\}$ in this computation, we perform this reduction via the computation of $f - \sum_{i=1}^{k} m_i g_{j_i}$ for some $m_i \in M, g_{j_i} \in G$. A matrix and Gaussian elimination are often introduced to explain how an F_4-style algorithm performs this polynomial reduction. However, the computation using this method and a matrix requires extensive memory since each polynomial $m_i g_{j_i}$ is expanded as a row of the matrix. Instead, the technique we implement prepares two regions h_1 and h_2 and iterate the following computations: $h_1 \leftarrow f, h_2 \leftarrow m_1 g_{j_1}, h_1 \leftarrow h_1 - h_2, \ldots, h_2 \leftarrow m_k g_{j_k}, h_1 \leftarrow h_1 - h_2$. This technique requires significantly less memory usage. The other technique we employ is based on the following strategy for avoiding computation of monomial multiplication as much as possible, since the computational cost of multiplication exceeds that of addition. For instance, when using $c_1 m_1 g_1, c_2 m_2 g_2, c_2 m_1 g_3, c_1 m_1 g_4, c_1 m_2 g_5, (c_1, c_2, \in \mathbb{F}_q, m_1, m_2 \in \mathcal{M}, g_1, \ldots g_5 \in G)$ for the full-reduction of $f \in \mathcal{R}$, we calculate $m_1(c_1(g_1 + g_4) + c_2 g_3) + m_2(c_2 g_2 + c_1 g_5)$.

5.2 Polynomials Compression

In this section, we introduce a method for storing polynomials on memories similar to that in [3]. This method is suitable for treating a dense polynomial set; for example, the set appearing in the computation for solving MQ problems from the Fukuoka MQ challenge by using Algorithm 5. Let $f \in H$ be a polynomial that appears in the computation at line 12. Then, the f is non-reducible by the G existing in line 12, and thus Mono(f) contains no monomial in LM(G). This means that we need the coefficients of non-reducible monomials by the G to express such an f.

This storing method is advantageous for SIMD. A polynomial $f \in \mathcal{R}$ is called tail-reducible by G if $f - \text{LM}(f)$ is reducible by G. To use this storing method, every $g \in G$ must not be tail-reducible by G. However, there are polynomials $g \in G$ that are tail-reducible by G in our proposal; for example, most of $g \in G^-$ in Algorithm 7 are tail-reducible by G. Therefore, we apply this storing method only to $g \in G$, which is used to reduce some polynomials, where this g is not tail-reducible by G. Although miscalculations may occur in solving some MQ problems with our algorithm, no miscalculations exist in our computation to solve the MQ problems from the MQ challenge project.

5.3   Benchmark

In our experiment, we implemented our proposal with gcc v7.3.0 and used a machine with Intel CPU Core i7-7820X 3.60 GHz and 64 GB RAM as a benchmark. Elements in $\mathbb{F}_{31}$ and $\mathbb{F}_{256}$ are represented by 1-byte values in our implementations. For $a, b \in \mathbb{F}_{31}$, the values of $a+b$ and $a \times b$ are respectively computed by $(a+b)\%31$ and $(a*b)\%31$. Meanwhile, for $a, b \in \mathbb{F}_{256}$, the computations of $a + b$ and $a \times b$ are respectively performed by $\mathrm{xor}(a, b)$ and $\mathrm{MultipleTable}(a, b)$ in our normal implementation. MultipleTable is stored the result of $a \times b$ before computing the Gröbner basis. We also generated optimized codes that can be easily implemented. We used AVX2 for $a+b$ ($a, b \in \mathbb{F}_{31}$ or $\mathbb{F}_{256}$) and did not use operator $\%$ in the calculation over $\mathbb{F}_{31}$.

The problems we used in the experiment are the MQ problem generated at random by Algorithm 1 in [8]. $\mathbb{F}_q = \mathbb{F}_{31}, \mathbb{F}_{256}$ and $m = 2n$ is the number of equations. We compared the proposed method with M4GB[2]. Since implementation of M4GB is parallelized, we thus parallelized our code. We measured the real time, CPU time, and memory usage of M4GB and our proposal (normal and optimized). In this context, real time is the time it took to compute, while CPU time is the operation time of CPU. CPU utilization is (CPU time)/((real time) $\times$ (the number of threads of the CPU)) in this paper, and the implementation has satisfactory parallelization performance if CPU utilization is high. The experimental results are as follows (Tables 1, 2 and Figs. 1, 2, 3).

Excepting the CPU time of Fig. 1, which is the computational time of our normal implementation for $\mathbb{F}_{31}$, every computation time for solving an MQ problem via our proposed method is less than that of the M4GB. Furthermore, regarding CPU utilization and memory usage, our implementation is more suitable to MQ problems than the M4GB. In the case of $\mathbb{F}_{256}$, memory usage of our optimized implementation is almost the same as that of our normal implementation; thus, we omit the results of our normal implementation in Fig. 3. Furthermore we experimentally confirm that memory usage over $\mathbb{F}_{31}$ is similar to that over $\mathbb{F}_{256}$. Therefore we print only the results over $\mathbb{F}_{256}$ for M4GB and our optimized code.

5.4   Record of Breaking Fukuoka MQ Challenge Problems

We implemented Algorithm 5 by using the techniques explained in Sects. 5.1 and 5.2 and succeeded in solving two Type II Fukuoka MQ challenge problems, which are defined over the finite field $\mathbb{F}_{256}$ using our implementation and machine with 4 x Intel Xeon CPU E5-4669 v4 2.20 GHz and 1 TB RAM. Our methods required about 25.2 days and about 200 GB of memory to solve the problem with $n = 36$ and $m = 72$, while that with $n = 37$ and $m = 74$ required about 75.7 days and 380 GB.

---

[2] https://github.com/cr-marcstevens/m4gb

Table 1. Benchmark for the $m = 2n$ over $\mathbb{F}_{31}$

n	Total real time (sec)			Total CPU time (sec)			CPU utilization		
	M4GB	Normal	Optimized	M4GB	Normal	Optimized	M4GB	Normal	Optimized
21	22.6	18.5	5.8	210	273	77	0.581	0.922	0.830
22	55.2	46.5	11.5	519	698	155	0.588	0.938	0.842
23	136.0	112.9	25.2	1302	1736	346	0.598	0.961	0.858
24	358.2	284.7	63.1	3766	4308	783	0.657	0.946	0.776
25	813.6	634.2	114.6	7725	9791	1503	0.593	0.965	0.820
26	2217.6	1592.7	226.4	19854	24660	3210	0.560	0.968	0.886
27	6640.5	4591.6	535.1	61788	72532	7910	0.582	0.987	0.924
28	18683.4	12790.4	1354.7	178569	202116	20522	0.597	0.988	0.947
29	53196.9	39646.0	4551.4	546976	630124	70315	0.643	0.993	0.966

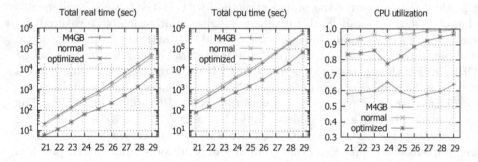

Fig. 1. Results for $m = 2n$ over $\mathbb{F}_{31}$

Table 2. Benchmark for the $m = 2n$ over $\mathbb{F}_{256}$

n	Total real time (sec)			Total CPU time (sec)			CPU utilization		
	M4GB	Normal	Optimized	M4GB	Normal	Optimized	M4GB	Normal	Optimized
21	21.8	9.5	7.1	195	136	97	0.559	0.895	0.854
22	52.2	21.2	14.5	473	313	203	0.566	0.923	0.875
23	128.7	52.4	35.6	1188	785	499	0.577	0.936	0.876
24	334.1	138.0	92.9	3403	1993	1227	0.637	0.903	0.825
25	751.3	291.0	177.0	6952	4337	2414	0.578	0.931	0.852
26	2102.1	683.2	348.8	18319	10421	5047	0.545	0.953	0.904
27	6040.5	1918.1	852.4	55086	30006	12834	0.570	0.978	0.941
28	17315.8	5236.8	2136.8	162366	82154	32557	0.586	0.980	0.952
29	49031.9	16690.7	7812.3	491964	263812	121082	0.627	0.988	0.969

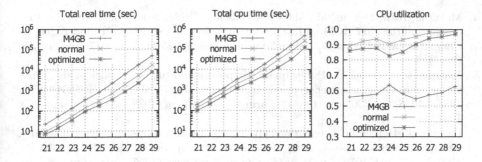

Fig. 2. Results for $m = 2n$ over $\mathbb{F}_{256}$

n	Memory usage (MB)	
	M4GB	optimized
21	118	44
22	229	67
23	360	102
24	755	281
25	1409	414
26	3331	638
27	6750	1091
28	14515	1830
29	28462	3447

Fig. 3. Benchmark for the $m = 2n$ over $\mathbb{F}_{256}$

6   Conclusion

In this paper, we propose the algorithm for solving MQ problems, by introducing three techniques into an F_4-style algorithm. The computational time and memory usage of our algorithm are less than those of M4GB when solving MQ problems. We succeeded in solving Type II of MQ problems provided by Fukuoka MQ challenge project, when the number of variables are 36 and 37, by our algorithm.

References

1. Becker, T., Weispfenning, V.: Gröbner Bases, a Computational Approach to Commutative Algebra. Graduate Texts in Mathematics. Springer, New York (1993). https://doi.org/10.1007/978-1-4612-0913-3
2. Faugère, J.C.: A new efficient algorithm for computing Gröbner bases (F_4). J. Pure Appl. Algebra **139**(1–3), 61–88 (1999)
3. Faugère, J., Gianni, P.M., Lazard, D., Mora, T.: Efficient computation of zero-dimensional Gröbner bases by change of ordering. J. Symb. Comput. **16**(4), 329–344 (1993)

4. Makarim, R.H., Stevens, M.: M4GB: an efficient Gröbner-basis algorithm. In: Proceedings of the 2017 ACM on International Symposium on Symbolic and Algebraic Computation, ISSAC 2017, Kaiserslautern, Germany, 25–28 July 2017, pp. 293–300 (2017)
5. Matsumoto, T., Imai, H.: Public quadratic polynomial-tuples for efficient signature-verification and message-encryption. In: Barstow, D., et al. (eds.) EUROCRYPT 1988. LNCS, vol. 330, pp. 419–453. Springer, Heidelberg (1988). https://doi.org/10.1007/3-540-45961-8_39
6. Patarin, J.: Hidden fields equations (HFE) and isomorphisms of polynomials (IP): two new families of asymmetric algorithms. In: Maurer, U. (ed.) EUROCRYPT 1996. LNCS, vol. 1070, pp. 33–48. Springer, Heidelberg (1996). https://doi.org/10.1007/3-540-68339-9_4
7. Sakumoto, K., Shirai, T., Hiwatari, H.: Public-key identification schemes based on multivariate quadratic polynomials. In: Rogaway, P. (ed.) CRYPTO 2011. LNCS, vol. 6841, pp. 706–723. Springer, Heidelberg (2011). https://doi.org/10.1007/978-3-642-22792-9_40
8. Yasuda, T., Dahan, X., Huang, Y., Takagi, T., Sakurai, K.: MQ challenge: Hardness evaluation of solving multivariate quadratic problems. IACR Cryptology ePrint Archive **2015**, 275 (2015)

How to Solve Multiple Short-Exponent Discrete Logarithm Problem

Kaoru Kurosawa$^{(\boxtimes)}$, Akinaga Ueda, Hayato Matsuhashi, and Yusuke Sakagami

Ibaraki University, Hitachi, Japan
kaoru.kurosawa.kk@vc.ibaraki.ac.jp

Abstract. Let $\mathbb{G}$ be a group of prime order p with a generator g. It is known that one can find $x_1, \ldots, x_L$ from $g^{x_1}, \ldots, g^{x_L}$ in time $O(\sqrt{Lp})$. On the other hand, suppose that $0 \leq x < w$. Then Pollard's kangaroo algorithm (or Pollard's lambda algorithm) can find x from g^x in time $O(\sqrt{w})$. It is used in the decryption algorithm of the homomorphic encryption scheme of Boneh, Goh and Nissim. Now suppose that $0 \leq x_i < w$ for $i = 1, \ldots, L$. This paper shows that we can find $x_1, \ldots, x_L$ from $g^{x_1}, \ldots, g^{x_L}$ in time $O(\sqrt{Lw})$. We further show an application of our algorithm to the model of preprocessing.

Keywords: Discrete log · Pollard's kangaroo algorithm · Multiple variant

1 Introduction

Let $\mathbb{G}$ be a group of prime order p with a generator g. The discrete logarithm problem (DLP) is to find x from g and g^x, and its hardness is a basis of many cryptographic schemes. It is well known that the DLP is solved in time $O(\sqrt{p})$.

A multiple variant of the DLP, the L DLP, is a problem to find $(x_1, \ldots, x_L)$ from $(g, g^{x_1}, \ldots, g^{x_L})$. Kuhn and Struik [8] showed a probabilistic algorithm which can solve the L DLP in time $O(\sqrt{Lp})$ by extending Pollard's rho algorithm. Fouque, Joux and Mavromati [5] showed an improvement of it. Kim (and Tibouchi) [7] showed a deterministic algorithm which can solve the L DLP in time $O(\sqrt{Lp})$ by extending the baby-step giant step algorithm.

Suppose that $0 \leq x < w$. Then the short-exponent DLP is a problem to find such x from g and $y = g^x$. Pollard [9] showed a probabilistic algorithm, called Pollard's kangaroo algorithm, which can solve this problem in time $O(\sqrt{w})$ and with $O(1)$ memory. This algorithm is used in the decryption algorithm of a 2-level homomorphic encryption scheme of Boneh, Goh and Nissim [3]. It is also used in the decryption algorithm of functional encryption schemes for inner products [1,2]. Applications of these encryptions schemes often involve decrypting multiple ciphertexts.

In this paper, we consider a multiple variant of the short-exponent DLP. Namely suppose that $0 \leq x_i < w$ for $i = 1, \ldots, L$. Then the L short-exponent

© Springer Nature Switzerland AG 2019
N. Attrapadung and T. Yagi (Eds.): IWSEC 2019, LNCS 11689, pp. 53–64, 2019.
https://doi.org/10.1007/978-3-030-26834-3_4

Table 1. Variants of DLP

Input	DLP	Short-exponent DLP
g, g^x	$O(\sqrt{p})$	$O(\sqrt{w})$
$g, g^{x_1}, \ldots, g^{x_L}$	$O(\sqrt{Lp})$	This paper

DLP is a problem to find $(x_1, \ldots, x_L)$ from $(g, y_1 = g^{x_1}, \ldots, y_L = g^{x_L})$. This problem has not been studied so far. See Table 1.

We show two algorithms which can solve this problem in time $O(\sqrt{Lw})$, a deterministic one and a probabilistic one. The former is an extension of the baby-step giant step algorithm, and the latter is an extension of Pollard's kangaroo algorithm. The memory space of our deterministic algorithm is $O(\sqrt{Lw})$, and that of our probabilistic algorithm is $O(L)$.

Further we show an application of our probabilistic algorithm to the model of preprocessing. Corrigan-Gibbs and Kogan [6] proved a lower bound of this model such as follows. Let A be a generic algorithm with preprocessing that solves the short-exponent discrete-log problem. If A records S bits as the advice tape in the preprocessing phase, and runs in time T in the online phase and succeeds with probability ϵ, then it must be that $ST^2 = \Omega(\epsilon w)$. We present an algorithm which meets this lower bound with logarithmic factor overhead.

1.1 Related Work

Bernstein and Lange [4] experimentally showed that the short-exponent DLP can be solved in time $O(w^{1/3})$ on average in the online phase if one computes and records a table of size $w^{1/3}$ in the preprocessing phase.

Shoup [10] showed that every generic algorithm which solves the DLP must run in time $\Omega(\sqrt{p})$. Yun [11] showed that every generic algorithm which solves the L DLP must run in time $\Omega(\sqrt{Lp})$.

2   Pollard's Kangaroo Algorithm

Suppose that it is known that $0 \le x < w$. Then Pollard's kangaroo algorithm (or Pollard's lambda algorithm) can find x from g^x in time $O(\sqrt{w})$.

The kangaroo algorithm relies on a deterministic pseudorandom walk. The steps in the walk are pictured as the gjumpsh of the kangaroo, and the group elements visited are the kangaroo's gfootprintsh.

We first generate a gtame kangaroohwhich is a sequence $a_0, \ldots, a_N$ of the footprints generated by the pseudorandom walk with $a_0 = g^w$. We record (a_N, e), where $a_N = g^e$.

We next generate a gwild kangarooh which is a sequence $b_0, b_1, \ldots$ of the footprints with $b_0 = g^x$. Eventually, a footprint of the wild kangaroo will hit a footprint of the tame kangaroo (this is called the gcollisionh). After this point, all the footprints of the two kangaroos are the same. Finally it will happen that

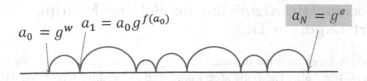

$a_0 = g^w$ $a_1 = a_0 g^{f(a_0)}$ $a_N = g^e$

Fig. 1. Tame kangaroo

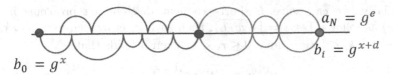

$a_N = g^e$

$b_i = g^{x+d}$

$b_0 = g^x$

Fig. 2. Wild kangaroo

$b_i = a_N$ for some i. Then we can compute x from $a_N = g^e$ and $b_i = g^{x+d}$, where e and d are known values.

Let $m = \lfloor \sqrt{w}/4 \rfloor$ and let $f : \mathbb{G} \to Z_{2m}$ be a pseudorandom function, which we can instantiate in practice using a standard hash function. We use the function f to define a pseudorandom walk on the elements of $\mathbb{G}$. Given a point $a \in \mathbb{G}$, the walk computes $r = f(a)$ and moves a to the point $a \cdot g^r$.

Let $N = \lfloor \sqrt{w} \rfloor$.

(Tame kangaroo generation)

1. Let $a_0 = g^w, e = w$.
2. For $i = 0, 1, \ldots, N - 1$, compute

$$a_{i+1} = a_i g^{f(a_i)}$$
$$e := e + f(a_i)$$

3. Record (a_N, e), where $a_N = g^e$.

(Wild kangaroo generation)

1. Let $b_0 = y \ (= g^x), d = 0$.
2. For $i = 0, 1, \ldots$, do
   (a) Compute

$$b_{i+1} = b_i g^{f(b_i)}$$
$$d := d + f(b_i)$$

   (b) If $b_i = a_N$, then it holds that

$$x + d = e$$

   Hence we can compute x.
   (c) If $d > e$, then output $fail$ and halts.

3 Deterministic Algorithm for Solving Multiple Short-Exponent DLP

If we allow large amount of memory, we can solve the discrete log problem in time $O(\sqrt{p})$ by using the baby step giant step algorithm. Kim (and Tibouchi) extended the baby step giant step algorithm to solve L discrete log problems in time $O(\sqrt{Lp})$ [7].

Similarly, we can solve L short-exponent discrete log problems in time $O(\sqrt{Lw})$ as follows. Let $s = \lceil \sqrt{w/L} \rceil$, then each x_i is written as $x_i = sk_i + r_i$ for some $0 \le k_i < \lceil \sqrt{wL} \rceil$ and $0 \le r_i < s$. Then it holds that

$$y_i = g^{x_i} = g^{sk_i + r_i}$$

and hence

$$y_i g^{-r_i} = g^{sk_i} \tag{1}$$

Therefore we first compute $L + 1$ lists such that

$$G = \{g^s, g^{2s}, \ldots, g^{\lceil \sqrt{wL} \rceil s}\}$$
$$B_i = \{y_i, y_i g^{-1}, \ldots, y_i g^{-(s-1)}\}$$

for $i = 1, \ldots, L$. Next we find $B_i \cap G$ for $i = 1, \ldots, L$, which gives a solution of Eq. (1)

We can compute G in time $O(\sqrt{wL})$, and $B_1, \ldots, B_L$ in time $O(L \times \sqrt{w/L}) = O(\sqrt{wL})$. Therefore we can solve this problem in time $O(\sqrt{wL})$. The memory space is

$$|G| + |B_1| + \ldots + |B_L| = O(\sqrt{wL} + L \times \sqrt{w/L}) = O(\sqrt{wL}).$$

4 Probabilistic Algorithm for Solving Multiple Short-Exponent DLP

In this section, we show a probabilistic algorithm which solves L short-exponent discrete log problems in time $O(\sqrt{Lw})$ by extending Pollard's kangaroo algorithm. The memory size is $O(L)$ only.

4.1 Algorithm

Let $m = \lfloor \sqrt{Lw} \rfloor$ and let $f : \mathbb{G} \to Z_{2m}$ be a pseudorandom function. Let $N = m/2L = \lfloor \sqrt{w/L}/2 \rfloor$.

iL tame kangaroos generation)
Let β be some positive integer (say, $\beta = 20$). [1] For $k = 1, \ldots, L$, do:

---
[1] We assume that Eq. (3) is executed at most $\beta - 1$ times.

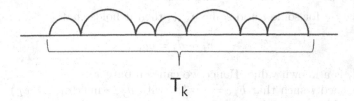

Fig. 3. T_k

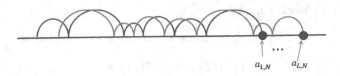

Fig. 4. $T_1, \ldots, T_L$

1. Let $a_{k,0} = g^{w+(k-1)\beta}$.
2. Generate the kth tame kangaroo

$$T_k = (a_{k,0}, \cdots, a_{k,N})$$

   by using the pseudorandom function f.
3. Ideally we want to do the following. If

$$T_k \cap (T_1 \cup \cdots \cup T_{k-1}) \neq \emptyset, \tag{2}$$

   then let $a_{k,0} := g \cdot a_{k,0}$ and goto 1.
   However, it takes a lot of memory to check Eq. (2). Hence we do the following.
   If

$$a_{k,i} \in \{a_{1,N}, \ldots, a_{k-1,N}\}$$

   for some $i \leq N$, then let

$$a_{k,0} := g \cdot a_{k,0} \tag{3}$$

   See Sect. 4.2 for the rationale.
4. Record the endpoint $a_{k,N}$ and e_k such that $a_{k,N} = g^{e_k}$.

   The above algorithm uses $O(L)$ memory.
   In what follows, we assume that all the footprints of $T_1, \ldots, T_L$ are distinct.

¿L wild kangaroos generation)
   For $j = 1, \ldots, L$, do:

1. Let $b_{j,0} = g^{x_j}$, where g^{x_j} is a given instance.
2. Generate the jth wild kangaroo

$$W_j = (b_{j,0}, b_{j,1}, \ldots) \tag{4}$$

   by using the pseudorandom function f.

3. If $b_{j,i} = a_{k,N}$ for some i and some $a_{k,N}$, then it holds that

$$x_j + d_j = e_k,$$

where d_j is a known value. Hence we can compute x_j.
4. If we reached i such that $b_{j,i} = g^{x_j + d_j}$ with $d_j > \max(e_1, \ldots, e_L)$, then we failed. In this case, let $b_{j,0} := g \cdot b_{j,0}$ and goto 1.

4.2   How to Check Eq. (2)

(a) If $a_{k,i} \in \{a_{1,N}, \ldots, a_{k-1,N}\}$ for some $i \leq N$, then it is clear that

$$T_k \cap (T_1 \cup \cdots \cup T_{k-1}) \neq \emptyset.$$

(b) Suppose that (a) does not happen. If $a_{k,i} = g^e$ and $e > \max(e_1, \ldots, e_{k-1})$, for some $i \leq N$, then it is clear that

$$T_k \cap (T_1 \cup \cdots \cup T_{k-1}) = \emptyset.$$

(c) Otherwise $a_{k,N} \notin \{a_{1,N}, \ldots, a_{k-1,N}\}$ and $e_k < \max(e_1, \ldots, e_{k-1})$, where $a_{k,N} = g^{e_k}$. In this case, we have two options.

Option 1. We assume that

$$T_k \cap (T_1 \cup \cdots \cup T_{k-1}) = \emptyset.$$

Option 2. We have the kth tame kangaroo jump N more steps. Hence it jumps $2N$ steps in total. If $a_{k,i} \notin \{a_{1,N}, \ldots, a_{k-1,N}\}$ for any $i \leq 2N$, then we can see that

$$T_k \cap (T_1 \cup \cdots \cup T_{k-1}) = \emptyset.$$

Otherwise we assume that

$$T_k \cap (T_1 \cup \cdots \cup T_{k-1}) \neq \emptyset.$$

We examined option 1 by computer simulation. The average running time of our algorithm with this option almost agreed with our theoretical one. Therefore we adopted option 1 because it is simpler and more efficient.

5   Analysis of Probabilistic Algorithm

We first show the following lemma for our tame kangaroos.

Lemma 1. *On Eq. (2), it holds that*

$$\Pr(T_k \cap (T_1 \cup \cdots \cup T_{k-1}) \neq \emptyset) < 1/2$$

for $k = 2, \ldots, L$.

Proof. We can assume that the value of $f(a)$ is uniformly distributed over $M = \{1, 2, \ldots, 2m\}$ because $f : G \to Z_{2m}$ be a pseudorandom function. For a footprint $a_{k,i} = g^{e_{k,i}}$ of the kth tame kangaroo, consider the next footprint $a_{k,i+1} = g^{e_{k,i+1}}$. Then $e_{k,i+1}$ is uniformly distributed over $X = \{e_{k,i} + 1, e_{k,i} + 2, \ldots, e_{k,i} + 2m\}$.

On the other hand, for $i = 1, \ldots, k - 1$, the step size of the ith kangaroo is also uniformly distributed over M. Hence the mean step size is m. Therefore, on average, there exist 2 footprints of the ith tame kangaroo T_i in X. Consequently there are $2(k - 1)$ footprints of $T_1, \ldots, T_{k-1}$ in X on average.

Now let p_k be the probability that $a_{k,i+1} = g^{e_{k,i+1}}$ does not coincide with any footprints of $T_1, \ldots, T_{k-1}$. Then it holds (heuristically) that

$$p_k = 1 - \frac{2(k-1)}{2m} \geq 1 - \frac{2L}{2m} = 1 - \frac{L}{m}$$

Therefore we have

$$\Pr(T_k \cap (T_1 \cup \cdots \cup T_{k-1}) = \emptyset)$$
$$= p_k^N$$
$$\geq (1 - \frac{L}{m})^N$$
$$\geq 1 - \frac{LN}{m} \quad \text{(by Bernoulli's inequality)}$$
$$= 1 - \frac{1}{2} \quad \text{(because } N = m/2L)$$
$$= \frac{1}{2}$$

Hence

$$\Pr(T_k \cap (T_1 \cup \cdots \cup T_{k-1}) \neq \emptyset) < 1/2.$$

$\square$

We obtain the following theorem from the above lemma.

Theorem 1. *Step 1 $\sim$ step 3 of the L tame kangaroos generation are repeated at most 2 times on average.*

We next show the following lemma for our wild kangaroos.

Lemma 2. *Suppose that W_j of Eq. (4) is generated in such a way that it jumps N more steps from its footprint just after g^w. Then*

$$\Pr[W_j \cap (T_1 \cup \cdots \cup T_L) = \emptyset] \simeq 0.6 \tag{5}$$

for $j = 1, \ldots, L$.

Proof. Without loss of generality, consider the first wild kangaroo W_1. Let $b_{1,i} = g^{d_{1,i}}$ be any footprint of W_1 such that $d_{1,j} > \max(e_1, \ldots, e_L)$. Then $d_{1,i+1}$ is uniformly distributed over $X = \{d_{1,i}+1, d_{1,i}+2, \ldots, d_{1,i}+2m\}$, where $b_{1,i+1} = g^{d_{1,i+1}}$.

Now as shown in the proof of Lemma 1, there are $2L$ footprints of $T_1, \ldots, T_L$ in X on average. Let q_j be the probability that $b_{1,i+1} = g^{d_{1,i+1}}$ does not coincide with any footprints of $T_1, \ldots, T_L$. Then it holds (heuristically) that

$$q_j = 1 - 2L/2m = 1 - L/m$$

Therefore we have

$$\Pr[W_j \cap (T_1 \cup \cdots \cup T_L) = \emptyset] = (1 - L/m)^N \le e^{(-L/m)N} = e^{-1/2} \simeq 0.6$$

because $N = m/2L$.

$\square$

We obtain the following theorem because $1/(1 - 0.6) = 2.5$.

Theorem 2. *Step 1 $\sim$ step 4 of the L wild kangaroos generation are repeated at most 2.5 times on average.*

The expected running time of our algorithm is given by the following theorem.

Theorem 3. *The expected running time of our algorithm is $O(\sqrt{Lw})$.*

Proof. From Theorem 1, the expected running time to generate our L tame kangaroos is given by

$$TIME_1 = L \times 2N$$
$$= m$$
$$= \sqrt{Lw}$$

because $N = m/2L$ and $m = \sqrt{Lw}$. From Theorem 2, the expected running time to generate a single wild kangaroo is given by

$$TIME_2 = 2.5 \times \left(\frac{w}{2m} + 2N\right)$$
$$= 2.5 \times \left(\frac{w}{2m} + \frac{m}{L}\right)$$
$$= 2.5 \times \left(\frac{w}{2\sqrt{Lw}} + \frac{\sqrt{Lw}}{L}\right)$$
$$= O(\sqrt{w/L}) \tag{6}$$

Therefore the total expected running time is given by

$$TIME_1 + L \times TIME_2 = \sqrt{Lw} + O(\sqrt{Lw})$$
$$= O(\sqrt{Lw})$$

$\square$

Finally the memory space is $O(L)$ because we record only the last footprints of the L tame kangaroos.

6 Simulation

6.1 Pseudorandom Function

We define a pseudorandom function $f : \mathbb{G} \to Z_{2m}$ as follows. First, choose $r_0, r_1, \ldots, r_{19}$ from $\{1, 2, \ldots, 2m\}$ randomly in such a way that

$$\frac{r_0 + \ldots + r_{19}}{20} = m \tag{7}$$

Second, define a hash function $H : \mathbb{G} \to \{0, 1, \ldots, 19\}$ as

$$H(a) = a \bmod 20.$$

Finally define $f(a)$ as follows.

1. Let $k = H(a)$.
2. Define $f(a) = r_k$.

In fact, we precompute $R_i = g^{r_i}$ for $i = 0, \ldots, 19$. Then we compute $ag^{f(a)}$ as follows.

1. $k = H(a)$
2. $ag^{f(a)} = aR_k$.

6.2 Time-Out for Wild Kangaroo Generation

If step 1 $\sim$ step 4 of the wild kangaroo generation algorithm are repeated c times for some positive integer c, we have our algorithm output *fail*.

6.3 Simulation Result

We executed our algorithm on a work station PowerEdgeT410 with CPU 2.4GHz and memory 32GB. We used CentOS6.10, C++11 and NTL.

Let p be a prime of 160 bits. For each parameter, we take the average over 100 experiments.

- Fix w as $w = 2^{20}$. Figure 5 shows the average running time for $c = 5, 10, 15, 20$. Figure 6 shows a comparison with our theoretical result (i.e., $\alpha\sqrt{L}$ for some α) for $c = 20$. In both figures, the horizontal axis is L.
- Fix L as $L = 10$. Figure 7 shows a comparison of the average running time with our theoretical result (i.e., $\alpha\sqrt{w}$ for some α) for $c = 20$, where the horizontal axis is the exponent part of w (i.e., $\log_2(w)$).
- Fig. 8 shows the failure probability for $w = 2^{20}$ and $c = 5, 10, 15, 20$.

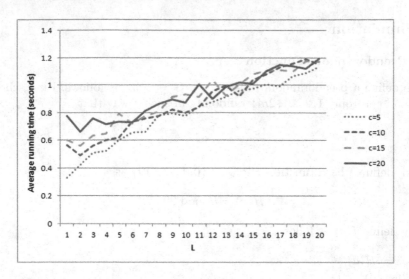

Fig. 5. Average running time for $w = 2^{20}$.

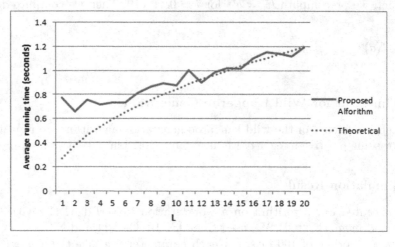

Fig. 6. Comparison with theory for $w = 2^{20}$ and $c = 20$

7 Application to the Model of Preprocessing

In this section, we show an application of our probabilistic algorithm to the model of preprocessing. Corrigan-Gibbs and Kogan [6] proved a lower bound of this model such as follows.

Let A be a generic algorithm with preprocessing that solves the short-exponent discrete-log problem. If A records S bits as the advice tape in the preprocessing phase, and runs in time T in the online phase and succeeds with

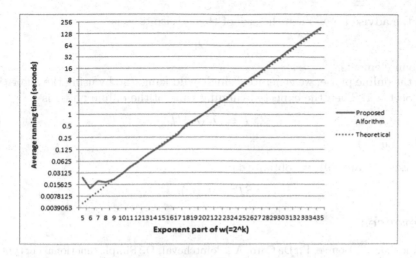

Fig. 7. Comparison with theory for $L = 10$

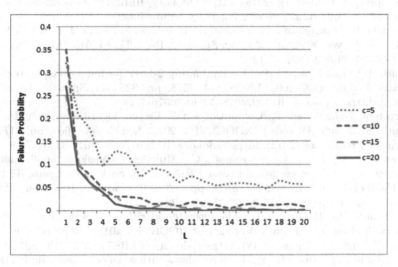

Fig. 8. Failure probability

probability ϵ, then it must be that

$$ST^2 = \Omega(\epsilon w).$$

We present an algorithm which meets this lower bound with logarithmic factor overhead.

1. In the preprocessing phase, we generate L tame kangaroos by using the algorithm of Sect. 4.1. Record the last footprints and their exponents

$$(a_{1,N}, e_1), \ldots, (a_{L,N}, e_L)$$

as the advise tape. Then the size of this advise tape is

$$\tilde{S} = O(L) \tag{8}$$

group elements.

2. In the online phase, we generate a single wild kangaroo by using the algorithm of Sect. 4.1. Then the expected running time of the online phase is

$$T = O(\sqrt{w/L}) \tag{9}$$

from Eq. (6).

From Eqs. (8) and (9), we obtain that

$$\tilde{S}T^2 = O(w).$$

References

1. Abdalla, M., Bourse, F., De Caro, A., Pointcheval, D.: Simple functional encryption schemes for inner products. In: Katz, J. (ed.) PKC 2015. LNCS, vol. 9020, pp. 733–751. Springer, Heidelberg (2015). https://doi.org/10.1007/978-3-662-46447-2_33
2. Agrawal, S., Libert, B., Stehlé, D.: Fully secure functional encryption for inner products, from standard assumptions. In: Robshaw, M., Katz, J. (eds.) CRYPTO 2016. LNCS, vol. 9816, pp. 333–362. Springer, Heidelberg (2016). https://doi.org/10.1007/978-3-662-53015-3_12
3. Boneh, D., Goh, E.-J., Nissim, K.: Evaluating 2-DNF formulas on ciphertexts. In: Kilian, J. (ed.) TCC 2005. LNCS, vol. 3378, pp. 325–341. Springer, Heidelberg (2005). https://doi.org/10.1007/978-3-540-30576-7_18
4. Bernstein, D.J., Lange, T.: Computing small discrete logarithms faster. In: Galbraith, S., Nandi, M. (eds.) INDOCRYPT 2012. LNCS, vol. 7668, pp. 317–338. Springer, Heidelberg (2012). https://doi.org/10.1007/978-3-642-34931-7_19
5. Fouque, P.-A., Joux, A., Mavromati, C.: Multi-user collisions: applications to discrete logarithm, even-mansour and PRINCE. In: Sarkar, P., Iwata, T. (eds.) ASIACRYPT 2014. LNCS, vol. 8873, pp. 420–438. Springer, Heidelberg (2014). https://doi.org/10.1007/978-3-662-45611-8_22
6. Corrigan-Gibbs, H., Kogan, D.: The discrete-logarithm problem with preprocessing. In: Nielsen, J.B., Rijmen, V. (eds.) EUROCRYPT 2018. LNCS, vol. 10821, pp. 415–447. Springer, Cham (2018). https://doi.org/10.1007/978-3-319-78375-8_14
7. Kim, T.: Multiple discrete logarithm problems with auxiliary inputs. In: Iwata, T., Cheon, J.H. (eds.) ASIACRYPT 2015. LNCS, vol. 9452, pp. 174–188. Springer, Heidelberg (2015). https://doi.org/10.1007/978-3-662-48797-6_8
8. Kuhn, F., Struik, R.: Random walks revisited: extensions of Pollard's Rho algorithm for computing multiple discrete logarithms. In: Vaudenay, S., Youssef, A.M. (eds.) SAC 2001. LNCS, vol. 2259, pp. 212–229. Springer, Heidelberg (2001). https://doi.org/10.1007/3-540-45537-X_17
9. Pollard, J.M.: Monte Carlo methods for index computation (mod p). Math. Comput. **32**(143), 918–924 (1978)
10. Shoup, V.: Lower bounds for discrete logarithms and related problems. In: Fumy, W. (ed.) EUROCRYPT 1997. LNCS, vol. 1233, pp. 256–266. Springer, Heidelberg (1997). https://doi.org/10.1007/3-540-69053-0_18
11. Yun, A.: Generic hardness of the multiple discrete logarithm problem. In: Oswald, E., Fischlin, M. (eds.) EUROCRYPT 2015. LNCS, vol. 9057, pp. 817–836. Springer, Heidelberg (2015). https://doi.org/10.1007/978-3-662-46803-6_27

Cryptographic Protocols 1

Secure Multiparty Matrix Multiplication Based on Strassen-Winograd Algorithm

Jean-Guillaume Dumas[1], Pascal Lafourcade[2], Julio Lopez Fenner[3],
David Lucas[1(✉)], Jean-Baptiste Orfila[5], Clément Pernet[1], and Maxime Puys[4]

[1] Univ. Grenoble Alpes, CNRS, Grenoble INP (Institute of Engineering), LJK,
38000 Grenoble, France
{jean-guillaume.dumas,david.lucas,clement.pernet,}@univ-grenoble-alpes.fr
[2] LIMOS, Université Clermont Auvergne, CNRS,
1, rue de Chebarde, 63178 Aubière, France
pascal.lafourcade@uca.fr
[3] Departamento De Ingenieria Matematica, Universidad de La Frontera,
Av. Francisco Salazar, 01145 Temuco, Chile
julio.lopez@ufrontera.cl
[4] Univ. Grenoble Alpes, CNRS, Grenoble INP (Institute of Engineering),
VERIMAG, 38000 Grenoble, France
maxime.puys@univ-grenoble-alpes.fr
[5] Wallix, 250 bis rue du Faubourg Saint-Honoré, 75008 Paris, France
jborfila@wallix.com

Abstract. This paper presents the first recursive secure multiparty computation protocol for matrix multiplication, based on Strassen-Winograd algorithm. We focus on the setting in which any given player knows only one row of both input matrices and learns the corresponding row of the resulting product matrix. Neither the player initial data, nor the intermediate values, even during the recurrence part of the algorithm, are ever revealed to other players. We use a combination of partial homomorphic encryption schemes and additive masking techniques together with a novel schedule for the location and encryption layout of all intermediate computations that preserves privacy. Compared to state of the art protocols, the asymptotic communication volume and computational time is reduced from $O(n^3)$ to $O(n^{2.81})$. This improvement in terms of communication volume arises with matrices of dimension as small as $n = 96$ which is confirmed by experiments.

1 Introduction

Secure multiparty computations (MPC) allows n players to compute together the output of some function, using private inputs without revealing them. This is useful, e.g., for a distributed evaluation of trust, as defined in [12,19]. In this

---

This work is partly funded by the OpenDreamKit Horizon 2020 European Research Infrastructures project (#676541) and the Cyber@Alps French National Research Agency program (ANR-15-IDEX-02).

N. Attrapadung and T. Yagi (Eds.): IWSEC 2019, LNCS 11689, pp. 67–88, 2019.
https://doi.org/10.1007/978-3-030-26834-3_5

context, players compute a confidence level by combining their mutual degrees of trust. This aggregation of trust among players can be represented as a matrix product $C = A \times B$, where each player knows one row of the matrix containing their partial trust towards their neighbors and the network has to compute a distributed matrix exponentiation, which reduces to several matrix multiplications. In this paper we thus focus on this particular layout of data, and on multiparty matrix multiplication of dimension $N \times N$ with N players.

Several tools exist to design MPC protocols, like Shamir's secret sharing scheme [29], homomorphic encryption [15], oblivious transfer [7] or using a Trusted Third Party [10]. Then, several MPC implementations are available[1]. Some of them are for two parties only and most of the others are generic and transform programs into circuits or use oblivious transfer [8,9,18,25,28]. For instance the symmetric system solving phase of the LINREG-MPC software is reported in [14] to take about 45 min for $n = 200$, while, in [13], a secure multiparty specific algorithm, YTP-SS, developed for matrix multiplication, requires about a hundred seconds to perform an $n = 200$ matrix multiplication. These timings, however, do not take into account communications, but for multiparty matrix multiplication, the number of communications and the number of operations should be within the same order of magnitude. Our goal is thus to improve on existing algorithms, primarily in terms of this number of communications (we do not minimize the number of messages, as in [17], but instead consider the overall volume). Our idea is to use an algorithm with a lower time and communication complexity for matrix multiplication. Strassen's algorithm [30] was the first sub-cubic time algorithm, with an exponent $\log_2 7 \approx 2.81$, with a complexity of $O(n^{2.81})$ and we hence construct an MPC protocol based Winograd's variant of this algorithm which carries this improvement over the communication volume.[2] [1, Ex. 6.5].

To preserve the inputs privacy during the computation of a matrix multiplication, the use of homomorphic encryption schemes appears to be natural. While we could use a fully homomorphic encryption scheme, it would slow down the protocol unreasonably. Instead, we will use partial homomorphic encryption scheme [5] as they allow to perform the operations we need, namely:

1. $D_{sk}(E_{pk}(m_1) \times E_{pk}(m_2)) = m_1 + m_2$ *(Additive homomorphism)*
2. $D_{sk}(E_{pk}(m_1)^{m_2}) = m_1 \times m_2$ *(Cipher/clear multiplicative homomorphism)*

Several cryptosystems do satisfy these, e.g., the ones designed by Naccache-Stern or Paillier [26,27]. The former is usually costlier than the latter. However, as the former allow parties to agree on a common message block size, which solves the issue of defining a consistent message space among them, we choose here to use the Naccache-Stern cryptosystem.

---

[1] http://www.multipartycomputation.com/mpc-software.

[2] The best value known to date, due to LeGall's [23], of approximately 2.3728639. However, only a few sub-cubic time algorithms are competitive in practice and used in software [3,11,21] (see also [22] and references therein), among which Strassen's algorithm and its variants stand out as a very effective one in practice.

Finally, Strassen-Winograd algorithm involves numerous additions and subtractions on parts of the A and B matrices that are held by different players. Security concerns require then that these entries should be encrypted from the start, contrarily to [13]. As a consequence, the classical matrix multiplication can no longer be used as stated in the latter reference, even for the base case of the recursive algorithm. We therefore propose an alternative base case. Its arithmetic cost is higher, but it involves an equivalent amount of communication. We shall show that this choice combined with our multiparty recursive Strassen-Winograd algorithm compares favorably to existing implementations in communication cost for matrices of dimensions larger than $N = 96$.

As Strassen-Winograd algorithm trades multiplications for additions, and as homomorphic additions are cheaper than multiplications, this algorithm is a very good candidate for a multiparty protocol using homomorphic techniques.

Hypotheses. In this paper, we will only consider the case of *semi-honest* (also called *honest-but-curious*) adversaries. Such adversaries, represented as probabilistic polynomial time machines, try to gather as many information as possible during the execution of the protocol, and can locally run any computation based on this information in order to deduce some private input. However, they strictly follow protocol specifications. We also consider that *communications are performed over secure channels*: this means transferred data is resistant to eavesdropping and that only the recipient will learn anything from communicated data.

Contributions. We propose an instance of Strassen-Winograd's algorithm in a secure multiparty computation setting, which, to our knowledge, will be the first recursive SMC protocol, where the input and output matrices are split and shared row-wise. More precisely, this paper presents the following contributions:

1. A reduction of the overall amount of communication from $O(N^3)$ to $O(N^{2.801})$ for the multiparty multiplication of $N \times N$ matrices;
2. A recursive protocol proven secure against one semi-honest adversary;
3. A schedule of the operations of Strassen-Winograd's algorithm and of a classic matrix multiplication algorithm compliant with a privacy-preserving location and encryption data-layout;
4. This improvement is confirmed by experiments showing advantages of this approach over alternative implementations of MPC matrix multiplication protocols.

The article proceeds as follows: Sect. 2 presents Strassen-Winograd and the competitor YTP-SS algorithms. There, we also define the dedicated data layout and the cryptographic tools we will use. Next, in Sect. 3, we first describe our building block protocols, with their security analysis. Second, we present in this Section a new cubic-time matrix multiplication algorithm on ciphered entries to be used as a base case. Section 4 describes the complete novel sub-cubic MPC Strassen-Winograd algorithm and details its theoretical communication cost. Finally, Sect. 5 closes with practical comparisons between our C++ and competitor implementations.

2 Preliminaries

2.1 Strassen-Winograd Algorithm

Strassen-Winograd algorithm computes $C = A \times B$ by splitting the input matrices in four quadrants of equal dimensions: $A = \left[\begin{smallmatrix} A_{11} & A_{12} \\ A_{21} & A_{22} \end{smallmatrix} \right]$ and $B = \left[\begin{smallmatrix} B_{11} & B_{12} \\ B_{21} & B_{22} \end{smallmatrix} \right]$. Each recursive call consists in 22 block operations:

- 8 additions:

$$S_1 \leftarrow A_{21} + A_{22} \quad S_2 \leftarrow S_1 - A_{11} \quad S_3 \leftarrow A_{11} - A_{21} \quad S_4 \leftarrow A_{12} - S_2$$
$$T_1 \leftarrow B_{12} - B_{11} \quad T_2 \leftarrow B_{22} - T_1 \quad T_3 \leftarrow B_{22} - B_{12} \quad T_4 \leftarrow T_2 - B_{21}$$

- 7 recursive multiplications:

$$R_1 \leftarrow A_{11} \times B_{11} \quad R_2 \leftarrow A_{12} \times B_{21} \quad R_3 \leftarrow S_4 \times B_{22} \quad R_4 \leftarrow A_{22} \times T_4$$
$$R_5 \leftarrow S_1 \times T_1 \quad R_6 \leftarrow S_2 \times T_2 \quad R_7 \leftarrow S_3 \times T_3$$

- 7 final additions:

$$U_1 \leftarrow R_1 + R_2 \quad U_2 \leftarrow R_1 + R_6 \quad U_3 \leftarrow U_2 + R_7 \quad U_4 \leftarrow U_2 + R_5$$
$$U_5 \leftarrow U_4 + R_3 \quad U_6 \leftarrow U_3 - R_4 \quad U_7 \leftarrow U_3 + R_5$$

- The result is the matrix: $C = \left[\begin{smallmatrix} U_1 & U_5 \\ U_6 & U_7 \end{smallmatrix} \right]$.

Although the recursion could be run down to products of 1×1 matrices, it is commonly stopped at a fixed dimension threshold, where a classical cubic time algorithm is then used, in order to reduce the overhead of recursion on small dimension instances. For the sake of simplicity, we consider henceforth that the initial input matrices are of dimension $N \times N$, with $N = b2^{\ell}$, so that up to ℓ recursive calls can be made without having to deal with padding with zeroes nor with peeling thin rows or columns.

2.2 Data Layout and Encryption

We consider the setting where the two input matrices A and B have dimension $N \times N$ and each of the N players stores one row of A and the corresponding row of B and learns the corresponding row of $C = A \times B$. In this setting, the YTP-SS Algorithm [13, Algorithm 15] can compute C by encrypting the rows of A only and then relying on homomorphic multiplications of encrypted coefficients of A by plain coefficients of B.

However, Strassen's algorithm, considered here, requires adding and subtracting submatrices of B of distinct row index sets (e.g. $T_3 \leftarrow B_{22} - B_{12}$). These operations on non-ciphered rows of B would automatically leak information. We therefore impose that the rows of both operands A and B, of the result C and of any intermediate matrix are encrypted by the public key of a player who is not the one hosting the row. We therefore introduce the notion of location and key sequences for a matrix, to identify the roles of the players in this data layout:

Definition 1. *An* $n \times n$ *matrix* A *of* ciphered values *has location sequence* $L = (l_1, l_2, \ldots, l_n)$ *and key sequence* $K = (k_1, k_2, \ldots, k_n)$ *if player* P_{l_i} *stores row* i *of* A, *that was encrypted with the public key* pk_{k_i} *of player* P_{k_i} *for all* $1 \leq i \leq n$.

Example 1. For $n = 3$, consider the location sequence $L = (2, 3, 1)$ and key sequence $K = (3, 1, 2)$. This means that player P_2 stores row 1 of A encrypted with the public key of player P_3; player P_3 stores row 2 of A encrypted with the public key of player P_1 and finally player P_1 stores row 3 of A encrypted with the public key of player P_2.

In the matrix multiplication algorithms presented in the later sections, the location and key sequences of operand A and C will always be identical. On the other hand the location and key sequences of B may equal those of A (in the first recursive call), or differ, but then they must have an empty intersection with those of A.

A recursive step in Strassen-Winograd algorithm splits the matrices A, B and C into four quadrants of equal dimensions. Hence their key and location sequences are split into two sub-sequences: for $X \in \{A, B, C\}$, $L_X = (L_{X_U}, L_{X_L})$ and $K_X = (K_{X_U}, K_{X_L})$ such that (L_{X_U}, K_{X_U}) are the location and key sequences for the upper half of X and (L_{X_L}, K_{X_L}) are the location and key sequences for the lower half of X.

Figure 1 summarizes the notations we use on the input/output operands in Strassen-Winograd algorithm.

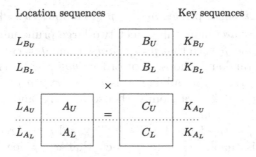

Fig. 1. Recursive splitting of the location and key sequences of the input and output operands in Strassen-Winograd algorithm.

More formally, we present in Definition 2 the two distinct data layouts used in our algorithms: one for the recursive levels of Strassen-Winograd, and one for its base case.

Definition 2. *Let* $N \in \mathbb{N}$, $n \leq N$ *and* A *and* B *two* $n \times n$ *matrices with location and key sequences* $(L_A, K_A) \in (\{1..N\}^n)^2$ *and* $(L_B, K_B) \in (\{1..N\}^n)^2$.

1. (L_A, K_A, L_B, K_B) *is a valid data layout if*
   (a) $\forall i \in \{1..n\}$, $L_A[i] \neq K_A[i]$ *and* $L_B[i] \neq K_B[i]$.

(b) $\forall i, j \in \{1..n\}$ with $i \neq j$, $L_A[i] \neq L_A[j]$ and $L_B[i] \neq L_B[j]$
(c) $\forall i, j \in \{1..n\}$ with $i \neq j$, $K_A[i] \neq K_A[j]$ and $K_B[i] \neq K_B[j]$

2. (L_A, K_A, L_B, K_B) is a base case or a 0-recursive data layout if it is a valid data layout and $(L_A \cup K_A) \cap (L_B \cup K_B) = \emptyset$.

3. (L_A, K_A, L_B, K_B) is a ℓ-recursive data layout if it is a valid data layout and
   (a) $(L_{A_U} \cup K_{A_U}) \cap (L_{A_L} \cup K_{A_L}) = \emptyset = (L_{B_U} \cup K_{B_U}) \cap (L_{B_L} \cup K_{B_L})$
   (b) $(L_{A_U}, K_{A_U}, L_{B_L}, K_{B_L})$ and $(L_{A_L}, K_{A_L}, L_{B_U}, K_{B_U})$ are both $(\ell - 1)$-recursive data layouts

Lemma 1. *For $N = b2^\ell$, the following values for the location and key sequences form an ℓ-recursive data layout according to Definition 2:*

$$\begin{cases} k_i & = i & \text{for } 0 \leq i < N \\ l_{ib+j} = ib + (j+1) \mod b) & \text{for } 0 \leq i < N/b, \text{ and } 0 \leq j < b \end{cases} \tag{1}$$

For instance, for a product of dimension 12, with base case dimension $b = 3$, this gives; $L_A = L_B = L_C = (1, 2, 0, 4, 5, 3, 7, 8, 6, 11, 9, 10)$ and $K_A = K_B = K_C = (0, 1, 2, 3, 4, 5, 6, 7, 8, 9, 10, 11)$.

2.3 Homomorphic Encryption

Naccache-Stern Cryptosystem. In the following, we use Naccache-Stern [26] partially homomorphic cryptosystem, with security parameter 1^λ, set up as follows:

Setup(1^λ): Select $2k$ small primes $p_1, \ldots, p_{2k}$; compute $u = \prod_{i=1}^{k} p_i$ and $v = \prod_{i=k+1}^{2k} p_i$; let $\sigma = u \cdot v$; uniformly select two large prime numbers a and b of size $\lambda/2$; find f_1 and f_2 such that $p = f_1 \cdot a \cdot u + 1$ and $q = f_2 \cdot b \cdot v + 1$ are primes; let $m = p \cdot q$ and randomly choose g of order $aubv$ in $\mathbb{Z}_m^*$. The private key is $SK = (p_1, \ldots, p_{2k}, p, q)$, the public key is $PK = (\sigma, g, m)$.

Encrypt$_{PK}(x)$: for $x \in \mathbb{Z}_\sigma$, randomly choose $r \in \mathbb{Z}_m$ and encrypt x as $c = E_{PK}(x) \equiv r^\sigma \cdot g^x \mod m$.

Decrypt$_{SK}(c)$: let $\phi = (p-1)(q-1)$, $c_i \equiv c^{\phi/p_i} \mod m$ and recover, by exhaustive search (p_i is small), $x_i \mod p_i$ such that $x_i = \log_{g^{\phi/p_i}}(c_i) \mod m$. Finally reconstruct x with the Chinese remaindering, $x \equiv CRT(\{x_i, p_i\}) \mod \sigma$.

In the following, cleartexts will be elements of $\mathbb{Z}_\sigma$ while ciphertexts are elements of $\mathbb{Z}_m$. Note that while σ is shared by all players, there is a distinct modulus $\mathbb{Z}_m$ for each player, otherwise they would have to share their private keys. Consequently a plain text matrix has coefficients in $\mathbb{Z}_\sigma$ but in a layout where each row is encrypted using a different key pk_i, its encryption is no longer a matrix but a sequence of rows over distinct rings $\mathbb{Z}_{m_{pk_i}}$. We will abusively refer to this ciphered data as the ciphered matrix.

Notations. Given some scalar u and a player A, we denote by $\{u\}_A$, as a shortcut to $\{u\}_{pk_A}$, the encryption of data u with the public key of A. This is an element of $\mathbb{Z}_{m_A}$. Similarly, we also denote by $E_A(u)$ the action of encrypting the data u using the public key of A (this means that the player generating this cipher-text knows the plaintext u. For a key sequence K and a matrix A over $\mathbb{Z}_\sigma$, the ciphered matrix obtained by encrypting row i of A by $K[i]$ is denoted by $\{A\}_K$. Row i of $\{A\}_K$ is over $\mathbb{Z}_{m_{K[i]}}$, where $m_{K[i]}$ is the modulus in the public key of player $P_{K[i]}$. We also denote by $r \xleftarrow{\$} D$ the operation of drawing uniformly at random r from a domain D.

2.4 Multiparty Protocols Security

Here, we recall some widely used notations and results for the security of multi-party protocols.

Definition 3 (from [16]). *Let f be a n-ary functionality, where $f_i(x_1, ..., x_n)$ denotes the ith element of $f(x_1, ..., x_n)$. For $I = \{i_1, ..., i_t\} \subset [n] = \{1, ..., n\}$, we denote by $f_I(x_1, ..., x_m)$ the subsequence $f_{i_1}(x_1, ..., x_n), ..., f_{i_t}(x_1, ..., x_n)$. We let $x_I = (x_{i_1}, ..., x_{i_t})$. Let Π be a n-party protocol for computing f. The view of the ith party during an execution of Π on $\overline{x} = (x_1, ..., x_n)$ is denoted $\text{view}_i^\Pi(\overline{x})$, and for I, we let $\text{view}_I^\Pi(\overline{x}) = (I, \text{view}_{i_1}^\Pi(\overline{x}), ..., \text{view}_{i_t}^\Pi(\overline{x}))$. We say that Π securely computes f if there exist a probabilistic polynomial time algorithm, such that for every $I \subset [n]$, we have: $\{S_I((x_I), f_I(\overline{x})), f(\overline{x})\}_{\overline{x}} \overset{C}{\equiv} \{\text{view}_I^\Pi(\overline{x}), \text{output}^\Pi(\overline{x})\}_{\overline{x}}$.*

Definition 4. *Let $f_1, ..., f_{p(n)}$ be functionalities, and let Π be a protocol. We say that the protocol Π is executed in the $f_1, ..., f_{p(n)}$-hybrid mode if Π uses ideal calls to a trusted party to compute $f_1, ..., f_{p(n)}$.*

Theorem 1 (from [24]). *Let $p(n)$ be a polynomial, let $f_1, ..., f_{p(n)}$ be functionalities, and let $\pi_1, ..., \pi_{p(n)}$ be protocols such that each π_i securely computes f_i in the presence of semi-honest adversaries. Let g be a functionality, and let Π be a protocol that securely computes g in the $f_1, ..., f_{p(n)}$-hybrid model. Then, the protocol $\Pi^{\pi_1, ..., \pi_{p(n)}}$ securely computes g in presence of semi-honest adversaries.*

We will also need a function, which, given a small input is able to securely and deterministically produce a stream of uniformly generated random values. We will achieve this by using classical **mask generation functions**, as defined in [20, Section 10.2]: a function which takes two parameters, a seed Z and a length l and returns a random string of length l. We will then split the output string in as many fragments as needed, and use each of these fragments as a mask. Such function achieve an output indistinguishable property: if the seed is unknown, it is impossible to distinguish between the output of an MGF and a truly random string. Such secure functions exist, see for instance the one given in [20] and in what follows, we will denote by MGF any function that have the aforementioned security properties. Finally, for the rest of this paper, our functionalities follow the input/output specification described in the protocols they realize.

2.5 Relaxing an Existing Algorithm: YTP-SS

The matrix multiplication algorithm using the secure dot-product protocol YTP-SS [13, Algorithm 15] is secure against semi-honest adversaries over insecure communication channels. In order to analyze the difference with our proposition, Protocol 7 MP-SW, we extract here the core of the former protocol, i.e., without the securization of the channel (that is we remove the protection of the players private elements by random values, and the final communications to derandomize the results). The resulting simplification is called MP-PDP and its costs are given in Theorem 2. More details can be found in [13, Algorithm 15]

Theorem 2. *For n players, [13, Algorithm 15], without the channel securization, requires $2(n-1)$ communications. When used to compute a classical matrix product, it requires $n^3 + n(n-1)$ operations overall.*

3 Toolbox

3.1 Initialization Phase

Before the actual computation, the involved parties need to agree on the location and key sequences they will use, generate their key pairs, share their associated public keys, cipher their input data and communicate it where needed. Parties know their identifier, which is the index of the row they own, and use Eq. (1) to compute the location/key sequences. Protocol 1 shows how the input data is initially ciphered and dispatched: each party, identified as $P_i, i \in \{1..N\}$ starts with the i-th row of A and B, and, after generating its own key pair, ciphers its row according to the key sequence.

Protocol 1. SW-Setup

Input: Two $N \times N$ matrices A and B over $\mathbb{Z}_\sigma$, where $N = b2^\ell$, such that party P_i knows the i-th row of A and the i-th row B for all $i \in \{1..N\}$. A location and a key sequence $L \in \{1..N\}^N$ and $K \in \{1..N\}^N$ such that (L, K, L, K) form an ℓ-recursive data layout, following Definition 2. All parties know a security parameter λ.

Output: For all $i \in \{1..N\}$, party $P_{L[i]}$ learns vectors $\{a_{i,*}\}_{K[i]}$ and $\{b_{i,*}\}_{K[i]}$ and learns the public key of every other party.

Goal: Generate key pairs for each party, cipher and distribute input matrices according to their respective location and key sequences.

1. **Key generation:** for all $i \in \{1..N\}$, each party P_i locally executes NaccacheSternSetup(1^λ) to generate a pair of keys (pk_i, sk_i).
2. **Broadcast keys:** for all $i \in \{1..N\}$, party P_i broadcasts its public key pk_i.
3. **Cipher inputs:** for all $i \in \{1..N\}$, for all $j \in [n]$, party P_i locally performs NaccacheSternEncrypt($pk_{K[i]}, a_{ij}$) and stores the result as a new vector $\{a_{i,*}\}_{K[i]}$. It does the exact same operation with $b_{i,*}$ to get $\{b_{i,*}\}_{K[i]}$.
4. **Distribute rows:**
   (a) **Rows of A:** for all $i \in \{1..N\}$, party P_i sends $\{a_{i,*}\}_{K[i]}$ to party $P_{L[i]}$.
   (b) **Rows of B:** for all $i \in \{1..N\}$, party P_i sends $\{b_{i,*}\}_{K[i]}$ to party $P_{L[i]}$.

Finally, the protocol sends the ciphered row to the party hosting this row, designated by the location sequence. For input matrices of size N, Protocol 1 requires $2N^2$ communications.

3.2 Multiparty Copy

In the various subroutines that compose our algorithm, we will often need to copy and recipher a vector from one Party to another following location and key sequences. For this, one could use proxy reencryption protocols, but it is simpler, in our setting, to instead mask and decrypt, using interaction. Protocol 2 describes protocol MP-COPY, performing this very operation for a given ciphered element x hosted by Bob and encrypted for Dan, to its new location at Alice and encrypted for Charlie. Here, Dan is in charge of performing the decryption and the re-encryption of the element. To prevent Dan from learning the value of x, Bob masks it additively with a random value. Bob therefore needs to clear out this random mask on the value re-encrypted by Dan, with Charlie's key, before sending it to Alice. This protocol uses a total of 3 communications.

Protocol 2. MP-COPY

Input: Four parties, Alice, Bob, Charlie and Dan. Bob knows a ciphered element $\{x\}_D \in \mathbb{Z}_m$ (for $x \in \mathbb{Z}_\sigma$), ciphered using Dan's public key.

Output: Alice learns the element $\{x\}_C$, ciphered using Charlie's public key.

Goal: Recipher from Dan to Charlie and transfer from Bob to Alice.

1. **Add masking**
   (a) **Random:** Bob samples uniformly at random $r \in \mathbb{Z}_\sigma$
   (b) **Mask:** Bob locally computes $\alpha = \{x\}_D \cdot g^r = \{x+r\}_D \in \mathbb{Z}_m$
   (c) **Communication:** Bob sends α to Dan.
2. **Recipher:**
   (a) **Decipher:** Dan computes $\beta = \texttt{NaccacheSternDecrypt}(sk_D, \alpha) = x + r \in \mathbb{Z}_\sigma$.
   (b) **Cipher:** Dan computes $\gamma = \texttt{NaccacheSternEncrypt}(pk_C, \beta) \in \mathbb{Z}_m$.
   (c) **Communication:** Dan sends γ to Bob.
3. **Remove masking:**
   (a) **Unmask:** Bob locally computes $\delta = \gamma \cdot g^{-r} = \{x\}_C \in \mathbb{Z}_m$
   (b) **Communication:** Bob sends δ to Alice.

3.3 Classical Matrix Multiplication Base Case

We describe in this section an algorithm to perform classical matrix multiplications in the data and encryption layout of Definition 2. It consists in n^2 scalar products in which, products of elements $a_{i,k}$ of A by elements $b_{k,j}$ of B are performed using the homomorphic multiplication between a ciphertext and a plaintext: $\{a_{i,k}\}_{PK}^{b_{k,j}} = \{a_{i,k}b_{k,j}\}_{PK}$, where PK is the public key that has been used to cipher the element. Therefore, the coefficient $b_{k,j}$ should first be deciphered, and to avoid leaking information, it should also be masked beforehand by some random value.

Protocol 3. `MaskAndDecrypt`

Input: Two parties, further denoted as Bob and Charlie. They both know their own private key, public keys of all the parties involved, the security parameter $\lambda \in \mathbb{N}$ and the modulus $m \in \mathbb{N}$. Moreover, Bob knows a seed $s_k \in \mathbb{N}$ and a ciphered vector of size n, $\{b_{k,*}\}_C$, whose elements $(b_{k,j}) \in \mathbb{Z}_\sigma^n$ have been ciphered using Charlie's public key.

Output: Charlie learns the additively masked plaintext of Bob's input vector.

Goal: Perform the additive masking of Bob's input vector, and let Charlie learn it.

1. **Mask Bob's input:**
    (a) **Generate randoms:** Bob performs $\mathrm{MGF}(s_k, \mathrm{bitsize}(\sigma) \times n)$ and splits the output in n shares of size $\mathrm{bitsize}(\sigma)$, denoted as $t_{k,j}$ for $j \in \{1..n\}$.
    (b) **Mask vector:** for $j \in \{1..n\}$, Bob computes $\beta_{k,j} = \{b_{k,j}\}_C \cdot g^{t_{k,j}} \in \mathbb{Z}_m$.
    (c) **Communication:** for $j \in \{1..n\}$, Bob sends $\beta_{k,j}$ to Charlie.
2. **Finalize:**
    (a) **Decipher:** for $j \in \{1..n\}$, Charlie performs `NaccacheSternDecrypt`$(sk_C, \beta_{k,j})$ and stores the results in $u_{k,j} = b_{k,j} + t_{k,j} \in \mathbb{Z}_\sigma$.

Protocol 4. `PointwiseProducts`

Input: Four parties, further denoted as Alice, Bob, Charlie and Dan. Alice knows a ciphered $\{a_{i,k}\}_D \in \mathbb{Z}_m$ for given i and k, ciphered using Dan's public key. Bob knows a seed $s_k \in \mathbb{N}$ and Charlie knows a masked vector $(u_{k,*}) \in \mathbb{Z}_\sigma^n$ (each coefficient is masked by a random value).

Output: Alice learns all the ciphertexts $\{a_{i,k}b_{k,j}\}_D$ for $j \in \{1..n\}$.

Goal: Compute the point-wise products for naive matrix product on a given row

1. **Communication:** Alice sends $\{a_{i,k}\}_D$ to Charlie
2. **Multiplication:** for $j \in \{1..n\}$, Charlie computes $\delta_{i,k,j} = \{a_{i,k}\}_D^{u_{k,j}}$, $\delta_{i,k,j} \in \mathbb{Z}_m$
3. **Communication:** for $j \in \{1..n\}$, Charlie sends $\delta_{i,k,j}$ to Alice.
4. **Send seed:** Bob sends s_k to Alice
5. **Generate and remove masks:** Alice performs $\mathrm{MGF}(s_k, \mathrm{bitsize}(\sigma) \times n)$ and splits the output in n shares of size σ, denoted as $t_{k,j}$ for $j \in \{1..n\}$.
    For $j \in \{1..n\}$, Alice computes:

$$\epsilon_{i,k,j} = \delta_{i,k,j} / \left(\{a_{i,k}\}_D^{t_{k,j}}\right) = \{a_{i,k}(b_{k,j} + t_{k,j}) - a_{i,k}t_{k,j}\}_D \in \mathbb{Z}_m.$$

Protocol 3 takes care of masking and deciphering a whole column of B. There, player Charlie is the only one able to decrypt the masked value $\beta_{k,j} = \{b_{k,j} + t_{k,j}\}_C$. For this we require a stream of uniformly random values $t_{k,j}$, that can be sent. To reduce communications, we here instead use a mask generating function (MGF) that generates this stream from a small seed. Then only the seed need to be communicated to remove the mask. All players have of course to agree beforehand on a choice for this mask generating function.

Protocol 4 shows how player Alice can then recover the ciphertext of one product $\{a_{i,k}b_{k,j}\}_D$. Alice sends her value $\{a_{i,k}\}_D$ to player Charlie who then performs the exponentiation, corresponding to a multiplication on the plaintexts, and sends it back to Alice. Meanwhile Alice has received the seed and generated the masking values $t_{k,j}$ to clean out the product. Finally each coefficient $\{c_{i,j}\}_D$

Protocol 5. BaseCase

Input: two $n \times n$ matrices $\{A\}_{K_A}$ and $\{B\}_{K_B}$ distributed and ciphered according to a base-case data layout $(L_A, K_A, L_B, K_B) \in (\{1..N\}^n)^4$ among parties $(P_1, \ldots, P_N)$ as in Definition 2,

Output: Matrix $C = A \times B$ is distributed and ciphered among parties $(P_1, \ldots, P_N)$ according to the location and key sequences (L_A, K_A).

Goal: Compute $C = A \times B$ distributed and ciphered in the same way as A is.

1. **Computation:**
   For all $k \in \{1..n\}$
   (a) **Choose a seed:** Party $P_{L_B[k]}$ samples uniformly at random a seed $s_k \in \mathbb{N}$ according to the security parameter λ.
   (b) Parties $P_{L_B[k]}$ and $P_{K_B[k]}$ run MaskAndDecrypt on vector $\{b_{k,*}\}_{K_B[k]}$
   (c) For all $i \in \{1..n\}$
       Parties $P_{L_A[i]}, P_{L_B[k]}, P_{K_B[k]}$ and $P_{K_A[i]}$ run PointwiseProducts where Parties $P_{L_A[i]}$ learn $\epsilon_{i,k,j} = \{a_{i,k}b_{k,j}\}_{K_A[i]}$ for all $j \in \{1..n\}$.
2. **Reduction:** for all $i \in \{1..n\}$ Party $P_{L_A[i]}$ computes $\{c_{i,j}\}_{K_A[i]} \leftarrow \prod_{k=1}^{n} \epsilon_{i,k,j}$

---

of the result is computed during a reduction step where player Alice simply multiplies together all corresponding point-wise products.

Overall, Protocol 5 schedules these three operations. In the calls to Protocols MaskAndDecrypt and PointwiseProducts, Alice is incarnated by Player $P_{L_A[i]}$, Bob by $P_{L_B[k]}$, Charlie by $P_{K_B[k]}$ and Dan by $P_{K_A[i]}$.

Theorem 3. *Protocol 5 correctly computes the product $C = A \times B$ in the specified layout. It requires a communication of $n^3 + 3n^2 + n$ modular integers.*

Proof. Correctness stems first from the fact that $c_{i,j} = \sum_{k=1}^{n} a_{i,k}b_{k,j}$ is obtained "in the exponents" by the homomorphic properties (1). Second the only masks applied, in Protocol 3, are all removed in Protocol 4. Now, the communication cost in number of ring element is n for Protocol 3 and $n + 1$ for Protocol 4. Protocol 3 and Protocol 4 also send one seed, which, for simplicity, we consider smaller than a modular integer. Overall this yields a communication cost lower than $n(n + 1) + n^2(n + 2) = n^3 + 3n^2 + n$ modular integers for Protocol 5. □

3.4 Security Analysis

From the formalization of the different protocols we can state the security of the overall base case for matrix multiplication in the following Theorem 4.

Theorem 4. *If players share a 0-data-layout, Protocol BaseCase is secure against one semi-honest adversary.*

The idea is to start by proving the security of the subprotocols and then use the composition theorem and the data layout to prove the security of the double loop of Protocol BaseCase. The full formal proof is given in Appendix A.1.

Protocol 6. MP-MAT-COPY

Input: an $n \times n$ matrix $\{A\}_{K_A}$ distributed and ciphered according to a location and a key sequence $(L_A, K_A) \in (\{1..N\}^n)^2$ among parties $(P_1, \ldots, P_N)$ following Definition 2 and a location-key sequence (L', K').

Output: A copy $\{A\}_{K'}$ is distributed and ciphered among parties $(P_1, \ldots, P_N)$ according to the location and key sequences (L', K').

For all $i, j \in \{1..n\}^2$
    Parties $P_{L'[i]}, P_{L[i]}, P_{K[i]}$ and $P_{K'[i]}$ run MP-COPY to copy $\{a_{i,j}\}_{K[i]}$ to $\{a_{i,j}\}_{K'[i]}$

---

4 Multiparty Strassen-Winograd

4.1 Operation Schedule in MP-SW

The 22 operations in a recursive step of Strassen-Winograd's algorithm is composed by 15 matrix additions and 7 recursive calls. The matrix additions are performed using component-wise homomorphic additions, denoted by HOM-MAT-ADD: each player performs locally a simple homomorphic addition of the rows of the two input operands that she stores. Homomorphic subtraction, denoted by HOM-MAT-SUB, works similarly. However, this requires that the two operands share the same key and location sequences. To ensure this, some matrices will be copied from one key-location sequence to another, using a multiparty matrix copy, denoted by MP-MAT-COPY. The location sequences of the input an output are non-intersecting (and therefore so are the related key sequences). These operations are achieved by n^2 instances of MP-COPY (Protocol 2) as shown in Protocol 6.

Theorem 5. *Assuming an l-data layout, Protocol MP-MAT-COPY is secure against one semi-honest adversary.*

We only give a sketch of the proof, since its very similar to the one for the MaskAndDecrypt protocol within the proof of Theorem 4.

Proof. First, we prove that MP-COPY is secure against one semi-honest adversary: from the data layout or the added randomness, each players only see ciphers or additively masked values so that it does not lean anything from the execution. Then, we prove the security in an hybrid model where calls to MP-COPY are replaced by an equivalent ideal functionality. Since the output is ciphered accordingly to the data layout, a simulation by ciphering random values is computationally indistinguishable from the real execution. Finally, by sequentially composing calls to the MP-COPY protocol, we apply the sequential composition theorem to conclude.   □

We propose in Protocol 7 a scheduling of these operations and data movement ensuring that all additions can be made homomorphically, that the key and location sequences for all seven recursive calls satisfy the requirements for a base-case data-layout (Definition 2) and finally that the output matrix also follows the location and key sequences of the first operand. The last three columns in

Protocol 7 indicate the location sequences of the input and output operands for each operation.

Protocol 7. MP-SW

Input: two $n \times n$ matrices $\{A\}_{K_A}$ and $\{B\}_{K_B}$, distributed and ciphered according to an ℓ-recursive data layout $(L_A, K_A, L_B, K_B) \in (\{1..N\}^n)^4$ among parties $(P_1, \ldots, P_N)$ following Definition 2, where $n = b2^\ell$.

Output: $\{C\}_{K_A} = \{A \times B\}_{K_A}$, distributed and ciphered among parties $(P_1, \ldots, P_N)$ according to the location and key sequences (L_A, K_A).

1. If $\ell = 0$: Parties in (L_A, K_A) and (L_B, K_B) run BaseCase on $\{A\}_{K_A}$ and $\{B\}_{K_B}$
2. Else

				In1 loc.	In2 loc.	Out loc.
$\{S_1\}_{K_{A_L}}$	$\leftarrow$ HOM-MAT-ADD	$(\{A_{21}\}_{K_{A_L}},$	$\{A_{22}\}_{K_{A_L}}$)	L_{A_L}	L_{A_L}	L_{A_L}
$\{A'_{11}\}_{K_{A_L}}$	$\leftarrow$ MP-MAT-COPY	$(\{A_{11}\}_{K_{A_U}},$	(L_{A_L}, K_{A_L}))	L_{A_U}		L_{A_L}
$\{S_2\}_{K_{A_L}}$	$\leftarrow$ HOM-MAT-SUB	$(\{S_1\}_{K_{A_L}},$	$\{A'_{11}\}_{K_{A_L}}$)	L_{A_L}	L_{A_L}	L_{A_L}
$\{S_3\}_{K_{A_L}}$	$\leftarrow$ HOM-MAT-SUB	$(\{A'_{11}\}_{K_{A_L}},$	$\{A_{21}\}_{K_{A_L}}$)	L_{A_L}	L_{A_L}	L_{A_L}
$\{S'_2\}_{K_{A_U}}$	$\leftarrow$ MP-MAT-COPY	$(\{S_2\}_{K_{A_L}},$	(L_{A_U}, K_{A_U}))	L_{A_L}		L_{A_U}
$\{S_4\}_{K_{A_U}}$	$\leftarrow$ HOM-MAT-SUB	$(\{A_{12}\}_{K_{A_U}},$	$\{S'_2\}_{K_{A_U}}$)	L_{A_U}	L_{A_U}	L_{A_U}
$\{T_1\}_{K_{B_U}}$	$\leftarrow$ HOM-MAT-SUB	$(\{B_{12}\}_{K_{B_U}},$	$\{B_{11}\}_{K_{B_U}}$)	L_{B_U}	L_{B_U}	L_{B_U}
$\{B'_{22}\}_{K_{B_U}}$	$\leftarrow$ MP-MAT-COPY	$(\{B_{22}\}_{K_{B_L}},$	(L_{B_U}, K_{B_U}))	L_{B_L}		L_{B_U}
$\{T_2\}_{K_{B_U}}$	$\leftarrow$ HOM-MAT-SUB	$(\{B'_{22}\}_{K_{B_U}},$	$\{T_1\}_{K_{B_U}}$)	L_{B_U}	L_{B_U}	L_{B_U}
$\{T_3\}_{K_{B_U}}$	$\leftarrow$ HOM-MAT-SUB	$(\{B'_{22}\}_{K_{B_U}},$	$\{B_{12}\}_{K_{B_U}}$)	L_{B_U}	L_{B_U}	L_{B_U}
$\{B'_{21}\}_{K_{B_U}}$	$\leftarrow$ MP-MAT-COPY	$(\{B_{21}\}_{K_{B_L}},$	(L_{B_U}, K_{B_U}))	L_{B_L}		L_{B_U}
$\{T_4\}_{K_{B_U}}$	$\leftarrow$ HOM-MAT-SUB	$(\{T_2\}_{K_{B_U}},$	$\{B'_{21}\}_{K_{B_U}}$)	L_{B_U}	L_{B_U}	L_{B_U}
$\{R_1\}_{K_{A_L}}$	$\leftarrow$ MP-SW	$(\{A'_{11}\}_{K_{A_L}},$	$\{B_{11}\}_{K_{B_U}}$)	L_{A_L}	L_{B_U}	L_{A_L}
$\{R_2\}_{K_{A_U}}$	$\leftarrow$ MP-SW	$(\{A_{12}\}_{K_{A_U}},$	$\{B_{21}\}_{K_{B_L}}$)	L_{A_U}	L_{B_L}	L_{A_U}
$\{R_3\}_{K_{A_U}}$	$\leftarrow$ MP-SW	$(\{S_4\}_{K_{A_U}},$	$\{B_{22}\}_{K_{B_L}}$)	L_{A_U}	L_{B_L}	L_{A_U}
$\{R_4\}_{K_{A_L}}$	$\leftarrow$ MP-SW	$(\{A_{22}\}_{K_{A_L}},$	$\{T_4\}_{K_{B_U}}$)	L_{A_L}	L_{B_U}	L_{A_L}
$\{R_5\}_{K_{A_L}}$	$\leftarrow$ MP-SW	$(\{S_1\}_{K_{A_L}},$	$\{T_1\}_{K_{B_U}}$)	L_{A_L}	L_{B_U}	L_{A_L}
$\{R_6\}_{K_{A_L}}$	$\leftarrow$ MP-SW	$(\{S_2\}_{K_{A_L}},$	$\{T_2\}_{K_{B_U}}$)	L_{A_L}	L_{B_U}	L_{A_L}
$\{R_7\}_{K_{A_L}}$	$\leftarrow$ MP-SW	$(\{S_3\}_{K_{A_L}},$	$\{T_3\}_{K_{B_U}}$)	L_{A_L}	L_{B_U}	L_{A_L}
$\{R'_1\}_{K_{A_U}}$	$\leftarrow$ MP-MAT-COPY	$(\{R_1\}_{K_{A_L}},$	(L_{A_U}, K_{A_U}))	L_{A_L}		L_{A_U}
$\{U_1\}_{K_{A_U}}$	$\leftarrow$ HOM-MAT-ADD	$(\{R'_1\}_{K_{A_U}},$	$\{R_2\}_{K_{A_U}}$)	L_{A_U}	L_{A_U}	L_{A_U}
$\{U_2\}_{K_{A_L}}$	$\leftarrow$ HOM-MAT-ADD	$(\{R_1\}_{K_{A_L}},$	$\{R_6\}_{K_{A_L}}$)	L_{A_L}	L_{A_L}	L_{A_L}
$\{U_3\}_{K_{A_L}}$	$\leftarrow$ HOM-MAT-ADD	$(\{U_2\}_{K_{A_L}},$	$\{R_7\}_{K_{A_L}}$)	L_{A_L}	L_{A_L}	L_{A_L}
$\{U_4\}_{K_{A_L}}$	$\leftarrow$ HOM-MAT-ADD	$(\{U_2\}_{K_{A_L}},$	$\{R_5\}_{K_{A_L}}$)	L_{A_L}	L_{A_L}	L_{A_L}
$\{U'_4\}_{K_{A_U}}$	$\leftarrow$ MP-MAT-COPY	$(\{U_4\}_{K_{A_L}},$	(L_{A_U}, K_{A_U}))	L_{A_L}		L_{A_U}
$\{U_5\}_{K_{A_U}}$	$\leftarrow$ HOM-MAT-ADD	$(\{U'_4\}_{K_{A_U}},$	$\{R_3\}_{K_{A_U}}$)	L_{A_U}	L_{A_U}	L_{A_U}
$\{U_6\}_{K_{A_L}}$	$\leftarrow$ HOM-MAT-SUB	$(\{U_3\}_{K_{A_L}},$	$\{R_4\}_{K_{A_L}}$)	L_{A_L}	L_{A_L}	L_{A_L}
$\{U_7\}_{K_{A_L}}$	$\leftarrow$ HOM-MAT-ADD	$(\{U_3\}_{K_{A_L}},$	$\{R_5\}_{K_{A_L}}$)	L_{A_L}	L_{A_L}	L_{A_L}

3. **End result** $\{C\}_{K_A} \leftarrow \begin{bmatrix} \{U_1\}_{K_{A_U}} & \{U_5\}_{K_{A_U}} \\ \{U_6\}_{K_{A_L}} & \{U_7\}_{K_{A_L}} \end{bmatrix}$

Note that the initial problem requires that both operands A and B share the same key and location sequences (so that matrix squaring is possible). However, the base case protocol (Protocol 5) requires that these sequences are non-intersecting. In order to satisfy these two constraints the recursive Strassen-Winograd algorithm is presented with a location and key sequence for A (L_A and K_A) and a location and key sequence for B (L_B and K_B). The algorithm does not require that they are non intersecting, but ensures that from the first recursive call, they will always be, so as to fit with the requirement of the base case, Protocol 5.

Lemma 2. *The total communication cost of a recursive level of MP-SW following the schedule defined Protocol 7, Step 2 is $18 \left(\frac{n}{2}\right)^2$ communications.*

Proof. The only communication are that of the 6 calls to MP-MAT-COPY, each accounting for $3(n/2)^2$ communication.   □

Finally, our main security result is that of the following Theorem 6. The full proof relies on a sequence of hybrid games, where each transition is based on indistinguishability and is given in Appendix A.2.

Theorem 6. *Assuming an ℓ-data layout, Protocol MP-SW is secure against one semi-honest adversary.*

4.2   Finalization Step

Finally, there remains to decipher and distribute each row of $\{C\}_{K_A}$ to the party who has to learn it. By setting the key sequence to $K_A = (1, 2, 3 \dots)$ as in Lemma 1, this player is able to perform the decryption himself. This finalization step is formally described in Protocol 8 and uses N^2 communications.

Protocol 8. SW-Finalize

Input: An $N \times N$ matrix $\{C\}_{K_C}$ distributed and ciphered according to the location and key sequences $(L_C, K_C) \in (\{1..N\}^N)^2$ among parties $P_1, \dots, P_N$, following Definition 1.

Output: Each party $P_{K_C[i]}$ learns the plaintext of the i-th row of C.

1. **Exchange rows:** For all $i \in \{1..N\}$, party $P_{L_C[i]}$ send row i of C to party $P_{K_C[i]}$.
2. **Decipher vector:** For all $i \in \{1..N\}$, for all $j \in \{1..N\}$, party $P_{K_C[i]}$ runs NaccacheSternDecrypt($sk_{K_C[i]}, (\{c_{i,j}\}_{K_C[i]})$) and stores the output values in a vector $c_{K_C[i]} \in \mathbb{Z}_\sigma^N$.

4.3   Cost and Security Analysis

From Lemma 2 and Theorem 3, the recurrence relation for communication complexity of MP-SW writes:

$$\begin{cases} C(n) = 7C\left(\frac{n}{2}\right) + 18\left(\frac{n}{2}\right)^2 & \text{for } n > b \\ C(b) = b^3 + 2b^2 & \text{for the base case} \end{cases} \qquad (2)$$

The threshold at which the recursive algorithm should switch to the base case algorithm is set by finding at which dimension b does the base case algorithm start to perform worse than one recursive level. In terms of communication cost, this means the following equation: $7((\frac{b}{2})^3 + 3(\frac{b}{2})^2 + 3(\frac{b}{2})) + 18(\frac{b}{2})^2 = b^3 + 3b^2 + b$ which comes from injecting the base case cost of Theorem 3 into the recurrence formula. It gives a threshold of $b = 56$.

Theorem 7. *For $N = b2^\ell$ parties $(P_i)_{i \in \{1..N\}}$ and two matrices $A, B \in \mathbb{Z}_\sigma^{N \times N}$, such that party P_i knows the i-th row of A and the i-th row B for all $i \in \{1..N\}$, the execution in sequence of algorithms (SW-Setup; MP-SW; SW-Finalize), using the ℓ-recursive data layout of Eq. (1), correctly computes $C = A \times B \in \mathbb{Z}_\sigma$ with $O(7^\ell b^3)$ communications in $O(\ell)$ rounds and is secure against one semi-honest adversary. When b is constant, then $\ell = O(\log_2(N))$, and the communication bound is $O(N^{\log_2(7)})$.*

Proof. Correctness of MP-SW is given by Theorem 3 for the basecase and that of Strassen-Winograd algorithm (Sect. 2.1). Then SW-Setup is just the set up of the keys and initial encipherings, while SW-Finalize is the associated decipherings. Then, the communication bound stems from Theorem 3 and Eq. (2), with $3N^2$ communications for SW-Setup and SW-Finalize. The non-recursive parts of each recursive level of MP-SW require a constant number of rounds, and so does the execution of the BaseCase, leading to a total of $O(\ell)$ rounds. For the security, again SW-Setup is just the communication of public keys and self-ciphered values, while SW-Finalize is also the communication of ciphered values to their legitimate locations. Finally, Theorem 6 asserts the security of MP-SW and the sequential execution of (SW-Setup; MP-SW; SW-Finalize) that of the whole process. □

We now compare the cost of MP-SW with the cost of MP-PDP, $C_{\text{MP-PDP}}(n) = n^3 + n(n-1)$. We also recall that the initialization step SW-Setup costs $C_{\text{init}} = 2n^2$ and the finalization step SW-Finalize costs $C_{\text{final}} = n^2$. The crossover point where our full algorithm improves over MP-PDP in communication cost is obtained by solving the equation: $C(n) + 3n^2 \leq n^3 + n(n-1)$ which yields $n > 94$, with one recursive call. This means that for any instance of dimension larger than 96, the proposed MP-SW algorithm has a better communication cost than MP-PDP.

5   Experiments

We implemented the algorithms under study[3] to demonstrate their behavior in practice and compared them to the state of the art implementations of other solutions. In the following $\text{SPD}\mathbb{Z}_{2^k}$ refers to a run of a textbook matrix multiplication algorithm performed with the general purpose library $\text{SPD}\mathbb{Z}_{2^k}$ [6][4], YTP-SS refers to n^2 applications of [13, Algorithm 15]; MP-PDP refers the relaxation and

---

[3] C++ source files, including benchmarks for YTP-SS and $\text{SPD}\mathbb{Z}_{2^k}$, are available on request via the PC chair and will be made publicly available if the paper is accepted.
[4] https://github.com/bristolcrypto/SPDZ-2.

improvement of this algorithm to the current setting; MP-SW refers to our implementation of Protocol 7 using Protocol 5 as a basecase with threshold set to
$n = 56$. The Naccache-Stern cryptosystem is set with public keys of size 2048
bits and message space of 224 bits (using 14 primes of 16 bits).

Please note that, while MP-PDP and MP-SW share the same security model,
YTP-SS and SPDZ$_{2^k}$ achieve better security: malicious adversaries over insecure
channels. Also, SPDZ$_{2^k}$ uses a different approach based on oblivious transfer and
secret sharing. However, as they were the only state of the art implementations
available, we still chose to include them in our comparisons.

Figure 2 presents the volume of communication performed by these four variants. Communication-wise, for $n = 100$ players, MP-SW is 4% cheaper than MP-PDP
(271 vs. 261 MB), but becomes 24% cheaper for $n = 400$ (15.3 vs. 11.7 GB) and
up to 27.8% for $n = 528$ (35.2 vs. 25.4 GB). Note that the cross-over point
of $n = 96$ between MP-PDP and MP-SW is confirmed experimentally. For SPDZ$_{2^k}$,
computations were performed for small matrices only because of computational
power requirements: on a workstation with 16 GB of RAM and an Intel i5-7300U
@2.60GHz, computations stalled for any matrices larger than 37×37.

To reach this communication improvement, the price to pay is that of some
computational slowdown, as shown in Table 1.

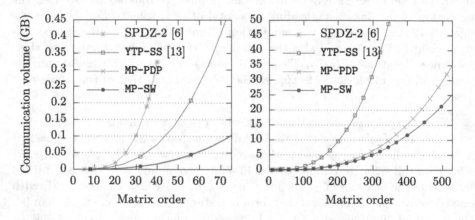

Fig. 2. Comparing communication volume for multiparty matrix multiplications.

Table 1. Computation time (in s) per player of Multiparty Strassen-Winograd MP-SW
compared to MP-PDP on an Intel Xeon E7-8860 2.2 Ghz.

Key size	1024			2048		
n	16	32	64	16	32	64
MP-PDP	0.58	2.68	11.01	4.54	18.05	69.80
MP-SW	2.87	6.19	13.27	23.63	49.22	196.24

However, with the same order of magnitude for the computational cost and the communication cost, communications should be largely dominant. Therefore, the improvement in communication volume is the one that matters.

6   Conclusion and Perspective

We have presented in this paper a novel secure multiparty matrix multiplication where each player owns one row of the different matrices. For this we use Strassen-Winograd algorithm and reduce for the first time the total communication volume from $O(N^3)$ to $O(N^{\log_2(7)})$. The improvement in communication cost over state of the art algorithms takes effect for dimension as small as 96.

The version of Strassen-Winograd we presented here is secure against semi-honest adversaries. However, as many of its building blocks have a stronger security level anyway, it would be interesting to see if it is possible to increase the security of the whole MP-SW protocol and how it would impact its performance.

Even if this paper is a about improving the communication cost while preserving security, several arithmetic cost improvements could be envisioned. For instance, removing the need for players to encrypt their share of the B matrix beforehand. While this is required in order to preserve security, a large part of the computing cost lies in the operations required to decipher and re-cipher that data. In particular, the MP-COPY protocol is actually a proxy re-encryption, and we want to further investigate how dedicated proxy re-encryption techniques like [2,4] could be used in this context. Another possibility would be to replace the Naccache-Stern by a faster cryptosystem. The difficulty is to be able to combine the masking schemes with the homomorphic encryption.

A   Security Proofs

A.1   Base Case Security Proof

Theorem 4 (From Sect. 3.4). *If players shares a 0-data-layout, Protocol BaseCase is secure against one semi-honest adversary.*

Proof. We start by proving that both subprotocols MaskAndDecrypt ($M\&D$) and PointwiseProducts (PWP) are secure against one semi-honest adversary.

Protocol MaskAndDecrypt is a 2-party protocol such that: $\text{output}^{M\&D}$ $((\{b_1\}_{P_2}, s_1), -) = (-, u_1)$, with $b_1 = b_{k,*}$, $s_1 = s_k$, $u_1 = \{u_{k,j}\}_{j \in \{1..n\}}$. The proof is then divided in two parts: one for each corruption case. We labeled P_1 the player providing the seeds as input.

P_1 *is corrupted.* The view of P_1 is: $\text{view}_{P_1}^{M\&D} = (t_1, \beta_1)$. From the inputs of P_1, the simulator is able to perfectly simulate the view of P_1.

P_2 *is corrupted.* The view of P_2 is: $\text{view}_{P_2}^{M\&D} = (\beta_1)$. From the output u_1 of P_2, the simulator S_2 ciphers each of its elements with the key of P_2. From the IND-CPA security, the simulated view is computationally indistinguishable from the real one.

Protocol `PointwiseProducts` is a 4-parties protocol. However, the 4th player does not have any input nor output: only its public key is used. In the same vein, P_2 only sends s_2 and does not interact otherwise. Its view is empty, so that its simulator is trivial. Therefore, the proof is only divided in two part. The output of the protocol is: $\text{output}^{PWP}(\{a_1\}_{P_4}, s_2, u_k, -) = (\epsilon, -, -, -)$ with $a_1 = a_{i,k}$, $u_k = u_{k,*}$ and $\epsilon = \{\epsilon_{i,k,j}\}_{j \in \{1..n\}}$.

P_1 *is corrupted.* The view of P_1 is: $\text{view}_{P_1}^{PWP} = (s_2, t_1, \delta_1)$. The simulator S_1 picks $s_2' \xleftarrow{\$} \mathbb{Z}_\sigma$ and computes t_1' as in the protocol. Then, from the output ϵ and the input $\{a_1\}_{P_4}$, it computes $\delta' = \epsilon * \{a_1\}_{P_4}^{t_1'}$ component wise. Since the δ values are ciphered with the key of P_4, and that s_1 is a random value, both views are indistinguishable.

P_3 *is corrupted.* We have $\text{view}_{P_3}^{PWP} = (\{a_1\}_{P_4}, \delta_1)$. S_3: $a_1' \xleftarrow{\$} \mathbb{Z}_\sigma$, then the value is ciphered with the public key of P_4 to obtain $\{a_1'\}_{P_4}$. Next, it computes δ_1' as in protocol using the simulated value $\{a_1'\}_{P_4}$. This simulation is computationally indistinguishable from the real view thanks to the IND-CPA security of the cryptosystem.

We denote by $F^{M\&D}$ (respectively F^{PWP}) the ideal functionalities associated to the protocol `MaskAndDecrypt` (resp. `PointwiseProducts`). If players shares a 0-data-layout, the `BaseCase` protocol is secure against one semi-honest adversary in the $(F^{M\&D}, F^{PWP})$-hybrid model.

`BaseCase` is a N-party protocol, where the view depends on which group the player belongs. Since players share a 0-data-layout, there are four distinct possibilities: $\{L_A, K_A, L_B, K_B\}$. The cases where $P_{K_A[i]}$ or $P_{L_B[i]}$ is corrupted are trivial, since their respective view are empty in the $(F^{M\&D}, F^{PWP})$-hybrid model.

$P_{L_A[i]}$ *is corrupted.* The view of $P_{L_A[i]}$ is: $\text{view}_{P_{L_A[i]}}^{\text{BaseCase}} = (\{\epsilon\} P_{K_A[i]})$ where ϵ_i is the output of a call to F^{PWP}. The simulator S_i executes: for each $k \in \{1..N\}$: from the `BaseCase` output int the ideal world, it picks $N-1$ random shares in $\mathbb{Z}_\sigma$ the (denoted $\epsilon_i', i \in \{1..N-1\}$), and ciphers them using $Pk_{K_A}[i]$. Then, it chooses the last share ϵ_n' such that: $\epsilon_n' * \prod_{k=1}^{n-1} \epsilon_i'$. If ϵ_n' belongs to $\mathbb{Z}_m$, then it outputs each component of ϵ', otherwise it redoes the process from the beginning for the kth step. The definition of the data layout ensures that $P_{L_A[i]} \neq P_{K_A[i]}$, so that ϵ_i and ϵ_i' are indistinguishable as long as the encryption scheme is IND-CPA. Moreover, since the choice of each share is consistent with the output of the protocol (i.e., their product is equal to the output), the adversary is not able to computationally distinguish between the real and the simulated execution.

$P_{L_B[i]}$ *is corrupted.* The view of $P_{L_B[i]}$ is: $\{\text{view}_{P_{L_B[i]}}^{\text{BaseCase}} = (u)\}$. The output of the protocol is empty for this player. The simulator picks n random values from $\mathbb{Z}_\sigma$, and outputs each of them to form u'. In the real world, each u_i is masked by a random value (unknown by $P_{L_B[i]}$ since $P_{L_B[i]} \neq P_{K_B[i]}$), so that u_i and u_i' are then perfectly indistinguishable.

Finally, we apply the composition Theorem 1: since we have proven the security of `BaseCase` protocol in the $(F^{M\&D}, F^{PWP})$-hybrid model, and that the protocols `PointwiseProducts` and `MaskAndDecrypt` are secure, and that each call to both of these protocols are sequentially made, we conclude that the `BaseCase` protocol is secure against one semi-honest adversary. Moreover, the 0-data layout ensures that the seed sharing does not leak information. □

A.2   Multiparty Strassen-Winograd Security Proof

Theorem 6 (From Section 4.1**).** *Assuming an ℓ-data layout, Protocol* `MP-SW` *is secure against one semi-honest adversary.*

Proof. First, we prove that `MP-SW` is secure in the $F^{\texttt{BaseCase}}, F^{Copy}, F_{N/2}^{\texttt{MP-SW}}$-hybrid model, where $F^{\texttt{BaseCase}}$, F^{Copy} and $F_{N/2}^{\texttt{MP-SW}}$ respectively denotes the ideal functionality associated to the protocol `BaseCase`, `MP-MAT-COPY`, and `MP-SW` with $N/2$ players. In this model, calls to `MP-MAT-COPY` are replaced by ideals calls to F^{Copy}. In the same vein, if $N \leq T$, the `MP-SW` calls are replaced by $F^{\texttt{BaseCase}}$, or by $F_{N/2}^{\texttt{MP-SW}}$ otherwise. e need to prove that for any corrupted player, its real view is indistinguishable from the simulated one.

From the inputs described as in `MP-SW` (implicit in the following), the outputs for the player $P_{L_{A_X[i]}}$ are the rows of the following matrices, ciphered with $Pk_{K_{A_X[i]}}$, with $X \in \{U, L\}$. $\text{output}_{A_U}^{\texttt{MP-SW}}(U_1, U_5)$ and $\text{output}_{A_L}^{\texttt{MP-SW}}(U_6, U_7)$. Using the same notations, we obtains the following views:

$$\text{view}_{L_{A_U}}^{\texttt{MP-SW}} = (S_2', S_4, R_1', R_2, R_3, U_4'),$$
$$\text{view}_{L_{A_L}}^{\texttt{MP-SW}} = (S_1, A_{11}', S_2, S_3, R_1, R_4, R_5, R_6, R_7, U_2, U_3, U_4),$$
$$\text{view}_{L_{B_U}}^{\texttt{MP-SW}} = (T_1, B_{22}', T_2, T_3, T_4), \quad \text{view}_{L_{B_L}}^{\texttt{MP-SW}} = (-).$$

We construct a generic simulator, where differences depending on the corrupted player are explicitly detailed. The simulator $S_{i \in \{1..N\}}$ takes two random matrices in α and β both in $\mathbb{Z}_\sigma^{(N*N)}$. Then, it replaces the rows for the corrupted player with its actual inputs (i.e., the rows of A and B owned by the corrupted player). The remaining coefficients are ciphered accordingly to the data layout. The first part of the protocol (i.e. the computation of S_i and T_i, $i \in \{1..4\}$) is simulated using the inputs and ideal calls to F^{Copy}. This simulates the views for the L_B cases. Then, there are two cases.

$P_{L_{A_U[i]}}$ is corrupted: From the output, the simulator $S_{L_{A_U[i]}}$ takes $N/2$ random values from $\mathbb{Z}_m$ to obtain the simulation of the row of U_4. Then, it computes the row of $R_3 = \texttt{HOM-MAT-SUB}(U_5, U_4)$. Similarly, it take the row R_1' at random, and computes $R_1 = \texttt{HOM-MAT-SUB}(U_1, R_1')$.

$P_{L_{A_L[i]}}$ is corrupted: $S_{L_{A_L[i]}}$ samples $3N/2$ random values from $\mathbb{Z}_m$ to simulate the row of U_2, R_1 and R_7. Next, it computes: $R_6 = \texttt{HOM-MAT-SUB}(U_2, R_1)$, $U_3 = \texttt{HOM-MAT-ADD}(U_2, R_7)$, $R_4 = \texttt{HOM-MAT-SUB}(U_3, U_6)$, $R_5 = \texttt{HOM-MAT-SUB}(U_7, U_3$ and $U_4 = \texttt{HOM-MAT-ADD}(U_2, R_5)$.

We now prove that the simulated view is indistinguishable from the real one. The proof relies on a sequence of hybrid games, where each transition is based on indistinguishability.

H_0: The first game represents the view of a real protocol execution in the $(F^{Copy}, F^{\texttt{BaseCase}}, F_{N/2}^{\texttt{MP-SW}})$-hybrid model.

H_1: for each call to F^{Copy}, we replace the output of the functionality by random numbers, accordingly ciphered with the data layout. i.e.: $\forall j \in \{1..N\}, r_i \xleftarrow{\$} \mathbb{Z}_\sigma$ and $\{r_j\}_{K_X[j]}$ with $X \in \{A_L, B_U\}$. As only one player is corrupted, and (L_A, K_A, L_B, K_B) is a 1-recursive data layout which verifies $(L_{X_U} \cup K_{X_U}) \cap (L_{X_L} \cup K_{X_L}) = \emptyset, X \in \{A, B\}$, then the player obtains ciphers which it cannot decipher. Then, the IND-CPA security of the cryptosystem ensures that H_0 and H_1 are indistinguishable.

H_2: this game, we replace the output obtained from: $F^{\texttt{BaseCase}}$ if $N \leq T$; or $F_{N/2}^{\texttt{MP-SW}}$ otherwise; by the previously detailed simulation for the R_i, $i \in \{1..N\}$. From the data layout, the corrupted player ($P_{L_{A_U}[i]}$ or $P_{L_{A_L}[i]}$) in the real case gets undecipherable values that cannot be guessed from the inputs of the adversary (which knows one row of each matrix in the worst case) so that the simulation is computationally indistinguishable. Then, $H_1 \overset{C}{\equiv} H_2'$.

H_3: In this game, we replace the U_i of the real view with the simulated ones U_i, $i \in \{2..4\}$. Each of the simulated values is directly computed from the output, so that as long as the adversary is not able to distinguish ciphers, the simulation is computationally indistinguishable from the real execution.

H_3 represents the simulated view for N players. We have then proven that MP-SW is secure against one semi-honest adversary in the (F^{Copy}, $F^{\texttt{BaseCase}}$, $F_{N/2}^{\texttt{MP-SW}}$)-model.

Second, we prove that if we assume a l-data layout between the players, the MP-SW protocol is secure against one semi-honest adversary under a sequential composition of the sub-protocols MP-MAT-COPY and BaseCase. By induction, we suppose that the protocol MP-SW is secure with $N/2$ players, and we show that the protocol MP-SW for N players.

Base Case: $N \leq T$. In this case, MP-SW calls are replaced by calls to BaseCase. By construction, the data layout is now 0-recursive. Then, the corrupted player cannot act as more than one player in the execution, so that the security of the protocol against one-semi honest is enough.

Induction: $N > T$. In this case, each call to the MP-SW protocol is assumed secure from the induction hypothesis. Then, each of these calls can be sequentially realized.

Then, since all sub-protocols calls can be realized sequentially, and since we have proven that MP-SW is secure in the $F^{\texttt{BaseCase}}$, F^{Copy}, $F_{N/2}^{\texttt{MP-SW}}$-hybrid model, the sequential composition theorem ensures that the protocol obtained by composition is also secure. Henceforth, by induction, we have proven that from $F_{N/2}^{\texttt{MP-SW}}$, we are able to construct a secure execution of MP-SW. In conclusion, the protocol MP-SW is secure against one semi-honest adversary. $\square$

References

1. Aho, A.V., Hopcroft, J.E., Ullman, J.D.: The Design and Analysis of Computer Algorithms (1974)
2. Blaze, M., Bleumer, G., Strauss, M.: Divertible protocols and atomic proxy cryptography. In: Nyberg, K. (ed.) EUROCRYPT 1998. LNCS, vol. 1403, pp. 127–144. Springer, Heidelberg (1998). https://doi.org/10.1007/BFb0054122

3. Boyer, B., Dumas, J.-G.: Matrix multiplication over word-size modular rings using approximateformulas. ACM Trans. Math. Softw. **42**, 20 (2016)

4. Castagnos, G., Imbert, L., Laguillaumie, F.: Encryption switching protocols revisited: switching modulo p. In: Katz, J., Shacham, H. (eds.) CRYPTO 2017. LNCS, vol. 10401, pp. 255–287. Springer, Cham (2017). https://doi.org/10.1007/978-3-319-63688-7_9

5. Cramer, R., Damgård, I.B., Nielsen, J.B.: Secure Multiparty Computation and Secret Sharing (2015)

6. Cramer, R., Damgård, I., Escudero, D., Scholl, P., Xing, C.: SPDZ$_{2^k}$: efficient MPC mod 2^k for dishonest majority. In: Shacham, H., Boldyreva, A. (eds.) CRYPTO 2018. LNCS, vol. 10992, pp. 769–798. Springer, Cham (2018). https://doi.org/10.1007/978-3-319-96881-0_26

7. Dagdelen, Ö., Venturi, D.: A multi-party protocol for privacy-preserving cooperative linear systems of equations. In: Ors, B., Preneel, B. (eds.) BalkanCryptSec 2014. LNCS, vol. 9024, pp. 161–172. Springer, Cham (2015). https://doi.org/10.1007/978-3-319-21356-9_11

8. Damgård, I., Nielsen, J.B., Nielsen, M., Ranellucci, S.: The tinytable protocol for 2-party secure computation, or: gate-scrambling revisited. In: Katz, J., Shacham, H. (eds.) CRYPTO 2017. LNCS, vol. 10401, pp. 167–187. Springer, Cham (2017). https://doi.org/10.1007/978-3-319-63688-7_6

9. Demmler, D., Schneider, T., Zohner, M.: ABY - a framework for efficient mixed-protocol secure two-party computation. In: NDSS (2015)

10. Du, W., Zhan, Z.: A practical approach to solve secure multiparty computation problems. In: NSPW 2002 (2002)

11. Dumas, J.-G., Giorgi, P., Pernet, C.: Dense linear algebra over word-size prime fields: The FFLAS andFFPACK packages. ACM Trans. Math. Softw. **35**, 19 (2008)

12. Dumas, J.-G., Hossayni, H.: Matrix powers algorithms for trust evaluation in public-key infrastructures. In: Jøsang, A., Samarati, P., Petrocchi, M. (eds.) STM 2012. LNCS, vol. 7783, pp. 129–144. Springer, Heidelberg (2013). https://doi.org/10.1007/978-3-642-38004-4_9

13. Dumas, J.-G., Lafourcade, P., Orfila, J.-B., Puys, M.: Dual protocols for private multiparty matrix multiplication and trustcomputations. Comput. Secur. **71**, 51–70 (2017)

14. Gascón, A., et al.: Privacy-preserving distributed linear regression on high-dimensional data. Proc. Priv. Enhancing Technol. **2017**, 345–364 (2017)

15. Goethals, B., Laur, S., Lipmaa, H., Mielikäinen, T.: On private scalar product computation for privacy-preserving data mining. In: Park, C., Chee, S. (eds.) ICISC 2004. LNCS, vol. 3506, pp. 104–120. Springer, Heidelberg (2005). https://doi.org/10.1007/11496618_9

16. Goldreich, O.: Foundations of Cryptography: Volume 2, Basic Applications (2004)

17. Ishai, Y., Mittal, M., Ostrovsky, R.: On the message complexity of secure multiparty computation. In: Abdalla, M., Dahab, R. (eds.) PKC 2018. LNCS, vol. 10769, pp. 698–711. Springer, Cham (2018). https://doi.org/10.1007/978-3-319-76578-5_24

18. Jarecki, S.: Efficient covert two-party computation. In: Abdalla, M., Dahab, R. (eds.) PKC 2018. LNCS, vol. 10769, pp. 644–674. Springer, Cham (2018). https://doi.org/10.1007/978-3-319-76578-5_22

19. Josang, A.: Probabilistic logic under uncertainty. In: 13th Computing: Australasian Theory Symposium (CATS 2007) (2007)

20. Kaliski, B., Staddon, J.: RSA Cryptography Specifications. RFC 2437 (1998)

21. Kaporin, I.: A practical algorithm for faster matrix multiplication. In: Numerical Linear Algebra with Applications (1999)
22. Karstadt, E., Schwartz, O.: Matrix multiplication, a little faster. In: SPAA 2017 (2017)
23. Le Gall, F.: Powers of tensors and fast matrix multiplication. In: ISSAC 2014 (2014)
24. Lindell, Y.: How to simulate it – a tutorial on the simulation proof technique. In: Lindell, Y. (ed.) Tutorials on the Foundations of Cryptography. ISC, pp. 277–346. Springer, Cham (2017). https://doi.org/10.1007/978-3-319-57048-8_6
25. Mishra, P.K., Rathee, D., Duong, D.H., Yasuda, M.: Fast secure matrix multiplications over ring-based homomorphic encryption. Cryptology ePrint, 2018/663
26. Naccache, D., Stern, J.: A new public key cryptosystem based on higher residues. In CCS 1998 (1998)
27. Paillier, P.: Public-key cryptosystems based on composite degree residuosity classes. In: Stern, J. (ed.) EUROCRYPT 1999. LNCS, vol. 1592, pp. 223–238. Springer, Heidelberg (1999). https://doi.org/10.1007/3-540-48910-X_16
28. Rindal, P., Rosulek, M.: Faster malicious 2-party secure computation with online/offline dual execution. In: USENIX Security Symposium (2016)
29. Shamir, A.: How to share a secret. ACM Commun. **22**, 612–613 (1979)
30. Strassen, V.: Gaussian elimination is not optimal. Numerische Mathematik (1969)

An Anonymous Credential System with Constant-Size Attribute Proofs for CNF Formulas with Negations

Ryo Okishima and Toru Nakanishi[✉]

Graduate School of Engineering, Hiroshima University,
Higashi-Hiroshima, Hiroshima, Japan
{m186746,t-nakanishi}@hiroshima-u.ac.jp

Abstract. To enhance the user's privacy in electronic ID, anonymous credential systems have been researched. In the anonymous credential system, a trusted issuing organization first issues a certificate certifying the user's attributes to a user. Then, in addition to the possession of the certificate, the user can anonymously prove only the necessary attributes. Previously, an anonymous credential system was proposed, where CNF (Conjunctive Normal Form) formulas on attributes can be proved. The advantage is that the attribute proof in the authentication has the constant size for the number of attributes that the user owns and the size of the proved formula. Thus, various expressive logical relations on attributes can be efficiently verified. However, the previous system has a limitation: the proved CNF formulas cannot include any negation. Therefore, in this paper, we propose an anonymous credential system with constant-size attribute proofs such that the user can prove CNF formulas with negations. For the proposed system, we extend the previous accumulator for the limited CNF formulas to verify CNF formulas with negations.

Keywords: Anonymous credentials · Accumulator · Pairing · Attributes

1 Introduction

1.1 Backgrounds

Electronic identity (eID) such as eID card is often used for physical user authentication for entering buildings, use of facilities and so on, and furthermore it can be used for network-based user authentication in Web services. In eID, in addition to the user's ID, the user's attributes such as gender, occupation, and birth date are authorized, and thus the attribute-based authentication using the eID can be performed. However, one of serious problem in the existing eID system is the user's privacy: Since the eID may reveal the user's unique ID, the verifier

© Springer Nature Switzerland AG 2019
N. Attrapadung and T. Yagi (Eds.): IWSEC 2019, LNCS 11689, pp. 89–106, 2019.
https://doi.org/10.1007/978-3-030-26834-3_6

can collect the user's history. As the solution, the anonymous credential system was proposed [9].

In the anonymous credential system, an issuer issues each user a certificate. The certificate is a proof of membership, qualification, or privilege, and ensures the user's own attributes. The user with the certificate can anonymously convince a service provider (SP) of the possession of the certificate. Additionally, the user can prove the possession of attributes, and furthermore a logical relation on the attributes. By the AND relation, the user can prove the possession of all attributes in the relation. By the OR relation, the user can prove the possession of one attribute from the attributes in the relation. As the advantage of the anonymous credential system with attribute proofs, it does not leak any other information beyond the satisfaction of the proved relation.

1.2 Previous Works

In [7,11,14], anonymous credential systems with attribute proofs have been proposed, where the proof size is constant for the number of user's attributes and the size of proved logical relation. However, available relations are only AND or OR relations on attributes. In [12], an anonymous credential system with attribute proofs of constant size has been proposed, where inner product relations on attributes can be proved. This means that CNF (Conjunctive Normal Form) and DNF (Disjunctive Normal Form) formulas are available by using polynomial-based encoding. However, this system has a problem of the computational cost: The proof generation requires the exponentiations depending on the number of OR literals in the proved formula. Thus, when the formula contains lots of OR literals, it requires large time on users' devices such as eID cards.

In the backgrounds, in [4], an efficient anonymous credential system with constant-size attribute proofs was proposed, where the user can prove CNF formulas on attributes. In this system, by newly constructing an efficient accumulator to verify CNF formulas and applying it to the system, the proof generation requires only the multiplications depending on the number of OR literals in the proved formula, and thus it is more efficient than [12]. However, this system has the problem that a user cannot directly prove any CNF relation with negations.

1.3 Our Contributions

In this paper, we construct an accumulator to verify CNF formulas with negations, and we apply it to the previous system [4] with the constant-size attribute proofs. In the proposed system, a user can prove any CNF formula with negations, where the proof generation cost is similar to the previous, i.e., the proof generation needs only multiplications depending on the number of OR literals.

In the previous accumulator [4] for the limited CNF formula without negations, the set relation $U \cap V_\ell \neq \emptyset$ can be verified for the user's attribute set U and the attribute set V_ℓ in the ℓ-th OR clause in the CNF formula, which implies that the user owns some attribute in each OR clause. In this paper, we consider non-limited CNF formulas of $\bigwedge_i \bigvee_j \breve{a}_{ij}$, where $\breve{a}_{ij}$ is a literal that is a non-negated attribute a_{ij} (the user owns the attribute) or a negated attribute a_{ij} (the user does not own the attribute). Any logical formula can be transformed to a CNF formula. In the proposed accumulator, in addition to $U \cap V_\ell^+ \neq \emptyset$ for the non-negated attribute set V_ℓ^+ in the ℓ-th OR clause, the relation $U \cap V_\ell^- \neq V_\ell^-$ can be verified for the negated attribute set V_ℓ^- in the ℓ-th OR clause. These means that the user owns some non-negated attribute or does not own some negated attribute, which implies the satisfaction of the CNF formula with negations.

1.4 Related Works

In [13], as the extension of [4], an anonymous credential system with the constant-size attribute proofs was proposed. The advantage is that a user can prove any monotone formula on attributes. However, in the system, negations are not available. Our idea is to support negations based on the previous accumulator [4] for the limited CNF formulas, and it does not work well in the accumulator of [13] for monotone formulas.

2 Preliminaries

2.1 Bilinear Maps

In this paper, we use the following bilinear groups with a bilinear map.

1. $\mathcal{G}_1, \mathcal{G}_2, \mathcal{T}$ are cyclic groups of prime order p.
2. g_1, g_2 are randomly chosen generators of $\mathcal{G}_1, \mathcal{G}_2$, respectively.
3. $e : \mathcal{G}_1 \times \mathcal{G}_2 \to \mathcal{T}$ is an efficiently calculated bilinear map satisfying
   (a) **Bilinearity:** for all $u \in \mathcal{G}_1$, $v \in \mathcal{G}_2, a, b \in \mathcal{Z}$, $e(u^a, v^b) = e(u, v)^{ab}$.
   (b) **Non-degeneracy:** $e(g_1, g_2) \neq 1_\mathcal{T}$ ($1_\mathcal{T}$ is the identity element of group $\mathcal{T}$).

The bilinear map e can be efficiently implemented with a pairing. There are two types of bilinear pairings, symmetric ($\mathcal{G}_1 = \mathcal{G}_2$) and asymmetric ($\mathcal{G}_1 \neq \mathcal{G}_2$). In the following descriptions, for simplicity, we adopt the symmetric one, i.e., e is defined as $\mathcal{G} \times \mathcal{G} \to \mathcal{T}$.

2.2 Assumptions

As in the previous system [4], the security of our system is based on the DLIN (Decision Linear) assumption, the q-SFP (Simultaneous Flexible Pairing) assumption, and n-DHE (DH Exponent) assumption. Hereafter, we use the notation $a \in_R A$ as sampling a from the set A according to the uniform distribution.

Definition 1 (DLIN assumption). *For all PPT algorithm* $\mathcal{A}$,

$$|Pr[\mathcal{A}(g, g^a, g^b, g^{ac}, g^{bd}, g^{c+d}) = 1] - Pr[\mathcal{A}(g, g^a, g^b, g^{ac}, g^{bd}, g^z) = 1]|$$

is negligible, where $g \in_R \mathcal{G}$ *and* $a, b, c, d, z \in_R Z_p$.

Definition 2 (q-SFP assumption). *For all PPT algorithm* $\mathcal{A}$, *the probability*

$$Pr[\mathcal{A}(g_z, h_z, g_r, h_r, a, \tilde{a}, b, \tilde{b}, \{(z_j, r_j, s_j, t_j, u_j, v_j, w_j)\}_{j=1}^q)$$
$$= (z^*, r^*, s^*, t^*, u^*, v^*, w^*) \in \mathcal{G}^7$$
$$\wedge e(a, \tilde{a}) = e(g_z, z^*)e(g_r, r^*)e(s^*, t^*)$$
$$\wedge e(b, \tilde{b}) = e(h_z, z^*)e(h_r, u^*)e(v^*, w^*)$$
$$\wedge z^* \neq 1_{\mathcal{G}} \wedge z^* \neq z_j \text{ for all } 1 \leq j \leq q]$$

is negligible, where $(g_z, h_z, g_r, h_r, a, \tilde{a}, b, \tilde{b}) \in \mathcal{G}^8$ *and all tuples* $\{(z_j, r_j, s_j, t_j, u_j, v_j, w_j)\}_{j=1}^q$ *satisfy*

$$e(a, \tilde{a}) = e(g_z, z_j)e(g_r, r_j)e(s_j, t_j) \wedge e(b, \tilde{b}) = e(h_z, z_j)e(h_r, u_j)e(v_j, w_j),$$

and $1_{\mathcal{G}}$ *is the identity element of group* $\mathcal{G}$.

Definition 3 (n-DHE assumption). *For all PPT algorithm* $\mathcal{A}$, *the probability*

$$Pr[\mathcal{A}(g, g^a, \ldots, g^{a^n}, g^{a^{n+2}}, \ldots, g^{a^{2n}}) = g^{a^{n+1}}]$$

is negligible, where $g \in_R \mathcal{G}$ *and* $a \in_R Z_p$.

2.3 AHO (Abe-Haralambiev-Ohkubo) Signatures

As in the previous system [4], we adopt AHO signatures [2] as the structure-preserving signatures, where multiple messages can be signed, and the verification using pairings can be proved by the following GS proofs. In this paper, we use it for a single message. As proved in [2], this signature is existentially unforgeable against the chosen message attacks under the q-SFP assumption.

AHOKeyGen: Select bilinear groups $\mathcal{G}, \mathcal{T}$ with a prime order p and bilinear map e. Select $g, G_r, H_r \in_R \mathcal{G}$, and $\mu_z, \nu_z, \mu, \nu, \alpha_a, \alpha_b \in_R Z_p$. Compute $G_z = G_r^{\mu_z}, H_z = H_r^{\nu_z}, G = G_r^{\mu}, H = H_r^{\nu}, A = e(G_r, g^{\alpha_a}), B = e(H_r, g^{\alpha_b})$. Output the public key as $pk = (\mathcal{G}, \mathcal{T}, p, e, g, G_r, H_r, G_z, H_z, G, H, A, B)$ and the secret key as $sk = (\alpha_a, \alpha_b, \mu_z, \nu_z, \mu, \nu)$.

AHOSign: The message M given as element of $\mathcal{G}$ is signed with the secret key sk. Choose $\beta, \epsilon, \eta, \iota, \kappa \in_R Z_p$, and compute $\theta_1 = g^{\beta}$ and

$$\theta_2 = g^{\epsilon - \mu_z \beta} M^{-\mu}, \qquad \theta_3 = G_r^{\eta}, \qquad \theta_4 = g^{(\alpha_a - \epsilon)/\eta},$$
$$\theta_5 = g^{\iota - \nu_z \beta} M^{-\nu}, \qquad \theta_6 = H_r^{\kappa}, \qquad \theta_7 = g^{(\alpha_b - \iota)/\kappa}.$$

Output the signature $\sigma = (\theta_1, \ldots, \theta_7)$.

AHOVerify: Given the message M and the signature $\sigma = (\theta_1, \ldots, \theta_7)$, accept these if the following equations hold:

$$A = e(G_z, \theta_1) \cdot e(G_r, \theta_2) \cdot e(\theta_3, \theta_4) \cdot e(G, M),$$
$$B = e(H_z, \theta_1) \cdot e(H_r, \theta_5) \cdot e(\theta_6, \theta_7) \cdot e(H, M).$$

2.4   GS (Groth-Sahai) Proofs

GS proofs [10] are Non-Interactive Witness Indistinguishable (NIWI) proofs for pairing relations. GS proofs need a CRS (Common Reference String) $(\boldsymbol{f}_1, \boldsymbol{f}_2, \boldsymbol{f}_3) \in (\mathcal{G}^3)^3$, where $\boldsymbol{f}_1 = (f_1, 1, g), \boldsymbol{f}_2 = (1, f_2, g)$ for $f_1, f_2 \in \mathcal{G}$. Two types of CRS are used. In the soundness setting, set $\boldsymbol{f}_3 = \boldsymbol{f}_1^{\xi_1} \cdot \boldsymbol{f}_2^{\xi_2}$ for $\xi_1, \xi_2 \in_R Z_p^*$. Compute the commitment to element X as $\boldsymbol{C} = (1, 1, X) \cdot \boldsymbol{f}_1^r \cdot \boldsymbol{f}_2^s \cdot \boldsymbol{f}_3^t$ for $r, s, t \in_R Z_p^*$. In this case, the commitment $\boldsymbol{C} = (f_1^{r+\xi_1 t}, f_2^{s+\xi_2 t}, X g^{r+s+t(\xi_1+\xi_2)})$ is a linear encryption [3]. Therefore, X can be extracted using the secret keys, $\log_g f_1, \log_g f_2$. On the other hand, in the Witness Indistinguishable (WI) setting, $\boldsymbol{f}_1, \boldsymbol{f}_2, \boldsymbol{f}_3$ are linearly independent, and thus $\boldsymbol{C}$ is perfectly hiding. Under the DLIN assumption, the two types of CRS are computationally indistinguishable.

In order to prove that committed values satisfy the pairing relation, the prover prepares the commitments and replaces variables in the relation with the commitments. By GS proof, we can prove the following pairing product equation.

$$\prod_{i=1}^{n} e(A_i, X_i) \cdot \prod_{i=1}^{n} \prod_{j=1}^{n} e(X_i, X_j)^{a_{ij}} = t$$

for variables $X_1, \ldots, X_n \in \mathcal{G}$ and constants $A_1, \ldots, A_n \in \mathcal{G}$, $a_{ij} \in Z_p$, $t \in \mathcal{T}$.

2.5   Set Membership Proof

As in the previous system [4], the set membership proof [6] is used to prove that an element is included in a set of elements, which is constructed from signatures, as follows. An issuer signs all elements of set A and publishes the signatures. To prove that an element a is included in set A, a prover proves the knowledge of a signature on a. Since the issuer does not publish the signatures on elements that are not included in A, $a \in A$ is guaranteed.

3   Accumulator to Verify CNF Formulas with Negations

3.1   Previous Accumulator and Problem

In [8], an efficient pairing-based accumulator using multiplications has been proposed. An accumulator is generated from a set of values, and we can confirm that a single value is included in the set. In the previous work [4], an extended accumulator has been proposed, where we can verify that $U \cap V_\ell \neq \emptyset$ $(1 \leq \ell \leq L)$ for sets U and $V_1, \ldots, V_L$. This verification is applied to the construction of the previous anonymous credential system [4] to verify CNF formulas on attributes. Let $V_1, \ldots, V_L$ be subsets of $\{1, \cdots, n\}$, and $\mathcal{V} = (\mathcal{V}_\infty, \ldots, \mathcal{V}_\mathcal{L})$. Let U be a subset of $\{1, \cdots, n\}$ that satisfies $U \cap V_\ell \neq \emptyset$ $(1 \leq \ell \leq L)$. In the attribute proof, U corresponds to the attribute set of an user. Each V_ℓ corresponds to the ℓ-th OR clause in the proved CNF formula. In the accumulator of [4], we can verify that $U \cap V_\ell \neq \emptyset$ for $1 \leq \ell \leq L$. This implies that some attribute of the user is included in all OR clauses, and so it can be verified that this user holds the attributes satisfying the CNF formula.

In the accumulator and the attribute proof using it in [4], we can not directly prove any CNF formula including a negation. To solve this problem, we can consider the following simple method without negations: Attributes can be divided into attribute types such as gender, age, and occupation. Then, to prove the non-possession of attribute a in an attribute type can be performed by proving the possession of one of other attributes in the type. However, this is undesirable for two reasons. One is to assign all attributes of the same type to the CNF formula as an OR clause, which increases the overhead of the proof. Secondly, any user must recognize all other attributes, but a user may be not aware of a newly added attribute to a attribute type. Therefore, we need an accumulator to directly verify CNF formulas with negations.

3.2 Construction Idea

In this paper, based on the previous accumulator [4], we extend it to verify the CNF formulas with negations. The accumulator acc_V of the previous scheme is computed as $acc_V = \prod_{1 \leq \ell \leq L} \left(\prod_{j \in V_\ell} g_{n+1-j} \right)^{c_\ell}$ for $g_i = g^{\gamma^i}$ (γ is secret) and some integers c_ℓ. On the other hand, in the proposed scheme, for a negated attribute $j \in V_\ell$, $g_{n+1-j}^{-c_\ell}$ is multiplied, instead of $g_{n+1-j}^{c_\ell}$. In the previous one, the verification is successful if $|U \cap V_\ell| \geq 1$ for the attribute set U of the user and the attribute set V_ℓ of the ℓ-th clause of the CNF formula. In the verification, for some witness W,

$$\frac{e(\prod_{i \in U} g_i, acc_V)}{e(g, W)} = z^{\delta_1 c_1 + \cdots + \delta_L c_L}, \text{ and } \delta_\ell \geq 1 \text{ for all } 1 \leq \ell \leq L$$

are checked. In the verification, $\delta_\ell = |U \cap V_\ell|$ holds. Thus, when U satisfies the CNF formula, which means $|U \cap V_\ell| \geq 1$, then the above $\delta_\ell \geq 1$ holds for all ℓ. In this previous scheme, c_ℓ is $|U \cap V_\ell|$ times added in the exponent of z for each ℓ in the left side of the verification equation. In the proposed scheme, each V_ℓ is partitioned to the non-negated attribute set V_ℓ^+ and the negated attribute set V_ℓ^-. For the attributes of V_ℓ^+ c_ℓ is added as in the previous scheme, but for the negated attributes of V_ℓ^-, c_ℓ is subtracted. Then, in the verification, the coefficient of c_ℓ in the exponent of z on the left side is $|U \cap V_\ell^+| - |U \cap V_\ell^-|$ for each ℓ, and by checking $\delta_\ell \geq 1 - |V_\ell^-|$, we can verify $|U \cap V_\ell^+| \geq 1$ or $|U \cap V_\ell^-| \neq |V_\ell^-|$. This means $U \cap V_\ell^+ \neq \emptyset$ or $U \cap V_\ell^- \neq V_\ell^-$ (for the detail, see the proof of Theorem 1). Thus, in each OR clause, it means that the user owns a non-negated attribute or does not own a negated attribute, and thus the CNF formula is satisfied. In the proposed scheme, since we only modify c_ℓ in the exponent to $-c_\ell$ for each negated attribute, it is expected that the processing time will remain.

3.3 Proposed Algorithms

AccSetup: This algorithm outputs public parameters. Set η_ℓ as the maximum value of $|V_\ell^+ \cup V_\ell^-|$ for all $1 \leq \ell \leq L$. Let $c_1 = 1$, $c_\ell = (\eta_{\ell-1} + 1) \cdot c_{\ell-1}$ ($2 \leq \ell \leq L$), $C = (c_1, \ldots, c_L)$. Here, it is assumed that $(\eta_L + 1) \cdot c_L < p$, as in the previous accumulator [4]. Select bilinear groups $\mathcal{G}, \mathcal{T}$ with prime order p and the bilinear map e. Select $g \in_R \mathcal{G}$. Choose $\gamma \in_R Z_p$. Compute and output the public parameters $(C, p, \mathcal{G}, \mathcal{T}, e, g, g_1 = g^{\gamma^1}, \ldots, g_n = g^{\gamma^n}, g_{n+2} = g^{\gamma^{n+2}}, \ldots, g_{2n} = g^{\gamma^{2n}}, z = e(g,g)^{\gamma^{n+1}})$.

AccGen: This algorithm, given the public parameters and $\mathcal{V} = (V_1^+, V_1^-, \ldots, V_L^+, V_L^-)$, outputs an accumulator for $\mathcal{V}$. Here, $V_\ell^+ \subseteq \{1, \ldots, n\}$ is the set of non-negated attributes in the ℓ-th OR clause, and $V_\ell^- \subseteq \{1, \ldots, n\}$ is the set of negated attributes. Accumulator $acc_\mathcal{V}$ is calculated as follows.

$$acc_\mathcal{V} = \prod_{1 \leq \ell \leq L} \left(\prod_{j \in V_\ell^+} g_{n+1-j} \right)^{c_\ell} \left(\prod_{j \in V_\ell^-} g_{n+1-j} \right)^{-c_\ell}$$

AccWitGen: This algorithm, given the public parameters, $\mathcal{V}$, and $U \subseteq \{1, \ldots, n\}$, outputs the witness W. W is calculated as follows.

$$W = \prod_{i \in U} \prod_{1 \leq \ell \leq L} \left(\prod_{\substack{j \in V_\ell^+ \\ j \neq i}} g_{n+1-j+i} \right)^{c_\ell} \left(\prod_{\substack{j \in V_\ell^- \\ j \neq i}} g_{n+1-j+i} \right)^{-c_\ell}$$

Furthermore, $\delta_\ell = |U \cap V_\ell^+| - |U \cap V_\ell^-|$ for all $1 \leq \ell \leq L$ are calculated and outputted as auxiliary parameters.

AccVerify: This algorithm, given the public parameters, $\mathcal{V}, acc_\mathcal{V}, U, W$, $\{\delta_\ell\}_{1 \leq \ell \leq L}$, verifies $U \cap V_\ell^+ \neq \emptyset$ or $U \cap V_\ell^- \neq V_\ell^-$ for all $1 \leq \ell \leq L$. Set $u = \delta_1 c_1 + \ldots + \delta_L c_L$. Accept if the following relations hold.

$$\frac{e(\prod_{i \in U} g_i, acc_\mathcal{V})}{e(g, W)} = z^u, \text{ and } 1 \leq \delta_\ell + |V_\ell^-| \leq \eta_\ell \text{ for all } 1 \leq \ell \leq L.$$

In this case, since $1 - |V_\ell^-| \leq \delta_\ell$, this verification means the check of $1 - |V_\ell^-| \leq |U \cap V_\ell^+| - |U \cap V_\ell^-|$, which implies $|U \cap V_\ell^+| - |U \cap V_\ell^-| \neq -|V_\ell^-|$, and thus $U \cap V_\ell^+ \neq \emptyset$ or $U \cap V_\ell^- \neq V_\ell^-$.

3.4 Security

At first, we show the correctness of the proposed accumulator.

Theorem 1. *Suppose that all parameters of* **AccSetup**, **AccGen**, *and* **Acc WitGen** *are calculated correctly. Then,* **AccVerify** *accepts* $\mathcal{V}$, $acc_\mathcal{V}, U, W$, $\{\delta_\ell\}_{1 \leq \ell \leq L}$ *that those algorithms output, if* $U \cap V_\ell^+ \neq \emptyset$ *or* $U \cap V_\ell^- \neq V_\ell^-$ *for all* $1 \leq \ell \leq L$.

Proof. Assume all parameters of **AccSetup**, **AccGen**, and **AccWitGen** are calculated correctly. Then, the left hand of the verification equation in **AccVerify** is transformed as follows.

$$
\frac{e(\prod_{i\in U} g_i, acc_\mathcal{V})}{e(g,W)} = \frac{e(\prod_{i\in U} g_i, \prod_{1\le\ell\le L}\left(\prod_{j\in V_\ell^+} g_{n+1-j}\right)^{c_\ell}\left(\prod_{j\in V_\ell^-} g_{n+1-j}\right)^{-c_\ell})}{e(g,\prod_{i\in U}\prod_{1\le\ell\le L}\left(\prod_{\substack{j\in V_\ell^+\\ j\ne i}} g_{n+1-j+i}\right)^{c_\ell}\left(\prod_{\substack{j\in V_\ell^-\\ j\ne i}} g_{n+1-j+i}\right)^{-c_\ell})}
$$

$$
= \frac{e(g,\prod_{i\in U}\prod_{1\le\ell\le L}\left(\prod_{j\in V_\ell^+} g_{n+1-j+i}\right)^{c_\ell}\left(\prod_{j\in V_\ell^-} g_{n+1-j+i}\right)^{-c_\ell})}{e(g,\prod_{i\in U}\prod_{1\le\ell\le L}\left(\prod_{\substack{j\in V_\ell^+\\ j\ne i}} g_{n+1-j+i}\right)^{c_\ell}\left(\prod_{\substack{j\in V_\ell^-\\ j\ne i}} g_{n+1-j+i}\right)^{-c_\ell})}
$$

$$
= e(g,\prod_{i\in U}\prod_{1\le\ell\le L}\left(\prod_{\substack{j\in V_\ell^+\\ j=i}} g_{n+1-j+i}\right)^{c_\ell}\left(\prod_{\substack{j\in V_\ell^-\\ j=i}} g_{n+1-j+i}\right)^{-c_\ell})
$$

Set $\delta_\ell = |U\cap V_\ell^+| - |U\cap V_\ell^-|$ for all $1\le\ell\le L$, and $u = \delta_1 c_1 + \ldots + \delta_L c_L$. Then, the above expression is equal to the right side of the verification equation as follows.

$$
e\left(g,\prod_{1\le\ell\le L} g_{n+1}^{\delta_\ell c_\ell}\right) = e(g,g_{n+1})^u = z^u
$$

Here, for $|U\cap V_\ell^+|$, the possible range is $0\le |U\cap V_\ell^+|\le |V_\ell^+|$, and for $|U\cap V_\ell^-|$, it is $0\le |U\cap V_\ell^-|\le |V_\ell^-|$, and thus

$$
-|V_\ell^-|\le |U\cap V_\ell^+| - |U\cap V_\ell^-|\le |V_\ell^+|.
$$

On the other hand, we have $U\cap V_\ell^+\ne\emptyset$ or $U\cap V_\ell^-\ne V_\ell^-$ for all $1\le\ell\le L$ as the condition in this theorem. In case that the condition of the theorem does not hold, for some ℓ, $|U\cap V_\ell^+| = 0$ and $|U\cap V_\ell^-| = |V_\ell^-|$, which means $|U\cap V_\ell^+| - |U\cap V_\ell^-| = -|V_\ell^-|$. Therefore, in case that the condition in this theorem holds, we obtain

$$
1 - |V_\ell^-|\le |U\cap V_\ell^+| - |U\cap V_\ell^-|\le |V_\ell^+|,
$$

for all $1\le\ell\le L$. From $\delta_\ell = |U\cap V_\ell^+| - |U\cap V_\ell^-|$, we have $1 - |V_\ell^-|\le\delta_\ell\le |V_\ell^+|$, and thus

$$
1\le\delta_\ell + |V_\ell^-|\le |V_\ell^+| + |V_\ell^-|\le\eta_\ell,
$$

for all $1 \leq \ell \leq L$. Therefore, **AccVerify** accepts these parameters.   □

Furthermore, as in the journal version [5] of the previous work [4], using the following lemma (the proof is in [5]), we show the security of the proposed accumulator in Theorem 2.

Lemma 1. *For any $\tilde{\ell}$ s.t. $2 \leq \tilde{\ell} \leq L$, it holds $c_{\tilde{\ell}} > \sum_{1 \leq \ell \leq \tilde{\ell}-1} n_\ell \cdot c_\ell$.*

Theorem 2. *Under n-DHE assumption, given the public parameters, any adversary cannot output $U, \mathcal{V} = \{V_\ell^+, V_\ell^-\}_{1 \leq \ell \leq L}, W, \{\delta_\ell\}_{1 \leq \ell \leq L}$ which satisfy the following with a non-negligible probability.*

- *For $acc_\mathcal{V}$ correctly computed from $\mathcal{V}$, **AccVerify** accepts $\mathcal{V}, acc_\mathcal{V}, U, W, \{\delta_\ell\}_{1 \leq \ell \leq L}$.*
- *There exists some ℓ s.t. $U \cap V_\ell^+ = \emptyset$ and $U \cap V_\ell^- = V_\ell^-$.*

Proof. Assume an adversary that outputs $U, \mathcal{V} = \{V_\ell^+, V_\ell^-\}_{1 \leq \ell \leq L}, W, \{\delta_\ell\}_{1 \leq \ell \leq L}$ s.t. **AccVerify** accepts them and $U \cap V_\ell^+ = \emptyset$ and $U \cap V_\ell^- = V_\ell^-$ for some ℓ with a non-negligible probability. Since **AccVerify** accepts them, we have

$$\frac{e(\prod_{i \in U} g_i, acc_\mathcal{V})}{e(g, W)} = z^u = e(g, g_{n+1})^u,$$

for $u = \delta_1 c_1 + \ldots + \delta_L c_L$. From the correctly computed

$$acc_\mathcal{V} = \prod_{1 \leq \ell \leq L} \left(\prod_{j \in V_\ell^+} g_{n+1-j} \right)^{c_\ell} \left(\prod_{j \in V_\ell^-} g_{n+1-j} \right)^{-c_\ell},$$

we have

$$\frac{e\left(\prod_{i \in U} g_i, \prod_{1 \leq \ell \leq L} \left(\prod_{j \in V_\ell^+} g_{n+1-j}\right)^{c_\ell} \left(\prod_{j \in V_\ell^-} g_{n+1-j}\right)^{-c_\ell}\right)}{e(g, W)} = e(g, g_{n+1})^u$$

$$e\left(g, \prod_{i \in U} \prod_{1 \leq \ell \leq L} \left(\prod_{j \in V_\ell^+} g_{n+1-j+i}\right)^{c_\ell} \left(\prod_{j \in V_\ell^-} g_{n+1-j+i}\right)^{-c_\ell}\right) = e(g, W g_{n+1}{}^u)$$

Thus, we obtain the followings.

$$\prod_{i \in U} \prod_{1 \leq \ell \leq L} \left(\prod_{j \in V_\ell^+} g_{n+1-j+i}\right)^{c_\ell} \left(\prod_{j \in V_\ell^-} g_{n+1-j+i}\right)^{-c_\ell} = W g_{n+1}{}^u$$

$$\prod_{1 \leq \ell \leq L} \prod_{i \in U} \left(\prod_{\substack{j \in V_\ell^+ \\ j \neq i}} g_{n+1-j+i}\right)^{c_\ell} \cdot \prod_{1 \leq \ell \leq L} g_{n+1}{}^{|U \cap V_\ell^+| c_\ell}$$

$$\cdot \prod_{1 \leq \ell \leq L} \prod_{i \in U} \left(\prod_{\substack{j \in V_\ell^- \\ j \neq i}} g_{n+1-j+i}\right)^{-c_\ell} \cdot \prod_{1 \leq \ell \leq L} g_{n+1}{}^{-|U \cap V_\ell^-| c_\ell}$$

$$= W g_{n+1}{}^u$$

By setting $\lambda_\ell = |U \cap V_\ell^+| - |U \cap V_\ell^-| + |V_\ell^-|$,

$$\prod_{1 \le \ell \le L} \prod_{i \in U} \left(\prod_{\substack{j \in V_\ell^+ \\ j \ne i}} g_{n+1-j+i} \right)^{c_\ell} \cdot \prod_{1 \le \ell \le L} \prod_{i \in U} \left(\prod_{\substack{j \in V_\ell^- \\ j \ne i}} g_{n+1-j+i} \right)^{-c_\ell}$$

$$= W g_{n+1}{}^{u - \sum_{1 \le \ell \le L}(\lambda_\ell - |V_\ell^-|)c_\ell} \tag{1}$$

Define $\Delta = u - \sum_{1 \le \ell \le L}(\lambda_\ell - |V_\ell^-|)c_\ell$. Then, we have

$$\Delta = \sum_{1 \le \ell \le L} \delta_\ell c_\ell - \sum_{1 \le \ell \le L} (\lambda_\ell - |V_\ell^-|)c_\ell$$

$$= \sum_{1 \le \ell \le L} (\delta_\ell - \lambda_\ell + |V_\ell^-|)c_\ell.$$

Here, divide $\{1,\ldots,L\}$ into $L^>, L^<$, and $L^=$, where $L^>$ consists of ℓ s.t. $\delta_\ell - \lambda_\ell + |V_\ell^-| > 0$, $L^<$ consists of ℓ s.t. $\delta_\ell - \lambda_\ell + |V_\ell^-| < 0$, and $L^=$ consists of ℓ s.t. $\delta_\ell - \lambda_\ell + |V_\ell^-| = 0$.

Using $L^>, L^<$, and $L^=$, the following equation can be obtained.

$$\Delta = \sum_{\ell \in L^>} (\delta_\ell - \lambda_\ell + |V_\ell^-|)c_\ell + \sum_{\ell \in L^<} (\delta_\ell - \lambda_\ell + |V_\ell^-|)c_\ell$$

Let $\tilde{\ell}$ be the maximum value of ℓ s.t. $\ell \notin L^=$ (i.e., $\tilde{\ell} \in L^>$ or $\tilde{\ell} \in L^<$). From **AccVerify** $= 1$, it holds $\delta_\ell + |V_\ell^-| \ge 1$ for all ℓ. On the other hand, since for some ℓ, $U \cap V_\ell^+ = \emptyset$ and $U \cap V_\ell^- = V_\ell^-$, we have $\lambda_\ell = |U \cap V_\ell^+| - |U \cap V_\ell^-| + |V_\ell^-| = 0$ for the ℓ. This implies that $\delta_\ell - \lambda_\ell + |V_\ell^-| \ne 0$ for the ℓ. Therefore, $\ell \notin L^=$ exists.

Next, we will prove $\Delta \ne 0 \pmod{p}$ for two cases (i) and (ii).

(i) **Case of $\tilde{\ell} \in L^<$ $(\delta_{\tilde{\ell}} - \lambda_{\tilde{\ell}} + |V_{\tilde{\ell}}^-| < 0)$:**

In this case, $(\delta_{\tilde{\ell}} - \lambda_{\tilde{\ell}} + |V_{\tilde{\ell}}^-|)c_{\tilde{\ell}} \le -c_{\tilde{\ell}}$, which implies

$$\Delta \le -c_{\tilde{\ell}} + \sum_{\ell \in L^>} (\delta_\ell - \lambda_\ell + |V_\ell^-|)c_\ell + \sum_{\ell \in L^<, \ell \ne \tilde{\ell}} (\delta_\ell - \lambda_\ell + |V_\ell^-|)c_\ell.$$

For $\ell \in L^>$, since $\lambda_\ell \ge 0$ and $\delta_\ell + |V_\ell^-| \le \eta_\ell$, we have $\delta_\ell - \lambda_\ell + |V_\ell^-| \le \eta_\ell$. For $\ell \in L^<$, we have $\delta_\ell - \lambda_\ell + |V_\ell^-| < 0$. Therefore,

$$\Delta < -c_{\tilde{\ell}} + \sum_{\ell \in L^>} \eta_\ell c_\ell.$$

From Lemma 1, we obtain $\Delta < 0$ due to $c_{\tilde{\ell}} > \sum_{\ell \in (L^> \cup L^<)} \eta_\ell c_\ell$.

On the other hand, from $\delta_\ell + |V_\ell^-| > 0$ and $\lambda_\ell = |U \cap V_\ell^+| - |U \cap V_\ell^-| + |V_\ell^-| \le |V_\ell^+ \cup V_\ell^-| \le \eta_\ell$,

$$\Delta = \sum_{1 \le \ell \le L} (\delta_\ell + |V_\ell^-|)c_\ell - \sum_{1 \le \ell \le L} \lambda_\ell c_\ell > - \sum_{1 \le \ell \le L} \eta_\ell c_\ell$$

From Lemma 1, we obtain $\sum_{1 \le \ell \le L-1} \eta_\ell c_\ell < c_L$, and thus

$$\sum_{1 \le \ell \le L} \eta_\ell c_\ell \; < \; c_L + \eta_L c_L \; = \; (\eta_L + 1)c_L \; < \; p.$$

This is why $\Delta > -p$. Therefore, in this case, $\Delta \ne 0 \pmod{p}$.

(ii) **Case of $\tilde{\ell} \in L^>$ $(\delta_{\tilde{\ell}} - \lambda_{\tilde{\ell}} + |V_{\tilde{\ell}}^-| > 0)$:**
In this case, $(\delta_{\tilde{\ell}} - \lambda_{\tilde{\ell}} + |V_{\tilde{\ell}}^-|)c_{\tilde{\ell}} \ge c_{\tilde{\ell}}$, which means

$$\Delta \ge c_{\tilde{\ell}} + \sum_{\ell \in L^>, \ell \ne \tilde{\ell}} (\delta_\ell - \lambda_\ell + |V_\ell^-|)c_\ell + \sum_{\ell \in L^<} (\delta_\ell - \lambda_\ell + |V_\ell^-|)c_\ell$$

From $\delta_\ell - \lambda_\ell + |V_\ell^-| > 0$ for any $\ell \in L^>$, we have

$$\Delta > c_{\tilde{\ell}} + \sum_{\ell \in L^<} (\delta_\ell - \lambda_\ell + |V_\ell^-|)c_\ell.$$

Here, from $\lambda_\ell \le \eta_\ell$ and $\delta_\ell + |V_\ell^-| \ge 0$, we have $\lambda_\ell - \delta_\ell - |V_\ell^-| \le \eta_\ell$. Thus, from $\tilde{\ell} > \ell$ for any $\ell \in L^<$ and Lemma 1, we obtain

$$c_{\tilde{\ell}} > \sum_{\ell \in L^<} \eta_\ell c_\ell \ge \sum_{\ell \in L^<} (\lambda_\ell - \delta_\ell - |V_\ell^-|)c_\ell$$

Therefore,

$$c_{\tilde{\ell}} + \sum_{\ell \in L^<} (\delta_\ell - \lambda_\ell + |V_\ell^-|)c_\ell > 0.$$

Namely, we can get $\Delta > 0$.
On the other hand, from $\lambda_\ell \ge 0$, $\delta_\ell + |V_\ell^-| \le \eta_\ell$, and Lemma 1,

$$\Delta = \sum_{1 \le \ell \le L} (\delta_\ell + |V_\ell^-|)c_\ell \; - \sum_{1 \le \ell \le L} \lambda_\ell c_\ell$$

$$\le \sum_{1 \le \ell \le L} (\delta_\ell + |V_\ell^-|)c_\ell \le \sum_{1 \le \ell \le L} \eta_\ell c_\ell = \sum_{1 \le \ell \le L-1} \eta_\ell c_\ell + \eta_L c_L \le c_L + \eta_L c_L.$$

Thus, $\Delta \le (\eta_L + 1)c_L < p$. Therefore, it also holds $\Delta \ne 0 \pmod{p}$ in this case.

Therefore, since $\Delta \ne 0 \pmod{p}$ in both cases, from Eq. (1), we obtain

$$g_{n+1} = \left(W^{-1} \cdot \prod_{1 \le \ell \le L} \prod_{i \in U} \left(\prod_{j \in V_\ell^+}^{j \ne i} g_{n+1-j+i} \right)^{c_\ell} \right.$$

$$\left. \cdot \prod_{1 \le \ell \le L} \prod_{i \in U} \left(\prod_{j \in V_\ell^-}^{j \ne i} g_{n+1-j+i} \right)^{-c_\ell} \right)^{1/\Delta}.$$

For any $i \in U$, any $j \in V_\ell^+$ and $j \in V_\ell^-$ s.t. $j \ne i$, it holds $g_{n+1-j+i} \ne g_{n+1}$. Therefore, we can calculate g_{n+1}, given $g_1, \ldots, g_n, g_{n+2}, \ldots, g_{2n}$, which contradicts the n-DHE assumption.   □

4   Syntax and Security Model of Anonymous Credential System

We adopt the syntax and security model of anonymous credential system with attribute proofs in the previous work [4]. It is the non-interactive anonymous credential system, where the user creates the attribute proof from his own certificate issued from an issuer, and the verifier can confirm the proof by himself. Since this concept is similar to the group signature scheme, the security model is derived from the group signature scheme, but concentrates on the security of attribute proofs. This is why the model considers the following two security requirements: misauthentication resistance and the anonymity.

4.1   Syntax

As in [4], each attribute values is indexed by an integer from $\{1, \ldots, n\}$ where n is the total number of attribute values. Use the indexes to describe a CNF formula Ψ (including negations) on attribute, as follows.

$$(\breve{a}_{11} \vee \breve{a}_{12} \vee \ldots) \wedge (\breve{a}_{21} \vee \breve{a}_{22} \vee \ldots) \wedge \cdots ,$$

where each literal $\breve{a}_{ij}$ is (non-negated) attribute index $a_{ij} \in \{1, \ldots, n\}$ or its negation $\neg a_{ij}$. The literal a_{ij} means that the user owns the attribute of the index, and the literal $\neg a_{ij}$ means that the user does not own the attribute of the index. Let V_ℓ^+ be the set of non-negated attribute indexes in the ℓ-th clause in CNF formula Ψ (i.e, $V_\ell^+ = \{a_{\ell j} | \breve{a}_{\ell j} = a_{\ell j}\}$). Let V_ℓ^- be the set of negated attribute indexes in the ℓ-th clause in CNF formula Ψ (i.e, $V_\ell^- = \{a_{\ell j} | \breve{a}_{\ell j} = \neg a_{\ell j}\}$).

Let U be a set of attribute indexes that the proving user owns. We assume that the upper bound of each clause size, i.e., $|V_\ell^+ \cup V_\ell^-|$, is η_ℓ for all $1 \le \ell \le L$. Also, we assume that the maximum number of clauses of CNF formulas is L.

Then, the satisfaction of the CNF formula Ψ with $(V_1^+, V_1^-, \ldots, V_\ell^+, V_\ell^-)$ by U is shown by $U \cap V_\ell^+ \ne \emptyset$ or $U \cap V_\ell^- \ne V_\ell^-$ for all $1 \le \ell \le L$.

The anonymous credential system consists of the following algorithms and protocol.

IssuerKeyGen: This algorithm, given $n, L, \{\eta_\ell\}_{1 \le \ell \le L}$, outputs the issuer's public key ipk and the issuer's secret key isk.

CertObtain: This is an interactive protocol between algorithm **CertObtain-$\mathcal{U}_k$** of the k-th user and algorithm **CertObtain-$\mathcal{I}$** of the issuer, where the issuer issues a certificate certifying the attributes to the user. **CertObtain-$\mathcal{U}_k$**'s inputs are ipk and $U_k \subset \{1, \ldots, n\}$ which are the user's attribute indexes, and its output is certificate $cert_k$ that guarantees the attributes of the user. On the other hand, **CertObtain-$\mathcal{I}$** is given ipk, isk and U_k as inputs.

ProofGen: This algorithm for the k-th user, given $ipk, U_k, cert_k, \Psi$ that is a proved CNF formula on attributes, outputs the attribute proof σ.

Verify: This algorithm for verification, given ipk, proof σ generated on U_k of the k-th user, and the proved CNF formula Ψ, outputs 'valid' if the attributes U_k satisfy Ψ (i.e., $U_k \cap V_\ell^+ \ne \emptyset$ or $U_k \cap V_\ell^- \ne V_\ell^-$ for all $1 \le \ell \le L$), and otherwise 'invalid'.

4.2   Security Model

The security model in [4] consists of *misauthentication resistance* and *anonymity*. The misauthentication resistance means the soundness of attribute proofs, i.e., any adversary $\mathcal{A}$ cannot forge an attribute proof for a CNF formula, where the formula is not satisfied by the attributes of any user who is corrupted by the adversary. The anonymity means the anonymity and unlinkability of proofs, which are similar to those of group signatures. Due to the page limitation, we omit the formal definitions (See [4]).

5   An Anonymous Credential System with Constant-Size Attribute Proofs for CNF Formulas with Negations

We extend the anonymous credential system [4] for limited CNF formulas without negations such that the user can prove any CNF formula with negations. In the previous system, in **IssuerKeyGen**, an issuer publishes the signatures on valid u's in the accumulator verification, which is based on the concept of the set membership proof. In **CertObtain**, to the user, the issuer issues a membership certificate which is the AHO signature on $P_k = \prod_{i \in U_k} g_i$ for the attribute set U_k of the user. In **ProofGen** and **Verify**, the user proves the verification of the AHO signature on P_k, and the equation of the accumulator verification by GS proofs. In addition, to show the range of each δ_ℓ in $u = \delta_1 c_1 + \ldots + \delta_L c_L$ in the accumulator verification, the user proves the verification of the AHO signature on u.

In our extension, **IssuerKeyGen** and **CertObtain** are the almost same as the previous system, where AHO signatures are published for the valid range of $u' = (\delta_1 + |V_1^-|)c_1 + \ldots + (\delta_L + |V_L^-|)c_L$. In **ProofGen** and **Verify**, the used accumulator is modified to our newly constructed accumulator in Sect. 3 for CNF formulas with negations. The user proves the verification equation of the accumulator, and the verification of the AHO signature on u' which means $1 \leq \delta_\ell + |V_\ell^-| \leq \eta_\ell$ for each ℓ. Thus, due to the accumulator, it is ensured that $U \cap V_\ell^+ \neq \emptyset$ or $U \cap V_\ell^- \neq V_\ell^-$ for all $1 \leq \ell \leq L$.

5.1   Construction

The algorithms and protocol of the proposed system is as follows.

IssuerKeyGen: Given n that is the total number of attribute values, L that is the maximum value of clauses of proved CNF formulas, and η_ℓ that is the upper bound of $|V_\ell^+ \cup V_\ell^-|$. This algorithm executes **AccSetup** to generate the public parameters of the proposed accumulator, and generates the key pair of AHO signatures, CRS for GS NIWI proofs, and AHO signatures for the set membership proof.

(i) Select prime order p, bilinear group $\mathcal{G}, \mathcal{T}$ and bilinear map e. Choose $g \in_R \mathcal{G}$.

(ii) Generate public parameters of the proposed accumulator for CNF formulas with negations: Calculate $c_1 = 1, c_\ell = (\eta_{\ell-1} + 1) \cdot c_{\ell-1}$ for $2 \leq \ell \leq L$, and set $\mathcal{C} = (c_1, \ldots, c_L)$. Choose $\gamma \in_R \mathbb{Z}_p$ and calculate

$$pk_{acc} = (\mathcal{C}, g_1 = g^{\gamma^1}, \ldots, g_n = g^{\gamma^n}, g_{n+2} = g^{\gamma^{n+2}}, \ldots, g_{2n} = g^{\gamma^{2n}}, z = (g,g)^{\gamma^{n+1}}).$$

(iii) For AHO signatures, generate the following two key pairs for $d = 0, 1$.

$$pk_{AHO}^{(d)} = (G_r^{(d)}, H_r^{(d)}, G_z^{(d)}, H_z^{(d)}, G^{(d)}, H^{(d)}, A^{(d)}, B^{(d)}),$$
$$sk_{AHO}^{(d)} = (\alpha_a^{(d)}, \alpha_b^{(d)}, \mu_z^{(d)}, \nu_z^{(d)}, \mu^{(d)}, \nu^{(d)}).$$

(iv) Generate CRS $\boldsymbol{f} = (\boldsymbol{f_1}, \boldsymbol{f_2}, \boldsymbol{f_3})$ for GS NIWI proof:

$$\boldsymbol{f_1} = (f_1, 1, g), \quad \boldsymbol{f_2} = (1, f_2, g), \quad \boldsymbol{f_3} = \boldsymbol{f_1}^{\xi_1} \cdot \boldsymbol{f_2}^{\xi_2},$$

where $f_1, f_2 \in_R \mathcal{G}$, $\xi_1, \xi_2 \in_R \mathbb{Z}_p^*$.

(v) Define set $\Phi = \{u' = \sum_{\ell=1}^{L} \delta'_\ell c_\ell | 1 \leq \delta'_\ell \leq \eta_\ell\}$. Then, $|\Phi| = \prod_{1 \leq \ell \leq L} \eta_\ell$. For all $u' \in \Phi$, we generate an AHO signature on $g_1^{u'}$ using $sk_{AHO}^{(0)}$. The signature is denoted as $\tilde{\sigma}_{u'} = (\tilde{\theta}_{u'1}, \ldots, \tilde{\theta}_{u'7})$.

(vi) As the public key and secret key of the issuer, output

$$ipk = (p, \mathcal{G}, \mathcal{T}, e, g, pk_{AHO}^{(0)}, pk_{AHO}^{(1)}, pk_{acc}, \boldsymbol{f}, \{\tilde{\sigma}_{u'}\}_{u' \in \Phi}),$$
$$isk = (sk_{AHO}^{(0)}, sk_{AHO}^{(1)}).$$

CertObtain: This is the protocol between **CertObtain-$\mathcal{U}_k$** (the k-th user) and **CertObtain-$\mathcal{I}$** (issuer). The input of **CertObtain-$\mathcal{U}_k$** consists of ipk and the set U_k of the user's attribute indexes. The inputs of **CertObtain-$\mathcal{I}$** are ipk, isk, and U_k. In this protocol, the issuer issues the user the certificate $cert_k$. Here, it is assumed that a special attribute value a_{SP} is introduced and all users owns a_{SP}.

(i) **CertObtain-$\mathcal{I}$**: Generate $P_k = \prod_{i \in U_k} g_i$.

(ii) **CertObtain-$\mathcal{I}$**: Use $sk_{AHO}^{(1)}$ to generate the AHO signature $\sigma_k = (\theta_1, \ldots, \theta_7)$ on P_k, where σ_k is sent to **CertObtain-$\mathcal{U}_k$** as the certificate.

(iii) **CertObtain-$\mathcal{U}_k$**: Compute $P_k = \prod_{i \in U_k} g_i$, and verify the AHO signature σ_k on P_k. Then, output $cert_k = (P_k, \sigma_k)$.

ProofGen: Given $ipk, U_k, cert_k$ and CNF formula $\Psi = (\breve{a}_{11} \vee \breve{a}_{12} \vee \ldots) \wedge (\breve{a}_{21} \vee \breve{a}_{22} \vee \ldots) \wedge \cdots (\breve{a}_{L'1} \vee \breve{a}_{L'2} \vee \ldots)$, where each literal $\breve{a}_{ij}$ is (non-negated) attribute index $a_{ij} \in \{1, \ldots, n\}$ or its negation $\neg a_{ij}$. Let V_ℓ^+ be the set of non-negated attributes in the ℓ-th OR clause, and let V_ℓ^- be the set of negated attributes. If $L' < L$, define $V_{L'+1}^+ = \ldots = V_L^+ = \{a_{SP}\}$ and $V_{L'+1}^- = \ldots = V_L^- = \emptyset$. This algorithm generates GS proofs to prove that P_k satisfies the accumulator verification for acc_Ψ corresponding to Ψ and that P_k is signed by the issuer using AHO signatures. In addition, the AHO signature on $g_1^{u'}$ is also used in the accumulator verification.

(i) Compute the accumulator of $\mathcal{V} = (V_1^+, V_1^-, \ldots)$:

$$acc_\mathcal{V} = \prod_{1 \leq \ell \leq L} \left(\prod_{j \in V_\ell^+} g_{n+1-j} \right)^{c_\ell} \left(\prod_{j \in V_\ell^-} g_{n+1-j} \right)^{-c_\ell}$$

(ii) Compute the witness $W_\mathcal{V}$:

$$W_\mathcal{V} = \prod_{i \in U} \prod_{1 \leq \ell \leq L} \left(\prod_{j \in V_\ell^+}^{j \neq i} g_{n+1-j+i} \right)^{c_\ell} \left(\prod_{j \in V_\ell^-}^{j \neq i} g_{n+1-j+i} \right)^{-c_\ell}$$

For all $1 \leq \ell \leq L$, set $\delta_\ell = |U \cap V_\ell^+| - |U \cap V_\ell^-|$ and set $u = \delta_1 c_1 + \ldots + \delta_L c_L$.

(iii) Set $\delta_\ell' = \delta_\ell + |V_\ell^-|$, $u' = \delta_1' c_1 + \ldots + \delta_L' c_L$, and $\tau_{u'} = g_1^{u'}$. From ipk, pick up $\tilde{\sigma}_{u'} = (\tilde{\theta}_{u'1}, \ldots, \tilde{\theta}_{u'7})$ that is the AHO signature on $g_1^{u'}$. Set $\tilde{u} = -(|V_1^-|c_1 + \ldots + |V_L^-|c_L)$ and $\tau_{\tilde{u}} = g_1^{\tilde{u}}$.

(iv) Compute $com_{P_k}, com_{W_\mathcal{V}}, com_{\tau_{u'}}$ as the GS commitments to $P_k, W_\mathcal{V}, \tau_{u'}$. Then, re-randomize the AHO signature σ_k by the method of [2] to obtain $\sigma_k' = \{\theta_1', \ldots, \theta_7'\}$. Compute the GS commitments $\{com_{\theta_i'}\}_{i \in \{1,2,5\}}$ to $\{\theta_i'\}_{i \in \{1,2,5\}}$. Similarly, re-randomize the AHO signature $\tilde{\sigma}_{u'}$ to obtain $\tilde{\sigma}_{u'}' = \{\tilde{\theta}_{u'1}', \ldots, \tilde{\theta}_{u'7}'\}$. Compute the GS commitments $\{com_{\tilde{\theta}_{u'i}'}\}_{i \in \{1,2,5\}}$ to $\{\tilde{\theta}_{u'i}'\}_{i \in \{1,2,5\}}$.

(v) Generate GS proofs $\{\pi_i\}_{i=1}^5$ to prove the following.

$$e(\tau_{\tilde{u}}, g_n)^{-1} = \quad e(P_k, acc_\mathcal{V}) \cdot e(g, W_\mathcal{V})^{-1} \cdot e(\tau_{u'}, g_n)^{-1}, \quad (2)$$

$$A^{(1)} \cdot e(\theta_3', \theta_4')^{-1} = \quad e(G_z^{(1)}, \theta_1') \cdot e(G_r^{(1)}, \theta_2') \cdot e(G^{(1)}, P_k), \quad (3)$$

$$B^{(1)} \cdot e(\theta_6', \theta_7')^{-1} = \quad e(H_z^{(1)}, \theta_1') \cdot e(H_r^{(1)}, \theta_5') \cdot e(H^{(1)}, P_k), \quad (4)$$

$$A^{(0)} \cdot e(\tilde{\theta}_{u'3}', \tilde{\theta}_{u'4}')^{-1} = \quad e(G_z^{(0)}, \tilde{\theta}_{u'1}') \cdot e(G_r^{(0)}, \tilde{\theta}_{u'2}') \cdot e(G^{(0)}, \tau_{u'}), \quad (5)$$

$$B^{(0)} \cdot e(\tilde{\theta}_{u'6}', \tilde{\theta}_{u'7}')^{-1} = \quad e(H_z^{(0)}, \tilde{\theta}_{u'1}') \cdot H_r^{(0)}, \tilde{\theta}_{u'5}') \cdot e(H^{(0)}, \tau_{u'}) \quad (6)$$

(vi) Output $\sigma = (\{\theta_i'\}_{i=3,4,6,7}, \{\tilde{\theta}_{u'i}'\}_{i=3,4,6,7}, com_{P_k}, com_{W_\mathcal{V}}, com_{\tau_{u'}}, \{com_{\theta_i'}\}_{i=1,2,5}, \{com_{\tilde{\theta}_{u'i}'}\}_{i=1,2,5}, \{\pi_i\}_{i=1}^5)$.

By substituting $P_k = \prod_{i \in U_k} g_i$, $\tau_{u'} = g_1^{u'}$, and $\tau_{\tilde{u}} = g_1^{\tilde{u}}$ in Eq. (2), it can be transformed into the verification equation of the accumulator as follows.

$$\frac{e(\prod_{i \in U_k} g_i, acc_\mathcal{V})}{e(g, W_\mathcal{V})} = e(g_1^{u'}, g_n) \cdot e(g_1^{\tilde{u}}, g_n)^{-1} = z^{u' - \tilde{u}}$$

Equations (3) and (4) prove the verification of the AHO signature on P_k. Equations (5) and (6) show the verification of the AHO signature on $\tau_{u'}$, which ensures that $u' = \delta_1' c_1 + \ldots + \delta_L' c_L$, where $1 \leq \delta_\ell' \leq \eta_\ell$. Then, we have $z^{u' - \tilde{u}} = z^{(\delta_1' - |V_1^-|)c_1 + \ldots + (\delta_L' - |V_L^-|)c_L}$ from $\tilde{u} = -(|V_1^-|c_1 + \ldots + |V_L^-|c_L)$, and

$1 - |V_\ell^-| \leq \delta_\ell' - |V_\ell^-| \leq \eta_\ell - |V_\ell^-|$. By setting $\delta_\ell = \delta_\ell' - |V_\ell^-|$, we obtain $z^{u'-\tilde{u}} = z^u$ and $1 - |V_\ell^-| \leq \delta_\ell \leq \eta_\ell - |V_\ell^-|$, i.e, $1 \leq \delta_\ell + |V_\ell^-| \leq \eta_\ell$. It is the verification of the accumulator in Chap. 3. Thus, $U_k \cap V_\ell^+ \neq \emptyset$ or $U_k \cap V_\ell^- \neq V_\ell^-$ for all $1 \leq \ell \leq L$ is verified.

Verify: Given ipk, the proof σ, and the proved CNF formula Ψ, verify the validity of σ as follows.

(i) As in **ProofGen**, compute the accumulator acc_V, and set $\tilde{u} = -(|V_1^-|c_1 + \ldots + |V_L^-|c_L)$ and $\tau_{\tilde{u}} = g_1^{\tilde{u}}$.

(ii) If the verification of all GS proofs $\{\pi_i\}_{i=1}^5$ succeeds, accept σ.

5.2   Efficiency Comparisons

Since the proposed system is similar to the previous system [4], it has the similar asymptotic efficiency. The size of the attribute proof σ is $O(1)$, and the size of the certificate $cert_k$ is also $O(1)$. But, the size of the issuer's public key ipk is different from the previous. In the previous system, the maximum number of $\zeta_\ell = |U \cap V_\ell|$ for V_ℓ (the attribute set of the ℓ-th clause in CNF formulas) is fixed in the setup. The number of the AHO signatures for Φ in ipk is $\prod_{1 \leq \ell \leq L} \zeta_\ell$. But, in our system, the number is $\prod_{1 \leq \ell \leq L} \eta_\ell$ where η_ℓ is the maximum number of the attributes in ℓ-th clause which corresponds to $|V_\ell|$. Due to $|U \cap V_\ell| \leq |V_\ell|$, ipk in our system is longer that in the previous system, which is a trade-off to the adaptation to negations in proved CNF formulas.

The computational costs are also similar to the previous system. In **Proof-Gen**, the computation of the witness W_V depends on the parameters (acc_V also depends on the parameters, but the cost of W_V is heavier). The cost is the same as the previous system, since the exponentiation of the integer c_ℓ is only changed to the exponentiation of $-c_\ell$ for the negated attributes, and the multiplications of OR literals remain.

5.3   Security Considerations

As in the journal version [5] of the previous system [4], we can prove that the proposed system satisfies the misauthentication resistance under the security of the AHO signatures and the proposed accumulator. The security proof of the previous system constructs two types of forgeries by interacting with an adversary winning the misauthentication resistance game and extracting committed secret values in the attribute proof σ forged by the adversary. One forgery is for AHO signatures, and another forgery is for the accumulator. As well as the previous system, in the proposed system, the attribute set U_k of the proving user is ensured by the AHO signature on $P_k = \prod_{i \in U_k} g_i$, and the user proves that U_k satisfies the proved CNF formula Ψ as $U_k \cap V_\ell^+ \neq \emptyset$ or $U_k \cap V_\ell^- \neq V_\ell^-$ for all $1 \leq \ell \leq L$ by the verification of the proposed accumulator, where the correctness of $\tau_{u'} = g_1^{u'}$ is ensured by an AHO signature. Thus, similarly to the proof for the previous system, we can prove the misauthentication resistance.

As for the anonymity, the security proof is also similar to that for the previous system, where the methodology of a sequence of games is used. For the original anonymity game, we can consider the modified game where the GS commitments are replaced by ones using the CRS in the WI setting. In this modified game, since the adversary has no information, the advantage of the adversary in the anonymity game is negligible. Furthermore, this modified game and the original game are indistinguishable due to the indistinguishability of CRS in the real protocol and the WI setting under the DLIN assumption. In our system, the attribute proof σ consists of the same components as those in the previous system, i.e., the re-randomized AHO signatures, GS commitments, and GS proofs. Thus, in the same proof as that for the previous system, we can prove the anonymity.

The security proofs in our system will be shown in the journal version of this paper.

6   Conclusions

In this paper, we have proposed an anonymous credential system with the constant-size attribute proofs, where any CNF formula with negations can be proved. As the key primitive, we have constructed an accumulator to verify the CNF formulas with negations, based on the previous accumulator [4] for limited CNF formulas without negations.

One of our future work is to apply the proposed system to eID systems.

Acknowledgments. This work was partially supported by JSPS KAKENHI Grant Number 19K11964.

References

1. Abe, M., Fuchsbauer, G., Groth, J., Haralambiev, K., Ohkubo, M.: Structure-preserving signatures and commitments to group elements. In: Rabin, T. (ed.) CRYPTO 2010. LNCS, vol. 6223, pp. 209–236. Springer, Heidelberg (2010). https://doi.org/10.1007/978-3-642-14623-7_12
2. Abe, M., Haralambiev, K., Ohkubo, M.: Singing on elements in bilinear groups for modular protocol design. Cryptology ePrint Archive, Report 2010/133 (2010). http://eprint.iacr.org/. (This was merged and presented in [1])
3. Boneh, D., Boyen, X., Shacham, H.: Short group signatures. In: Franklin, M. (ed.) CRYPTO 2004. LNCS, vol. 3152, pp. 41–55. Springer, Heidelberg (2004). https://doi.org/10.1007/978-3-540-28628-8_3
4. Begum, N., Nakanishi, T., Funabiki, N.: Efficient proofs for CNF formulas on attributes in pairing-based anonymous credential system. In: Kwon, T., Lee, M.-K., Kwon, D. (eds.) ICISC 2012. LNCS, vol. 7839, pp. 495–509. Springer, Heidelberg (2013). https://doi.org/10.1007/978-3-642-37682-5_35
5. Begum, N., Nakanishi, T., Funabiki, N.: Efficient proofs for CNF formulas on attributes in pairing-based anonymous credential system. IEICE Trans. Fundam. **96-A**(12), 2422–2433 (2013)

6. Camenisch, J., Chaabouni, R., Shelat, A.: Efficient protocols for set membership and range proofs. In: Pieprzyk, J. (ed.) ASIACRYPT 2008. LNCS, vol. 5350, pp. 234–252. Springer, Heidelberg (2008). https://doi.org/10.1007/978-3-540-89255-7_15
7. Camenisch, J., Groß, T.: Efficient attributes for anonymous credentials. In: Proceedings of the ACM Conference on Computer and Communications Security (ACM CCS 2008), pp. 345–356 (2008)
8. Camenisch, J., Kohlweiss, M., Soriente, C.: An accumulator based on bilinear maps and efficient revocation for anonymous credentials. In: Jarecki, S., Tsudik, G. (eds.) PKC 2009. LNCS, vol. 5443, pp. 481–500. Springer, Heidelberg (2009). https://doi.org/10.1007/978-3-642-00468-1_27
9. Camenisch, J., Lysyanskaya, A.: Dynamic accumulators and application to efficient revocation of anonymous credentials. In: Yung, M. (ed.) CRYPTO 2002. LNCS, vol. 2442, pp. 61–76. Springer, Heidelberg (2002). https://doi.org/10.1007/3-540-45708-9_5
10. Groth, J., Sahai, A.: Efficient non-interactive proof systems for bilinear groups. In: Smart, N. (ed.) EUROCRYPT 2008. LNCS, vol. 4965, pp. 415–432. Springer, Heidelberg (2008). https://doi.org/10.1007/978-3-540-78967-3_24
11. Hanser, C., Slamanig, D.: Structure-preserving signatures on equivalence classes and their application to anonymous credentials. In: Sarkar, P., Iwata, T. (eds.) ASIACRYPT 2014. LNCS, vol. 8873, pp. 491–511. Springer, Heidelberg (2014). https://doi.org/10.1007/978-3-662-45611-8_26
12. Izabachène, M., Libert, B., Vergnaud, D.: Block-wise P-signatures and non-interactive anonymous credentials with efficient attributes. In: Chen, L. (ed.) IMACC 2011. LNCS, vol. 7089, pp. 431–450. Springer, Heidelberg (2011). https://doi.org/10.1007/978-3-642-25516-8_26
13. Sadiah, S., Nakanishi, T., Funabiki, N.: Anonymous credential system with efficient proofs for monotone formulas on attributes. In: Tanaka, K., Suga, Y. (eds.) IWSEC 2015. LNCS, vol. 9241, pp. 262–278. Springer, Cham (2015). https://doi.org/10.1007/978-3-319-22425-1_16
14. Sudarsono, A., Nakanishi, T., Funabiki, N.: Efficient proofs of attributes in pairing-based anonymous credential system. In: Fischer-Hübner, S., Hopper, N. (eds.) PETS 2011. LNCS, vol. 6794, pp. 246–263. Springer, Heidelberg (2011). https://doi.org/10.1007/978-3-642-22263-4_14

Symmetric-Key Primitives

More Results on Shortest Linear Programs

Subhadeep Banik[1]([✉]), Yuki Funabiki[2], and Takanori Isobe[3,4]

[1] LASEC, École Polytechnique Fédérale de Lausanne, Lausanne, Switzerland
subhadeep.banik@epfl.ch
[2] Sony Corporation, Tokyo, Japan
yuki.funabiki@sony.com
[3] National Institute of Information and Communications Technology, Tokyo, Japan
[4] University of Hyogo, Kobe, Japan
takanori.isobe@ai.u-hyogo.ac.jp

Abstract. At the FSE conference of ToSC 2018, Kranz et al. presented their results on shortest linear programs for the linear layers of several well known block ciphers in literature. Shortest linear programs are essentially the minimum number of 2-input xor gates required to completely describe a linear system of equations. In the above paper the authors showed that the commonly used metrics like d-xor/s-xor count that are used to judge the "lightweightedness" do not represent the minimum number of xor gates required to describe a given MDS matrix. In fact they used heuristic based algorithms of Boyar/Peralta and Paar to find implementations of MDS matrices with even fewer xor gates than was previously known. They proved that the AES mixcolumn matrix can be implemented with as little as 97 xor gates. In this paper we show that the values reported in the above paper are not optimal. By suitably including random bits in the instances of the above algorithms we can achieve implementations of almost all matrices with lesser number of gates than were reported in the above paper. As a result we report an implementation of the AES mixcolumn matrix that uses only 95 xor gates.

In the second part of the paper, we observe that most standard cell libraries contain both 2 and 3-input xor gates, with the silicon area of the 3-input xor gate being smaller than the sum of the areas of two 2-input xor gates. Hence when linear circuits are synthesized by logic compilers (with specific instructions to optimize for area), most of them would return a solution circuit containing both 2 and 3-input xor gates. Thus from a practical point of view, reducing circuit size in presence of these gates is no longer equivalent to solving the shortest linear program. In this paper we show that by adopting a graph based heuristic it is possible to convert a circuit constructed with 2-input xor gates to another functionally equivalent circuit that utilizes both 2 and 3-input xor gates and occupies less hardware area. As a result we obtain more lightweight implementations of all the matrices listed in the ToSC paper.

ⓒ Springer Nature Switzerland AG 2019
N. Attrapadung and T. Yagi (Eds.): IWSEC 2019, LNCS 11689, pp. 109–128, 2019.
https://doi.org/10.1007/978-3-030-26834-3_7

1   Introduction

Shortest linear programs are essentially the minimum number of 2-input xor gates required to completely describe a linear system of equations. The advantages to having a short linear program solution of a given matrix over $GF(2)$ are obvious. Since such linear matrices are used in the diffusion layer of block ciphers, they lead to more lightweight implementations of the block cipher circuit in hardware.

There has been extensive study on construction of lightweight diffusion layers with Maximum diffusion property [GR15, SKOP15, SS16, SS17, LS16, LW16, BKL16, JPST17] that guarantees optimal diffusion of differentials across the linear layer. MDS matrices ensure that the sum of the number of active cells before and after the linear layer is at least equal to one more than the number of rows/columns of the matrix. The advent of recursive constructions for MDS matrices [AF14, GPV17], made block cipher and hash function circuits more compact as was evidenced in the designs of LED [GPPR11] and Photon [GPP11]. Recent years have seen MDS matrices being constructed using several underlying structures like Toeplitz matrices, Hadamard matrices Cauchy matrices, Vandermonde matrices etc. The end goal for all these approaches is to minimize the xor gate count of the matrices. However since the problem of finding the minimal xor gate count of any linear system of equations is known to be NP-complete [BMP08], the authors resorted to heuristic methods of evaluating the gate count of such matrices. Some such metrics like d-xor and s-xor count have been proposed earlier [JPST17]. However, in [KLSW18b], the authors showed that such heuristic metrics do not reflect accurately the minimum number of xor gates required to completely describe any linear system. Instead, the approach followed in [KLSW18b], was to try and find the shortest linear program of a given matrix by using approximation algorithms like the one proposed by Boyar-Peralta [BP10] and Paar [Paa97]. As a result, they proposed instantiations of several well known matrices in crypto-literature with a smaller number of xor gates than was previously known. In particular, they proposed a circuit for the AES mixcolumn matrix with only 97 xor gates, which was considerably lower than the best construction of 103 gates known at the time [JMPS17].

Shortest linear program is a well known hard problem in computer science. It is known that the problem is NP-complete (polynomially reducible to the Vertex-Cover problem): in fact it was proven in [BMP08], the problem is MAX-SNP complete, which roughly means that there are no good approximation algorithms for the problem unless P = NP. Nevertheless, over the years there have been many attempts at proposing approximation algorithms to solve the problem when the size of the input matrix is limited. One of the first such attempts was by Paar in [Paa97]. The algorithm is a essentially a greedy one, which at every stage finds the pair of operands that appear most frequently in the set of equations and replaces them with a new variable. The process continues until all operands appear exactly once. For obvious reasons, the algorithm only produces cancellation-free solutions to the problem. This basically means that if one takes any two intermediate operands in the algorithm and writes out the expression of each operand as a linear equation of the input variables, then the two expressions will not contain any common term. It is well-known that cancellation-free solutions are sub-optimal. There have been attempts to solve the problem using SAT solvers [FS10]. The authors of this paper showed that the problem can be formulated as a SAT instance, i.e. if one wants to know if a given linear system can be described using t xor gates, one may frame the problem in such a manner so that a solution returned by the SAT solver would be a unique encoding of the underlying t-xor gate circuit. An optimal solution is reached when the solver returns a solution for some value of t but finds the instance unsatisfiable for $t - 1$. SAT based solutions have been used before to minimize gate complexities of Sboxes [Sto16] using similar approaches. But the problem is that the running time of the solver itself is exponential in the size of the input and for input sizes larger than 10, it is difficult to get a solution from the solver in reasonable time. Another algorithm for the problem is due to Boyar-Peralta [BP10]. Unlike Paar's method, the algorithm may produce solutions with cancellation.

1.1   Contribution and Organization

In this paper we first show that both the Boyar-Peralta and the Paar algorithm can be executed with additional randomness to produce shorter linear programs for any given matrix. We explain how to efficiently incorporate additional randomness and give an intuitive explanation of why our approach works. As a result we produce shorter programs for almost all the matrices listed in [KLSW18b]. In particular, we propose an implementation of the AES mixcolumn matrix that takes only 95 2-input xor gates.

As mentioned in the abstract, most standard cell libraries contain dedicated two input and three input xor gates. The hardware area of the 3-input xor gate is generally smaller than the sum of the areas of two 2-input xor gates. And if a logic synthesizer is presented with a functional description of any linear system in any hardware description language like VHDL or Verilog, and asked to produce a circuit that is optimized for area, it generally comes up with a circuit that utilizes both types of xor gates. In such a scenario, minimizing the area of the circuit implementing the linear system can no longer be achieved by computing the SLP solution. Indeed the solution that minimizes the hardware area would depend on the individual areas of the 2-input and 3-input xor gates, and this does not appear to be easier to solve than the SLP problem. In the second part of the paper, we present a graph based approximation algorithm that does the following: it takes as input an SLP solution and then encodes it as a directed graph. It then recursively alters the edges of the graph till a certain stopping criterion is reached. In the end we obtain a solution comprising both 2 and 3-input xor gates, which is smaller in area than the initial SLP solution that we started with. As a result we provide improved circuit implementation of all the matrices listed in [KLSW18b].

The rest of the paper is organized in the following manner. In Sect. 2, we give a brief description of the Boyar-Peralta and Paar algorithms and explain how randomness can be incorporated in the algorithm execution to produce shorter linear programs for a given linear system. In Sect. 3, we explain the working of our graph based approximation algorithm that produces a circuit for a given linear system utilizing both 2 and 3-input xor gates. Section 4, concludes the paper.

2   Approximation Algorithms

2.1   Boyar-Peralta Method [BP10]

Before we proceed let us take a look at the Boyar-Peralta algorithm. The problem is to find a short linear program that computes $f(x) = Mx$ where M is an $m \times n$ matrix over $GF(2)$. The basic idea is as follows. A "base" S of known linear functions is first constructed. Initially S is just the set of input variables $x_1, x_2, \ldots, x_n$. The vector $Dist[\cdot]$ is the set of distances from S to the linear functions given by the rows of M. That is, if f_i is the linear function given by the ith row of M then $Dist[i]$ represents the minimum number of functions from S that can add to give f_i. Consequently, we have that initially, $Dist[i]$ is just one less than the hamming weight of row i. The following steps are then performed in a loop:

- Choose a new base element by adding two existing base elements and add it to S.
- Update $Dist[i]$ since S has been modified.
- Do the above until $Dist[i] = 0$ for all i.

At any stage if the size of S is t there are $\binom{t}{2}$ options to choose a new base. The criterion for picking the new base element is

1. Pick one that minimizes the sum of elements of the updated $Dist[\cdot]$ array.
2. If there is a tie between two choices of the new base element, then resolve it by choosing the base element that maximizes the Euclidean norm of updated $Dist[\cdot]$ array.

This tie resolution criterion, may seem counter-intuitive. The basic idea is that a distance vector like 0, 0, 3, 1 is preferred to one like 1, 1, 1, 1. In the latter case, we would need 4 more gates to finish. In the former, 3 might do it. The bulk of the time of the heuristic is spent on picking the new base element.

Example 1. Before proceeding it may be instructive to look at a small example of the working of the above algorithm using an example take directly form [BP10]. Suppose we need a circuit that computes the system of equations defined as follows. This is equivalent to finding a circuit for multiplication by the 6×5 matrix, M given on the left.

$$
\begin{aligned}
x_0 \oplus x_1 \oplus x_2 &= y_0 \\
x_1 \oplus x_3 \oplus x_4 &= y_1 \\
x_0 \oplus x_2 \oplus x_3 \oplus x_4 &= y_2 \\
x_1 \oplus x_2 \oplus x_3 &= y_3 \\
x_0 \oplus x_1 \oplus x_3 &= y_4 \\
x_1 \oplus x_2 \oplus x_3 \oplus x_4 &= y_5
\end{aligned}
\Rightarrow
\begin{bmatrix}
1 & 1 & 1 & 0 & 0 \\
0 & 1 & 0 & 1 & 1 \\
1 & 0 & 1 & 1 & 1 \\
0 & 1 & 1 & 1 & 0 \\
1 & 1 & 0 & 1 & 0 \\
0 & 1 & 1 & 1 & 1
\end{bmatrix}
\cdot
\begin{bmatrix}
x_0 \\ x_1 \\ x_2 \\ x_3 \\ x_4
\end{bmatrix}
=
\begin{bmatrix}
y_0 \\ y_1 \\ y_2 \\ y_3 \\ y_4 \\ y_5
\end{bmatrix}
$$

The target functions to be computed are given rows of M. The initial base is given by $\{x_0, x_1, x_2, x_3, x_4\}$, which corresponds to $S = \{10000, 01000, 00100, 00010, 00001\}$. The initial distance vector is $Dist = [2, 2, 3, 2, 2, 3]$. The algorithm finds two base vectors whose sum, when added to the base, minimizes the sum of the new distances. It turns out the right choice is to calculate $t_5 = x_1 \oplus x_3$. So the new base S is expanded to contain the signal 01010. The new distance vector is $Dist = [2, 1, 3, 1, 1, 2]$.

Step 1. According to the algorithm we have a choice between $x_1 \oplus x_2$ and $x_0 \oplus t_5$. The updated $Dist$ vectors for the above choices are respectively $[1, 1, 3, 1, 1, 2]$ and $[2, 1, 3, 1, 0, 2]$, both of which sum to 9. However the second choice gives a Euclidean norm of $\sqrt{19}$. So we choose $t_6 = x_0 \oplus t_5 = y_4$.
Step 2. $t_7 = x_2 \oplus t_5 = y_3$, new $Dist = [2, 1, 3, 0, 0, 1]$.
Step 3. $t_8 = x_4 \oplus t_5 = y_1$, new $Dist = [2, 0, 3, 0, 0, 1]$.
Step 4. $t_9 = x_2 \oplus t_8 = y_5$, new $Dist = [2, 0, 2, 0, 0, 0]$.
Step 5. $t_{10} = x_0 \oplus x_1$, new $Dist = [1, 0, 1, 0, 0, 0]$.
Step 6. $t_{11} = x_2 \oplus t_{10} = y_0$, new $Dist = [0, 0, 1, 0, 0, 0]$.
Step 7. $t_{12} = t_8 \oplus t_{11} = y_2$, new $Dist = [0, 0, 0, 0, 0, 0]$.

This therefore gives a circuit with eight gates.

2.2   Our Experiments

The authors of [KLSW18b] were kind enough to make all the codes used by them freely available in the public domain [KLSW18a]. We downloaded the C++ code for the Boyar-Peralta algorithm which is based on the code available at [BP18] written by the authors of [BP10]. We ran the code for the AES mixcolumn matrix and found that it returned a solution with **96** xor gates. This was surprising for us, since the authors of [KLSW18b] claim that their implementation of the AES mixcolumn matrix takes 97 xor gates. Initially we concluded that it must have been an error by the authors of [KLSW18b]. But on closer inspection we started to make a sense of why the discrepancy arose.

In the code used by [KLSW18a], the ordering of the input byte in terms of bits is as follows: $[x_0, x_1, x_2, \dots, x_7]$ which essentially means that they place the least significant bit first, whereas the ordering we used is $[x_7, x_6, x_5, \dots, x_0]$ which essentially means most significant bit first and arranging bits in decreasing index order. This means that the AES mixcolumn matrices we and the authors of [KLSW18b] have used in our respective experiments would be column and row shuffled versions of each other. However there is nothing in the steps of the Boyar-Peralta algorithm that suggests that if we present column/row shuffled instances of the same matrix to the algorithm, it would output different solutions. In fact the algorithm picks out a new base element at each step which minimizes the sum of given distance vector, and computes a Euclidean norm to resolve ties. Since this sum or norm should not change no matter how the columns/rows are arranged, there is every reason to believe that the output of the algorithm should be independent of how the matrix is arranged, if the underlying linear system is unchanged.

However as it turns out, the way in which the algorithm has been implemented in [KLSW18a], it **does** output different results when different column shuffled instances of the same matrix is input. The reason this happens is as follows. Following is a snippet of the C++ code where the algorithm implements resolution of ties via Euclidean norm:

```cpp
MinDistance = BaseSize*NumTargets; //i.e. something big
OldNorm = 0; //i.e. something small
for (int i = 0; i < BaseSize - 1; i++) {
        for (int j = i+1; j < BaseSize; j++) {
            NewBase = Base[i] ^ Base[j];

            ThisDist = TotalDistance();//also calculates NDist[]
            if (ThisDist <= MinDistance) {
                //calculate Norm
                ThisNorm = 0;
                for (int k = 0; k < NumTargets; k++) {
                    d = NDist[k];
                    ThisNorm = ThisNorm + d*d;
                }
                //resolve tie in favor of largest norm
                if((ThisDist < MinDistance)||(ThisNorm > OldNorm))

                {
                    besti = i;
                    bestj = j;
                    TheBest = NewBase;
                    for (int uu = 0; uu < NumTargets; uu++) {
                        BestDist[uu] = NDist[uu];
                    }
                    MinDistance = ThisDist;
                    OldNorm = ThisNorm;
                }
            }
        }
    }
    //update Dist array
```

```
NewBase = TheBest;
for (int i = 0; i < NumTargets; i++) {
    Dist[i] = BestDist[i];
}
//update Base with TheBest
Base[BaseSize] = TheBest;
```

The above code is intuitively easy to understand and follow. We describe it briefly. The variable `BaseSize` stores the current size of S. The algorithm then loops over all choices of the new base element. A candidate base element is placed in the global variable `NewBase`, and then the code computes the temporary updated distance vector `NDist[]` via the function `TotalDistance` which returns the sum of `NDist[]` in `ThisDist`. If `ThisDist` is less than or equal to the current minimum stored in `MinDistance`, the code then computes the Euclidean norm of `NDist[]` in `ThisNorm`. A final choice of new base element is made in the variable `TheBest`, depending on whether the current candidate produces a sum that is absolutely less than the current minimum `MinDistance` or it produces a Euclidean norm strictly greater than the current maximum norm `OldNorm`. Consider what happens when two candidates for the new base element say for i=i_0,j=j_0 and i=i_1,j=j_1 produce identical values of `ThisDist` and `ThisNorm`. According to the code, the new candidate would be the one which appears first lexicographically in the double loop traversal of i,j. In general if such a situation appears for n choices for the new candidate base element, the code all always chooses the one that appears first in the double loop traversal. Thus it becomes clearer why the order in which the columns are arranged matrix is crucial: shuffling of columns essentially means we shuffle the order of input variables to the system, which in turn implies we shuffle the initial placement of elements of S. This has a direct effect on how new candidates are chosen to be added to S and takes the program execution in different directions.

2.3   New Idea

In the paper [BP10], the authors suggest other methods to resolve ties including choosing random candidate elements. We did not take this approach for two reasons: one it may not necessarily lead to optimal solutions and second it is not necessarily straightforward to adapt the code snippet to accommodate random candidate choices. However since the order of rows/columns seems to bring about a change in the output of this particular code execution: we tried the following idea. We take the target matrix M and multiply with randomly generated permutation matrices P and Q to get $M_R = P \cdot M \cdot Q$. This only shuffles the rows and columns of the matrix and so keeps the underlying linear system unchanged. We use M_R as input to the C++ code and extract a solution. The code could be run multiple number of times with random permutation matrices until we get a solution better than previously obtained.

We started our experiment with the AES mixcolumn matrix. After around 4 hours of execution we obtained a solution with 95 xor gates. The solution is presented in Table 1. Note that the permutation matrices P, Q has been listed as a table. For example, $PT[0] = 4$ implies that in the 0th row of P, the element in the 4th column is 1 and the rest are 0.

2.4 Paar's Algorithm

Paar's algorithm is essentially a greedy one, which at every stage finds the pair of operands that appear most frequently in the set of equations and replaces them with a new variable. The process continues until all operands appear exactly once. The algorithm however returns cancellation-free solutions that are known to be not always optimal. But it is always useful to use this algorithm to decrease the gate count of larger matrices for which the Boyar-Peralta method is unable to return a solution in practical time.

Let us look at the details of the algorithm. Let M be the matrix whose gate count is to be minimized. Then the algorithm performs the following steps:

Step 1. Find columns whose bitwise AND has largest weight. This essentially finds two operands x_i, x_j whose xor occurs most number of times in the underlying linear system.

Step 2. Extend matrix M, by adding the above product column *newcol* to the matrix.

Step 3. For the two previous columns do *oldcol* ← *oldcol·newcol*. The above two steps adds the xor gate $v = x_i \oplus x_j$ to the gate list and by adding the product column to M creates a new input variable v. By doing *oldcol* ← *oldcol·newcol*, the algorithm removes extra xors in the matrix structure, which are no longer needed after the addition of the new column.

Example 2. It is again instructive to understand the algorithm with a small example. Given the following linear system.

$$
\begin{aligned}
x_1 \oplus x_2 &= y_1 \\
x_1 \oplus x_2 \oplus x_3 &= y_2 \\
x_1 \oplus x_2 \oplus x_3 \oplus x_4 &= y_3 \\
x_2 \oplus x_3 \oplus x_4 &= y_4
\end{aligned}
\Rightarrow
\begin{bmatrix} 1&1&0&0 \\ 1&1&1&0 \\ 1&1&1&1 \\ 0&1&1&1 \end{bmatrix} \cdot \begin{bmatrix} x_1 \\ x_2 \\ x_3 \\ x_4 \end{bmatrix} = \begin{bmatrix} y_1 \\ y_2 \\ y_3 \\ y_4 \end{bmatrix}
$$

In this example, the product of the second and third column has largest weight. We have $v_1 = x_2 + x_3$. The new column to be added is $(1\ 1\ 1\ 1) \cdot (0\ 1\ 1\ 1) = (0\ 1\ 1\ 1)$, and after the *oldcol* ← *oldcol · newcol* step we have the following system.

$$
\begin{aligned}
x_1 \oplus x_2 &= y_1 \\
x_1 \oplus v_1 &= y_2 \\
x_1 \oplus x_4 \oplus v_1 &= y_3 \\
x_4 \oplus v_1 &= y_4
\end{aligned}
\Rightarrow
\begin{bmatrix} 1&1&0&0&0 \\ 1&0&0&0&1 \\ 1&0&0&1&1 \\ 0&0&0&1&1 \end{bmatrix} \cdot \begin{bmatrix} x_1 \\ x_2 \\ x_3 \\ x_4 \\ v_1 \end{bmatrix} = \begin{bmatrix} y_1 \\ y_2 \\ y_3 \\ y_4 \end{bmatrix}
$$

The above steps are continued until all targets are achieved.

Table 1. AES mixcolumn using 95 xor gates

#	Gate	#	Gate	#	Gate
1	t0 = x0 + x2	33	t32 = x9 + t3	65	t64 = x1 + t0
2	t1 = x10 + x24	34	y21 = t9 + t32	66	t65 = t6 + t13
3	t2 = x0 + x10	35	t34 = x19 + t6	67	y4 = t64 + t65
4	t3 = x2 + x24	36	y20 = t2 + t34	68	t67 = t10 + t32
5	t4 = x3 + x5	37	t36 = t1 + t9	69	t68 = x31 + t34
6	t5 = x4 + x11	38	y18 = t34 + t36	70	y5 = t67 + t68
7	t6 = x9 + x20	39	t38 = x20 + t9	71	t70 = y18 + y4
8	t7 = x16 + x29	40	y26 = t0 + t38	72	y27 = t67 + t70
9	t8 = x6 + x23	41	t40 = x11 + t8	73	t72 = x13 + t1
10	t9 = x19 + x21	42	y9 = t14 + t40	74	t73 = t15 + t16
11	t10 = x1 + x7	43	t42 = x13 + t5	75	y14 = t72 + t73
12	t11 = x12 + x26	44	t43 = x6 + x17	76	t75 = x15 + t2
13	t12 = x8 + x30	45	y15 = t42 + t43	77	t76 = x27 + t16
14	t13 = x18 + x31	46	t45 = x11 + y10	78	t77 = t0 + t17
15	t14 = x13 + x14	47	y16 = t29 + t45	79	t78 = t14 + t77
16	t15 = x17 + x28	48	t47 = x12 + t12	80	y24 = x28 + t78
17	t16 = x15 + x22	49	y28 = t13 + t47	81	t80 = t75 + t76
18	t17 = x25 + x27	50	t49 = x18 + t11	82	t81 = x17 + t14
19	t18 = x2 + t1	51	t50 = x1 + y28	83	y2 = t80 + t81
20	y8 = t7 + t18	52	y7 = t49 + t50	84	t83 = t3 + t11
21	t20 = x16 + t2	53	t52 = x7 + x8	85	y3 = t76 + t83
22	t21 = x2 + t2	54	y30 = t49 + t52	86	t85 = t12 + t17
23	y29 = t4 + t21	55	t54 = x18 + t10	87	y1 = t75 + t85
24	t23 = x3 + y8	56	y12 = t36 + t54	88	t87 = y14 + t78
25	y25 = t20 + t23	57	t56 = x23 + t5	89	y13 = t80 + t87
26	t25 = x5 + x24	58	y17 = t15 + t56	90	t89 = x26 + x30
27	y23 = t20 + t25	59	t58 = x28 + y9	91	t90 = t77 + t89
28	t27 = x5 + t7	60	y19 = t42 + t58	92	y6 = t76 + t90
29	y10 = t8 + t27	61	t60 = x29 + t4	93	t92 = x25 + t83
30	t29 = x23 + t4	62	y31 = t5 + t60	94	t93 = y1 + y6
31	t30 = x4 + x16	63	t62 = x30 + t10	95	y0 = t92 + t93
32	y11 = t29 + t30	64	y22 = t11 + t62		

$PT = [4,12,11,28, 22,30,20,5, 16,26,9,17, 6,27,3,18, 1,10,7,2, 15,31,13,24, 19,8,23,14, 29,0,21,25]$

$QT = [24,5,11,14, 15,12,31,19, 10,3,6,28, 22,8,1,21, 0,29,23,17, 27,30,7,9, 2,16,4,13, 25,26,18,20]$

Again, there are no steps in the above algorithm that suggest that different results would be output if the input matrices are row/column shuffled. However again due to the C++ implementation of the above algorithm in [KLSW18a], column shuffled versions of the same matrix do produce different outcomes. The reasons due too are quite similar: for candidate column pairs C_{i_0}, C_{j_0} and C_{i_1}, C_{j_1} both of whose products have the same hamming weight, the code in [KLSW18a] chooses the one which occurs first lexicographically during a standard double loop search over every pair of columns. Thus shuffling of columns of M directly impacts the outcome. Again we could multiply with randomly generated permutation matrices P and Q to get $M_R = P \cdot M \cdot Q$. The code is run multiple number of times with random permutation matrices until we get a solution better than previously obtained.

Note that in the original paper [Paa97], two algorithms were proposed of which we have discussed the first one. The second algorithm recurses on all possible choices of candidate intermediate steps and thus will output the optimal result. The probabilistic version suggested in this paper is thus something in between the two original algorithms. We did not try to implement Paar's second algorithm as it took a lot of time to run on the computing systems we had access to.

2.5   Results

We ran the modified algorithms for all the matrices listed in [KLSW18b]. For smaller 32×32 matrices the Boyar-Peralta algorithm can be executed efficiently in reasonable time. For 64×64 and larger matrices we used the modified Paar algorithm as the Boyar-Peralta took an unreasonable amount of time just to execute the optimization of one shuffled version of the target matrix M. The results are given in Tables 2 and 3. Table 2 contains matrices proposed in recent literature, whereas Table 3 contains matrices used in some cryptographic constructions. For almost all matrices we have improved the results of [KLSW18b].

3   Optimization with 3-Input Xor Gates

One of the motivations of constructing circuits with lower number of xor gates is that it makes for a more lightweight implementation in hardware. However most standard cell libraries of CMOS logic processes have dedicated gates that support both the 2-input and the 3-input xor functionality. Generally the area of a 3-input xor gate is lower than the area of two 2-input xor gates. Take for example, the standard cell library CORE90GPHVT v 2.1.a of the STM 90 nm CMOS logic process. It has two types of gates

- 2-input xor gate with area: 2 GE
- 3-input xor gate with area: 3.25 GE

where GE refers to Gate equivalents which is the area of a two input NAND gate. Our experiments started with the AES mixcolumn matrix. We presented

Table 2. Comparison of gate counts for matrices available in literature

#	Matrix	Type	Gate count in [KLSW18b]	Gate count in this paper
4×4 matrices over $GF(2^4)$				
1	[SKOP15]	Hadamard	48	46
2	[LS16]	Circulant	44	44
3	[LW16]	Circulant	44	44
4	[BKL16]	Circulant	42	42
5	[SS16]	Toeplitz	43	42
6	[JPST17]		43	42
7	[SKOP15]	Hadamard, Involutary	48	47
8	[LW16]	Hadamard, Involutary	48	46
9	[SS16]	Involutary	42	40
10	[JPST17]	Involutary	47	46
4×4 matrices over $GF(2^8)$				
11	[SKOP15]	Subfield	98	94
12	[LS16]	Circulant	112	110
13	[LW16]		102	102
14	[BKL16]	Circulant	110	108
15	[SS16]	Toeplitz	107	104
16	[JPST17]	Subfield	86	86
17	[SKOP15]	Subfield, Involutary	100	94
18	[LW16]	Hadamard, Involutary	91	90
19	[SS16]	Involutary	100	98
20	[JPST17]	Subfield, Involutary	91*	92
8×8 matrices over $GF(2^4)$				
21	[SKOP15]	Hadamard	194	192
22	[SS17]	Toeplitz	204	203
23	[SKOP15]	Hadamard, Involutary	217	212
8×8 matrices over $GF(2^8)$				
24	[SKOP15]	Hadamard	467	460
25	[LS16]	Circulant	447	443
26	[BKL16]	Circulant	498	497
27	[SS17]	Toeplitz	438	436
28	[SKOP15]	Hadamard, Involutary	428	419
29	[JPST17]	Hadamard, Involutary	599	591

*On running the code from [KLSW18a] on our PC, we got solution 92 for this matrix

Table 3. Comparison of gate counts for matrices used in cryptographic constructions

#	Cipher	Type	Gate count	
			[KLSW18b]	This paper
4×4 matrices over $GF(2^8)$				
1	AES [DR02]	Circulant	97	95
2	ANUBIS [BR00a]	Hadamard, Involutary	113	102
3	CLEFIA M_0* [SSA+07]	Hadamard, Involutary	106	102
4	CLEFIA M_1 [SSA+07]	Hadamard	111	110
5	FOX MU4 [JV04]		137	131
6	TWOFISH [SKW+98]		129	125
8×8 matrices over $GF(2^8)$				
7	FOX MU8 [JV04]		594	592
8	GRØSTL [GKM+09]	Circulant	475	460
9	KHAZAD [BR00b]	Hadamard, Involutary	507	492
10	WHIRLPOOL [BR11]	Circulant	465	464
4×4 matrices over $GF(2^4)$				
11	JOLTIK [JNP13]	Hadamard, Involutary	48	47
12	SMALLSCALE AES [CMR05]	Circulant	47	45
8×8 matrices over $GF(2^4)$				
13	WHIRLWIND M_0 [BNN+10]	Hadamard, Subfield	212	210
14	WHIRLWIND M_1 [BNN+10]	Hadamard, Subfield	235	234
Non MDS matrices				
15	QARMA128 [Ava17]	Circulant (4×4 over $GF(2^8)$)	48	48
16	ARIA [KKP+03]	Involutary (16×16 over $GF(2^8)$)	416	392
17	MIDORI [BBI+15]	Involutary (4×4 over $GF(2^4)$)	24	24
18	PRINCE M_0, M_1 [BCG+12]	(16×16 over $GF(2)$)	24	24
19	PRIDE L_0-L_3 [ADK+14]	(16×16 over $GF(2)$)	24	24
20	QARMA64 [Ava17]	Circulant (4×4 over $GF(2^4)$)	24	24
21	SKINNY64 [BJK+16]	(4×4 over $GF(2^4)$)	12	12

*ANUBIS and CLEFIA M_0 matrices are the same. [KLSW18b] gives different results for them.
It might have been an error.

a functional description of the matrix written in VHDL to the Synopsys design compiler and instructed it to compile a circuit optimized for area. It returned a solution with 39 3-input xor and 31 2-input xor gates. The area of the above circuit is $39 * 3.25 + 31 * 2 = 188.75$ GE which is less than $2 * 95 = 190$ GE (the area of 95 2-input xor gates).

However the situation is different for another library CORE65GPHVT v 5.1 which is based on the STM 65 nm CMOS logic process. It has two types of xor gates listed as follows:

- 2-input xor gate with area: 1.981 GE
- 3-input xor gate with area:: 3.715 GE

If we took the previous solution and tried to apply it to this library the gate area would be $39 * 3.715 + 31 * 1.981 = 206.296$ GE which is much more than $95 * 1.981 = 188.195$ GE that would be obtained by using only the 2-input xor gate. In fact when we repeated the exercise for this library and asked the design compiler to synthesize an area optimized circuit it returned a solution with 38 3-input xors and 32 2-input xors which amounts to 204.56 GE. The experiments bring out three crucial facts: (a) The SLP solution does not always represent the optimal circuit area when the circuit compiler can additionally use 3-input xor gates, (b) the optimal solution is heavily dependent on the target standard cell library, a solution that is optimal for a given library may not be optimal for a different library, (c) the solutions returned by circuit compilers may also not represent the optimal solution in terms of circuit area.

3.1   Incremental Graph Based Technique

Since a single 3-input xor is smaller in area than two 2-input xors, we started with the rule of thumb that, given any matrix, we should convert all instances of two 2-input xors to a single 3-input xor wherever possible. However, consider the following linear system before proceeding.

Example 3. $y_1 = x_1 \oplus x_2 \oplus x_3$, $y_2 = x_2 \oplus x_3 \oplus x_4$.

One could solve the above problem in a straightforward manner by using two 3-input xor gates that would cost 6.5 GE in the 90 nm library and around 7.4 GE in the 65 nm library. However an SLP based solution that reuses the sum $x_2 \oplus x_3$ could give us a solution using three 2-input xors, that would cost around 6 GE in both libraries.

- Solution: $t_1 = x_2 \oplus x_3$, $y_2 = t_1 \oplus x_4$ and $y_1 = x_1 \oplus t_1$.

Let us say we already have a SLP solution for a given matrix obtained by either the Boyar-Peralta or the Paar method and we want to take this solution as a starting point and make incremental modifications to it to get a circuit that uses both 2 and 3-input xor gates. The standard way to do this would be to check if there are pairs of 2-input xors in the original SLP solution that could be replaced with a 3-input xor gate thereby reducing the area of the circuit. This approach has an additional advantage that the final solution of this approach is guaranteed to have less area than the corresponding SLP solution, irrespective of the library of synthesis. Given the information in the above example, a handy way to proceed is to check if the output of a particular 2-input xor gate is used multiple times in the circuit. If so then it is best to avoid removing this xor gate from the SLP solution to facilitate insertion of another 3-input xor gate. Let us formalize this intuitive approach.

Let L be the SLP solution for an underlying linear system given by the matrix M. Each line of L represents a 2-input xor gate used to implement the circuit. Define a directed graph $G = (V, E)$ in the following manner. Each line of L is a vertex in the graph: thus the size of $|V|$ is simply the length of L. Two vertices v_i, v_j are connected by a directed edge in E, if the output of the xor gate represented by v_i is an input to the xor gate represented by v_j. In such a graph, a node with outdegree strictly equal to 1 are those whose outputs are used only once. Nodes with outdegree 0 represent the gates which produce the output bits of the linear system, although it may be possible that nodes with larger outdegree produces output bits of the system. All other nodes are those that are used multiple number of times. Thus our strategy would be as follows:

1. Make a list of all nodes of outdegree 1 and 0, and additionally those nodes that produce output bits but have outdegree larger than 0.
2. If there exist two nodes v_i, v_j such that $(v_i, v_j) \in E$ and outdegree $(v_i) = 1$ and v_i does not produce an output of the underlying linear system then merge them to form a new node X that represents a 3-xor gate in the following manner: the incoming edges of v_i and v_j are made the incoming edges of X and if the outdegree of v_j is 1, the outgoing edge of v_j is made the outgoing edge of X.
3. Essentially what the above step does is as follows: if v_i represents the 2-input xor gate $t = x \oplus y$ and v_j represents the 2-input xor gate $u = t \oplus z$, then the outdegree of $v_i = 1$, guarantees that t does not appear elsewhere in the SLP solution. We merge them to a 3-input xor node X representing $u = x \oplus y \oplus z$. Note that if $t = x \oplus y$ was an output of the system then the above merge procedure would have proven counter-productive because we would have lost the output signal t after the merge procedure.
4. The algorithm is recursively executed until all nodes of outdegree 1 of the required property are exhausted.

The algorithm starts with an SLP solution for a given matrix obtained by either the Boyar-Peralta or the Paar method, and runs the above steps iteratively until a solution is found. Since permutation matrices P, Q for which we get the optimal SLP solution for $M_R = P \cdot M \cdot Q$, may not necessarily lead to the optimal area after running the above algorithm, we run the above algorithm for a number of randomly generated P, Q till a solution is obtained. In particular, for the AES mixcolumn matrix we were able to get a solution with 39 2-input xor and 28 3-input xor gates. This gives an area of 169 GE with the CORE90GPHVT v 2.1.a library and 181.3 GE with CORE65GPHVT v 5.1. This is well below the hardware area of the corresponding SLP solution.

Table 4. Comparison of areas for matrices available in literature. Lib1 and Lib2 refer to `CORE90GPHVT v 2.1.a` and `CORE65GPHVT v 5.1` respectively.

#	Matrix	Type	# 2-xor	#3-xor	Area in GE		
					SLP	Lib 1	Lib 2
4×4 matrices over $GF(2^4)$							
1	[SKOP15]	Hadamard	26	10	92.0	84.5	88.7
2	[LS16]	Circulant	20	12	88.0	79.0	84.2
3	[LW16]	Circulant	20	12	88.0	79.0	84.2
4	[BKL16]	Circulant	18	12	84.0	75.0	80.2
5	[SS16]	Toeplitz	18	12	84.0	75.0	80.2
6	[JPST17]		13	15	84.0	74.8	81.5
7	[SKOP15]	Hadamard, Involutary	16	16	94.0	84.0	91.1
8	[LW16]	Hadamard, Involutary	13	15	86.0	74.8	81.5
9	[SS16]	Involutary	20	10	80.0	72.5	76.8
10	[JPST17]	Involutary	16	15	92.0	80.8	87.4
4×4 matrices over $GF(2^8)$							
11	[SKOP15]	Subfield	45	25	188.0	171.3	182.0
12	[LS16]	Circulant	28	42	220.0	192.5	211.5
13	[LW16]		31	35	204.0	175.8	191.4
14	[BKL16]	Circulant	40	34	216.0	190.5	205.6
15	[SS16]	Toeplitz	26	40	208.0	182.0	200.1
16	[JPST17]	Subfield	26	30	172.0	149.5	163.0
17	[SKOP15]	Subfield, Involutary	32	32	188.0	168.0	182.3
18	[LW16]	Hadamard, Involutary	48	21	180.0	164.3	173.1
19	[SS16]	Involutary	44	27	196.0	175.8	187.5
20	[JPST17]	Subfield, Involutary	36	28	184.0	163.0	175.3
8×8 matrices over $GF(2^4)$							
21	[SKOP15]	Hadamard	78	57	384.0	341.3	366.2
22	[SS17]	Toeplitz	87	58	406.0	362.5	387.8
23	[SKOP15]	Hadamard, Involutary	90	61	424.0	378.3	404.8
8×8 matrices over $GF(2^8)$							
24	[SKOP15]	Hadamard	181	141	920.0	820.3	882.2
25	[LS16]	Circulant	181	141	920.0	820.3	882.2
26	[BKL16]	Circulant	157	144	886.0	782.0	845.8
27	[SS17]	Toeplitz	153	144	872.0	782.0	837.9
28	[SKOP15]	Hadamard, Involutary	167	126	838.0	743.5	798.8
29	[JPST17]	Hadamard, Involutary	205	193	1182.0	1037.3	1022.9

Table 5. Comparison of areas for matrices used in cryptographic constructions. Lib1 and Lib2 refer to `CORE90GPHVT v 2.1.a` and `CORE65GPHVT v 5.1` respectively.

#	Matrix	Type	#2-xor	#3-xor	Area in GE		
					SLP	Lib 1	Lib 2
4×4 matrices over $GF(2^8)$							
1	AES [DR02]	Circulant	39	28	190.0	169.0	181.3
2	ANUBIS [BR00a]	Hadamard and Involutary	60	20	200.0	185.0	193.2
3	CLEFIA M_0 [SSA+07]	Hadamard Involutary	60	20	200.0	185.0	193.2
4	CLEFIA M_1 [SSA+07]	Hadamard	38	36	220.0	193.0	209.0
5	FOX MU4 [JV04]		46	43	262.0	231.8	250.9
6	TWOFISH [SKW+98]		43	42	250.0	222.5	241.2
8×8 matrices over $GF(2^8)$							
7	FOX MU8 [JV04]		212	190	1184.0	1041.5	1125.8
8	GRØSTL [GKM+09]	Circulant	190	129	920.0	799.3	855.6
9	KHAZAD [BR00b]	Hadamard and Involutary	224	134	984.0	883.5	941.6
10	WHIRLPOOL [BR11]	Circulant	154	155	928.0	811.8	880.9
4×4 matrices over $GF(2^4)$							
11	JOLTIK [JNP13]	Hadamard and Involutary	16	16	94.0	84.0	91.1
12	SMALLSCALE AES [CMR05]	Circulant	19	13	90.0	80.3	85.9
8×8 matrices over $GF(2^4)$							
13	WHIRLWIND M_0 [BNN+10]	Hadamard and Subfield	82	64	420.0	372.0	400.2
14	WHIRLWIND M_1 [BNN+10]	-do-	96	69	468.0	416.3	446.5
Non MDS matrices							
15	QARMA128 [Ava17]	Circulant (4×4 over $GF(2^8)$)	34	7	96.0	90.8	93.4
16	ARIA [KKP+03]	Involutary (16×16 over $GF(2^8)$)	136	128	784.0	688.0	744.8
17	MIDORI [BBI+15]	Involutary (4×4 over $GF(2^4)$)	16	4	48.0	45.0	46.6
18	PRINCE M_0, M_1[BCG+12]	(16×16 over $GF(2)$)	16	4	48.0	45.0	46.6
19	PRIDE L_0-L_3 [ADK+14]	(16×16 over $GF(2)$)	16	4	48.0	45.0	46.6
20	QARMA64 [Ava17]	Circulant (4×4 over $GF(2^4)$)	16	4	48.0	45.0	46.6
21	SKINNY64 [BJK+16]	(4×4 over $GF(2^4)$)	12	0	24.0	24.0	24.0

3.2   Results

We applied the above algorithm to all the SLP solutions that are listed above in Sect. 2. For all the matrices that we experimented with, we obtained a circuit implementation smaller in area than the area of the corresponding SLP solution. The results are presented in Tables 4 and 5. We compare the area of the circuit obtained after running the algorithm with the corresponding area of the SLP solution (for the sake of conciseness we fix this value to 2 times the length of SLP solution, in GE). Results for both the libraries `CORE90GPHVT v 2.1.a` and `CORE65GPHVT v 5.1` are tabulated.

4   Conclusion

In this paper we took another look at the shortest linear program problem for implementing linear systems. We found implementation issues that may result in a situation where the order of appearance of columns in a matrix affect the outcome of heuristic based algorithms like the ones due to Boyar-Peralta and Paar. We showed that by suitably including randomness in the execution of these algorithms it is possible to obtain even more efficient solutions to the SLP problem. We applied our method to the diffusion layer matrices of well known constructions in literature. We were able to improve the number of xor gates required for the implementations for most of these matrices. We have also reported an implementation of the AES mixcolumn matrix that uses only 95 xor gates which is 2 gates better than the currently known best implementation.

In the second part of the paper, we observed that most standard cell libraries contain both 2 and 3-input xor gates, with the silicon area of the 3-input xor gate being smaller than the sum of the areas of two 2-input xor gates. Hence when linear circuits are synthesized by logic compilers (with specific instructions to optimize for area), most of them would return a solution circuit containing both 2 and 3-input xor gates. Thus from a practical point of view, reducing circuit size in presence of these gates was not equivalent to solving the shortest linear program. In this paper we showed that by adopting a graph based heuristic it is possible to convert a circuit constructed with 2-input xor gates to another functionally equivalent circuit that utilizes both 2 and 3-input xor gates and occupies less hardware area. As a result we obtain more lightweight implementations of all the matrices listed in first half of the paper.

Acknowledgments. Subhadeep Banik is supported by the Ambizione Grant PZ00P2_179921, awarded by the Swiss National Science Foundation (SNSF). Takanori Isobe is supported by Grant-in-Aid for Scientific Research (B) (KAKENHI 19H02141) for Japan Society for the Promotion of Science.

References

[ADK+14] Albrecht, M.R., Driessen, B., Kavun, E.B., Leander, G., Paar, C., Yalçın, T.: Block ciphers – focus on the linear layer (feat. PRIDE). In: Garay, J.A., Gennaro, R. (eds.) CRYPTO 2014. LNCS, vol. 8616, pp. 57–76. Springer, Heidelberg (2014). https://doi.org/10.1007/978-3-662-44371-2_4

[AF14] Augot, D., Finiasz, M.: Direct construction of recursive MDS diffusion layers using shortened BCH codes. In: Cid, C., Rechberger, C. (eds.) FSE 2014. LNCS, vol. 8540, pp. 3–17. Springer, Heidelberg (2015). https://doi.org/10.1007/978-3-662-46706-0_1

[Ava17] Avanzi, R.: The QARMA block cipher family: almost MDS matrices over rings with zero divisors, nearly symmetric even-mansour constructions with non-involutory central rounds, and search heuristics for low-latency s-boxes. IACR Trans. Symmetric Cryptol. **2017**(1), 4–44 (2017)

[BBI+15] Banik, S., et al.: Midori: a block cipher for low energy. In: Iwata, T., Cheon, J.H. (eds.) ASIACRYPT 2015. LNCS, vol. 9453, pp. 411–436. Springer, Heidelberg (2015). https://doi.org/10.1007/978-3-662-48800-3_17

[BCG+12] Borghoff, J., et al.: PRINCE – a low-latency block cipher for pervasive computing applications. In: Wang, X., Sako, K. (eds.) ASIACRYPT 2012. LNCS, vol. 7658, pp. 208–225. Springer, Heidelberg (2012). https://doi.org/10.1007/978-3-642-34961-4_14

[BJK+16] Beierle, C., et al.: The SKINNY family of block ciphers and its low-latency variant MANTIS. In: Robshaw, M., Katz, J. (eds.) CRYPTO 2016. LNCS, vol. 9815, pp. 123–153. Springer, Heidelberg (2016). https://doi.org/10.1007/978-3-662-53008-5_5

[BKL16] Beierle, C., Kranz, T., Leander, G.: Lightweight multiplication in $GF(2^n)$ with applications to MDS Matrices. In: Robshaw, M., Katz, J. (eds.) CRYPTO 2016. LNCS, vol. 9814, pp. 625–653. Springer, Heidelberg (2016). https://doi.org/10.1007/978-3-662-53018-4_23

[BMP08] Boyar, J., Matthews, P., Peralta, R.: On the shortest linear straight-line program for computing linear forms. In: Ochmański, E., Tyszkiewicz, J. (eds.) MFCS 2008. LNCS, vol. 5162, pp. 168–179. Springer, Heidelberg (2008). https://doi.org/10.1007/978-3-540-85238-4_13

[BNN+10] Barreto, P.S.L.M., Nikov, V., Nikova, S., Rijmen, V., Tischhauser, E.: Whirlwind: a new cryptographic hash function. Des. Codes Cryptogr. **56**(2–3), 141–162 (2010)

[BP10] Boyar, J., Peralta, R.: A new combinational logic minimization technique with applications to cryptology. In: Festa, P. (ed.) SEA 2010. LNCS, vol. 6049, pp. 178–189. Springer, Heidelberg (2010). https://doi.org/10.1007/978-3-642-13193-6_16

[BP18] Boyar, J., Peralta, R.: C++ implementation of SLP algorithm (2018). http://www.imada.sdu.dk/~joan/xor/Improved2.cc

[BR00a] Barreto, P.S.L.M., Rijmen, V.: The anubis block cipher (2000). Submission to NESSIE project. https://www.cosic.esat.kuleuven.be/nessie/workshop/submissions/anubis.zip

[BR00b] Barreto, P.S.L.M., Rijmen, V.: The khazad legacy-level block cipher (2000). Submission to NESSIE project. https://www.cosic.esat.kuleuven.be/nessie/workshop/submissions/khazad.zip

[BR11] Barreto, P.S.L.M., Rijmen, V.: Whirlpool. In: van Tilborg, H.C.A., Jajodia, S. (eds.) Encyclopedia of Cryptography and Security, 2nd edn, pp. 1384–1385. Springer, Boston (2011). https://doi.org/10.1007/978-1-4419-5906-5_626

[CMR05] Cid, C., Murphy, S., Robshaw, M.J.B.: Small scale variants of the AES. In: Gilbert, H., Handschuh, H. (eds.) FSE 2005. LNCS, vol. 3557, pp. 145–162. Springer, Heidelberg (2005). https://doi.org/10.1007/11502760_10

[DR02] Daemen, J., Rijmen, V.: The Design of Rijndael: AES - The Advanced Encryption Standard. Springer, Berlin (2002). https://doi.org/10.1007/978-3-662-04722-4

[FS10] Fuhs, C., Schneider-Kamp, P.: Synthesizing shortest linear straight-line programs over GF(2) using SAT. In: Strichman, O., Szeider, S. (eds.) SAT 2010. LNCS, vol. 6175, pp. 71–84. Springer, Heidelberg (2010). https://doi.org/10.1007/978-3-642-14186-7_8

[GKM+09] Gauravaram, P., et al.: Grøstl - a SHA-3 candidate. In: Symmetric Cryptography, 11–16 January 2009 (2009)

[GPP11] Guo, J., Peyrin, T., Poschmann, A.: The PHOTON family of lightweight hash functions. In: Rogaway, P. (ed.) CRYPTO 2011. LNCS, vol. 6841, pp. 222–239. Springer, Heidelberg (2011). https://doi.org/10.1007/978-3-642-22792-9_13

[GPPR11] Guo, J., Peyrin, T., Poschmann, A., Robshaw, M.: The LED block cipher. In: Preneel, B., Takagi, T. (eds.) CHES 2011. LNCS, vol. 6917, pp. 326–341. Springer, Heidelberg (2011). https://doi.org/10.1007/978-3-642-23951-9_22

[GPV17] Gupta, K.C., Pandey, S.K., Venkateswarlu, A.: Towards a general construction of recursive MDS diffusion layers. Des. Codes Cryptogr. 82(1–2), 179–195 (2017)

[GR15] Kishan Chand Gupta and Indranil Ghosh Ray: Cryptographically significant MDS matrices based on circulant and circulant-like matrices for lightweight applications. Cryptogr. Commun. 7(2), 257–287 (2015)

[JMPS17] Jean, J., Moradi, A., Peyrin, T., Sasdrich, P.: Bit-sliding: a generic technique for bit-serial implementations of SPN-based primitives. In: Fischer, W., Homma, N. (eds.) CHES 2017. LNCS, vol. 10529, pp. 687–707. Springer, Cham (2017). https://doi.org/10.1007/978-3-319-66787-4_33

[JNP13] Jean, J., Nikolić, I., Peyrin, T.: Joltik v1.3 (2013). Submission to caesar competition. https://competitions.cr.yp.to/round2/joltikv13.pdf

[JPST17] Jean, J., Peyrin, T., Sim, S.M., Tourteaux, J.: Optimizing implementations of lightweight building blocks. IACR Trans. Symmetric Cryptol. 2017(4), 130–168 (2017)

[JV04] Junod, P., Vaudenay, S.: FOX: a new family of block ciphers. In: Handschuh, H., Hasan, M.A. (eds.) SAC 2004. LNCS, vol. 3357, pp. 114–129. Springer, Heidelberg (2004). https://doi.org/10.1007/978-3-540-30564-4_8

[KKP+03] Kwon, D., et al.: New block cipher: ARIA. In: Lim, J.-I., Lee, D.-H. (eds.) ICISC 2003. LNCS, vol. 2971, pp. 432–445. Springer, Heidelberg (2004). https://doi.org/10.1007/978-3-540-24691-6_32

[KLSW18a] Kranz, T., Leander, G., Stoffelen, K., Wiemer, F.: Github repository: shorter linear SLPs for MDS matrices (2018). https://github.com/rub-hgi/shorter_linear_slps_for_mds_matrices

[KLSW18b] Kranz, T., Leander, G., Stoffelen, K., Wiemer, F.: Shorter linear straight-line programs for MDS matrices. IACR Trans. Symmetric Cryptol. 2018(4), 188–211 (2018)

[LS16] Liu, M., Sim, S.M.: Lightweight MDS generalized circulant matrices. In: Peyrin, T. (ed.) FSE 2016. LNCS, vol. 9783, pp. 101–120. Springer, Heidelberg (2016). https://doi.org/10.1007/978-3-662-52993-5_6

[LW16] Li, Y., Wang, M.: On the construction of lightweight circulant involutory MDS matrices. In: Peyrin, T. (ed.) FSE 2016. LNCS, vol. 9783, pp. 121–139. Springer, Heidelberg (2016). https://doi.org/10.1007/978-3-662-52993-5_7

[Paa97] Paar, C.: Optimized arithmetic for Reed-Solomon encoders. In: Proceedings of IEEE International Symposium on Information Theory, p. 250, June 1997

[SKOP15] Sim, S.M., Khoo, K., Oggier, F., Peyrin, T.: Lightweight MDS involution matrices. In: Leander, G. (ed.) FSE 2015. LNCS, vol. 9054, pp. 471–493. Springer, Heidelberg (2015). https://doi.org/10.1007/978-3-662-48116-5_23

[SKW+98] Schneier, B., Kelsey, J., Whiting, D., Wagner, D., Hall, C., Ferguson, N.: Twofish: a 128-bit block cipher (1998). https://www.schneier.com/academic/paperfiles/paper-twofish-paper.pdf

[SS16] Sarkar, S., Syed, H.: Lightweight diffusion layer: importance of toeplitz matrices. IACR Trans. Symmetric Cryptol. **2016**(1), 95–113 (2016)

[SS17] Sarkar, S., Syed, H.: Analysis of toeplitz MDS matrices. In: Pieprzyk, J., Suriadi, S. (eds.) ACISP 2017. LNCS, vol. 10343, pp. 3–18. Springer, Cham (2017). https://doi.org/10.1007/978-3-319-59870-3_1

[SSA+07] Shirai, T., Shibutani, K., Akishita, T., Moriai, S., Iwata, T.: The 128-bit blockcipher CLEFIA (extended abstract). In: Biryukov, A. (ed.) FSE 2007. LNCS, vol. 4593, pp. 181–195. Springer, Heidelberg (2007). https://doi.org/10.1007/978-3-540-74619-5_12

[Sto16] Stoffelen, K.: Optimizing S-box implementations for several criteria using SAT solvers. In: Peyrin, T. (ed.) FSE 2016. LNCS, vol. 9783, pp. 140–160. Springer, Heidelberg (2016). https://doi.org/10.1007/978-3-662-52993-5_8

Tweakable TWINE: Building a Tweakable Block Cipher on Generalized Feistel Structure

Kosei Sakamoto[1(✉)], Kazuhiko Minematsu[2], Nao Shibata[3], Maki Shigeri[3], Hiroyasu Kubo[3], Yuki Funabiki[4], Andrey Bogdanov[5], Sumio Morioka[6], and Takanori Isobe[1,7]

[1] University of Hyogo, Kobe, Japan
aa18s502@ai.u-hyogo.ac.jp
[2] NEC Corporation, Tokyo, Japan
k-minematsu@ah.jp.nec.com
[3] NEC Solution Innovators, Tokyo, Japan
[4] Sony corporation, Tokyo, Japan
[5] Technical University of Denmark, Lyngby, Denmark
[6] Interstellar Technologies, Obihiro, Japan
[7] National Institute of Information and Communications Technology, Tokyo, Japan
takanori.isobe@ai.u-hyogo.ac.jp

Abstract. Tweakable block cipher (TBC) is an extension of conventional block cipher. We study how to build a TBC based on generalized Feistel structure (GFS), a classical block cipher construction. While known dedicated TBC proposals are based on substitution-permutation network (SPN), GFS has not been used for building TBC. In particular, we take 64-bit GFS block cipher TWINE and try to make it tweakable with a minimum change. To find a best one from a large number of candidates, we performed a comprehensive search with a help of mixed integer linear programming (MILP) solver. As a result, our proposal Tweakable TWINE is quite efficient, has the same number of rounds as TWINE with extremely simple tweak schedule.

1 Introduction

Tweakable Block Cipher. Tweakable block cipher (TBC) is an extension of a conventional block cipher. An encryption of TBC is a function takes a public input called tweak T in addition to key K and plaintext M, and the pair (K, T) specifies the permutation over the message space. Since its inception by Liskov et al. [17] TBC has been extensively studied, and now it is widely acknowledged as a powerful primitive to build efficient and highly-secure symmetric-key modes of operations. For example, the seminal OCB authenticated encryption [14, 24, 25] scheme can be seen as a mode of TBC with TBC instantiated as a block cipher mode called XEX [24].

As proposed by Liskov et al., TBCs can be built on block ciphers. Typical examples are LRW and XEX modes of operations. They are efficient, as it

© Springer Nature Switzerland AG 2019
N. Attrapadung and T. Yagi (Eds.): IWSEC 2019, LNCS 11689, pp. 129–145, 2019.
https://doi.org/10.1007/978-3-030-26834-3_8

requires few block cipher calls for one TBC encryption/decryption. For security, they have provable security guarantee up to around $2^{n/2}$ queries for TBC of n-bit block. Unfortunately, this level of security is not always enough, in particular when a TBC is used by modes of operation achieving "beyond-the-birthday-bound" (BBB) security. Some modes of operations to achieve BBB security have been proposed [15,16], however, they are usually much more costlier than the simple LRW/XEX.

Another approach, which is our focus, is a dedicated construction. To our knowledge the earliest proposal is HPC (where tweak is called "spice") proposed for AES competition [23]. In recent years, dedicated TBCs are becoming popular, such as Threefish [21], Deoxys-BC [12], SKINNY [2] and QARMA [1]. One strong advantage of dedicated construction is one can expect the full security when properly designed. While dedicated TBCs are possible in principle, by somehow absorbing tweak in the ordinary block cipher structures such as SPN or Feistel, but the challenge is how to make it efficient, in a small number of rounds, while keeping the sufficient security. Tweakey flamework [11] is one prominent methodology to SPN-based dedicated TBCs. However, in general, the constructions of TBCs are far less studied than those for block ciphers or fixed-key permutations.

Building TBC on GFS. In this paper, we study how to build a TBC on generalized Feistel structure (GFS) [22,30], one of the classical structures for block ciphers. GFS has been adopted by a number of block cipher proposals [9,27]. However, it has never been used to build a TBC, to the best of our knowledge. Goldenberg et al. [7] and Mitsuda and Iwata [19] studied GFS-based TBC constructions from the viewpoint of provable security, where the round functions are instantiated by PRFs and the focus is to evaluate (S)PRP security of GFS. While these results give us a baseline, they tell little about the design and security of concrete TBCs. GFS has a large freedom regarding the choice of sub-block permutation. Suzaki and Minematsu [26] showed a comprehensive study on the effect of permutation, including the diffusion, the number of differential/linear active S-boxes, etc. Subsequently Suzaki et al. proposed 64-bit block cipher TWINE [27]. It uses a permutation over 16 nibbles selected from the result of [26] for achieving the best characteristics.

To build a TBC on GFS, we set our primary goal to reduce the cost of design, security evaluation, and implementation. Consequently, we choose to reuse TWINE as much as possible. We design an extremely simple tweak scheduling based on SKINNY's tweakey schedule [2] and attach it to TWINE. This reusing approach to dedicated TBC is useful for both designers and users, and we think our approach itself has some novelties (of course, some of the aforementioned work convert a block cipher into a TBC, but they are provably secure constructions). We evaluated linear/differential/impossible/integral characteristics for single-key, related-key and chosen-tweak setting. For finding the best parameter of tweak schedule against these attacks, we extensively used Mixed Integer Linear Programming (MILP) solver, which is now quite common for designing ciphers. With these efforts, our proposal, called Tweakable TWINE (or

T-TWINE), becomes quite efficient: it has 64-bit tweak (the same as the block size) and has *the same number of 36 rounds* as the original. Key schedule and tweak schedule are independent, which will be useful for some use cases, e.g, when a key is hardwired. Tweakable TWINE is obtained by adding few nibble XORs to TWINE, therefore the hardware cost is essentially the same as TWINE except the registers for tweak. We also show basic hardware implementation results to verify this claim.

1.1   Organization of This Paper

For simplicity (and not to describing almost the same algorithms twice), we first present our proposal Tweakable TWINE at Sect. 2. At Sect. 3 we show our design goals and tweak schedule function. Section 4 shows the security evaluation on our proposal. We present hardware implementation results at Sect. 5, and conclude at Sect. 6.

2   Specification

Tweakable TWINE is based on TWINE [27], which is a 64-bit block cipher supporting two key lengths of 80 bits and 128 bits. Tweakable TWINE takes a 64-bit tweak value T as an additional input, and consists of a data processing part, a key scheduling function and a tweak scheduling function. The data processing part and the key scheduling function are the same as those of TWINE except additional inputs of tweaks in the data processing part. We, hereafter, refer Tweakable TWINE [27] with an 80-bit key and a 128-bit key to T-TWINE-80 and T-TWINE-128, respectively.

2.1   Notation

A bitwise exclusive-OR is denoted by $\oplus$. For binary strings, x and y, $x\|y$ denotes their concatenation. Let $|x|$ denote the bit length of x. If $|x| = m$, we may write $x_{(m)}$ to emphasize its bit length. If $|x| = 4c$ for a positive integer c, we write $x \rightarrow (k_0\|k_1\|\cdots\|k_{c-1})$, where $|k_i| = 4$, is the partition operation into the 4-bit sub-blocks. The opposite operation, $(k_0\|k_1\|\cdots\|k_{c-1}) \rightarrow x$, is similarly defined. The partition operation may be implicit, i.e., we may simply write x_i to denote the i-th 4-bit subsequence for any $4c$-bit string x.

2.2   Data Processing Part

The data processing part is based on a variant of Type-2 GFS with 16 4-bit nibbles [26]. The round function consists of a 4-bit S-box S, a round-key XOR, a round-tweak XOR and a nibble shuffle operation π, which permutes 16 nibbles as shown in Fig. 1. The S-box S and the nibble shuffle operation π are described in Fig. 2. The number of rounds for both of T-TWINE-80 and T-TWINE-128 is 36, where the nibble shuffle operation in the last round is omitted.

132   K. Sakamoto et al.

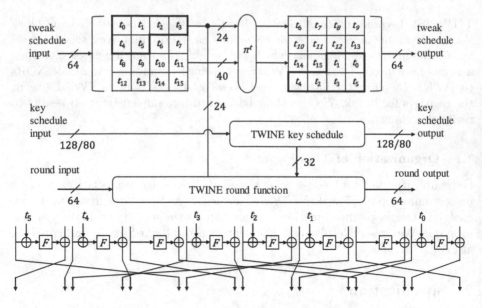

Fig. 1. Overview of Tweakable TWINE

x	0	1	2	3	4	5	6	7	8	9	A	B	C	D	E	F
$S(x)$	C	0	F	A	2	B	9	5	8	3	D	7	1	E	6	4

h	0	1	2	3	4	5	6	7	8	9	10	11	12	13	14	15
$\pi[h]$	5	0	1	4	7	12	3	8	13	6	9	2	15	10	11	14
$\pi^{-1}[h]$	1	2	11	6	3	0	9	4	7	10	13	14	5	8	15	12

Fig. 2. S-box S and nibble shuffle π

For $i = 1, \ldots, 36$, i-th round uses a 32-bit (8 nibbles) round key RK^i, which is derived from the secret key $K_{(n)}$ with $n \in \{80, 128\}$, using the key scheduling function, and i-th round also uses a 24-bit (6 nibbles) round tweak RT^i, which is derived from the 64-bit tweak T using the tweak scheduling function. The detailed algorithm of encryption and decryption is given as Fig. 3. The key scheduling function is described in Appendix B.

2.3 Tweak Scheduling Function

The tweak scheduling function produces $RT_{(24 \times 36)}$ from the 64-bit tweak T. It is a permutation-based function as shown in Fig. 1. In each round, all nibbles are shifted by 6 nibbles, and 6 nibbles which are inserted to a round function are shuffled using a 6-nibble permutation π^t, s.t. $(0, 1, 2, 3, 4, 5) \to (1, 0, 4, 2, 3, 5)$. The detailed algorithm is given as Fig. 4.

Algorithm $Enc(P_{(64)}, RK_{(32\times36)}, RT_{(24\times36)}, C_{(64)})$

1. $X^1_{0(4)} \| X^1_{1(4)} \| \cdots \| X^1_{15(4)} \leftarrow P$
2. $RK^1_{(32)} \| RK^2_{(32)} \| \cdots \| RK^{36}_{(32)} \leftarrow RK_{(32\times36)}$
3. $RT^1_{(24)} \| RT^2_{(24)} \| \cdots \| RT^{36}_{(24)} \leftarrow RT_{(24\times36)}$
4. **for** $i = 1$ **to** 36 **do**
   $RK^i_{0(4)} \| \cdots \| RK^i_{7(4)} \leftarrow RK^i_{(32)}, \; RT^i_{0(4)} \| \cdots \| RT^i_{5(4)} \leftarrow RT^i_{(24)}$
   $X^i_1 \leftarrow S(X^i_0 \oplus RK^i_0 \oplus RT^i_5) \oplus X^i_1, \; X^i_3 \leftarrow S(X^i_2 \oplus RK^i_1 \oplus RT^i_4) \oplus X^i_3,$
   $X^i_5 \leftarrow S(X^i_4 \oplus RK^i_2) \oplus X^i_5, \; X^i_7 \leftarrow S(X^i_6 \oplus RK^i_3 \oplus RT^i_3) \oplus X^i_7,$
   $X^i_9 \leftarrow S(X^i_8 \oplus RK^i_4 \oplus RT^i_2) \oplus X^i_9, \; X^i_{11} \leftarrow S(X^i_{10} \oplus RK^i_5 \oplus RT^i_1) \oplus X^i_{11},$
   $X^i_{13} \leftarrow S(X^i_{12} \oplus RK^i_6) \oplus X^i_{13}, \; X^i_{15} \leftarrow S(X^i_{14} \oplus RK^i_7 \oplus RT^i_0) \oplus X^i_{15},$
   If $i \le 35$ **for** $h = 0$ **to** 15 **do** $X^{i+1}_{\pi[h]} \leftarrow X^i_h$
5. $C \leftarrow X^{36}_0 \| X^{36}_1 \| \cdots \| X^{36}_{15}$

Algorithm $Dec(C_{(64)}, RK_{(32\times36)}, RT_{(24\times36)}, P_{(64)})$

1. $X^{36}_{0(4)} \| X^{36}_{1(4)} \| \cdots \| X^{36}_{15(4)} \leftarrow C$
2. $RK^1_{(32)} \| \cdots \| RK^{36}_{(32)} \leftarrow RK_{(32\times36)}$
3. $RT^1_{(24)} \| RT^2_{(24)} \| \cdots \| RT^{36}_{(24)} \leftarrow RT_{(24\times36)}$
4. **for** $i = 36$ **down to** 1 **do**
   $RK^i_{0(4)} \| RK^i_{1(4)} \| \cdots \| RK^i_{7(4)} \leftarrow RK^i_{(32)}, \; RT^i_{0(4)} \| \cdots \| RT^i_{5(4)} \leftarrow RT^i_{(24)}$
   $X^i_1 \leftarrow S(X^i_0 \oplus RK^i_0 \oplus RT^i_5) \oplus X^i_1, \; X^i_3 \leftarrow S(X^i_2 \oplus RK^i_1 \oplus RT^i_4) \oplus X^i_3,$
   $X^i_5 \leftarrow S(X^i_4 \oplus RK^i_2) \oplus X^i_5, \; X^i_7 \leftarrow S(X^i_6 \oplus RK^i_3 \oplus RT^i_3) \oplus X^i_7,$
   $X^i_9 \leftarrow S(X^i_8 \oplus RK^i_4 \oplus RT^i_2) \oplus X^i_9, \; X^i_{11} \leftarrow S(X^i_{10} \oplus RK^i_5 \oplus RT^i_1) \oplus X^i_{11},$
   $X^i_{13} \leftarrow S(X^i_{12} \oplus RK^i_6) \oplus X^i_{13}, \; X^i_{15} \leftarrow S(X^i_{14} \oplus RK^i_7 \oplus RT^i_0) \oplus X^i_{15},$
   If $i \ge 2$ **for** $h = 0$ **to** 15 **do** $X^{i-1}_{\pi^{-1}[h]} \leftarrow X^i_h$
5. $P \leftarrow X^1_0 \| X^1_1 \| \cdots \| X^1_{15}$

Fig. 3. Encryption and decryption of Tweakable TWINE

Algorithm $TweakScheduling(T_{(64)}, RT_{(24\times36)})$

1. $t^1_{0(4)} \| t^1_{1(4)} \| \cdots \| t^1_{16(4)} \leftarrow T$

2. **for** $i = 1$ **to** 36 **do**
   $RT^r_{(24)} \leftarrow t^i_0 \| t^i_1 \| t^i_2 \| t^i_3 \| t^i_4 \| t^i_5 \|$
   for $h = 0$ **to** 5 **do** $t^i_{\pi^t[h]} \leftarrow t^i_h$
   for $h = 0$ **to** 15 **do** $t^{i+1}_{(h-6) \bmod 16} \leftarrow t^i_h$
3. $RK_{(24\times36)} \leftarrow RT^1 \| RT^2 \| \cdots \| RT^{36}$

Fig. 4. Tweak scheduling function of Tweakable TWINE

3   Design Decision

In this section, we describe design goals of Tweakable TWINE, and explain how to design the tweak key scheduling function and choose its parameters.

3.1   Design Goals

Our primal motivation is to build a dedicated TBC on GFN, which is one of the classical structures for block ciphers. To minimize design and evaluation costs, we decide to choose a lightweight block cipher TWINE, which is based on GFN, as an underlying cipher. Then we are able to focus on how to design a tweak scheduling function, and to add it to TWINE. Our design goals of Tweakable TWINE are as follow.

1. Reuse the core of original TWINE.
2. Minimize additional H/W cost, especially area.
3. Keep a nice S/W performance of TWINE by SIMD instructions.
4. Minimize additional rounds to keep throughput of TWINE as possible.

Following the requirement 1, we choose a tweak scheduling function that is independent from the key scheduling function unlike the tweakey framework of SKINNY [2] so that Tweakable TWINE is realized by only adding the new tweak scheduling function to TWINE in software and hardware. Besides, the security in the single-key setting and the related-key setting is reduced to that of TWINE. Thus, we can focus on only the security evaluation in the chosen-tweak setting where the adversary can control of the value of a tweak for Tweakable TWINE.

Following the requirements 2 and 3, we choose a permutation-based tweak scheduling function that outputs d nibble out of 16 nibbles as round tweak nibbles and permutes 16 nibbles in each round as shown in Fig. 5. While the independence of key and tweak schedule is differs from Tweakey framework, our tweak scheduling function itself has a similarity to tweakey scheduling of SKINNY. We further simplify it by removing nibble LFSRs and observe no noticeable security loss. It is well known that the H/W cost (esp. gate size) of the permutation-based scheduling is very small as shuffle layers are implemented by cost-free wire operations in hardware. In software, such shuffle operations are executed by shuffle instructions of SIMD.

3.2   How to Design Permutation-Based Tweak Scheduling Function

To achieve the requirement 4, we properly design the permutation-based scheduling function. Specifically, we need to carefully choose the patterns of the permutation and the locations where tweak nibbles are inserted in the round function, and the number of tweak nibbles to be inputted to each round. As a criteria for finding the best tweak scheduling function, we use *the number of differentially active S-boxes*.

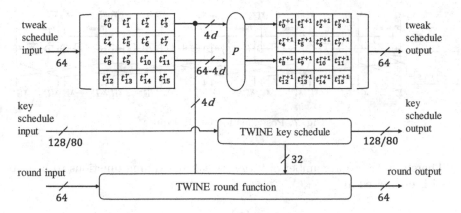

Fig. 5. Permutation-based tweak scheduling function

Permutation. Since the number of possible 16-nibble permutations is $16! \approx 2^{44}$, it is computationally infeasible to evaluate the number of active S-boxes for all permutations. To reduce the search space, we choose the SKINNY-type scheduling function [2] such that in each round, d nibbles which are inserted to a round function are shuffled and all nibbles are shifted by d nibbles as shown in Fig. 6, because the SKINNY-type permutation guarantees that each nibble is included in every $\lceil 16/d \rceil$ round. The total number of candidates of this-type permutation is estimated as $\sum_{d=1}^{8}(d!)$

An example of $d = 4$ is given as follows. In the figure, we first shuffle the first four nibbles and then shift all 16 nibbles by 4.

$$P_4 : (0, 1, 2, 3, 4, 5, 6, 7, 8, 9, 10, 11, 12, 13, 14, 15) \rightarrow$$
$$(4, 5, 6, 7, 8, 9, 10, 11, 12, 13, 14, 15, 3, 1, 0, 2)$$

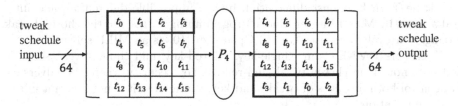

Fig. 6. Permutation of $d = 4$

Position of Tweak Inputs in the Round Function. In each round function, we add d nibble-wise tweak inputs before S-boxes as shown in Fig. 7. Thus, the number of candidates of the positions of round tweak inputs is estimated as $\binom{8}{d}$.

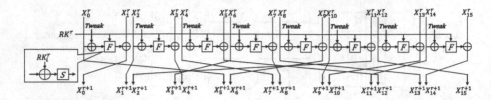

Fig. 7. Positions for tweak inputs

Therefore, the total number of target tweak scheduling functions to be evaluated is estimated as

$$\sum_{d=1}^{8} (d! \times \binom{8}{d}) \approx 2^{16.7}.$$

For these all candidates, we have evaluated the lower bounds on the number of active S-boxes in each round by the MILP-aided autormatic search algorithm (See Sect. 4.1 for details), and then find the optimal one of Sect. 2.3. It takes about 40 days by the computer with 44 cores. To be more specific, when $d = 6$, the number of rounds to achieve 32 active S-boxes is the smallest, namely 19 rounds. There are 32 permutations having 32 active S-boxes in 19 rounds (see Table 4). Among them, we choose the one having more active S-boxes of than the others in each number (1 in Table 4).

4   Security Evaluation

As mentioned in Sect. 3, the security of Tweakable TWINE in the single-key and related-key settings is reduced to that of TWINE. This section focuses on the security of Tweakable TWINE in the chosen-tweak setting where the adversary fully controls values of a 64-bit tweak. Specifically, we evaluate the security of Tweakable TWINE against differential, linear, impossible differential, and integral attacks by Mixed-Integer Linear Programming (MILP) in the chosen-tweak setting. Our evaluation uses Gurobi Optimizer [10] as an MILP solver.

Tweakable TWINE claims single-key, related-key, and chosen-tweak security and does not claim chosen-tweak-and-related-key security where the adversary can control both of values of tweaks and key relations as it is not relevant in our target application.

4.1   Differential/Linear Attack

Differential and linear attacks were proposed by Biham et al. [5] and Matsui [18], respectively. To evaluate the security against differential and linear attacks, we obtain the lower bound on the number of differentially and linearly active S-boxes by the MILP-aided automatic search method, which is proposed by

Mouha et al. [20]. Since Tweakable TWINE is based on nibble-wise operations, we evaluate all nibble-wise differential and linear trails.

Table 1 shows our search results up to 25 rounds in each setting, where AS^D_{SK}, $AS^D_{RK_{80}}$, $AS^D_{RK_{128}}$, AS^D_{CT}, $AS^D_{CTRK_{80}}$ and $AS^D_{CTRK_{128}}$, and AS^L_{CT} are the number of differentially active S-boxes in the single-key setting, the related-key setting (80-bit key), the related-key setting (128-bit key), the chosen-tweak setting, the chosen-tweak-and-related-key setting (80-bit key) and the chosen-tweak-and-related-key settings (128-bit key), respectively, and AS^L_{CT} denotes the number of linearly active S-boxes in the chosen-tweak setting.

Since the maximum differential and linear probability of the S-box is 2^{-2}, 32 active S-boxes $(2^{-2 \cdot 32} = 2^{-64})$ are sufficient to guarantee the security against differential and linear attacks. In the chosen-tweak setting, T-TWINE-80 and T-TWINE-128 has at least 32 active S-boxes in 19 rounds. Note that the linear mask in the round function is not canceled by the input linear mask from the tweak schedule. Thus AS^L_{RT} in the chosen tweak setting is the same as the number of active S-boxes in the single-key setting. Therefore, we expect that the full-round Tweakable TWINE has enough immunity against differential and linear attacks in the chosen-tweak setting.

In the chosen-tweak-and-related-key setting, 25 rounds are required to achieve 32 active S-boxes for T-TWINE-80 and T-TWINE-128. Although we do not claim the chosen-tweak-and-related-key security, if it is needed, for the reason that the number of rounds to achieve 32 active S-boxes increase 6 rounds from the chosen-tweak setting, we recommend to add 6 more rounds.

Table 1. Lower bound on the number of differentially and linearly active S-boxes in each model

Round	1	2	3	4	5	6	7	8	9	10	11	12	13	14	15	16	17	18	19	20	21	22	23	24	25
AS^D_{SK}	0	1	2	3	4	6	8	11	14	18	22	24	27	30	**32**	-	-	-	-	-	-	-	-	-	-
$AS^D_{RK_{80}}$	0	0	0	0	0	1	3	5	6	8	10	13	16	18	21	23	25	28	**32**	35	-	-	-	-	-
$AS^D_{RK_{128}}$	0	0	0	0	0	1	2	3	4	6	8	10	14	18	20	21	24	26	28	**33**	-	-	-	-	-
AS^D_{CT}	0	0	0	0	2	3	4	6	8	10	12	15	18	21	23	25	28	30	**32**	34	-	-	-	-	-
$AS^D_{CTRK_{80}}$	0	0	0	0	0	0	0	1	3	4	6	9	11	13	15	18	19	21	23	24	25	27	29	30	**32**
$AS^D_{CTRK_{128}}$	0	0	0	0	0	0	1	2	3	5	7	8	10	12	14	15	17	19	21	23	25	27	29	31	**32**
AS^L_{CT}	0	1	2	3	4	6	8	11	14	18	22	24	27	30	**32**	-	-	-	-	-	-	-	-	-	-

4.2 Impossible Differential Attack

Generally, the cryptanalysis with impossible differentials, which is proposed by Biham et al. [4], is one of the most powerful attacks against Feistel and GFS-based ciphers. By the miss-in-the-middle approach, we search the impossible differential characteristics that have one active nibble in the 16 tweak nibbles and one active nibble in 16 ciphertext nibbles at the decryption side. Therefore, we explore the space of $2^4(1 + 2^4)$ inputs. As a result, we find an 18-round impossible differential characteristic in the chosen tweak setting as shown in

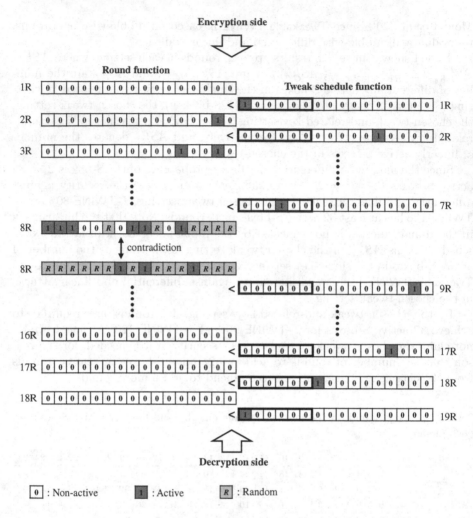

Fig. 8. 18-round impossible differential characteristic

Fig. 8. We remark that we do not have to search the input patterns with one active nibble in the 16 plaintext nibbles (and no active nibble in the tweak) because they already have been studied by the original paper of TWINE, showing 64 instances of 14-round characteristic as the longest possible ones among them, in the single-key setting. Due to the structure of Tweakable TWINE, this result is directly applicable to ours. Thus, by controlling tweak inputs, the adversary can improve an impossible differential characteristic by 4 rounds. Since we have 36 rounds, we expect that the full-round Tweakable TWINE has enough immunity against impossible differential attacks.

4.3 Integral Attack

The integral attack was first proposed by Daemen et al. [6], and then it was formalized by Knudsen and Wagner [13]. After that, it is generalized to the division property by Todo [28], and is defined as follows.

ALL ($\mathcal{A}$). The set contains all possible taken values the same number of times.
CONSTANT ($\mathcal{C}$). All values in the set are equal.
BALANCE ($\mathcal{B}$). The XOR of all values in the set is zero.
UNKNOWN ($\mathcal{U}$). Each value in the set is random.

To evaluate the nibble-based division property, we use an MILP-aided automatic search method which is proposed by Xiang et al. [29], which enable us to efficiently explore the propagation of the division property in the chosen tweak setting. In our evaluation, the division property of plaintext is fixed to all $\mathcal{C}$ and division property of tweak is freely chosen from 2^{16} nibble-wise candidates.

As a result, we find the 11-round integral distinguisher in the chosen tweak setting as shown in Fig. 9. Thus, we expect that the full-round Tweakable TWINE has enough immunity against integral attack in the chosen plaintext setting and chosen tweak setting.

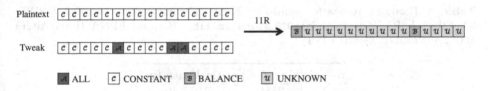

Fig. 9. 11-round integral characteristic

5 Hardware Implementation Results

We evaluated ASIC implementation of Tweakable TWINE and compared it with TWINE. See Table 2. We used Yosys ver. 0.7^1 with osu018_stdcells.lib process

Table 2. Hardware results for round-based, enc-only implementations.

TBC	Yosys (GE)	Known results (GE)	Library used by known results
T-TWINE-80	2180	–	–
SKINNY-64-128	–	1696 [2]	UMCL18G212T3 standard cell library
CRAFT-128	–	1193 [3]	130 nm standard cell library
BC	Yosys (GE)	Known results (GE)	Library used by Known results
TWINE-80	1627	1503 [27]	90 nm standard cell library
PRESENT-80	1841	1570 [27]	90 nm standard cell library
LED-80	3029	1040 [8]	UMCL18G212T3 standard cell library

---

[1] http://www.clifford.at/yosys/.

library. This process library is comparable to TSMC 0.18 μm. To see the validity of the tool, we also list some known results. We warn that this consists of several different synthesis environments. Unfortunately, we were not able to compile Tweakable TWINE using tools other than Yosis. We emphasize that, unlike the results of [27], we did not use Scan FF for registers which will reduce total GE counts if available.

The difference between TWINE-80 and T-TWINE-80 are around 550 GEs. Our library has 4 GEs for 1-bit DFF and 3-1 MUX, and 2.3 GEs for 1-bit XOR, thus an implementation of tweak schedule needs 64-bit DFF and 64-bit 3-1 MUX, and 24-bit XOR which amounts to 567 GEs. Thus the difference in size is almost from the additional tweak schedule function.

The results of Table 2 imply that T-TWINE-80 requires more GEs than the other tweakable block ciphers listed in the table. However, we focus on how to build a TBC on TWINE while minimizing the additional cost and keeping the security, which is basically a different goal from building a small TBC from scratch (even though TWINE has an excellent hardware performance). Regarding our goal, and that the additional cost is close to be what we can do, we consider that the hardware performance of T-TWINE-80 is reasonably good.

Table 3. Hardware results for multi-round, enc-only implementation of T-TWINE-80. (Top) ASIC (Yosys with `osu018_stdcells.lib`) (Bottom) FPGA (Intel/Altera 10CL120YF780I7G, Quartus 18.1)

rnd/clk	Size (GE)	critical path (ps)
1	2180	1077.46
2	2752	1907.98
3	3300	3048.44
4	3793	3717.95
6	4559	5483.03
9	6368	8369.95
12	8795	9947.94
18	20789	13095.40
36	40850	26254.36

rnd/clk	Size (LE)	Fmax (MHz)	critical path (ns)
1	325	343.88	2.9
2	442	244.68	4.1
3	534	158.91	6.3
4	618	124.63	8.0
6	835	85.22	11.7
9	1147	62.50	16.0
12	1449	46.78	21.4
18	2059	31.81	31.4
36	4072	13.12	76.2

We also evaluated multi-round implementations of T-TWINE-80 as shown in Table 3. The fact that Tweakable TWINE has 36 rounds enables a very flexible choice for multi-round implementations with small overhead, which is a property inherited from the original.

6 Conclusion

With a motivation of designing a tweakable block cipher based on generalized Feistel structure, we have presented Tweakable TWINE, a tweakable variant of lightweight block cipher TWINE. Our primary design goal is to build a TBC with minimum cost for both design and implementation, so we use TWINE as is and attach an extremely lightweight tweak schedule to it. The design challenge was how to find the best tweak schedule in terms of security and efficiency, and we extensively used Mixed integer linear programming (MILP) solver for this purpose. Consequently, Tweakable TWINE maintains TWINE's efficiency by keeping the same number of rounds, with very little (almost unavoidable) overhead due to the existence of tweak. One of the possible future directions is to apply the same methodology to other block ciphers, and see how efficiently we can turn them into tweakable block ciphers.

Acknowledgement. Takanori Isobe is supported by Grant-in-Aid for Scientific Research (B)(KAKENHI 19H02141) for Japan Society for the Promotion of Science.

A   Test Vectors

We give test vectors of T-TWINE for each key length. The data are represented in hexadecimal form.

A. T-TWINE-80

Plaintext	:	0123456789abcdef
Key	:	00112233445566778899
Tweak	:	fedcba9876543210
Ciphertext	:	fbb33219433a42f2

B. T-TWINE-128

Plaintext	:	0123456789abcdef
Key	:	00112233445566778899aabbccddeeff
Tweak	:	fedcba9876543210
Ciphertext	:	ce9e755fffeca2f8

B   Key Scheduling Function

The key schedule produces $RK_{(32\times36)}$ from the secret key, $K_{(n)}$, for $n \in \{80, 128\}$. It is a variant of GFS with few S-boxes, which is the same as one used at the data processing. The 80-bit key schedule uses 6-bit round constants, $CON^i_{(6)} = CON^i_{H(3)} \| CON^i_{L(3)}$ for $i = 1$ to 35.

The 80-bit and 128-bit key schedules are shown in Fig. 10. Here, $\text{Rot}\mathbf{z}(x)$ means $\mathbf{z}$-bit left cyclic shift of x. We note that CON^i corresponds to z^i in $GF(2^6)$ with primitive polynomial $z^6 + z + 1$.

Algorithm $KeySchedule - 80(K_{(80)}, RK_{(32\times36)})$

1. $WK_{0(4)} \| WK_{1(4)} \| \cdots \| WK_{19(4)} \leftarrow K$
2. **for** $r = 1$ **to** 35 **do**
3. $\quad RK^r_{(32)} \leftarrow WK_1 \| WK_3 \| WK_4 \| WK_6 \| WK_{13} \| WK_{14} \| WK_{15} \| WK_{16}$
4. $\quad WK_1 \leftarrow WK_1 \oplus S(WK_0)$
5. $\quad WK_4 \leftarrow WK_4 \oplus S(WK_{16})$
6. $\quad WK_7 \leftarrow WK_7 \oplus 0 \| CON^r_H$
7. $\quad WK_{19} \leftarrow WK_{19} \oplus 0 \| CON^r_L$
8. $\quad WK_0 \| \cdots \| WK_3 \leftarrow \text{Rot4}(WK_0 \| \cdots \| WK_3)$
9. $\quad WK_0 \| \cdots \| WK_{19} \leftarrow \text{Rot16}(WK_0 \| \cdots \| WK_{19})$
10. $RK^{36}_{(32)} \leftarrow WK_1 \| WK_3 \| WK_4 \| WK_6 \| WK_{13} \| WK_{14} \| WK_{15} \| WK_{16}$
11. $RK \leftarrow RK^1 \| RK^2 \| \cdots \| RK^{36}$

Algorithm $KeySchedule - 128(K_{(128)}, RK_{(32\times36)})$

1. $WK_{0(4)} \| WK_{1(4)} \| \cdots \| WK_{31(4)} \leftarrow K$
2. **For** $r = 1$ **to** 35 **do**
3. $\quad RK^r_{(32)} \leftarrow WK_2 \| WK_3 \| WK_{12} \| WK_{15} \| WK_{17} \| WK_{18} \| WK_{28} \| WK_{31}$
4. $\quad WK_1 \leftarrow WK_1 \oplus S(WK_0)$
5. $\quad WK_4 \leftarrow WK_4 \oplus S(WK_{16})$
6. $\quad WK_{23} \leftarrow WK_{23} \oplus S(WK_{30})$
7. $\quad WK_7 \leftarrow WK_7 \oplus 0 \| CON^r_H$
8. $\quad WK_{19} \leftarrow WK_{19} \oplus 0 \| CON^r_L$
9. $\quad WK_0 \| \cdots \| WK_3 \leftarrow \text{Rot4}(WK_0 \| \cdots \| WK_3)$
10. $\quad WK_0 \| \cdots \| WK_{31} \leftarrow \text{Rot16}(WK_0 \| \cdots \| WK_{31})$
11. $RK^{36}_{(32)} \leftarrow WK_2 \| WK_3 \| WK_{12} \| WK_{15} \| WK_{17} \| WK_{18} \| WK_{28} \| WK_{31}$
12. $RK_{(32\times36)} \leftarrow RK^1 \| RK^2 \| \cdots \| RK^{36}$

---

i	1	2	3	4	5	6	7	8	9	10	11	12	13	14	15	16	17	18
CON^i	01	02	04	08	10	20	03	06	0C	18	30	23	05	0A	14	28	13	26
i	19	20	21	22	23	24	25	26	27	28	29	30	31	32	33	34	35	
CON^i	0F	1E	3C	3B	35	29	11	22	07	0E	1C	38	33	25	09	12	24	

Fig. 10. Key schedules of TweakableTWINE, for 80-bit and 128-bit keys. S-box S is the same as Fig. 3, and key schedule constants, CON^i, are described in the bottom.

Table 4. The number of active S-box of each round for 32 tweak scheduling functions with $d = 6$ that achieve 32 active Sbox in 19 rounds.

Round	1	2	3	4	5	6	7	8	9	10	11	12	13	14	15	16	17	18	19	20
1	0	0	0	0	2	3	4	6	8	10	12	15	18	21	23	25	28	30	32	34
2	0	0	0	0	1	2	3	4	7	9	11	13	16	20	21	24	27	29	32	34
3	0	0	0	0	1	2	4	5	6	8	10	12	15	18	22	24	26	28	32	33
4	0	0	0	0	1	3	4	5	6	7	8	10	12	14	18	23	27	29	32	34
5	0	0	0	0	1	2	3	5	7	8	9	12	16	17	20	22	24	27	32	33
6	0	0	0	0	2	2	4	5	6	8	11	15	17	20	22	24	26	29	32	34
7	0	0	0	0	2	3	4	6	8	9	11	13	15	18	21	24	26	30	32	34
8	0	0	0	0	1	2	4	6	8	10	12	14	16	19	21	23	26	28	32	33
9	0	0	0	0	1	2	3	5	8	10	13	15	17	18	22	24	26	29	32	33
10	0	0	0	0	1	3	4	5	7	9	11	14	17	20	22	23	25	28	32	34
11	0	0	0	0	2	3	5	6	7	8	10	13	16	19	23	25	27	29	32	33
12	0	0	0	0	1	2	3	5	7	10	12	15	16	19	22	25	27	30	32	33
13	0	0	0	0	1	3	4	6	7	9	11	14	16	19	22	23	27	29	32	33
14	0	0	0	0	1	2	3	5	7	9	12	14	17	20	22	25	26	30	32	33
15	0	0	0	0	2	3	4	6	7	9	11	13	15	18	21	25	26	29	32	34
16	0	0	0	0	2	3	3	6	8	10	12	14	17	19	21	25	28	29	32	34
17	0	0	0	0	1	2	4	5	7	8	10	12	15	17	20	23	26	29	32	34
18	0	0	0	0	1	2	3	5	6	8	11	14	16	18	21	24	27	29	32	34
19	0	0	0	0	1	3	4	5	6	9	12	15	16	19	22	24	27	30	32	34
20	0	0	0	0	1	3	5	6	7	8	10	12	15	18	21	24	26	29	32	33
21	0	0	0	0	1	2	3	5	6	8	10	12	15	19	21	24	26	29	32	33
22	0	0	0	1	1	3	4	6	8	10	11	13	15	16	20	24	26	29	32	33
23	0	0	0	1	1	2	3	5	6	8	11	13	15	19	22	24	26	30	32	33
24	0	0	0	0	1	2	4	5	7	9	11	13	16	18	21	23	26	29	32	33
25	0	0	0	0	1	3	4	5	6	8	11	15	18	21	22	25	27	29	32	34
26	0	0	0	0	1	2	3	5	6	9	11	14	17	20	23	24	27	29	32	33
27	0	0	0	0	1	2	3	5	7	9	12	15	17	19	22	24	27	29	32	33
28	0	0	0	0	2	3	4	5	6	9	11	13	16	19	20	23	26	29	32	34
29	0	0	0	0	1	3	4	6	8	10	11	13	16	18	20	23	26	29	32	34
30	0	0	0	0	2	2	2	5	6	7	9	11	15	18	22	25	27	30	32	33
31	0	0	0	0	1	2	3	5	6	7	9	12	16	18	22	24	27	29	32	34
32	0	0	0	1	1	2	3	4	6	8	11	14	15	17	20	23	26	29	32	34

References

1. Avanzi, R.: The QARMA block cipher family. IACR Trans. Symmetric Cryptol. **2017**(1), 4–44 (2017)
2. Beierle, C., et al.: The SKINNY family of block ciphers and its low-latency variant MANTIS. In: Robshaw, M., Katz, J. (eds.) CRYPTO 2016. LNCS, vol. 9815, pp. 123–153. Springer, Heidelberg (2016). https://doi.org/10.1007/978-3-662-53008-5_5
3. Beierle, C., Leander, G., Moradi, A., Rasoolzadeh, S.: CRAFT: lightweight tweakable block cipher with efficient protection against DFA attacks. IACR Trans. Symmetric Cryptol. **2019**, 5–45 (2019)
4. Biham, E., Biryukov, A., Shamir, A.: Cryptanalysis of skipjack reduced to 31 rounds using impossible differentials. In: Stern, J. (ed.) EUROCRYPT 1999. LNCS, vol. 1592, pp. 12–23. Springer, Heidelberg (1999). https://doi.org/10.1007/3-540-48910-X_2
5. Biham, E., Shamir, A.: Differential cryptanalysis of DES-like cryptosystems. In: Menezes, A.J., Vanstone, S.A. (eds.) CRYPTO 1990. LNCS, vol. 537, pp. 2–21. Springer, Heidelberg (1991). https://doi.org/10.1007/3-540-38424-3_1
6. Daemen, J., Knudsen, L., Rijmen, V.: The block cipher square. In: Biham, E. (ed.) FSE 1997. LNCS, vol. 1267, pp. 149–165. Springer, Heidelberg (1997). https://doi.org/10.1007/BFb0052343
7. Goldenberg, D., Hohenberger, S., Liskov, M., Schwartz, E.C., Seyalioglu, H.: On tweaking Luby-Rackoff blockciphers. In: Kurosawa, K. (ed.) ASIACRYPT 2007. LNCS, vol. 4833, pp. 342–356. Springer, Heidelberg (2007). https://doi.org/10.1007/978-3-540-76900-2_21
8. Guo, J., Peyrin, T., Poschmann, A., Robshaw, M.: The LED block cipher. In: Preneel, B., Takagi, T. (eds.) CHES 2011. LNCS, vol. 6917, pp. 326–341. Springer, Heidelberg (2011). https://doi.org/10.1007/978-3-642-23951-9_22
9. Hong, D., et al.: HIGHT: a new block cipher suitable for low-resource device. In: Goubin, L., Matsui, M. (eds.) CHES 2006. LNCS, vol. 4249, pp. 46–59. Springer, Heidelberg (2006). https://doi.org/10.1007/11894063_4
10. Gurobi Optimization Inc.: Gurobi optimizer 6.5 (2015). http://www.gurobi.com/
11. Jean, J., Nikolić, I., Peyrin, T.: Tweaks and keys for block ciphers: the TWEAKEY Framework. In: Sarkar, P., Iwata, T. (eds.) ASIACRYPT 2014. LNCS, vol. 8874, pp. 274–288. Springer, Heidelberg (2014). https://doi.org/10.1007/978-3-662-45608-8_15
12. Peyrin, T., Seurin, Y., Jean, J., Nikolić I.: Deoxys v1.41. Submitted to CAESAR (2016)
13. Knudsen, L., Wagner, D.: Integral cryptanalysis. In: Daemen, J., Rijmen, V. (eds.) FSE 2002. LNCS, vol. 2365, pp. 112–127. Springer, Heidelberg (2002). https://doi.org/10.1007/3-540-45661-9_9
14. Krovetz, T., Rogaway, P.: The software performance of authenticated-encryption modes. In: Joux, A. (ed.) FSE 2011. LNCS, vol. 6733, pp. 306–327. Springer, Heidelberg (2011). https://doi.org/10.1007/978-3-642-21702-9_18
15. Lampe, R., Seurin, Y.: Tweakable blockciphers with asymptotically optimal security. In: Moriai, S. (ed.) FSE 2013. LNCS, vol. 8424, pp. 133–151. Springer, Heidelberg (2014). https://doi.org/10.1007/978-3-662-43933-3_8
16. Landecker, W., Shrimpton, T., Terashima, R.S.: Tweakable blockciphers with beyond birthday-bound security. In: Safavi-Naini, R., Canetti, R. (eds.) CRYPTO 2012. LNCS, vol. 7417, pp. 14–30. Springer, Heidelberg (2012). https://doi.org/10.1007/978-3-642-32009-5_2

17. Liskov, M., Rivest, R.L., Wagner, D.: Tweakable block ciphers. In: Yung, M. (ed.) CRYPTO 2002. LNCS, vol. 2442, pp. 31–46. Springer, Heidelberg (2002). https://doi.org/10.1007/3-540-45708-9_3

18. Matsui, M.: Linear cryptanalysis method for DES cipher. In: Helleseth, T. (ed.) EUROCRYPT 1993. LNCS, vol. 765, pp. 386–397. Springer, Heidelberg (1994). https://doi.org/10.1007/3-540-48285-7_33

19. Mitsuda, A., Iwata, T.: Tweakable pseudorandom permutation from generalized feistel structure. In: Baek, J., Bao, F., Chen, K., Lai, X. (eds.) ProvSec 2008. LNCS, vol. 5324, pp. 22–37. Springer, Heidelberg (2008). https://doi.org/10.1007/978-3-540-88733-1_2

20. Mouha, N., Wang, Q., Gu, D., Preneel, B.: Differential and linear cryptanalysis using mixed-integer linear programming. In: Wu, C.-K., Yung, M., Lin, D. (eds.) Inscrypt 2011. LNCS, vol. 7537, pp. 57–76. Springer, Heidelberg (2012). https://doi.org/10.1007/978-3-642-34704-7_5

21. Schneier, B., et al.: The SKEIN hash function family (2010). http://www.skein-hash.info

22. Nyberg, K.: Generalized feistel networks. In: Kim, K., Matsumoto, T. (eds.) ASIACRYPT 1996. LNCS, vol. 1163, pp. 91–104. Springer, Heidelberg (1996). https://doi.org/10.1007/BFb0034838

23. Schroeppel, R.: An overview of the hasty pudding cipher (1998). http://www.cs.arizona.edu/~rcs/hpc

24. Rogaway, P.: Efficient instantiations of tweakable blockciphers and refinements to modes OCB and PMAC. In: Lee, P.J. (ed.) ASIACRYPT 2004. LNCS, vol. 3329, pp. 16–31. Springer, Heidelberg (2004). https://doi.org/10.1007/978-3-540-30539-2_2

25. Rogaway, P., Bellare, M., Black, J., Krovetz, T.: OCB: a block-cipher mode of operation for efficient authenticated encryption. In: ACM CCS 2001, pp. 196–205. ACM Press, November 2001

26. Suzaki, T., Minematsu, K.: Improving the generalized feistel. In: Hong, S., Iwata, T. (eds.) FSE 2010. LNCS, vol. 6147, pp. 19–39. Springer, Heidelberg (2010). https://doi.org/10.1007/978-3-642-13858-4_2

27. Suzaki, T., Minematsu, K., Morioka, S., Kobayashi, E.: *TWINE* : a lightweight block cipher for multiple platforms. In: Knudsen, L.R., Huapeng, W. (eds.) SAC 2012. LNCS, vol. 7707, pp. 339–354. Springer, Heidelberg (2013)

28. Todo, Y.: Structural evaluation by generalized integral property. In: Oswald, E., Fischlin, M. (eds.) EUROCRYPT 2015. LNCS, vol. 9056, pp. 287–314. Springer, Heidelberg (2015). https://doi.org/10.1007/978-3-662-46800-5_12

29. Xiang, Z., Zhang, W., Bao, Z., Lin, D.: Applying MILP method to searching integral distinguishers based on division property for 6 lightweight block ciphers. In: Cheon, J.H., Takagi, T. (eds.) ASIACRYPT 2016. LNCS, vol. 10031, pp. 648–678. Springer, Heidelberg (2016). https://doi.org/10.1007/978-3-662-53887-6_24

30. Zheng, Y., Matsumoto, T., Imai, H.: Impossibility and optimality results on constructing pseudorandom permutations. In: Quisquater, J.-J., Vandewalle, J. (eds.) EUROCRYPT 1989. LNCS, vol. 434, pp. 412–422. Springer, Heidelberg (1990). https://doi.org/10.1007/3-540-46885-4_41

Malware Detection and Classification

Correlating High- and Low-Level Features:
Increased Understanding of Malware Classification

Sergii Banin[✉] and Geir Olav Dyrkolbotn

Department of Information Security and Communication Technology,
NTNU, Gjøvik, Norway
sergii.banin@ntnu.no

Abstract. Malware brings constant threats to the services and facilities used by modern society. In order to perform and improve anti-
malware defense, there is a need for methods that are capable of malware categorization. As malware grouped into categories according to its
functionality, dynamic malware analysis is a reliable source of features
that are useful for malware classification. Different types of dynamic features are described in literature [5,6,13]. These features can be divided
into two main groups: high-level features (API calls, File activity, Network activity, etc.) and low-level features (memory access patterns, high-
performance counters, etc). Low-level features bring special interest for
malware analysts: regardless of the anti-detection mechanisms used by
malware, it is impossible to avoid execution on hardware. As hardware-
based security solutions are constantly developed by hardware manu-
facturers and prototyped by researchers, research on low-level features
used for malware analysis is a promising topic. The biggest problem with
low-level features is that they don't bring much information to a human
analyst. In this paper, we analyze potential correlation between the low-
and high-level features used for malware classification. In particular, we
analyze n-grams of memory access operations found in [6] and try to
find their relationship with n-grams of API calls. We also compare performance of API calls and memory access n-grams on the same dataset
as used in [6]. In the end, we analyze their combined performance for
malware classification and explain findings in the correlation between
high- and low-level features.

Keywords: Malware analysis · Malware classification ·
Information security · Low-level features · Hardware-based features

1 Introduction

Malware, or malicious software, is one of the threats that modern digitized
society faces every day. The use of malware ranges from showing ads to users,

The research leading to these results has received funding from the Center for Cyber
and Information Security, under budget allocation from the Ministry of Justice and
Public Security.

spreading spam and stealing of private data, to attacks on power grids, transportation and banking facilities [19,23]. The more severe consequences of malware use, the more likely they are a part of malicious campaign performed by an APT: Advanced Persistent Threat [9], an organization or a human that performs stealthy, adaptive, targeted and data focused [8] attack. APTs utilize different methods, tools and techniques to achieve their goals. Malware can be used at the different steps of APT kill-chain [6]: from reconnaissance and denial-of-service attacks to data stealing and creation of backdoors (for remote access) in the victim system. Since malware can be used for the variety of purposes, it is not only important to detect it, but also to be able to categorize it into different categories based on certain properties.

Malware classification (categorization) is an important step for understanding goals and methods of adversaries [1], analyzing security of systems and operations as well as for improving defense and security mechanisms. Static malware detection may fail due to obfuscation and encryption techniques used by the creators of malware. Because of this dynamic, or behavior-based detection methods are used. Moreover, malware samples are categorized into *types* and *families* by anti-virus vendors based on their behavior [6]. Hence, it is possible to assume that the use of features derived from *malware behavior* for malware classification can outperform static methods due to the nature of categories. Both static and dynamic methods need predefined sets of *features*: properties derived from a malicious file itself or its behavior.

We can divide features for dynamic analysis into two main groups: high-level (API and system calls, network activity, etc.) and low-level (memory access operation, opcodes, operations on hard-drive, etc). Generally speaking, we consider low-level features as those that directly emerge from the system's hardware [6,14,18]. Malware authors can try to conceal their malware and its behavior from anti-malware solutions and malware analysts by utilizing different techniques such as obfuscation, encryption, polymorphism or anti-debug. Despite their attempts, they can not avoid execution on the systems hardware [6,17]. That's why hardware-based, or low-level, features (since they are behavior features) are a reliable source of information for malware detection [7,18] and classification [6]. Different low-level features have been used for malware detection and classification: Hardware Performance Counters [5], frequencies of memory reads and writes [17], memory access patterns [6,7], architectural and micro-architectural events [22]. To the author's knowledge, there are no attempts to explain how particular low-level features correspond to high-level activity. Hardware-based features describe behavior of an executable on a very fine-grained level, so it is hard, by looking at the low-level feature itself, to explain which role in the behavior of an executable it has. Therefore, in this paper, we made an attempt to explain how memory access patterns correlate with the behavior of malware described by high-level features. This will make it easier for a human analyst to understand what exactly makes malware samples to be distinctive.

In order to describe our problem more generally we use an approach pictured on the Figure 1. Assume we have a dataset that contains N samples and the task is to classify them into M classes. From the dataset we can extract features of types A (e.g. low-level features) and B (e.g. high-level features). Different feature types are derived from different sources of information: different ways to describe properties of samples in the dataset. After feature selection, features of both types can be independently used for classification of samples from the dataset. Here we suggest a hypothesis that features from feature sets A and B can correlate with each other. In this paper, we focus on finding a correlation between n-grams of memory access operations and API calls. To address this problem we take paper [6] as baseline. In their paper authors used patterns of memory access operations to classify malware into 10 malware families and 10 malware types. The best 29 n-grams of memory access operations are selected, and we reuse them in our case since our datasets are identical. As the high-level, or human understandable, features we decided to use n-grams of API calls since they are shown to be a reliable source of information for malware detection [4] and classification [13]. To get the most complete picture of possible correlations between memory access operations and API calls we need to search for *all-to-all* correlations. However, such an exhaustive search is computationally infeasible. In order to be able to carry out the search, we had to adjust the method, as described in Subsect. 4.7. We record an execution flow of malware samples that contains memory access operations performed by single instructions as well as calls to the API functions (more details in Sect. 4). First, we perform classification and feature selection for n-grams of API calls. Our goal is not to study the performance of API calls for malware classification, but rather to find good and relatively short feature set of API calls n-grams as it will be more useful for research and analysis purposes. This feature set is later used in an attempt to find a possible relationship between memory access patterns and API calls, which existence or non-existence will help to reveal nature of memory access patterns that were successfully used for the same classification task.

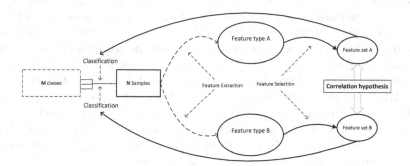

Fig. 1. Generalized problem description

The key findings of our paper are following. Our results show no significant correlation between information relevant for multinomial malware classification represented by best API-calls and best memory access patterns. This is important, as it shows that memory access patterns are not redundant to the higher level features such as API calls. As the result, feature set combined from memory access patterns and API calls show improved classification performance. This contributes to better malware detection and classification as well as to the potential hardware-based security solutions.

This paper is a proof of concept, and our main goal is to address challenges and possibility of a high-level explanation of low-level events as well as creation of a stepping stone towards an explanation of a performance of low-level features in malware classification context. The remainder of the paper is arranged as follows. In Sect. 2 we provide an overview of the related studies and focus on the baseline paper [6]. In Sect. 3 we describe our problem more specifically and describe an approach for validating of our hypothesis. In Sect. 4 we describe our experimental design, analysis environment, methods used for feature extraction and selection, explain how we search for correlation between features of different types as well as provide terms, definitions and assumptions important for our study. Finally, in Sect. 5 we present results, analyze them and provide conclusions in Sect. 6.

2 Background

In this section, we present a short overview of articles that are related to features and methods we use in this paper. There are many papers that use hardware-based features for malware detection or categorization. For example in [5] a real-time dynamic malware detection with the use of special-purpose registers of modern CPUs as a source of features is proposed. Special-purpose registers, or hardware performance counters, are used for CPU scheduling, performance monitoring, integrity checking or workload pattern identification. In their paper, authors used four different events to construct features: retiring of a branch, load and store instructions as well as mispredicted branch instructions. With the use of various machine learning algorithms, they achieved up to 96% accuracy when classifying malicious and benign executables. Even though their dataset is small, consisting of only 20 benign and 11 malicious samples, their paper shows that hardware-based (or low-level) features can be used for malware detection.

In [17] Ozsoy et al. propose so-called malware-aware processors: processors that has a built-in hardware module that is capable of malware detection. In their work authors also mention hardware performance counters, but choose slightly different features to be used in malware detection: frequency of memory reads and writes, immediate and taken branches as well as unaligned memory accesses. They implemented a malware-aware processor in an FPGA emulator and state that their system is capable of malware detection with detection rates up to 94% and false positive rates of up to 7%. As they didn't achieve low-enough false positive rates, they propose to use malware-aware processor together with a software-based solution. They also emphasize the importance of malware-aware processor to be always on, so that it is hard to avoid detection from it.

Paper [7] is of particular interest for us, since it proposes a novel method for malware detection based on memory access pattern. In their work Banin et al. recorded sequences of memory access operations produced by malicious and benign executables. They didn't take into account addresses and values used by these operations but utilized only a type of operation: read or write. Each sample in their dataset was launched under surveillance of specially crafted Intel Pin [12] tool and was made to produce up to 10 millions of memory access operations. Later, larger sequences of memory access operations were split into a set of overlapping sub-sequences - n-grams of a size from 16 to 96. With the use of a feature selection and various machine learning algorithms they achieved a classification accuracy of up to 98%. Results showed, that 800 memory access n-grams are enough to achieve the highest accuracy on their dataset of 455 benign and 759 malicious executables. They claimed, that n-grams of memory access operations of a size 96 extracted from only the first million of memory access operations performed by executables are reliable features for malware against benign classification. Later, in [6] they evaluated performance of 96-grams derived from the first million of memory access operations for the malware classification task. They used two different datasets, one consisted of 952 malware samples and was label according to malware types while the other had 983 malicious executables that were labeled according to malware families. With the use of feature selection, they compared results from feature sets of a size 50,000 and 29. Even though machine learning algorithms showed a decline in performance while given 29 features instead of 50000, this decline was only of a 5%. With only 29 features they achieved a classification accuracy of up to 78% for malware families and 66% for types. Even though it was far from the 98% from their previous paper they stated, that 78% can be considered good enough for 10-class classification problem. They also compared their results to the results from a paper [20], where authors used the same malware families and types but on the different dataset. In [20] Shalaginov et al. used static features, and achieved lower true positive and higher false positive rates. As we stated in the Sect. 1 we use paper [6] as a baseline: we use the same datasets, execution environment (Virtual Machine) and use their feature set as low-level features which origin we tend to explain. We will elaborate more on the similarities between our data collection processes in the Sect. 4.

Finally, we will look at some articles that make use of API-calls performed by malware during its execution for malware detection and classification. In their paper [13] Islam et al. used frequencies of occurrence of API calls during the execution of malware to detect malware and categorize into one of the 9 malware families. They also carve several static-based features such as lengths of functions or printable strings. Combining dynamic and static features they created so-called *integrated feature vector* and evaluated the classification performance of different features separately and together. They achieved a classification accuracy of up to 97% and showed that integrated feature vector can outperform other feature vectors. On its turn, Lim et al. in [16] proposed to use *k-grams* (special modification of n-grams derived from behavior automatons) of API-calls for malware detection. Even though authors didn't clearly picture the performance of their algorithm, they explained how small sequences of API calls can be used to measure the similarity between the behavior of different malware samples.

Shijo et al. [21] (similarly to [13]) utilized integrated feature vector constructed from dynamic and static features. As dynamic features, they used API calls n-grams of a size 3 and 4. With the use of only dynamic features they achieved a classification accuracy of up to 97% for malware against benign classification. Integrated feature vector allowed them to gain an increase in classification accuracy of up to 1%. The last paper we want to mention is [4] where Alazab et al. used API calls n-grams of a size 1 to 5 for malware detection. With the use of Support Vector Machines they achieved a classification accuracy of up to 96% and concluded, that for their dataset the best features were actually 1-grams or unigrams: n-grams of a size 1.

As we have seen, different high- and low-level features are used for malware detection and classification. Our goal in this paper is to find possible correlation between memory access patterns (low-level features) and API calls (high-level features).

3   Problem Description

From the literature overview, we can state that low-level features (despite difficulties with their extraction) can be a reliable source of information for malware detection and classification. However, system counters, opcodes and memory access patterns don't give much information about malware functionality to the security analyst. An n-gram of opcodes of a size 4, when given out of context, does not reveal what it was used for by itself. The same can be said about sequence of memory access operations: it is challenging to grasp which goals were achieved by malware when a certain sequence of memory access operations was performed. For example, a typical n-gram of a size 96 of memory access operations found in [6] looks like this: $WRWRRRRR...WWWRRRRRW$. It is obvious, that such features, even if they can be effectively used for malware classification, do not bring much useful information about malware's behavior. As different papers describe the use of low-level features for malware detection and classification, to the author's knowledge there have been no attempts to find a relationship between low-level activity and high-level events such as API-calls. Because of everything said above, first, we propose two following statements:

1. N-grams of memory access operations can be used for malware classification (shown in [6]).
2. N-grams of API calls can be used for malware classification (shown in e.g. [21]).

Based on statements 1 and 2 we propose the following hypothesis: if statements 1 and 2 are true, then it should be possible to find a correlation between some of the features from both feature spaces. An approach for validating this hypothesis is described in Subsect. 4.7. For example, we assume that some memory access n-grams might originate in API call n-grams. If we are able to validate this hypothesis then we will find a way to correlate sequences of memory access operations to the events of higher level which are more human understandable. If our hypothesis is rejected, then API calls and memory access n-grams are independent features, thus combining them into an integrated feature vector should increase overall classification accuracy. Generally speaking, our goal is to check whether sequences of memory access operations that were successfully used for multinomial malware classification can be attributed to certain sequences of API calls, thus can be explained with high-level events and become more human understandable.

4   Experimental Design

In this section, we present terms and definitions, provide the assumptions used and describe experimental setup and properties of datasets. Later on, we explain methods used for data collection and processing, list the machine learning and feature selection algorithms and describe the way we were searching for correlation between high- and low-level event.

4.1   Terms, Definitions and Assumptions

In this subsection, we provide terms and definitions and assumptions used during this study. We begin with the definitions:

- **N-gram.** An n-gram is a sub-sequence of length n of an original sequence of length L. For example if an original sequence of length $L = 6$ [RRWRWW] is split into n-grams of length $n = 4$ (4-grams) then our n-grams set will be: RRWR, RWRW, WRWW [6]. In this example, similarly to baseline paper [6], and our paper we use overlapping n-grams: the next n-gram begins from the second element of the preceding one.
- **Memory access operations:** when an executable is *reading* from virtual memory, *read* (or R) memory operation is recorded. When *writing* to virtual memory performed by an executable, *write* (or W) memory operation is recorded.
- **API call:** or Application Programming Interface call is a call to a function provided by the operating system (Windows 7 in our case). API calls are usually used by malware and goodware to perform network, file, process and other kinds of activity.
- **Malware types and families.** Malware *types* and *families* are different ways to divide malware into categories. Malware *types* describe *general* functionality of malware: *what* it does, which *goals* it pursues. Malware *families* describe *particular* functionality of malware: which *methods* it use and *how* it pursues its goals [6]. For example, *virus, worm* and *backdoor* are malware types, while *hupigon, vundo* and *zlob* are malware families.

We continue with the following assumptions:

1. We assume that for the research and analytic purposes it is better to use smaller feature sets even if their performance in terms of classification accuracy is slightly lower [6]. For example, it is way easier to understand feature set of a size 33 that brings classification accuracy of around 70% than the one of a size 20000 with classification accuracy 73%.
2. We assume that if features from different sources (memory access operations and API calls) are related to each other, then this relationship can be found among small sets of the best features.

4.2 Experimental Flow

In this subsection, we will describe our experimental flow. On the Fig. 2 we picture a schematic view of our experiment. By running malware samples from two datasets (see Subsect. 4.3), we collect data (memory access operations and API calls, Subsect. 4.5) and perform feature construction (n-grams of API calls), later on, we use feature selection to reduce feature space and train machine learning algorithms in order to assess quality of a newly built feature vectors (Subsect. 4.6). For the consistency (to the baseline paper) reasons, we run malware samples until they generate 1,000,000 of memory access operations. Some samples stop execution before they generate the desired amount of memory access operations, but we keep such data as is since this is a real-world scenario where one can't expect malware to produce as much traces as needed. While running malware, we record memory access operations and API calls (if present) for every executed instruction. From the literature review we understood, that API call n-grams of a size 3 and 4 are the most promising features. However, we also decided to use n-grams of length 8 in order to get a slightly more complete picture of API calls n-grams capabilities for malware classification. This also gives us more data to use in the search for correlation between memory access patterns and API calls. The number of n-grams is quite big, so in order to pursue one of our goals (shorter and more understandable feature set) we perform **feature selection** to reduce the dataset. As well as authors of [6] we used Correlation Based feature selection [11] from machine learning tool Weka [3] as it showed quite good performance while reducing the size of a feature set in several times of magnitude. After getting a reduced feature set, we store data in the format that can be used for training of machine learning models. In our case, similarly to the baseline paper, as feature values, we store only the fact of presence (1 or 0) of a certain feature in the behavior of a malicious sample. The logic here is similar to [6]: in contrast to other articles, where authors rely on frequencies of appearance of certain features, we want to find features that work regardless the time malicious executable has run. Our data looks like a **bitmap** of presence, where each row represents a single malicious sample, first column represents a category of a sample (family or type) and the rest of the columns represent features. Cells contain *1* if a certain feature is present in the behavior of malware and *0* if not. The bitmap of presence is later used for training the **machine**

learning models (see Subsect. 4.6), which classification performance (classification accuracy) is compared with the one from baseline paper. Having API call n-grams as features, we later search through the entire records or behavior data from each malware sample in order to find whether these n-grams are related to the 29 memory access n-grams derived by authors of [6]. We elaborate on the search technique in the Subsect. 4.7.

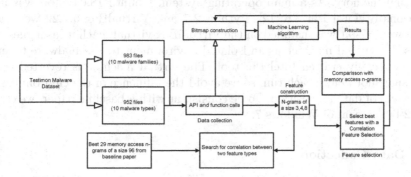

Fig. 2. Detailed experimental flow

4.3   Dataset

Similarly to [6], our two datasets are derived from the original dataset collected under the initiative of Testimon [10] research group. It consists of 400k malware samples: malicious PE32 executables gathered from VirusShare [2]. Initial dataset was used for research purposes and is described in [20]. Both our datasets are the same as in baseline paper [6]. The authors of a baseline paper provide a detailed description of their datasets, while we focus only on the most important properties of these datasets. First of all, one dataset (952 files) has malware samples that are labeled according to ten types: *backdoor, pws, rogue, trojan, trojandownloader, trojandropper, trojanspy, virtool, virus, worm.* Secondly, another dataset (983 files) has its malware samples label according to ten families: *agent, hupigon, obfuscator, onlinegames, renos, small, vb, vbinject, vundo, zlob.* The choice of categories was made by the simple rule: 10 most prevalent categories in the original dataset were chosen. To simplify automated malware analysis (see Sect. 4.4) sample were chosen to be without anti-VM and anti-Debug features. As described in [6], dealing with anti-analysis functionality of malware is out of scope in such research, since their goal was to study a possibility of malware classification with memory access patterns as features. The distributions of categories within datasets are almost uniform, so we assume that datasets are nearly balanced, so there is no need to study the influence of categories distribution on the results of an assessment of machine learning models.

4.4   Analysis Environment

Our analysis environment was almost identical to the one in [6], apart from different versions of host OS and VirtualBox. We assume that these changes will not influence the results of the experiments since hardware and guest OS are identical. We run our experiments on Virtual Dedicated Server (VDS) with Intel Core CPU running at 3.60 GHz, 4 cores, SSD RAID storage and 32 GB of virtual memory. As a main operating system, Ubuntu 18.04 64bit was used. Additionally, Intel Pin 3.6 [12], Python 2.7 and VirtualBox 5.2.22 were used. Windows 7 32-bit was installed on the VirtualBox virtual machine as a guest OS. We used a virtual machine as an isolated environment to run malware together with a specially crafted Intel Pin tool. The virtual machine is reverted to the same snapshot before each run, so we avoid the influence of the environment on the results of data acquisition. To be consistent with a baseline paper, we choose the 32-bit version of Windows 7.

4.5   Data Collection

We focus on "correlating" the n-grams of memory access operations with n-grams of API calls. We need to: (a) record memory access operations produced by malware (b) record calls to API functions. The first task is the easiest one. With the use of dynamic binary instrumentation framework Intel Pin, one can put instrumentation on each executed instruction and record memory access operations performed by it. For the consistency reasons, we chose the same amount of memory access operations to record as was used in [6]. A malicious executable run until it produces 1 million of memory access operations. As it was shown in the previously published papers, this is not only enough to reveal maliciousness of an executable [7] but also to perform multinomial classification of malware into categories and types [6]. The second task is more difficult. When a *call* instruction is performed it only contains an address of a function. In order to get its name from a library, one should find which one of the export symbols correspond to a certain address. Moreover, some native Windows libraries perform inter- and intra-modular calls not to the functions themselves (a call to a first instruction of a function) but to the subroutines within these functions. Most of the papers that use dynamic API call sequences do not describe how they treat such calls: it is not clear whether they record or just ignore them. In this paper, we treat a call to a first instruction of an API function and a call to a subroutine in an API function equally. Our reason for this is that if a logic of an executable requires such calls to be done and we can collect this information, it may improve the understanding of malware's current execution goals and context.

The call instruction can be used to invoke internal (to an executable itself) function. It is usually impossible to derive a name of an internal function of an executable (unless you have debug file, which is not the case in malware analysis), so we store a name of a section where a function of interest is placed. We also keep this information and treat such calls equally to the API calls.

Having raw data recorded, we split a sequence of API calls generated by each malicious sample into **n-grams**.

For better analysis capabilities as well as future work we record additional information for *each* instruction executed after launching a malware sample. A real example of raw data is present in the Listing 2 in Appendix A. In order to record this data, we created an Intel Pin based tool that is launched together with each sample from a dataset. A tool records all data into a file and stops if an executable generated 1 million of memory access operations. Some samples generate less memory activity than others, but we consider it a real-world scenario where one can't rely on malware to generate a particular amount of data.

From the raw data we extract names of the called functions, store them into the sequence according to their execution order and split the sequence into n-grams of a different size. For example, one of the API call n-grams of a size 4 derived from malware families dataset looks as following: *memset, GetModule-HandleW, ferror, _freea.* From the raw data, we extract API calls and memory access operations, that are later used in training the machine learning models and searching for mutual correlation.

4.6   Machine Learning Algorithms and Feature Selection

For the consistency reasons, we chose the same machine learning (ML) algorithms as in [6]: k-Nearest Neighbors (kNN), RandomForest (RF), Decision Trees (J48), Support Vector Machines (SVM), Naive Bayes (NB) and Artificial Neural Network (ANN). The following parameters (default for Weka [3] package) were used for ML algorithms: kNN used $k = 1$; RF had 100 random trees; J48 used pruning confidence of 0.25 and a minimum split number of 2; SVM used radial basis as function of kernel; NB used 100 instances as the preferred batch size; ANN used 500 epochs, learning rate 0.3 and a number of hidden neurons equal to half of the sum of a number of classes and a number of attributes. In order to assess the quality of machine learning models we used 5-fold cross validation, and chose accuracy (number of correctly classified instances) as the measure of evaluation. To reduce the feature set we used Correlation Based feature selection from Weka. Correlation-based feature selection [11] is an algorithm that chooses a subset of features that have the highest correlation with classes, lowest correlation with each other and give the best merit among other possible subsets. First reason to choose this feature selection method as it helped authors of a baseline paper to go from 50 thousands of features to just 29, so we wanted to get a number of features of nearly the same magnitude. Second reason is that one of our goals is to have relatively short feature set that can be easily analyzed by a human analyst.

4.7   Correlating Features Derived from Different Sources

In this section, we present a method to validate our hypothesis presented in Sect. 3. There are several approaches that can be used to validate our hypothesis.

The first one is the most obvious: create the *entire* feature sets for memory access operations and API calls n-grams and find correlations between them (*all-to-all* approach). This approach will reveal the full picture of correlation between the two feature types. But it also has one major drawback, that makes its use almost impossible. The entire feature space of memory access n-grams in [6] consists of 15 millions distinctive features for malware families dataset. Finding their correlation with around 12 thousands of API calls 3-grams (see Subsect. 5.1) can not be finished in feasible time. Slightly less time consuming variant is to search for correlation between the best memory access operations features and the entire feature space of API calls n-grams (*best-to-all* approach). This method would provide a less complete overview over the possible correlations, but would still be very time consuming, and is left for the future work. To some initial results we used a *best-to-best* approach: instead of taking the entire feature sets of memory access operations and API calls, we use only the best features out of both feature spaces. This approach allowed us to finish the experiments in feasible time, but also has some limitations that will be discussed in the following sections. As this paper is aiming to provide a proof of concept for searching for correlations, we believe that this approach properly fits our purposes.

One of the challenges we met during this research is how to correlate a certain n-gram of memory access operations to an n-gram (n-grams) of API calls. First of all, we need to locate a place in a raw data, where a certain n-gram of memory access operations is found. To do this, we iterate over the raw data, collect memory access operation into a buffer of a size 96 (see Sect. 2) and check if the pattern in the buffer is found among one of the features taken from the baseline paper. If match occurs - we save the position where memory n-grams starts and begin the search for API call n-gram. There can be various approaches to this and we selected the following one, as it brings wider coverage of execution flow. To state that a certain memory access n-gram is related to an API call n-gram we use the following criteria:

1. If the beginning of memory access n-gram lays after first call in API calls n-gram and before the call that follows current n-gram - these memory and API call n-grams correlate. In this case we assume that memory access n-gram is correlated to an API calls n-gram.
2. For any other case we state, that memory access and API call n-grams are not correlated.

The above mentioned criteria works as shown in Fig. 3 where we present a simplified version of our data. On this Figure, memory access n-gram of a size 96 correlates with API calls 3-grams [APIcall_1, APIcall_2, APIcall_3], [APIcall_2, APIcall_3, APIcall_4] and [APIcall_3, APIcall_4, APIcall_5] but does not correlate with [APIcall_4, APIcall_5, APIcall_6].

5   Results and Analysis

In this section we provide the results of feature selection and classification for API calls n-grams, compare them to the results achieved with memory access

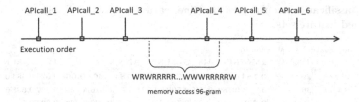

Fig. 3. Correlation between API calls and memory access n-grams

n-grams from [6] and evaluate our findings in correlating these two types of features.

5.1 API Call n-grams for Malware Classification

From the raw captured data we extracted 12818 3-grams, 17407 4-grams and 33900 8-grams in the malware family dataset and 17252 3-grams, 24054 4-grams and 49513 8-grams in the malware types dataset. Using correlation based feature selection allowed us to reduce number of features to the following: 23 3-grams, 33 4-grams and 47 8-grams in the malware family dataset and 52 3-grams, 62 4-grams and 76 8-grams in the malware types dataset. The reduction of feature vectors worked similarly to the baseline paper: we went down from *tens of thousands* to *less than hundred* features. As assessment of classification performance of API call n-grams is not the main goal of this paper, we provide only the results for reduced feature sets. However, we performed classification on the full feature sets and their classification accuracy was only a few percents higher then in reduced feature sets. It is again similar to [6], so we assume that it is possible to compare newly acquired feature set with the one from [6]. In the Table 1 the classification accuracy achieved by different machine learning algorithms is presented. On the left and right sides of the table we present the results achieved on malware families and malware types datasets respectively. First row represent results achieved with n-grams of memory access operations of a size 96 from [6]. We name this feature type *Mem96*. Rows from 2 to 4 represent results achieved with API calls n-grams of sizes 3,4, and 8. We name them *API3, API4* and *API8* respectively. As we can see, most of the time API calls n-grams performed on the same or even higher level then memory access n-grams for the malware families dataset. In contrast, performance of API calls n-grams for malware types dataset most of the time was lower then the one by memory access n-grams. These results help us to prove Statement 2 from Sect. 3. In the Table 1 we use bold font in order to underline best classification accuracy for a certain type of features. It is also worth mentioning, that in general API calls n-grams of a size 4 performed better then other types of n-grams. We have to draw an important conclusion from the results we achieved with API calls n-grams. Classification performance of less then a hundred API calls n-grams are comparable to those achieved with tens of thousands of memory access n-grams in [6].

Table 1. Classification accuracy for baseline feature set, API call n-grams feature sets and combined feature sets.

#	Feature type	Feature set size		Families						Types					
		Fam.	Typ.	kNN	RF	J48	SVM	NB	ANN	kNN	RF	J48	SVM	NB	ANN
1	Mem96	29	29	**0.784**	0.781	0.769	0.740	0.724	**0.784**	**0.668**	**0.668**	0.626	0.584	0.498	0.617
2	API3	23	36	0.775	0.780	0.746	0.709	0.652	0.774	0.616	0.631	0.587	0.533	0.521	0.607
3	API4	33	46	**0.813**	0.810	0.792	0.765	0.677	0.805	0.636	0.636	0.604	0.541	0.566	0.616
4	API8	47	67	0.799	0.801	0.784	0.751	0.694	0.797	0.643	**0.660**	0.605	0.537	0.562	0.615
5	API3+Mem96	52	65	0.834	0.856	0.817	0.781	0.711	0.845	0.680	**0.700**	0.641	0.573	0.556	0.682
6	API4+Mem96	62	75	0.838	**0.859**	0.824	0.786	0.716	0.842	0.680	0.694	0.662	0.580	0.566	0.676
7	API8+Mem96	76	96	0.832	0.845	0.801	0.773	0.717	0.835	0.667	0.687	0.649	0.586	0.575	0.686

5.2   Correlating Memory Access and API Call n-grams

The results we got were quite surprising. With the feature selection, we used and feature correlation search method we described in Subsect. 4.7 we found no correlation between memory access n-grams and API call n-grams for malware *types* dataset. For malware *types* dataset our hypothesis about the correlation between features derived from different sources was rejected. Results for malware *families* dataset was not much different. One memory access n-gram was found to be related to a certain API calls 3-gram in different malicious samples, and the other was found to be related to two API calls 4-grams in different malicious samples as shown in Listing 1.1. So our initial hypothesis was mostly rejected for malware *families* dataset as well. Having this information we decided to create integrated feature sets by combining memory n-grams feature set with API call n-grams feature sets. We analyze the performance of an integrated feature set in the next subsection.

5.3   Performance of Integrated Feature Sets

We found an idea about combining features of different types into an integrated feature vector from [16]. In the Table 1 we present classification accuracy achieved with integrated feature vectors. In the rows 5 to 7 results of combining memory n-grams feature vector with all API call n-gram feature vectors are present. As we can see, with several exceptions, most of the time integrated feature vector outperform separate feature vectors. Moreover, with an integrated feature vector (which size didn't exceed 100) we achieved a classification accuracy of 85.9% for families and 70% for types, which are higher than respective 84.5% and 66.8% achieved in [6] with use of 50,000 memory access n-grams. This indicates that combining API call and memory access n-grams does not bring redundant information which often results in lower classification accuracy [15]. Even though our hypothesis was rejected, the increased classification accuracy of an integrated feature set show that our correlation search method (Subsect. 4.7) was correct.

5.4   Discussion and Analysis of Correlation Findings

As we already said, for the two entire datasets, we found only two memory access n-grams that we found to be related to the API call n-grams from a reduced feature set. In the Listing 1.1 we show found relationships of memory access n-grams and API call n-grams. As we can see, for our family dataset, a memory access n-gram is related to only one API call 3-gram. However, the relationship between memory access n-gram and API 4-grams can look a little bit more complicated. We found that the same memory access n-gram can originate from different API call n-grams. But this can be easily explained after analysis of the API 4-grams themselves. As we can see, these two API call 4-grams can easily overlap: last three API calls of the first 4-gram can be the first three API calls in the second 4-gram. And as we described in Subsect. 4.7 if the beginning of memory access n-gram lays between first and last call in the API call n-gram - these memory and API call n-grams are related. So it is easy to understand now, that if selected API call n-grams are overlapping - the same memory access n-gram can originate from both of them.

```
Memory ngram WWWRRRRRRRWRRWRRWWWWRRWWWWRWRRRRRRWRRWWRWWR
    ↪ RRWWWRRRWWRRRRWRWRRRRRRWRRRRRRRRRRWRWWRWWWWWRRRWRRRWW
is related to the following API call 3-gram: RtlTryEnterCriticalSection,
    ↪ RtlLeaveCriticalSection,memset

Memory ngram WRWRRRRRRWRRWRWRRRWRRRRRRWRRRWRWRRRRRWRRR
    ↪ RRRRRWRWRWRRRWWWRRWWRWRRRRRWRWWRWRWWRRWWRWRWRWWWWRRRRRW
is related to the following API call 4-grams: RtlEnterCriticalSection,
    ↪ RtlEnterCriticalSection,RtlEnterCriticalSection,
    ↪ RtlCompareUnicodeStrings
and RtlEnterCriticalSection,RtlEnterCriticalSection,RtlCompareUnicodeStrings,
    ↪ RtlCompareUnicodeStrings
```

Listing 1.1. Memory access n-grams and correlated API call n-grams from malware families dataset

As a way to improve our search technique it is possible to split a sequence of API calls into *non-overlapping* n-grams. However, in some rare cases, it might result in several memory trace n-grams to be related to a single API call n-gram. Another reason of small correlation findings can be a *best-to-best* approach that we chose for correlation search. Utilizing a *best-to-all* approach together with an in-depth explanation of correlated API calls n-grams is one of the priority goals for the future work.

There is one thing that is important to look at after presenting relatively poor correlation findings. As we have written above, we trace the execution of malware samples until they generate 1 million of memory access operations. Some samples produce less than the expected number of memory access operations. It is important to understand, that the execution of PE file does not start from the main module of a file. Instead, different API calls are invoked by an operating system (they still executed under the process of malware, so we trace them anyway) in order to prepare an execution environment. The amount and type of calls performed before execution of main logic (main module) of a malware depends on the way an executable was compiled and the resources it needs for execution. It is important to notice, that even if an API call is made from the main module of an executable, its instructions will be corresponded to the external module (e.g. ntdll.dll). To go deeper into this problem first we counted the number of instructions executed by malware from its main module and divided it by the total number of instructions in the trace. Amount of instructions performed from the main module (defined by the malware directly) ranges from 0% to 99.9% with an average of around 20%. It means that some samples didn't even reach to the execution of their main module. From first glance, it should have led to the sample being indistinguishable from each other. Nevertheless, as we already said, this platform-specific (PE is an executable format used in Windows) preamble depends on the properties of the file. Another thing that we checked was the percentage of *call* instructions executed from the main module. These numbers range from 0% to 8% with an average of up to 1.5%. From what was said above, and from additional data analysis, it is possible to draw the following conclusion: most of the API calls in our experiments didn't originate from the main modules of executables. Moreover, as the number of instructions performed from the main modules is relatively low, the memory access n-grams from [6] also did not originate from main modules either. The first conclusion that can be drawn from this is that some malicious executables can be categorized into families and types (with an accuracy we achieved) based on the activity they produce before executing their main logic. On the first hand, these are very promising results since detection mechanisms based on the features used in this paper can potentially detect malware before anything malicious is done. However, we didn't study what changes to our victim system our malicious samples did. So this is clearly a question for future research. On the other hand we might have actually detected malicious behavior by itself: there are known malware samples that achieve its goals from TLS callbacks or by inserting malicious code into legitimate DLLs or executables (other than malware's main modules) and performing direct jumps or calls to the infected parts of legitimate DLL's or executables.

As a final remark to this subsection we suggest the following solution to the questions we outlined in the beginning. To understand if API calls that actually produce memory access patterns from [6] can be useful for malware classification we have to use only a certain amount of API calls made around a place from where memory access n-gram is originated from. Based on these API call sequences we may try to find features that are relevant for malware classification. This is planned to be done in the future work, as the amount of "API calls made around a place from where memory access n-gram is originated from" has to be found after a number of experiments. Also, the type of features in this future case has to be discussed as well.

6   Conclusions

In this paper, we examined the nature of memory access n-grams that were successfully used for malware classification by authors of [6]. We also attempted to understand the relationship between those low-level features and high-level activity patterns such as API call n-grams. Our findings showed no significant correlation between the best n-grams of memory access operations and the best n-grams of API calls (at least under our experimental design). We also showed that API calls n-grams can be used for malware classification on the dataset from [6] and found that combining features derived from different sources (low- and high-level activity) can bring improvement in classification accuracy. While analyzing our data we concluded, that both low- and high-level features used in our experiments often have their origin outside of the main module of an executable. This paper brings important findings and outlines the direction of future research about the use of low-level features in malware analysis.

Appendix A.   Raw Data Sample

In this Appendix we present a sample of a raw data gather during our experiments. We also explain each field included in the data.

1. Opcode id: each opcode is given a unique identifier. If this opcode is executed again (e.g. in a loop), it will receive the same id.
2. Module name: a name of a module where current instruction is executed, It can be a name of a library or a name of an executable itself.
3. Section name: a name of a section in executable file or library where current instruction is executed. Often it will be *.text* or *CODE*, however it some cases (especially with malware) a name of an executable section can be different from standard.
4. Current function name: if a function name of a current instruction can be found we record it to understand *which* function performed a certain part of logic.
5. Opcode: text representation of an assembly instruction together with arguments but without arguments values.
6. Type of module: whether an instruction is executed from the main module of executable under analysis or from the external library.
7. Memory operations: memory operations performed by an instruction. Only *read* or *write* without addresses and values.
8. Name of a function being called: if a current instruction is *call* - a name of a function is being stored.

A real example of raw data is present in the Listing 2. The first line represents header: names of fields are in the same order as in the list above.

```
OPID;MODULE;SECTION;ROUTINE;OPCODE;MODULETYPE;MEMOPS;ROUTINETOCALL
6712;C:\Windows\SYSTEM32\ntdll.dll;.text;RtlInitializeExceptionChain;xor ecx,
 ↪    ecx;isNotMainModule;;
6713;C:\Windows\SYSTEM32\ntdll.dll;.text;RtlInitializeExceptionChain;call eax
 ↪    ;isNotMainModule;W;BaseThreadInitThunk
6369;C:\Windows\system32\kernel32.dll;.text;BaseThreadInitThunk;mov edi, edi;
 ↪    isNotMainModule;;
6370;C:\Windows\system32\kernel32.dll;.text;BaseThreadInitThunk;push ebp;
 ↪    isNotMainModule;W;
6371;C:\Windows\system32\kernel32.dll;.text;BaseThreadInitThunk;mov ebp, esp;
 ↪    isNotMainModule;;
6372;C:\Windows\system32\kernel32.dll;.text;BaseThreadInitThunk;test ecx, ecx
 ↪    ;isNotMainModule;;
```

```
6373;C:\Windows\system32\kernel32.dll;.text;BaseThreadInitThunk;jnz 0
 ↪ x76f4853d;isNotMainModule;;
6374;C:\Windows\system32\kernel32.dll;.text;BaseThreadInitThunk;push dword
 ↪ ptr [ebp+0x8];isNotMainModule;RW;
6375;C:\Windows\system32\kernel32.dll;.text;BaseThreadInitThunk;call edx;
 ↪ isNotMainModule;W;unnamedImageEntryPoint
6714;C:\Users\win7\Documents\malware_PE32\1b6142e3c80362a3f49666856f330510;.
 ↪ duciuni;unnamedImageEntryPoint;inc ebx;isMainModule;;
6715;C:\Users\win7\Documents\malware_PE32\1b6142e3c80362a3f49666856f330510;.
 ↪ duciuni;unnamedImageEntryPoint;pushad ;isMainModule;W;
```

Listing 2. Raw data sample

References

1. Types of malware. https://usa.kaspersky.com/resource-center/threats/types-of-malware. Accessed 17 Mar 2019
2. Virusshare.com. https://virusshare.com/. Accessed 12 Mar 2019
3. Weka: Data mining software in Java (2019). http://www.cs.waikato.ac.nz/ml/weka/. Accessed 12 Mar 2019
4. Alazab, M., Layton, R., Venkataraman, S., Watters, P.: Malware detection based on structural and behavioural features of api calls (2010)
5. Bahador, M.B., Abadi, M., Tajoddin, A.: HPCMalHunter: behavioral malware detection using hardware performance counters and singular value decomposition. In: 2014 4th International eConference on Computer and Knowledge Engineering (ICCKE), pp. 703–708. IEEE (2014). https://doi.org/10.1109/iccke.2014.6993402
6. Banin, S., Dyrkolbotn, G.O.: Multinomial malware classification via low-level features. Digit. Invest. **26**, S107–S117 (2018). https://doi.org/10.1016/j.diin.2018.04.019
7. Banin, S., Shalaginov, A., Franke, K.: Memory access patterns for malware detection. (NISK) 96–107 (2016). Norsk informasjonssikkerhetskonferanse
8. Cole, E.: Advanced Persistent Threat: Understanding the Danger and How to Protect Your Organization. Newnes, Amsterdam (2012)
9. Hoglund, G.: What APT Means To Your Enterprise (2011). https://pdfs.semanticscholar.org/d0a0/47c6b19fc3645973f8f300b507886b54196a.pdf
10. Group, T.R.: Testimon research group (2017). https://testimon.ccis.no/
11. Hall, M.A.: Correlation-based feature subset selection for machine learning. Ph.D. thesis, University of Waikato, Hamilton, New Zealand (1998)
12. IntelPin: A dynamic binary instrumentation tool (2019)
13. Islam, R., Tian, R., Batten, L.M., Versteeg, S.: Classification of malware based on integrated static and dynamic features. J. Netw. Comput. Appl. **36**(2), 646–656 (2013). https://doi.org/10.1016/j.jnca.2012.10.004
14. Khasawneh, K.N., Ozsoy, M., Donovick, C., Abu-Ghazaleh, N., Ponomarev, D.: Ensemble learning for low-level hardware-supported malware detection. In: Bos, H., Monrose, F., Blanc, G. (eds.) RAID 2015. LNCS, vol. 9404, pp. 3–25. Springer, Cham (2015). https://doi.org/10.1007/978-3-319-26362-5_1
15. Kononenko, I., Kukar, M.: Machine Learning and Data Mining: Introduction to Principles and Algorithms. Horwood Publishing, Cambridge (2007)
16. Lim, H.I.: Detecting malicious behaviors of software through analysis of api sequence k-grams i (2016). https://doi.org/10.13189/csit.2016.040301
17. Ozsoy, M., Donovick, C., Gorelik, I., Abu-Ghazaleh, N., Ponomarev, D.: Malware-aware processors: a framework for efficient online malware detection. In: 2015 IEEE 21st International Symposium on High Performance Computer Architecture (HPCA), pp. 651–661. IEEE (2015). https://doi.org/10.1109/hpca.2015.7056070

18. Ozsoy, M., Khasawneh, K.N., Donovick, C., Gorelik, I., Abu-Ghazaleh, N., Pono-marev, D.: Hardware-based malware detection using low-level architectural fea-tures. IEEE Trans. Comput. **65**(11), 3332–3344 (2016). https://doi.org/10.1109/tc.2016.2540634

19. Reuters: Ukraine's power outage was a cyber attack: Ukrenergo (2017). https://www.reuters.com/article/us-ukraine-cyber-attack-energy/ukraines-power-outage-was-a-cyber-attack-ukrenergo-idUSKBN1521BA

20. Shalaginov, A., Grini, L.S., Franke, K.: Understanding neuro-fuzzy on a class of multinomial malware detection problems. In: 2016 International Joint Conference on Neural Networks (IJCNN), pp. 684–691. IEEE (2016). https://doi.org/10.1109/ijcnn.2016.7727266

21. Shijo, P., Salim, A.: Integrated static and dynamic analysis for malware detection. Procedia Comput. Sci. **46**, 804–811 (2015). https://doi.org/10.1016/j.procs.2015.02.149

22. Tang, A., Sethumadhavan, S., Stolfo, S.J.: Unsupervised anomaly-based malware detection using hardware features. In: Stavrou, A., Bos, H., Portokalidis, G. (eds.) RAID 2014. LNCS, vol. 8688, pp. 109–129. Springer, Cham (2014). https://doi.org/10.1007/978-3-319-11379-1_6

23. The Verge: the petya ransomware is starting to look like a cyberattack in dis-guise (2017). https://www.theverge.com/2017/6/28/15888632/petya-goldeneye-ransomware-cyberattack-ukraine-russia

Towards Efficient Detection of Malicious VBA Macros with LSI

Mamoru Mimura$^{(\boxtimes)}$ and Taro Ohminami

National Defense Academy, Yokosuka, Japan
mim@nda.ac.jp

Abstract. Targeted email attacks are one of main threats for organizations of all sizes and across every field. In targeted email attacks, malicious VBA (Visual Basic for Applications) macros are often contained in the attachment files to exploit the target computers. These malicious VBA macros are obfuscated in several ways to evade detection. Hence, pattern-based detection has a limitation in detecting these new malicious VBA macros. To detect new malicious VBA macros, some methods with machine learning techniques have been proposed. A method extracts words from the source code, and constructs a language model to represent VBA macros for machine learning techniques. This method, however, constructs a language model from all the extracted words. Therefore, this model might contain unnecessary words to classify. To construct an efficient language model, we focus on LSI (Latent Semantic Indexing). LSI is one of the foundational techniques in topic modeling, and calculates similarity of documents. Our method uses LSI to construct an efficient language model, which produces more accuracy and efficiency. To the best of our knowledge, our method is the first method to detect new malicious VBA macros with LSI. Our method extracts words from the source code and converts into feature vectors with some Natural Language Processing techniques. Our method trains a classifier with benign and malicious VBA macros and detects new malicious VBA macros. Several thousands of samples for evaluation are obtained from Virus Total. The experimental result shows that our method can detect new malicious VBA macros more accurately and efficiently. The best F-measure achieves 0.95.

Keywords: VBA macro · SVM · NLP · Bag-of-Words · TFIDF · LSI

1 Introduction

Targeted email attacks are one of main threats for organizations of all sizes and across every field. In targeted email attacks, malicious VBA macros are often contained in the attachment files to exploit the target computers. According to a report, Microsoft (MS) document files account for a large percentage of the attachments in targeted email attacks, and the most of the MS document files contain malicious VBA macros [6]. VBA (Visual Basic for Applications) is the

© Springer Nature Switzerland AG 2019
N. Attrapadung and T. Yagi (Eds.): IWSEC 2019, LNCS 11689, pp. 168–185, 2019.
https://doi.org/10.1007/978-3-030-26834-3_10

programming language of Office programs and enables to automate tasks in MS document files. These malicious VBA macros are obfuscated in several ways to evade detection. Some attackers confirm that the obfuscated VBA macro is not detected by anti-virus programs with the latest definitions in advance. In fact, main anti-virus programs with the latest definitions barely detect new malware samples [9,14]. Hence, pattern-based detection has a limitation in detecting these new malicious VBA macros. Moreover, malicious VBA macros do not require vulnerabilities to compromise a computer.

To detect new malicious VBA macros, some methods with machine learning techniques have been proposed [7,11,16,17]. Due to the restricted evaluation methods, the practical performance and long-term effect are still open to discussion. A method extracts words from the source code, and constructs a language model to represent VBA macros for machine learning techniques [13,16,17]. Thereafter, these represented feature vectors are classified by the trained models such as SVM (Support Vector Machine). This method, however, constructs a language model from all the extracted words. Thus, this model might contain unnecessary words to classify. For instance, common words included in most VBA macros are not useful to classify VBA macros as benign or malicious. Conversely, very rare words hardly appear in VBA macros, thus, might be not useful.

Our method assumes VBA macros are written by a natural language. To construct a more efficient language model, our method uses Latent Semantic Indexing (LSI). LSI is a natural language processing technique for extracting semantics of words in documents. This model assumes that words that are close in meaning will occur in similar pieces of documents, and reduces the number of words while preserving the similarity structure by singular value decomposition (SVD). Our method extracts words from the source code and converts into feature vectors with some Natural Language Processing (NLP) techniques such as LSI. Our method trains a model with benign and malicious VBA macros, and detects new malicious VBA macros with the trained model. Our method requires benign and malicious samples for training. We obtain several thousands of benign and malicious samples from Virus Total [4], one of the most popular sites which share malware samples. To evaluate the practical performance and long-term effect against new malicious VBA macros, the time series of samples is very important. The datasets for evaluation are constructed, considering the time series. The experimental result shows that our method can detect new malicious VBA macros containing new malware families. The best F-measure achieves 0.95.

To the best of our knowledge, our method is the first method to detect new malicious VBA macros with LSI. Likewise, the previous works do not reveal the effectiveness of LSI in VBA macros nor evaluate the long-term effect of their methods. Even though required time is an essential part to evaluate practical performance, these works did not pay attention to required time either. This paper provides the following contributions:

1. Propose a more accurate and efficient method to detect new malicious VBA macros with LSI.
2. Reveal the effectiveness of LSI in VBA macros.
3. Evaluate the long-term effect by time series analysis with actual VBA macros.
4. Our method requires only the time for almost one third or one quarter of the previous method.

The structure of this paper is shown below. Section 2 describes related work. Section 3 describes malicious VBA macros, and Sect. 4 provides NLP techniques. Section 5 presents our method, and Sect. 6 demonstrates the performance. Finally, we discuss the results and conclude this paper.

2   Related Work

Our method examines MS document files without executing files on a real or virtual computer. Several methods without dynamic analysis are proposed to examine MS document files.

2.1   MS Document File

OfficeMalScanner is a basic tool to detect malicious MS document files [8]. This tool scans the entire MS document file for generic shellcode patterns or embedded objects, and the malicious index rating can be used for automated analysis as threshold values. Mimura et al. proposed a method to extract the executable files embedded in a document file [14]. This method can detect new malicious document files with known obfuscation methods. Otsubo et al. developed a tool to detect anomaly file structure of document files containing executable files [19]. They examined hundreds of malicious document files and found these document files do not conform to the file format strictly.

The similar idea has been extended to XML-based Office documents. Cohen et al. presented a novel structural feature extraction method for XML-based Office documents [9]. This method extracts discriminative features from malicious documents based on their structure, and detects malicious document files with machine learning algorithms. Nissim et al. created a detection model that detects new malicious docx files [18]. In this model, detection relies upon their structural feature extraction methodology [9].

Another approach is a visualization based method for malware detection [10]. In this approach, the target file is converted into an image to examine. Deep learning methods have brought outstanding performance on image classification. Mimura et al. proposed some methods to detect malicious document files with Convolutional Neural Network (CNN) [15]. This method converts a document file into an image, and attempts to detect shellcode with CNN.

These methods examine document files and detect new malicious document files. Some methods might detect malicious document files which contain VBA macros. These methods, however, do not examine the contents of VBA macros.

2.2   VBA Macro

Bearden et al. proposed a method of classifying MS Office files containing macros as malicious or benign using the K-Nearest Neighbors machine learning algorithm [7]. This method extracts important features from p-code opcode (translated VBA macro code) with TFIDF. Our method uses raw VBA macro code, and constructs a LSI model from the TFIDF scores. Kim et al. focused on the obfuscation techniques and proposed an obfuscated macro code detection method using machine learning classifiers [11]. To train these classifiers, their method uses 15 discriminant static features, taking into account the characteristics. Because cross-validation is not valid for time series models, the practical performance and long-term effect are still open to discussion.

Miura et al. proposed a method to detect new malicious VBA macros with Doc2Vec [16,17]. Doc2Vec learns fixed-length feature representations from variable-length pieces of texts, such as documents [12]. This method extracts words from the source code, and constructs a Doc2Vec model to represent VBA macros for classifiers. This method, however, constructs a language model from all the extracted words. Hence, this model might contain unnecessary words to classify.

3   Malicious VBA Macro

3.1   Behavior

Malicious VBA macros are mainly contained in MS document files conform to Compound File Binary (CFB) file format or Office Open XML (OOXML) file format. CFB file format is the binary file format used by Microsoft Office 2003 and earlier. OOXML stores a document as a collection of separate files and folders in a compressed zip package, and is used by Microsoft Word 2007 and later. Many extensions conform to both file formats support VBA macros. VBA is a programming language running with Office programs, and provides useful functions. VBA macros are a series of commands that can be run automatically to perform a task. The following sample code shows how to run a VBA macro automatically.

```
1: Sub Auto_Open()
2: Msgbox "Hello World!"
3: End Sub
```

This simple example shows a welcome message with specific text. Thus, attackers abuse this useful functions to compromise other computers. They code a malicious VBA macro into a MS document file, and send it to the target by e-mail. Malicious VBA macros mainly could be used to drop malware and download malware. The former is called dropper and the latter is called downloader. Once a malicious document file is opened, only a single click is required for the malicious VBA macro to activate.

Dropper contains and extracts the main body from itself. The main body is encoded or obfuscated by various methods. Thus, dropper enables persistent access to the computer without Internet connection. Downloader downloads the main body from the Internet as its name suggests. Thus, downloader requires Internet connection to gain persistent access to the computer. Downloader does not contain the main body. Hence, the size tends to be less than dropper's.

As described in this section, malicious VBA macros tend to contain functions to download or extract the main body in the source code. Traditional approach attempted to represent these features manually. In contrast, our method attempts to detect these features automatically with NLP techniques.

3.2   Obfuscation

Malicious VBA macros are often obfuscated by various methods such as Base64. The typical obfuscation techniques are summarized in Table 1.

Table 1. Typical obfuscation techniques

	Method	Example
1	Encode strings	Convert to ASCII code
2	Replace strings	Replace with random strings
3	Split strings	Divide strings into characters

Encode strings is converting parameters with reversible algorithms. Several functions are used for encoding strings. For instance, some functions such as Asc(), Hex(), and Chr() change characters to the number of the ASCII code. These functions convert strings into numerous numerical characters. Therefore, malicious VBA macros tend to contain these functions and formatted numerical characters.

Replace strings is replacing strings with random strings. Several functions are used for replacing strings. For instance, some functions such as Replace(), Right(), or Left() are used to replace strings to other random strings. These functions mainly convert function names and variable names into random strings. Therefore, malicious VBA macros tend to contain these functions and random strings.

Split strings is dividing strings into other characters. This technique is effective to avoid signature-based anti-virus programs. The divided characters are restored to its original strings by join operators such as "and" or "plus".

As described in this section, malicious VBA macros tend to contain these functions and characteristic strings. Kim et al. extracted these features manually to use machine learning classifiers [11]. Our method does not extract these fixed features. Our method expects that NLP techniques extract these features automatically.

4   NLP Technique

4.1   Bag-of-Words

Bag-of-Words (BoW) is a basic method to extract feature vectors from documents. BoW represents the frequency of a word in a document, and extracts matrix from documents. In this matrix, each row corresponds to each document, and each column corresponds to each unique word in documents. This method does not consider word order or meaning. In this method, the number of unique words corresponds to the dimension of matrix. Thus, the more number of unique words increases, the more dimension of matrix increases. Therefore, methods to adjust the number of dimensions are required. To adjust the number of dimensions, important words have to be selected.

4.2   Term Frequency-Inverse Document Frequency

Term Frequency-Inverse Document Frequency (TFIDF) is one of the most popular methods to define word importance. TFIDF value is calculated as follows.

$$TFIDF_{i,j} = frequency_{i,j} \times \log_2 \frac{D}{document\_frequency_i}$$

The $frequency_{i,j}$ is the frequency of a word i in a document j. The $document\_frequency_i$ is the frequency of documents in which the word i appears. The TF is the $frequency_{i,j}$. The IDF is the logarithm of a value in which D (the number of total documents) is divided by the $document\_frequency_i$. TFIDF value is a value which is the multiplication of TF and IDF. Finally, TFIDF values are normalized. In this model, if a word appears rarely in an entire corpus and appears frequently in a document, the TFIDF value increases.

4.3   Latent Semantic Indexing

Latent Semantic Indexing (LSI) is one of the foundational techniques in topic modeling. The core idea is to take a matrix of documents and words, and decompose it into a separate document-topic matrix and a topic-word matrix. LSI is used for classifying documents, data clustering and calculating similarity of documents. Given m documents and n words in our vocabulary, we can construct an m x n matrix $\mathbf{T}$ in which each row represents a document and each column represents a word. $\mathbf{T}$ is described as follows.

$$\mathbf{T} = \begin{bmatrix} tf_{11} & \cdots & tf_{1n} \\ \vdots & \ddots & \vdots \\ tf_{m1} & \cdots & tf_{mn} \end{bmatrix}$$

In this matrix, a row will be a vector corresponding to a word, giving its relation to each document. Likewise, a column in this matrix will be a vector corresponding to a document, giving its relation to each word. In the simplest version of LSI, each entry can simply be a raw count of the number of times the j-th word appeared in the i-th document. In practice, however, raw counts do not work particularly well because they do not account for the significance of each word in the document. In all likelihood, T is sparse and redundant across its many dimensions. As a result, to find the few latent topics that capture the relationships among the words and documents, we want to perform dimensionality reduction on T. Dimensionality reduction can be performed using truncated Singular Value Decomposition (SVD). From the theory of linear algebra, there exists a decomposition of $\mathbf{T}$ such that $\mathbf{D}$ and $\mathbf{W}$ are orthogonal matrices and $\mathbf{V}$ is a diagonal matrix. Matrix $\mathbf{T}'$ is calculated from $\mathbf{T}$ by SVD using TFIDF as follows.

$$\mathbf{T}' = \mathbf{DVW} \approx \begin{bmatrix} d_1 \\ \vdots \\ d_r \end{bmatrix} \begin{bmatrix} v_1 & & 0 \\ & \ddots & \\ 0 & & v_r \end{bmatrix} \begin{bmatrix} w_1 \cdots w_r \end{bmatrix}$$

An element of $\mathbf{V}$ corresponds to each topic of all the documents. A row of $\mathbf{D}$ corresponds to each document. A column of $\mathbf{W}$ corresponds to each word. Thus, SVD reduces dimensionality by selecting only the r largest singular values, and only keeping the first r columns or rows of D and W. To select the largest values, we can use TFIDF scores. In this case, r is a hyper parameter we can select and adjust to reflect the number of topics. In our method, this parameter is used to reduce dimensionality while keeping the significance of each word in the document.

5   Proposed Method

5.1   Outline

This paper proposes a method to detect new malicious VBA macros with LSI. Our method requires benign and malicious VBA macros as training data. The outline of our method is shown in Fig. 1.

In training phase, our method extracts words from their source code, and constructs a LSI model. Thereafter, our method extracts feature vectors, and trains a classifier with the feature vectors and labels. In test phase, our method extracts feature vectors from unknown samples with the LSI model, and detects malicious VBA macros with the trained classifier.

5.2   Training Phase

In training phase, our method requires benign and malicious VBA macros as training data. These samples are obtained from web pages such as Virus Total [4]. First, our method extracts VBA macros from benign and malicious MS

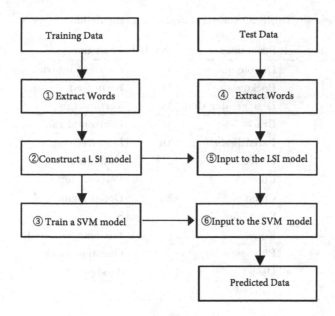

Fig. 1. Proposed method

document files. Thereafter, our method divides their source code into words (①). Special characters shown in Table 2 are used as the delimiter.

Second, our method constructs a LSI model from these words extracted from all the samples (②). The LSI model converts benign and malicious VBA macros into feature vectors. The dimension of feature vectors is compressed into the number of topics. Finally, a SVM classifier is trained by these feature vectors with their labels (③). SVM is a supervised learning model that assigns new examples to one category or the other.

5.3   Test Phase

In test phase, our method investigates unknown samples. These unknown samples are assumed as the attachments in targeted email attacks. First, our method extracts words from MS document files in the same way (④). Second, these words are converted into feature vectors by the LSI model (⑤) which was constructed in training phase. Finally, the trained classifier investigates these feature vectors, and predicts the label (⑥).

5.4   Implementation

We implemented our method with Python2.7 in an environment as shown in Table 3. Our method uses olevba [2] to extract VBA macros from MS document files. Olevba is a script to parse OLE and OpenXML files such as MS document files to detect VBA macros and extract their source code in clear text. Our

Table 2. Special characters as the delimiter

Symbol	Pronounce	Symbol	Pronounce
"	Double quote	\r	Carriage return
'	Backquote	\f	Form feed
<>	Less/greater than	\v	Vertical tab.
{}	Brace	\t	Horizontal tab.
()	Parenthesis	\n	Line feed
.	Period	_	Underline
,	Comma	%	Percent sign
:	Colon	$	Dollar sign
;	Semicolon	/	Slash
=	Equals	!	Exclamation mark
+	Plus	?	Question mark
-	Dash	@	At sign
*	Asterisk		

Table 3. Environment

CPU	IntelCorei7 (3.40 GHz)
Memory	16 GB
OS	Windows 10 home

method uses scikit-learn-0.19.2 [3] to implement SVM. Scikit learn is a machine learning library and has many classification algorithms. The parameters are provided from grid search, which exhaustively generates candidates from a grid of parameter values. We used gensim-3.4.0 [1] to implement a LSI model. Gensim has many functions related to NLP techniques such as BoW or LSI. Moreover, we implemented the previous methods [16,17] with BoW and Doc2Vec. In this paper, the same parameters are chosen for comparison in a fair condition.

6   Evaluation

6.1   Dataset

To evaluate our method, actual VBA macros were obtained from Virus Total [4]. These VBA macros contain both benign and malicious VBA macros. Table 4 shows the number of samples.

Table 4. The number of samples obtained from Virus Total

2015		2016		2017	
benign	malicious	benign	malicious	benign	malicious
622	870	1200	1150	2220	1083

We selected all MS document files containing VBA macros. Their file extensions are doc, docx, xls, xlsx, ppt, and pptx. These samples were uploaded to Virus Total between April 2015 and March 2018 for the first time. Each year in the Table corresponds to fiscal year from April to March. In general, unknown samples are investigated as soon as possible. Hence, we assume these samples appeared at the time. In targeted email attacks, anti-virus programs with the latest definitions barely detect new malware samples [9,14]. This fact means some anti-virus programs cannot detect malicious samples correctly. Hence, we determined to use malicious samples, which are judged malicious by a rate of more than 50 % anti-virus vendors. The benign samples are judged benign by all anti-virus vendors. We compared the hash values and removed duplicated samples.

Table 5 shows the main malware families in each dataset.

Table 5. Main malware families in each dataset

Dataset	Family name
2015	TrojanDownloader:O97M/Donoff
	TrojanDownloader:O97M/Adnel
	TrojanDownloader:O97M/Bartallex
	TrojanDownloader:W97M/Adnel
	TrojanDownloader:W97M/Donoff
2016	TrojanDownloader:O97M/Donoff
	Virus:W97M/Thus.GB
	Trojan:Win32/Tiggre!rfn
	Virus:X97M/Metcol.A
	Trojan:Win32/Occamy.C
2017	TrojanDownloader:O97M/Donoff
	Trojan:O97M/Madeba.A!det
	TrojanDownloader:JS/Swabfex.P
	Virus:W97M/Thus.GB
	TrojanDownloader:O97M/Donoff.CD

These names are defined by Windows Defender Antivirus [5]. Thus, each dataset is adequately distributed and contains a wide variety of malware samples. Furthermore, the consecutive datasets contain new malware families, which are not defined yet.

6.2 Evaluation Metrics

To evaluate accuracy, we use Accuracy, Precision, Recall, and F-measure as metrics. These metrics are defined as follows.

$$Accuracy = \frac{TP + TN}{TP + FP + FN + TN}$$

$$Precision = \frac{TP}{TP + FP}$$

$$Recall = \frac{TP}{TP + FN}$$

$$F - measure = \frac{2 Recall \times Precision}{Recall + Precision}$$

Table 6 shows the confusion matrix.

Table 6. Confusion matrix

		Actual value	
		True	False
Predicted result	Positive	TP	FP
	False	FN	TN

In this experiment, TP means detecting malicious VBA macros correctly.

6.3 Experimental Method

To reveal the performance and long-term effect against new VBA macros, the time series of samples is very important. The purpose of our method is detecting new malicious VBA macros. In practical use, many methods which contain our method can only use previous samples for training, and the test samples should not be the previous samples. If test samples contain previous samples, it is not possible to evaluate the performance appropriately. Hence, cross-validation is not appropriate in this case. Therefore, the datasets for evaluation are constructed, considering the time series.

First, we conduct a preliminary experiment to find the optimum value of a hyper parameter. As described in the previous section, this hyper parameter is the number of topics, and is used to reduce dimensionality while keeping the significance of each word in the document. In this preliminary experiment, we conduct 10-fold cross-validation with the 2015's dataset. We trace changes to the value of the dimension. Since this preliminary experiment, subsequent experiments will be conducted with the optimum value.

Next, we conduct 10-fold cross-validation with 2015's and 2016's datasets to confirm the generalization performance.

Finally, we conduct time series analysis to reveal the performance and long-term effect. The combinations of the training data and test data are shown in Table 7.

Table 7. The combinations of the training data and test data

	1	2	3	4
Training data	2015	2015	2016	2015 + 2016
Test data	2016	2017	2017	2017

To compare with the previous method [16,17], we perform the first combination with the previous method and our method. Other combinations are performed to reveal the long-term effect.

6.4   Result

Figure 2 shows the result of the preliminary experiments.

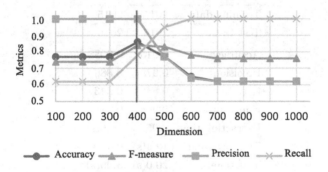

Fig. 2. Results of the preliminary experiments

The horizontal axis corresponds to the dimensions, and the vertical axis corresponds to each metrics. The dimensions are adjusted by varying the parameter described in the previous section. As described in Fig. 2, the precision and recall are in the relationship of trade-off. The accuracy and F-measure are maximized at 400 dimensions. Thus, we determined the optimum value, and fix the number of topics to 400 in subsequent experiments.

Table 8 shows generalization performance of the 10-fold cross-validation with 2015's and 2016's datasets.

Table 8. Generalization performance of the 10-fold cross-validation with 2015's and 2016's datasets

Metrics	Score	Range
Accuracy	0.79	± 0.21
Precision	0.74	± 0.20
Recall	0.98	± 0.04
F-measure	0.84	± 0.13

The recall has produced better results than precision. Owing to the unstable performances, the average precision is less than recall. In each time, however, the recall achieves at least 0.94. This suggests that benign samples are biased. Therefore, we conclude that the generalization performance is appropriate.

Table 9 shows performance of the time series analysis with the previous method.

Table 9. Performance of the time series analysis with the previous method

	BoW	Doc2Vec
Training data	2015	2015
Test Data	2016	2016
Accuracy	0.915	0.908
Precision	0.979	0.886
Recall	0.846	0.943
F-measure	0.908	0.918
Extracting time	6.05(s)	29.6(s)
Training time	12.4(s)	0.46(s)
Test time	20.0(s)	3.99(s)
Total time	60.8(s)	82.3(s)

In the previous method, Doc2Vec produced better performance than BoW. Doc2Vec requires more time for extracting words, that includes constructing a language model. Doc2Vec, however, does not demand much time for detecting. Overall, Doc2Vec is better than BoW in the previous method.

Table 10 shows generalization performance of the time series analysis with each combination.

Table 10. Performance of the time series analysis with each combination

	1	2	3	4
Training data	2015	2015	2016	2015 + 2016
Test data	2016	2017	2017	2017
Accuracy	0.949	0.886	0.814	0.833
Precision	0.981	0.816	0.682	0.691
Recall	0.914	0.842	0.809	0.885
F-measure	0.946	0.829	0.740	0.776
Extracting time	8.05(s)	8.75(s)	21.1(s)	29.6(s)
Training time	0.795(s)	0.625(s)	1.68(s)	4.46(s)
Test time	1.24(s)	1.39(s)	2.28(s)	3.56(s)
Total time	21.9(s)	20.4(s)	40.7(s)	60.0(s)

In the combination 1, our method produced better performance than the previous method, the F-measure achieves almost 0.95. Our method requires only less than half the time for detecting. Thereafter, our method is more effective than the previous method. In the combination 2, the performance is slightly reduced due to aging. The training samples were discovered over a year ago, nevertheless the F-measure maintains almost 0.83. Hence, the performance of our method does not become excessively reduced due to aging. In the combination 3 and 4, there is no great difference in the performances. This suggests new and much samples are not always appropriate for training.

7   Discussion

7.1   Accuracy

In practical use, many methods with machine learning techniques cannot use following samples for training. These methods should be evaluated with the previous samples. In the time series analysis, our method used only previous samples for training. The best F-measure achieves almost 0.95. Thus, our method is effective to new VBA macros. Despite the training samples were discovered over a year ago, the F-measure maintains almost 0.83. Hence, our method is accurate, and the performance does not become excessively reduced due to aging.

Next, Table 11 shows detection rate of known and unknown malware families.

Each detection rate is in almost the same range. Therefore, our method is effective to not only known families, but also unknown malware families.

Several samples were detected incorrectly by our method. We analyzed these samples, and counted the unique words included in only benign and malicious files. Table 12 show numbers of the unique words in the files detected incorrectly.

The overlooked malicious samples (FN) tend to contain more words included in only benign files than other samples. Therefore, these malicious samples were

Table 11. Each detection rate of known and unknown malware families

Dataset	2016		2017	
Total number	1150		1083	
Each number	Known	Unknown	Known	Unknown
	850	300	542	541
Detection count	779	272	466	446
Detection rate (%)	91.6	90.7	82.3	86.1

Table 12. Number of the unique words in the files detected incorrectly

	FN	FP
Number of words included in only benign files	4118	2384
Number of words included in only malicious files	3195	1955

classified as benign. The detected benign samples (FP) also tend to contain words included in only benign files. However, the words included in only malicious file are relatively numerous. We conclude that is why these benign samples were classified as malicious.

7.2 Topic Vector

We analyzed the contents of the topic vectors to reveal the effectiveness of LSI. Some examples of the words classified by LSI are shown in Table 13.

Table 13. Some examples of the words classified by the topic vector

Topic	Parts of the contents
1	epcrazkwlscpbqm, ipathwdinj, ylabbu, ynvneqrhdqazxz, vxqhus, ubepnlsziosn
2	wlijflsdkj, ghrj32, 2k3h, sdlkjfwhfe, rkj23, njqkwndjwqd
3	qs8juqb1am, qa94, zyprern, e5iqj, twkk, zytologischen
4	control, checkbox, range, click, cells, sheets
5	range, selection, select, activewindow, long, macro
6	lirdifqhvefomgkmsysaqvqrpufmtkkkzqskk ujphtxxljdvsoljplwzpklvf fcyityvgxyuvedjncjpiqgmhiglvowacmdhjbadhsocwne smgytipxywbmgnqedtxarqgyiqsnquisnbobbxwzgy

The topic 1, 2, 3, and 6 consist of random strings, which are often contained in obfuscated malicious VBA macros. Each topic has regularity such as alphabetical character, alphanumeric character, numerical character or the length. The topic 4 and 5 contain meaningful words. Some words are related with VBA macros. Thus, LSI classifies related words into each topic vector. This enables to reduce dimensions without lowering classification accuracy. Therefore, LSI represents VBA macros efficiently, and produces more accuracy.

7.3 Comparison

There are several methods to detect malicious VBA macros.

Bearden et al. conducted 10-fold cross-validation with several dozens of samples to evaluate their method [7]. The number of malicious VBA macros is only 40. Kim et al. conducted 10-fold cross-validation with several thousands of samples to evaluate their method [11]. Nevertheless, they used 90% of samples for training, the detection rate was no more than 0.915. Moreover, they did not describe the details of malware samples. As we described before, cross-validation is not appropriate to evaluate the performance for detecting new malicious VBA macros. Because, training samples could contain only previous samples. Therefore, it is not clear that their method could detect new malicious VBA macros in practical environment. We used only previous samples for training from more than ten thousand of samples. The training samples account for almost 25% of our samples. As a result, our method could detect new malicious VBA macros. Furthermore, this paper described the details of malware samples.

Miura et al. evaluated their method with several thousand of samples for 2 years [13,16,17]. The best F-measure achieved 0.93. However, they did not evaluate the long-term effect of their methods. We obtained 6 thousands of samples for 3 years from Virus Total. We categorized these samples into each year, and evaluated the long-term effect by time series analysis. Moreover, the best F-measure achieved almost 0.95. Previous works did not evaluate required time of their methods either. Required time is an essential part to evaluate practical performance. Our method requires only the time for almost one third or one quarter of the previous method. Furthermore, we compared each detection rate of known and unknown malware families. This revealed that our method was effective to detect not only known families, but also unknown malware families.

7.4 Ethics

Our method requires benign and malicious samples which can be collected from the Internet. Our method is light-weight and easy to implement. We used malware samples obtained from a commercial web site. We indicated clear conditions to choose malware samples from the web site. The details of samples were described and investigated. Hence, our method is reproducible and has high transparency.

8 Conclusion

In this paper, we propose a more accurate and efficient method to detect new malicious VBA macros with LSI. Our method extracts words from the source code and converts into feature vectors with a LSI model. To the best of our knowledge, our method is the first method to detect new malicious VBA macros with LSI. Previous works do not reveal the effectiveness of LSI in VBA macros nor evaluate the long-term effect of their methods. The experimental results reveal the effectiveness of LSI in VBA macros. Furthermore, we evaluate the long-term effect by time series analysis with actual VBA macros. The best F-measure achieves almost 0.95. Hence, our method is more accurate and can detect new malware families.

Our method is light-weight and investigates VBA macros without requiring much time. Thus, one of future work is to implement real time detection system. We can implement our method on a mail server or proxy server to investigate files in real time.

References

1. gensim topic modelling for humans. https://radimrehurek.com/gensim/
2. olevba. https://github.com/decalage2/oletools/wiki/olevba
3. scikit-learn machine learning in Python. https://scikit-learn.org/
4. Virus total. https://www.virustotal.com/
5. Windows defender antivirus. https://www.microsoft.com/en-us/windows/windows-defender/
6. Wolf in sheep's clothing: a SophosLabs investigation into delivering malware via VBA. https://nakedsecurity.sophos.com/2017/05/31/wolf-in-sheeps-clothing-a-sophoslabs-investigation-into-delivering-malware-via-vba/
7. Bearden, R., Lo, D.C.T.: Automated microsoft office macro malware detection using machine learning. In: Nie, J.Y., et al. (eds.) 2017 IEEE International Conference on Big Data, BigData 2017, Boston, MA, USA, 11–14 December 2017, pp. 4448–4452. IEEE (2017). http://ieeexplore.ieee.org/xpl/mostRecentIssue.jsp?punumber=8241556
8. Boldewin, F.: Analyzing msoffice malware with officemalscanner, 30 July 2009
9. Cohen, A., Nissim, N., Rokach, L., Elovici, Y.: SFEM: structural feature extraction methodology for the detection of malicious office documents using machine learning methods. Expert Syst. Appl. **63**, 324–343 (2016)
10. Kancherla, K., Mukkamala, S.: Image visualization based malware detection. In: 2013 IEEE Symposium on Computational Intelligence in Cyber Security (CICS), pp. 40–44, April 2013
11. Kim, S., Hong, S., Oh, J., Lee, H.: Obfuscated VBA macro detection using machine learning. In: DSN, pp. 490–501. IEEE Computer Society (2018). http://ieeexplore.ieee.org/xpl/mostRecentIssue.jsp?punumber=8415926
12. Le, Q.V., Mikolov, T.: Distributed representations of sentences and documents. In: Proceedings of the 31th International Conference on Machine Learning, ICML 2014, Beijing, China, 21–26 June 2014, pp. 1188–1196 (2014). http://jmlr.org/proceedings/papers/v32/le14.html
13. Mimura, M., Miura, H.: Detecting unseen malicious VBA macros with NLP techniques. J. Inf. Process. (JIP) **27** (2019, in press)
14. Mimura, M., Otsubo, Y., Tanaka, H.: Evaluation of a brute forcing tool that extracts the rat from a malicious document file. In: AsiaJCIS, pp. 147–154. IEEE Computer Society (2016). http://ieeexplore.ieee.org/xpl/mostRecentIssue.jsp?punumber=7781470

15. Mimura, M., Otsubo, Y., Tanaka, H., Goto, A.: Is emulating "binary grep in eyes" possible with machine learning? In: CANDAR, pp. 337–343. IEEE Computer Society (2017). http://ieeexplore.ieee.org/xpl/mostRecentIssue.jsp?punumber=8338657
16. Miura, H., Mimura, M., Tanaka, H.: Discovering new malware families using a linguistic-based macros detection method. In: 2018 Sixth International Symposium on Computing and Networking Workshops (CANDARW), pp. 431–437, November 2018
17. Miura, H., Mimura, M., Tanaka, H.: Macros finder: do you remember LOVELET-TER? In: Su, C., Kikuchi, H. (eds.) ISPEC 2018. LNCS, vol. 11125, pp. 3–18. Springer, Cham (2018). https://doi.org/10.1007/978-3-319-99807-7_1
18. Nissim, N., Cohen, A., Elovici, Y.: ALDOCX: detection of unknown malicious microsoft office documents using designated active learning methods based on new structural feature extraction methodology. IEEE Trans. Inf. Forensics Secur. **12**(3), 631–646 (2017)
19. Otsubo, Y., Mimura, M., Tanaka, H.: O-checker : detection of malicious documents through deviation from file format specifications. In: Black Hat USA (2016)

Intrusion Detection and Prevention

IDS Alert Priority Determination Based on Traffic Behavior

Shohei Hiruta[1]([✉]), Satoshi Ikeda[1], Shigeyoshi Shima[1], and Hiroki Takakura[2]

[1] NEC Security Research Laboratories, Kanagawa, Japan
s-hiruta@cb.jp.nec.com, s-ikeda@fd.jp.nec.com, shima@ap.jp.nec.com
[2] National Institute of Informatics, Tokyo, Japan
takakura@nii.ac.jp

Abstract. With the increase in the variety of devices connected to the Internet, each with their own vulnerabilities, we are currently observing an explosion of cyber attacks patterns. Furthermore, the overwhelming number of alerts from security sensors, such as intrusion detection systems (IDSs), makes it impossible to take appropriate countermeasures against attacks. A method to prioritize IDS alerts is therefore required for the next generation of security operation centers (SOCs). To this end, we have developed an IDS alert priority determination method that combines IDS alert information with traffic behavior and uses the difference in the distribution of traffic behavior to determine the priority of the alerts. We performed experiments with 2 million IDS alerts and 20 billion traffic flows in a real large-scale environment over two months and found that our method could identify 553 IDS alerts out of 2 million as high priority, which is a small enough number for SOC analysts to investigate them in detail.

Keywords: Intrusion detection and prevention · Alert prioritization · Traffic behavior analysis

1 Introduction

Security operation centers (SOCs) play a key role in the cyber security domain. A SOC monitors the traffic on the boundary between an organization and the Internet to detect cyber attacks and sends notifications as soon as a risky threat is found. Among the various security sensors used in a SOC, the intrusion detection system (IDS) is one of the most important [1]. The IDS detects cyber attacks by performing either pattern matching with the signatures it has [2] or anomaly detection by learning normal behavior [3]. An SOC typically uses IDS alerts as the starting point for cyber attack investigation.

As the number and types of cyber attacks increase, the IDS issues more alerts. Therefore, many SOCs reduce the number of IDS alerts by monitoring only alerts identified as high severity by IDS. However, it is becoming impossible for SOC analysts to deal with the number of alerts even after they have been

© Springer Nature Switzerland AG 2019
N. Attrapadung and T. Yagi (Eds.): IWSEC 2019, LNCS 11689, pp. 189–206, 2019.
https://doi.org/10.1007/978-3-030-26834-3_11

reduced. Moreover, the insufficient number of SOC analysts also makes it difficult to deal with the increase of alerts. In addition, various types of devices, each of which has its own specific vulnerabilities, are now connected to the Internet, which means that a huge amount of signatures are frequently provided. This makes it nearly impossible for analysts to understand all the vulnerabilities and determine if detailed analysis of the corresponding alerts is necessary or not. To solve these problems, it is necessary to determine the priority of alerts.

Security information and event management (SIEM) systems that determine the priority of IDS alerts by combining with various logs are used in SOCs. However, due to computer resources and storage capacity issues, SIEM systems do not make good use of the logs so that they actually determine the priority by only using alert information. Furthermore, SIEM systems must manually define rules for each threat, and can't reuse the rules for other threats. For these reasons, it is now crucial to come up with a general method to determine the priority of IDS alerts combined with other logs.

In actual operation, SOCs are attempting to solve these problems by analyzing the traffic behavior of attacks. In this paper, we propose an IDS alert priority determination method based on traffic behavior. Our method identifies IDS alerts that have suspicious traffic behavior as high priority and notifies SOC analysts so that they can preferentially analyze them in detail. To achieve this goal, our main concern is what kind of IDS alert traffic behavior should be considered high priority. We developed a method based on our definition of this and on the opinions of SOC analysts. We then evaluated our method with experiments using data in a real large-scale environment.

The main contributions of this paper are:

1. We propose a general IDS alert priority determination method based on traffic behavior. We came up with the method on the basis of our own experience and the opinions of SOC analysts.
2. We experimented and evaluated our method in a real large-scale environment.

In Sect. 2 of this paper, we provide an overview of related works. Sect. 3 presents our definition of high priority IDS alerts, and Sect. 4 describes the details of our method. We report the experimental results in Sect. 5 and discuss them in greater detail in Sect. 6. We conclude in Sect. 7 with a brief summary and mention of future work.

2   Related Work

Many IDS alert reduction methods based on alert correlation have been proposed. Lv et al. proposed an alert correlation algorithm called *TPPrefixSpan* that is based on the sequence pattern mining of IDS alerts [4]. They focused on the relationship between alerts and time sequence and found that considering these relationships improved the *PrefixSpan* algorithm [5]. In addition, methods using alert sequences based on graphs [6], codebooks [7], Markov models [8,9], Bayesian networks [10] have been proposed. The common point of these methods is that similar alert sequences are regarded as the same threat. However, in an SOC, we still need to further determine the priority among the reduced alerts.

Shittu et al. proposed *OutMet* which measures the degree to which an alert belongs to anomalous behavior [11]. Firstly, they perform alert correlation based on four perspectives: *Time Proximity*, which represents the time proximity between two alerts, *Common Prefix*, which means that two alerts are from the same attacker or/and target the same destination, *Crossed Common Prefix*, which represents two alerts in correspondence, and *Port Similarity*, which indicates that the destination port numbers of two alerts are the same. Secondly, based on the results of the alert correlation, they generate a *meta-alert* consisting of all the low level IDS alerts that are part of the same or a similar attack. Finally, they identify outliers from multiple *meta-alerts* and define them as high priority. Other methods that have been proposed include one using clustering to gather similar alerts [12,13] and one using alert correlation based on entropy [14]. However, even if IDS alerts have high correlation with each other or belong to the same cluster, if all we have is the IDS alert information, it is still not enough to determine if they are the same.

In response to the problems of the above methods, an IDS alert prioritizing method that combines IDS alerts with other information has been proposed. Gupta et al. proposed a post-processor for IDS alerts using knowledge-based evaluation (*PIKE*) [15], which combines an IDS alert, host information, and vulnerabilities. Firstly, *PIKE* gathers the information about the OS and services/applications running on a particular host. Then, it collects vulnerability information on the OS and services/applications. Secondly, it extracts the attack target host and the signature from the IDS alert. Finally, it matches the signature with the vulnerability of the attack target host and determines the priority of the IDS alert as follows: If the OS of the attack target host and the target OS of the vulnerability are different, it decides the priority is low and ignores it. Otherwise, it determines the priority based on the *CVSSv2* score [16]. However, collecting the information of all hosts is very expensive. In addition, some attackers intentionally insert dummy codes into their programs to cause false positive alerts. Because such alerts report the existence of vulnerabilities that are frequently meaningless to the actual targets, the analysts can be deceived into misjudgment. When an IDS alert that is different between the attack target host OS and the target OS of the vulnerability is prioritized as low, such attacks will be missed.

Our method differs from the ones above in that it prioritizes IDS alerts on the basis of traffic behavior.

3   Definition of High Priority IDS Alert

Our research goal is to notify the SOC analysts of IDS alerts that must be analyzed in detail by determining their priority on the basis of traffic behavior. To achieve this, we must define what kind of IDS alert traffic behavior is high priority. We investigated the traffic behavior and came up with the following definitions based on our own experience and the opinions of SOC analysts.

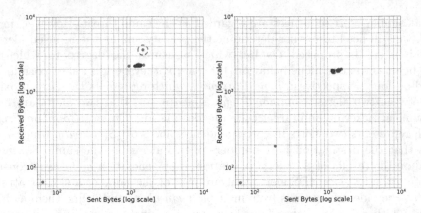

Fig. 1. 2D scatter plots of SSH BruteForce from same attack source on different days. Most points are clustered together, but the received byte size of only one point (surrounded by red line circle) on the left figure is bigger than the others. (Color figure online)

1. A small amount of traffic is different from a large amount of traffic in a short period of time. Figure 1 shows a 2D scatter plot of the traffic sizes of *Secure Shell (SSH) BruteForce* from the same attack source on different days. As shown on the left side of the figure, only one attack shows different behavior from the others, i.e., large traffic sizes (about 3.6×10^3 bytes). In such a case two scenarios can be considered:

   (a) **Successful attack:** To put it simply, there is a possibility that the attack is successful. Intuitively, when an attack is failing, the features of the related traffic are similar, and when an attack succeeds, the traffic features may become different. For example, in the case of *SSH BruteForce* attack, if a login has failed, a SSH server always returns the same phrase. Also, most SSH servers disconnect if there are three login failures in a row, so the traffic sizes typically remain uniform. However, if the login is successful, the servers return a login shell, so the traffic sizes increase. In addition, attackers continue their attacks to hide the success log in the failure cases even if they succeeded in the attack. Therefore, the difference in traffic between successful and unsuccessful attacks becomes significant.

   (b) **Attack with smokescreen:** According to SOC analysts, if a large number of attacks occur in a short period of time, most of them can be considered smokescreens intended to conceal the real attack. Attackers often use this technique to deceive SOC analysts. In this case, there is a high possibility that only a small amount of the traffic is for the true purpose.

2. The traffic behavior of an attack is different from past attacks even though they were detected by the same signature. In this case, three scenarios can be considered:

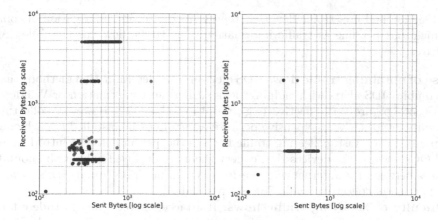

Fig. 2. 2D scatter plot of traffic behavior of SQLMAP. Left: Successful attack. Right: Fail attack.

(a) **Successful attack:** Attackers often use tools to attack mechanically and automatically. Therefore, we expect that traffic behavior when an attack is successful will be different from when it is a failure. Figure 2 shows the traffic behavior when we tested the SQLMAP tool[1] in our own environment. A successful attack is shown on the left and a failed one on the right. As we can see, the traffic behavior is completely different between successful and unsuccessful attacks.

(b) **Changing attack methods:** Various tools are used in attacks. When such tools are updated or new tools are released, the traffic behavior may change from past ones even if an attack is targeting the same vulnerabilities. In such a case, it is necessary to ask SOC analysts to check early.

(c) **Completely different threats:** According to SOC analysts, threats detected by IDS may be different from actual threats. There are two possible cases here. The first is when tools or exploit code that attack a new vulnerability have diverted from past ones and IDS detects it as a past threat. Since IDS performs matching with signatures, there is a possibility of mistakenly divert them as past threats. The second is when attackers intentionally insert the past exploit code into their code so that IDS mistakenly determines them as past threats. This technique is also used for the purpose of misleading SOC analysts.

Since an IDS alert contains no information on the traffic sizes and does not issue alerts for all traffic related to an attack, alert priority determination methods using only alerts such as [4–14] cannot correctly determine the priority of the alerts. In order to define these alerts as high priority, it is necessary to use traffic information.

---

[1] SQLMAP: http://sqlmap.org.

Our method uses traffic flow that represents the session information of communications per line as traffic information. The traffic flow has the following features:

Ease of obtaining traffic flows: IDS alert priority determination methods that combine IDS alerts with endpoint logs such as host information or Windows Event Log are very effective (e.g., Gupta et al.'s [15]). However, collecting endpoint logs is very expensive because agents must be installed at each endpoint. In contrast, collecting traffic flows is cheaper and easy to introduce to SOCs because the devices that collect them are deployed only at the boundary between the Internet and the intranet. In addition, recent IDSs have a function of collecting traffic flows as a standard.

Difficulty of falsifying traffic flows: If attackers successfully intrude on an endpoint, the endpoint logs can be easily falsified by simple commands. However, in order to falsify traffic flows, attackers have to search for the devices or servers that collect the logs, and then intrude on them and falsify logs. This is very expensive for attackers.

No payload information: Using payload to prioritize or reduce the number of IDS alerts is useful. However, there are two problems when it comes to using them. The first problem is payload encryption. More than 50% of Internet traffic is encrypted and recent malware uses encrypted communication [17,18], so it is impossible to investigate payloads without a specific method for doing so. The most popular method currently is a wildcard certification installed into all end hosts by which a proxy server can decrypt payloads, but it is often unacceptable in many environments. The second problem is log size. All traffic must be captured and recorded in order to analyze payloads, and the bigger the organization to be monitored is, the bigger the log size becomes, which makes it is very expensive to prepare adequate storages. In contrast, since traffic flow does not include payload information, it can be used even if the payload is encrypted. Also, traffic flow represents session information, so the log size is smaller.

4   IDS Alert Priority Determination

Our method determines the priority of IDS alerts on the basis of traffic behavior. Firstly, we introduce the items of the IDS alerts and traffic flows that we use for our method. An IDS alert consists of many items, but we focus only on some of them. Each alert is represented using a 7-tuple $A = (a_{sn}, a_{sc}, a_{sip}, a_{dip}, a_{sport}, a_{dport}, a_{time})$ where each element is as follows: a_{sn} is signature name, a_{sc} is signature category, a_{sip} is source IP address, a_{dip} is destination IP address, a_{sport} is source port number, a_{dport} is destination port number, and a_{time} is date-time. Traffic flow represents information from the start to the end of a session per line. Traffic flow also consists of many fields, but we focus only on some of them. Each traffic flow is represented using 8-tuple $F = (f_{sip}, f_{dip}, f_{sport}, f_{dport}, f_{sbyte}, f_{dbyte}, f_{time}, f_{dur})$ where each element is as follows: f_{sip} is source IP address, f_{dip} is destination IP address, f_{sport} is source port number, f_{dport} is destination port number, f_{sbyte} is sent traffic size (in bytes), f_{dbyte} is received traffic size (in bytes), f_{time} is date-time, and f_{dur} is duration (in seconds). We use the traffic flow feature $f = (f_{sbyte}, f_{dbyte}, f_{dur})$, and we perform base-10 logarithmic transform on each element of f. We also use the source and destination IP addresses, source and destination port numbers, and date-time for matching with IDS alerts.

Secondly, we introduce the two phases comprising our method: the training phase and the test phase. When a signature name set is $\mathbb{S}$, both phases are performed for each element in $\mathbb{S}$. In the test phase, our method assigns an IDS alert one of the following six priorities:

1. High priority: *suspicious, new pattern, outlier*
2. Low priority: *failed*
3. Undetermined: *new signature, no flow*

For the two "undetermined" priorities, *new signature* means the signature name does not exist in the training phase and *no flow* means there is no traffic flow that matches the source and destination IP addresses and source and destination port numbers of the alert. We describe *new signature* in detail when we explain the test phase and discuss *no flow* in Sect. 6.

4.1   Training Phase

In this phase, our method builds the training data for determining the priority of IDS alerts in the test phase. When an IDS alert set is $\mathbb{A}$, we use an IDS alert set $\mathbb{A}_S$ of each element $S \in \mathbb{S}$:

$$\mathbb{A}_S = \{A \in \mathbb{A} | a_{sn} = S\} \tag{1}$$

We also use a traffic flow set $\mathbb{F}$, and when an IDS alert $A \in \mathbb{A}_S$ is given, the traffic flow set $\mathbb{F}_A$ is used:

$$\mathbb{F}_A = \{F \in \mathbb{F} | a_{time} - \beta \le f_{time} \le a_{time} + \alpha, f_{sip} = a_{sip}, f_{dip} = a_{dip}, f_{dport} = a_{dport}\} \tag{2}$$

where α, β are minutes and may be fixed values or variables, respectively.

We introduce the training phase in detail. This phase applies the following three steps: *Clustering, Distribution Generation,* and *Sub Clustering based on Distribution.*

Step 1 Clustering. In this step, we perform clustering using the traffic flow features f of $F \in \mathbb{F}_A$ where $f_{sip} = a_{sip}, f_{dip} = a_{dip}, f_{sport} = a_{sport}$, and $f_{dport} = a_{dport}$ for each element $A \in \mathbb{A}_S$. We use *DBSCAN*, which is a non-hierarchical clustering methods based on density [19]. Compared with other clustering methods, *DBSCAN* does not need to predefine the number of clusters and only needs two parameters, *eps* and *minPts*. *DBSCAN* adds points less than the distance *eps* from a certain point to the cluster and repeats this process on the added points. If the number of points belonging to the cluster is less than *minPts*, these points are considered outliers. Figure 3 shows the results of clustering with f responding to a certain signature name of IDS. We display the 2D plot of sent and received traffic sizes because the 3D plot is very hard to see. As shown, the red cluster is far from the others despite having the same signature name. Even in the case of the same signature name, the *Distribution Generation* and the *Sub Clustering based on Distribution* steps must be performed for each cluster since the traffic flow features of attacks are different.

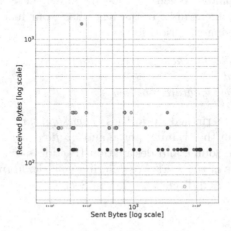

Fig. 3. 2D scatter plot of traffic flows of a certain signature. Only the received size of the red cluster is bigger than 10^3 bytes despite belonging to the same threat. (Color figure online)

Step 2 Distribution Generation. In this steps, we generate the distribution of traffic flow features f of each element $F \in \mathbb{F}_A$. As shown in Fig. 2, traffic behavior may be different even with the same signature name. Our method must determine a distribution like the one on the left side of Fig. 2 as high priority because this one shows the attack success behavior and SOC analysts have to deal with it immediately. In order to distinguish such behavioral differences, our method calculates the distribution differences. The distribution is represented using *kernel density estimation (KDE)* to calculate the distribution differences in the next step. *KDE* is a non-parametric method to estimate the probability density function of a random variable. When a set $\mathbb{X} = \{x_1, x_2, ..., x_n\}$, where x is d-dimensional feature and n is the number of elements of $\mathbb{X}$, is given as input, the probability density function is calculated as:

$$\hat{f}(x) = \frac{1}{nh^d} \sum_{i=1}^{n} K(\frac{x - x_i}{h})$$ (3)

where h is a smoothing parameter called *bandwidth* and K is the *kernel function*. When a traffic flow features of Fig. 2 is given as input, the distribution by Eq. (3) can be represented as shown in Fig. 4 (since it is difficult to illustrate the KDE applied to 3D data, we show the *KDE* applied to 2D data here). As shown in Fig. 4, our method can represent the distribution of the traffic behavior.

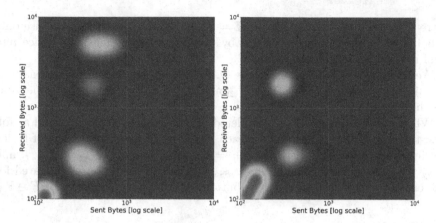

Fig. 4. KDEs applied to traffic behaviors in Fig. 2. Left: Successful attack. Right: Failed attack.

Step 3 Sub Clustering Based on Distribution. In this steps, we generate sub clusters with similar distribution based on *KDE* for each cluster. Our method uses the *Kullback-Leibler divergence* to calculate the distribution difference. The divergence is a measure of the difference between two probability densities. Here, we represent the distribution of traffic behavior with probability density functions based on *KDE*, so that we can use it to calculate the difference. When the probability density functions to be compared are $p(x)$ and $q(x)$, the divergence D_{KL} is calculated as:

$$D_{KL}(P||Q) = \int p(x)log\frac{p(x)}{q(x)}dx \qquad (4)$$

where P and Q are the probability distributions and $D_{KL}(P||Q) \geq 0$. A value close to 0 for D_{KL} means that the distributions are similar. In our case, the traffic flow feature is 3-dimensional, so let x, y, and z be random variables representing sent traffic size, received traffic size, and duration respectively, D_{KL} is as follows:

$$D_{KL}(P||Q) = \int \int \int p(x,y,z)log\frac{p(x,y,z)}{q(x,y,z)}dxdydz \qquad (5)$$

Furthermore, D_{KL} is asymmetric, $D_{KL}(P||Q) \neq D_{KL}(Q||P)$, and x, y, z are discrete values. Therefore, when two probability distributions $P(x,y,z)$ and

$Q(x, y, z)$ which are KDEs obtained in *Distribution Generation* step are given, we estimate divergence D as follows:

$$D = \frac{1}{2} \sum_{x \in \mathbb{X}} \sum_{y \in \mathbb{Y}} \sum_{z \in \mathbb{Z}} \left[P(x, y, z) log \frac{P(x, y, z)}{Q(x, y, z)} + Q(x, y, z) log \frac{Q(x, y, z)}{P(x, y, z)} \right] \quad (6)$$

where $\mathbb{X}, \mathbb{Y} = \{1.0, 1.1, ..., 10.0\}$ and $\mathbb{Z} = \{1.0, 1.1, ..., 3.5\}$. That is, we use only probabilities at grid points obtained by dividing the 3-dimensional space into equal intervals in logarithmic scale.

We generate sub clusters using the D. We set a threshold, Th_Δ, and assume that distributions with D less than Th_Δ are similar and assign them to the same sub cluster.

When the training phase is completed, the training data is consisted as follows: the clusters are generated for each signature name on the basis of traffic flow features f of $F \in \mathbb{F}_A$, where $f_{sip} = a_{sip}, f_{dip} = a_{dip}, f_{sport} = a_{sport}$, and $f_{dport} = a_{dport}$ for each element $A \in \mathbb{A}_S$, and the sub clusters are generated for each cluster on the basis of the distribution of traffic flow features f of $F \in \mathbb{F}_A$.

4.2   Test Phase

We introduce how to determine the priority of IDS alerts by using the training data for each signature name $S \in \mathbb{S}$. Our method determines the priority of IDS alerts every γ (in minutes) and uses IDS alert set $\mathbb{A}'_S$ within the interval I as follows:

$$\mathbb{A}'_S = \{A \in \mathbb{A} | I_{min} \leq a_{time} \leq I_{max}, a_{sn} = S\} \quad (7)$$

where I_{min} and I_{max} are the minimum and maximum date-times in the interval I. Also, when we determine the priority at date-time T and IDS alert $A' = (a'_{sn}, a'_{sc}, ..., a'_{time})$ is given, the traffic flow set $\mathbb{F}_{A'}$ is:

$$\mathbb{F}_{A'} = \{F \in \mathbb{F} | I_{min} - \beta \leq f_{time} \leq I_{max} + \alpha, f_{sip} = a'_{sip}, f_{dip} = a'_{dip}, f_{dport} = a'_{dport}\} \quad (8)$$

$$I_{max} + \alpha \leq T - \gamma \quad (9)$$

where α and β are minutes and may be fixed values or variables respectively.

This phase applies the following four steps: *Outlier Detection, Distance Calculation, Distribution Difference Calculation*, and *Verification*. However, if the signature category of IDS alert is *brute-force*, this phase only applies *Outlier Detection* because the success or failure of a *brute-force* attack can be determined by outlier detection and there is no need to compare with past traffic behavior. This phase determines the priority of IDS alerts for each signature name $S \in \mathbb{S}$.

Step 1 Outlier Detection. In this step, we perform outlier detection in the traffic flow set $\mathbb{F}_{A'}$. This step is used differently depending on if the signature category is *brute-force* or not.

Brute-force: As mentioned in Sect. 3, since the traffic sizes of the login success and failure are different and most of the login attempts fail, determining the priority of *brute-force* alerts can be done just with the outlier detection. Our method performs *DBSCAN* (described in Sect. 4.1) with traffic flow features f of $F \in \mathbb{F}_{A'}$. We do not use only the traffic flows that perfectly match each item of IDS alert A' because IDS detects *brute-force* by the frequency of login attempts, so it does not issue alerts to all login attempts related to *brute-force*. As a result of the clustering, if there is an outlier with an amount of data is less than the *minPts* parameter, the traffic flow belonging to it is suspected of successful login and our method determines A' as *suspicious*. If there is no outlier, our method determines A' as *failed*.

In other categories: This step is intended to find outliers, as shown in Fig. 3. As mentioned in Sect. 3, if attacks from the same source IP address are detected by the same signature but few attacks with different traffic flow features are involved, there are two possible scenarios: a successful attack or an attack with smokescreen. Outlier detection effective for finding such outliers. This step is also intended to eliminate scan activities, which are performed in large quantities in a short time against the same IP address ranges. Therefore, IDS issues a huge number of alerts and it is pointless to analyze all of them. Scan activities are performed mechanically and automatically, and most of them seem to fail, so we assume we should investigate only those that are outliers. We use outlier detection for this. Our method uses the traffic flow features f of $F \in \mathbb{F}_{A'}$ where $f_{sip} = a'_{sip}$, $f_{dip} = a'_{dip}$, $f_{sport} = a'_{sport}$, and $f_{dport} = a'_{dport}$ for each element $A' \in \mathbb{A}'_S$, and performs *DBSCAN* with traffic flow features for each combination of a'_{sip} and a'_{dport} of $\mathbb{A}'_S$. The reason each combination is clustered is that attacks detected by the same signature and from the same source IP address to the same destination port number of multiple destination IP addresses are likely to be scan activities. Therefore, our method finds outliers of a large number of scan activities and only analyzes these ones in detail. As a result of the clustering, if there are outliers, the traffic flows belonging to them are considered suspicious and our method analyzes them in detail in the *Distance Calculation* step. If there are no outliers, those attacks are considered to be failures and the priority of IDS alerts is set as *failed*.

Step 2 Distance Calculation. In this step, we perform distance calculation between traffic flow features belonging to the outlier and each one belonging to the clusters of the same signature name generated in the *Clustering* step of the training phase. This step is intended to confirm whether or not the outlier is actually an outlier compared to the past behavior. If the traffic flow features are different from the past ones despite having the same signature name, these attacks may be successful or different threats. Therefore, IDS alerts corresponding to such traffic flows are considered high priority and must be analyzed immediately by the SOC analysts. Our method calculates the Euclidean distances between the traffic flow features f belonging to an outlier and each one belonging to the clusters of the same signature name and obtains the minimum distance. We set a threshold Th_d, and define the priority of the corresponding IDS alert as *suspicious* if the minimum distance is greater than Th_d. If the minimum distance is equal to or less than Th_d, we take the nearest cluster and go to the *Distribution Difference Calculation* step.

Step 3 Distribution Difference Calculation. In this step, we calculate the distribution difference between the distributions of traffic behavior and past ones of the same signature name. As mentioned in Sect. 3, when an IDS alert indicates that the traffic behavior is completely different from that of past ones even though they are detected by the same signature, there are three possible scenarios: a successful attack, changing attack methods, or a completely different threat. Our method uses the traffic flow features f of $F \in \mathbb{F}_{A'}$ of the IDS alert A'. Firstly, we generate the distribution of the traffic flow features based on Eq. (3). Secondly, we also generate the past distributions of the traffic flow features of the IDS alerts belonging to each sub cluster in the nearest cluster obtained in the *Distance Calculation* step. Thirdly, we calculate the differences between the distribution and each past distribution based on Eq. (6) and obtain the minimum difference. Finally, we set a threshold Th_Δ, and define the priority of the corresponding IDS alert A' as *new pattern* if the minimum difference is greater than Th_Δ. If it is less than Th_Δ, we take the nearest sub cluster and go to the *Verification* step.

Step 4 Verification. In this step, we determine whether there is any unknown behavior in the traffic behavior, including past ones. Our method represents traffic behavior as a distribution based on *KDE*. However, *KDE* might not be able to represent the distribution well if there is bias in the number of elements. For example, some of the outliers (especially data where sent traffic size is about 1.9×10^3 and received traffic size is about 1.8×10^3) on the left side of Fig. 2 are not represented in the distribution on the left side of Fig. 4. If these outliers do not exist in the past traffic behavior of the same signature name, we define the priority as high because this is suspicious behavior. Our method achieves this by using the traffic flow features f of $F \in \mathbb{F}_{A'}$ of IDS alert A' and the past ones of the nearest sub cluster obtained in the *Distribution Difference Calculation* step. Our method runs *DBSCAN* on all the traffic flow features described above. If one of the f is an outlier, we define the priority of IDS alert A' as *outlier*. Otherwise, we define it as *failed*.

Finally, we describe how to deal with an IDS alert that appears in the test phase when its signature name does not exist in the training phase. In such a case, we perform the same processing as the training phase for one day from the time it first appeared to generate the training data for the test phase. During this process, we output *new signature* as the priority of IDS alert. We determine the priority of the IDS alert in the same way as the test phase using the generated data from the next day. In actual operation, it is necessary to fully test the training data before it is used for the test phase.

5   Experiments

To evaluate the effectiveness of our method, we performed experiments using IDS alerts and traffic flows from the real network of a large-scale environment. This network has over a million hosts and its traffic rate is 5 Gbps on average. The experiments were performed using data collected over roughly two months.

5.1   Experimental Data

IDS alerts and traffic flows were collected from *Palo Alto Networks PA-5060* deployed at the boundary between the Internet and the organization being monitored. Data from October 25 to December 31, 2018 were used. Among them, data from the first week were utilized for training considering our machine specs and the rest for testing. IDS alerts in the following six signature categories were used in these experiments: *autogen, brute-force, code-execution, info-leak, overflow,* and *sql-injection,* as these account for over 99% of all signature categories. To avoid side effect caused by well-known institute, i.e., *Shodan, Rapid7,* and *Shadowserver*[2], we eliminated IDS alerts whose source IP addresses belong to them. The IDS alerts and traffic flows used in our experiments are listed in Table 1.

Table 1. Numbers of IDS alerts and traffic flows from October 25 to December 31, 2018.

	IDS alerts	Traffic flows
Training	20,802	2,049,588,595
Test	2,067,888	18,591,128,533

In our method, we set the following parameters: $\alpha = 30.0$ min, $\beta = 30.0$ min, $\gamma = 30.0$ min, $I = 30.0$ min, $Th_d = 0.173$, $Th_\Delta = 0.30$, $eps = 0.173$, $minPts = 5$, $bandwidth = 0.30$, $K = Gaussian$. These parameters weren't based on equations but rather were determined manually, they may not be the optimum values.

5.2   Result

The results of our method are shown in Table 2. It defined 553(0.0267%) IDS alerts as high priority and $1,960,603(94.7\%)$ as low priority. It is considered that 553 high priority alerts are small enough for analysts to investigate in detail and our method is effective as one of the general priority determination

---

[2] Shodan: https://www.shodan.io
  Rapid7: https://www.rapid7.com
  Shadowserver: https://shadowserver.org/wiki.

method in SIEM. However, our method was unable to determine the priority of $108,303(5.24\%)$ of the IDS alerts. We will discuss these results in detail in Sect. 6

Table 2. Results of IDS alert priority determination.

Priority	High			Low	Undetermined	
Type	Suspicious	New pattern	Outlier	Failed	New signature	No flow
Autogen	4	7	0	76	3	3
Brute-force	47	0	0	669	0	0
Code-execution	214	143	0	1,953,723	1,853	3,286
Info-leak	9	2	0	1,193	391	102,734
Over-flow	25	79	0	3,320	0	24
Sql-injection	15	8	0	51	9	0
Total	553			1,959,032	108,303	
	314	239	0		2,256	106,047

We were not able to evaluate the effectiveness by SOC analysts for 553 IDS alerts that were high priority. Therefore, we investigated the all destination IP addresses (214 IP addresses) of the alerts for the existence of vulnerability, which is one of the analyst's point of view. We searched for these addresses on *SHODAN* on January 15, 2019. Information on 70 IP addresses could not be found, and 58 IP addresses had some vulnerabilities at the time of the investigation. We also randomly extracted $1,000$ IP addresses from $65,656$ unique destination IP addresses of IDS alerts that were low priority and investigated the existence of vulnerability. We found that three of the IP addresses had some vulnerabilities. These results clearly demonstrate that our method can effectively extract suspicious IDS alerts of attacks on vulnerable servers.

6   Discussion

Firstly, we discuss the possibility of false positives of the result by our method. Signature *Microsoft IIS WebDAV ScStrongPathFromUrl Buffer Overflow Vulnerability(30464)*[3] detected 104 IDS alerts out of 553. Figure 5 shows the traffic behavior distributions of this signature. The left side of Fig. 5 was determined as *new pattern*, the center of Fig. 5 was determined as *failed*, and the right of Fig. 5 shows the distribution in training data determined to be most similar to them by our method. At first glance, the distributions of the left and center are quite similar and we actually confirmed that both cases were failure ones. However, divergence D between the left and right was 0.335 and between the center and right was 0.206. Because Th_Δ was defined as 0.30, the former was mistakenly

---

[3] Signature name provided by Palo Alto Networks.

judged as *new pattern* and the latter was judged as *failed*. This is because the distribution shown on the left is bigger in overall received bytes than other distributions and D reacts sensitively to the deviation of distributions. To solve this problem, it is necessary to adjust the parameters. In this case, we can change the values of T_Δ and *bandwidth*. If T_Δ is bigger than 0.335, the left one is determined as existing traffic behavior. If we increase the range of distribution by increasing the *bandwidth*, D gets smaller. However, it is difficult to apply this solution because if T_Δ or *bandwidth* are increased, other alerts correctly determined as *new pattern* may be incorrectly determined as *failed*. Another solution is to change the algorithm to calculate the distribution difference. For example, we could change D to an algorithm that calculates the difference based on the shape of the distribution, or to a combination of both.

new pattern   failed   training data

Fig. 5. Distributions of traffic behavior concerning Microsoft IIS WebDAV ScStrong-PathFromUrl Buffer OverflowVulnerability(30464).

Secondly, we discuss the false positive alerts of IDS. According to *FireEye* report, more than 50% of alerts that most organizations received are false positives [20]. There is a possibility that the false positive alerts exist in the alerts determined as *new pattern*. However, we consider that such alerts can be covered by operation. Because our method determined 533 alerts as high priority for two months data and SOC analysts can analyze them in detail. If the analysts determine that the alert is false positive, they can add the relevant traffic flows of the alert to the training data. Then, the alerts showing the same traffic behavior will not be determined as *new pattern*. However, if the traffic behavior of the successful attacks and the traffic behavior of the false positive alerts are similar, this solution cannot be applied. Therefore, careful investigation is required before adding traffic flows to training data.

Thirdly, we discuss *no flow* alerts. As shown in Table 2, the alerts of the *info-leak* signature category accounted for the majority of *no flow* alerts. After investigating these in detail, we found that they were detected by signature *RPC Portmapper Dump Request detected(32796)*. The 120 alerts per day on average were determined as *no flow*, but $91,187(85.9\%)$ were determined in two days. This is due to the limitation on the IDS that reports an alert together with its corresponding traffic flow. If the IDS raises an enormous amount of alerts in a short period, it cannot have enough resources to handle the traffic flows. Therefore, our approach could not determine the priorities because there were IDS alerts but no traffic flows matching them. To solve this problem, it is necessary to adopt a method that determines the priority of alerts or reduces the number of alerts without using the traffic behavior, such as the ones introduced in Sect. 2. Since our method takes a totally different approach from these, it can be combined with them.

Finally, we discuss the application of our method to practical operation. In the experiments, we collected traffic flows for a certain period time and then prioritized the alerts in order to simplify the experiment. However, in practical operation, the time at which the SOC analysts must deal with an attack after the IDS detects it will vary depending on the case. To solve this problem, we need an algorithm that changes the priority of IDS alerts in accordance with elapsed time. Such an algorithm would first determine the priority of the alert by using the traffic behavior prior to the IDS detection, and then re-determine the priority in the same way every specific time. Even if the first priority determination result is high, if the priority decreases with each re-determination, the alert will be moved to a lowerpriority and the analyst can put off the analysis. Conversely, if the priority gets higher with elapsed time, the analyst must prioritize the analysis. Our method can easily change the time for priority determination, and as such, can flexibly deal with actual operation.

7   Conclusion and Future Work

In this paper, we proposed an general IDS alert priority determination method based on traffic behavior. We defined what kind of traffic behavior in an IDS alert indicates high priority based on our own experiences and the opinions of SOC analysts. We developed a method to judge IDS alerts that have defined traffic behavior as high priority using outlier detection and distribution difference calculation. The proposed method was evaluated with experiments using 2 million IDS alerts and 20 billion traffic flows on a real large-scale environment over two months. Results showed that our method defined that 553 IDS alerts as high priority, which is a small number for SOC analysts to investigate in detail. Our method is expected to be more effective when combined with other existing method.

For future work, we plan to investigate how changing the parameters affects the result and examine the IDS alerts determined as high priority in more detail cooperate with SOC analysts. We will also devise a method to detect attacks that can't currently be detected by IDS because the real threats are attacks that IDS can't detect.

References

1. Denning, D.E.: An intrusion-detection model. J. IEEE Trans. Softw. Eng. **13**, 222–232 (1987)
2. Lunt, T.F., Jagannathan, R., Lee, R., Whitehurst, A., Listgarten, S.: Knowledge-based intrusion detection. In: AI Systems in Government Conference, Washington, USA, pp. 102–107 (1989)
3. Garcia-Teodoro, P., Diaz-Verdejp, J., Macia-Fernandez, G., Vazquez, E.: Anomaly-based network intrusion detection: techniques, systems and challenges. J. Comput. Secur. **28**, 18–28 (2009)
4. Lv, Y., Xiang, S., Geng, J., Li, Y., Xia, C.: An alert correlation algorithm based on the sequence pattern mining. In: 2015 IEEE Advanced Technology, Electronic and Automation Control Conference, Chongqing, China, pp. 1146–1151 (2015)
5. Pei, J., Han, J., Mortazavi-Asl, B., Chen, Q., Dayal, U., Hsu, M.-C.: PrefixSpan: mining sequential patterns efficiently by prefix-projected pattern growth. In: 17th International Conference on Data Engineering, Heidelberg, Germany, pp. 215–224 (2001)
6. Wang, L., Liu, A., Jajodia, S.: Using attack graphs for correlating, hypothesizing, and predicting intrusion alerts. J. Comput. Commun. **29**, 2917–2933 (2006)
7. Yemini, S.A., Kliger, S., Mozes, E., Yemini, Y., Ohsie, D.: High speed and robust event correlation. J. IEEE Commun. Mag. **34**, 82–90 (1996)
8. Zan, X., Gao, F., Han, J., Sun, Y.: A hidden Markov model based framework for tracking and predicting of attack intention. In: 2009 International Conference on Multimedia Information Networking and Security, Hubei, China, pp. 498–501 (2009)
9. Zhicai, S., Yongxiang, X.: A novel hidden Markov model for detecting complicate network attacks. In: 2010 IEEE International Conference on Wireless Communications, Networking and Information Security, Beijing, China, pp. 312–315 (2010)
10. Steinder, M., Sethi, A.S.: Probabilistic fault localization in communication systems using belief networks. J. IEEE/ACM Trans. Netw. **12**, 809–822 (2004)
11. Shittu, R., Healing, A., Ghanea-Hercock, R., Bloomfield, R., Muttukrishnan, R.: OutMet: a new metric for prioritising intrusion alerts using correlation and outlier analysis. In: 39th Annual IEEE Conference on Local Computer Networks, Edmonton, Canada, pp. 322–330 (2014)
12. Njogu, H.W., Jiawei, L.: Using alert cluster to reduce IDS alerts. In: 2010 3rd International Conference on Computer Science and Information Technology, Chengdu, China, pp. 467–471 (2010)
13. Vaarandi, R., Podins, K.: Network IDS alert classification with frequent itemset mining and data clustering. In: 2010 International Conference on Network and Service Management, Niagara Falls, Canada, pp. 451–456 (2010)
14. GhasemiGol, M., Ghaemi-Bafghi, A.: A new alert correlation framework based on entropy. In: 3rd International eConference on Computer and Knowledge Engineering, Mashhad, Iran, pp. 184–189 (2013)
15. Gupta, D., Joshi, P.S., Bhattacharjee, A.K., Mundada, R.S.: IDS alerts classification using knowledge-based evaluation. In: 2012 Fourth International Conference on Communication Systems and Networks, Bangalore, India, pp. 1–8 (2012)
16. Mell, P., Scarfone, K., Romansky, S.: A Complete Guide to the Common Vulnerability Scoring System Version 2.0, National Infrastracture Advisory Council. https://ws680.nist.gov/publication/get_pdf.cfm?pub_id=51198. Accessed 15 Feb 2019

17. The Global Internet Phenomena Report. https://www.sandvine.com/hubfs/downloads/phenomena/2018-phenomena-report.pdf. Accessed 15 Feb 2019
18. Uncovering Hidden Threats within Encrypted Traffic. https://www.a10networks.com/sites/default/files/A10-EB-14106-EN.pdf. Accessed 15 Feb 2019
19. Evangelos, S., Jiawei, H., Usama, M.F.: A density-based algorithm for discovering clusters in large spatial databases with noise. In: The Second International Conference on Knowledge Discovery and Data Mining, Oregon, USA, pp. 226–231 (1996)
20. How many Alerts is Too Many to Handle?. https://www2.fireeye.com/StopTheNoise-IDC-Numbers-Game-Special-Report.html. Accessed 5 Jun 2019

(Short Paper) Effectiveness of Entropy-Based Features in High- and Low-Intensity DDoS Attacks Detection

Abigail Koay[1]($\boxtimes$), Ian Welch[2], and Winston K. G. Seah[2]

[1] University of Waikato, Hamilton, New Zealand
abigail.koay@waikato.ac.nz
[2] Victoria University of Wellington, Wellington, New Zealand
{ian.welch,winston.seah}@ecs.vuw.ac.nz

Abstract. DDoS attack detection using entropy-based features in network traffic has become a popular approach among researchers in the last five years. The use of traffic distribution features constructed using entropy measures has been proposed as a better approach to detect Distributed Denial of Service (DDoS) attacks compared to conventional volumetric methods, but it still lacks in the generality of detecting various intensity DDoS attacks accurately. In this paper, we focus on identifying effective entropy-based features to detect both high- and low-intensity DDoS attacks by exploring the effectiveness of entropy-based features in distinguishing the attack from normal traffic patterns. We hypothesise that using different entropy measures, window sizes, and entropy-based features may affect the accuracy of detecting DDoS attacks. This means that certain entropy measures, window sizes, and entropy-based features may reveal attack traffic amongst normal traffic better than the others. Our experimental results show that using Shannon, Tsallis and Zhou entropy measures can achieve a clearer distinction between DDoS attack traffic and normal traffic than Rényi entropy. In addition, the window size setting used in entropy construction has minimal influence in differentiating between DDoS attack traffic and normal traffic. The result of the effectiveness ranking shows that the commonly used features are less effective than other features extracted from traffic headers.

Keywords: DDoS · Entropy · Traffic features

1 Introduction

Denial of Service (DoS) is a popular type of cyber attack that has remained a problem for users of the Internet for over twenty years. This attack is popular for its ability to effectively cripple servers and networks [6]. Now, DoS attacks are often distributed where it is called Distributed Denial of Service (DDoS) attack. In a recent case, a DDoS attack disrupted GitHub.com, a highly used

© Springer Nature Switzerland AG 2019
N. Attrapadung and T. Yagi (Eds.): IWSEC 2019, LNCS 11689, pp. 207–217, 2019.
https://doi.org/10.1007/978-3-030-26834-3_12

site for code repository and version control using a powerful DDoS attack that peaked at 1.35Tbps [5]. The increasing severity of DDoS attacks has motivated increased efforts to develop solutions to counter the attack.

Entropy-based features are a popular measure to detect DDoS attacks [10]. Generally, entropy-based features are computed by applying entropy measures such as Shannon entropy [11] to raw traffic attributes. Entropy measures are algorithms used to calculate the uncertainty of these raw traffic attributes. Typically these attributes are packet header fields such as source and destination IP addresses, source and destination port numbers, and protocol. Entropy-based features provide a distributional view of the network traffic where it shows the variations of raw traffic attributes. For example, a high entropy value computed using the source IP address attribute indicates that there is a high variation in the origin of the traffic whereas a low entropy value indicates a smaller variation in the traffic packets' origins. This is useful for attack detection since a typical DDoS attack with a large number of attack sources targeting a single or small set of devices usually has a high variation in the source IP addresses and low variation in destination IP addresses as compared to normal traffic [7].

The usage of entropy-based features is more appealing to researchers and security professionals compared to the traditional volumetric based approaches in DDoS attack detection because they provide the following advantages: simple calculation, high sensitivity, and independence from the level of network utilisation. However, most existing approaches [4,9,10,13] use a limited set of entropy-based features for detection that is only effective for specific DDoS attacks and may fail to detect different types of DDoS attacks accurately. Choosing the right set of entropy-based features to detect all types of DDoS attacks is a hard problem where it requires a deep understanding of each feature and their effectiveness in distinguishing between various attack and normal traffic. In addition, it is also important to understand the effect of entropy measures and window size used in constructing entropy-based features on the effectiveness of detecting DDoS attacks, in particularly in high- and low-intensity DDoS attacks.

The main contribution of this paper is the evaluation of a set of useful entropy-based features based upon two types of investigation: (1) exploration of the effectiveness of alternative entropy measures such as Tsallis, Rényi and Zhou as opposed to the more commonly used Shannon entropy for highlighting DDoS attack traffic patterns and (2) understanding the tradeoffs between detection window size and detection accuracy of entropy-based features to construct effective entropy-based features.

2   Related Work

Most recent existing work on DDoS Detection concentrates on using entropy-based features [4,7,10,14]. Most research focused on using a single entropy-based feature for detecting anomalies in the network rather than multiple entropy features [7]. In most entropy-based DDoS attack detection systems, Shannon entropy [11] measure is used. Gu *et al.* [2] proposed a maximum entropy and relative entropy approach based on Shannon entropy to detect network traffic anomalies in the network traffic. The reported experimental results showed that this approach is highly accurate in achieving very low false positive and false negative rates. In another approach, Zhang et al. [14] proposed an advanced entropy-based method using Shannon entropy that splits variable rate attacks into different fields and treats each field with different methods to detect Low-rate DoS (LDoS) attacks. However, the method has a significantly longer response time and uses substantially more resources than prior entropy-based approaches.

Other entropy measures such as Tsallis or Rényi entropies have also been used. For example, Ma et al. [7] proposed a DDoS detection method using Tsallis entropy with an exponent separation detection algorithm based upon a variation of Lyapunov Exponent. Their method measures the rate of exponent separation between the source and destination IP addresses where the rate of exponent separation in attack traffic tends to be much higher than normal traffic. Bhuyan et al. [1] used an extended entropy metric based on Rényi entropy to calculate the entropy difference between two traffic samples taken at different times for detecting DDoS attacks. However, their method only analyses sample traffic where important information or evidence of DDoS attack might be missed, especially in low-intensity DDoS attacks.

Apart from entropy measures, DDoS attack detection approaches also adopt different window sizes to detect DDoS attack traffic. For example, Mousavi et al. [8] chose 50 packets as the window size by calculating the entropy of 50 new incoming packets that are sent to the software-defined network controller. Their approach is able to detect the presence of DDoS attack traffic after observing only the first five window periods. Another study [7] on the various window sizes, using a single dataset, found that 50 s window size yields the best result.

3   Entropy-Based Features

To construct the entropy-based features, we used the UNB ISCX 2012 intrusion detection evaluation dataset (ISCXIDS2012) [12], a recent widely used dataset. This dataset contains seven days (Monday through to Sunday) of network activities which include high-. and low-intensity attack traffic. IRC Botnet DDoS attack traffic represents the high-intensity DDoS attack and HTTP Denial of Service attack traffic represents the low-intensity DDoS attack traffic. Each day has a different combination of attacks.

Entropy-based features can be constructed using two steps: (1) extract features from the raw dataset, (2) compute entropy values based on pre-defined entropy measures using a specific time interval.

3.1   Step 1 - Extract Features from the Raw Dataset

All possible traffic features that can be extracted from packet header information (Table 1) are used to construct entropy-based features except redundant features (i.e., Absolute time, resolved/unresolved addresses) or features that contain null values (i.e., Cisco VSAN, 802.1Q VLAN id, Expert Info Severity).

Table 1. List of regular entropy-based features constructed

Regular entropy-based features	
Delta time (D.Time)	Protocol identifier (Protocol)
Source IP address (S.IP)	Destination IP address (D.IP)
Source port address (S.Port)	Destination port address (D.Port)
Source MAC address (S.MAC)	Destination MAC address (D.MAC)
Source network address (S.Net)	Destination network address (D.Net)
Packet length (P.Length)	IP DSCP value (DSCP)
TCP sequence number (Seq)	TCP window length (W.Length)
TCP payload (Payload)	

3.2 Step 2 - Compute Entropy Values

In the second step, the entropy value of each feature is calculated based on a pre-defined entropy measure and window size. Entropy value can be calculated using several different entropy measures, namely Shannon, Tsallis, Rényi and Zhou entropies. On the other hand, the window size is defined as the distance between two time points. For example, a window size of 60 s means that the entropy of each feature of all packets within the 60 s time frame will be calculated.

Two types of entropy-based features are computed: *regular entropy-based features* (Table 1) created by calculating the entropy of a single traffic features and *entropy variation features* (Table 2) created by calculating the variation between two distinct *regular entropy-based features*.

Table 2. List of Entropy variation features constructed

Entropy variation features	
Separation IP address (V.IP)	Separation port number (V.Port)
Separation MAC address (V.MAC)	Separation network address (V.Net)
Separation TCP information (V.TCP)	

4 Influence of Entropy Measures in Traffic Patterns

This section examines the influence of different entropy algorithms on the accuracy of detecting DDoS attack traffic. We compare the traffic patterns generated using four different entropy measures, namely, Shannon, Tsallis, Rényi and Zhou entropy measures in both high- and low-intensity DDoS attack traffic. Due to space constraint, we did not show patterns of commonly used features such as S.IP, D.IP, S.Port, D.Port and Protocol.

4.1   Network Traffic Containing High-Intensity DDoS Attack

The Tuesday's network activities in the ISCXIDS2012 dataset contains the IRC Botnet based DDoS attack traffic. This dataset is used as a representation of network traffic containing high-intensity DDoS attack traffic.

Figure 1 shows entropy values generated using Shannon, Tsallis and Zhou entropy measures; Rényi entropy shows a different traffic pattern from the others. Since Tsallis and Zhou entropies are a generalisation of Shannon entropy, traffic patterns generated will be similar.

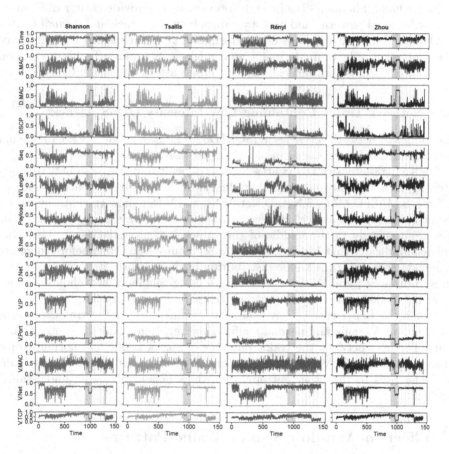

Fig. 1. Different entropy measures of entropy-based features with high-intensity attack traffic; grey area shows the period of the DDoS attack.

We observe that it is possible to distinguish high-intensity DDoS attack traffic from normal traffic quite easily when entropy measures are applied to most of the traffic features except for entropy measures calculated using the Seq field as shown in Fig. 1. This is because for most of the entropy-based features generated, the entropy values of attack traffic have a much smaller range than normal traffic.

For example, the attack traffic entropy values of the DSCP feature, using the Shannon entropy algorithm, lie between 0.1 to 0.35 whereas the normal traffic entropy values of the same entropy lie between 0.05 to 0.95.

The differences between these entropies represent the distributional differences between attack and normal traffic. There is not much of a difference in the distributional patterns of attack and normal traffic using entropy-based features constructed using Rényi entropy, which may not be useful in identifying stealthy DDoS attacks. This is because the differences between attack and normal traffic entropy values are too small to be noticeable and can be easily misclassified. On the other hand, Shannon, Tsallis and Zhou entropies provide clearer differences in distributional patterns and entropy values between attack and normal traffic.

Overall, Rényi entropy does not perform well at distinguishing high-intensity DDoS attack traffic from normal traffic whereas Shannon, Tsallis and Zhou entropies perform better and can identify DDoS attack traffic relatively well.

4.2   Network Traffic Containing Low-Intensity DDoS Attack

The Monday's network activities in ISCXIDS2012 dataset contains HTTP Denial of Service attack traffic, an example of low-intensity DDoS attack (Fig. 2.)

Unlike high-intensity DDoS attacks, it is difficult to distinguish between low-intensity attack traffic and normal traffic. Most entropy-based features such as D.Time, S.MAC, D.MAC, S.Net, D.Net, V.IP, and V.Net show the entropy values decreases during the attack. However, this is true for only a small part of the attack, specifically in the middle of the attack (i.e. around 1200 s). This phenomenon indicates that low-intensity attacks require some time before there are significant changes in the traffic distribution in the network. Entropy-based features such as Seq and W. Length entropies using Shannon and Zhou entropies show a clear distinction between attack traffic and normal traffic.

Similar to Rényi entropy gives almost no difference in the traffic patterns between attack traffic and normal traffic. However, Rényi entropy shows significant differences between the traffic patterns of attack traffic and normal traffic when applied to V.IP, V.Port and V.Net entropy features, in which it shows similar differences to the other entropy algorithms (Zhou, Shannon, and Tsallis) examined.

5   Effects of Window Size in Traffic Patterns

This section examines the influence of window size in calculating entropy values for DDoS detection on network traffic. If the window size is set too large, DDoS attacks that lasted for a shorter period than the window size may be hidden and the entropy value computed may not show the distinct difference between attack traffic and normal traffic. However, if the window size is set too small, entropy values generated may be too sensitive to the changes in the traffic. This means that a slight change in the network can be regarded as an attack even though it is not. In this case, a lot of false alarms may occur.

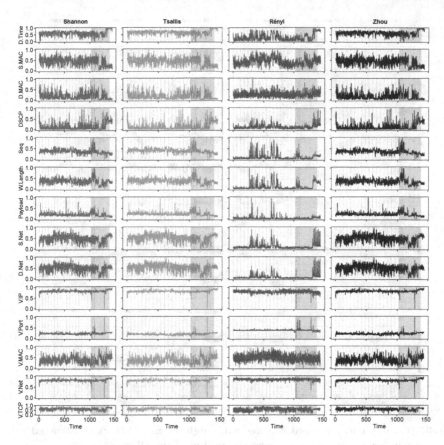

Fig. 2. Different entropy measures of entropy-based features with low-intensity attack traffic; grey area shows the period of the DDoS attack.

We compared six different window sizes (30, 60, 90, 120, 150, and 180 s) and observe the traffic patterns generated. Traffic patterns based on the entropy values of traffic features in high-intensity DDoS attack scenarios are shown in Fig. 3. We observe that all features have similar traffic patterns even though different window intervals are applied.

Furthermore, there is almost no difference in traffic patterns between these four window intervals. Entropy is being calculated more frequently in the 30-s interval compared to the 60-s interval, but both gave similar traffic patterns. The lack of differences in attack traffic and normal traffic patterns (also observed in low-intensity DDoS attack scenarios) suggest that the window size used for generating traffic feature entropy values only has a slight effect on the accuracy of DDoS attack detection.

214   A. Koay et al.

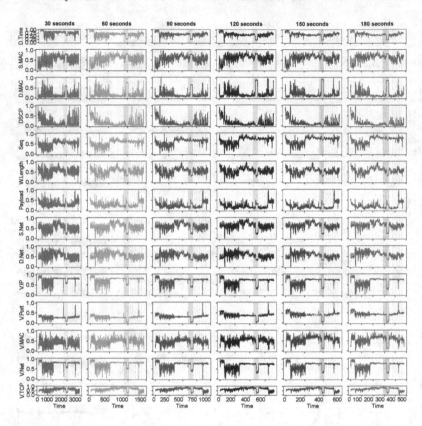

Fig. 3. Shannon entropy-based features with high-intensity attack constructed using different window sizes; grey area shows the period of the DDoS attack.

6 Effectiveness of Individual Entropy-Based Features

We analysed the effectiveness of each feature by using Pearson's Correlation, gain ratio, and information gain techniques found in the WEKA tool [3]. Table 3 shows the effectiveness ranking (correlation, information gain, and gain ratio) of entropy-based features in detecting low-intensity DDoS attacks based on 10-fold cross-validation on a single seed (seed = 1). D.Time, Protocol, W.Length, Payload, V.MAC, and V.TCP are consistently ranked within the top five in at least two out of three feature selection algorithms. These features, except for protocol, are not one of the commonly used features on most DDoS detection systems.

Table 4 shows the effectiveness ranking of entropy-based features in detecting high-intensity DDoS attacks. The top features in the high-intensity DDoS attack dataset are D.Port, D.MAC, Protocol, P.Length, Seq, V.Port and V.MAC. Unlike the results for low-intensity DDoS attack dataset, the top features that are effective in detecting high-intensity DDoS attacks include one of the normally used in DDoS attack detection systems as the attack used in this dataset focused on attacking the victim using the same destination port address.

Table 3. Effectiveness ranking in detecting low-intensity DDoS attacks

Feature	Correlation	Information gain	Gain ratio
D.Time	**3.5 ± 0.5**	17.6 ± 0.49	**3.3 ± 2.37**
S.IP	14.4 ± 0.66	9.9 ± 0.83	14.4 ± 0.66
D.IP	9.9 ± 0.3	12.4 ± 1.11	17.5 ± 0.5
S.Port	16.2 ± 0.4	6.9 ± 0.3	6.8 ± 0.75
D.Port	19 ± 0	15.9 ± 0.54	10.9 ± 1.22
S.MAC	8.2 ± 0.6	14.7 ± 0.64	13.7 ± 1.62
D.MAC	6 ± 0	8.1 ± 0.3	12.5 ± 0.5
S.Net	16.8 ± 0.4	13.5 ± 1.96	12.1 ± 4.04
D.Net	11 ± 0	13 ± 1.34	17.5 ± 0.5
Protocol	**5 ± 0**	6.3 ± 0.64	**1 ± 0**
P.Length	18 ± 0	10.5 ± 1.91	15 ± 1.41
DSCP	8.9 ± 0.3	18.5 ± 1.02	19 ± 0
Seq	7 ± 0	16.6 ± 3.93	9.2 ± 0.6
W.Length	**3.5 ± 0.5**	1 ± 0	**2.8 ± 0.6**
Payload	12.5 ± 0.5	2 ± 0	**5.4 ± 0.49**
V.IP	12.7 ± 0.78	11 ± 1	11.3 ± 0.46
V.Port	14.4 ± 0.66	3.6 ± 0.49	8.4 ± 0.8
V.MAC	**1 ± 0**	**3.4 ± 0.49**	**5.4 ± 1.2**
V.TCP	**2 ± 0**	**5.1 ± 0.3**	**3.8 ± 0.6**

Table 4. Effectiveness ranking in detecting high-intensity DDoS attacks

Feature	Correlation	Information gain	Gain ratio
D.Time	15 ± 0.77	**2 ± 0**	**2 ± 0**
S.IP	18.9 ± 0.3	8.4 ± 0.49	7.5 ± 1.86
D.IP	12 ± 0.77	11.7 ± 0.9	7.2 ± 1.4
S.Port	2.8 ± 0.4	14.9 ± 0.3	15.3 ± 0.46
D.Port	**4 ± 0**	**4 ± 0**	**4 ± 0**
S.MAC	14.3 ± 0.46	8.2 ± 0.98	9.3 ± 1.68
D.MAC	6 ± 0	**1 ± 0**	**1 ± 0**
S.Net	17 ± 0	7 ± 0.89	8.5 ± 1.75
D.Net	10.9 ± 0.83	10.6 ± 0.8	7.9 ± 1.37
Protocol	15.7 ± 0.46	**3 ± 0**	**3 ± 0**
P.Length	5 ± 0	11.6 ± 1.11	13.9 ± 0.54
DSCP	18.1 ± 0.3	14.1 ± 0.3	9.4 ± 1.36
Seq	7.9 ± 0.54	5 ± 0	13.2 ± 0.6
W.Length	10.9 ± 1.04	16 ± 0	16.7 ± 0.46
Payload	7.2 ± 0.4	6.4 ± 0.49	12.2 ± 0.4
V.IP	8.9 ± 0.3	19 ± 0	18.6 ± 0.66
V.Port	**1 ± 0**	12.1 ± 1.04	**5.3 ± 0.64**
V.MAC	2.2 ± 0.4	17.6 ± 0.49	18.3 ± 0.46
V.TCP	12.2 ± 1.08	17.4 ± 0.49	15.8 ± 1.54

From the results, we found several features that are more effective than the commonly used entropy-based features. We also found that D.Time and Protocol are the top features for detecting both high- and low-intensity DDoS attacks.

7 Summary of the Usefulness of Entropy-Based Features

In this paper, we examined the usefulness of entropy-based features in detecting DDoS attacks by analysing each entropy-based feature as shown in Fig. 1 to Fig. 3. We found that entropy-based features such as Protocol, and P.Length can show a more distinct difference between attack and normal traffic (refer Fig. 1). Our effectiveness ranking based on three feature selection algorithms shows that uncommon features such as D.Time, V.Port and V.MAC entropy-based features are the most effective in detecting both high- and low-intensity based DDoS attacks.

Although some entropy-based features can be effective in detecting a DDoS attack, they may not be effective for all types of DDoS attack. For example, Payload can be effective against DDoS attacks that transmit attack traffic at a low-intensity rate but may not be effective against DDoS attacks that send attack traffic at a high-intensity rate. D.IP is effective against DDoS attacks that send attack traffic to the same IP Address but may not be effective against DDoS attacks that send attack traffic to multiple IP addresses. An attacker can easily defeat the detection scheme based on single entropy features by randomising the attack traffic sending rate and IP addresses.

Also, at the earlier stage of an attack, the temporal change of a single entropy feature may be too small to be noticed by the detection scheme, especially when it is observed close to the attack source. Temporal changes are changes that could be observed over time. Entropy values before an attack and during an attack could be different based on the characteristics of attack traffic and its differences with normal traffic. These differences might not be noticeable in the early stage of an attack before the aggregated attack traffic meets at the aggregation point, but become more noticeable after some time where attack volumes are increasing over time.

8   Conclusion and Future Work

This paper evaluated a set of useful entropy-based features by exploring the effectiveness of entropy measures in detecting DDoS attacks and understanding the tradeoffs between detecting window size and detection accuracy of entropy-based features to construct effective entropy-based features. Our experiments showed that not all regular entropy-based features provide a clear distinction between attack and normal traffic patterns and window size used in entropy construction has minimal impact on overall accuracy. We also found that several uncommon features are more effective than the commonly used features in DDoS attack detection. In the future, we plan to work on the following items to further enhance the accuracy and generality of this approach:

- *Sliding window intervals.* In this paper, we only used a single fixed window interval. We plan to optimise the detection results by adopting a sliding window interval approach.
- *New machine learning classifier.* We found the top features that are effective and useful in detecting both high- and low-intensity DDoS attacks. We plan to further investigate the best machine learning classifier using those features to improve the results of DDoS detection.
- *Newer type of attacks.* Our evaluation dataset uses older types of DDoS attack. We plan to test the approach with newer and more recent of DDoS attacks such as NTP reflection attacks and DNS Amplification attacks.

References

1. Bhuyan, M.H., Bhattacharyya, D., Kalita, J.: E-LDAT: a lightweight system for DDoS flooding attack detection and IP traceback using extended entropy metric. Secur. Commun. Netw. **9**(16), 3251–3270 (2016)
2. Gu, Y., McCallum, A., Towsley, D.: Detecting anomalies in network traffic using maximum entropy estimation. In: Proceedings of the 5th ACM SIGCOMM Conference on Internet Measurement, p. 32. USENIX Association (2005)
3. Hall, M., Frank, E., Holmes, G., Pfahringer, B., Reutemann, P., Witten, I.H.: The WEKA data mining software: an update. ACM SIGKDD Explor. Newslett. **11**(1), 10–18 (2009)
4. Jun, J.H., Ahn, C.W., Kim, S.H.: DDoS attack detection by using packet sampling and flow features. In: Proceedings of the 29th Annual ACM Symposium on Applied Computing, pp. 711–712. ACM (2014)
5. Kottler, S.: February 28th DDoS Incident Report (2018). https://githuben gineering.com/ddos-incident-report/

6. Loukas, G., Öke, G.: Protection against denial of service attacks: a survey. Comput. J. **53**, 1020–1037 (2009)
7. Ma, X., Chen, Y.: DDoS detection method based on chaos analysis of network traffic entropy. IEEE Commun. Lett. **18**(1), 114–117 (2014)
8. Mousavi, S.M., St-Hilaire, M.: Early detection of DDoS attacks against SDN controllers. In: Proceedings of the International Conference on Computing, Networking and Communications (ICNC), pp. 77–81. IEEE (2015)
9. Nychis, G., Sekar, V., Andersen, D.G., Kim, H., Zhang, H.: An empirical evaluation of entropy-based traffic anomaly detection. In: Proceedings of the 8th ACM SIGCOMM Conference on Internet Measurement, pp. 151–156 (2008)
10. Özçelik, İ., Brooks, R.R.: Deceiving entropy based DoS detection. Comput. Secur. **48**, 234–245 (2015)
11. Shannon, C.E.: Communication theory of secrecy systems. Bell Labs Tech. J. **28**(4), 656–715 (1949)
12. Shiravi, A., Shiravi, H., Tavallaee, M., Ghorbani, A.A.: Toward developing a systematic approach to generate benchmark datasets for intrusion detection. Comput. Secur. **31**(3), 357–374 (2012)
13. Zhang, C., Cai, Z., Chen, W., Luo, X., Yin, J.: Flow level detection and filtering of low-rate DDoS. Comput. Netw. **56**(15), 3417–3431 (2012)
14. Zhang, J., Qin, Z., Ou, L., Jiang, P., Liu, J., Liu, A.: An advanced entropy-based DDoS detection scheme. In: Proceedings of the International Conference on Information Networking and Automation (ICINA), vol. 2, pp. V2–67 (2010)

Web and Usable Security

API Usability of Stateful Signature Schemes

Alexander Zeier$^{(\boxtimes)}$ ⓘ, Alexander Wiesmaier ⓘ, and Andreas Heinemann ⓘ

Darmstadt University of Applied Sciences,
Haardtring 100, 64295 Darmstadt, Germany
{alexander.zeier,alexander.wiesmaier,andreas.heinemann}@h-da.de

Abstract. The rise of quantum computers poses a threat to asymmetric cryptographic schemes. With their continuing development, schemes such as DSA or ECDSA are likely to be broken in a few years' time. We therefore must begin to consider the use of different algorithms that would be able to withstand powerful quantum computers. Among the considered algorithms are hash-based signature schemes, some of which, including XMSS, are stateful. In comparison to stateless algorithms, these stateful schemes pose additional implementation challenges for developers, regarding error-free usage and integration into IT systems. As the correct use of cryptographic algorithms is the foundation of a secure IT system, mastering these challenges is essential.

This work proposes an easy-to-use API design for stateful signature schemes, using XMSS(MT) as an example. Our design is based on findings from literature as well as on a series of interviews with software developers. It has been prototypically implemented and evaluated in small-scale user-studies. Our results show that the API can manage the stateful keys in a way that is transparent to the user. Furthermore, a preliminary online-study has shown that the API's documentation and applicability are comprehensible. However, due to the transparent state management, many of the study's participants were unaware of using a stateful scheme. This might lead to possible obstacles. Our current API design will serve as the basis for a larger user-study in order to review our preliminary findings in the next step.

Keywords: Post-quantum cryptography · API usability ·
Stateful signature schemes · Cryptographic agility

1 Introduction

1.1 The Need for Post-quantum Crypto Schemes

Quantum computers are the subject of ongoing research. With sufficient performance, they will be able to break the asymmetric schemes currently in use, such as RSA, DSA, ECDSA, and ECDH [10]. Their security is based on the prime factorization of large numbers and on the calculation of discrete logarithms,

© Springer Nature Switzerland AG 2019
N. Attrapadung and T. Yagi (Eds.): IWSEC 2019, LNCS 11689, pp. 221–240, 2019.
https://doi.org/10.1007/978-3-030-26834-3_13

respectively. For conventional computers, these are sufficiently difficult to solve if the parameters are suitably selected. However, this will no longer be the case when Shor's algorithms [28] are used on a sufficiently large quantum computer. The need for post-quantum cryptography (PQC), i.e. schemes secure enough to withstand a large quantum computer, is therefore evident.

In 2016, the National Institute of Standards and Technology (NIST) initiated a standardization process for PQC schemes.[1] These schemes are based on mathematical principles which are believed not to be vulnerable to quantum computer attacks. Hash-based schemes including XMSS [15], LMS [20] or SPHINCS [4] are possible candidates for post-quantum-secure algorithms. These schemes use hash functions to sign data and each signature requires a one-time key. Therefore, the private key contains a set of one-time keys. To record which keys have already been used, XMSS and LMS require a state. SPHINCS does not use a state and is therefore not considered within this work.

1.2   The Need for Usable Crypto APIs

The wrong usage of cryptographic functionality bears great risks and may lead to the leakage of personal data or identity theft. Therefore, the usage of cryptographic tools is indicated, if not for other reasons at least to be compliant with regulations such as GDPR[2]. This leads to an increasing integration of cryptographic functionality in software, including every-day applications such as instant messaging. Thus, more and more programmers, usually from other fields than cryptography, are using these APIs. Since these programmers are often unfamiliar with the required cryptographic principles, they struggle with the current APIs, which are too low-level for their needs [23]. Prior work shows that developers encounter problems using cryptographic APIs correctly [3,23,30]. Incorrect use of cryptographic APIs leads to insecure code, which in turn leads to an insecure application [11]. Therefore, easy-to-use APIs are playing an increasingly important role. Lazar et al. [19] have analyzed the vulnerabilities listed in the CVE database[3] and found that 83% of those vulnerabilities were caused by the incorrect use of cryptographic libraries, e.g. unsafe algorithms or hash functions were unknowingly applied, especially when using the default values provided by the API. Other errors included the use of weak random generators or private keys specified in the code.

Nadi et al. [23] have carried out 4 studies to point out typical problems regarding the use of cryptographic Java APIs. Problems included the time required to read resources such as the documentation, finding the correct sequence to call individual methods and insufficient knowledge about the domain. Similar to Acar et al. [3], the authors have identified good documentation, which should include examples for frequent tasks, as an important characteristic of a usable API. Many participants also mentioned the API design itself. The developers wish for

---

[1] https://csrc.nist.gov/Projects/Post-Quantum-Cryptography (2019-02-12).

[2] https://eugdpr.org (2019-06-07).

[3] https://cve.mitre.org (2019-03-09).

a *high-level* API that allows solving frequent tasks with only few method calls. Likewise, many developers requested tools to automatically detect faulty code and to provide code templates.

Stateful signature schemes introduce new challenges to the developer. In contrast to conventional signature schemes, the state of the private key changes with each signature. This property puts an extra burden to developers on their way to create secure applications. Even experienced developers may struggle with this new concept, as it differs from their experience and mental model. Our approach is to design an appropriate library that is easy to use from the developer's perspective. As to our knowledge, current implementations of stateful signature schemes (e.g. the XMSS implementation of Bouncy Castle[4]) do not automatically handle the states of the keys. How and whether the state is managed at all is entirely up to the developer, which indicates insufficient usability.

1.3 Goal and Approach

The goal of this paper is to design a cryptoagile, easy-to-use API for stateful and stateless signature schemes, focusing on a novel approach to handle the state of the private key.

To reach this goal, we investigate general design recommendations through literature research and conduct interviews with software developers (experts and non-experts) to collect a first set of requirements for our API. With these requirements, a prototype API for digital signatures, including the stateful scheme XMSS(MT), is designed and implemented. We evaluate our API in multiple iterations of small scale laboratory- and online-studies, improving our design with each iteration. These evaluation steps will provide us with an initial version of our API, ready to be used in a future, large-scale user-study.

The remainder of this work is structured as follows: we discuss related work (Sect. 2) as well as a new API layer for non-experts (Sect. 3), introduce our easy-to-use API for digital signatures, including stateful schemes (Sect. 4) and evaluate our API in user studies (Sect. 5). Section 6 concludes the paper and provides an outlook.

2   Related Work

Due to our interdisciplinary work, we discuss related work regarding stateful signature schemes and the management of their states (Sect. 2.1), the concept of cryptographic agility (Sect. 2.2), general recommendations for good API design (Sect. 2.3), research aiming to improve the usability of (cryptographic) APIs (Sect. 2.4) and methodology of online and laboratory studies (Sects. 2.5 and 2.6, respectively).

---

[4] https://www.bouncycastle.org/docs/docs1.5on/org/bouncycastle/pqc/jcajce/provider/xmss/package-frame.html (2019-02-21).

2.1   Stateful Signature Schemes and State Management

Buchmann et al. [8] describe the *eXtended Merkle Signature Scheme* (XMSS), an extension of the *Merkle Signature Scheme* (MSS) [22]. In XMSS, as well as in other hash-based signature schemes, the private key contains a limited set of one-time keys. As the name implies, these one-time keys can only be used once and therefore, only a limited amount of signatures can be performed with a single private key. The so-called state of the private key contains the information about which of the one-time keys have already been used. A further extension of XMSS is XMSSMT (*XMSS Multi Tree*). Through the introduction of subtrees in several layers, a practically unlimited number of signatures can be generated with comparable performance. Both schemes (XMSS and XMSSMT) are an Internet standard by the *IETF* [15].

Besides the reference implementation in C[5], a Java implementation for Bouncy Castle[6] exists as a lightweight API since version 1.57 and as a provider[7] implementation since version 1.58. Since we are using Java for our prototype implementation, we use the BC provider API as the basis to implement our own API (see Sect. 4). As of now, this is the only existing Java implementation for XMSS(MT).

McGrew et al. [21] investigate which measures must be taken to securely manage the states of hash-based signature schemes. They point out the danger of *cloning* in particular, especially by copying a virtual machine (VM) and with it the contained key material. A private key contained therein would then exist in two independent instances and could be used by both without synchronization.

Their work also mentions the risk of a *synchronization failure* in case the private key stored in the persistent storage fails to update at the same time or before the private key in RAM does, e.g. due to an application crash.

The authors consider the secure use of stateful signature methods possible in scenarios with dedicated hardware, but propose a hybrid scheme for general use. This includes scenarios that take the occurrence of *cloning* into account.

The paper also presents a strategy to increase efficiency by reserving states. The stateful private key is persistently stored n states in advance. Thus n keys are reserved for signing. Only if all reserved keys were used, the persistent storage would have to be accessed again.

We will take these considerations into account when designing our own API, by measures taken either in the implementation or in the documentation.

2.2   Cryptographic Agility

In order to respond to the constantly improving attacks on cryptographic schemes and primitives, APIs, cryptographic system components, and supporting libraries must be designed in a crypto-agile manner.

---

[5] https://github.com/joostrijneveld/xmss-reference (2019-03-09).

[6] https://www.bouncycastle.org (2019-03-09).

[7] https://docs.oracle.com/javase/8/docs/api/java/security/Provider.html   (2019-03-09).

In RFC7696 [14] the agility of algorithms is described as follows: *"Algorithm agility is achieved when a protocol can easily migrate from one algorithm suite to another more desirable one, over time"*. RFC6421 [24] offers a similar definition.

Schneider described cryptographic agility in a more general way: *"Cryptographic agility refers to how easy it is to evolve or replace the hardware, software, or entire information technology (IT) systems being used to implement cryptographic algorithms or protocols (and, in particular, whether the resulting systems remain "interoperable")"* (opening remarks at a workshop on Cryptographic Agility and Interoperability [17]).

The replacement of algorithms is necessary, for example, if weaknesses are found in the algorithms or their implementation. But also simply the age of the algorithms and the increasing processing power of modern computers will make the use of more advanced algorithms a necessary step [14]. A faulty protocol design can also lead to weaknesses. However, in general, an simple exchange of cryptographic algorithms does not solve the problem. Instead, the protocol itself has to be adapted [14].

The crypto-agile integration of stateful schemes into IT systems poses a challenge. Compared to classical schemes, additional steps have to be performed in order to manage the state of the private key. Our goal is to take the above mentioned factors into account when designing our own API, providing a crypto-agile solution for stateful and stateless cryptographic schemes.

2.3 API Design

Several authors formulate usability principles for APIs or for systems in general [5,13,25]. We designed our API according to the following principles, as they best fit our use case and provide a good starting point: *easy to learn, easy to use, hard to misuse, safe default values, good documentation, easy to read and to maintain code, easily extensible.*

2.4 Usability of (cryptographic) APIs

Acar et al. [1] investigate the usability of cryptographic APIs in Python. Their work compares 5 of such APIs, 3 of which state to have good usability. The results show that simpler APIs usually lead to more secure code. Auxiliary functions, e.g. for storing the key material, should also be part of the API, although often this is not the case. Good official documentation was also considered as crucial. If no clear documentation is provided, the developer may turn to other sources (e.g. *StackOverflow*[8]), resulting in erroneous code [3].

Acar et al. [1] also introduced a new usability scale that better fits for the evaluation of APIs than the *System Usability Scale* (SUS, [6]). This new scale correlates with the *SUS*. 11 statements (see Appendix) about an API's usability are used to calculate a score between 0 and 100, where higher values represent a better usability. The statements have to be rated by the participants of a

---

[8] https://stackoverflow.com (2019-03-09).

usability study from *1 = strongly disagree* to *5 = strongly agree*. We make use of this usability scale during our small-scale user-studies.

Google is developing the cryptographic API *Tink*[9] with focus on usability. Accordingly, the API is *"secure, easy to use correctly, and hard(er) to misuse"*. *Tink* is the (unofficial) successor to *Keyczar*[10]. Currently, however, *Tink* does not support stateful signature schemes. The design and development of such APIs, as it is carried out in the work at hand, is therefore still necessary. To the best of our knowledge, scientific literature on Tink, especially on usability tests of the API, does not (yet) exist.

CogniCrypt is an extension for the Eclipse IDE [18]. It provides a wizard for secure code generation and static code analysis to continuously ensure the correctness of the code. While this helps the developer to create and maintain secure code, the usability of the cryptographic API itself is not improved. In contrast, our goal is to address the problem in an earlier phase by designing an easy-to-use cryptographic API, independent from any IDE or platform used by the developer. Tools like *CogniCrypt* may further be used complementary to further improve the process of code creation and maintenance.

2.5   Related Online Studies

Acar et al. [1] conducted their online study using a specifically developed online test environment which is described in detail by Stransky et al. [29]. The participants, most of whom were acquired from GitHub[11], were asked to solve a number of cryptographic problems using a randomly assigned API. After completing the tasks, they were asked to participate in an online survey. Gorski et al. [12] use a similar methodology, including test environment and participant acquisition, evaluating the integration of security warnings into the API.

For our own study, we are using the same test environment as mentioned above. While our methodology is similar, we focus on the usability of stateful signature schemes in particular. To our knowledge, this is the first work that examines the usability of such schemes.

2.6   Related Laboratory Studies

Scheller and Kühn [26,27] have conducted various laboratory studies to investigate factors that influence the usability of an API's methods and classes and to compare different configuration-based design concepts. For this purpose, participants were invited into a laboratory environment in which they were asked to solve a number of programming tasks. Screen recordings were made to analyze the results. These recordings made it possible to determine, for example, precise time values required to perform various steps, such as reading a specific section

---

[9] https://github.com/google/tink (2019-03-09).
[10] https://github.com/google/keyczar (2019-03-17).
[11] These were sent invitations by e-mail that had previously been extracted from git commits.

of the tutorial or documentation, or initializing a required class. In [27] there were three groups of 9 participants each. All groups were asked to solve a series of tasks with a different design concept. The time required for these tasks was analyzed and evaluated in combination with other collected information. In [26] a total of 20 participants took part in the study. They were divided into 2 groups of 10 participants each. For each group, a different API was provided to solve a number of tasks. Both studies were moderated by a supervisor sitting next to the participant during the entire execution period, giving explanations on each task.

As mentioned before, the online studies discussed in Sect. 2.5 served as an orientation as we use their methodology to evaluate our own API.

To summarize, we create and evaluate a crypto-agile, easy-to-use API design for digital signature schemes, including stateful ones, using various methods and principles described in this section.

3 A New Layer for Non-experts

There are established Crypto-APIs providing standardized access to cryptographic functionality. Prominent examples are the Microsoft Cryptography API: Next Generation[12] (CNG) for MS Windows applications and the Java Cryptography Architecture[13] (JCA) for Java-based applications. These are used by professional programmers to implement cryptography code in the respective language for the given platforms.

While these APIs provide very flexible access to cryptographic functionality, they also demand a detailed understanding of the underlying mechanisms. On the one hand, this allows the experienced developer to make detailed decisions on how to implement their IT security measurements; a possibility that is surely needed when out-of-the-box solutions do not fit. On the other hand, this also leaves much room for errors, especially when the programmer is not skilled in the use of cryptography; errors that should be avoided, especially when out-of-the-box solutions suffice.

In order to provide suitable cryptographic APIs for both, experts with the need for detailed tweaking and inexperienced programmers with everyday needs, our design consists of a new abstraction layer.

Figure 1 shows the conceptual integration of our new layer on top of the JCA. On the right hand side, the expert user directly accesses the JCA API as it comes with the Java Development Kit[14] (JDK). On the left hand side, the non-expert user employs an easy-to-use API that provides out-of-the-box cryptography methods for common cryptography tasks. The easy-to-use API in

---

[12] https://docs.microsoft.com/en-us/windows/desktop/seccng (2019-02-27).

[13] https://docs.oracle.com/en/java/javase/11/security/java-cryptography-architecture-jca-reference-guide.html (2019-02-21).

[14] https://www.oracle.com/technetwork/java/javase/downloads/jdk11-downloads-5066655.html (2019-02-21).

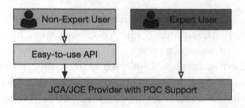

Fig. 1. Conceptual layer integration

turn, makes use of the JCA API. Note that the same design model can also be built upon other underlying standard APIs, e.g. CNG.

Besides providing a solution to the above described requirement of an expert API and to the demand for an error-proof API, this layered design comes with some additional advantages. Firstly, programmers that are already used to (and confident in) using the existing API (e.g. JCA or CNG) can continue to do so, they are not forced to use or learn an additional API. Secondly, the implementation of the easy-to-use API (by expert programmers) may be based (as in the example at hand) on an existing standard that already provides a suitable level of abstraction, especially regarding the exchange of underlying cryptographic algorithms. This way, our API inherits the cryptographic agility of that standard (see also Sect. 4.2).

4   EasySigner API

This section describes the *EasySigner* API[15], an easy-to-use API for digital signatures, providing a uniform interface for stateful and stateless signature schemes, both classical and post-quantum. A first prototype of this API, focusing on stateful signature schemes, is implemented in order to conduct small-scale usability tests (see Sect. 5). For the time being, we focus on a Java implementation of the API. We chose Java, as it is one of the most popular programming languages[16].

4.1   Requirements

Section 2 dealt with general design recommendations for (cryptographic) APIs. These were taken into account for the design of the *EasySigner* API.

Additionally, the results of four interviews with software developers from different German institutions were taken into account. These interviews were conducted to gain a deeper insight into the specific requirements for stateful signature schemes, also providing ideas and inspirations for the required methods, their naming and their placement. As is common in usability research, these

---

[15] Source code available at https://github.com/azeier-ucs/EasySigner-API.

[16] It was the most popular programming language in the StackOverflow developer survey 2018: https://insights.stackoverflow.com/survey/2018/ (2019-03-07).

interviews are intended to ensure that the API design meets the requirements and wishes of potential users.

Two of the interviewees were experienced Java developers with good knowledge of XMSS(MT) and cryptography in general (both rating their own Java (J) and crypto (C) knowledge with *high* or *very high*), working professionally with Java for 17 and 2 years, mostly on cryptographic tasks. The other two developers are less familiar with cryptography (C: *very low*, J: *medium*) or Java (J: *low*, C: *high*), respectively. All interviewees were acquaintances of the authors of this paper. The participation was voluntary and no incentive was given. These developers were chosen in order to gain insights from users with different skill sets. We will elaborate on the interviews in the following.

Interview Conduction. After familiarizing the interviewees with the topic at hand, they were asked about the challenges of using cryptographic APIs in general and stateful APIs in particular. In case of the two participants that were already familiar with the Bouncy Castle XMSS(MT) implementation, example code was presented at this point. For the other two participants, this was done at a later point during the interview. Here, the interviewees were asked to point out code fragments they felt were well or badly implemented. They were asked for example whether certain method calls appeared intuitive or whether the interviewees were unsure about their meaning. If an interviewee had already used the XMSS(MT) Java Provider, they could also report their own experiences.

Furthermore the interviewees were asked to write down their own ideas for an easy-to-use API for digital signatures, this way providing ideas for method names and required parameters as well as for the call sequence of related methods.

Interview Findings. According to all interviewees, a cryptographic API should be easy to use, even without any knowledge of cryptography or IT security, should provide secure default values that make it difficult to use the API incorrectly as well as a good documentation. In the following, several aspects are discussed in more detail:

Regarding the API's documentation, the interviewees stated missing examples for typical use cases. Instead, Google and StackOverflow are used, often resulting in insecure code, as already shown by Acar et al. [2].

In order to provide secure default values, *usage profiles* were suggested by some interviewees. Depending on the use case, e.g. for a Certification Authority (CA) or for code signatures, the respective usage profile contains *predefined values*[17] to be used by the developer. For some algorithms, suitable parameters already exist in literature. Hülsing et al. describe XMSS(MT) parameters for the use cases *Document and Code Signing* and *Communication Protocol* [16].

All interviewees preferred an automatic key management that does not require any interaction with the developer. This means the update of the key state is performed by the API with each signature. This requires the API to interact with the persistent storage of the key material.

---

[17] They are referred to as *predefined values* within the API's documentation, since the term profiles proved to be confusing in the first iteration of our usability tests.

Furthermore, backup strategies and parallel signing (which are also mentioned by Butin et al. [9]) were discussed. These aspects will not be considered further in this work, but will be part of future work.

Summarized Requirements. To summarize, Table 1 shows the requirements for the *EasySigner* API as determined through literature research and interviews. Additionally, the table states the source of each requirement and whether it was integrated in our prototype implementation (see Sect. 4.2).

Table 1. Requirements for the *EasySigner* API

	Requirements	Source	Prototype
Functional requirements	Usage profiles containing predefined values, e.g. for key generation	Interview	Yes
	Storing and loading key pairs from various storage formats, e.g. KeyStore file or HSM	Interview & Literature	Only KeyStore
	Automatic management of the key material, i.e. updating and persistent storage with every signature generation	Interview & Literature	Yes
	Reservation of states as described in Sect. 2.1	Literature	Yes
	Providing support for backups and parallel signing	Interview & Literature	No
Non-functional requirements	Easy to use for both experts and non-experts	Interview & Literature	Yes
	Good and complete documentation, including code examples	Interview & Literature	Yes
	In spite of the automated administration of the stateful key, the user should be aware that he is working with stateful keys and about the resulting risks	Interview & Literature	Yes

4.2 Design

We implemented a prototype of the *EasySigner* API. Since we are interested in the usability of stateful schemes in particular, only XMSS(MT) was implemented. We created dummy classes for RSA and ECDSA to demonstrate how stateless schemes fit within the API. This was also necessary to generate additional documentation and thus to be able to conduct a more realistic user-study.

We introduce a common abstraction layer for stateful and stateless signature schemes as presented in Sect. 3, meaning the state of a key will be handled by the API without any necessary actions from the developer. While other APIs, e.g. Java JCA, already provide ways to exchange the used algorithms in a modular way, we extend this ability to the exchange of stateless and stateful schemes. Therefore, the administration of the states must be within the scope of the API. Otherwise, additional method calls for stateful methods would be necessary. As our research show, this is also in the interest of the interviewed developers.

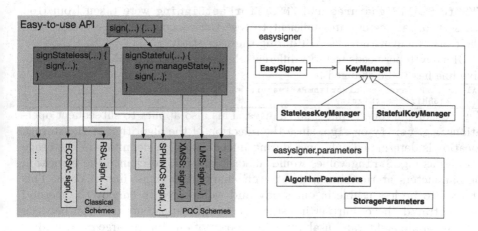

Fig. 2. API design   **Fig. 3.** API overview

For our implementation, we focus on non-expert users, trying to provide a high level API with the priority on easy usability. A JCA/JCE provider implementation, aiming at more experienced users, will be part of future work. Figure 2 shows a first design of the API. Depending on the signature scheme in use, the API calls the signing method for stateless or stateful schemes.

Figure 3 shows an overview of the *EasySigner* API. The API consists of the main class `EasySigner` that contains all methods needed for signing and verification. The class `KeyManager` is responsible for the management of the cryptographic keys. During initialization, the `EasySigner` object is given a `KeyManager` object, or has alternatively to be provided with the required parameters in order to create a `KeyManager` object by itself. There are two types of parameters: `AlgorithmParameters` and `StorageParameters`.

To give an example, the code to create a new XMSS key pair, stored in a `KeyStore`, looks like this:

```
AlgorithmParameters algorithmParameters = AlgorithmParameters.
    XMSSforSmallSignatures();
StorageParameters storageParameters = new KeystoreParameters("pathToFile",
    password);
EasySigner signer = EasySigner.withNewKeyPair(algorithmParameters,
    storageParameters);
```

This example uses *predefined values* for XMSS signatures. These default parameters ensure secure programming even for developers who lack the knowledge about which parameters to choose. These parameters may change over time, but can be renewed simply by updating the API or a corresponding configuration file. Changing any code is not necessary. This will be investigated further in future work. Nevertheless, by calling e.g.

```
AlgorithmParameters algorithmParameters = new XMSSParameters(20,
    XMSSParameters.SHA512);
```

the developer regains full control of the used parameters.

For the prototypical implementation of the API, the two *predefined values* `XMSSforSmallSignatures` and `XMSSMTforFastSigning` were taken from [16]. These two parameters are sufficient to test the concept of usage profiles and their placement within the API during the user study.

If a developer needs to use a different algorithm (e.g. XMSSMT), the respective line has to be changed to

```
AlgorithmParameters algorithmParameters = AlgorithmParameters.
    XMSSMTforFastSigning();
```

The rest of the code requires no changes. This also applies to subsequent operations, e.g. `verify` or `sign`, since the selection of the algorithm or the storage location is determined only once during initialization. A definition of the usage profiles as e.g. `String` values would make it possible to change the algorithm or parameters at runtime, without even changing a single line of code. This showed to be less usable in our study and we decided to employ the method demonstrated above. Further investigation of this (apparent) trade-off between cryptographic agility and usability will be part of our future large-scale study.

In case the `sign` method is called, either the `signStateless()` or `signStateful()` method will be executed depending on which algorithm is used (stateless or stateful). This is depicted in the architecture proposal in Fig. 2. To prevent corruption of the state, for example by multi-threading, `signStateful()` contains a *synchronized*[18] block for obtaining the current key as well as updating and storing the new key on the persistent storage. For this, the new updated key must first be stored before the old key is used. Otherwise a *synchronization failure* might occure (see Sect. 2.1).

The methods of the `KeyManager` class `createNewKeyPair()` and `loadKeyPair()` can either be called directly or by using the methods `withNewKeyPair()` and `withExistingKeyPair()` of the `EasySigner` class. These are *Factory* methods returning so-called *Singletons*. This prevents the initialization of several independent handles to the same Keypair. Once a new `KeyManager` is created with

---

[18] https://docs.oracle.com/javase/tutorial/essential/concurrency/syncmeth.html (2019-03-13).

the same Keypair as an existing one, the method returns the earlier created object. The Keypair is identified by its path.

For the `StorageParameters` only `KeystoreParameters` were implemented in the context of this work. The use of other formats or HSMs to store the key material will not be discussed any further.

The storage location is indicated by the `StorageParameters`. These can be for example `KeystoreParameters`, in which case a Java `KeyStore` object is used to store the key material on the hard disk. The `KeystoreParameters` object therefore contains at least the path to the file and the password to the `KeyStore`. For other parameters, such as the aliases for public and private keys as well as for the certificate, predefined values are assumed. If the actual values differ, for example from an already existing key pair, another constructor, also allowing the specification of these parameters, may be used.

Depending on what `AlgorithmParameters` are passed to the `KeyManager` during initialization, the `KeyManager` automatically creates and returns an instance of the subclass `StatefulKeyManager` or `StatelessKeyManager`. The main difference between these subclasses is the management of the key material. The `StatefulKeyManager` ensures that the stateful key is updated and persistently stored again before each signature automatically. This prevents the user from making mistakes during the implementation of his application, which might result in the key material not being updated correctly. Furthermore, the same code can be executed regardless of the chosen scheme, without any adjustments for stateful methods. Exchanging the algorithm, in our case the `Algorithm-Parameters`, is enough. This supports our goal of cryptographic agility.

For the realization of the state reservation strategy (see Sect. 2.1) the methods `signMultipleData()` in the `EasySigner` class and `updateKeyInAdvance()` in the `KeyManager` class were implemented. While `signMultipleData()` can be used for both stateful and stateless schemes, `updateKeyInAdvance()` is meaningful only with the use of stateful schemes, since otherwise no key updates are necessary. Nevertheless, for the sake of cryptographic agility, this method should also be available for stateless schemes, while calling it will have no effect.

5   User-Studies

To evaluate the usability of the designed API, a total of three iterations of small-scale user-studies were performed. Two in a laboratory setting with a total of 8 participants and one online study with 9 participants. After each iteration, the API was adjusted based on the results of the respective iteration. At the same time, we evaluated and adjusted the tasks, test environment and survey questions, leaving us prepared for our future large-scale study.

We conducted moderated laboratory studies. Since we had to change the location for almost each participant and therefore had to use a mobile laboratory setup, a non-moderated execution was not possible. The online study on the other hand was non-moderated, so we were able to gain results for both kinds of study. In the following, we will first present the procedures of the studies and then discuss the summarized results in a separate section.

Tasks. The user-study tasks were selected to test the complete functional range of the designed API. This includes the following API functions: Generating a key pair, storing and loading a key pair, creating a signature, verifying a signature, and increasing efficiency by reducing disk access.

Another crucial goal was to find out whether the participants were aware of working with stateful keys during the tasks.

For the first iteration, 4 tasks were given, each of them designed to cover at least one of the functions above. For the sake of a more realistic scenario and to save time, in the second iteration the same functions were tested within a single task. For the online study that same single task was used. Only the task's description was modified, adding details to better fit the online scenario and to compensate for the missing moderator.

Exit Survey. After completing the task(s), the participants were asked to answer questions about the API's usability. This was done to gain better insight into the difficulties that were encountered while solving the tasks and to receive further feedback. For the laboratory studies, this was done in form of an interview. In the online study, the participants were forwarded to a survey. Besides closed-ended questions, in which the participants could rate e.g. the correctness and security of their code and state whether they were aware of using a stateful scheme, they were also able to report usability issues in free text form.

In all iterations the participants were asked to rate a number of statements, leading to a usability score (see Sect. 2.4).

5.1   Laboratory Study

In the first two iterations of the evaluation, moderated usability tests were carried out with a total of 8 software developers. All developers had experience using Java, varying from only 2–3 years over 6–8 years to a maximum of 17 years. The experience with cryptography also varied from very high to almost non-existent. Before the study, none of the developers were familiar with XMSS(MT).

Furthermore, ethical considerations had to be taken into account. There were no ethical concerns regarding the laboratory study as the participation did cause no disadvantages of any kind. All participants took part in our study during their working hours with their employer's permission. No further risks were involved.

5.2   Online Study

After the completion of the laboratory studies, an online study was carried out to increase the number of participants and gain more significant data.

Setup. The online study was strongly based on the online studies conducted in [1,12]. From these studies, the test environment (*Developer Observatory*[19]),

---

[19] *Developer Observatory*, including setup guide, is available for download at https://github.com/developer-observatory/developer-observatory (2019-03-09).

including the consent form and introductory texts, was reused and only modified according to the deviating test subject.

Since *Developer Observatory* was originally implemented to test Python code, a few adjustments had to be made. In *Developer Observatory* the *Jupyter*[20] editor is used, which supports various programming languages via different kernels. For our online study the *SciJava*[21] kernel was chosen, because it worked most reliably during testing and allows the integration of custom JAR files.

Acquisition of Participants. Invitations to the online study were sent to mailing lists focusing on cryptography and online forums as well as posted to reddit boards about software, especially Java, development. As an incentive, three Amazon vouchers at a value of 100€ each were offered and randomly assigned to three participants after the study had been completed. Initially, there were no participants, presumably because of the required time to solve the task (about 1,5 hours was given as an estimate in the invitation) and the incentive not being guaranteed. Due to the lack of participants, additional invitations were sent to students and former students of our university. As a result, a total of 9 participants eventually completed the task (together with the exit survey). This is a sufficient amount for our pre-study, giving us a first insight into the current state of our API. The participants showed a broad variety regarding Java and cryptography knowledge, most of them being students or software developers.

5.3   Results

After each iteration the participants were asked to answer the API usability score in order to compare the results.

The result of the first iteration indicates a mediocre usability with an average of *68,06*. After integrating the feedback (e.g. about naming or method placement) into the API, a much better result could be achieved in the second iteration with an average of *87,08*. After the second iteration, only a small number of adjustments had to be made. In the following we will present the results of our online study in more detail. Since this was the latest study we conducted, all previous findings had been already integrated in the API's design, and therefore represents our current end result.

Table 2 (see Appendix) shows the determined API usability score of the *EasySigner* API. The table contains the 11 statements as described in Sect. 2.4. The score of *72,56* is slightly above the average value of *68* [7]. However, with a standard deviation of *12,86* there is also a strong dispersion of the results. In the following, the individual aspects of the score are discussed.

Comprehension. Statements 1–4 were rated mostly average or negative. These refer to the participant's comprehension of the API. Hence, the mere use of the API does not lead to a clear understanding of its functionality. The laboratory

---

[20] http://jupyter.org (2019-03-09).
[21] https://github.com/scijava/scijava-jupyter-kernel (2019-03-09).

studies showed that the documentation is hardly and rather reluctantly read, which may be a reason for the poor comprehension.

The lack of understanding of the API's functionality also leads to the fact that the participants were partly uncertain whether they had securely solved the task. They answered the question about the security of their solution with an average of $3,63/5$ wherein half of the participants answered with a 3 or less.

Of the 9 participants, 6 did not realize they were working with a stateful signature scheme, even though it was mentioned in various places in the documentation and in a console output when generating or loading the key pair. This seems to confirm the assumption that most participants did not carefully read the documentation.

Documentation. The documentation was consistently perceived as helpful. With an average of 4, a satisfactory result was achieved. Two faulty examples in the documentation were pointed out in the commentary by a participant, explaining his mediocre assessment of the documentation.

Also the *API Usability Score.* clearly shows that the documentation was perceived by the participants as very positive and helpful. They were able to find useful help easily (statement 7: $4,22$), helpful explanations (statement 8: $4,56$) and code examples (statement 9: $4,56$).

Naming and Usage. With an average of $4,89$, a nearly perfect score was achieved regarding naming. The usage of the API for solving the task was evaluated with an average of $4,11$. Analyzing the code written by the participants revealed that all of them had correctly and securely solved the task. As the survey showed, the participants themselves were confident about their solution.

Error Messages/Exceptions. Any error messages that occurred were also assessed as largely comprehensive by the participants (statement 10: $4,13$, statement 11: $4,5$, each with a minimum of 3).

6 Conclusion and Outlook

In this paper, we present an easy-to-use API design for signature schemes, introducing a novel approach to handle stateful signature schemes such as XMSS(MT). The design is based on a literature review and findings from interviews, conducted with software developers (experts and non-experts). We evaluate our design through small-scale laboratory and online studies, using a prototypical Java implementation of our API. We achieved our goal as it was described in Sect. 1.3. We were able to achieve very good results regarding the documentation and the usage of the API (ratings of the respective statements of the *API Usability Score* with an average >4 out of 5). Among the participants of the online study, however, the use of the API only resulted in a mediocre understanding of its functions and the used algorithms (average ratings of the respective statements ≈ 3 out of 5). This also includes the developers' awareness about working with stateful schemes. Most participants did not realize that they were using stateful keys. This may lead to security-critical errors. While the API ensures the update and persistent storage of the key material, it cannot prevent the key material from being duplicated outside the application or API. This could result in multiple use of a single state, ultimately compromising the key material. If the developer is not aware of this fact, he cannot assess whether or not such a scheme is suitable for a particular application.

Therefore, future work will investigate ways to make sure the developer fully aware of the statefulness of the schemes. This may include further improvement of the API's documentation or changing the API in a way that the statefulness is not transparent to the user, while still providing a crypto-agile solution.

Throughout the paper, various aspects for future work were mentioned. We summarize them here: (a) Investigating the possible trade-off between usability and cryptographic agility regarding the full fledged parameterization of the API, (b) Designing an update mechanism for the predefined values in our usage profiles, (c) Enhancing the API to support advanced functionality such as backing up the key material and perform parallel signing, (d) Transferring our key management approach to a JCA provider implementation.

The API will also be the subject of further improvements, including more usability tests at a larger scale. Part of these tests will be a comparison to other cryptographic APIs, e.g. regarding the time needed to solve certain tasks. It will be put into a larger context, being part of a comprehensive library for classical and post-quantum cryptography methods.

Acknowledgements. This project (HA proj. no. 633/18-56) is financed with funds of LOEWE – Landes-Offensive zur Entwicklung Wissenschaftlich-ökonomischer Exzellenz, Förderlinie 3 (State Offensive for the Development of Scientific and Economic Excellence). We thank our reviewers and the shepherd for their valuable feedback.

Appendix.   API Usability Score of the Online Study

Table 2. API usability score of the online study.

Statement	O1	O2	O3	O4	O5	O6	O7	O8	O9	∅	σ
1: I had to understand how most of the assigned library works in order to complete the tasks	5	3	3	4	2	2	2	5	2	3,11	1,27
2: It would be easy and require only small changes to change parameters or configuration later without breaking my code	4	2	4	5	4	4	4	3	5	3,89	0,93
3: After doing these tasks, I think I have a good understanding of the assigned library overall	2	1	4	2	3	3	3	3	3	2,67	0,87

(*continued*)

238   A. Zeier et al.

Table 2. (*continued*)

Statement	O1	O2	O3	O4	O5	O6	O7	O8	O9	∅	σ
4: I only had to read a little of the documentation for the assigned library to understand the concepts that I needed for these tasks	3	2	5	2	5	2	5	2	3	3,22	1,39
5: The names of classes and methods in the assigned library corresponded well to the functions they provided	4	5	5	5	5	5	5	5	5	4,89	0,33
6: It was straightforward and easy to implement the given tasks using the assigned library	3	4	5	3	5	4	5	3	5	4,11	0,93
7: When I accessed the assigned library documentation, it was easy to find useful help	4	5	5	4	4	2	5	5	4	4,22	0,97
8: In the documentation, I found helpful explanations	4	5	5	4	4	4	5	5	5	4,56	0,53
9: In the documentation, I found helpful code examples	4	5	5	4	5	4	5	4	5	4,56	0,53
10: When I made a mistake, I got a meaningful error message/exception	4	3	5	0	4	4	4	5	4	4,13	0,64
11: Using the information from the error message/exception, it was easy to fix my mistake	4	3	5	0	5	5	4	5	5	4,50	0,76
Result	57,5	62,5	90	60,5	82,5	65	87,5	65	82,5	72,56	12,81

∅ = average
σ = standard deviation

References

1. Acar, Y., et al.: Comparing the usability of cryptographic APIs. In: 2017 IEEE Symposium on Security and Privacy (SP), pp. 154–171 (2017). https://doi.org/10.1109/SP.2017.52
2. Acar, Y., Backes, M., Fahl, S., Kim, D., Mazurek, M.L., Stransky, C.: You get where you're looking for: the impact of information sources on code security. In: 2016 IEEE Symposium on Security and Privacy (SP), pp. 289–305 (2016). https://doi.org/10.1109/SP.2016.25
3. Acar, Y., Stransky, C., Wermke, D., Weir, C., Mazurek, M.L., Fahl, S.: Developers need support, too: a survey of security advice for software developers. In: 2017 IEEE Cybersecurity Development (SecDev), pp. 22–26 (2017). https://doi.org/10.1109/SecDev.2017.17
4. Bernstein, D., et al.: SPHINCS: practical stateless hash-based signatures. In: Oswald, E., Fischlin, M. (eds.) EUROCRYPT 2015. LNCS, vol. 9056, pp. 368–397. Springer, Heidelberg (2015). https://doi.org/10.1007/978-3-662-46800-5_15
5. Bloch, J.: Slides on how to design a good API and why it matters. In: Companion to the 21st ACM SIGPLAN Symposium on Object-Oriented Programming Systems, Languages, and Applications. ACM (2006)
6. Brooke, J.: SUS - a quick and dirty usability scale. Usability Eval. Ind. **189**(194), 4–7 (1996)
7. Brooke, J.: SUS: retrospective. J. Usability Stud. **8**(2), 29–40 (2013)
8. Buchmann, J., Dahmen, E., Hülsing, A.: XMSS - a practical forward secure signature scheme based on minimal security assumptions. In: Yang, B.-Y. (ed.) PQCrypto 2011. LNCS, vol. 7071, pp. 117–129. Springer, Heidelberg (2011). https://doi.org/10.1007/978-3-642-25405-5_8

9. Butin, D., Wälde, J., Buchmann, J.: Post-quantum authentication in OpenSSL with hash-based signatures. In: 2017 Tenth International Conference on Mobile Computing and Ubiquitous Network (ICMU), pp. 1–6. IEEE (2017). https://doi.org/10.23919/ICMU.2017.8330093

10. Chen, L., et al.: Report on Post-Quantum Cryptography. US Department of Commerce, National Institute of Standards and Technology (2016). https://doi.org/10.6028/NIST.IR.8105

11. Fahl, S., Harbach, M., Muders, T., Baumgärtner, L., Freisleben, B., Smith, M.: Why Eve and Mallory Love Android: an analysis of Android SSL (in) security. In: Proceedings of the 2012 ACM Conference on Computer and Communications Security, pp. 50–61. ACM (2012). https://doi.org/10.1145/2382196.2382205

12. Gorski, P.L., et al.: Developers deserve security warnings, too: on the effect of integrated security advice on cryptographic API misuse. In: Fourteenth Symposium on Usable Privacy and Security, SOUPS 2018, pp. 265–281. USENIX Association (2018)

13. Green, M., Smith, M.: Developers are not the enemy!: the need for usable security APIs. IEEE Secur. Priv. **14**(5), 40–46 (2016). https://doi.org/10.1109/MSP.2016.111

14. Housley, R.: Guidelines for Cryptographic Algorithm Agility and Selecting Mandatory-to-Implement Algorithms. BCP 201, RFC Editor (2015)

15. Hülsing, A., Butin, D., Gazdag, S., Rijneveld, J., Mohaisen, A.: XMSS: eXtended Merkle Signature Scheme. RFC 8391, RFC Editor, May 2018

16. Hülsing, A., Rausch, L., Buchmann, J.: Optimal parameters for $XMSS^{MT}$. In: Cuzzocrea, A., Kittl, C., Simos, D.E., Weippl, E., Xu, L. (eds.) CD-ARES 2013. LNCS, vol. 8128, pp. 194–208. Springer, Heidelberg (2013). https://doi.org/10.1007/978-3-642-40588-4_14

17. Johnson, A.F., Millett, L.I. (eds.): Cryptographic Agility and Interoperability: Proceedings of a Workshop. The National Academies Press, Washington, DC (2017). https://doi.org/10.17226/24636

18. Krüger, S., et al.: CogniCrypt: supporting developers in using cryptography. In: Proceedings of the 32nd IEEE/ACM International Conference on Automated Software Engineering, pp. 931–936. IEEE Press (2017). https://doi.org/10.1109/ASE.2017.8115707

19. Lazar, D., Chen, H., Wang, X., Zeldovich, N.: Why does cryptographic software fail? A case study and open problems. In: Proceedings of 5th Asia-Pacific Workshop on Systems, pp. 1–7. ACM Press (2014). https://doi.org/10.1145/2637166.2637237

20. McGrew, D., Curcio, M., Fluhrer, S.: Leighton-Micali Hash-Based Signatures. RFC 8554, RFC Editor, April 2019

21. McGrew, D., Kampanakis, P., Fluhrer, S., Gazdag, S.-L., Butin, D., Buchmann, J.: State management for hash-based signatures. In: Chen, L., McGrew, D., Mitchell, C. (eds.) SSR 2016. LNCS, vol. 10074, pp. 244–260. Springer, Cham (2016). https://doi.org/10.1007/978-3-319-49100-4_11

22. Merkle, R.C.: A certified digital signature. In: Brassard, G. (ed.) CRYPTO 1989. LNCS, vol. 435, pp. 218–238. Springer, New York (1990). https://doi.org/10.1007/0-387-34805-0_21

23. Nadi, S., Krüger, S., Mezini, M., Bodden, E.: Jumping through hoops: why do Java developers struggle with cryptography APIs? In: Proceedings of the 38th International Conference on Software Engineering, pp. 935–946. ACM Press (2016). https://doi.org/10.1145/2884781.2884790

24. Nelson, D.: Crypto-Agility Requirements for Remote Authentication Dial-In User Service (RADIUS). RFC 6421, RFC Editor (2011)

25. Nielsen, J.: Usability Engineering. Elsevier, Amsterdam (1994)
26. Scheller, T., Kuhn, E.: Influencing factors on the usability of API classes and methods. In: 2012 IEEE 19th International Conference and Workshops on Engineering of Computer-Based Systems, pp. 232–241 (2012). https://doi.org/10.1109/ECBS.2012.27
27. Scheller, T., Kühn, E.: Usability evaluation of configuration-based API design concepts. In: Holzinger, A., Ziefle, M., Hitz, M., Debevc, M. (eds.) SouthCHI 2013. LNCS, vol. 7946, pp. 54–73. Springer, Heidelberg (2013). https://doi.org/10.1007/978-3-642-39062-3_4
28. Shor, P.W.: Polynomial-time algorithms for prime factorization and discrete logarithms on a quantum computer. SIAM J. Comput. **26**(5), 1484–1509 (1997). https://doi.org/10.1137/S0097539795293172
29. Stransky, C., et al.: Lessons learned from using an online platform to conduct large-scale, online controlled security experiments with software developers. In: 10th USENIX Workshop on Cyber Security Experimentation and Test, CSET 2017 (2017)
30. Xie, J., Lipford, H.R., Chu, B.: Why do programmers make security errors? In: 2011 IEEE Symposium on Visual Languages and Human-Centric Computing (VL/HCC), pp. 161–164 (2011). https://doi.org/10.1109/VLHCC.2011.6070393

(Short Paper) Method for Preventing Suspicious Web Access in Android WebView

Masaya Sato$^{(\boxtimes)}$, Yuta Imamura, Rintaro Orito, and Toshihiro Yamauchi$^{(\boxtimes)}$

Graduate School of Natural Science and Technology, Okayama University,
Okayama 700-8530, Japan
{sato,yamauchi}@cs.okayama-u.ac.jp

Abstract. WebView is commonly used by applications on the Android OS. Given that WebView is used as a browsing component on applications, they can be attacked via the web. Existing security mechanisms mainly focus on web browsers; hence, securing WebView is an important challenge. We proposed and implemented a method for preventing suspicious web access in Android WebView. Attackers distribute their malicious content including malicious applications, potentially unwanted programs, and coin miners, by inserting contents into a web page. Because loading malicious content involves HTTP communication, our proposed method monitors HTTP communication by WebView and blocks suspicious web accesses. To apply the proposed method to widely used applications, we implemented our method inside WebView. We also evaluated the proposed method with some popular applications and confirmed that the method can block designated web content without impeding the functionality of applications.

Keywords: WebView · Android · Web access ·
HTTP communication · Content blocking

1 Introduction

Android is a widely used operating system for mobile devices. As of February 2019, approximately 74% of mobile devices in the world run Android [1]. Many Android applications use WebView, which is a framework to embed a browser component inside applications. Developers can insert a web page within an application using WebView. This means developers can create applications content using HTML and JavaScript by using WebView [2]. This implies that a web-based attack can be effective against Android applications. For example, JavaScript code for mining cryptocurrency can be executed on applications using WebView. Although many existing attacks exploit vulnerabilities in applications or operating systems [3], web-based attacks present a significant opportunity for attackers. Security researchers statically and dynamically analyze applications to find and remove vulnerabilities. WebView is a browser component, i.e., the

© Springer Nature Switzerland AG 2019
N. Attrapadung and T. Yagi (Eds.): IWSEC 2019, LNCS 11689, pp. 241–250, 2019.
https://doi.org/10.1007/978-3-030-26834-3_14

content in applications is dynamically loaded during run-time. Thus, static analysis is useless for detecting attacks via WebView. Even though dynamic analysis is effective for analyzing applications using WebView, it is difficult to prevent malicious or suspicious content from being loaded. While the same versions of applications and operating systems are used, web content is changed dynamically. Therefore, security analysts cannot guarantee that the web content loaded via WebView is secure, thus run-time protection for dynamic content is required.

Google's safe browsing technology can protect users from suspicious webpages [4]. Web browsers can check if the accessing URL is secure using the safe browsing API. The safe browsing lists are maintained by Google. The list holds the hash values of unsafe URLs including malware, unwanted software, and social engineering. Safe browsing is employed by the Chrome web browser. Following this, safe browsing features have been added to WebView for Android 8.0 and above. Since WebView 66, safe browsing is turned on by default in all applications using WebView. However, the detection rate for safe browsing is not high. In our survey, safe browsing only detects 34 out of 100 phishing sites and cannot detect a fake alert window. In addition, safe browsing only blocks content based on URL information. If the URL corresponding to a malicious web site is changed, it is no longer detected as malicious.

Herein, we propose a method for preventing suspicious communication on Android WebView. The proposed method monitors HTTP requests within the WebView framework and blocks suspicious content based on a blacklist. Given that the proposed method only blocks HTTP requests to suspicious content, the functionality of the application itself is not affected. We modified WebView to apply the proposed method to various applications. To verify the effectiveness of the proposed method, we conducted experiments to detect and block malicious web sites and found that the proposed method successfully blocked the content.

2   WebView

WebView is a framework to insert web contents within applications running on Android. Developers can create portable application components with HTML and JavaScript. In addition, developers can change the design and content of applications by changing the content loaded by WebView without updating the application itself. Conventionally, WebView is a component in the Android Framework. Since Android 5.0, WebView has been independent of the Android Framework and has been implemented as a system application. This enables us to update WebView without updating the entire Android system.

Figure 1 shows the overview of a process for accessing a web page via WebView. First, an application calls the WebView API. The Android framework receives the call and calls a method inside the WebView application. The Java layer of the WebView application receives the request and calls the URLRequest API, which is implemented as a C/C++ layer of the WebView application. Finally, the C/C++ component layer requests communication with the Linux kernel.

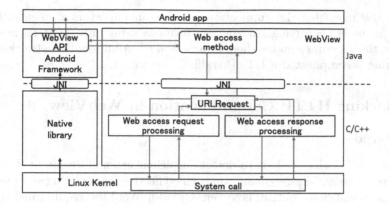

Fig. 1. Overview of WebView

3 Related Work

3.1 Run-Time Detection of Malicious Behavior

MADAM is a malware detection tool for Android [5]. MADAM monitors multiple behaviors in Android at four levels and five groups of features including system calls, SMS messages, critical APIs, user activities, and application metadata. Combining multiple features at multiple levels and various groups, MADAM enables run-time detection anomalous behaviors. Although MADAM is an efficient and accurate detection method for an Android system as a whole, we mainly focus on its behavior of WebView. Hence complicated analysis combining multiple features is not required. This simplifies our approach and makes it easier to integrate multiple components. AdCapsule is a sandboxing technique specifically aimed at advertisements in Android applications [6]. AdCapsule intercepts APIs have privacy issues without modification to applications' code and Android framework using the Java dynamic proxy mechanism. This technique enables hooking APIs called by in-app ad libraries. Zhu et al. implemented two types of sandboxes for isolating untrusted ad libraries from the application considering permissions and file operations [6]. Although AdCapsule also covers WebView and does not requires rooting, it can only acquire information related to observable APIs. Because our approach modifies WebView's code, more information can be acquired before calling APIs. Furthermore, our approach focuses not only on the ad but also on other communication.

3.2 Network-Based Blocking

Detecting malicious web access by network monitoring is a conventional and effective approach. Although host-based approaches strongly depend on the software and hardware of the device, network-based approaches are not affected by the device. This means that the monitor cannot distinguish the software or devices being used. Because various applications are installed on Android devices, distinguishing the applications used is an important challenge. Some studies focus on identifying Android applications using only TCP/IP headers; however, their accuracy makes them impractical [7]. Additionally, network-based monitoring is complicated if HTTP traffic is encrypted.

4   Blocking HTTP Communication in WebView

4.1   Purpose

The main goal of this study is to detect suspicious communication of WebView and prevent access. Thus, dynamic analysis is effective for detecting and preventing access to malicious content; however, exploring WebView requires insight into the processing of WebView. Because modules are abstracted and isolated, gaining insights into WebView from the outside incurs a high cost. Network-based detection and blocking are effective without extensive knowledge of WebView; however, they cannot determine which communications are triggered by WebView. Thus, detecting and blocking communication in WebView is required.

4.2   Requirements

There are two requirements for preventing web access in WebView.

R1. Detect web access triggered by WebView
R2. Control web access based on a policy

To prevent access to malicious web sites, detecting web access in WebView is required. Thus, the present study applied a method presented in a previous study to detect web access in WebView [8].

To decide which access must be prevented, web access must be controlled based on some information after detection. For example, if only some of the content on a web page is malicious, it is better to prevent loading just the malicious parts. A naive approach, such as this is effective; however, it reduces usability. A more fine-grained control for web access is required.

Moreover, maintaining usability is necessary. A security mechanism that disturbs usability is not preferable, especially for smartphone use; hence, a mechanism that does not affect functionality of the application and has a low overhead is required.

4.3   Detecting Communication

We developed and implemented WebView Monitor, a web access monitoring mechanism for Android WebView to monitor web access by WebView on Android [8]. It is implemented as a modified WebView; thus, it is possible to install WebView Monitor by simply replacing the WebView system application on an Android device. We modified WebView's C++ layer to monitor web access including HTTP/1, HTTP/1.1, SPDY, and HTTP/2 via WebView on Android.

The modified part is web access request processing and web access response processing, as shown in Fig. 1. The monitor detects web access on WebView and logs the following information:

1. Time stamp
2. The package name of an application
3. HTTP request header
4. URL
5. IP address
6. Port number of the web server
7. HTTP request body
8. HTTP response header
9. HTTP response body

Information of items 1 to 6 can be acquired immediately after generation of the HTTP request header. Information of item 7 can be acquired before sending the HTTP request body. Information of item 8 can be acquired after reception of the HTTP response header. Information of item 9 can be acquired after reception of the HTTP response body. Using WebView Monitor, R1 is fulfilled.

4.4 Blocking Communication

Certain triggers are considered as a step to block web access in WebView. The triggers and acquirable information can be summarized as:

1. Immediately after generation of the HTTP request header
   WebView first constructs the request header. In this phase, the proposed method can acquire the time stamp, package name of an application, HTTP request header, URL, IP address, and the port number of the web server.
2. Before sending the HTTP request body
   WebView sends the HTTP request body after sending the request header based on the constructed header. In this phase, the proposed method can acquire the HTTP request body.
3. After reception of the HTTP response header
   WebView receives the HTTP response header before receiving a response body. In this phase, the proposed method can acquire the HTTP response header.
4. After reception of the HTTP response body
   WebView receives the HTTP response body from the web server. In this phase, the proposed method can acquire the HTTP response body.

From the viewpoint of fine-grained inspection and control of web access, triggers 1 and 4 fulfill R2. It is difficult to control web access in triggers 2 and 3 because acquirable information is less characteristic. Because the proposed method can acquire various information using trigger 1, several types of control policies can be considered. Moreover, controlling and blocking web access after reception of the HTTP response body is not suitable for R2 and maintaining usability. Inspecting and removing malicious parts of the web content after reception of the HTTP response body would enable improved control for users; however, this requires a fully functional interpreter for the web content. This requires a comprehensive analysis and a long time. Compared to this, controlling the web access in trigger 1 requires no connection to the servers because the proposed method can control before establishing the connection. There is no need to wait for the reception of a HTTP response body from the server; therefore, no delay occurs. In addition, the size of information that can be acquired in trigger 1 is typically constant compared to the HTTP response body. Thus, comprehension of the information acquirable in trigger 1 takes a short time. It is beneficial for retaining usability. For this reason, we employed trigger 1 for controlling web access in WebView.

The proposed method controls web access in trigger 1, using the above mentioned acquirable information. In particular, as the URL and IP address are characteristic and commonly used in detection for malicious web sites, we employed them for policy construction. Construction of prevention policy is described in Sect. 5.2.

5   Implementation

5.1   Blocking HTTP Request

WebView supports various protocols including HTTP/1, HTTP/1.1, SPDY, and HTTP/2. Methods for these protocols are not shared and are defined in various source codes. To summarize, we implemented the proposed method in HttpStreamParser and SpdyHttpStream interfaces for HTTP/1.1 and SPDY, respectively. However, the basic structure of each implementation is similar; therefore, we describe the implementation in the HTTP case.

Some implementation methods are considered to block HTTP access: if a method fails, a failed value is returned, or stops calling the method from the first. The former two implies an interrupt for the method. This may cause unexpected side effects on the application; hence, it could lead to a crash or reduction of usability of the application. HTTP requests in particular are invoked in an asynchronous manner in Android WebView. Interrupting or causing a call to fail will result in an unexpected situation. In contrast, giving up calling a method for the HTTP request has no effect. Thus, WebView stops calling a method for HTTP requests when the constructed HTTP request header is detected as potentially malicious. For this reason, the proposed method stops calling a method for the HTTP request when the acquired information matches the blacklist.

5.2   Prevention Policy

In our prototype, we defined domain names and IP addresses as a key to determine what access to block. For example, URLs of phishing web sites are frequently changed and have a short lifetime to avoid detection [9]. Therefore, prevention based on just URL is not effective. For covering a wider range web sites, we added an IP address as an entry of prevention policy. IP addresses correspond to web sites for phishing or malware distribution have a longer lifetime compared to URLs [10]. Thus, prevention via IP addresses in addition to URLs is more effective for detecting and preventing access to malicious web sites.

Other information, that can be acquired using the proposed method would help to construct a more effective blacklist. For example, the port number of the web server or HTTP response header/body will help us find characteristics of malicious web sites. Constructing a prevention policy with this additional information and experiments with malicious web sites will be addressed in the future.

5.3   Limitation

To install modified WebView the original WebView must be removed. While the proposed method is simple and powerful, it requires the Android device to be rooted. Installing new applications into devices does not require rooting; however, WebView is a system application. Android requires rooting when replacing system applications.

6   Evaluation

6.1   Experimental Detection and Prevention

To verify the effectiveness of the proposed method, we performed experiments to detect and block loading of suspicious content. Because our prototype just accepts blacklists with URLs and IP addresses, we experimented blocking based on URLs and IP addresses.

We chose two types of malicious web pages: coin miners and fake alerts. Coin miner is a program to mine cryptocurrency. Cryptomining has become popular not only for legitimate use but also in criminal activities [11]. One of the most famous coin miner application was hosted by Coinhive [12] and 52% of organizations were affected [13]. Coinhive executes a small chunk of JavaScript code instead of displaying an advertisement to the website visitor. This makes it possible to mine "Monero", which is a cryptocurrency, with the processing power of their devices, and earn money. However, Coinhive can be injected by attackers without the web site owner's knowledge or permission. Thus, Coinhive can be used to mine "Monero," illegally [14]. As of March 2018, it has been reported that Coinhive is running on 32,000 websites [15]. Although Coinhive is no longer operational, other similar services can be used in the same manner.

In addition to coin miners, we also verified the detection of fake alerts. Fake alerts are mainly used to lead users to click ads or malicious links by inciting a sense of danger. A fake ad suddenly appears on the web site and redirects users to malicious web sites. Viewers were alarmed when they saw the alert claiming that their smartphone was not secure or sensitive data has been leaked. Then,

[info]timestamp: 2018_12_12_16_14_55_899932
app: com.twitter.android
[request_info]
url: https://coinhive.com/lib/coinhive.min.js
ip: 104.20.209.59
port: 443
method: GET
[request_headers]
Host: coinhive.com
Connection: keep-alive
User-Agent: Mozilla/5.0 (Linux; Android 6.0; Android SDK built for x86
Build/MASTER; wv) AppleWebKit/537.36 (KHTML, like Gecko) Version/4.0
Chrome/60.0.3094.2 Safari/537.36 TwitterAndroid
Accept: */*
Referer: http://mortgagespeak.com/
Accept-Encoding: gzip, deflate
Accept-Language: en-US
X-Requested-With: com.twitter.android

Fig. 2. Communication log of installing Coinhive.

they would click the ad showing security applications, ignoring its reliability. To make matters worse, the JavaScript code within the fake alerts automatically redirects the page to malicious contents. Consequently, viewers load malicious JavaScript exploiting vulnerabilities or download malicious applications.

We verified the proposed method from the following viewpoints:

1. Detection and prevention of loading JavaScript codes hosted by Coinhive
2. Detection and prevention of sending mining results to the Coinhive server
3. Detection and prevention of loading fake alerts

To prevent loading of mining JavaScript code, we added the domain name of Coinhive to the blacklist. This also prevents sending mining results to the Coinhive server. Although the JavaScript code is not loaded from the Coinhive server, embedded scripts can mine "Monero." The mining results must be submitted to the Coinhive server; thus, it is also necessary to prevent mining results from being sent. In addition to blocking based on domain names, we also added the IP address of a server, which was hosting fake alerts.

Figure 2 shows the communication log of downloading JavaScript of Coinhive. This result shows that the proposed method can detect and prevent downloading the JavaScript code of Coinhive. Moreover, all web access to the Coinhive server, including the establishment of a mining pool, was prevented as the download was blocked.

Figure 3 shows the communication log of sending mining result to Coinhive server. This result shows that the proposed method can detect and prevent establishing connections to send the mining results to the Coinhive server. Additionally, the complete mining pool was not established by blocking this access using the Coinhive domain.

We also confirmed that no fake alert or redirections to malicious web sites occurred when accessing the web page showing fake alerts in regular access. In summary, the experimental results show that blocking with domain names and IP addresses was successful and the functionality of the application was not lost.

[info]timestamp: 2018_12_12_16_4_22_448400
app: com.twitter.android
[request_info]
url: wss://ws022.coinhive.com/proxy
ip: 37.187.167.69
port: 443
method: GET
[request_headers]
Host: ws022.coinhive.com
Connection: Upgrade
Pragma: no-cache
Cache-Control: no-cache
Upgrade: websocket
Origin: http://mortgagespeak.com
Sec-WebSocket-Version: 13
User-Agent: Mozilla/5.0 (Linux; Android 6.0; Android SDK built for x86
Build/MASTER; wv) AppleWebKit/537.36 (KHTML, like Gecko) Version/4.0
Chrome/60.0.3094.2 Safari/537.36 TwitterAndroid
Accept-Encoding: gzip, deflate
Accept-Language: en-US
X-Requested-With: com.twitter.android
Sec-WebSocket-Key: rqUj68NQ/UJTZnbJdocgTw==
Sec-WebSocket-Extensions: permessage-deflate; client_max_window_bits

Fig. 3. Communication log of sending mining result to Coinhive server.

6.2 Performance Measurement

We also evaluated the overhead of the proposed method. We measured the performance for accessing the Coinhive server per Request/Response with the proposed method. The evaluation results showed that the overheads in detecting and preventing access to Coinhive server using HTTP and SPDY protocols was 0.017 ms and 0.015 ms, respectively. These overheads are very small, and the total effect on the performance of WebView itself is limited; thus, the proposed method can detect and prevent such access without reducing usability.

7 Conclusion

We proposed a method to detect and prevent access to suspicious web pages on Android WebView. We modified WebView to monitor HTTP, HTTPS, and SPDY access to web pages and match its domain names and IP addresses with a blacklist. Because applications using WebView calls a system WebView application, replacing the WebView application with the modified version enables us to apply the proposed method to all applications using WebView. We evaluated the effectiveness of the proposed method using the Coinhive mining JavaScript and fake alerts. The evaluation results showed that the proposed method successfully prevented loading of the Coinhive JavaScript, sending mining results, and displaying fake alerts. The performance evaluation showed that the proposed method does not reduce usability. Further experiments on malicious web sites will be performed in the future.

Acknowledgement. The research results have been achieved by "WarpDrive: Web-based Attack Response with Practical and Deployable Research InitiatiVE," the Commissioned Research of National Institute of Information and Communications Technology (NICT), Japan.

References

1. StatCounter: Mobile operating system market share worldwide. http://gs.statcounter.com/os-market-share/mobile/worldwide. Accessed 2 Apr 2019
2. Acar, Y., Backes, M., Bugiel, S., Fahl, S., McDaniel, P., Smith, M.: Sok: Lessons learned from android security research for appified software platforms. In: 2016 IEEE Symposium on Security and Privacy (SP), pp. 433–451. IEEE (2016)
3. Hur, J.B., Shamsi, J.A.: A survey on security issues, vulnerabilities and attacks in android based smartphone. In: 2017 International Conference on Information and Communication Technologies (ICICT), pp. 40–46. IEEE (2017). https://doi.org/10.1109/ICICT.2017.8320163
4. Google: Safe Browsing. https://safebrowsing.google.com/. Accessed 2 Apr 2019
5. Chin, E., Wagner, D.: Bifocals: analyzing webview vulnerabilities in android applications. In: Kim, Y., Lee, H., Perrig, A. (eds.) WISA 2013. LNCS, vol. 8267, pp. 138–159. Springer, Cham (2014). https://doi.org/10.1007/978-3-319-05149-9_9
6. Zhu, X., Li, J.: AdCapsule: Practical confinement of advertisements in android applications. In: IEEE Transactions on Dependable and Secure Computing. IEEE (2018). https://doi.org/10.1109/TDSC.2018.2814999
7. Alan, H.F., Kaur, J.: Can android applications be identified using only TCP/IP headers of their launch time traffic? In: Proceedings of the 9th ACM Conference on Security & Privacy in Wireless and Mobile Networks, pp. 61–66. ACM (2016). https://doi.org/10.1145/2939918.2939929
8. Imamura, Y., Uekawa, H., Ishihara, Y., Sato, M., Yamauchi, T.: Web access monitoring mechanism for android webview. In: Proceedings of the Australasian Computer Science Week Multiconference, pp. 1:1–1:8. ACM (2018). https://doi.org/10.1145/3167918.3167942
9. Dou, Z., Khalil, I., Khreishah, A., Al-Fuqaha, A., Guizani, M.: Systematization of knowledge (SoK): a systematic review of software-based web phishing detection. IEEE Commun. Surv. Tutor. **19**(4), 2797–2819 (2017). https://doi.org/10.1109/COMST.2017.2752087
10. Lever, C., Kotzias, P., Balzarotti, D., Caballero, J., Antonakakis, M.: A lustrum of malware network communication: evolution and insights. In: 2017 IEEE Symposium on Security and Privacy (SP), pp. 788–804. IEEE (2017)
11. Rüth, J., Zimmermann, T., Wolsing, K., Hohlfeld, O.: Digging into browser-based crypto mining. In: Proceedings of the Internet Measurement Conference 2018, pp. 70–76. ACM (2018). https://doi.org/10.1145/3278532.3278539
12. Coinhive: Coinhive. https://coinhive.com/. Accessed 3 Dec 2018
13. Check Point: 2017 Global Cyber Attack Trends Report. https://research.checkpoint.com/cyber-attack-trends-mid-year-report/. Accessed 2 Apr 2019
14. Segura, J.: Drive-by cryptomining campaign targets millions of Android users. https://blog.malwarebytes.com/threat-analysis/2018/02/drive-by-cryptomining-campaign-attracts-millions-of-android-users/. Accessed 2 Apr 2019
15. Krebs, B.: Who and what is coinhive? https://krebsonsecurity.com/2018/03/who-and-what-is-coinhive/. Accessed 2 Apr 2019

Public-Key Primitives 2

Equivalence Between Non-malleability Against Replayable CCA and Other RCCA-Security Notions

Junichiro Hayata[1,3]([✉]), Fuyuki Kitagawa[2], Yusuke Sakai[3], Goichiro Hanaoka[3], and Kanta Matsuura[1]

[1] The University of Tokyo, Tokyo, Japan
{hayata,kanta}@iis.u-tokyo.ac.jp
[2] NTT Secure Platform Laboratories, Tokyo, Japan
fuyuki.kitagawa.yh@hco.ntt.co.jp
[3] National Institute of Advanced Industrial Science and Technology (AIST), Tokyo, Japan
{yusuke.sakai,hanaoka-goichiro}@aist.go.jp

Abstract. Replayable chosen ciphertext (RCCA) security was introduced by Canetti, Krawczyk, and Nielsen (CRYPTO 03) in order to handle an encryption scheme that is "non-malleable except tampering which preserves the plaintext". RCCA security is a relaxation of CCA security and a useful security notion for many practical applications such as authentication and key exchange. Canetti et al. defined non-malleability against RCCA (NM-RCCA), indistinguishability against RCCA (IND-RCCA), and universal composability against RCCA (UC-RCCA). Moreover, they proved that these three security notions are equivalent when considering a PKE scheme whose plaintext space is super-polynomially large. Among these three security notions, NM-RCCA seems to play the central role since RCCA security was introduced in order to capture "non-malleability except tampering which preserves the plaintext." However, their definition of NM-RCCA is not a natural extension of that of classical non-malleability, and it is not clear whether their NM-RCCA captures the requirement of classical non-malleability. In this paper, we propose definitions of indistinguishability-based and simulation-based non-malleability against RCCA by extending definitions of classical non-malleability. We then prove that these two notions of non-malleability and IND-RCCA are equivalent regardless of the size of plaintext space of PKE schemes.

Keywords: Public-key encryption · Non-malleability · Replayable chosen ciphertext security

1 Introduction

1.1 Background

Non-malleability [1] is one of the most fundamental security requirement for public key encryption (PKE). Non-malleability guarantees that an adversary

© Springer Nature Switzerland AG 2019
N. Attrapadung and T. Yagi (Eds.): IWSEC 2019, LNCS 11689, pp. 253–272, 2019.
https://doi.org/10.1007/978-3-030-26834-3_15

cannot modify the plaintext of a given ciphertext. For example, consider the electronic bidding using a PKE scheme played by companies A and B. Suppose that the company A places its bid of $1,000,000 by sending an encryption c of $1,000,000 generated by the PKE scheme over the internet. In this case, if the PKE scheme does not satisfy non-malleability, the company B might be able to intercept c, make an encryption of $1,500,000 by modifying c, and use it as its bid. In order to prevent such kind of malicious activities, the PKE scheme should satisfy non-malleability. There are both simulation-based and indistinguishability-based definitions of non-malleability for PKE. Bellare and Sahai [8] showed these two definitions are equivalent when considering each of chosen plaintext attack (CPA), non-adaptive chosen ciphertext attack (CCA1), and adaptive chosen ciphertext attack (CCA2). In this work, we study non-malleability against *replayable chosen ciphertext attacks (RCCA)* [3].

The notion of RCCA security was introduced by Canetti, Krawczyk, and Nielsen [3] in order to handle an encryption scheme that is "non-malleable except tampering which preserves the plaintext". RCCA security is a relaxation of CCA security and a useful security notion for many practical applications such as authentication and key exchange. To formulate "non-malleability except tampering which preserves the plaintext", in the security experiment of RCCA security, the decryption oracle returns a symbol "Test" when an adversary queries an encryption of m_0 and m_1, where m_0 and m_1 are challenge messages. Canetti et al. defined non-malleability against RCCA (NM-RCCA), indistinguishability against RCCA (IND-RCCA), and universal composability against RCCA (UC-RCCA). Moreover, they proved that these three security notions are equivalent when considering a PKE scheme whose plaintext space is super-polynomially large.

As noted above, RCCA security was introduced in order to handle an encryption scheme that is non-malleable except tampering which preserves the plaintext. To clarify whether a security notion against RCCA such as IND-RCCA captures non-malleability except tampering which preserves the plaintext, we should consider the equivalence between the security notion and NM-RCCA. Therefore, NM-RCCA seems to play the central role among security notions against RCCA.

However, the definition of NM-RCCA proposed by Canetti et al. is not a natural extension of that of classical non-malleability, and it is not clear whether the definition plays the above required role. More specifically, in the security experiment of their NM-RCCA, an adversary is required to make an encryption of m_{1-b} given an encryption of m_b, where b is the challenge bit and (m_0, m_1) are challenge messages. It is not clear whether this definition captures the requirement of classical non-malleability that given an encryption of some message m, an adversary cannot generate that of any message related to m. In fact, Canetti et al. claimed the validity of the definition of their NM-RCCA relying on the equivalence between NM-RCCA and UC-RCCA, but it does not hold when considering an encryption scheme the size of whose plaintext space is polynomial. For this reason, we need to study non-malleability against RCCA more

deeply and propose a definition of it that captures the requirement of classical
non-malleability.

1.2   Our Contribution

In this paper, we propose simulation-based and indistinguishability-based definitions of non-malleability against RCCA. The proposed definitions are natural
extensions of that of classical non-malleability, and thus they have the same
spirit as classical definitions capturing the intuition that given an encryption of
some message m, an adversary cannot generate that of any message related to
m. Moreover, we prove that these two security notions and IND-RCCA security
proposed by Canetti et al. [3] are all equivalent regardless of the size of plaintext
space.

   While we can easily formalize indistinguishability-based non-malleability by
naturally extending the definition of IND-RCCA proposed by Canetti et al.,
there is a problem when formalizing simulation-based non-malleability. The most
non-trivial point is what decryption oracle we should allow an adversary to access
when we formalize a simulation-based security against RCCA. At first glance,
the decryption oracle in RCCA environment seems to leak less information than
the decryption oracle in CCA environment. However, compared to the ordinary
CCA, the decryption oracle seems to leak much more information about messages when considering RCCA due to the special symbol "Test" returned by
the decryption oracle. Thus, when formalizing a simulation-based security under
RCCA environment, we need to formalize the intuition that an adversary cannot
obtain any information about the plaintext encrypted in the ciphertext except
information leaked from the decryption oracle. To capture the intuition, we use
a predicate in the definition of simulation-based non-malleability against RCCA.
See Sect. 3.1 for more details.

   We can see the usefulness of using a predicate when formalizing RCCA security from the following fact. We can define semantic security under RCCA by
using a predicate in a similar way as the definition of simulation-based non-
malleability against RCCA. Then, we can prove the semantic security under
RCCA is equivalent to IND-RCCA proposed by Canetti et al. In Appendix A,
we show the definition of semantic security under RCCA and its equivalence to
IND-RCCA.

   We summarize our results in Fig. 1.

1.3   Related Work

Goldwasser and Micali [6] proved the equivalence between semantic security and
indistinguishability against CPA. Watanabe et al. [7] proved the equivalence
between semantic security and indistinguishability against CCA1 and CCA2.
Bellare et al. [2] proved the equivalence between indistinguishability and non-
malleability under CCA2 environment. Bellare and Sahai [8] proved equivalence
between simulation based non-malleability and indistinguishability based non-
malleability. In addition to above, Pass et al. [4] considered the situation that

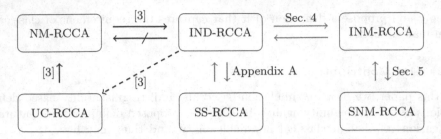

Fig. 1. The summary of our results and previous results regarding security notions against RCCA. SNM-RCCA and INM-RCCA indicate proposed definitions of simulation-based and indistinguishability-based non-malleability, respectively. SS-RCCA indicates proposed definition of semantic security. Solid arrows indicate implications. Red arrows indicate our results. Dashed arrows indicate implication for a PKE scheme whose plaintext space is super polynomially large. The slashed arrow from IND-RCCA to NM-RCCA indicates that there exists IND-RCCA secure but not NM-RCCA secure PKE scheme the size of whose plaintext space is polynomial. (Color figure online)

an adversary outputs a ciphertext which is decrypted to $\perp$ in the experiment, and proved the relation of simulation based non-malleability and indistinguishability based non-malleability under the condition they considered. Specifically, they proved that those two definitions are equivalent for a PKE scheme that allows efficient sampling of a ciphertext decrypted to $\perp$. On the other hand, they proved a separation scheme exists between the two definitions in the case that a PKE scheme does not allow efficient sampling of a ciphertext decrypted to $\perp$. Katz and Yung [5] proved relations among notions of security for symmetric-key encryption.

Several studies on the construction of RCCA secure PKE schemes have been done since RCCA security was proposed by Canetti et al. [3]. Also, there are studies that consider RCCA security for various cryptographic primitives such as proxy re-encryption, hybrid encryption, signcryption and steganography [9–15]. A specific construction of a rerandomizable PKE scheme satisfying a weaker variant of RCCA security was proposed by Groth [16]. Subsequently, a construction of a rerandomizable PKE scheme satisfying RCCA security using non-standard cryptographic groups was proposed by Prabhakaran et al. [17]. In addition, a construction of a rerandomizable PKE scheme satisfying RCCA security from a standard assumption was proposed by Chase et al. [18], and Libert et al. [19] improved the efficiency of their construction.

1.4 Organization

In Sect. 2, we review the definition of PKE and IND-RCCA defined by Canetti et al. [3]. In Sect. 3, we then give our simulation-based definition of non-malleability against RCCA (SNM-RCCA) and indistinguishability-based one

(INM-RCCA). In Sect. 4, we prove the equivalence of IND-RCCA and INM-RCCA. In Sect. 5, we also prove the equivalence of INM-RCCA and SNM-RCCA. In Sect. 6, we state the conclusion of this work. In Appendix A, we give our definition of semantic security against RCCA, and prove that it is equivalent to IND-RCCA.

2   Preliminaries

Notations. We denote probabilistic polynomial time algorithm by PPTA, and for an algorithm A, we denote the procedure that A is given input a and outputs b by $b \leftarrow A(a)$. In addition, for a set $\mathcal{S}$, we denote the cardinality of $\mathcal{S}$ by $\|\mathcal{S}\|$.

2.1   Public Key Encryption

We define public key encryption (PKE). In this work, we consider PKE schemes whose plaintext space is binary, that is, $\{0,1\}^\ell$, where ℓ is a polynomial of the security parameter.

Definition 1 (Public key encryption). *A PKE scheme Σ is a tuple* (Gen, Enc, Dec) *of PPT algorithms. Below, let the message space of Σ be $\{0,1\}^\ell$, where ℓ is a polynomial of the security parameter.*

- *The key generation algorithm* Gen, *given a security parameter 1^λ, outputs a public key pk and a secret key sk.*
- *The encryption algorithm* Enc, *given a public key pk and message $m \in \{0,1\}^\ell$, outputs a ciphertext c.*
- *The decryption algorithm* Dec, *given a secret key sk and ciphertext c, outputs a plaintext $\tilde{m} \in \{\bot\} \cup \{0,1\}^\ell$.*

Correctness. *We require* $\mathsf{Dec}(sk, \mathsf{Enc}(pk, m)) = m$ *for every* $m \in \{0,1\}^\ell$ *and* $(pk, sk) \leftarrow \mathsf{Gen}(1^\lambda)$.

2.2   Definition of IND-RCCA

We review the definition of IND-RCCA security introduced by Canetti et al. [3]. They formalized RCCA security by letting the decryption oracle in the second phase $\mathcal{O}_2$ return a special symbol "Test" when an adversary queries a ciphertext of m_0 or m_1, where m_0 and m_1 are the challenge messages. The formulation that $\mathcal{O}_2$ returns "Test" relaxes CCA security. For example, even if an adversary queries a ciphertext generated by rerandomizing the challenge ciphertext to $\mathcal{O}_2$, the adversary cannot obtain any information about the challenge bit in the experiments of RCCA security.

Then we give a formal definition of the IND-RCCA security. Let $\Sigma = $ (Gen, Enc, Dec) be a PKE scheme, and $\mathcal{A} = (\mathcal{A}_1, \mathcal{A}_2)$ be a pair of PPTAs. We consider the following experiments IND-RCCA-b ($b = 0, 1$):

$$\frac{\mathrm{Exp}_{\Sigma,\mathcal{A}}^{\text{IND-RCCA-}b}(\lambda)}{\begin{aligned}&(pk, sk) \leftarrow \mathsf{Gen}(1^\lambda);\\&(m_0, m_1, st_1) \leftarrow \mathcal{A}_1^{\mathcal{O}_1}(pk);\\&c^* \leftarrow \mathsf{Enc}(pk, m_b);\\&b' \leftarrow \mathcal{A}_2^{\mathcal{O}_2}(c^*, st_1);\\&\text{output } b'\end{aligned}}$$

where,

$$\mathcal{O}_1(c) = \mathsf{Dec}(sk, c),$$

$$\mathcal{O}_2(c) = \begin{cases} \mathsf{Test} & (\mathsf{Dec}(sk, c) \in \{m_0, m_1\}) \\ \mathsf{Dec}(sk, c) & (\text{otherwise}). \end{cases}$$

We define the advantage $\mathsf{Adv}_{\Sigma,\mathcal{A}}^{\text{IND-RCCA}}(\lambda)$ as $\mathsf{Adv}_{\Sigma,\mathcal{A}}^{\text{IND-RCCA}}(\lambda) :=$
$|\mathrm{Pr}[\mathrm{Exp}_{\Sigma,\mathcal{A}}^{\text{IND-RCCA-0}}(\lambda) \to 1] - \mathrm{Pr}[\mathrm{Exp}_{\Sigma,\mathcal{A}}^{\text{IND-RCCA-1}}(\lambda) \to 1]|.$

Definition 2 (IND-RCCA). *We say that Σ is IND-RCCA secure if* Adv
$_{\Sigma,\mathcal{A}}^{IND\text{-}RCCA}(\lambda)$ *is negligible for any pair of PPTAs $\mathcal{A}$.*

3   Definitions of SNM-RCCA and INM-RCCA

In this section, we introduce our definitions of simulation-based and indistinguishability-based non-malleability against RCCA.

3.1   Definition of SNM-RCCA

We give our definition of simulation-based non-malleability under RCCA environment (SNM-RCCA) as follows.

Let $\Sigma = (\mathsf{Gen}, \mathsf{Enc}, \mathsf{Dec})$ be a PKE scheme, $\mathcal{A} = (\mathcal{A}_1, \mathcal{A}_2)$ and $\mathcal{S} = (\mathcal{S}_1, \mathcal{S}_2)$ be pairs of PPTAs, and h be a polynomial time computable function. We consider the following experiments SNM-RCCA-0 and SNM-RCCA-1:

$$\frac{\mathrm{Exp}_{\Sigma,\mathcal{A},h}^{\text{SNM-RCCA-0}}(\lambda)}{\begin{aligned}&(pk, sk) \leftarrow \mathsf{Gen}(1^\lambda);\\&(\mathcal{M}, \boldsymbol{P}(\cdot, \cdot), st_1) \leftarrow \mathcal{A}_1^{\mathcal{O}_1}(pk);\\&m \leftarrow \mathcal{M};\\&c^* \leftarrow \mathsf{Enc}(pk, m);\\&(c_1, \ldots, c_n, st_2) \leftarrow \mathcal{A}_2^{\mathcal{O}_2}(c^*, h(m), st_1);\\&\text{For } i = 1 \text{ to } n\\&\quad d_i := \begin{cases} \mathsf{Test} & (\boldsymbol{P}(m, \mathsf{Dec}(sk, c_i)) = 1) \\ \mathsf{Dec}(sk, c_i) & (\text{otherwise}) \end{cases}\\&\text{output } (\mathcal{M}, m, \boldsymbol{P}(\cdot, \cdot), d_1, \ldots, d_n, st_2)\end{aligned}}$$

$$\frac{\mathrm{Exp}_{\Sigma,\mathcal{S},h}^{\text{SNM-RCCA-1}}(\lambda)}{\begin{aligned}&(pk, sk) \leftarrow \mathsf{Gen}(1^\lambda);\\&(\mathcal{M}, \boldsymbol{P}(\cdot, \cdot), st_1) \leftarrow \mathcal{S}_1(pk);\\&m \leftarrow \mathcal{M};\\&(c_1, \ldots, c_n, st_2) \leftarrow \mathcal{S}_2^{\boldsymbol{P}(m, \cdot)}(h(m), st_1);\\&\text{For } i = 1 \text{ to } n\\&\quad d_i := \begin{cases} \mathsf{Test} & (\boldsymbol{P}(m, \mathsf{Dec}(sk, c_i)) = 1 \\ & \quad \lor c_i = \mathsf{Test}) \\ \bot & (c_i = \bot) \\ \mathsf{Dec}(sk, c_i) & (\text{otherwise}) \end{cases}\\&\text{output } (\mathcal{M}, m, \boldsymbol{P}(\cdot, \cdot), d_1, \ldots, d_n, st_2)\end{aligned}}$$

where, the predicate P should satisfy $P(m,m) = 1$ for any m which is included in the support of $\mathcal{M}$, and

$$\mathcal{O}_1(c) = \mathsf{Dec}(sk, c),$$

$$\mathcal{O}_2(c) = \begin{cases} \mathsf{Test} & (P(m, \mathsf{Dec}(sk, c)) = 1) \\ \mathsf{Dec}(sk, c) & (\text{otherwise}). \end{cases}$$

In the above two experiments, $\mathcal{M}$ is a distribution over the plaintext space.

We define the advantage $\mathsf{Adv}_{\Sigma,\mathcal{A},\mathcal{S},\mathcal{D},h}^{\mathsf{SNM\text{-}RCCA}}(\lambda)$ as $\mathsf{Adv}_{\Sigma,\mathcal{A},\mathcal{S},\mathcal{D},h}^{\mathsf{SNM\text{-}RCCA}}(\lambda) :=$ $|\Pr[\mathcal{D}(\mathsf{Exp}_{\Sigma,\mathcal{A},h}^{\mathsf{SNM\text{-}RCCA\text{-}0}}(\lambda)) \to 1] - \Pr[\mathcal{D}(\mathsf{Exp}_{\Sigma,\mathcal{S},h}^{\mathsf{SNM\text{-}RCCA\text{-}1}}(\lambda)) \to 1]|.$

Definition 3 (SNM-RCCA security). *We say that Σ is SNM-RCCA secure if for any polynomial time computable function h and for any pair of PPTAs $\mathcal{A}$, there exists a pair of PPTAs $\mathcal{S}$ such that* $\mathsf{Adv}_{\Sigma,\mathcal{A},\mathcal{S},\mathcal{D},h}^{\mathsf{SNM\text{-}RCCA}}(\lambda)$ *is negligible for any PPTA $\mathcal{D}$.*

When formalizing SNM-RCCA, we refer to the formulation of Pass et al. [4]. They considered the case where an adversary outputs challenge ciphertext directly in the experiment of simulation-based and indistinguishability-based non-malleability under CCA environment. They allowed a simulator to output the symbol "COPY" and formulated it. Similarly to the definitions of Pass et al., we allow a simulator to output special symbols in order to handle replays of ciphertexts.

On the Use of Predicate. We use a predicate in the definition of SNM-RCCA above. The reason is as follows. When we formalize the simulation-based RCCA security, it is not trivial what decryption oracle we should allow an adversary to access. For example, suppose that we allow an adversary to access the decryption oracle which returns "Test" only when he queries a ciphertext of m, where m is the plaintext chosen in the experiment as the target of tampering. Then, this decryption oracle seems to leak m entirely to the adversary in some cases. In fact, when the size of the plaintext space is polynomial, by querying a ciphertext of all plaintexts contained in the plaintext space, the adversary can learn m by the decryption oracle's response "Test".

In this way, in RCCA environment, the decryption oracle leaks the information of the plaintext m chosen in the experiment. Thus, when we formalize simulation-based RCCA security, we need to formalize it by capturing the intuition that an adversary cannot obtain any information about the plaintext encrypted in the ciphertext except the information leaked from the decryption oracle. To capture the intuition, in our definition, we make an adversary output a predicate that determines whether a decryption result of a decryption query is "Test" or not. In other words, this predicate indicates which kind of tampering is considered to be success. More importantly, we allow a simulator to access the predicate oracle in order to give him the same information leaked from the decryption oracle which the adversary accesses. We see that if such a simulator can simulate an adversary, the adversary does not obtain any information of the plaintext from the ciphertext except information leaked from the decryption oracle.

We can observe the usefulness of using a predicate when formalizing RCCA security from the following fact. We can define semantic security under RCCA environment using a predicate in a similar way as the definition of SNM-RCCA. Then, we can prove semantic security under RCCA is equivalent to IND-RCCA security proposed by Canetti et al. [3]. In Appendix A, we show the definition of semantic security under RCCA and its equivalence to IND-RCCA.

3.2 Definition of INM-RCCA

We give our definition of indistinguishability-based non-malleability under RCCA environment (INM-RCCA) as follows.

Let $\Sigma = (\mathsf{Gen}, \mathsf{Enc}, \mathsf{Dec})$ be a PKE scheme, and $\mathcal{A} = (\mathcal{A}_1, \mathcal{A}_2, \mathcal{A}_3)$ be a triple of PPTAs. We consider the following experiments INM-RCCA-b ($b = 0, 1$):

$$
\begin{array}{l}
\underline{\mathrm{Exp}_{\Sigma,\mathcal{A}}^{\mathrm{INM\text{-}RCCA}\text{-}b}(\lambda)} \\[4pt]
(pk, sk) \leftarrow \mathsf{Gen}(1^\lambda); \\
(m_0, m_1, st_1) \leftarrow \mathcal{A}_1^{\mathcal{O}_1}(pk); \\
c^* \leftarrow \mathsf{Enc}(pk, m_b); \\
(c_1, \ldots, c_n, st_2) \leftarrow \mathcal{A}_2^{\mathcal{O}_2}(c^*, st_1); \\
\text{For } i = 1 \text{ to } n \\
\quad d_i := \begin{cases} \mathsf{Test} & (\mathsf{Dec}(sk, c_i) \in \{m_0, m_1\}) \\ \mathsf{Dec}(sk, c_i) & (\text{otherwise}) \end{cases} \\
b' \leftarrow \mathcal{A}_3(d_1, \ldots, d_n, st_2); \\
\text{output } b'
\end{array}
$$

where,

$$
\mathcal{O}_1(c) = \mathsf{Dec}(sk, c),
$$

$$
\mathcal{O}_2(c) = \begin{cases} \mathsf{Test} & (\mathsf{Dec}(sk, c) \in \{m_0, m_1\}) \\ \mathsf{Dec}(sk, c) & (\text{otherwise}). \end{cases}
$$

We define the advantage $\mathsf{Adv}_{\Sigma,\mathcal{A}}^{\mathrm{INM\text{-}RCCA}}(\lambda)$ as $\mathsf{Adv}_{\Sigma,\mathcal{A}}^{\mathrm{INM\text{-}RCCA}}(\lambda) := |\Pr[\mathrm{Exp}_{\Sigma,\mathcal{A}}^{\mathrm{INM\text{-}RCCA}\text{-}0}(\lambda) \to 1] - \Pr[\mathrm{Exp}_{\Sigma,\mathcal{A}}^{\mathrm{INM\text{-}RCCA}\text{-}1}(\lambda) \to 1]|$.

Definition 4 (INM-RCCA security). *We say that Σ is INM-RCCA secure if $\mathsf{Adv}_{\Sigma,\mathcal{A}}^{\mathrm{INM\text{-}RCCA}}(\lambda)$ is negligible for any triple of PPTAs $\mathcal{A}$.*

4   Equivalence of IND-RCCA and INM-RCCA

We can prove the equivalence between IND-RCCA and INM-RCCA. Specifically, the following two theorems, Theorems 1 and 2 hold.

Theorem 1. *If a PKE scheme $\Sigma = (\mathsf{Gen}, \mathsf{Enc}, \mathsf{Dec})$ is INM-RCCA secure, then Σ is IND-RCCA secure.*

$\mathcal{B}_1^{O_1}(pk)$	$\mathcal{B}_2^{O_2}(c^*, st_1)$
$(m_0, m_1, st_1') \leftarrow \mathcal{A}_1^{O_1}(pk)$	$b' \leftarrow \mathcal{A}_2^{O_2}(c^*, st_1')$
$st_1 := (m_0, m_1, st_1')$	c : empty string
output (m_0, m_1, st_1)	$st_2 := b'$
	output (c, st_2)
$\mathcal{B}_3(d, st_2)$	
output b'	

Fig. 2. The constructions of $\mathcal{B}$ used in Theorem 1

Proof. We assume that for any INM-RCCA adversary $\mathcal{B} = (\mathcal{B}_1, \mathcal{B}_2, \mathcal{B}_3)$, $\mathsf{Adv}_{\Sigma,\mathcal{B}}^{\text{INM-RCCA}}(\lambda)$ is negligible. Then, we show $\mathsf{Adv}_{\Sigma,\mathcal{A}}^{\text{IND-RCCA}}(\lambda)$ is negligible for any IND-RCCA adversary $\mathcal{A} = (\mathcal{A}_1, \mathcal{A}_2)$.

We construct an INM-RCCA adversary $\mathcal{B} = (\mathcal{B}_1, \mathcal{B}_2, \mathcal{B}_3)$ who uses internally $\mathcal{A}$ as in Fig. 2. When $\mathcal{A}_2$ queries a ciphertext c to $\mathcal{B}_2$, $\mathcal{B}_2$ sends c to the decryption oracle that he can access. Then $\mathcal{B}_2$ sends the response from the oracle to $\mathcal{A}_2$.

By the construction of $\mathcal{B}$ as in Fig. 2, $\mathcal{B}$ simulates IND-RCCA-0 experiment for $\mathcal{A}$ when $\mathcal{B}$ receives an encryption of m_0. Moreover, $\mathcal{B}$ outputs 1 only when $\mathcal{A}$ outputs 1, and thus it holds that $\Pr[\mathsf{Exp}_{\Sigma,\mathcal{B}}^{\text{INM-RCCA-0}}(\lambda) \to 1] = \Pr[\mathsf{Exp}_{\Sigma,\mathcal{A}}^{\text{IND-RCCA-0}}(\lambda) \to 1]$. Likewise, it holds that $\Pr[\mathsf{Exp}_{\Sigma,\mathcal{B}}^{\text{INM-RCCA-1}}(\lambda) \to 1] = \Pr[\mathsf{Exp}_{\Sigma,\mathcal{A}}^{\text{IND-RCCA-1}}(\lambda) \to 1]$.

Therefore, we can derive

$$\mathsf{Adv}_{\Sigma,\mathcal{A}}^{\text{IND-RCCA}}(\lambda) = |\Pr[\mathsf{Exp}_{\Sigma,\mathcal{A}}^{\text{IND-RCCA-1}}(\lambda) \to 1] - \Pr[\mathsf{Exp}_{\Sigma,\mathcal{A}}^{\text{IND-RCCA-0}}(\lambda) \to 1]|$$

$$= |\Pr[\mathsf{Exp}_{\Sigma,\mathcal{B}}^{\text{INM-RCCA-0}}(\lambda) \to 1] - \Pr[\mathsf{Exp}_{\Sigma,\mathcal{B}}^{\text{INM-RCCA-1}}(\lambda) \to 1]|$$

$$= \mathsf{Adv}_{\Sigma,\mathcal{B}}^{\text{INM-RCCA}}(\lambda).$$

Since we assume Σ is INM-RCCA secure, it is negligible. $\square$

Theorem 2. *If a PKE scheme* $\Sigma = (\mathsf{Gen}, \mathsf{Enc}, \mathsf{Dec})$ *is IND-RCCA secure, then* Σ *is INM-RCCA secure.*

Proof. We assume that for any IND-RCCA adversary $\mathcal{B} = (\mathcal{B}_1, \mathcal{B}_2)$, $\mathsf{Adv}_{\Sigma,\mathcal{B}}^{\text{IND-RCCA}}(\lambda)$ is negligible. Then, we show $\mathsf{Adv}_{\Sigma,\mathcal{A}}^{\text{INM-RCCA}}(\lambda)$ is negligible for any INM-RCCA adversary $\mathcal{A} = (\mathcal{A}_1, \mathcal{A}_2, \mathcal{A}_3)$.

We construct an IND-RCCA adversary $\mathcal{B} = (\mathcal{B}_1, \mathcal{B}_2)$ who uses internally $\mathcal{A}$ as in Fig. 3. When $\mathcal{A}_2$ queries a ciphertext c to $\mathcal{B}_2$, $\mathcal{B}_2$ sends c to the decryption oracle that he can access. Then $\mathcal{B}_2$ sends the response from the oracle to $\mathcal{A}_2$.

By the construction of $\mathcal{B}$ as in Fig. 3, $\mathcal{B}$ simulates INM-RCCA-0 experiment for $\mathcal{A}$ when $\mathcal{B}$ runs in IND-RCCA-0 experiment. Moreover, $\mathcal{B}$ outputs 1 only when $\mathcal{A}$ outputs 1. Therefore, we have $\Pr[\mathsf{Exp}_{\Sigma,\mathcal{B}}^{\text{IND-RCCA-0}}(\lambda) \to 1] = \Pr[\mathsf{Exp}_{\Sigma,\mathcal{A}}^{\text{INM-RCCA-0}}(\lambda) \to 1]$. Similarly, it holds that $\Pr[\mathsf{Exp}_{\Sigma,\mathcal{B}}^{\text{IND-RCCA-1}}(\lambda) \to 1] = \Pr[\mathsf{Exp}_{\Sigma,\mathcal{A}}^{\text{INM-RCCA-1}}(\lambda) \to 1]$.

$\mathcal{B}_1^{\mathcal{O}_1}(pk)$	$\mathcal{B}_2^{\mathcal{O}_2}(c^*, st_1)$
$(m_0, m_1, st_1') \leftarrow \mathcal{A}_1^{\mathcal{O}_1}(pk)$	$(c_1, \ldots, c_n, st_2') \leftarrow \mathcal{A}_2^{\mathcal{O}_2}(c^*, st_1')$
$st_1 := st_1'$	For $i = 1$ to n
output (m_0, m_1, st_1)	$\quad d_i := \mathcal{O}_2(c_i)$
	$b' \leftarrow \mathcal{A}_3(d_1, \ldots, d_n, st_2')$

Fig. 3. The constructions of $\mathcal{B}$ used in Theorem 2

Therefore, we can derive

$$\mathsf{Adv}_{\Sigma,\mathcal{A}}^{\text{INM-RCCA}}(\lambda) = |\Pr[\mathsf{Exp}_{\Sigma,\mathcal{A}}^{\text{INM-RCCA-1}}(\lambda) \to 1] - \Pr[\mathsf{Exp}_{\Sigma,\mathcal{A}}^{\text{INM-RCCA-0}}(\lambda) \to 1]|$$
$$= |\Pr[\mathsf{Exp}_{\Sigma,\mathcal{B}}^{\text{IND-RCCA-0}}(\lambda) \to 1] - \Pr[\mathsf{Exp}_{\Sigma,\mathcal{B}}^{\text{IND-RCCA-1}}(\lambda) \to 1]|$$
$$= \mathsf{Adv}_{\Sigma,\mathcal{B}}^{\text{IND-RCCA}}(\lambda).$$

Since we assume Σ is IND-RCCA secure, it is negligible. □

5 Equivalence of SNM-RCCA and INM-RCCA

In this section, we prove the equivalence between SNM-RCCA and INM-RCCA proposed in this paper.

5.1 INM-RCCA Implies SNM-RCCA

We prove that INM-RCCA implies SNM-RCCA by a case analysis. We can consider two cases where the size of the plaintext space which a PKE scheme Σ supports is polynomial or not. We consider the case that the size of the plaintext space is polynomial at first, and give a proof. After that, we consider the other case, and give a proof.

Theorem 3. *If a PKE scheme $\Sigma = (\mathsf{Gen}, \mathsf{Enc}, \mathsf{Dec})$ is INM-RCCA secure, and the size of the plaintext space of Σ is polynomial, then Σ is SNM-RCCA secure.*

Proof. We assume $\mathsf{Adv}_{\Sigma,\mathcal{B}}^{\text{INM-RCCA}}(\lambda)$ is negligible for any INM-RCCA adversary $\mathcal{B} = (\mathcal{B}_1, \mathcal{B}_2, \mathcal{B}_3)$. Then, we show for any SNM-RCCA adversary $\mathcal{A} = (\mathcal{A}_1, \mathcal{A}_2)$ and for any polynomial time computable function h, there exists a simulator $\mathcal{S} = (\mathcal{S}_1, \mathcal{S}_2)$ such that $\mathsf{Adv}_{\Sigma,\mathcal{A},\mathcal{S},\mathcal{D},h}^{\text{SNM-RCCA}}(\lambda)$ is negligible for any distinguisher $\mathcal{D}$. To give a proof, we use a sequence of games (Game 0 to Game 3), and the construction of $\mathcal{S}$ is as in Fig. 4.

We define Game 0 to Game 3 as follows:

Game 0: Game 0 is the same as SNM-RCCA-0 for $\mathcal{A}$ and $\mathcal{D}$. We denote the plaintext sampled in SNM-RCCA-0 as m_0.

$\mathcal{S}_1(pk)$	$\mathcal{S}_2^{P(m_0,\cdot)}(h(m_0), st_1)$
$(pk', sk') \leftarrow \mathsf{Gen}(1^\lambda)$	$m_1 \leftarrow \mathcal{P}_{m_0}$
$(\mathcal{M}, P(\cdot,\cdot), st_1') \leftarrow \mathcal{A}_1^{\mathcal{O}_1'}(pk')$	$c^* \leftarrow \mathsf{Enc}(pk', m_1)$
$st_1 := (pk, pk', sk', st_1')$	$(c_1', \ldots, c_n', st_2') \leftarrow \mathcal{A}_2^{\mathcal{O}_2'}(c^*, h(m_0), st_1')$
output $(\mathcal{M}, P(\cdot,\cdot), st_1)$	$st_2 := st_2'$
	For $i = 1$ to n
	$d_i' := \begin{cases} \mathsf{Test} & (m_i' \leftarrow \mathsf{Dec}(sk', c_i'), P(m_0, m_i') = 1) \\ \mathsf{Dec}(sk', c_i') & (\text{otherwise}) \end{cases}$
	$c_i := \begin{cases} \mathsf{Test} & (d_i' = \mathsf{Test}) \\ \bot & (d_i' = \bot) \\ \mathsf{Enc}(pk, d_i') & (\text{otherwise}) \end{cases}$
	output $(c_1, \ldots, c_n, st_2)$

Fig. 4. The construction of $\mathcal{S}$ used in Theorem 3

Game 1: The difference from Game 0 is to create $(pk', sk') \leftarrow \mathsf{Gen}(1^\lambda)$ newly and change the game so that (pk', sk') are used throughout the game. The input to $\mathcal{A}_1$ is changed to pk', the challenge ciphertext is generated using pk', and the oracles $\mathcal{O}_1$ and $\mathcal{O}_2$ that $\mathcal{A}$ accesses are changed to the oracles that use sk'. In addition, the secret key used to decrypt ciphertexts c_i ($i = 1, \ldots, n$) output by $\mathcal{A}_2$ is changed to sk'.

Game 2: The difference from Game 1 is that $m_1 \leftarrow \mathcal{P}_{m_0}$ is sampled in addition to m_0, where $\mathcal{P}_{m_0}$ is the uniform distribution over all plaintexts m' such that $P(m_0, m') = 1$. In addition, the challenge ciphertext $c^* \leftarrow \mathsf{Enc}(pk', m_0)$ is changed to $c^* \leftarrow \mathsf{Enc}(pk', m_1)$.

Game 3: Game 3 is the same as SNM-RCCA-1 under PPTA $\mathcal{S}$ and pk.

We can sample efficiently from $\mathcal{P}_{m_0}$ which is used in Game 2 and $\mathcal{S}_2$. This is because, since the size of the plaintext space is polynomial, by inputting all plaintexts to $P(m_0, \cdot)$, we can identify all plaintexts m' which satisfy $P(m_0, m') = 1$. Note that there always exists at least one plaintext m' satisfying $P(m_0, m') = 1$ because m_0 satisfies $P(m_0, m_0)$.

Let T_i be the event that 1 is output in Game i.

Lemma 1. *It holds that* $\Pr[T_1] = \Pr[T_0]$.

Proof. Game 1 is SNM-RCCA-0 under (pk', sk'), and (pk, sk) is not used. Since $(pk, sk) \leftarrow \mathsf{Gen}(1^\lambda)$ is not input to $\mathcal{A}$ in Game 1, Game 0 and Game 1 are equivalent from $\mathcal{A}$'s view. Thus, it holds that $\Pr[T_1] = \Pr[T_0]$. □

Lemma 2. *There exists* $\mathcal{B}$ *as in Fig. 5 such that* $|\Pr[T_2] - \Pr[T_1]| = \mathsf{Adv}_{\Sigma,\mathcal{B}}^{INM\text{-}RCCA}(\lambda)$.

Proof. We construct a reduction $\mathcal{B}$ that breaks INM-RCCA security from $\mathcal{A}$. We construct INM-RCCA adversary $\mathcal{B} = (\mathcal{B}_1, \mathcal{B}_2, \mathcal{B}_3)$ under (pk', sk') who uses internally $\mathcal{A}$ and $\mathcal{D}$ as in Fig. 5. When $\mathcal{A}_2$ queries a ciphertext c to $\mathcal{B}_2$, $\mathcal{B}_2$ sends

$\mathcal{B}_1^{\mathcal{O}_1'}(pk')$	$\mathcal{B}_2^{\mathcal{O}_2'}(c^*, st_1)$
$(\mathcal{M}, \boldsymbol{P}(\cdot, \cdot), st_1') \leftarrow \mathcal{A}_1^{\mathcal{O}_1'}(pk')$	$(c_1', \ldots, c_n', st_2') \leftarrow \mathcal{A}_2^{\mathcal{O}_2'}(c^*, st_1')$
$m_0 \leftarrow \mathcal{M}, m_1 \leftarrow \mathcal{P}_{m_0}$	$st_2 := (m_0, m_1, \mathcal{M}, \boldsymbol{P}(\cdot, \cdot), st_2')$
$st_1 := (m_0, m_1, \mathcal{M}, \boldsymbol{P}(\cdot, \cdot), st_1')$	output $(c_1', \ldots, c_n', st_2)$
output (m_0, m_1, st_1)	
$\mathcal{B}_3(d_1, \ldots, d_n, st_2)$	
By using m_0 and $\boldsymbol{P}(\cdot, \cdot)$, check the value of $\boldsymbol{P}(m_0, d_i)$ for each d_i	
d_i that satisfies $\boldsymbol{P}(m_0, d_i) = 1$ is set as $d_i :=$ "Test" by the above procedure	
$b' \leftarrow \mathcal{D}(\mathcal{M}, m_0, \boldsymbol{P}(\cdot, \cdot), d_1, \ldots, d_n, st_2')$	
output b'	

Fig. 5. The construction of $\mathcal{B}$ used in Lemma 2

c to the decryption oracle that he can access. Then, $\mathcal{B}_2$ receives m or "Test" from the oracle. After that, if $\boldsymbol{P}(m_0, m) = 1$ or $\mathcal{B}_2$ receives "Test", then $\mathcal{B}_2$ sends "Test" to $\mathcal{A}_2$. Otherwise, $\mathcal{B}_2$ sends m to $\mathcal{A}_2$. Since the plaintext m_1 which is generated in $\mathcal{B}_1$ satisfies $\boldsymbol{P}(m_0, m_1) = 1$, $\mathcal{B}_2$ can simulate the decryption oracle correctly. Likewise, $\mathcal{B}_2$ can simulate the sequence of d_i which is input to $\mathcal{D}$ correctly.

When $\mathcal{B}$ runs in INM-RCCA-0, $\mathcal{B}$ simulates Game 1 for $\mathcal{A}$ and $\mathcal{D}$. Moreover, $\mathcal{B}$ outputs 1 only when $\mathcal{D}$ outputs 1. Therefore, we have $\Pr[\mathsf{Exp}_{\Sigma, \mathcal{B}}^{\text{INM-RCCA-0}}(\lambda) \to 1] = \Pr[T_1]$. Similarly, we have $\Pr[\mathsf{Exp}_{\Sigma, \mathcal{B}}^{\text{INM-RCCA-1}}(\lambda) \to 1] = \Pr[T_2]$.

Therefore, we can derive

$$|\Pr[T_2] - \Pr[T_1]| = |\Pr[\mathsf{Exp}_{\Sigma, \mathcal{B}}^{\text{INM-RCCA-1}}(\lambda) \to 1] - \Pr[\mathsf{Exp}_{\Sigma, \mathcal{B}}^{\text{INM-RCCA-0}}(\lambda) \to 1]|$$
$$= \mathsf{Adv}_{\Sigma, \mathcal{B}}^{\text{INM-RCCA}}(\lambda).$$

$\square$

Lemma 3. *It holds that* $\Pr[T_3] = \Pr[T_2]$.

Proof. In Game 3, $\mathcal{S}$ uses $\mathcal{A}$ internally as in Fig. 4. Since Game 3 is SNM-RCCA-1, $\mathcal{S}$ cannot access to the decryption oracle. However, $\mathcal{S}$ generates (pk', sk') internally, and he can access the predicate oracle $\boldsymbol{P}(m_0, \cdot)$. In addition, an input to $\mathcal{A}$ is pk' as in Game 2, and thus $\mathcal{S}_2$ can respond to decryption queries from $\mathcal{A}$ by using sk' and $\boldsymbol{P}(m_0, \cdot)$.

$\mathcal{S}_2$ inputs a ciphertext of m_1 which is generated internally in $\mathcal{S}_2$ to $\mathcal{A}_2$, and $\mathcal{A}_2$ outputs a sequence of ciphertexts. $\mathcal{S}_2$ decrypts them using sk'. After that, each d_i is encrypted by using pk, and the encrypted sequence is the output of $\mathcal{S}_2$. All ciphertexts are decrypted using sk after $\mathcal{S}_2$ outputs, and these sequence is input to $\mathcal{D}$. Here, the distributions of the inputs to $\mathcal{D}$ in Game 2 and Game 3 are identical. Thus, it holds that $\Pr[T_3] = \Pr[T_2]$. $\square$

By using Lemma 1 to Lemma 3, we can derive

$$\mathsf{Adv}^{\text{SNM-RCCA}}_{\Sigma,\mathcal{A},\mathcal{S},\mathcal{D},h}(\lambda)$$

$$= |\Pr[\mathcal{D}(\mathsf{Exp}^{\text{SNM-RCCA-0}}_{\Sigma,\mathcal{A},h}(\lambda)) \to 1] - \Pr[\mathcal{D}(\mathsf{Exp}^{\text{SNM-RCCA-1}}_{\Sigma,\mathcal{A},h}(\lambda)) \to 1]|$$

$$= |\Pr[T_0] - \Pr[T_3]| = |\Pr[T_1] - \Pr[T_2]|$$

$$= \mathsf{Adv}^{\text{INM-RCCA}}_{\Sigma,\mathcal{B}}(\lambda).$$

Therefore, for any $\mathcal{A}$, there exists $\mathcal{S}$ as in Fig. 4 such that $\mathsf{Adv}^{\text{SNM-RCCA}}_{\Sigma,\mathcal{A},\mathcal{S},\mathcal{D},h}(\lambda)$ is negligible for any $\mathcal{D}$. □

Theorem 4. *If a PKE scheme* $\Sigma = (\mathsf{Gen},\mathsf{Enc},\mathsf{Dec})$ *is INM-RCCA secure, and the size of the plaintext space of* Σ *is super polynomially large, then* Σ *is SNM-RCCA secure.*

Proof. Let the plaintext space of Σ be $\{0,1\}^\ell$. We assume $\mathsf{Adv}^{\text{INM-RCCA}}_{\Sigma,\mathcal{B}}(\lambda)$ is negligible for any INM-RCCA adversary $\mathcal{B} = (\mathcal{B}_1,\mathcal{B}_2,\mathcal{B}_3)$. Then, we show for any SNM-RCCA adversary $\mathcal{A} = (\mathcal{A}_1,\mathcal{A}_2)$ and for any polynomial time computable function h, there exists a simulator $\mathcal{S} = (\mathcal{S}_1,\mathcal{S}_2)$ such that $\mathsf{Adv}^{\text{SNM-RCCA}}_{\Sigma,\mathcal{A},\mathcal{S},\mathcal{D},h}(\lambda)$ is negligible for any distinguisher $\mathcal{D}$. To give a proof, we use a sequence of games (Game 0 to Game 5), and the construction of $\mathcal{S}$ is as in Fig. 6.

We define Game 0 to Game 5 as follows:

Game 0: Game 0 is the same as SNM-RCCA-0 for $\mathcal{A}$ and $\mathcal{D}$. We denote the plaintext sampled in SNM-RCCA-0 as m_0.

Game 1: The difference from Game 0 is to create $(pk',sk') \leftarrow \mathsf{Gen}(1^\lambda)$ newly and change the game so that (pk',sk') are used throughout the game. The input to $\mathcal{A}_1$ is changed to pk', the challenge ciphertext is generated using pk', and the oracles $\mathcal{O}_1$ and $\mathcal{O}_2$ that $\mathcal{A}$ accesses are changed to oracles that use sk'. In addition, the secret key used to decrypt ciphertexts c_i ($i = 0,\ldots,n$) output by $\mathcal{A}_2$ is changed to sk'.

Game 2: The difference from Game 1 is that $m_1 \leftarrow \{0,1\}^\ell$ is sampled in addition to m_0. In additon, when decrypting c'_i, if $\boldsymbol{P}(m_0,\mathsf{Dec}(sk',c'_i)) = 1 \vee m_1 = \mathsf{Dec}(sk',c'_i)$, then let d_i be "Test".

Game 3: The difference from Game 2 is that $\mathcal{O}'_2$ returns "Test" when a ciphertext of m_1 is queried or a ciphertext of m satisfying $\boldsymbol{P}(m_0,m) = 1$ is queried.

Game 4: The difference from Game 3 is that the challenge ciphertext $c^* \leftarrow \mathsf{Enc}(pk',m_0)$ is changed to $c^* \leftarrow \mathsf{Enc}(pk',m_1)$.

Game 5: Game 5 is the same as SNM-RCCA-1 under PPTA $\mathcal{S}$ and pk.

Let T_i be the event that 1 is output in Game i.

Lemma 4. *It holds that* $\Pr[T_1] = \Pr[T_0]$.

Proof. Game 1 is SNM-RCCA-0 under (pk',sk'), and (pk,sk) is not used. Since $(pk,sk) \leftarrow \mathsf{Gen}(1^\lambda)$ is not input to $\mathcal{A}$ in Game 1, Game 0 and Game 1 are equivalent from $\mathcal{A}$'s view. Thus, it holds that $\Pr[T_1] = \Pr[T_0]$. □

$$
\begin{array}{|l|l|}
\hline
\begin{aligned}
&\mathcal{S}_1(pk)\\
&(pk', sk') \leftarrow \mathsf{Gen}(1^\lambda)\\
&(\mathcal{M}, \boldsymbol{P}(\cdot, \cdot), st_1') \leftarrow \mathcal{A}_1^{\mathcal{O}_1'}(pk')\\
&st_1 := (pk, pk', sk', st_1')\\
&\text{output } (\mathcal{M}, \boldsymbol{P}(\cdot, \cdot), st_1)
\end{aligned}
&
\begin{aligned}
&\mathcal{S}_2^{P(m_0, \cdot)}(h(m_0), st_1)\\
&m_1 \leftarrow \{0,1\}^\ell\\
&c^* \leftarrow \mathsf{Enc}(pk', m_1)\\
&(c_1', \ldots, c_n', st_2') \leftarrow \mathcal{A}_2^{\mathcal{O}_2'}(c^*, h(m_0), st_1')\\
&st_2 := st_2'\\
&\text{For } i = 1 \text{ to } n
\end{aligned}\\
\hline
\end{array}
$$

$$
d_i' := \begin{cases} \mathsf{Test} & (m_i' \leftarrow \mathsf{Dec}(sk', c_i'), \boldsymbol{P}(m_0, m_i') = 1 \\ & \vee m_i' = m_1) \\ \mathsf{Dec}(sk', c_i') & (\text{otherwise}) \end{cases}
$$

$$
c_i := \begin{cases} \mathsf{Test} & (d_i' = \mathsf{Test}) \\ \bot & (d_i' = \bot) \\ \mathsf{Enc}(pk, d_i') & (\text{otherwise}) \end{cases}
$$

$$
\text{output } (c_1, \ldots, c_n, st_2)
$$

Fig. 6. The construction of $\mathcal{S}$ used in Theorem 4

Lemma 5. *It holds that* $|\Pr[T_2] - \Pr[T_1]| < \frac{poly(\lambda)}{2^\ell}$.

Proof. Game 1 and Game 2 are identical if $\mathcal{A}_2$ does not output a ciphertext of m_1. Here, m_1 is chosen at uniformly random from $\{0,1\}^\ell$. Since the number of ciphertexts that $\mathcal{A}_2$ outputs is polynomial, it holds that $|\Pr[T_2] - \Pr[T_1]| < \frac{poly(\lambda)}{2^\ell}$ using the difference lemma and the union bound. □

Lemma 6. *It holds that* $|\Pr[T_3] - \Pr[T_2]| < \frac{poly(\lambda)}{2^\ell}$.

Proof. Game 2 and Game 3 are identical if $\mathcal{A}_2$ does not query a ciphertext of m_1 as a decryption query. Here, m_1 is chosen at uniformly random from $\{0,1\}^\ell$. Since the number of ciphertexts that $\mathcal{A}_2$ queries is polynomial, it holds that $|\Pr[T_3] - \Pr[T_2]| < \frac{poly(\lambda)}{2^\ell}$ using the difference lemma and the union bound. □

Lemma 7. *There exists* $\mathcal{B}$ *such that* $|\Pr[T_4] - \Pr[T_3]| = \mathsf{Adv}_{\Sigma,\mathcal{B}}^{INM\text{-}RCCA}(\lambda)$.

Proof. We construct a reduction $\mathcal{B}$ that breaks INM-RCCA security from $\mathcal{A}$. We construct an INM-RCCA adversary $\mathcal{B} = (\mathcal{B}_1, \mathcal{B}_2, \mathcal{B}_3)$ who uses internally $\mathcal{A}$ and $\mathcal{D}$ as in Fig. 7. When, $\mathcal{A}_2$ queries a ciphertext c to $\mathcal{B}_2$, $\mathcal{B}_2$ sends c to the decryption oracle that he can access. Then, $\mathcal{B}$ receives m or "Test" from the oracle. After that, if $\boldsymbol{P}(m_0, m) = 1 \vee m = m_1$ or $\mathcal{B}_2$ receives "Test", then $\mathcal{B}_2$ sends "Test" to $\mathcal{A}_2$. Otherwise, $\mathcal{B}_2$ sends m to $\mathcal{A}_2$. We see that $\mathcal{B}$ simulate the decryption oracles in Game 3 and Game 4 for $\mathcal{A}$. Likewise, $\mathcal{B}_2$ can simulate the sequence of d_i which is input to $\mathcal{D}$ correctly.

When $\mathcal{B}$ runs in INM-RCCA-0, $\mathcal{B}$ simulates Game 3 for $\mathcal{A}$ and $\mathcal{D}$. Moreover, $\mathcal{B}$ outputs 1 only when $\mathcal{D}$ outputs 1. Therefore, we have $\Pr[\mathsf{Exp}_{\Sigma,\mathcal{B}}^{INM\text{-}RCCA\text{-}0}(\lambda) \to 1] = \Pr[T_3]$. Similarly, we have $\Pr[\mathsf{Exp}_{\Sigma,\mathcal{B}}^{INM\text{-}RCCA\text{-}1}(\lambda) \to 1] = \Pr[T_4]$.

$\mathcal{B}_1^{\mathcal{O}_1'}(pk')$	$\mathcal{B}_2^{\mathcal{O}_2'}(c^*, st_1)$
$(\mathcal{M}, \boldsymbol{P}(\cdot,\cdot), st_1') \leftarrow \mathcal{A}_1^{\mathcal{O}_1'}(pk')$	$(c_1', \ldots, c_n', st_2') \leftarrow \mathcal{A}_2^{\mathcal{O}_2'}(c^*, st_1')$
$m_0 \leftarrow \mathcal{M}, m_1 \leftarrow \{0,1\}^\ell$	$st_2 := (m_0, m_1, \mathcal{M}, \boldsymbol{P}(\cdot,\cdot), st_2')$
$st_1 := (m_0, m_1, \mathcal{M}, \boldsymbol{P}(\cdot,\cdot), st_1')$	output $(c_1', \ldots, c_n', st_2)$
output (m_0, m_1, st_1)	

$\mathcal{B}_3(d_1, \ldots, d_n, st_2)$

By using m_0 and $\boldsymbol{P}(\cdot,\cdot)$, check the value of $\boldsymbol{P}(m_0, d_i)$ for each d_i
d_i that satisfies $\boldsymbol{P}(m_0, d_i) = 1 \vee d_1 = m_1$ is set as $d_i :=$ "Test" by the above procedure
$b' \leftarrow \mathcal{D}(\mathcal{M}, m_0, \boldsymbol{P}(\cdot,\cdot), d_1, \ldots, d_n, st_2')$
output b'

Fig. 7. The construction of $\mathcal{B}$ used in Lemma 7

Therefore, we can derive

$$|\Pr[T_4] - \Pr[T_3]| = |\Pr[\mathrm{Exp}_{\Sigma,\mathcal{B}}^{\mathrm{INM\text{-}RCCA\text{-}1}}(\lambda) \to 1] - \Pr[\mathrm{Exp}_{\Sigma,\mathcal{B}}^{\mathrm{INM\text{-}RCCA\text{-}0}}(\lambda) \to 1]|$$
$$= \mathsf{Adv}_{\Sigma,\mathcal{B}}^{\mathrm{INM\text{-}RCCA}}(\lambda). \qquad \square$$

Lemma 8. *It holds that* $\Pr[T_5] = \Pr[T_4]$.

Proof. In Game 5, $\mathcal{S}$ uses $\mathcal{A}$ internally as in Fig. 6. Since Game 5 is SNM-RCCA-1, $\mathcal{S}$ cannot access to the decryption oracle. However, $\mathcal{S}$ generates (pk', sk') internally, and he can access predicate oracle $\boldsymbol{P}(m_0, \cdot)$. In addition, an input to $\mathcal{A}$ is pk' as in Game 4, and thus $\mathcal{S}_2$ can respond the decryption query from $\mathcal{A}$ by using sk' and $\boldsymbol{P}(m_0, \cdot)$.

$\mathcal{S}_2$ inputs a ciphertext of m_1 which is generated internally in $\mathcal{S}_1$ to $\mathcal{A}_2$, and $\mathcal{A}_2$ outputs a sequence of ciphertexts. $\mathcal{S}_2$ decrypts them by using sk'. After that, each d_i is encrypted by using pk, and the encrypted sequence is output of $\mathcal{S}_2$. All ciphertexts are decrypted by using sk after $\mathcal{S}_2$ outputs them, and these sequence is input to $\mathcal{D}$. Here, the distributions of the inputs to $\mathcal{D}$ in Game 4 and Game 5 are identical. Thus, it holds that $\Pr[T_5] = \Pr[T_4]$. $\square$

By using Lemma 4 to Lemma 8, we can derive

$$\mathsf{Adv}_{\Sigma,\mathcal{A},\mathcal{S},\mathcal{D},h}^{\mathrm{SNM\text{-}RCCA}}(\lambda)$$
$$= |\Pr[\mathcal{D}(\mathrm{Exp}_{\Sigma,\mathcal{A},h}^{\mathrm{SNM\text{-}RCCA\text{-}0}}(\lambda)) \to 1] - \Pr[\mathcal{D}(\mathrm{Exp}_{\Sigma,\mathcal{A},h}^{\mathrm{SNM\text{-}RCCA\text{-}1}}(\lambda)) \to 1]|$$
$$= |\Pr[T_0] - \Pr[T_5]|$$
$$= |\Pr[T_1] - \Pr[T_4]|$$
$$= |\Pr[T_1] - \Pr[T_2] + \Pr[T_2] - \Pr[T_3] + \Pr[T_3] - \Pr[T_4]|$$
$$\leq |\Pr[T_1] - \Pr[T_2]| + |\Pr[T_2] - \Pr[T_3]| + |\Pr[T_3] - \Pr[T_4]|$$
$$\leq \frac{poly(\lambda)}{2^\ell} + \frac{poly(\lambda)}{2^\ell} + \mathsf{Adv}_{\Sigma,\mathcal{B}}^{\mathrm{INM\text{-}RCCA}}(\lambda).$$

Since we assume that 2^ℓ is super polynomially large and Σ is INM-RCCA secure, for any $\mathcal{A}$, there exists $\mathcal{S}$ as in Fig. 6 such that $\mathsf{Adv}^{\text{SNM-RCCA}}_{\Sigma,\mathcal{A},\mathcal{S},\mathcal{D},h}(\lambda)$ is negligible for any $\mathcal{D}$. $\qquad\square$

The following theorem holds from Theorems 3 and 4.

Theorem 5. *If a PKE scheme* $\Sigma = (\mathsf{Gen}, \mathsf{Enc}, \mathsf{Dec})$ *is INM-RCCA secure, then* Σ *is SNM-RCCA secure.*

5.2 SNM-RCCA Implies INM-RCCA

We prove that SNM-RCCA implies INM-RCCA.

Theorem 6. *If a PKE scheme* $\Sigma = (\mathsf{Gen}, \mathsf{Enc}, \mathsf{Dec})$ *is SNM-RCCA secure, then* Σ *is INM-RCCA secure.*

Proof. We denote $\mathsf{Exp}^{\text{INM-RCCA}}_{\Sigma,\mathcal{A}}$ as the experiment that chooses the challenge bit b randomly and execute INM-RCCA-b. Without loss of generality, we can assume $\Pr[\mathsf{Exp}^{\text{INM-RCCA}}_{\Sigma,\mathcal{A}}(\lambda) \to b] \geq 1/2$ for any INM-RCCA adversary $\mathcal{A}$. It is because if $\Pr[\mathsf{Exp}^{\text{INM-RCCA}}_{\Sigma,\mathcal{A}}(\lambda) \to b] < 1/2$, then we consider the adversary $\mathcal{A}'$ whose output is the reverse of $\mathcal{A}$'s output. Then, the advantage of $\mathcal{A}'$ is same as $\mathcal{A}$, and it holds $\Pr[\mathsf{Exp}^{\text{INM-RCCA-}b}_{\Sigma,\mathcal{A}'}(\lambda) \to b] \geq 1/2$. Thus, if we can bound the advantage of $\mathcal{A}'$, it means we can bound the advantage of $\mathcal{A}$ at the same time.

We assume that for any SNM-RCCA adversary $\mathcal{B} = (\mathcal{B}_1, \mathcal{B}_2)$ and for any polynomial time computable function h, there exists a simulator $\mathcal{S} = (\mathcal{S}_1, \mathcal{S}_2)$ such that $\mathsf{Adv}^{\text{SNM-RCCA}}_{\Sigma,\mathcal{B},\mathcal{D},h}(\lambda)$ is negligible for any distinguisher $\mathcal{D}$. Then, we show $\mathsf{Adv}^{\text{INM-RCCA}}_{\Sigma,\mathcal{A}}(\lambda)$ is negligible for any INM-RCCA adversary $\mathcal{A} = (\mathcal{A}_1, \mathcal{A}_2, \mathcal{A}_3)$.

We consider the SNM-RCCA-0 experiment with $h : m \mapsto \epsilon$, where ϵ is the empty string, and we construct an SNM-RCCA adversary $\mathcal{B}$ and a distinguisher $\mathcal{D}$ who uses $\mathcal{A}$ internally as in Fig. 8. When $\mathcal{A}_2$ submits a decryption query c to $\mathcal{B}_2$, $\mathcal{B}_2$ submits c to the decryption oracle that $\mathcal{B}_2$ can access. Then $\mathcal{B}_2$ sends the response from the oracle to $\mathcal{A}_2$.

By the construction of $\mathcal{B}$ and $\mathcal{D}$ above, $\mathcal{D}$ outputs 1 when $\mathcal{A}$ guesses bit b which is chosen in the experiment correctly. Thus, we can derive

$$\Pr[\mathcal{D}(\mathsf{Exp}^{\text{SNM-RCCA-0}}_{\Sigma,\mathcal{B},h}(\lambda)) \to 1] = \Pr[\mathsf{Exp}^{\text{INM-RCCA-}b}_{\Sigma,\mathcal{A}}(\lambda) \to b].$$

Let E be the event that $\mathcal{S}$ outputs $\mathcal{M}$ and $\mathcal{S}$ such that $\|\mathcal{M}\| = 2$ and $\boldsymbol{P}(m, m_0) = 1 \wedge \boldsymbol{P}(m, m_1) = 1$, and p be the probability that E occurs in SNM-RCCA-1, where $[\{m_0, m_1\}, \Pr(m_0) = \Pr(m_1) = 1/2] = \mathcal{M}$. When the event E occurs in SNM-RCCA-1, $\mathcal{S}$ does not receive the challenge ciphertext, and he cannot obtain any information about the choice of m_0 and m_1 even if he access the predicate oracle. Thus, since $\|\mathcal{M}\| = 2$ when E occurs, it holds that

$$\Pr\left[\mathcal{D}\left(\mathsf{Exp}^{\text{SNM-RCCA-1}}_{\Sigma,\mathcal{S},h}(\lambda)\right) \to 1\right] = \Pr\left[\mathcal{D}\left(\mathsf{Exp}^{\text{SNM-RCCA-1}}_{\Sigma,\mathcal{S},h}(\lambda)\right) \to 1 \Big| E\right] \cdot \Pr[E]$$

$$= \frac{p}{2} \leq \frac{1}{2}. \tag{1}$$

$\mathcal{B}_1^{\mathcal{O}_1}(pk)$	$\mathcal{B}_2^{\mathcal{O}_2}(c^*, st_1)$
$(m_0, m_1, st_1') \leftarrow \mathcal{A}_1^{\mathcal{O}_1}(pk)$	$(pk, sk) \leftarrow \mathsf{Gen}(1^\lambda)$
$\mathcal{M} := [\{m_0, m_1\}, \Pr(m_0) = \Pr(m_1) = 1/2]$	$(c_1, \ldots, c_n, st_2') \leftarrow \mathcal{A}_2^{\mathcal{O}_2}(c^*, st_1')$
$\boldsymbol{P}(m, m') := \begin{cases} 1 & (m' \in \{m_0, m_1\}) \\ 0 & (\text{otherwise}) \end{cases}$	$st_2 := (m_0, m_1, \boldsymbol{P}(\cdot, \cdot), st_2')$
$st_1 := (m_0, m_1, \boldsymbol{P}(\cdot, \cdot), st_1')$	$\text{output } (c_1, \ldots, c_n, st_2)$
$\text{output } (\mathcal{M}, \boldsymbol{P}(\cdot, \cdot), st_1)$	

$\mathcal{D}(\mathcal{M}, m, \boldsymbol{P}(\cdot, \cdot), d_1, \ldots, d_n, st_2)$
if $\|\mathcal{M}\| \neq 2$, then output 0
else if $\boldsymbol{P}'(m, m_0) = 0 \vee \boldsymbol{P}'(m, m_1) = 0$, then output 0,
$\quad$ where $[\{m_0, m_1\}, \Pr(m_0) = \Pr(m_1) = 1/2] = \mathcal{M}$
else if $b' \leftarrow \mathcal{A}_3(d_1, \ldots, d_n, st_2') \wedge m = m_{b'}$, then output 1
else then output 0

Fig. 8. The constructions of $\mathcal{B}$ and $\mathcal{D}$ used in Theorem 6

Here, $\mathsf{Adv}_{\Sigma, \mathcal{A}}^{\text{INM-RCCA}}(\lambda)$ can be rewritten as follows.

$$\mathsf{Adv}_{\Sigma, \mathcal{A}}^{\text{INM-RCCA}}(\lambda) = |\Pr[\mathsf{Exp}_{\Sigma, \mathcal{A}}^{\text{INM-RCCA-0}}(\lambda) \to 1] - \Pr[\mathsf{Exp}_{\Sigma, \mathcal{A}}^{\text{INM-RCCA-1}}(\lambda) \to 1]|$$
$$= |2 \cdot \Pr[\mathsf{Exp}_{\Sigma, \mathcal{A}}^{\text{INM-RCCA}}(\lambda) \to b] - 1|.$$

Then, it holds that

$$\mathsf{Adv}_{\Sigma, \mathcal{A}}^{\text{INM-RCCA}}(\lambda)$$
$$= |2 \cdot \Pr[\mathsf{Exp}_{\Sigma, \mathcal{A}}^{\text{INM-RCCA}}(\lambda) \to b] - 1|$$
$$= |2 \cdot \Pr[\mathcal{D}(\mathsf{Exp}_{\Sigma, \mathcal{B}, h}^{\text{SNM-RCCA-0}}(\lambda)) \to 1] - 1|$$
$$\leq |2 \cdot \Pr[\mathcal{D}(\mathsf{Exp}_{\Sigma, \mathcal{B}, h}^{\text{SNM-RCCA-0}}(\lambda)) \to 1] - 2 \cdot p/2|$$
$$= 2(|\Pr[\mathcal{D}(\mathsf{Exp}_{\Sigma, \mathcal{B}, h}^{\text{SNM-RCCA-0}}(\lambda)) \to 1] - \Pr[\mathcal{D}(\mathsf{Exp}_{\Sigma, \mathcal{S}, h}^{\text{SNM-RCCA-1}}(\lambda)) \to 1])$$
$$= 2 \cdot \mathsf{Adv}_{\Sigma, \mathcal{B}, \mathcal{D}, h}^{\text{SNM-RCCA}}(\lambda).$$

The transformation of the third equality is derived from the fact that we can assume the advantage of $\mathcal{A}$ is greater than 1/2. Therefore, for any PPTA $\mathcal{A}$, $\mathsf{Adv}_{\Sigma, \mathcal{A}}^{\text{INM-RCCA}}(\lambda)$ is negligible. $\square$

6   Conclusion

NM-RCCA proposed by Canetti et al. [3] as non-malleability under RCCA environment is not a natural extension of classical non-malleability. Canetti et al. argued that the validity of their definition is evidenced by its equivalence to the universal composability against RCCA, but this equivalence does not hold when the size of the plaintext space is polynomial. Therefore, the validity of their formulation of NM-RCCA is not clear. In this paper, we formulated simulation based non-malleability and indistinguishability based non-malleability under RCCA environment by extending classical definitions of non-malleability. In addition to this, we prove that these two proposed security notions and IND-RCCA proposed by Canetti et al. are all equivalent regardless of the size of plaintext space.

Acknowledgments. The third and fourth authors are supported by JST CREST Grant Number JPMJCR19F6, Japan.

A Definition of SS-RCCA and Its Equivalence with IND-RCCA

We give our definition of semantic security under RCCA environment (SS-RCCA) as follows.

Let $\Sigma = (\mathsf{Gen}, \mathsf{Enc}, \mathsf{Dec})$ be a PKE scheme, $\mathcal{A} = (\mathcal{A}_1, \mathcal{A}_2)$ and $\mathcal{S} = (\mathcal{S}_1, \mathcal{S}_2)$ be a pair of PPTAs, and h and f be polynomial time computable function. We consider the following experiments SS-RCCA-0 and SS-RCCA-1:

$\mathrm{Exp}_{\Sigma,\mathcal{A},h,f}^{\mathrm{SS\text{-}RCCA\text{-}0}}(\lambda)$	$\mathrm{Exp}_{\Sigma,\mathcal{S},h,f}^{\mathrm{SS\text{-}RCCA\text{-}1}}(\lambda)$
$(pk, sk) \leftarrow \mathsf{Gen}(1^\lambda);$	$(pk, sk) \leftarrow \mathsf{Gen}(1^\lambda);$
$(\mathcal{M}, \boldsymbol{P}(\cdot, \cdot), st_1) \leftarrow \mathcal{A}_1^{\mathcal{O}_1}(pk);$	$(\mathcal{M}, \boldsymbol{P}(\cdot, \cdot), st_1) \leftarrow \mathcal{S}_1(pk);$
$m \leftarrow \mathcal{M};$	$m \leftarrow \mathcal{M};$
$c^* \leftarrow \mathsf{Enc}(pk, m);$	$c^* \leftarrow \mathsf{Enc}(pk, m);$
$v \leftarrow \mathcal{A}_2^{\mathcal{O}_2}(c^*, h(m), st_1);$	$v \leftarrow \mathcal{S}_2^{\boldsymbol{P}(m,\cdot)}(h(m), st_1);$
If $v = f(m)$, then $\beta := 1$	If $v = f(m)$, then $\beta := 1$
Else $\beta := 0$	Else $\beta := 0$
output $(\mathcal{M}, \boldsymbol{P}(\cdot, \cdot), \beta)$	output $(\mathcal{M}, \boldsymbol{P}(\cdot, \cdot), \beta)$

where, a predicate $\boldsymbol{P}$ satisfies $\boldsymbol{P}(m, m) = 1$ for any m which is included in support of $\mathcal{M}$, and

$$\mathcal{O}_1(c) = \mathsf{Dec}(sk, c),$$

$$\mathcal{O}_2(c) = \begin{cases} \mathsf{Test} & (\boldsymbol{P}(m, \mathsf{Dec}(sk, c)) = 1) \\ \mathsf{Dec}(sk, \cdot) & (\text{otherwise}). \end{cases}$$

In above two experiments, $\mathcal{M}$ is a distribution over the plaintext space.

We define the advantage $\mathsf{Adv}_{\Sigma,\mathcal{A},\mathcal{S},\mathcal{D},h,f}^{\mathrm{SS\text{-}RCCA}}(\lambda)$ as $\mathsf{Adv}_{\Sigma,\mathcal{A},\mathcal{S},\mathcal{D},h,f}^{\mathrm{SS\text{-}RCCA}}(\lambda) :=$ $|\Pr[\mathcal{D}(\mathrm{Exp}_{\Sigma,\mathcal{A},h,f}^{\mathrm{SS\text{-}RCCA\text{-}0}}(\lambda)) \to 1] - \Pr[\mathcal{D}(\mathrm{Exp}_{\Sigma,\mathcal{S},h,f}^{\mathrm{SS\text{-}RCCA\text{-}1}}(\lambda)) \to 1]|.$

Definition 5 (SS-RCCA security). *We say that Σ is SS-RCCA secure if for any polynomial time computable function h and f, and for any pair of PPTAs $\mathcal{A}$, there exists a simulator $\mathcal{S}$ such that $\mathsf{Adv}_{\Sigma,\mathcal{A},\mathcal{S},\mathcal{D},h,f}^{\mathrm{SS\text{-}RCCA}}(\lambda)$ is negligible for any PPTA $\mathcal{D}$.*

A.1   IND-RCCA Implies SS-RCCA

We prove that IND-RCCA implies SS-RCCA by a case analysis. Like as proofs of Theorems 3 and 4, we consider two cases that the size of the plaintext space which a PKE scheme Σ supports is polynomial or not.

Theorem 7. *If a PKE scheme $\Sigma = (\mathsf{Gen}, \mathsf{Enc}, \mathsf{Dec})$ is IND-RCCA secure, and the size of plaintext space of Σ is polynomial, then Σ is SS-RCCA secure.*

We omit proof of the theorem.

Theorem 8. *If a PKE scheme $\Sigma = (\mathsf{Gen}, \mathsf{Enc}, \mathsf{Dec})$ is IND-RCCA secure, and the size of the plaintext space of Σ is super polynomially large, then Σ is SS-RCCA secure.*

We omit proof of the theorem.

The following theorem holds from Theorems 7 and 8.

Theorem 9. *If a PKE scheme $\Sigma = (\mathsf{Gen}, \mathsf{Enc}, \mathsf{Dec})$ is IND-RCCA secure, then Σ is SS-RCCA secure.*

A.2   SS-RCCA Implies IND-RCCA

Theorem 10. *If a PKE scheme $\Sigma = (\mathsf{Gen}, \mathsf{Enc}, \mathsf{Dec})$ is SS-RCCA secure, then Σ is IND-RCCA secure.*

We omit proof of the theorem.

References

1. Dolev, D., Dwork, C., Naor, M.: Non-malleable cryptography (extended abstract). In: STOC, pp. 542–552 (1991)
2. Bellare, M., Desai, A., Pointcheval, D., Rogaway, P.: Relations among notions of security for public-key encryption schemes. In: Krawczyk, H. (ed.) CRYPTO 1998. LNCS, vol. 1462, pp. 26–45. Springer, Heidelberg (1998). https://doi.org/10.1007/BFb0055718
3. Canetti, R., Krawczyk, H., Nielsen, J.B.: Relaxing chosen-ciphertext security. In: Boneh, D. (ed.) CRYPTO 2003. LNCS, vol. 2729, pp. 565–582. Springer, Heidelberg (2003). https://doi.org/10.1007/978-3-540-45146-4_33
4. Pass, R., Shelat, A., Vaikuntanathan, V.: Relations among notions of non-malleability for encryption. In: Kurosawa, K. (ed.) ASIACRYPT 2007. LNCS, vol. 4833, pp. 519–535. Springer, Heidelberg (2007). https://doi.org/10.1007/978-3-540-76900-2_32
5. Katz, J., Yung, M.: Characterization of security notions for probabilistic private-key encryption. J. Cryptol. **19**(1), 67–95 (2006)
6. Goldwasser, S., Micali, S.: Probabilistic encryption. J. Comput. Syst. Sci. **28**(2), 270–299 (1984)

7. Watanabe, Y., Shikata, J., Imai, H.: Equivalence between semantic security and indistinguishability against chosen ciphertext attacks. In: Desmedt, Y.G. (ed.) PKC 2003. LNCS, vol. 2567, pp. 71–84. Springer, Heidelberg (2003). https://doi.org/10.1007/3-540-36288-6_6

8. Bellare, M., Sahai, A.: Non-malleable encryption: equivalence between two notions, and an indistinguishability-based characterization. IACR Cryptology ePrint Archive 2006/228 (2006)

9. Chen, Y., Dong, Q.: RCCA security for KEM+DEM style hybrid encryptions and a general hybrid paradigm from RCCA-secure KEMs to CCA-secure encryptions. Secur. Commun. Netw. **7**(8), 1219–1231 (2014)

10. Libert, B., Vergnaud, D.: Unidirectional chosen-ciphertext secure proxy re-encryption. In: Cramer, R. (ed.) PKC 2008. LNCS, vol. 4939, pp. 360–379. Springer, Heidelberg (2008). https://doi.org/10.1007/978-3-540-78440-1_21

11. Li, K., Wang, J., Zhang, Y., Ma, H.: Key policy attribute-based proxy re-encryption and RCCA secure scheme. J. Internet Serv. Inf. Secur. **4**(2), 70–82 (2014)

12. Dai, H., Wang, D., Chang, J., Xu, M.: On the RCCA security of hybrid signcryption for internet of things. Wirel. Commun. Mob. Comput. **2018**, 8646973:1–8646973:11 (2018)

13. Lu, R., Lin, X., Shao, J., Liang, K.: RCCA-secure multi-use bidirectional proxy re-encryption with master secret security. In: Chow, S.S.M., Liu, J.K., Hui, L.C.K., Yiu, S.M. (eds.) ProvSec 2014. LNCS, vol. 8782, pp. 194–205. Springer, Cham (2014). https://doi.org/10.1007/978-3-319-12475-9_14

14. Backes, M., Cachin, C.: Public-key steganography with active attacks. In: Kilian, J. (ed.) TCC 2005. LNCS, vol. 3378, pp. 210–226. Springer, Heidelberg (2005). https://doi.org/10.1007/978-3-540-30576-7_12

15. Abe, M., Gennaro, R., Kurosawa, K.: Tag-KEM/DEM: a new framework for hybrid encryption. J. Cryptol. **21**(1), 97–130 (2008)

16. Groth, J.: Rerandomizable and replayable adaptive chosen ciphertext attack secure cryptosystems. In: Naor, M. (ed.) TCC 2004. LNCS, vol. 2951, pp. 152–170. Springer, Heidelberg (2004). https://doi.org/10.1007/978-3-540-24638-1_9

17. Prabhakaran, M., Rosulek, M.: Rerandomizable RCCA encryption. In: Menezes, A. (ed.) CRYPTO 2007. LNCS, vol. 4622, pp. 517–534. Springer, Heidelberg (2007). https://doi.org/10.1007/978-3-540-74143-5_29

18. Chase, M., Kohlweiss, M., Lysyanskaya, A., Meiklejohn, S.: Malleable proof systems and applications. In: Pointcheval, D., Johansson, T. (eds.) EUROCRYPT 2012. LNCS, vol. 7237, pp. 281–300. Springer, Heidelberg (2012). https://doi.org/10.1007/978-3-642-29011-4_18

19. Libert, B., Peters, T., Qian, C.: Structure-preserving chosen-ciphertext security with shorter verifiable ciphertexts. In: Fehr, S. (ed.) PKC 2017. LNCS, vol. 10174, pp. 247–276. Springer, Heidelberg (2017). https://doi.org/10.1007/978-3-662-54365-8_11

Cocks' Identity-Based Encryption in the Standard Model, via Obfuscation Techniques (Short Paper)

Xin Wang[1,2], Shimin Li[1,2], and Rui Xue[1,2(✉)]

[1] State Key Laboratory of Information Security, Institute of Information Engineering, Chinese Academy of Sciences, Beijing, China
[2] School of Cyber Security, University of Chinese Academy of Sciences, Beijing, China
{wangxin9076,lishimin,xuerui}@iie.ac.cn

Abstract. Identity-based encryption (IBE) is an attractive primitive in modern cryptography. Cocks first gave an elegant construction of IBE under Quadratic Residuosity (QR) assumption. Unfortunately, its security works only in the Random Oracle (RO) model. In this work, we aim at providing Cock's scheme with provable security in the *standard* model. Specifically, we modify Cocks' scheme by explicitly instantiating the hash function using indistinguishability obfuscation in two different ways which yield two variants of Cocks' scheme. Their security are promised under well-defined selective-ID and adaptive-ID model respectively. As an additional contribution, we adapt the same method into the Boneh, LaVigne, Sabin (BLS) e^{th} residuosity based IBE cryptosystem and obtain an adaptive chosen-ID secure scheme under Modified e^{th} Residuosity (MER) assumption.

Keywords: Identity-based encryption · Cocks' scheme · Random oracle

1 Introduction

Identity-Based Encryption (IBE), first initiated by Shamir [13], offers an alternative way to implement public key infrastructure and sheds light on deriving a user's public key from arbitrary string together with a common public parameter. The early constructions mainly grounded on the structure of a bilinear group where a pairing operation is allowed. This ramification, known as pairing-based IBE, first achieved provable security in the Random Oracle (RO) model [2] and later developed in the standard model [3–5]. In recent years, lattices has become a candidate algebraic structure for designing cryptographic primitives including IBE [1,9]. An entirely different method to build IBE was due to Cocks [7]. The construction takes place in a well investigated group $\mathbb{Z}_N^*$ and merely depends on simple and efficient number-theoretic operations. The security is proved under

© Springer Nature Switzerland AG 2019
N. Attrapadung and T. Yagi (Eds.): IWSEC 2019, LNCS 11689, pp. 273–283, 2019.
https://doi.org/10.1007/978-3-030-26834-3_16

a well-known assumption called Quadratic Residuosity (QR) assumption [10] in the random oracle model. Cocks' scheme, in comparison with the other two types of constructions (pairing-based and lattice-based), has many advantages such as working in a standard composite-order group, relying on quite basic mathematics, and so forth. But it is hard to do any security proof in the standard model. In Cocks' scheme, the public key corresponding to an identity is designated as the hash value of this identity, which is a quadratic residue and the secret key of the identity is a square root of it. When trying to reduce the security to QR assumption, the simulator needs to respond to the adversary's secret key queries. The tricky part naturally appears: how to compute square root of a quadratic residue, even without the factorization of a public modulus? With the help of random oracle heuristic, this obstacle could be tackled, in a reverse direction. The simulator maintains an empty list that stores entries of hash value and square roots. It randomly picks a uniform distributed value within a certain group and then squares it to be the hash value whenever a query comes. In this way the key extraction issue no longer bothers since the simulator always knows a root of hash value of any identity except the challenge one.

Our Results. In this paper, we dedicate to investigating Cocks' scheme in the standard model. As was mentioned in [11], their techniques for proving security of a certain signature scheme are applicable for Boneh-Franklin IBE scheme so that it can be proved both selectively and adaptively secure in the standard model under different paring-based assumptions. Yet no explicit evidence reveals that the QR-based scheme could have such results in the standard model. Inspired by the work of [11], which provides a subtle framework of instantiating random oracle using indistinguishability obfuscation in full domain hash signature schemes, we inspected Cocks' scheme and carefully examined the feasibility of establishing concrete hash functions in the group $\mathbb{Z}_N^*$. Specifically, we instantiate the hash function in two different ways using indistinguishability obfuscation and reach the goal of basing the security of Cocks' scheme on QR assumption in commonly accepted selective-ID and adaptive-ID security model. As our first attempt, we give a selectively secure scheme, namely Cocks' Variant I. In this scheme, we could securely map a bitstring to a quadratic residue within $\mathbb{Z}_N^*$ using indistinguishability obfuscation together with puncturable pseudorandom function and security proof works in a very natural way. To get adaptive security, we combine indistinguishability obfuscation with admissible hash function to implement the hash function, which derives Cocks' Variant II. For security, we take advantage of the techniques appeared in [11].

As an additional contribution, we adapt the constructing and proving methods into the Boneh, LaVigne, Sabin (BLS) e^{th} residuosity based IBE cryptosystem [6] and obtain an adaptive chosen-ID secure scheme.

2   Preliminaries

Let $N = pq$ be the product of two primes p and q. The set of integers with Jacobi symbol 1 is denoted by $\mathbb{J}_N$. The quadratic residues form a subgroup $\mathbb{QR}_N$. The set of quadratic non-residues with Jacobi symbol $+1$ is denoted by $\mathbb{QNR}^+$.

Definition 1 (Quadratic Residuosity Assumption [10]). *Let* RSAGen *be an algorithm that, given a security parameter λ, outputs primes p, q and their product $N = pq$. The Quadratic Residuosity (QR) assumption relative to* RSAGen *asserts that the probability below is negligible for any p.p.t distinguisher $\mathcal{D}$:*

$$\left| \Pr[\mathcal{D}(v, N) = 1 \mid v \leftarrow \mathbb{QR}_N] - \Pr[\mathcal{D}(v, N) = 1 \mid v \leftarrow \mathbb{QNR}^+] \right|.$$

Assuming that *strong* primes are sufficiently dense [8], the QR assumption also implies that if p, q are strong primes, the distinguishing task above will be computationally infeasible too. In this case, we call the modulus as an *strong RSA modulus* for convenience. Next, we will introduce some useful notions in higher residue case. We follow the notations in [6].

Let $e \geq 2$ be an integer and $N = pq$ be an RSA modulus with $p, q \equiv 1 \mod e$. The eth power residue symbol of an integer a modulo N is written as $\left(\frac{a}{N}\right)_e$. The symbol will always yield an eth root of unity. The trivial e^{th} root of unity is 1. Some e^{th} roots of unity are called degenerate since if they are leaked, the factorization of N is easy to get. $\mathcal{Z}$ denotes the set of nontrivial, non-degenerate e^{th} roots of unity in $\mathbb{Z}_N$. The set of eth residues in $\mathbb{Z}_N^*$ is denoted by $\mathbb{ER}_N$ and the set of elements that have symbol 1 is represented by $\mathbb{PR}_N$. Boneh et al. [6] formalized the Modified e^{th} Residuosity (MER) assumption which posits that given an integer which has symbol 1 with a non-degenerate e^{th} root of unity published, it is hard to tell whether it is an eth residue or not.

2.1   Admissible Hash Functions

Definition 2 ([4,11]). *Let ℓ, n and θ be efficiently computable univariate polynomials. Let $h : \{0,1\}^{\ell(\lambda)} \rightarrow \{0,1\}^{n(\lambda)}$ be an efficiently computable function and* AdmSample *a p.p.t algorithm that takes as input 1^λ and an integer Q, and outputs $u \in \{0, 1, \perp\}^{n(\lambda)}$. For any $u \in \{0, 1, \perp\}^{n(\lambda)}$, define $P_u : \{0,1\}^{\ell(\lambda)} \rightarrow \{0,1\}$ as follows:*

$$P_u(x) = \begin{cases} 1 & \text{if } \exists j \leq n(\lambda), \ u_j = h(x)_j \\ 0 & \text{if } \forall j \leq n(\lambda), \ u_j \neq h(x)_j, \end{cases}$$

where $u_j, h(x)_j$ denote the j-th bit of $u, h(x)$ respectively.

We say that $(h, \mathsf{AdmSample})$ is θ-admissible if the following condition holds: For any efficiently computable polynomial Q, for all $x_1, \ldots, x_{Q(\lambda)}, x^* \in \{0,1\}^{\ell(\lambda)}$, where $x^* \notin \{x_i\}_{i=1}^{Q(\lambda)}$, $\Pr[(\forall i \leq Q(\lambda), P_u(x_i) = 1) \wedge P_u(x^*) = 0] \geq \frac{1}{\theta(Q(\lambda))}$, where the probability is taken over $u \leftarrow \mathsf{AdmSample}(1^\lambda, Q(\lambda))$.

2.2   Identity-Based Encryption

Definition 3 (Identity-Based Encryption [5]). *An identity-based encryption scheme with message space $\mathcal{M}$ and ciphertext space $\mathcal{C}$ consists of four algorithms* (Setup, KeyGen, Enc, Dec):

- Setup(1^λ): *Inputs a security parameter λ and outputs public parameters* mpk *and a master secret key* msk.
- KeyGen(msk, id): *Inputs* msk *and an arbitrary* id $\in \{0,1\}^*$, *and outputs a corresponding secret key* $\mathsf{sk}_{\mathsf{id}}$.
- Enc(mpk, id, m): *Inputs* mpk, id, *and* $m \in \mathcal{M}$, *and outputs a ciphertext* $c \in \mathcal{C}$.
- Dec(c, $\mathsf{sk}_{\mathsf{id}}$): *Inputs* $c \in \mathcal{C}$, *and a user secret key* $\mathsf{sk}_{\mathsf{id}}$, *and outputs* $m \in \mathcal{M}$.

Definition 4 (IND-aID-CPA security [5]). *We say that an identity-based encryption scheme Π has indistinguishable encryptions against adaptive chosen-ID, chosen plaintext attack (IND-aID-CPA) if no p.p.t adversary $\mathcal{A}$ has a non-negligible advantage over the Challenger in the following* IND-aID-CPA *game:*

Setup: *A challenger runs the* Setup *algorithm. It gives $\mathcal{A}$ the resulting public parameters* mpk *and keeps the corresponding master secret key* msk.

Phase 1: *$\mathcal{A}$ issues key extraction queries* $\mathsf{id}_1, \ldots, \mathsf{id}_{n_1}$. *The challenger responds by running algorithm* KeyGen *to generate user secret key* $\mathsf{sk}_{\mathsf{id}_i}$ *corresponding to identity* id_i. *It sends* $\mathsf{sk}_{\mathsf{id}_i}$ *to $\mathcal{A}$. These queries may be asked adaptively.*

Challenge: *Once $\mathcal{A}$ decides that Phase 1 is over it outputs two equal length messages $m_0, m_1 \in \mathcal{M}$ and an identity* id^* *on which it wishes to be challenged subject to the constraint that* $\mathsf{id}^* \neq \mathsf{id}_i$ *for $1 \le i \le n_1$. The challenger picks a random bit b and sends* $C^* = $ Enc(mpk, id^*, m_b) *as the challenge to $\mathcal{A}$.*

Phase 2: *$\mathcal{A}$ issues more key extraction queries* $\mathsf{id}_{n_1+1}, \ldots, \mathsf{id}_n$ *where* $\mathsf{id}_i \neq \mathsf{id}^*$ *for $n_1 + 1 \le i \le n$. The challenger responds as in Phase 1.*

Guess: *Finally, $\mathcal{A}$ outputs a guess b' and wins the game if $b' = b$.*

We refer to such an adversary $\mathcal{A}$ as an IND-aID-CPA *adversary. We define the advantage of it against the IBE scheme Π as*

$$\mathrm{Adv}_{\mathcal{A}}^{\Pi} = \left| \Pr[b' = b] - \frac{1}{2} \right|.$$

3   Cocks' Variant I (Selectively Secure)

We instantiate the hash function in Cocks' scheme with an obfuscated program that returns square of an output of puncturable PRF.

- Setup(1^λ): Generate an RSA modulus $N = pq$. Next, sample a key K for the puncturable PRF $F(K, \cdot) : \{0,1\}^\ell \to \{0,1\}^n$ where $n = \log N$. Then build an obfuscation of the program id-to-qr hash (Fig. 1). The size of this program is padded to the maximum of itself and the program id-to-qr hash* (Fig. 2). This obfuscated program is used as the hash function $\mathcal{H} : \{0,1\}^\ell \to \mathbb{QR}_N$. The master public key mpk is $(N, \mathcal{H})$. The master secret key msk is (p, q).

Input: Identity id
Constants: RSA modulus N, punctured PRF key K

1. Compute $a = F(K, \text{id})$.
2. Output $a^2 \bmod N$.

Fig. 1. Program id-to-qr hash

Input: Identity id
Constants: RSA modulus N, punctured PRF key $K(\{\text{id}^*\})$, $\text{id}^* \in \{0,1\}^\ell$, $v \in \mathbb{J}_N$

1. If id $=$ id*, output v.
2. Else output $a^2 \bmod N$ where $a = F(K(\{\text{id}^*\}), \text{id})$.

Fig. 2. Program id-to-qr hash*

- KeyGen(msk, id): Compute $r_{\text{id}} = \mathcal{H}(\text{id})^{1/2} \bmod N$. Return key $\text{sk}_{\text{id}} = r_{\text{id}}$.
- Enc(mpk, id, m): To encrypt a message $m \in \{\pm 1\}$ to user whose identity is id $\in \{0,1\}^\ell$, choose random $t \in \mathbb{Z}_N$ such that $\left(\frac{t}{N}\right) = m$. Then compute $c = t + \frac{\mathcal{H}(\text{id})}{t} \bmod N$. Return ciphertext c.
- Dec(c, sk_{id}): The message m is recovered as $m = \left(\frac{c+2r_{\text{id}}}{N}\right)$.

Theorem 1. *If the obfuscation scheme is indistinguishably secure, F is a secure puncturable PRF, and QR assumption holds in $\mathbb{Z}_N^*$, then Cocks' Variant I is selectively secure.*

The proof is straightforward and can be found in the full version.

4   Cocks' Variant II (Adaptively Secure)

We build the hash function for Cocks' scheme more subtly to prove adaptive security. The only difference compared with the selective case is how to setup:

- Setup(1^λ): Generate a *strong* RSA modulus $N = pq$. Next, pick n pairs of integers $(a_{1,0}, a_{1,1}), \ldots, (a_{n,0}, a_{n,1})$, uniformly at random from the range $[1, \phi(N)/4 - 1]$. Sample $v \leftarrow \mathbb{QR}_N$. Then build an obfuscation of the program Admissible Hash (Fig. 3). The size of this program is padded to the maximum of itself and the program Admissible Hash* (Fig. 4). This obfuscated program is used as the hash function $\mathcal{H} : \{0,1\}^\ell \rightarrow \mathbb{QR}_N$. The master public key mpk is composed of $(N, \mathcal{H})$. The master secret key msk is (p, q).

Theorem 2. *If the obfuscation scheme is indistinguishably secure, and the QR assumption holds in $\mathbb{Z}_N^*$, then Cocks' Variant II is IND-aID-CPA.*

Input: Identity id
Constants: RSA modulus N, $(a_{1,0}, a_{1,1}), \ldots, (a_{n,0}, a_{n,1}) \in [1, \frac{\phi(N)}{4} - 1]$, $v \in \mathbb{QR}_N$

1. Compute $\mathsf{id}' = h(\mathsf{id})$.
2. Output $v^{\prod_{i \in [n]} a_{i, \mathsf{id}'_i}} \bmod N$.

Fig. 3. Program Admissible Hash

Input: Identity id
Constants: RSA modulus N, $(c_{1,0}, c_{1,1}), \ldots, (c_{n,0}, c_{n,1})$ chosen as in Game_2, $v \in \mathbb{QR}_N$

1. Compute $\mathsf{id}' = h(\mathsf{id})$.
2. Output $v^{\prod_{i \in [n]} c_{i, \mathsf{id}'_i}} \bmod N$.

Fig. 4. Program Admissible Hash*

Suppose there is a p.p.t IND-aID-CPA adversary $\mathcal{A}$ against Cocks' Variant II. We list a sequence of games to bound its advantage ε. Let Suc_i be the event that $\mathcal{A}$ succeeds in Game_i and Q denote an upper bound of key extraction queries.

- Game_0: The original IND-aID-CPA security game. Specifically,
    1. The challenger sets $N = pq$ where $p = 2p' + 1, q = 2q' + 1$ are safe primes.
    2. The challenger chooses n pairs of integers, $(a_{1,0}, a_{1,1}), \ldots, (a_{n,0}, a_{n,1})$, uniformly at random from $[1, \phi(N)/4 - 1]$. It also samples $v \leftarrow \mathbb{QR}_N$.
    3. The hash function $\mathcal{H}(\cdot)$ is created as an obfuscation of the program Admissible Hash. The master public key mpk is $(N, \mathcal{H})$.
    4. The adversary queries the key extraction oracle a polynomial number of times on $\mathsf{id} \neq \mathsf{id}^*$. The challenger answers by computing $\mathcal{H}(\mathsf{id})^{1/2}$ through its knowledge of factorization of N. Once this phase is over, the adversary announces target identity id^*.
    5. During the challenge phase, the challenger first samples a bit $b \leftarrow \{0, 1\}$, then samples $t \leftarrow \mathbb{Z}_N$ such that $\left(\frac{t}{N}\right) = (-1)^b$ and finally outputs a challenge ciphertext $C^* = t + \frac{\mathcal{H}(\mathsf{id}^*)}{t} \bmod N$.
    6. The adversary receives C^* and could still issue key extraction queries for polynomial times with the same restriction that $\mathsf{id} \neq \mathsf{id}^*$, finally it outputs b' as its guess of b. If $b' = b$, the game outputs 1, else outputs 0.
- Game_1: The same as Game_0 except that the challenger begins by sampling $\mathsf{AdmSample}(1^\lambda, Q) \to u$. Suppose that $\mathcal{A}$ made $\eta \leq Q$ queries on identities $\mathsf{id}_1, \ldots, \mathsf{id}_\eta$. Whenever any of the adversary's queries and its target identity fail to satisfy the condition $P_u(\mathsf{id}_1) = P_u(\mathsf{id}_2) = \cdots = P_u(\mathsf{id}_\eta) = 1 \wedge P_u(\mathsf{id}^*) = 0$, the challenger aborts and chooses a random bit $\beta \leftarrow \{0, 1\}$. If the challenger aborts, $\mathcal{A}$ succeeds if $\beta = 1$. By definition, we already have a non-negligible lower bound on the probability of successfully partitioning:

$$\Pr[(\forall i \leq Q, P_u(\mathsf{id}_i) = 1) \wedge P_u(\mathsf{id}^*) = 0] \geq \frac{1}{\theta(Q)} = \zeta_{\min}.$$

Artificial Abort. Besides, the challenger needs to perform an artificial abort step [14] to even out the probability of abort over all possible sequences of queries. Let the sequence of queries issued by $\mathcal{A}$ be denoted as $\overrightarrow{\text{id}} = \{\text{id}_1, \ldots, \text{id}_Q, \text{id}^*\}$, and $\zeta(\overrightarrow{\text{id}})$ be the probability that the challenger does not abort on this set of issued queries. After $\mathcal{A}$ terminates, the queried sequence $\overrightarrow{\text{id}}$ is well-defined, therefore the challenger estimates the probability of not aborting $\zeta(\overrightarrow{\text{id}})$ as ζ' by freshly sampling $w \leftarrow \mathsf{AdmSample}(1^\lambda, Q)$ T-times (where T will be defined later in Lemma 1), and checking whether for all $j \in [1, Q], P_w(\text{id}_j) = 1$ and $P_w(\text{id}^*) = 0$. Finally, the challenger artificially aborts with probability $\max(0, 1 - \zeta_{\min}/\zeta')$. If it aborts then it chooses a random bit $\beta \leftarrow \{0, 1\}$, and $\mathcal{A}$ wins if $\beta = 1$. Otherwise, $\mathcal{A}$ wins if $b' = b$. Note that this does not require running the adversary again.

- Game$_2$: The same as Game$_1$ except for a few changes. First $y_{i,b}$ is picked uniformly at random from $[1, \frac{N-1}{4}]$. The challenger computes

$$c_{i,b} = \begin{cases} 2 \cdot y_{i,b} & \text{if } b = u_i \\ 2 \cdot y_{i,b} + 1 & \text{if } b \neq u_i. \end{cases}$$

Set $a_{i,b} = (c_{i,b} \mod \frac{\phi(N)}{4})$ for $i \in [n]$ and $b \in \{0, 1\}$. In this game, we change the way that the challenger responding to key extraction queries. When the adversary requests an identity id, the challenger simply computes $h(\text{id})$ and finds an index i such that $h(\text{id})_i = u_i$. The challenger computes and returns $v^{y_{i,\text{id}'_i}} \prod_{j \in ([n] \setminus \{i\})} c_{j,\text{id}'_j} \mod N$ to the adversary as sk$_\text{id}$. Note that factorization of N is no longer needed for the challenger.

- Game$_3$: The same as Game$_2$ except that the hash function $\mathcal{H}(\cdot)$ is created as an obfuscation of the program Admissible Hash* using the values $(c_{1,0}, c_{1,1}), \ldots, (c_{n,0}, c_{n,1})$ formed as in Game$_2$.
- Game$_4$: The same as Game$_3$ except that the challenger samples $v \leftarrow \mathsf{QNR}^+$.

We next analyze the above game sequence. Game$_0$ is the IND-aID-CPA security game, thus we have $|\Pr[\mathsf{Suc}_0] - \frac{1}{2}| = \varepsilon$. We prove the following lemmas which together conclude Theorem 2.

Lemma 1. *If $(h, \mathsf{AdmSample})$ is θ-admissible, then $|\Pr[\mathsf{Suc}_1] - \frac{1}{2}| \geq \frac{3\zeta_{\min}}{8}\varepsilon$.*

Proof. During the artificial abort step in Game$_1$, the challenger takes $T = O(\varepsilon^{-2} \ln(\varepsilon^{-1}) \zeta_{\min}^{-1} \ln(\zeta_{\min}^{-1}))$ samples to approximate the abort probability $\zeta(\overrightarrow{\text{id}})$. Let abort be the event that the challenger aborts. Using standard techniques appeared previously in [12, 14], we get the useful bounds below:

$$\Pr[\mathsf{abort}] \geq 1 - \zeta_{\min} - \zeta_{\min}\frac{3\varepsilon}{8}, \quad \Pr[\overline{\mathsf{abort}}] \geq \zeta_{\min}(1 - \frac{\varepsilon}{4}).$$

Then the probability of Suc$_1$ can be analyzed using these bounds in a similar way like [12]. We conclude that $|\Pr[\mathsf{Suc}_1] - \frac{1}{2}| \geq \frac{3\zeta_{\min}}{8}|\Pr[\mathsf{Suc}_0] - \frac{1}{2}|$. $\square$

Lemma 2. *The success probability of any p.p.t adversary in Game$_1$ is negligibly close to that in Game$_2$.*

Proof. The main difference between Game_1 and Game_2 is the choice of the $a_{i,b}$ values. We next show that these values are statistically indistinguishable. In Game_1, $a_{i,b}$ values are uniformly distributed from $[1, \phi(N)/4 - 1]$. In Game_2, $y_{i,b}$ is uniformly chosen from $[1, \frac{N-1}{4}]$, which is statistically close to the uniform distribution over the range $[1, \frac{\phi(N)}{4} - 1]$. Then, the output distribution of any $a_{i,b}$ value derived from the distributions $(2 \cdot y_{i,b} \bmod \frac{\phi(N)}{4})$ and $(2 \cdot y_{i,b} + 1 \bmod \frac{\phi(N)}{4})$ is statistically close to $[1, \phi(N)/4 - 1]$, which is promised by that $\gcd(2, \phi(N)/4) = 1$. This tells us that $\Pr[\mathsf{Suc}_1] \approx \Pr[\mathsf{Suc}_2]$. $\square$

Lemma 3. *If the obfuscation scheme is indistinguishably secure, then the success probability of any p.p.t adversary in* Game_2 *is negligibly close to* Game_3.

Proof. We build two algorithms Samp and $\mathcal{D}$ to give a reduction to the indistinguishability of the obfuscator.

$\mathsf{Samp}(1^\lambda)$ algorithm first invokes the adversary $\mathcal{A}$ to get its state σ', then runs the Setup algorithm as in the scheme to get $N = pq$. It picks an integer $v \leftarrow \mathbb{QR}_N$. It chooses $(c_{1,0}, c_{1,1}), \ldots, (c_{n,0}, c_{n,1})$ and $(a_{1,0}, a_{1,1}), \ldots, (a_{n,0}, a_{n,1})$ derived from them, as in Game_2. It sets $\sigma = (N, p, q, (c_{1,0}, c_{1,1}), \ldots, (c_{n,0}, c_{n,1}), (a_{1,0}, a_{1,1}), \ldots, (a_{n,0}, a_{n,1}), v, \sigma')$ and builds C_0 as the program for Admissible Hash, and C_1 for Admissible Hash*. We show that the functionality of programs C_0 and C_1 are always the same on every input. Since $v \leftarrow \mathbb{QR}_N$, it is of order $\phi(N)/4$ w.h.p. If so we have $v^{\prod_{i \in [n]} c_{i,\mathsf{id}_i'}} = v^{\left(\prod_{i \in [n]} c_{i,\mathsf{id}_i'}\right) \bmod \phi(N)/4} = v^{\prod_{i \in [n]} \left(c_{i,\mathsf{id}_i'} \bmod \phi(N)/4\right)} = v^{\prod_{i \in [n]} a_{i,\mathsf{id}_i'}}$. This concludes the equivalence between two programs.

We now set up algorithm $\mathcal{D}$. It takes as input σ and $i\mathcal{O}(\lambda, C_d)$ where $d \in \{0,1\}$. $\mathcal{D}$ runs $\mathcal{A}$ and when $\mathcal{A}$ asks for an identity id, it returns $v^{2^{-1} \prod_{j \in [n]} c_{j,\mathsf{id}_j'}} \bmod N$ through its knowledge of v and $c_{i,b}$ values within σ. Once $\mathcal{A}$ submits an identity id^*, $\mathcal{D}$ picks a random bit b, chooses $t \leftarrow \mathbb{Z}_N$ s.t. $\left(\frac{t}{N}\right) = (-1)^b$ and forwards $C^* = t + \frac{\mathcal{H}(\mathsf{id}^*)}{t} \bmod N$ to $\mathcal{A}$. $\mathcal{D}$ answers the extraction queries as above. When $\mathcal{D}$ has received $\mathcal{A}$'s guess b', it outputs 1 if $b' = b$, or 0 otherwise.

By observation, when $d = 0$, i.e. $i\mathcal{O}(\lambda, C_0) = \mathcal{H}(\cdot)$, the environment $\mathcal{D}$ simulated for $\mathcal{A}$ is exactly the same as Game_2. As a result, $\Pr[\mathcal{D}(\sigma, i\mathcal{O}(\lambda, C_0)) = 1] = \Pr[\mathsf{Suc}_2]$. Similarly, $\Pr[\mathcal{D}(\sigma, i\mathcal{O}(\lambda, C_1)) = 1] = \Pr[\mathsf{Suc}_3]$. Due to the indistinguishability of $i\mathcal{O}$, we have

$$\left| \Pr[\mathcal{D}(\sigma, i\mathcal{O}(\lambda, C_0)) = 1] - \Pr[\mathcal{D}(\sigma, i\mathcal{O}(\lambda, C_1)) = 1] \right| \leq \varepsilon_{i\mathcal{O}},$$

where $\varepsilon_{i\mathcal{O}}$ is a negligible function. Thus $\left| \Pr[\mathsf{Suc}_2] - \Pr[\mathsf{Suc}_3] \right| \leq \varepsilon_{i\mathcal{O}}$. $\square$

Lemma 4. *If* QR *assumption holds in* $\mathbb{Z}_N^*$, *then the success probability of any p.p.t adversary in* Game_3 *is negligibly close to that in* Game_4.

Proof. We set up algorithm $\mathcal{B}$ to solve the QR problem. $\mathcal{B}$ takes as input (N, v). It simulates the game for an IND-aID-CPA adversary $\mathcal{A}$. Initially, $\mathcal{B}$ samples $u \leftarrow \mathsf{AdmSample}(1^\lambda, Q)$. Then it sets integers $(c_{1,0}, c_{1,1}), \ldots, (c_{n,0}, c_{n,1})$ in the following way. For $i \in [n]$ and $b \in \{0,1\}$, if $b = u_i$, choose $y_{i,b}$ uniformly at random in $[1, \frac{N-1}{4}]$, and set $c_{i,b} = 2 \cdot y_{i,b}$. Otherwise, set $c_{i,b} = 2 \cdot y_{i,b} + 1$. Next $\mathcal{B}$ creates an obfuscation of the program Admissible Hash* as the hash function $\mathcal{H}(\cdot)$ using the values $(c_{1,0}, c_{1,1}), \ldots, (c_{n,0}, c_{n,1})$ and the challenge (N, v) it received. So far, the Setup phase of Game$_3$ (or Game$_4$) is perfectly simulated. $\mathcal{B}$ then invokes $\mathcal{A}$ using the above generated parameters. $\mathcal{B}$ responds to the key extraction queries as in Game$_2$. In the challenge phase, if the identity output by $\mathcal{A}$ satisfies $h(\mathsf{id}^*)_j \neq u_j$ for $j \in [n]$, $\mathcal{B}$ samples $b \leftarrow \{0,1\}$ and $t \leftarrow \mathbb{Z}_N$ s.t. $\left(\frac{t}{N}\right) = (-1)^b$. $\mathcal{B}$ constructs the challenge ciphertext $C^* = t + \frac{\mathcal{H}(\mathsf{id}^*)}{t} \mod N$ and sends it to $\mathcal{A}$. Finally, $\mathcal{A}$ outputs a bit b'. If $b' = b$, $\mathcal{B}$ outputs 1, otherwise 0.

If $v \in \mathbb{QR}_N$, the environment $\mathcal{B}$ simulated for $\mathcal{A}$ is exactly the same as Game$_3$. Thus, $\Pr[\mathcal{B}(N,v) = 1 \mid v \leftarrow \mathbb{QR}_N] = \Pr[\mathsf{Suc}_3]$. Else if $v \in \mathbb{QNR}^+$, $\mathcal{A}$ interacts with $\mathcal{B}$ as in Game$_4$. Therefore, $\Pr[\mathcal{B}(N,v) = 1 \mid v \leftarrow \mathbb{QNR}^+] = \Pr[\mathsf{Suc}_4]$. The distinguishing advantage of $\mathcal{B}$ is computed as: $|\Pr[\mathcal{B}(N,v) = 1 \mid v \leftarrow \mathbb{QR}_N] - \Pr[\mathcal{B}(N,v) = 1 \mid v \leftarrow \mathbb{QNR}^+]|$, which must be bounded by a negligible $\varepsilon_{\mathsf{QR}}$ by QR assumption. This leads to $|\Pr[\mathsf{Suc}_3] - \Pr[\mathsf{Suc}_4]| \leq \varepsilon_{\mathsf{QR}}$.   □

Lemma 5. *The advantage of any p.p.t adversary in* Game$_4$ *is negligible.*

Proof. It was noted [7] that if $\mathcal{H}(\mathsf{id}^*) \in \mathbb{QNR}^+$, then the challenge ciphertext C^* leaks no information about the bit encrypted. We will show that it's exactly the case in Game$_4$. Remember that the identity id^* submitted by the adversary will satisfy $\forall i \in [n], h(\mathsf{id}^*)_i \neq u_i$. As a result, in Game$_4$, the $c_{i,h(\mathsf{id}^*)_i}$ values will always be generated as odd integers as shown in Game$_2$. Therefore, $\mathcal{H}(\mathsf{id}^*) = v^{\prod_{i \in [n]} c_{i,h(\mathsf{id}^*)_i}} \mod N$ must be in $\mathbb{QNR}^+$. So $\Pr[\mathsf{Suc}_4] \leq \frac{1}{2}$.   □

5   BLS Variant (Adaptively Secure)

- Setup(1^λ): Generate an RSA modulus $N = pq$ where $e|(p-1)$ and $e|(q-1)$. Next, pick $(a_{1,0}, a_{1,1}), \ldots, (a_{n,0}, a_{n,1})$, uniformly at random from the range $[1, \phi(N)/e^2 - 1]$. Sample an element $v \leftarrow \mathbb{ER}_N$. Next choose a non-degenerate primitive e^{th} root of unity $\zeta \in \mathcal{Z}$. Then build an obfuscation of the program id-to-e^{th} residue Hash (Fig. 5). The size of this program is padded to the maximum of itself and the program id-to-e^{th} residue Hash* (Fig. 6). This obfuscated program is used as the hash function $\mathcal{H} : \{0,1\}^\ell \to \mathbb{ER}_N$. The master public key mpk is composed of $(N, e, \zeta, \mathcal{H})$. The master secret key msk is (p, q).
- KeyGen(msk, id): Set $v = \mathcal{H}(\mathsf{id})$. Compute e^{th} root of v using p, q, which is denoted by $r_{\mathsf{id}} = v^{1/e} \mod N$. Return secret key $\mathsf{sk}_{\mathsf{id}} = r_{\mathsf{id}}$.
- Enc(mpk, id, m): Let $v = \mathcal{H}(\mathsf{id})$. To encrypt a message $m \in \{0, \ldots, e-1\}$, choose a random $e-1$ degree polynomial $f(x) \leftarrow \mathbb{Z}_N^*[x]$ and $t \leftarrow \mathbb{Z}_N$. Compute $g(x) = f^e(x) \mod x^e - v$. Then derive the polynomial $c(x) = \frac{g(x)}{t}$. Let $M = \zeta^m$. Return ciphertext $C := (c(x), M \cdot \left(\frac{t}{N}\right)_e)$.
- Dec(C, $\mathsf{sk}_{\mathsf{id}}$): Parse C as $(c(x), d)$. Using $\mathsf{sk}_{\mathsf{id}} = r = v^{1/e}$, compute $c(r) = \frac{g(r)}{t}$. Then compute $M = d \cdot \left(\frac{c(r)}{N}\right)$ and recover the message by finding an integer $m \in \{0, \ldots, e-1\}$ such that $\zeta^m = M$.

Input: Identity id
Constants: RSA modulus N, $(a_{1,0}, a_{1,1}), \ldots, (a_{n,0}, a_{n,1}) \in [1, \frac{\phi(N)}{e^2} - 1]$, $v \in \mathbb{ER}_N$

1. Compute $id' = h(id)$.
2. Output $v^{\prod_{i \in [n]} a_{i,id'_i}} \bmod N$.

Fig. 5. Program id-to-e^{th} residue Hash

Input: Identity id
Constants: RSA modulus N, $(c_{1,0}, c_{1,1}), \ldots, (c_{n,0}, c_{n,1})$ chosen as in Game_2, $v \in \mathbb{ER}_N$

1. Compute $id' = h(id)$.
2. Output $v^{\prod_{i \in [n]} c_{i,id'_i}} \bmod N$.

Fig. 6. Program id-to-e^{th} residue Hash*

Theorem 3. *If the obfuscation scheme is indistinguishably secure, and the* MER *assumption holds in* $\mathbb{Z}_N^*$, *the BLS Variant scheme is* IND-aID-CPA.

The security proof is analogous to the process of acquiring adaptive security of Cocks' Variant II scheme. We list the game sequence in the full version.

Acknowledgments. The authors would like to thank anonymous reviewers for their helpful comments and suggestions. This work was supported by National Natural Science Foundation of China (Grants 61772514,61602061), and National Key R&D Program of China (2017YFB1400700).

References

1. Agrawal, S., Boneh, D., Boyen, X.: Efficient lattice (H)IBE in the standard model. In: Gilbert, H. (ed.) EUROCRYPT 2010. LNCS, vol. 6110, pp. 553–572. Springer, Heidelberg (2010). https://doi.org/10.1007/978-3-642-13190-5_28
2. Bellare, M., Rogaway, P.: Random oracles are practical: A paradigm for designing efficient protocols. In: CCS (1993)
3. Boneh, D., Boyen, X.: Efficient selective-ID secure identity-based encryption without random oracles. In: Cachin, C., Camenisch, J.L. (eds.) EUROCRYPT 2004. LNCS, vol. 3027, pp. 223–238. Springer, Heidelberg (2004). https://doi.org/10.1007/978-3-540-24676-3_14
4. Boneh, D., Boyen, X.: Secure identity based encryption without random oracles. In: Franklin, M. (ed.) CRYPTO 2004. LNCS, vol. 3152, pp. 443–459. Springer, Heidelberg (2004). https://doi.org/10.1007/978-3-540-28628-8_27
5. Boneh, D., Franklin, M.: Identity-based encryption from the weil pairing. In: Kilian, J. (ed.) CRYPTO 2001. LNCS, vol. 2139, pp. 213–229. Springer, Heidelberg (2001). https://doi.org/10.1007/3-540-44647-8_13
6. Boneh, D., LaVigne, R., Sabin, M.: Identity-based encryption with eth residuosity and its incompressibility. In: TRUST (2013)

7. Cocks, C.: An identity based encryption scheme based on quadratic residues. In: Honary, B. (ed.) Cryptography and Coding 2001. LNCS, vol. 2260, pp. 360–363. Springer, Heidelberg (2001). https://doi.org/10.1007/3-540-45325-3_32

8. Cramer, R., Shoup, V.: Universal hash proofs and a paradigm for adaptive chosen ciphertext secure public-key encryption. In: Knudsen, L.R. (ed.) EUROCRYPT 2002. LNCS, vol. 2332, pp. 45–64. Springer, Heidelberg (2002). https://doi.org/10.1007/3-540-46035-7_4

9. Gentry, C., Peikert, C., Vaikuntanathan, V.: Trapdoors for hard lattices and new cryptographic constructions. In: STOC (2008)

10. Goldwasser, S., Micali, S.: Probabilistic encryption. J. Comput. Syst. Sci. $\mathbf{28}(2)$, 270–299 (1984)

11. Hohenberger, S., Sahai, A., Waters, B.: Replacing a random oracle: full domain hash from indistinguishability obfuscation. In: Nguyen, P.Q., Oswald, E. (eds.) EUROCRYPT 2014. LNCS, vol. 8441, pp. 201–220. Springer, Heidelberg (2014). https://doi.org/10.1007/978-3-642-55220-5_12

12. Hohenberger, S., Waters, B.: Constructing verifiable random functions with large input spaces. In: Gilbert, H. (ed.) EUROCRYPT 2010. LNCS, vol. 6110, pp. 656–672. Springer, Heidelberg (2010). https://doi.org/10.1007/978-3-642-13190-5_33

13. Shamir, A.: Identity-based cryptosystems and signature schemes. In: Blakley, G.R., Chaum, D. (eds.) CRYPTO 1984. LNCS, vol. 196, pp. 47–53. Springer, Heidelberg (1985). https://doi.org/10.1007/3-540-39568-7_5

14. Waters, B.: Efficient identity-based encryption without random oracles. In: Cramer, R. (ed.) EUROCRYPT 2005. LNCS, vol. 3494, pp. 114–127. Springer, Heidelberg (2005). https://doi.org/10.1007/11426639_7

Cryptanalysis on Symmetric-Key Primitives

Finding Ordinary Cube Variables
for Keccak-MAC with Greedy Algorithm

Fukang Liu[✉], Zhenfu Cao, and Gaoli Wang

Shanghai Key Laboratory of Trustworthy Computing,
East China Normal University, Shanghai, China
liufukangs@163.com

Abstract. In this paper, we introduce an alternative method to find ordinary cube variables for Keccak-MAC by making full use of the key-independent bit conditions. First, we select some potential candidates for ordinary cube variables by properly adding key-independent bit conditions, which do not multiply with the chosen conditional cube variables in the first two rounds. Then, we carefully determine the ordinary cube variables from the candidates to establish the conditional cube tester. Finally, based on our new method to recover the 128-bit key, the conditional cube attack on 7-round Keccak-MAC-128/256/384 is improved to 2^{71} and 6-round Keccak-MAC-512 can be attacked with at most 2^{40} calls to 6-round Keccak internal permutation. It should be emphasized that our new approach does not require sophisticated modeling. As far as we know, it is the first time to clearly reveal how to utilize the key-independent bit conditions to select ordinary cube variables for Keccak-MAC.

Keywords: Hash function · Keccak · Keccak-MAC · Ordinary cube variables · Conditional cube attack

1 Introduction

In 2007, the U.S. National Institute of Standards and Technology (NIST) announced a public contest aiming at the selection of a new standard for a cryptographic hash function after Wang et al. made a break-through in MD-SHA hash family [14,15]. After five years of intensive scrutiny, Keccak was selected as the new SHA-3 standard [2].

Due to the low algebraic degree of a Keccak round, algebraic cryptanalysis has been deeply studied for Keccak, including cube attack [5], cube-attack-like cryptanalysis [3,5,11], conditional cube attack [8,9,12], linear structures for preimage attack [7], one/two/three-round connector for collision attack [4,10,13].

Recently, the application of cube attack on Keccak keyed mode has attracted researchers' interest and several results have been obtained [3,5,8,9,11,12]. Cube attack was first proposed by Dinur and Shamir at Eurocrypt 2009 [6], where a primitive is treated as a black-box polynomial in terms of plaintext and secret

© Springer Nature Switzerland AG 2019
N. Attrapadung and T. Yagi (Eds.): IWSEC 2019, LNCS 11689, pp. 287–305, 2019.
https://doi.org/10.1007/978-3-030-26834-3_17

key. The first application of cube attack to Keccak keyed mode was presented at Eurocrypt 2015 [5]. Two years later, at Eurocrypt 2017, Huang et al. introduced the conditional cube attack [8] on round-reduced Keccak keyed modes based on the pioneer work, i.e. cube attack [5,6] and cube tester [1]. Cube tester was first proposed by Aumasson et al. [1], aiming at detecting the non-random behaviour e.g. the cube sums are always equal to zero. Conditional cube tester detects a non-random behaviour (the cube sums are zero) only when some conditions hold. Therefore, once the key is involved in the conditions, conditional cube tester can be utilized to mount key-recovery attack. Indeed, conditional cube tester can be viewed as a key-dependent distinguisher.

At Eurocrypt 2017, Huang et al. firstly applied the conditional cube tester to mount key-recovery attack on 5/6/7-round Keccak-MAC-512/384/256 [8]. Later at Asiacrypt 2017, an MILP-based method [9] was proposed to identify good parameters for the conditional cube tester. Therefore, the conditional cube attack on Keccak-MAC-512/384 was extended by one more round. However, it seems that the modelling in [9] did not capture all factors influencing the performance of attack. Consequently, by taking more factors into consideration, Song et al. developed a new general MILP approach for Keccak-based primitives at Asiacrypt 2018 [12] and presented many applications. Despite that Song et al. claimed that 64-dimensional cube variables with only 2 key-dependent bit conditions were found, the details of the 64-dimensional cube variables were not reported in [12]. For the new modeling in [12], it seems sophisticated at the first glance. However, since more factors are taken into account, it is more general and powerful to mount new or improved attack on many Keccak-based constructions.

Due to the limited number of bits of Keccak-MAC-512 that can be controlled for an attacker, it is very difficult to find 64-dimensional cube variables under the conditional cube attack framework proposed by Huang et al. [8]. However, cube-attack-like cryptanalysis works quite well for Keccak-MAC-512 and attack on 7-round Keccak-MAC-512 was first achieved in [3], which was later slightly improved in [11].

Up until now, the improvement for [8] are all based on the MILP approach [9,12], which sometimes requires sophisticated modeling. This motivates us to consider whether there exist other simple approaches to find sufficient cube variables to establish the conditional cube tester.

Our Contributions. In this paper, we present an alternative method to find ordinary cube variables for Keccak-MAC-512/384. First, we observe that there are many potentially useful key-independent conditions to slow down the propagation of ordinary cube variables, which will help determine the candidates for ordinary cube variables. Then, we introduce a clever way to choose the ordinary cube variables from the candidates by considering their relations in the first round. With such a method, sufficient ordinary cube variables can be discovered to establish the conditional cube tester for 6-round Keccak-MAC-512 and 7-round Keccak-MAC-384. Meanwhile, the number of key-dependent bit conditions is minimum. It should be stressed that we do not use any specific greedy algorithms but use the idea of greedy algorithm. Specifically, we determine a small region of potential candidates at first and then select the final candidates from these potential candidates. As far as we know, it is the first time to clearly reveal how to utilize the key-independent bit conditions to select ordinary cube variables for Keccak-MAC.

Moreover, we observe that there are many unnecessary iterations of the conditional cube tester to recover the full key in [8]. Therefore, an optimal procedure to recover the full key for 7-round Keccak-MAC-256/128 based on the conditional cube tester in [8] is proposed and the new key-recovery attack is twice faster. Such an optimal approach is applied to the newly discovered 64-dimensional cube variables for 7-round Keccak-MAC-384. Consequently, conditional cube attack on 7-round Keccak-MAC-384 is improved to 2^{71} from 2^{75}. By carefully choosing the order to recover the full key, we can recover the 128-bit key for 6-round Keccak-MAC-512 with at most 2^{40} calls to 6-round Keccak internal permutation, while it costs $\lceil \frac{128}{3} \rceil \times 2^{2^5+3} = \lceil \frac{128}{3} \rceil \times 2^{35} \approx 2^{40.4}$ calls in [12]. The results are summarized in Table 1.

Table 1. Related results of Keccak-MAC

Attack type	Capacity	Rounds	Time	Ref.
Conditional cube attack	256/512	7	2^{72}	[8]
	768	7	2^{75}	[9]
	1024	6	$2^{40.4}$	[12]
	256/512/768	7	2^{71}	Sect. 4
	1024	6	2^{40}	Sect. 5
Cube-attack-like cryptanalysis	1024	7	$2^{112.6}$	[3]
	1024	7	2^{111}	[11]

Organization. The rest of the paper is organized as follows. The preliminaries of this paper will be presented in Sect. 2. In Sect. 3, our tracing algorithm will be introduced. Then, we will show our method to find enough ordinary cube variables for Keccak-MAC-384 and Keccak-MAC-512 in Sects. 4 and 5 respectively. Next, a slightly improved key-recovery method will be given in Sect. 6. The difference between our work and previous work is explained in Sect. 7. At last, we summarize the paper in Sect. 8.

2   Preliminaries

In this section, we will introduce the details of Keccak-MAC and some related techniques such as cube tester and conditional cube tester.

2.1 Description of Keccak-MAC

Keccak is a family of hash functions and Keccak-MAC is based on Keccak. The Keccak internal permutations denoted by Keccak-p$[b, n_r]$ are specified by two parameters, which are the width of permutation in bits b and the number of rounds n_r. There are many choices for b, i.e. $b = 25 \times 2^l$ with $l \in \{0, 1, 2, 3, 4, 5, 6\}$. Keccak-p$[b, n_r]$ works on a b-bit state A and iterates an identical round function $\mathbf{R}$ for n_r times. The state A can be viewed as a three-dimensional array of bits, namely $A[5][5][w]$ with $w = 2^l$. The expression $A[x][y][z]$ represents the bit with (x, y, z) coordinate. At lane level, $A[x][y]$ represents the w-bit word located at the xth column and the yth row. In this paper, the coordinates are considered within modulo 5 for x and y and within modulo w for z. The round function $\mathbf{R}$ consists of five operations $\mathbf{R} = \iota \circ \chi \circ \pi \circ \rho \circ \theta$ as follows.

$$\theta : A[x][y] = A[x][y] \oplus (\bigoplus_{y'=0}^{4} A[x-1][y']) \oplus (\bigoplus_{y'=0}^{4} (A[x+1][y'] \lll 1)).$$

$$\rho : A[x][y] = A[x][y] \lll r[x, y].$$

$$\pi : A[y][2x + 3y] = A[x][y].$$

$$\chi : A[x][y] = A[x][y] \oplus (\overline{A[x+1][y]} \wedge A[x+2][y]).$$

$$\iota : A[x][y] = A[x][y] \oplus RC.$$

According to the above definition of θ operation, it could be seen that if certain variable in every column of state has even parity, the variable will not diffuse to other columns. In Keccak specification [2], this property is called **column parity kernel, CP kernel** for short.

The construction of Keccak-MAC-n is illustrated in Fig. 1. For the sake of convenience, we denote the state A after θ, ρ, and π in round i ($i \geq 0$) by A_θ^i, A_ρ^i and A_π^i respectively. The input state of round i is denoted by A^i. The 128-bit key is denoted by k, where k_i represents the ith bit of k.

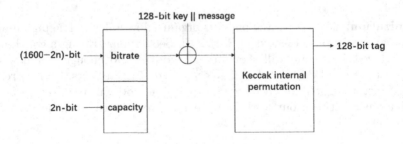

Fig. 1. Construction of Keccak-MAC-n

For Keccak-MAC-n, where $n \in \{128, 256, 384, 512\}$, the size of the internal state is 1600 bits and the 128-bit key is placed at $A^0[0][0]$ and $A^0[1][0]$. Specifically, k_i is placed at $A^0[0][0][i]$ and k_{i+64} is placed at $A^0[1][0][i]$, where $0 \leq i \leq 63$. Therefore, we can obtain Observation 1.

Observation 1. *Since*

$$A_\theta^0[3][i] = A^0[3][i] \oplus \left(\bigoplus_{y=0}^{4} A^0[2][y]\right) \oplus \left(\bigoplus_{y=0}^{4}(A^0[4][y] \lll 1)\right)$$

for $0 \le i \le 4$, $A_\theta^0[3][i]$ is independent of the 128-bit key. In other words, if we add bit conditions on $A_\theta^0[3][i]$, all of them are key-independent.

Then, we consider the influence of $\pi \circ \rho$ operation as shown in Fig. 2. Consequently, Observation 2 can be obtained.

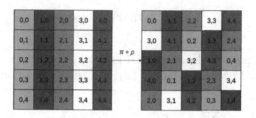

Fig. 2. $\pi \circ \rho$ operation

Observation 2. *After $\pi \circ \rho$ operation, $A_\theta^0[2][i]$ and $A_\theta^0[4][t]$ are next to $A_\theta^0[3][j]$ in each row, where $(i, j, t) \in \{(2,3,4),(4,0,1),(1,2,3),(3,4,0),(0,1,2)\}$.*

Our approach to determine the candidates for ordinary cube variables is heavily based on the two observations.

2.2   Cube Tester

Cube tester was first proposed by Aumasson et al. at FSE 2009 [1] after Dinur et al. introduced cube attack at Eurocrypt 2009 [6]. Different from standard cube attack, which aims at key extraction, cube tester performs non-randomness detection. In our paper, we only concentrate on a specific non-random behaviour, i.e. the cube sums are zero. To describe cube tester, we first recall the concept of cube attack as follows.

Theorem 1 [6]. *Given a polynomial f: $\{0,1\}^n \to \{0,1\}$ of degree d. Suppose $0 < k < d$ and t denotes the monomial $x_0 \ldots x_{k-1}$. Then, f can be written as*

$$f = t \cdot P_t(x_k, \ldots, x_{n-1}) + Q_t(X),$$

where none of the terms of $Q_t(X)$ is divisible by t. Then the sum of f over all values of the cube (defined by t) is

$$\sum_{x' \in C_t} f = \sum_{x' \in C_t} f(x', x_k, \ldots, x_{n-1}) = P_t(x_k, \ldots, x_{n-1}).$$

If there exists such a cube C_t that the following equation always hold, then C_t can be viewed as one type of cube tester [1], i.e. the sum over it always equals zero.

$$\sum_{x' \in C_t} f = \sum_{x' \in C_t} f(x', x_k, \ldots, x_{n-1}) = P_t(x_k, \ldots, x_{n-1}) = 0.$$

For example, consider the following polynomial f:

$$f(x_0, x_1, x_2, x_3) = x_0 x_1 + x_1 x_2 + x_2 x_4 + x_1 x_3 + x_1 x_2 x_4.$$

Then, the following equation always hold:

$$\sum_{(x_0, x_3) \in \{0,1\}^2} f(x_0, x_1, x_2, x_3) = 0.$$

The reason is that none of the monomial in $f(x_0, x_1, x_2, x_3)$ is divisible by $x_0 x_3$. However, if we sum f over all values of (x_1, x_2), then we can obtain the following equation:

$$\sum_{(x_1, x_2) \in \{0,1\}^2} f(x_0, x_1, x_2, x_3) = 1 + x_4.$$

That is, the sum is dependent on the value of x_4.

2.3   Conditional Cube Tester

The concept of conditional cube tester was firstly proposed by Huang et al. [8] at Eurocrypt 2017. Their goal is to construct a key-dependent distinguisher. Therefore, they have to overcome the obstacle of how to involve the key information into the distinguisher. Motivated by this, they firstly classify the cube variables into two types: conditional cube variable and ordinary cube variable. The classification is based on the multiplying relations of the cube variables in the first two rounds as follows.

- *Conditional cube variables can not multiply with each other after the second round.*
- *Ordinary cube variables can not multiply with each other after the first round.*
- *Ordinary cube variables can not multiply with conditional cube variables after the second round.*

Then, they develop a theorem to confirm the number of each type of the cube variables in order to establish a conditional cube tester, as specified below, whose proof is based on the relations of the cube variables in the first two rounds as above.

Theorem 2 [8]. *For $(n+2)$-round Keccak sponge function $(n > 0)$, if there are p conditional cube variables $v_0, v_1, \ldots, v_{p-1}$ and $q = 2^{n+1} - 2p + 1$ ordinary cube variables $v_p, v_{p+1}, \ldots, v_{p+q-1}$, then the term $v_0 v_1 \ldots v_{p+q-1}$ will not appear in the output polynomials of $(n+2)$-round Keccak sponge function.*

To make conditional cube tester work, it is essential to introduce some conditions which will influence the above multiplying relations between the conditional cube variable and ordinary cube variable in the first two round. Specifically, only when all the introduced conditions hold will their multiplying relations be satisfied, thus making **Theorem 2** work. Among the introduced conditions, the key-independent conditions can always be satisfied by controlling the input. For the key-dependent conditions, whether they are satisfied is detected by the conditional cube tester based on **Theorem 2**. To be more specific, the attack procedure can be briefly divided into three steps.

Step 1: Except for the cube variables in the input state, the attacker assigns a random value to the remaining part of it, while keeping the key-independent bit conditions satisfied.

Step 2: The attacker starts to exhaust all possible values of the cube variables and calculates the sum of all outputs.

Step 3: If the sum is zero, then the attacker knows that the key-dependent bit conditions are satisfied with an overwhelming probability and therefore he can extract some equations for the involved key bits. Otherwise, the attacker knows the key-dependent bit conditions do not hold. For this case, the attacker will flip some bits involved in the key-dependent bit conditions and located in the controllable part of the input state. Then, he goto Step 2 again.

The above procedure is only used to extract a small number of equations for the key bits. To recover the full key, the attacker will repeat the above procedure by changing the parameters of the conditions cube tester to extract more equations for the key bits. Finally, the attacker can solve the obtained equation system to recover some key bits. The remaining key bits can be recovered by brute force.

3   Tracing Algorithm

Several algorithms to determine the relations of cube variables in the first two rounds have been presented in [8]. In this section, we introduce a new method to achieve the same goal. We do not claim that our new method have any advantages over [8]. The purpose to use this new method is only to suit our programming. Before introducing how to determine the candidates for ordinary cube variables, we firstly describe how to trace the propagation of a variable in A_θ^0 to A_π^1.

Since θ, ρ, π are all linear transformations, an equivalent linear transformation matrix $M \in F_2^{1600 \times 1600}$ can be derived to express these three consecutive operations $\pi \circ \rho \circ \theta$. From the definitions of the three operations, it can be known that for each row of M, there are only 11 non-zero elements, whose values are all 1. To reduce the size of M, we can only record the positions of M where the corresponding value is 1 in a smaller matrix SM of size 1600×11. Specifically, suppose $M[i][J] = 1$ $(J \in \{j_0, \ldots, j_{10}\})$, then we construct a smaller matrix SM where $SM[i][t] = j_t$ for $0 \le t \le 10$. Moreover, since the operation $\pi \circ \rho$

is equivalent to a permutation of bit positions, an equivalent permutation P of size 1600 can be derived to express it.

To make the tracing algorithm more explicit, we should consider the internal state as a boolean vector denoted by V rather than a three-dimensional array. In addition, assume the internal state is an 1600-bit variable. For other sizes of the internal state, the procedure to trace the propagation is similar. For the sake of convenience, we denote the state V after θ, ρ, and π in round i ($i \geq 0$) by V_θ^i, V_ρ^i and V_π^i respectively. The input state of round i is denoted by V^i.

Now we describe how to trace the propagation of the variable in A_θ^0 to A_π^1.

Step 1. Suppose $A_\theta^0[x][y][z]$ contains a variable, we record $t_0 = (5x+y) \times 64 + z$.

Step 2. Calculate how the variable in $V_\theta^0[t_0]$ propagates through $\pi \circ \rho$ operation with P. Consequently, we record $t_1 = P[t_0]$.

Step 3. According to the definition of χ, after $\iota \circ \chi$ operation, three bits of V^1 will contain the variable from $V_\pi^0[t_1]$. We denote the corresponding three bit positions by t_2, t_3 and t_4. Among the three bits, one bit will always contain this variable. The other two bits contain this variable depending on bit conditions. We classify these three bits into three types. The first type is the bit that always contains the variable. The second type is the bit that contains the variable depending on a key-independent bit condition. The third type is the bit that contains the variable depending on a key-dependent bit condition. Then, for each of the three bits, we trace how the variable in $V^1[pos]$ ($pos \in \{t_2, t_3, t_4\}$) propagates to V_π^1 with Algorithm 1. The bit positions of V_π^1 containing the variable from $V^1[pos]$ are stored in the array $finalPosition$.

Algorithm 1. Tracing the influenced bit positions after $\pi \circ \rho \circ \theta$ operation

---

```
1:  for row in (0...1599) do
2:      for col in (0...10) do
3:          if SM[row][col] = pos then
4:              finalPosition.push_back(row)
5:              break
```

Up until now, the propagation of the variable in A_θ^0 to A_π^1 is known, i.e. the bit positions of A_π^1 containing the variable from A_θ^0 are known and are classified into three types. At last, we only need focus on how the cube variable in A^0 propagates to A_θ^0, which can be easily finished by considering the influence of θ operation.

Once knowing and recording how a variable propagates in the first two rounds with or without bit conditions to slow down this propagation, it is quite easy to determine their multiplying relations in the first two rounds. For example, suppose we know that $A_\pi^0[x][y][z]$ contains a variable v' and $A_\pi^0[x-1][y][z]$ contains a different variable v'', then v'' will multiply with v' after the first round. In the same way, suppose we know that $A_\pi^1[x][y][z]$ contains a variable v' and

$A_\pi^1[x-1][y][z]$ contains a different variable v'', then v'' will multiply with v' after the second round.

4   Finding Ordinary Cube Variables for Keccak-MAC-384

In this section, we will expand on the procedure to find sufficient ordinary cube variables for Keccak-MAC-384. First, the potential candidates for ordinary cube variables will be determined by carefully adding key-independent bit conditions to slow down its propagation. Then, we consider the multiplying relations of these candidates after the first round and deduce some contradictions. As will be shown, from these contradictions, we can efficiently determine how many ordinary cube variables can eventually survive.

4.1   Determining Candidates for Keccak-MAC-384

The initial state of Keccak-MAC-384 is shown in Fig. 3 with 12 lanes set to 0. In the same way as [8,9,12], $A[2][0][0] = A[2][1][0] = v_0$ is chosen as the conditional cube variable with four bit conditions ($A_\theta^0[1][4][60] = 1$, $A_\theta^0[1][0][5] = 1$, $A_\theta^0[3][1][7] = 0$, $A_\theta^0[3][2][45] = 0$) to slow down its propagation. Then, the ordinary cube variables are set in the CP kernel. The complete procedure is as follows.

Fig. 3. Initial state of Keccak-MAC-384

- For the first column, we exhaust all 64 possible variables $A[0][1][i] = A[0][2][i]$ ($0 \leq i \leq 63$). Based on **Observations** 1 and 2, if we add bit conditions to slow down the propagation of the variables in this case, all of them are key-dependent bit conditions. Therefore, we do not add bit conditions. For each of these 64 possible variables, the tracing algorithm is applied to determine its multiplying relation with the chosen conditional cube variable in the first two rounds. Only those are selected as candidates that they do not multiply with v_0 in the first two rounds.
- For the second column, we exhaust all 64 possible variables $A[1][1][i] = A[1][2][i]$ ($0 \leq i \leq 63$) and process in the same way as the first column.

- For the third column, we exhaust 63×3 possible variables $A[2][0][i] = A[2][1][i]$, $A[2][0][i] = A[2][2][i]$ and $A[2][1][i] = A[2][2][i]$ ($1 \leq i \leq 63$). Based on **Observations** 1 and 2, we can add key-independent bit conditions on $A_\theta^0[3][t]$ ($0 \leq t \leq 4$) to slow down the propagation of the variables. To remove the redundant conditions, we add a condition only when it is necessary. In other words, if such a condition is not added and the variable satisfies the required relation with v_0 in the first two rounds, this condition is not necessary and redundant. Moreover, if such a condition is added, the variable still does not satisfy the requirement, we filter this variable.
- For the forth column, we exhaust all 64 possible variables $A[3][0][i] = A[3][1][i]$ ($0 \leq i \leq 63$) and process in the same way as the first column since there are no key-independent bit conditions to slow the propagation of variables.
- For the fifth column, we exhaust 64 possible variables $A[4][0][i] = A[4][1][i]$ ($0 \leq i \leq 63$). Based on **Observations** 1 and 2, we can add key-independent bit conditions to slow down the propagation of variables as the third column.

The candidates found with our method are presented in Table 2.

4.2   Discussion

Adding some bit conditions on $A_\theta^0[3][t]$ ($0 \leq t \leq 4$) as described above will cause the following bad cases.

Case 1: Contradiction of conditions will occur. Specifically, for the third column, the bit condition on a certain bit i of $A_\theta^0[3][t_0]$ is $A_\theta^0[3][t_0][i] = 0$. However, for the fifth column, the bit condition on a certain bit j of $A_\theta^0[3][t_1]$ is $A_\theta^0[3][t_1][j] = 1$. If $i = j$ and $t_0 = t_1$, the contradiction of conditions is detected. In other words, we can not choose both of their corresponding variables as the final ordinary cube variables. Moreover, if $A_\theta^0[3][y_0][z_0]$ and $A_\theta^0[3][y_1][z_0]$ are added on different bit conditions for $y_0 > 1, y_1 > 1$, this is also a contradiction since $A[3][y][z_0]$ is set to a constant 0 for Keccak-MAC-384 for $y > 1$.

Case 2: Contradiction between conditions and ordinary cube variables will occur. Specifically, for the forth column, some of $A[3][0][i] = A[3][1][i]$ ($0 \leq i \leq 63$) will be chosen as candidates. The bad case is that $A[3][0][t] = A[3][1][t]$ is chosen as a candidate and $A_\theta^0[3][0][t]$ or $A_\theta^0[3][1][t]$ is added on a condition.

Indeed, the second case can be processed in a simple way. After the candidates are determined, if a contradiction in the second case is detected, it implies that two ordinary variables multiplies with each other in the first round. For example, supposing $A_\theta^0[3][0][t]$ is added on a condition and $A[3][0][t] = A[3][1][t]$ is chosen as a candidate, it implies a variables set in $A[2][4]$ or $A[4][1]$ is chosen as a candidate, which will multiply with the variable set to $A[3][0][t]$ after the first round. This can be seen from the $\pi \circ \rho$ operation in Fig. 2. Thus, the second case is equivalent to the case that two ordinary cube variables multiply with each other in the first round. Benefiting from this new property, we do not have to

Table 2. Candidates for Keccak-MAC-384, where c is an adjustable constant over GF(2) for each variable.

$A[0][1][i] = A[0][2][i] + c$								
i	15	22	28	34	37	46	47	58	59
Variable	v_1	v_2	v_3	v_4	v_5	v_6	v_7	v_8	v_9

$A[1][1][i] = A[1][2][i] + c$										
i	7	15	20	26	30	38	39	40	52	54	57
Variable	v_{10}	v_{11}	v_{12}	v_{13}	v_{14}	v_{15}	v_{16}	v_{17}	v_{18}	v_{19}	v_{20}

$A[2][0][i] = A[2][1][i] + c$																		
i	1	8	12	14	15	20	23	25	28	41	42	43	45	50	52	53	61	62	63
Variable	v_{21}	v_{22}	v_{23}	v_{24}	v_{25}	v_{26}	v_{27}	v_{28}	v_{29}	v_{30}	v_{31}	v_{32}	v_{33}	v_{34}	v_{35}	v_{36}	v_{37}	v_{38}	v_{39}

Condition:
$i=1$: $A_\theta^0[3][2][46] = 0$ — $i=14$: $A_\theta^0[3][1][21] = 0$
$i=15$: $A_\theta^0[3][1][22] = 0$ — $i=23$: $A_\theta^0[3][2][4] = 0$
$i=25$: $A_\theta^0[3][1][32] = 0$ — $i=42$: $A_\theta^0[3][1][49] = 0$
$i=50$: $A_\theta^0[3][2][31] = 0$ — $i=52$: $A_\theta^0[3][1][59] = 0$
$i=63$: $A_\theta^0[3][1][6] = 0$, $A_\theta^0[3][2][44] = 0$

$A[3][0][i] = A[3][1][i] + c$												
i	3	4	9	13	15	23	30	35	39	40	46	56	57
Variable	v_{40}	v_{41}	v_{42}	v_{43}	v_{44}	v_{45}	v_{46}	v_{47}	v_{48}	v_{49}	v_{50}	v_{51}	v_{52}

$A[4][0][i] = A[4][1][i] + c$																		
i	3	5	8	10	12	14	20	22	25	30	31	35	38	41	47	57	58	62	63
Variable	v_{53}	v_{54}	v_{55}	v_{56}	v_{57}	v_{58}	v_{59}	v_{60}	v_{61}	v_{62}	v_{63}	v_{64}	v_{65}	v_{66}	v_{67}	v_{68}	v_{69}	v_{70}	v_{71}

Condition:
$i=3$: $A_\theta^0[3][0][59] = 1$ — $i=8$: $A_\theta^0[3][0][0] = 1$
$i=20$: $A_\theta^0[3][0][12] = 1$ — $i=22$: $A_\theta^0[3][0][14] = 1$
$i=25$: $A_\theta^0[3][0][17] = 1$ — $i=30$: $A_\theta^0[3][4][1] = 1$, $A_\theta^0[3][0][22] = 1$
$i=35$: $A_\theta^0[3][4][6] = 1$, $A_\theta^0[3][0][27] = 1$ — $i=38$: $A_\theta^0[3][4][9] = 1$
$i=41$: $A_\theta^0[3][0][33] = 1$ — $i=57$: $A_\theta^0[3][0][49] = 1$

$A[2][0][i] = A[2][2][i] + c$																				
i	1	5	6	14	15	16	20	21	27	30	33	38	39	40	41	46	51	52	57	61	62
Variable	v_{72}	v_{73}	v_{74}	v_{75}	v_{76}	v_{77}	v_{78}	v_{79}	v_{80}	v_{81}	v_{82}	v_{83}	v_{84}	v_{85}	v_{86}	v_{87}	v_{88}	v_{89}	v_{90}	v_{91}	v_{92}

Condition:
$i=1$: $A_\theta^0[3][3][23] = 0$ — $i=14$: $A_\theta^0[3][1][21] = 0$, $A_\theta^0[3][3][36] = 0$
$i=15$: $A_\theta^0[3][1][22] = 0$ — $i=20$: $A_\theta^0[3][3][42] = 0$
$i=30$: $A_\theta^0[3][1][37] = 0$ — $i=33$: $A_\theta^0[3][3][55] = 0$
$i=38$: $A_\theta^0[3][1][45] = 0$ — $i=40$: $A_\theta^0[3][1][47] = 0$
$i=46$: $A_\theta^0[3][1][53] = 0$ — $i=52$: $A_\theta^0[3][1][59] = 0$
$i=57$: $A_\theta^0[3][1][0] = 0$ — $i=62$: $A_\theta^0[3][3][20] = 0$

$A[2][1][i] = A[2][2][i] + c$														
i	1	11	14	15	18	19	20	24	41	52	56	58	61	62
Variable	v_{93}	v_{94}	v_{95}	v_{96}	v_{97}	v_{98}	v_{99}	v_{100}	v_{101}	v_{102}	v_{103}	v_{104}	v_{105}	v_{106}

Condition:
$i=1$: $A_\theta^0[3][2][46] = 0$, $A_\theta^0[3][3][23] = 0$ — $i=14$: $A_\theta^0[3][3][36] = 0$
$i=18$: $A_\theta^0[3][2][63] = 0$ — $i=20$: $A_\theta^0[3][3][42] = 0$
$i=56$: $A_\theta^0[3][3][14] = 0$ — $i=62$: $A_\theta^0[3][3][20] = 0$

process the second bad case and only need concentrate on the relation of the candidates in the first round as well as the contradiction caused by conditions.

4.3 Deducing Contradictions

The contradictions of candidates are deduced from two cases. The first case is that variables multiply with each other in the first round. The second case is that there is contradiction of conditions. The contradictions deduced are displayed in Table 3. In this table, $v_i\{v_{j_0}, \ldots, v_{j_n}\}$ means v_i can not be chosen with any of $\{v_{j_0}, \ldots, v_{j_n}\}$ as the final candidates at the same time. We count the times that each variable appears in these contradictions and do not choose the one which appears more than one time as marked in red and blue. However, although some variables appear two times as marked in green in this table, we can still choose them. Therefore, for the obtained contradictions, at most 28 variables can be derived. Moreover, there are 56 fully free variables, i.e. there are no contradictions on them.

Table 3. Contradictions of candidates

$v_1\{v_{70}\}$	$v_2\{v_{54},\ v_{63}\}$	$v_3\{v_{19}\}$	$v_5\{v_{59}\}$	$v_7\{v_{62}\}$
$v_8\{v_{12},v_{53},v_{66}\}$	$v_{11}\{v_{77}\}$	$v_{12}\{v_{79}\}$	$v_{13}\{v_{80}\}$	$v_{15}\{v_{84}\}$
$v_{16}\{v_{85}\}$	$v_{17}\{v_{86},v_{101}\}$	$v_{20}\{v_{104}\}$	$v_{22}\{v_{44}\}$	$v_{27}\{v_{46}\}$
$v_{29}\{v_{47}\}$	$v_{34}\{v_{52}\}$	$v_{37}\{v_{41}\}$	$v_{41}\{v_{57},v_{91}\}$	$v_{43}\{v_{74}\}$
$v_{45}\{v_{63},v_{77}\}$	$v_{46}\{v_{65}\}$	$v_{48}\{v_{67}\}$	$v_{49}\{v_{82}\}$	$v_{50}\{v_{84}\}$

Observe that we consider the third column under three cases, which will cause two problems. Specifically, if $A[2][0][t] = A[2][1][t] + c$, $A[2][0][t] = A[2][2][t] + c$ and $A[2][1][t] = A[2][2][t]+c$ are chosen simultaneously, only two variables rather than three variables can be obtained. In this case, we should change the variables as $A[2][0][t] = v_{x_0}, A[2][1][t] = v_{x_1}, A[2][2][t] = v_{x_0} + v_{x_1} + c$. This is due to that the ordinary cube variables are set in the CP kernel. According to Table 2, there are 8 possible values for t and they are $\{1,14,15,20,41,52,61,62\}$. Therefore, for the worst case, we can finally obtain $28+56-8 = 76$ ordinary cube variables, which is much larger than the required number (63) to mount key-recovery attack on 7-round Keccak-MAC-384.

On the other hand, if two of $A[2][0][t] = A[2][1][t]+c$, $A[2][0][t] = A[2][2][t] + c$, $A[2][1][t] = A[2][2][t] + c$ are chosen simultaneously, we should change the variables as $A[2][0][t] = v_{x_0}, A[2][1][t] = v_{x_1}, A[2][2][t] = v_{x_0} + v_{x_1} + c$.

One choice of the 64-dimensional cube variables to establish the conditional cube tester is displayed in Table 4.

5   Finding Ordinary Cube Variables for Keccak-MAC-512

Although 32-dimensional cube variables have been found with MILP to establish the 6-round conditional cube tester for Keccak-MAC-512 and the time complexity is practical, we want to explain how to apply our method to achieve the same goal. This is for a better understanding of the differences between our method and others based on MILP. Now, we expand on how to find sufficient cube variables for Keccak-MAC-512.

In a similar way for Keccak-MAC-384, 32 candidates for ordinary cube variables are discovered as displayed in Table 5. The corresponding contradictions are as follows.

$$v_2\{v_{24}\},\ v_7\{v_{26}\},\ v_9\{v_{27}\},\ v_{14}\{v_{32}\},\ v_{17}\{v_{21}\}.$$

Table 4. One choice of ordinary cube variables for Keccak-MAC-384

Free ordinary cube variables ($56 - 6 = 50$ in total)	v_4, v_6, v_9, v_{10}, v_{14}, v_{18}, v_{21}, v_{23}, v_{24}, v_{25}, v_{26}, v_{28}, v_{30}, v_{31}, v_{32}, v_{33}, v_{35}, v_{36}, v_{38}, v_{39}, v_{40}, v_{42}, v_{51}, v_{55}, v_{56}, v_{58}, v_{60}, v_{61}, v_{64}, v_{68}, v_{69}, v_{71}, v_{72}, v_{73}, v_{75}, v_{76}, v_{78}, v_{81}, v_{83}, v_{87}, v_{88}, v_{89}, v_{90}, v_{92}, v_{93}, v_{94}, v_{95}, v_{96}, v_{97}, v_{98}, v_{99}, v_{100}, v_{102}, v_{103}, v_{105}, v_{106} $\{v_{21}, v_{72}, v_{93}\}$, $\{v_{24}, v_{75}, v_{95}\}$, $\{v_{25}, v_{76}, v_{96}\}$ $\{v_{26}, v_{78}, v_{99}\}$, $\{v_{35}, v_{89}, v_{102}\}$ and $\{v_{38}, v_{92}, v_{106}\}$ provide two variables respectively
Ordinary cube variables derived from contradictions (13 in total)	v_1, v_{54}, v_{63}, v_3, v_5, v_7, v_{53}, v_{66}, v_{11}, v_{79}, v_{13}, v_{15}, v_{16}
Conditional cube variable	v_0
Key-dependent conditions	$A_\theta^0[1][4][60] = 1, A_\theta^0[1][0][5] = 1$
Key-independent conditions for v_0	$A_\theta^0[3][1][7] = 0, A_\theta^0[3][2][45] = 0$
Other key-independent conditions for ordinary cube variables	Refer to Table 3 according to the chosen variables

Table 5. Candidates for Keccak-MAC-512, where c is an adjustable constant over $GF(2)$ for each variable.

$A[2][0][i] = A[2][1][i] + c$																			
i	1	8	12	14	15	20	23	25	28	41	42	43	45	50	52	53	61	62	63
Variable	v_1	v_2	v_3	v_4	v_5	v_6	v_7	v_8	v_9	v_{10}	v_{11}	v_{12}	v_{13}	v_{14}	v_{15}	v_{16}	v_{17}	v_{18}	v_{19}
Condition	detail below																		

Condition:
- $i=1$: $A_\theta^0[3][2][46] = 0$
- $i=15$: $A_\theta^0[3][1][22] = 0$
- $i=25$: $A_\theta^0[3][1][32] = 0$
- $i=50$: $A_\theta^0[3][2][31] = 0$
- $i=63$: $A_\theta^0[3][1][6] = 0, A_\theta^0[3][2][44] = 0$
- $i=14$: $A_\theta^0[3][1][21] = 0$
- $i=23$: $A_\theta^0[3][2][4] = 0$
- $i=42$: $A_\theta^0[3][1][49] = 0$
- $i=52$: $A_\theta^0[3][1][59] = 0$

$A[3][0][i] = A[3][1][i] + c$												
i	3	4	9	13	15	23	30	35	39	40	46	56	57
Variable	v_{20}	v_{21}	v_{22}	v_{23}	v_{24}	v_{25}	v_{26}	v_{27}	v_{28}	v_{29}	v_{30}	v_{31}	v_{32}

Therefore, there will be $32 - 5 = 27$ possible ordinary cube variables in total if the ordinary cube variables are set only in the CP kernel. As a result, we can not mount key-recovery attack on 6-round Keccak-MAC-512, which requires 31 ordinary cube variables if only v_0 is chosen to be the conditional cube variable.

Based on [12], the variables which multiply with v_0 only in the second round can be leveraged as well. For an intuitive example, suppose one variable v_{x_0} multiplies with v_0 only in the second round and the multiplying bit position is p_0. If another variable v_{x_1} multiplies with v_0 only in the second round and the multiplying bit position is p_0 as well, then setting $v_{x_0} = v_{x_1}$ will cause the already filtered two variables become one possible variable. Then, the goal becomes how to find these possible variables.

Suppose $A_\theta^0[i][j][k]$ contains a variable, then after χ operation, three bits will contain this variable. Based on the definition of χ operation, among the three bits, one bit will always contain this variable and the other two bits contain this variable depending on the conditions. We classify the three bits into three types.

Type-1: It always contains this variable.
Type-2: It contains this variable depending on a key-independent bit condition.
Type-3: It contains this variable depending on a key-dependent bit condition.

Then, we trace how the three bits propagate to the second round with the tracing algorithm. Specifically, we trace the **Type-1** bit and record the influenced bits of A_π^1 multiplying with v_0 in the second round. For the **Type-2** and **Type-3** bits, we process in the same way. The recorded bits for **Type-1**, **Type-2** and **Type-3** are defined as core bits, independent-key bits and key-dependent bits. Since our focus is the minimal key-dependent conditions, once the key-dependent bits are detected, the corresponding variable should not be chosen as a candidate.

With the above method, we reconsider the filtered ordinary cube variables set in the CP kernel. Besides, the variables set to a single bit are also considered. The final result obtained is displayed in Table 6.

For a better understanding of this table, we take the variable $A[3][1][8]$ as instance. For the first column, it means $A[3][1][8]$ is set to be a variable. For the second column, it means 5 bits of A_π^1 will multiply with v_0 only in the second round. For the third column, $\{656,1003\}$ means the two bits of A_π^1, i.e. $A_\pi^1[0][2][16]$ and $A_\pi^1[0][3][43]$, will multiply with v_0 only in the second round depending on the same key-independent bit condition. The last column means $A[3][1][8]$ can not be chosen as a variable with any of v_1 and v_{31} in Table 5 simultaneously.

According to Table 6, at most three more possible ordinary cube variables can be obtained. One choice is as follows:

$$A[3][0][58] = A[3][1][58] = A[2][0][24] = A[2][1][24] = v_{e_0},$$
$$A[3][0][61] = v_{e_1}, A[3][1][61] = v_{e_2},$$
$$A[2][0][26] = A[2][1][26] = v_{e_3}, v_{e_3} = v_{e_2} + v_{e_1}$$
$$A[2][0][46] = A[2][1][46] = v_{e_2}.$$
Condition : $A_\theta^0[3][3][20] = 0, A_\theta^0[3][4][21] = 0, A_\theta^0[3][1][53] = 0.$

According to Table 6, adding $A[2][0][37] = A[2][1][37] = v_{e_2}$ to the above variables and converting the bit condition $A_\theta^0[3][1][53] = 0$ into $A_\theta^0[3][1][53] = 1$ is also possible. However, it can not help improve the number of possible variables. In fact, there are many interesting cases. For example, if $A[3][0][60] = A[3][1][60]$ does not multiply with v_{16} in the first round, we can obtain one more candidate. For the third row, if $\{652, 1109\}$ does not depend on the same condition, then we can add one key-independent bit condition to prevent the propagation to the 652-nd bit and another key-independent bit condition to allow the propagation to the 1109-th bit of A_π^1.

Then we test whether v_{e_i} $(0 \leq i \leq 3)$ multiplies with each other in the first round and check whether the three bit conditions to slow down the propagation of v_{e_1} and v_{e_2} are contradict with the conditions in Table 5. It is shown that the

Table 6. Possible candidates for Keccak-MAC-512

Possible variables	Core bits	Key-independent bits	Contradictions
$A[2][0][4] = A[2][1][4]$	1540		
$A[2][0][5] = A[2][1][5]$	1109	{652, 1109}	
$A[2][0][9] = A[2][1][9]$	848, 467	{656, 1003}	
$A[2][0][13] = A[2][1][13]$	652, 1109		
$A[2][0][16] = A[2][1][16]$	1472	515	v_{25}
$A[2][0][24] = A[2][1][24]$	515		
$A[2][0][26] = A[2][1][26]$	665		
$A[2][0][29] = A[2][1][29]$	71, 1032	241	
$A[2][0][33] = A[2][1][33]$	491		v_{29}
$A[2][0][35] = A[2][1][35]$	1131, 42	1242	
$A[2][0][37] = A[2][1][37]$	1040		
$A[2][0][46] = A[2][1][46]$	903	1040	
$A[2][0][51] = A[2][1][51]$	767, 1160		
$A[2][0][54] = A[2][1][54]$	1510		
$A[2][0][57] = A[2][1][57]$	170	205	
$A[2][0][60] = A[2][1][60]$	1280	1540	v_{20}
$A[3][0][41] = A[3][1][41]$	113		
$A[3][0][43] = A[3][1][43]$	848		
$A[3][0][50] = A[3][1][50]$	42		v_{12}
$A[3][0][58] = A[3][1][58]$	515		
$A[3][0][60] = A[3][1][60]$	665		v_{16}
$A[3][0][61] = A[3][1][61]$	903		
$A[3][1][8]$	170, 848, 467, 1382, 1003	{656,1003}, {903}, {1237}	v_1, v_{31}
$A[3][0][32]$	491, 903, 1382	{13}, {848}, {775}	v_{29}
$A[3][0][61]$	665	{42}, {1348}	
$A[3][1][61]$	903, 665	{42}, {1348}	

three variables are all valid. Therefore, we can obtain at most $32 - 5 + 3 = 30$ ordinary cube variables without key-dependent bit conditions. It reveals in a way why [12] can only discover the same number of such ordinary variables with a solver. However, to mount key-recovery attack on 6-round Keccak-MAC-512, we need 31 ordinary cube variables. Thus, we try to search ordinary cube variables set in the CP kernel with only one key-dependent bit condition, which satisfy the required relation with v_0 and the chosen $32 + 4 = 36$ candidates for ordinary cube variables. Our searching result is displayed in Table 7. Thus, there are many possible choices for 31 ordinary cube variables, i.e. at least $2^5 \times 12$. The verification can be found at https://github.com/Crypt-CNS/Keccak_ConditionalCubeAttack.git.

6   Recovering Full Key

In this section, a new slightly improved way to recover 128-bit key for Keccak-MAC is presented by removing unnecessary iterations of conditional cube tester.

Table 7. Candidates for Keccak-MAC-512 with one key-dependent bit condition

Variable	Conditions
$A[2][0][11] = A[2][1][11]$	$A_\theta^0[1][4][7] = 1$
$A[2][0][19] = A[2][1][19]$	$A_\theta^0[1][4][15] = 1$
$A[2][0][21] = A[2][1][21]$	$A_\theta^0[1][0][26] = 1$, $A_\theta^0[3][2][2] = 0$
$A[2][0][22] = A[2][1][22]$	$A_\theta^0[1][0][27] = 1$
$A[2][0][30] = A[2][1][30]$	$A_\theta^0[3][1][37] = 0$, $A_\theta^0[1][0][35] = 1$
$A[2][0][34] = A[2][1][34]$	$A_\theta^0[1][0][39] = 1$, $A_\theta^0[3][2][15] = 0$
$A[2][0][44] = A[2][1][44]$	$A_\theta^0[3][1][51] = 0$, $A_\theta^0[1][0][49] = 1$
$A[2][0][56] = A[2][1][56]$	$A_\theta^0[1][4][52] = 1$, $A_\theta^0[3][1][63] = 0$
$A[3][0][12] = A[3][1][12]$	$A_\theta^0[4][1][20] = 0$
$A[3][0][20] = A[3][1][20]$	$A_\theta^0[4][2][36] = 0$
$A[3][0][29] = A[3][1][29]$	$A_\theta^0[2][4][60] = 1$
$A[3][0][34] = A[3][1][34]$	$A_\theta^0[2][4][1] = 1$

In [8], 64 iterations of the conditional cube tester were used to recover the 128-bit key for Keccak-MAC-256. For each iteration, it costs $2^{64+2} = 2^{66}$ to recover 2-bit key. Observe that once there are only a few key bits to be recovered, there is no need to iterate the conditional cube tester since each iteration is costly and only 2 bits are recovered.

Taking Keccak-MAC-128/256 for instance, for the 64-dimensional cube variable [8], after 31 iterations in z-axis of the conditional cube tester, 62 bits of key can be recovered. Then, the remaining 66 bits can be recovered by brute force. Therefore, the time complexity is improved to $2^{66} \times 31 + 2^{66} = 2^{71}$ from 2^{72}. Similarly, for the 64-dimensional cube variables in Table 4, we can recover the 128-bit key for 7-round Keccak-MAC-384 with time complexity 2^{71}.

For the conditional cube attack on 6-round Keccak-MAC-512, we choose $A[2][0][11] = A[2][1][11]$ in Table 7 as the ordinary cube variable with one key-dependent bit condition $A_\theta^0[1][4][7] = 1$, while $A[2][0][19] = A[2][1][19]$ is chosen in [12]. For our choice, only 31 iterations in z-axis is enough. Then, $3 \times 31 = 93$ bits can be recovered with time complexity $2^{32+3} \times 31 = 2^{35} \times 31$. The remaining $128 - 93 = 35$ bits can be recovered by brute force. The order to recover 93 bits of key with conditional cube tester is shown in Table 8. Therefore, the total time complexity becomes $2^{35} \times 31 + 2^{35} = 2^{40}$. However, the time complexity is estimated as $\lceil \frac{128}{3} \rceil \times 2^{2^5+3} = \lceil \frac{128}{3} \rceil \times 2^{35} = 2^{40.4}$ in [12], which implies 64 iterations of the conditional cube tester are used to recover the 128-bit key.

7   Comparison with Previous Work

Our work is heavily based on [8]. However, Huang et al. did not consider the potentially useful key-independent bit conditions to slow down the propagation of ordinary cube variables [8].

Table 8. The order to recover 93 bits of key with conditional cube tester

$(k_0, k_{53}, k_{62} \oplus k_{126})$, $(k_1, k_{54}, k_{63} \oplus k_{127})$, $(k_2, k_{55}, k_0 \oplus k_{64})$, $(k_3, k_{56}, k_1 \oplus k_{65})$,
$(k_4, k_{57}, k_2 \oplus k_{66})$, $(k_5, k_{58}, k_3 \oplus k_{67})$, $(k_6, k_{59}, k_4 \oplus k_{68})$, $(k_7, k_{60}, k_5 \oplus k_{69})$,
$(k_8, k_{61}, k_6 \oplus k_{70})$, $(k_9, k_{62}, k_7 \oplus k_{71})$, $(k_{10}, k_{63}, k_8 \oplus k_{72})$, $(k_{22}, k_{11}, k_{20} \oplus k_{84})$,
$(k_{23}, k_{12}, k_{21} \oplus k_{85})$, $(k_{24}, k_{13}, k_{22} \oplus k_{86})$, $(k_{25}, k_{14}, k_{23} \oplus k_{87})$, $(k_{26}, k_{15}, k_{24} \oplus k_{88})$,
$(k_{27}, k_{16}, k_{25} \oplus k_{89})$, $(k_{28}, k_{17}, k_{26} \oplus k_{90})$, $(k_{29}, k_{18}, k_{27} \oplus k_{91})$, $(k_{30}, k_{19}, k_{28} \oplus k_{92})$,
$(k_{31}, k_{20}, k_{29} \oplus k_{93})$, $(k_{32}, k_{21}, k_{30} \oplus k_{94})$, $(k_{44}, k_{33}, k_{42} \oplus k_{106})$, $(k_{45}, k_{34}, k_{43} \oplus k_{107})$,
$(k_{46}, k_{35}, k_{44} \oplus k_{108})$, $(k_{47}, k_{36}, k_{45} \oplus k_{109})$, $(k_{48}, k_{37}, k_{46} \oplus k_{110})$, $(k_{49}, k_{38}, k_{47} \oplus k_{111})$,
$(k_{50}, k_{39}, k_{48} \oplus k_{112})$, $(k_{51}, k_{40}, k_{49} \oplus k_{113})$, $(k_{52}, k_{41}, k_{50} \oplus k_{114})$.

As for [9], it seems that the key-independent bit conditions have been considered. However, it is strange that Li et al. found 63 ordinary cube variables with 6 key-dependent bit conditions for Keccak-MAC-384, while we can find much more ordinary cube variables without key-dependent bit conditions, i.e. at least 76 variables. Besides, Li et al. only found 25 ordinary cube variables set in the CP kernel for Keccak-MAC-512, while we can find $32 - 5 = 27$ ordinary cube variables set in the CP kernel. Therefore, we guess that the key-independent bit conditions were not fully leveraged in [9].

As for [12], minimum key-dependent bit conditions is considered in the model. In that paper, one instance of 31 ordinary cube variables for Keccak-MAC-512 was presented, which is almost the same with what we found. However, it is strange that there are 18 key-independent bit conditions to slow down the propagation of the ordinary cube variables. With our approach, there are at most $10 + 3 + 1 = 14$ key-independent bit conditions for ordinary cube variables. If we choose the same cube variables as [12], only $9 + 3 = 12$ key-independent bit conditions are sufficient. Indeed, we can reach the minimum key-independent bit conditions, which is $8 + 3 = 11$. Thus, we guess the redundancy in key-independent bit conditions are not well processed in the modeling in [12]. It should be noted that the redundancy of key-independent bit conditions will not affect the time complexity to recover the key. However, from the scientific point, if there is a more accurate answer, why not choose it?

In addition, a new slightly improved approach to recover the 128-bit key is introduced. This is based on the observation that many iterations of the conditional cube tester are costly once a few bits of key are left. Consequently, we improve the conditional cube attack on 7-round Keccak-MAC-128/256/384 and 6-round Keccak-MAC-512.

8   Conclusion

An algorithm to search ordinary cube variables for Keccak-MAC is developed. The first step is to identify a small region of potential candidates by making full use of the key-independent bit conditions. Then, these candidates are further filtered according to their relations after the first round with an efficient approach. In this way, sufficient ordinary cube variables can be discovered to establish the conditional cube tester. Combined with the new slightly improved way to recover the key, the time complexity of the conditional cube attack on 7-round Keccak-MAC-128/256/384 and 6-round Keccak-MAC-512 are improved to 2^{71} and 2^{40} respectively.

Acknowledgement. We thank the anonymous reviewers of IWSEC 2019 for their insightful comments and suggestions. Fukang Liu and Zhenfu Cao are supported by National Natural Science Foundation of China (Grant No.61632012, 61672239). Gaoli Wang is supported by the National Natural Science Foundation of China (No. 61572125) and National Cryptography Development Fund (No. MMJJ20180201).

References

1. Aumasson, J.-P., Dinur, I., Meier, W., Shamir, A.: Cube testers and key recovery attacks on reduced-round MD6 and trivium. In: Dunkelman, O. (ed.) FSE 2009. LNCS, vol. 5665, pp. 1–22. Springer, Heidelberg (2009). https://doi.org/10.1007/978-3-642-03317-9_1
2. Bertoni, G., Dacmen, J., Peeters, M., Van Assche, G.: The Keccak reference (2011). http://keccak.noekeon.org
3. Bi, W., Dong, X., Li, Z., Zong, R., Wang, X.: MILP-aided cube-attack-like cryptanalysis on Keccak keyed modes. Cryptology ePrint Archive, Report 2018/075 (2018). https://eprint.iacr.org/2018/075
4. Dinur, I., Dunkelman, O., Shamir, A.: New attacks on Keccak-224 and Keccak-256. In: Canteaut, A. (ed.) FSE 2012. LNCS, vol. 7549, pp. 442–461. Springer, Heidelberg (2012). https://doi.org/10.1007/978-3-642-34047-5_25
5. Dinur, I., Morawiecki, P., Pieprzyk, J., Srebrny, M., Straus, M.: Cube attacks and cube-attack-like cryptanalysis on the round-reduced Keccak sponge function. In: Oswald, E., Fischlin, M. (eds.) EUROCRYPT 2015. LNCS, vol. 9056, pp. 733–761. Springer, Heidelberg (2015). https://doi.org/10.1007/978-3-662-46800-5_28
6. Dinur, I., Shamir, A.: Cube attacks on tweakable black box polynomials. In: Joux, A. (ed.) EUROCRYPT 2009. LNCS, vol. 5479, pp. 278–299. Springer, Heidelberg (2009). https://doi.org/10.1007/978-3-642-01001-9_16
7. Guo, J., Liu, M., Song, L.: Linear structures: applications to cryptanalysis of round-reduced KECCAK. In: Cheon, J.H., Takagi, T. (eds.) ASIACRYPT 2016. LNCS, vol. 10031, pp. 249–274. Springer, Heidelberg (2016). https://doi.org/10.1007/978-3-662-53887-6_9
8. Huang, S., Wang, X., Xu, G., Wang, M., Zhao, J.: Conditional cube attack on reduced-round Keccak sponge function. In: Coron, J.-S., Nielsen, J.B. (eds.) EUROCRYPT 2017. LNCS, vol. 10211, pp. 259–288. Springer, Cham (2017). https://doi.org/10.1007/978-3-319-56614-6_9
9. Li, Z., Bi, W., Dong, X., Wang, X.: Improved conditional cube attacks on Keccak keyed modes with MILP method. In: Takagi, T., Peyrin, T. (eds.) ASIACRYPT 2017. LNCS, vol. 10624, pp. 99–127. Springer, Cham (2017). https://doi.org/10.1007/978-3-319-70694-8_4
10. Qiao, K., Song, L., Liu, M., Guo, J.: New collision attacks on round-reduced Keccak. In: Coron, J.-S., Nielsen, J.B. (eds.) EUROCRYPT 2017. LNCS, vol. 10212, pp. 216–243. Springer, Cham (2017). https://doi.org/10.1007/978-3-319-56617-7_8

11. Song, L., Guo, J.: Cube-attack-like cryptanalysis of round-reduced Keccak using MILP. IACR Trans. Symmetric Cryptol. **2018**(3), 182–214 (2018)
12. Song, L., Guo, J., Shi, D., Ling, S.: New MILP modeling: improved conditional cube attacks on Keccak-based constructions. In: Peyrin, T., Galbraith, S. (eds.) ASIACRYPT 2018. LNCS, vol. 11273, pp. 65–95. Springer, Cham (2018). https://doi.org/10.1007/978-3-030-03329-3_3
13. Song, L., Liao, G., Guo, J.: Non-full sbox linearization: applications to collision attacks on round-reduced KECCAK. In: Katz, J., Shacham, H. (eds.) CRYPTO 2017. LNCS, vol. 10402, pp. 428–451. Springer, Cham (2017). https://doi.org/10.1007/978-3-319-63715-0_15
14. Wang, X., Yin, Y.L., Yu, H.: Finding collisions in the full SHA-1. In: Shoup, V. (ed.) CRYPTO 2005. LNCS, vol. 3621, pp. 17–36. Springer, Heidelberg (2005). https://doi.org/10.1007/11535218_2
15. Wang, X., Yu, H.: How to break MD5 and other hash functions. In: Cramer, R. (ed.) EUROCRYPT 2005. LNCS, vol. 3494, pp. 19–35. Springer, Heidelberg (2005). https://doi.org/10.1007/11426639_2

Preimage Attacks on Reduced Troika with Divide-and-Conquer Methods

Fukang Liu[1,3(✉)] and Takanori Isobe[2,3]

[1] East China Normal University, Shanghai, China
liufukangs@163.com
[2] National Institute of Information and Communications Technology, Tokyo, Japan
[3] University of Hyogo, Hyogo, Japan
takanori.isobe@ai.u-hyogo.ac.jp

Abstract. Troika is a recently proposed sponge-based hash function for IOTA's ternary architecture and platform, which is developed by CYBERCRYPT. In this paper, we introduce the preimage attack on 2 and 3 rounds of Troika with a divide-and-conquer approach. Instead of directly matching a given hash value, we propose equivalent conditions to determine whether a message is the preimage before computing the complete hash value. As a result, for the two-round hash value that can be generated with one block, we can search the preimage only in a valid space and efficiently enumerate the messages which can satisfy most of the equivalent conditions with a guess-and-determine technique. For the three-round preimage attack, an MILP-based method is applied to separate the one-block message space into two parts in order to obtain the best advantage over brute force. Our experiments show that the time complexity of the preimage attack on 2 (out of 24) rounds of Troika can be improved to 3^{79}, which is 3^{164} times faster than the brute force. For the preimage attack on 3 (out of 24) rounds of Troika, we can obtain an advantage of $3^{25.7}$ over brute force. In addition, how to construct the second preimage for two-round Troika in seconds is presented as well. Our attacks do not threaten the security of Troika.

Keywords: Hash function · Troika · Preimage ·
Guess-and-determine · Divide-and-conquer · MILP

1 Introduction

IOTA and CYBERCRYPT announced a new lightweight ternary cryptographic hash function named Troika as well as the competition for cryptanalysts to evaluate Troika with a € 200,000 prize pool for breaking its round-reduced variants on December 20, 2018 [1]. The motivation to design Troika is to develop suitable new lightweight hash function for the ternary architecture of the IOTA protocol. Since the announcement of this competition, practical collisions for one/two-round Troika with two blocks have been found by Virginie Lallemand.

© Springer Nature Switzerland AG 2019
N. Attrapadung and T. Yagi (Eds.): IWSEC 2019, LNCS 11689, pp. 306–326, 2019.
https://doi.org/10.1007/978-3-030-26834-3_18

The one-round preimage challenge was solved by Håvard Raddum, John-Petter Indrøy and Morten Øygarden.

Troika [3] is a hash function $h : F_3^* \to F_3^{243}$ mapping arbitrary-length inputs to hash values of 243 trits. It follows the sponge construction with a rate of 243 and a capacity of 486 trits, yielding a total state of 729 trits, as shown in Fig. 1. Furthermore, the rate part of the state of Troika is overwritten by the input instead of added to it, in order to enable distributed hashing where only the capacity part of the state (486 trits) needs to be sent instead of the entire state (729 trits). Troika has to satisfy the following three requirements in order to be considered secure.

- Preimage resistance: No preimage attack of non-negligible success probability with a complexity of less than 3^{243} queries.
- Second preimage resistance: No second preimage attack of non-negligible success probability with a complexity of less than 3^{243} queries.
- Collision resistance: No collision attack of non-negligible success probability with a complexity of less than $3^{243/2}$ queries.

Although Troika shares many similarities with Keccak [4], which is the winner of SHA-3, the nonlinear transform is placed before the linear transform in Troika. Moreover, the algebraic degree of one-round Troika is 4 while it is 2 for Keccak. Cryptanalysts are obviously aware of the low algebraic degree of one-round Keccak. As a result, the linearizing techniques are widely exploited in the collision attack and preimage attack on Keccak [5,7,8,10,11]. However, the disadvantage of such linearizing techniques is the fast consumption of degree of freedom.

Considering the high algebraic degree of one-round Troika, it is not wise to use similar linearizing techniques since the degree of freedom will be faster utilized. Therefore, we will use a different strategy to achieve linearization without consuming degree of freedom. In addition, we observe that the length of hash value is almost equal to the length of one-block message, i.e. the padding rule must be satisfied. This motivates us to investigate whether it is possible to search the preimage only in a smaller potential space when the preimage can be generated with one block. As will be shown, invalid preimages can be efficiently discarded and no degree of freedom are consumed with our method.

Our Contributions. Firstly, we propose equivalent conditions to pre-determine whether a message is the preimage of a given hash value. As a consequence, when the hash value can be derived from one block, the search for the preimage of two-round Troika can be limited in a much smaller space, which can be further accelerated with a guess-and-determine approach. Indeed, it is expected that our algorithm to find the preimage of two-round Troika can be applied to arbitrary hash value, as shown in our partially solving the two-round preimage challenge [1], though it is difficult to give an accurate estimation of the time complexity. Moreover, we can construct several second preimages for arbitrary messages in seconds for two-round Troika.

Table 1. Summary of preimage and collision attack on Troika

Attack type	Rounds	Time	Generic	Ref.
Collision	1	Practical	$3^{243/2}$	[1]
	2	Practical	$3^{243/2}$	[1]
Preimage	1	Practical	3^{243}	[1]
	2	3^{79}	3^{243}	Section 4
	3	$3^{217.3}$	3^{243}	Section 5
Second preimage	2	3^6	3^{243}	Section 4.6

For the preimage attack on three rounds of Troika, the variables set at the rate part of input state can be separated into two parts with an MILP-based method, one of which is used to verify some equivalent conditions. Only those conditions are satisfied will we start guessing the values for the variables in another part. Due to the sufficient diffusion of three-round Troika permutation, we expect our approach can be applied to arbitrary hash value. All our results are displayed in Table 1.

Organization. The paper is organized as follows. The description of Troika is presented at Sect. 2. Then, we introduce how to derive equivalent conditions to match a given hash value in Sect. 3. The preimage attack on two and three rounds of Troika are displayed in Sects. 4 and 5 respectively. Finally, the paper is summarized in Sect. 6.

2   Description of Troika

The hash function Troika $h : F_3^* \rightarrow F_3^{243}$ maps arbitrary-length inputs to hash values of 243 trits [3]. It should follow the sponge construction with a rate of 243 and a capacity of 486 trits, yielding a total state of 729 trits as shown in Fig. 1. The state is initially initialized with all zeros. A message $m \in F_3^*$ is firstly padded with a trit "1" and non-negative number of "0" until the trit length of the padded message becomes multiple of 243. Then, the padded message is divided into n blocks of 243 trits each. Each block will be loaded in the rate part before processed. Formally, Troika operates on a state $A \in F_3^{729}$, which is organized as a $9 \times 3 \times 27$ cuboid of trits $A \in F_3^{9 \times 3 \times 27}$.

The individual trits of the state are identified as $A[x][y][z]$ via their x, y, z coordinates where $0 \leq x < 9$, $0 \leq y < 3$ and $0 \leq z < 27$. as illustrated in Fig. 2. $A[\cdot][y][z]$ composed of 9 trits is called a row of A, $A[x][\cdot][z]$ composed of 3 trits is called a column, $A[x][y][\cdot]$ composed of 27 trits is called a lane, and $A[\cdot][\cdot][z]$ composed of 27 trits is called a slice, and $A[\cdot][y][\cdot]$ composed of 243 trits is called a plane. The rate part is $A[\cdot][\cdot][z]$ ($0 \leq z < 9$) and the capacity part is $A[\cdot][\cdot][z]$ ($9 \leq z < 27$).

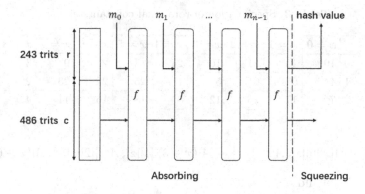

Fig. 1. Overview of Troika's Sponge Structure

Fig. 2. Coordinate

The internal permutation of Troika consists of 24 rounds. Each round is composed of five operations: **SubTrytes**, **ShiftRows**, **ShiftLanes**, **AddColumn-Parity** and **AddRoundConstant**, where only **SubTrytes** is the nonlinear transform.

SubTrytes. The SubTrytes mapping consists of the application of a 3-trit S-box $S : F_3^3 \to F_3^3$ to each tryte of the state as follows:

$$(a_2, a_1, a_0) \leftarrow S(9A[3i][y][z] + 3A[3i+1][y][z] + A[3i+2][y][z]),$$
$$(A[3i][y][z], A[3i+1][y][z], A[3i+2][y][z]) \leftarrow (a_2, a_1, a_0),$$

where $0 \le i < 3$, $0 \le y < 3$, $0 \le z < 27$ and $t_i \in F_3$ ($0 \le i \le 2$). The lookup table of the S-box is specified in Table 2.

Table 2. Lookup table for the tryte S-box

x	0	1	2	3	4	5	6	7	8	9	10	11	12	13	14	15	16	17	18	19	20	21	22	23	24	25	26
$S(x)$	6	25	17	5	15	10	4	20	24	0	1	2	9	12	26	18	16	14	3	13	23	7	11	12	8	21	19

ShiftRows. The ShiftRows provides diffusion along the x-axis in each row by shifting entire trytes cyclically to the right as follows:

Table 3. Specification of rotational constants $r[x][y]$

	$x=0$	$x=1$	$x=2$	$x=3$	$x=4$	$x=5$	$x=6$	$x=7$	$x=8$
$y=0$	19	13	21	10	24	15	2	9	3
$y=1$	14	0	6	5	1	25	22	23	2
$y=2$	7	17	26	12	8	18	16	11	4

$$A[x][0][z] \leftarrow A[x][0][z], A[x][1][z] \leftarrow A[(x-3)][1][z], A[x][2][z] \leftarrow A[(x-6)][2][z],$$

where $0 \leq x < 9$ and $0 \leq z < 27$.

ShiftLanes. ShiftLanes is to provide diffusion along the z-axis in each lane by shifting trits cyclically to the right as follows:

$$A[x][y][z] \leftarrow A[x][y][(z - r[x][y])\%27],$$

where $0 \leq x < 9$, $0 \leq y < 3$ and $0 \leq z < 27$. The specification of $r[x][y]$ can be referred to Table 3.

AddColumnParity. AddColumnParity provides diffusion along columns by adding to each column $A[x][\cdot][z]$ the parities of the two adjacent columns $A[x-1][\cdot][z]$ and $A[x+1][\cdot][z+1]$, where indices are taken modulo their respective dimensions:

$$A[x][y][z] \leftarrow A[x][y][z] + \Sigma_{y'=0}^{2}A[x-1][y'][z] + \Sigma_{y'=0}^{2}A[x+1][y'][z+1],$$

where $0 \leq x < 9$, $0 \leq y < 3$ and $0 \leq z < 27$.

AddRoundConstant. The operation AddRoundConstant only works on the first plane $A[\cdot][0][\cdot]$ in each round. Suppose RC_i represents the round constant in round i, which is a vector of size 243 then, the internal state A is updated as follows:

$$A[x][0][z] \leftarrow A[x][0][z] + RC_i[x + 9z],$$

where $0 \leq x < 9$ and $0 \leq z < 27$.

For convenience, we denote these five operations by ST, SR, SL, AP and AC respectively and define $L = AP \circ SL \circ SR$ and $L^{-1} = SR^{-1} \circ SL^{-1} \circ AP^{-1}$. For simplicity, we denote the input state of round i by A^i ($0 \leq i \leq 23$). The states after ST, SR, SL, AP and AC in round i are denoted by A_{ST}^i, A_{SR}^i, A_{SL}^i, A_{AP}^i and A_{AC}^i respectively. Obviously, the state A can be viewed as a trit vector of size 729 as well. When it is viewed as a trit vector, $A[x][y][z]$ will correspond to the $(27z + 9y + x)$-th trit in the vector. The complete description of Troika can be found at [3].

3   Equivalent Conditions to Find the Preimage

In this section, we introduce equivalent conditions to determine whether an input state is the preimage of a given hash value. Given a hash value of $(t+1)$-round $(0 \le t \le 23)$ Troika permutation, 243 trits in the rate part of A_{AC}^t are constants. Set variables to the remaining 486 trits in the capacity part of A_{AC}^t and construct an equation system

$$L^{-1} \cdot A_{AC}^t = A_{ST}^t.$$

Note that such an equation system must have solutions to A_{AC}^t. Otherwise, it is impossible to obtain the given hash value. Therefore, we define a space S satisfying the following two constraints:

Constraint 1. For each A_{ST}^t belonging to S, the equation system $L^{-1} \cdot A_{AC}^t = A_{ST}^t$ must have solutions to A_{AC}^t.
Constraint 2. For those A_{ST}^t not belonging to S, the equation system $L^{-1} \cdot A_{AC}^t = A_{ST}^t$ must not have solutions to A_{AC}^t.

Obviously, $A_{ST}^t \in S$ is a necessary but not sufficient condition to obtain the $(t+1)$-round preimage of the given hash value with one block. This is due to that the capacity part of the input state is fixed. However, when we start from a random input state A^0 with a correct fixed capacity part and compute forward until A_{ST}^t, the corresponding A^0 must be the preimage of the given hash value if $A_{ST}^t \in S$. As a result, the equivalent condition to match a given hash value with one block can be stated as follows.

The Equivalent Condition. *To find the preimage of $(t+1)$-round Troika, when starting from a random input state with a correct fixed capacity part, the preimage is found only when A_{ST}^t belongs to a specific space S satisfying* **Constraints 1** *and 2.*

3.1   Deriving the Space S

Let $A_{AC}^t = (C||V)$, where C is a 243-trit constant dependent on the hash value and V is a 486-trit variable. Then, the equation becomes

$$L^{-1} \cdot (C||V) = L^{-1} \cdot (C||0) + L^{-1} \cdot (0||V) = A_{ST}^t.$$

Let $T = A_{ST}^t - L^{-1} \cdot (C||0)$, we have

$$L^{-1} \cdot (0||V) = T.$$

Define a matrix SL^{-1}, where $SL^{-1}[i][j] = L^{-1}[i][j + 243]$ for $(0 \le i < 729, 0 \le j < 486)$, we obtain

$$SL^{-1} \cdot V = T.$$

Suppose there is a space TS, which is used to store all valid T that make the equation system $SL^{-1} \cdot V = T$ have solutions to V. Then, the space S used to store all valid A_{ST}^t can be trivially derived since $A_{ST}^t = T + L^{-1} \cdot (C||0)$.

The space TS can be easily calculated based on Gauss elimination. Then, a linear equation system ET in terms of T can be derived to store all valid values of T which can make $SL^{-1} \cdot V = T$ have solutions to V. Apply Gauss elimination to ET, the solution structure of T can be determined. Such a structure is good for attackers since it reveals that some trits of T are fixed as shown in Table 8 (see Appendix A), implying that the some trits of A_{ST}^t must be constants in order to match a given hash value. The space TS is obviously the set of T satisfying the conditions in Table 8.

Taking into account the equivalent condition to determine whether an input state is the preimage, instead of computing until A^{t+1}, we can only compute until A_{ST}^t and check whether these conditions on A_{ST}^t hold. If they do not hold, such an input state must not be the preimage and we can try another input state. Such a strategy is ultimately exploited in our preimage attack on two/three rounds of Troika.

To make this paper clear, we define some terms. A tryte is called a **conditional tryte** if this tryte can not take arbitrary values. A trit is called a **conditional trit** if its value is fixed to a constant. A condition is called a **single-tryte condition** if only one tryte is involved in it. A condition is called a **multi-tryte condition** if more than one tryte are involved in it. A condition is called a **single-trit/two-trit/three-trit condition** if it is imposed on a conditional tryte, where one/two/three trits of this tryte are fixed to constants. According to Table 8, there are 162 conditional trytes, 216 conditional trits, 162 single-tryte conditions, 115 single-trit conditions (marked in black), 40 two-trit conditions (marked in blue), 7 three-trit conditions (marked in red) and 27 multi-tryte conditions.

4   Preimage Attack on Two-Round Troika

To find the preimage for two-round Troika, according to Table 8, there are 7 three-trit conditions and 40 two-trit conditions on A_{ST}^1. If we can guess the message in a proper way to ensure these conditions always hold, an advantage over brute force is achieved. This motivates us to investigate the property of an S-box.

4.1   Linearizing the Inputs of an S-Box

Denote the input and output of an S-box by $(x_0, x_1, x_2) \in F_3^3$ and $(y_0, y_1, y_2) \in F_3^3$ respectively. If (y_0, y_1, y_2) is a constant, then (x_0, x_1, x_2) is a constant as well. When two trits of (y_0, y_1, y_2) are fixed, there are $3 \times 3^2 = 27$ patterns for (y_0, y_1, y_2) since it take values from F_3^3. We list all these 27 cases in Table 7 (see Appendix A). Based on this table, we observe **Property 1**.

Property 1. *When two trits of the output of an S-box are fixed, at least one linear equation of its corresponding input can be derived. In other words, the two-trit condition on the output hold with a probability of at least 3^{-1} if the inputs are linearized with such linear equations.*

4.2 Naive Preimage Attack on Two-Round Troika

Since there are 7 three-trit conditions and 40 two-trit conditions on A^1_{ST}, if we linearize the corresponding inputs of the S-box in A^1 based on Table 7, the probability that these conditions hold is improved to at least 3^{-40} from $3^{-21-80} = 3^{-101}$.

Observe that the nonlinear transform (**SubTrytes**) in the first round can be fully peeled off. In other words, we start from the state A^0_{ST} and set variables V_1 to $A^0_{ST}[\cdot][\cdot][z]$ ($0 \le z \le 8$). After linearizing some inputs of the S-box in A^1 as discussed above, there are at least $3 \times 7 + 40 = 61$ linear equations in terms of A^1 in order to satisfy the 7 three-trit conditions and 40 two-trit conditions. Since A^1 is linear with V_1, these linear equations are converted to the linear equations in terms of V_1 and form a linear equation system. Then, we can arbitrary choose V_1 from the solution space of this linear equation system and test whether the hash value is matched. In this way, we can gain an advantage of at least 3^{61} over brute force to find the preimage of two-round Troika.

4.3 Improved Preimage Attack on Two-Round Troika

Only the three-trit and two-trit conditions on A^1_{ST} are exploited in the above naive two-round preimage attack. Indeed, the single-trit conditions on A^1_{ST} can be utilized as well to significantly improve the attack.

In the same way, we start from the middle state A^0_{ST} and set variables at $A^0_{ST}[\cdot][\cdot][z]$ ($0 \le z \le 8$). Formally, let $A^0_{ST} = (V_1||P)$, where P is a 486-trit constant representing the capacity part of A^0_{ST} and V_1 is a 243-trit variable. Consider the following relation:

$$L \cdot (V_1||P) = L \cdot (V_1||0) + L \cdot (0||P) = A^0_{AP}.$$

Let $V_0 = A^0_{AP} - L \cdot (0||P)$, we have

$$L \cdot (V_1||0) = V_0.$$

To leverage all the single-tryte conditions on A^1_{ST}, we can firstly compute all valid inputs of the S-box for the corresponding conditional trytes in A^1_{ST}. For example, there is a single-trit condition on $(A^1_{ST}[0][2][0], A^1_{ST}[1][2][0], A^1_{ST}[2][2][0])$ (see Table 8). As a result, the tryte $(A^1[0][2][0], A^1[1][2][0], A^1[2][2][0])$ can only take 9 possible values, thus resulting that $(A^0_{AP}[0][2][0], A^0_{AP}[1][2][0], A^0_{AP}[2][2][0])$ can only take 9 possible values as well. Note that $V_0 = A^0_{AP} - L \cdot (0||P)$ and $L \cdot (0||P)$ is a constant for a fixed capacity part of the input state. Therefore, the corresponding tryte in V_0 can also only take 9 possible values. Similarly, for each conditional tryte in A_{ST}^1, we store the valid values for the corresponding tryte in V_0 in a two-dimensional dynamic array PV.

However, due to the non-full diffusion of L, there are 15 trits in A_{AP}^0 as listed below, which only depend on P. Therefore, before storing each valid value, we firstly check whether it is contradictory with the values of these 15 trits. Only those values that are consistent with these 15 trits will be stored. If there is no valid value for a specific conditional tryte, it implies that such a fixed capacity P can never lead to the given hash value. In this case, it is essential to generate another value for the capacity part of A^0 by compressing random messages until there is at least one valid value for each conditional tryte in A_{ST}^1.

$$A_{AP}^0[8][1][5], A_{AP}^0[6][1][7], A_{AP}^0[6][2][7], A_{AP}^0[7][1][12], A_{AP}^0[7][1][13],$$
$$A_{AP}^0[7][1][14], A_{AP}^0[7][1][15], A_{AP}^0[3][1][16], A_{AP}^0[3][1][17], A_{AP}^0[3][1][18],$$
$$A_{AP}^0[3][0][19], A_{AP}^0[3][1][19], A_{AP}^0[3][0][20], A_{AP}^0[3][1][20], A_{AP}^0[2][1][26].$$

According to the equivalent condition in Sect. 3, if we can find a solution V_1 such that $V_0 = L \cdot (V_1 || 0)$ can be contained in PV, then we ensure all the single-tryte conditions on A_{ST}^1. Since only the 162 single-tryte conditions are considered at this phase, we only need compute the corresponding 162 trytes in V_0. Consequently, we only need to focus on the $162 \times 3 = 486$ linear equations between V_1 and V_0. Denote the equation system composed of these 486 linear equations by S_1: $SL \cdot V_1 = V_0'$, where SL is the coefficient matrix of size 486×243 and V_0' is of size 486×1. Note that all valid values for the trytes in V_0' have been stored in PV.

With Gauss elimination, it is easy to derive a linear equation system S_0 in terms of V_0', which is used to store all valid values of V_0' that makes the equation system S_1: $SL \cdot V_1 = V_0'$ have solutions to V_1. If we can find a value for V_0' such that it is not only a solution of S_0 and but also contained in PV, then V_1 is found to satisfy all the single-tryte conditions. In next parts, we will expand on how to find such V_0' with a guess-and-determine approach. Before searching for such V_0', a preprocessing phase is necessary to pre-determine whether it can be found.

Note that all single-trit/two-trit/three-trit conditions have been taken into account. Therefore, for different trytes in V_0', the number of their valid values stored in PV will be different. Specifically, some trytes in V_0' can only take a unique value if they correspond to a three-trit condition. Some trytes in V_0' can only take at most 3 values if they correspond to a two-trit condition. And some trytes in V_0' can take at most 9 values if they correspond to a single-trit condition. For the trytes taking 1 or 3 values, it has been discussed previously that at least 61 linear equations in terms of V_0' can be derived.

Therefore, after obtaining S_0, we derive linear equations for each tryte of V_0' based on its valid values stored in PV as far as possible and add them to S_0. Once new equations are introduced in S_0, more variables in S_0 will become fixed. As a result, it is possible to remove invalid values for some trytes in V_0' from PV, which can be proceeded by checking whether each valid value is contained in the solution space of the updated S_0 via Gauss elimination. As invalid values are removed, the number of valid values for some trytes will decrease, thus having the potential to be linearized. Such a procedure is repeated until S_0 becomes stable, which means the size of the solution space S_0 will not be changed when adding the derived linear equations to it.

Observe that it is possible that none valid values for some trytes in V_0' are left after removing operation. In this case, it implies that such a fixed capacity P can never lead to the given hash value and it is necessary to generate another P by compressing arbitrary message.

4.4   Guess-and-Determine Method to Find the Preimage

After obtaining the stable linear equation system S_0, whose coefficient matrix is the row simplest form matrix, instead of naively exhausting the solution space of S_0 and checking whether it is contained in PV, we use a guess-and-determine technique to find V_0' which is not only contained in PV but also contained in the solution space of S_0.

As is known, for the coefficient matrix of S_0, each non-zero row will correspond to an equation

$$\alpha_0 V_0'[0] + \alpha_1 V_0'[1] + \cdots + \alpha_{485} V_0'[485] = \alpha_{486},$$

where $\alpha_i \in F_3$ ($0 \le i \le 486$). Since it corresponds to a non-zero row, there must exists $\alpha_i \ne 0$ ($0 \le i \le 485$). Suppose $\alpha_i \ne 0$ and $\alpha_j = 0$ ($j < i \le 485$), if there exists $\alpha_k \ne 0$ ($i < k \le 485$), then we define $V_0'[k]$ as the free variable in the equation system S_0. Moreover, we define this equation as the equation on the trit $V_0'[i]$.

Note that the coefficient matrix of S_0 is the row simplest form matrix. If we guess the values for V_0' in the order that

$$(V_0'[485], V_0'[484], V_0'[483]) \to (V_0'[482], V_0'[481], V_0'[480]) \to$$
$$(V_0'[3i+2], V_0'[3i+1], V_0'[3i]) \to \cdots \to (V_0'[2], V_0'[1], V_0'[0]),$$

we can always verify the equations on $(V_0'[3i+2], V_0'[3i+1], V_0'[3i])$ ($0 \le i \le 161$) when $(V_0'[3i+2], V_0'[3i+1], V_0'[3i])$ ($0 \le i \le 161$) is guessed. In other words, when choosing a valid value from PV for the tryte $(V_0'[3i+2], V_0'[3i+1], V_0'[3i])$ ($0 \le i \le 161$), we can verify whether it is contained in the solution space of S_0 before guessing the remaining free variables. If it is not contained, such a guess for this tryte is obviously wrong. Following such an order to guess, there are several advantages over simply exhausting the solution space of S_0 when properly using the guess-and-determine technique below.

How to Guess. Firstly, note that each tryte of V_0' can take at most 9 possible values. If all the three trits in a tryte are free variables, we have to try 27 possible values of this tryte when simply exhausting the solution space of S_0. However, if we only choose valid values from PV for the three trits, we only need to guess at most 9 times, thus obtaining an advantage of at least 3^1. If two trits in a tryte are free variables, we can obtain an advantage by guessing values from PV for this tryte when the number of valid values for this tryte stored in PV is smaller than 9, which is possible to occur. If only one trit in a tryte is a variable, advantages can be gained when the number of valid values for this tryte stored in PV is smaller than 3. Otherwise, we simply guess this free variable and determine the whole tryte and then check whether it is contained in the corresponding PV. The last case is that no trit in a tryte is a variable. In this case, according to the guess order, the value for this tryte can be computed based on the corresponding three equations on them. Then, we simply check whether the computed value for this tryte is contained in the corresponding PV, which can be finished in 1 time.

Local Test. When guessing a value for a tryte from PV, it is necessary to check whether such a guessed value is contained in the solution space of S_0. This can be efficiently checked by verifying the equations on this tryte due to the guess order. If a guessed value can not pass the test, i.e. the equations on this tryte do not hold, there is no need to move ahead to next tryte from this guessed value, thus reducing the search space further more.

Look-Ahead and Fast Backtracking. Although local test can provide early stop in a way, it is possible to occur that one value of a first guessed tryte will always lead to a contradiction for a later guessed tryte. In this case, there will be a lot of unnecessary backtracking if the two trytes locate far from each other since the guess order is predetermined. To improve the efficiency of looking ahead, we can construct a table for each tryte, which is used to record the trytes to be checked when this tryte is guessed. Only when all trytes in the recorded table can pass the local test can we move ahead to guess another tryte. In this case, for each checked tryte, the index of the first valid value in PV are recorded in order to remove redundant operations when the search actually reach these trytes.

Although look-ahead can be used to achieve faster early stop, another bad case may occur, which causes many unnecessary backtracking. Specifically, we can ensure that there is at least one valid value for a later guessed tryte with the look-ahead strategy. However, when we actually reach this tryte, we have to look ahead from this tryte as far as possible. It is possible that there is no valid value for this tryte that can pass look-ahead. As a result, backtracking starts. However, there will be many unnecessary backtracking if the value of this tryte is only influenced by a pre-guessed tryte that locates far from it. Obviously, if we can immediately backtrack to this pre-guessed tryte, the backtracking between this tryte and the pre-guessed tryte is removed, thus further reducing the search space on the whole. To achieve efficiency of fast backtracking, we construct a table for each tryte, which is used to record the tryte to be backtracked when this tryte fails to move ahead.

4.5 Complexity Evaluation

When a valid V_0' is found with the guess-and-determine approach, start exhausting the solution space of $SL \cdot V_1 = V_0'$ and check whether the given hash value can be generated with V_1. The size of the solution space of $SL \cdot V_1 = V_0$ is 3^6 based on our analysis, which is only related to the fixed coefficient matrix SL.

According to our guess-and-determine technique above, the found V_0' can only ensure the single-tryte conditions on A_{ST}^1. Therefore, each solution of the equation system $SL \cdot V_1 = V_0'$ can also only ensure the single-tryte conditions on A_{ST}^1. For the multi-tryte conditions on A_{ST}^1, they are not taken into account in our guess-and-determine technique to find a valid V_0'. To remove unnecessary enumeration of V_1 for each found V_0', when a valid V_0' is found, we firstly check some multi-tryte conditions composed of the trits that can be computed based on the fully determined V_0'. There are 8 such multi-tryte conditions. Only when they are satisfied will we start exhausting the solution space of $SL \cdot V_1 = V_0'$. Consequently, the time complexity to find a preimage with one block is equivalent to the time complexity to enumerate all valid V_0' with our guess-and-determine technique.

To calculate the time complexity to enumerate all valid V_0', we firstly omit the influence of local test, look-ahead and fast backtracking and only focus on the size of solution space if adopting our method to guess values for each tryte. Initialize a counter $cnt = 0$. After a stable S_0 is obtained, we check the positions of free variables. Suppose there are f_0 free variables in a tryte of V_0' and the number of valid values for this tryte stored in PV is f_1. For each of the 162 trytes of V_0', update cnt based on the following relations between f_0 and f_1.

$$
cnt = \begin{cases}
cnt & \text{(if } f_0 = 0) \\
cnt + log_3(f_1) & \text{(if } f_0 = 1 \text{ and } f_1 \le 3) \\
cnt + 1 & \text{(if } f_0 = 1 \text{ and } 3 < f_1 \le 9) \\
cnt + log_3(f_1) & \text{(if } f_0 = 2) \\
cnt + log_3(f_1) & \text{(if } f_0 = 3)
\end{cases}
$$

We generate hundreds of thousands of hash values used as the inputs to the program with random one-block messages. After a stable equation system S_0 and PV are obtained, start computing cnt. Among all these values for cnt, the largest one is $cnt = 92$. However, the effect of local test, look-ahead and fast backtracking has not been taken into account. It is reasonable to estimate that these early stop strategies can at least reduce the whole search space by a factor of 3^{13} according to our experiments. Specifically, when it is computationally feasible, we exhaust all possible values from the first guessed tryte to a certain later tryte. Then, record the total trying times in order to enumerate all valid solutions until this tryte. Meanwhile, the number of valid solutions is recorded as well. Suppose the total trying times is 3^{cnt_0}, the number of valid solutions is 3^{cnt_1} and the search space is 3^{cnt_2} without early stop strategy. In this way, we can reduce the whole search space by a factor of at least $3^{cnt_2 - cnt_1}$. As a consequence, for the hash value of two-round Troika that can be generated with one block, the time complexity to find its preimage is upper bounded by

$3^{92-13} = 3^{79}$, which is 3^{164} times faster than brute force. Due to this significant advantage over brute force as well as our algorithm to predetermine whether a hash value can be generated with one block, it is expected that our algorithm can be applied to arbitrary hash values.

Attempt to Solve the Two-Round Preimage Challenge. For the two-round preimage challenge [1], our algorithm shows that one block is not sufficient to generate this hash value. Therefore, we append random message blocks before the last block to generate a suitable capacity part for the last block. Such a capacity part can pass the test of our algorithm to determine whether it is potential to match the given hash value by using the degree of freedom of the last block. Then, the guess-and-determine technique will be applied to enumerate all valid V_0' and the corresponding V_1. The appended message block M_{app} we found is shown in Table 4. With such an appended message block, the two-round preimage challenge can be partially solved. Specifically, we found a solution M_{last} for the last block in seconds. There are only 40 different trits between the two-round preimage challenge and the hash value computed from $M_{app}||M_{last}$, as displayed in Table 4.

4.6 Second Preimage Attack on Two-Round Troika

To find the preimage of two-round Troika with one block, two linear equation systems S_0 in terms of V_0' and S_1: $SL \cdot V_1 = V_0'$ are constructed. The goal is to find a valid V_0'. After it is found, start exhausting the solution space of S_1: $SL \cdot V_1 = V_0'$. However, when given a message M_0 and its corresponding hash value H_0 after two-round Troika permutation, the corresponding value for V_0' computed from M_0 is known! To find the second preimage for (M_0, H_0), we simply set V_0' the same with that computed from M_0. Then, we start exhausting the solution space S_1: $SL \cdot V_1 = V_0'$. Note that there is at least one solution to V_1 that can lead to the hash value H_0, which exactly corresponds to M_0. However, our program suggests that there are several V_1 that can lead to the same hash value H_0. For the sake of correctness, we generate many random messages and compute the corresponding hash value. Our program suggests that there are always several V_1 which can lead to the same given hash value. Since the size of the solution space of S_1 is 3^6, the time complexity to find the second preimage is upper bounded by 3^6. To support our approach, we randomly generate a value for M_0 and compute the corresponding hash value H_0. Then we found that there are many second preimages for H_0. Due to the space limit, we only list 6 second preimages $(M_1, M_2, M_3, M_4, M_5, M_6)$ in Table 9 (see Appendix A).

Table 4. Partially solving the two-round preimage challenge

Two-round preimage challenge
100222202111012011001001110100211221021212210220201121
111111211000221112102012121212121020210211112202122212
111112221020112011200112222202010020010022022101020202
220012011012010000111111120102011222212011022121011122
121111111001201002212110012

M_{app}
202112201010011210202110200210010222102000011201012021
022111110012202011112121220100010202122201111210120102
201022100200121011102101112102001221101221011102120100
000221212011102001211211120212110102011220111021020212
011101122101212011000210021

M_{last}
211110012221000010020000220200212201102120112202022000
212102222210010022100012222020110212101010001211111000
110120212012222100222102102101110100210000021101110211
212011111021210011221122121221211102221201222211202100
001121000001112121210022100

Hash value computed from $M_{app}\|M_{last}$
200222202110120111010011101012112210022122102212011221201121
111111211000221112102012121212121020210211112202122212
111112221020112011200112222202010020010022022101020202
210012010002010002101111122102111202211111002021111102
222101002002100221111211200

5 Preimage Attack on Three-Round Troika

The preimage attack on two-round Troika can be viewed as the interaction between two linear equation systems. As the attacked round increases, it is almost impossible to establish similar linear equation systems. However, we can still construct two interacting systems to find the preimage of three-round Troika. Such an idea is much inspired from the cube-attack-like cryptanalysis of Keccak-MAC by Dinur et al. [6].

Note that an equivalent condition to match a given hash value has been proposed in Sect. 3. Specifically, when starting from a state with a correct fixed capacity part, matching a three-round hash value is equivalent to satisfying the 243 trit conditions on A_{ST}^2 as displayed in Table 8. The main technique is to separate the 243 variables set at $A_{ST}^0[\cdot][\cdot][z]$ ($0 \le z \le 8$) into two parts PA_1 and PA_2. Then, exhaust all possible values of the variables at PA_1 and compute some trytes in A_{ST}^2. Only when the equivalent conditions on these trytes hold can we start exhausting all possible values of the variables in PA_2. When all variables in PA_1 and PA_2 are guessed, the one-block message is fixed and we can determine whether it is the preimage of the three-round hash value.

As has been mentioned in [3], after three-round Troika permutation, the computation of one S-box requires the knowledge of all S-boxes in the first round. Therefore, it is reasonable to assume that three-round Troika provides sufficient diffusion and the 243 trits of the three-round hash value are independent from each other. In other words, suppose the capacity part of A_{ST}^0 is fixed and there are 243 variables at $A_{ST}^0[\cdot][\cdot][z]$ ($0 \leq z \leq 8$), we expect that one hash value only corresponds to one value of these 243 variables. Note that matching a given hash value is equivalent to satisfying the 243 conditions on A_{ST}^2 when starting from a correct fixed capacity part. Suppose the 243 trit conditions are not independent from each other, it may occur that more than one values of the variables can make the all the 243 trit conditions on A_{ST}^2 hold, suggesting that one hash value may correspond to more than one value of the 243 variables. Consequently, we can assume the 243 conditions on A_{ST}^2 are independent based on the assumption that three-round Troika provides sufficient diffusion.

If there are t_0 trit conditions on A_{ST}^2 that can be tested by only guessing all the t_1 variables at PA_1, based on the assumption that these trit conditions are independent, we can expect that only $3^{t_1-t_0}$ valid values are left for these t_1 variables after 3^{t_1} computations. Then, for each of the $3^{t_1-t_0}$ valid values, exhaust the remaining $(243 - t_1)$ variables and compute the three-round hash value. As a result, with time complexity $3^{t_1} + 3^{243-t_0}$, we can exhaust all possible one-block messages. Suppose the given hash value can be generated with only one block, the preimage must be found. When it can not be generated with only one block, we can append random blocks before the last block to generate a valid capacity part of the last block and exhaust all possible values of the last block with the above method. As a result, with at most $3 \times (3^{t_1} + 3^{243-t_0})$ computations, we can expect to find the preimage of three-round Troika.

Based on the above analysis, achieving the optimal time complexity is equivalent to finding the optimal separation of the 243 variables. As will be shown, such a problem can be solved with MILP (Mixed-Integer Linear Programming), which was firstly introduced to cryptanalysis in [9].

5.1   Finding Optimal Separation with MILP

Our attack starts from the middle state A_{ST}^0 and the 243 variables $(v_0, ..., v_{242})$ are set at $A_{ST}^0[\cdot][\cdot][z]$ ($0 \leq z \leq 8$), i.e. $v_{27z+9y+x} = A_{ST}^0[x][y][z]$. First of all, for each conditional tryte CT_i ($0 \leq i \leq 161$) at A_{ST}^2, record the corresponding variables in $(v_0, ..., v_{242})$ that need knowing in order to compute this conditional tryte, which can be easily finished with the linear transform matrix L. Suppose the recorded variables for the conditional tryte CT_i are $(v_{j_0}, v_{j_1}, ..., v_{j_r})$, then we construct the following inequalities to ensure that when CT_i needs to be determined, each of $(v_{j_0}, v_{j_1}, ..., v_{j_r})$ must be guessed:

$$TV_i - VV_{j_s} \leq 0, \quad s \in \{0, 1, .., r\},$$

where $TV_i = 1$ $(0 \leq i \leq 161)$ denotes that the tryte CT_i needs to be determined and $VV_i = 1$ $(0 \leq i \leq 242)$ denotes that the variable v_i belongs to PA_1, while $TV_i = 0$ $(0 \leq i \leq 161)$ denotes that the tryte CT_i does not need to be determined and $VV_i = 0$ $(0 \leq i \leq 242)$ denotes that the variable v_i belongs to PA_2. In this way, as many as 16305 inequalities can be derived.

The objective function of the MILP model is set as

$$\text{MAX} \sum_{i=0}^{161} c_i \cdot TV_i,$$

where c_i denotes the number of conditional trits in the conditional tryte CT_i.

To ensure that the number of variables in PV_1 is not too large, we adaptively add the following inequality to the constraints

$$\sum_{i=0}^{242} VV_i \leq bd,$$

where bd is used to constrain the number of variables in PA_1. To obtain optimal time complexity of the preimage attack on three-round Troika, bd should be as small as possible while the objective function should be as large as possible. Therefore, we adaptively choose values for bd and record the results of the objective function returned by the Gurobi solver [2]. Some results are displayed in Table 5.

Table 5. Results for different bd

bd	Result of obj.	Time complexity of attack
124	5	$3 \times (3^{124} + 3^{238})$
160	10	$3 \times (3^{160} + 3^{233})$
170	13	$3 \times (3^{170} + 3^{230})$
190	18	$3 \times (3^{190} + 3^{225})$
200	20	$3 \times (3^{200} + 3^{223})$
210	24	$3 \times (3^{210} + 3^{219})$
215	27	$3 \times (3^{215} + 3^{216})$

Based on the results displayed in Table 5, the optimal value for bd is 215. For $bd = 215$, the corresponding separation of the variables $(v_0, ..., v_{242})$ and the conditional trits in A_{ST}^2 to be checked are listed in Table 6. Therefore, the time complexity of the preimage attack on three-round Troika is $3^{217.3}$, which is $3^{25.7}$ times faster than brute force.

Table 6. The optimal separation of variables to achieve best time complexity

PA_1
v_0, v_1, v_2, v_3, v_4, v_5, v_6, v_8, v_9, v_{11}, v_{12}, v_{13}, v_{14}, v_{15}, v_{16},
v_{17}, v_{18}, v_{20}, v_{21}, v_{22}, v_{23}, v_{24}, v_{25}, v_{26}, v_{27}, v_{28}, v_{29}, v_{30}, v_{31}, v_{32},
v_{33}, v_{34}, v_{35}, v_{36}, v_{38}, v_{39}, v_{40}, v_{41}, v_{42}, v_{43}, v_{44}, v_{45}, v_{46}, v_{47}, v_{48},
v_{51}, v_{52}, v_{53}, v_{54}, v_{55}, v_{57}, v_{58}, v_{59}, v_{60}, v_{63}, v_{64}, v_{65}, v_{66}, v_{67}, v_{69},
v_{70}, v_{71}, v_{72}, v_{73}, v_{74}, v_{75}, v_{76}, v_{77}, v_{78}, v_{79}, v_{80}, v_{82}, v_{83}, v_{84}, v_{85},
v_{86}, v_{87}, v_{88}, v_{89}, v_{90}, v_{91}, v_{92}, v_{93}, v_{94}, v_{95}, v_{97}, v_{98}, v_{99}, v_{100}, v_{101},
v_{102}, v_{103}, v_{104}, v_{105}, v_{106}, v_{107}, v_{108}, v_{109}, v_{110}, v_{111}, v_{113}, v_{114}, v_{115}, v_{116}, v_{117},
v_{118}, v_{119}, v_{120}, v_{121}, v_{122}, v_{123}, v_{124}, v_{125}, v_{126}, v_{128}, v_{129}, v_{130}, v_{131}, v_{132}, v_{133},
v_{134}, v_{135}, v_{137}, v_{138}, v_{140}, v_{141}, v_{142}, v_{143}, v_{144}, v_{145}, v_{146}, v_{147}, v_{148}, v_{149}, v_{150},
v_{151}, v_{152}, v_{153}, v_{155}, v_{156}, v_{157}, v_{158}, v_{159}, v_{160}, v_{161}, v_{162}, v_{163}, v_{165}, v_{166}, v_{167},
v_{168}, v_{170}, v_{171}, v_{172}, v_{173}, v_{174}, v_{175}, v_{177}, v_{178}, v_{179}, v_{180}, v_{181}, v_{182}, v_{183}, v_{185},
v_{187}, v_{188}, v_{190}, v_{192}, v_{193}, v_{194}, v_{195}, v_{197}, v_{198}, v_{199}, v_{200}, v_{201}, v_{202}, v_{203}, v_{204},
v_{205}, v_{206}, v_{207}, v_{208}, v_{209}, v_{210}, v_{212}, v_{213}, v_{214}, v_{215}, v_{216}, v_{217}, v_{218}, v_{220}, v_{221},
v_{222}, v_{223}, v_{224}, v_{225}, v_{226}, v_{227}, v_{228}, v_{229}, v_{230}, v_{232}, v_{233}, v_{234}, v_{235}, v_{236}, v_{237},
v_{238}, v_{239}, v_{240}, v_{241}, v_{242}.
27 conditional trits on A_{ST}^2 to be checked
$A_{ST}^2[4][0][3]$, $A_{ST}^2[5][2][3]$, $A_{ST}^2[6][0][4]$, $A_{ST}^2[8][0][4]$, $A_{ST}^2[7][1][4]$, $A_{ST}^2[2][0][6]$, $A_{ST}^2[1][1][6]$, $A_{ST}^2[2][1][6]$, $A_{ST}^2[4][0][7]$, $A_{ST}^2[3][1][7]$, $A_{ST}^2[4][1][7]$, $A_{ST}^2[5][1][7]$, $A_{ST}^2[4][0][8]$, $A_{ST}^2[3][1][8]$, $A_{ST}^2[4][1][8]$, $A_{ST}^2[5][1][8]$, $A_{ST}^2[5][2][8]$, $A_{ST}^2[4][0][9]$, $A_{ST}^2[3][1][9]$, $A_{ST}^2[4][1][9]$, $A_{ST}^2[5][1][9]$, $A_{ST}^2[5][0][13]$, $A_{ST}^2[5][1][13]$, $A_{ST}^2[4][2][13]$, $A_{ST}^2[0][1][23]$, $A_{ST}^2[1][2][23]$, $A_{ST}^2[2][2][23]$.

6 Conclusion and Future Work

By discovering some equivalent conditions to pre-determine whether a message is the preimage of a given hash value, invalid messages can be filtered at an early stage and the search can be limited to a smaller potential space. To speed up the search in this potential smaller space for two-round preimage attack, two interacting linear equation systems are constructed. Then, a guess-and-determine technique involving fast cutting branches to efficiently enumerate valid solutions for one of the equation systems is proposed. Consequently, the time complexity to find the preimage of two-round Troika with one block is at most 3^{79}, which is 3^{164} times faster then brute force. Moreover, with the divide-and-conquer method, the one-block message space is separated in an optimal way with MILP so as to achieve optimal time complexity of the preimage attack on three-round Troika. As a result, the preimage of three-round Troika can be found with time complexity $3^{217.3}$.

Our algorithm shows that the second preimage for two-round Troika can be found with pretty small time complexity. In other words, we can efficiently enumerate several two-round differential characteristics which can lead to a collision for two-round Troika with only one block. To construct a collision for three-round Troika, we have placed the obtained two-round differential characteristic in the last two rounds and computed backward by one round to obtain the actual input difference. However, there is always difference in the capacity part of the input, which implies that we cannot find a three-round differential characteristic to generate a collision with only one block. We also have tested whether the obtained two-round differential characteristics for collision can be extended to three rounds. However, it is shown that there is always difference in the rate part of the output. Our future work is to improve the strategy to search the (second) preimage for two-round Troika and see whether it is possible to actually solve the three-round collision challenge and two-round preimage challenge.

Acknowledgement. We thank the anonymous reviewers of IWSEC 2019 for their insightful comments and suggestions. We also thank the Troika Group for the discussion. Fukang Liu is supported by Invitation Programs for Foreigner-based Researchers of the National Institute of Information and Communications Technology (NICT). Takanori Isobe is supported by Grant-in-Aid for Scientific Research (B) (KAKENHI 19H02141) for Japan Society for the Promotion of Science.

A   Some Tables and Example

Table 7. Linearizing the input of an S-box

Output (y_0, y_1, y_2)	Inputs (x_0, x_1, x_2)	Equations
(-, 0, 0)	(1, 0, 0), (1, 1, 0), (1, 2, 0)	$x_0 = 1, x_2 = 0$
(-, 0, 1)	(0, 1, 2), (1, 0, 1), (2, 2, 2)	$x_0 + x_1 = 1$
(-, 0, 2)	(0, 2, 1), (1, 0, 2), (2, 1, 1)	$x_0 - x_1 = 1$
(-, 1, 0)	(2, 0, 0), (2, 1, 2), (2, 2, 1)	$x_0 = 2, x_1 + x_2 = 0$
(-, 1, 1)	(0, 2, 0), (1, 1, 1), (2, 0, 1)	$x_0 + x_1 = 2$
(-, 1, 2)	(0, 1, 0), (1, 2, 2), (2, 0, 2)	$x_0 - x_1 = 2$
(-, 2, 0)	(0, 0, 0), (0, 1, 1), (0, 2, 2)	$x_0 = 0, x_1 - x_2 = 0$
(-, 2, 1)	(0, 0, 1), (1, 2, 1), (2, 1, 0)	$x_0 + x_1 = 0$
(-, 2, 2)	(0, 0, 2), (1, 1, 2), (2, 2, 0)	$x_0 - x_1 = 0$
(0, -, 0)	(0, 0, 0), (1, 0, 0), (2, 0, 0)	$x_1 = 0, x_2 = 0$
(0, -, 1)	(0, 2, 0), (1, 0, 1), (2, 1, 0)	$x_0 - x_1 = 1$
(0, -, 2)	(0, 1, 0), (1, 0, 2), (2, 2, 0)	$x_0 + x_1 = 1$
(1, -, 0)	(0, 1, 1), (1, 1, 0), (2, 1, 2)	$x_1 = 1, x_0 + x_2 = 1$
(1, -, 1)	(0, 1, 2), (1, 2, 1), (2, 0, 1)	$x_0 - x_1 = 2$
(1, -, 2)	(0, 0, 2), (1, 2, 2), (2, 1, 1)	$x_0 + x_1 = 0$
(2, -, 0)	(0, 2, 2), (1, 2, 0), (2, 2, 1)	$x_1 = 2, x_0 - x_2 = 1$
(2, -, 1)	(0, 0, 1), (1, 1, 1), (2, 2, 2)	$x_0 - x_1 = 0$
(2, -, 2)	(0, 2, 1), (1, 1, 2), (2, 0, 2)	$x_0 + x_1 = 2$
(0, 0, -)	(1, 0, 0), (1, 0, 1), (1, 0, 2)	$x_0 = 1, x_1 = 0$
(0, 1, -)	(0, 1, 0), (0, 2, 0), (2, 0, 0)	$x_2 = 0$
(0, 2, -)	(0, 0, 0), (2, 1, 0), (2, 2, 0)	$x_2 = 0$
(1, 0, -)	(0, 1, 2), (1, 1, 0), (2, 1, 1)	$x_1 = 1, x_0 - x_2 = 1$
(1, 1, -)	(1, 2, 2), (2, 0, 1), (2, 1, 2)	$x_0 + x_1 - x_2 = 1$
(1, 2, -)	(0, 0, 2), (0, 1, 1), (1, 2, 1)	$x_0 - x_1 - x_2 = 1$
(2, 0, -)	(0, 2, 1), (1, 2, 0), (2, 2, 2)	$x_1 = 2, x_0 + x_2 = 1$
(2, 1, -)	(1, 1, 1), (2, 0, 2), (2, 2, 1)	$x_0 - x_1 + x_2 = 1$
(2, 2, -)	(0, 0, 1), (0, 2, 2), (1, 1, 2)	$x_0 + x_1 + x_2 = 1$

Table 8. Conditions on T

Slice: 0	Slice: 1	Slice: 2	Slice: 3	Slice: 4
--- --- 0-0	--- --- 0-0	--- --- 0-0	--- -0- 0-0	--- -0- 0-0
00- --- -00	00- --- -00	000 --- -0-	-00 --- -0-	-00 -0- -0-
--0 0-- ---	--0 --0 ---	--0 --0 ---	--0 --0 ---	--- --0 ---

Slice: 5	Slice: 6	Slice: 7	Slice: 8	Slice: 9
--- -0- 0--	--0 -0- ---	--0 -0- ---	0-0 -0- ---	0-0 -0- ---
-00 00- -0-	-00 00- -0-	--0 000 -0-	--0 000 ---	--0 000 ---
--- --0 ---	--- --0 ---	--- --0 ---	--- --0 ---	--- --- --0

Slice: 10	Slice: 11	Slice: 12	Slice: 13	Slice: 14
0-0 -0- ---	0-0 --- ---	0-0 --0 ---	0-0 --0 ---	00- --0 ---
--- 000 ---	--- 000 ---	--- 0-0 ---	--- --0 0--	--- --0 0--
--- -0- --0	0-- -0- --0	0-- -0- --0	0-- -0- --0	0-- -0- --0

Slice: 15	Slice: 16	Slice: 17	Slice: 18	Slice: 19
00- --0 ---	-0- --0 ---	-0- 0-0 ---	-0- 0-0 -0-	-0- 0-0 -0-
--- --- 0--	--- --- 0--	--- --- 0--	--- --- 0--	--- --- 0--
0-- -0- 0-0	00- --0 0-0	00- --0 0--	00- --- 0--	-0- --- 00-

Slice: 20	Slice: 21	Slice: 22	Slice: 23	Slice: 24
-0- 0-- -0-	-0- 0-- -0-	--- 0-- -0-	--- 0-- -0-	--- 0-- -00
--- --- 0--	--- --- --0	0-- --- --0	0-- --- --0	0-- --- --0
-0- 0-- 00-	-0- 0-- 00-	-0- 0-- 00-	-00 0-- -0-	--0 0-- -0-

Slice: 25	Slice: 26
--- --- 000	--- --- 0-0
0-- --- --0	00- --- --0
--0 0-- -0-	--0 0-- -0-

Multi-tryte conditions

$T[7] + T[364] + T[531] + T[694] = 0$, $T[25] + T[308] + T[512] + T[572] = 0$,
$T[48] + 2T[582] = 0$, $T[52] + T[226] + T[328] + T[678] = 0$,
$T[71] + 2T[380] = 0$, $T[75] + T[419] + T[459] + T[609] = 0$,
$T[90] + 2T[678] = 0$, $T[98] + T[293] + T[407] + T[595] = 0$,
$T[117] + T[380] + T[672] + T[705] = 0$, $T[128] + 2T[419] = 0$,
$T[143] + 2T[419] = 0$, $T[155] + T[170] + T[446] + T[709] = 0$,
$T[168] + 2T[531] = 0$, $T[195] + T[390] + T[545] + T[558] = 0$,
$T[199] + T[308] + T[512] + T[572] = 0$, $T[232] + 2T[595] = 0$,
$T[259] + T[535] + T[582] + T[622] = 0$, $T[266] + 2T[380] = 0$,
$T[281] + 2T[545] = 0$, $T[301] + T[308] + T[512] + T[572] = 0$,
$T[337] + 2T[709] = 0$, $T[363] + 2T[531] = 0$, $T[432] + 2T[582] = 0$,
$T[485] + 2T[545] = 0$, $T[508] + 2T[595] = 0$, $T[645] + 2T[678] = 0$,
$T[667] + 2T[709] = 0$.

Table 9. Instances of second preimage

M_0	01011101012001200222221102000101122101120111111010202101122011210211200101200011022000021102221211222022120002222000210011000001201120201021221211221120121200211102110200011220212012001020020200010212021121021201222200221011120001120020220010
H_0	20112200210222001220100112111200211010210121001001000021102012101111122201120102122021221001102202010101122020201022221011210121202010211120211221100022002101212212222000002022202121010202101012212012211112222102220111001121202121022122002211
M_1	01011101002201200222221102000101122111020111111010202101122011210211200101200011022000021102221211222102212000221020111001100000120112020101102121122112012120021110211020001122021201200102002020001021202112102120122220022101112000112002022001 01
M_2	01011101002201200222221102000101122111020111111010202101122011210211200101200011022000021102221211222102212000221020111001100001100112020101102011221120121200211102110200011220212012001020020200010212021121021201222200221011120001120020220010 1
M_3	01011101002201200222221102000101122111020111111010202101122011210211200101200011022000021102221211222022120002210200021001100000120112020101102121122112012120021110211020001122021201200102002020001021202112102120122220022101112000112002022001 01
M_4	01011101012001200222221102000101122101120111111010202101122011210211200101200011022000021102221211222102212000222200111001100000120112020102122121122112012120021110211020001122021201200102002020001021202112102120122220022101112000112002022001 01
M_5	01011101012001200222221102000101122101120111111010202101122011210211200101200011022000021102221211222022120002222000210011000011001120201021220111221120121200211102110200011220212012001020020200010212021121021201222200221011120001120020220010 1
M_6	01011101012001200222221102000101122121220111111010202101122011210211200101200011022000021102221211222022120002222000210011000011001120201001120111221120121200211102110200011220212012001020020200010212021121021201222200221011120001120020220010 1

References

1. Cybercrypt. https://www.cyber-crypt.com/troika-challenge/
2. Gurobi. https://www.gurobi.com/
3. Troika: a ternary hash function (2018). https://www.cyber-crypt.com/wp-content/uploads/2018/12/20181221.iota_.troika-reference.v1.0.1.pdf
4. Bertoni, G., Daemen, J., Peeters, M., Van Assche, G.: The Keccak reference (2011). http://keccak.noekeon.org
5. Dinur, I., Dunkelman, O., Shamir, A.: New attacks on Keccak-224 and Keccak-256. In: Canteaut, A. (ed.) FSE 2012. LNCS, vol. 7549, pp. 442–461. Springer, Heidelberg (2012). https://doi.org/10.1007/978-3-642-34047-5_25
6. Dinur, I., Morawiecki, P., Pieprzyk, J., Srebrny, M., Straus, M.: Cube attacks and cube-attack-like cryptanalysis on the round-reduced keccak sponge function. In: Oswald, E., Fischlin, M. (eds.) EUROCRYPT 2015. LNCS, vol. 9056, pp. 733–761. Springer, Heidelberg (2015). https://doi.org/10.1007/978-3-662-46800-5_28
7. Guo, J., Liu, M., Song, L.: Linear structures: applications to cryptanalysis of round-reduced KECCAK. In: Cheon, J.H., Takagi, T. (eds.) ASIACRYPT 2016. LNCS, vol. 10031, pp. 249–274. Springer, Heidelberg (2016). https://doi.org/10.1007/978-3-662-53887-6_9
8. Li, T., Sun, Y., Liao, M., Wang, D.: Preimage attacks on the round-reduced Keccak with cross-linear structures. IACR Trans. Symmetric Cryptol. **2017**(4), 39–57 (2017)
9. Mouha, N., Wang, Q., Gu, D., Preneel, B.: Differential and linear cryptanalysis using mixed-integer linear programming. In: Wu, C.-K., Yung, M., Lin, D. (eds.) Inscrypt 2011. LNCS, vol. 7537, pp. 57–76. Springer, Heidelberg (2012). https://doi.org/10.1007/978-3-642-34704-7_5
10. Qiao, K., Song, L., Liu, M., Guo, J.: New collision attacks on round-reduced Keccak. In: Coron, J.-S., Nielsen, J.B. (eds.) EUROCRYPT 2017. LNCS, vol. 10212, pp. 216–243. Springer, Cham (2017). https://doi.org/10.1007/978-3-319-56617-7_8
11. Song, L., Liao, G., Guo, J.: Non-full sbox linearization: applications to collision attacks on round-reduced KECCAK. In: Katz, J., Shacham, H. (eds.) CRYPTO 2017. LNCS, vol. 10402, pp. 428–451. Springer, Cham (2017). https://doi.org/10.1007/978-3-319-63715-0_15

Cryptographic Protocols 2

VSS Made Simpler

Yvo Desmedt[2] and Kirill Morozov[1(✉)]

[1] Department of Computer Science and Engineering, University of North Texas, Denton, USA
Kirill.Morozov@unt.edu
[2] Department of Computer Science, The University of Texas at Dallas, Richardson, USA
Yvo.Desmedt@utdallas.edu

Abstract. Verifiable secret sharing (VSS) allows honest parties to ensure consistency of their shares even if a dealer and/or a subset of parties are corrupt. We focus on perfect VSS, i.e., those providing perfect privacy, correctness and commitment with zero error, in the unconditional (information-theoretic) security setting where no assumption on the computational power of the participants is imposed.

Our study is motivated by both practical and theoretical considerations. For the practical side, MPC with perfect security is now being implemented. Multi-cloud storage has been implemented by IBM. Modern users rely on smartphones with limited internet connectivity, limited battery power, etc. We focus on such a user outsourcing her data to multi-clouds with the capability to have these multi-clouds participate on her behalf in MPC protocols. We show that in the case of VSS based on the replicated secret sharing scheme, there is no need for that user to be involved in any interaction. In addition, this scheme has an optimal number of rounds. This construction is derived from Maurer's VSS based on the replicated secret sharing scheme.

A disadvantage of the replicated scheme is that it generally requires a considerable amount of randomness. We address this issue by showing a VSS scheme based on Shamir's secret sharing, where the dealer does not need any randomness at all.

Keywords: Secret sharing · Verifiable secret sharing ·
Round complexity · Randomness complexity

1 Introduction

Secret sharing [5,35] allows a *dealer* to share a secret among n parties such that certain "access" sets of them will be able to reconstruct it, while certain other "forbidden" sets will not. *Verifiable secret sharing (VSS)* [10] allows the honest parties to reliably reconstruct the secret even in the presence of active adversary who may corrupt both the dealer and a forbidden set of parties. VSS

© Springer Nature Switzerland AG 2019
N. Attrapadung and T. Yagi (Eds.): IWSEC 2019, LNCS 11689, pp. 329–342, 2019.
https://doi.org/10.1007/978-3-030-26834-3_19

finds numerous applications in cryptography, most notably for secure multi-party computations [3,9,20].

In this work, we focus on unconditionally secure VSS, where no assumption is made on the computational power of the participants [3,9]. A number of VSS schemes in this setting, starting from [3], were constructed that tolerate the so-called Q^3 adversary – this condition requires that no union of any three forbidden sets covers the set of all parties.[1] Two important directions in the studies on VSS can be identified: (1) Characterization of (ordinary) secret sharing schemes that can be transformed into VSS; (2) Optimization of the existing constructions in terms of their round, communication, and computation complexities. In the first line of research, Cramer, Damgård and Maurer (Eurocrypt'00) [11] proposed a general transformation from any linear secret sharing scheme (LSSS) into VSS (we will call this protocol the CDM scheme), however it requires $O(k^2)$ random field elements, where k is the number of random field elements used by the underlying LSSS. Fehr and Maurer (Crypto'02) [16] presented a purely algebraic condition on whether a given secret sharing scheme can be used as VSS.

Recent research on optimizing VSS [12,17,18,25,34] seems somewhat unbalanced in the sense that it is mainly devoted to reducing round complexity. At the same time, reducing randomness complexity appears to be an important goal, in the light of recent discoveries [21,28] showing that proper generation and management of randomness is by far a non-trivial task.

We focus on the "error-free" scenario, where robustness against Q^3 adversary is achieved in the perfect sense (see Definition 1). There exist other variants of verifiable secret sharing, see, e.g., [19,32,34], in which correctness and/or commitment are not error-free – they are out of scope of this work.

1.1 Motivation

We provide the following motivations for our work, the first two are practical, and the other is theoretical:

1. Consider a cloud storage scenario, where the data are secret-shared and placed onto the cloud (or the cloud of clouds). Now, if one wants to run multi-party computation (MPC) with such data as an input, then consistency of the shares must be verified first. Note that the VSS schemes considered so far either use some special form of secret sharing, or require interaction with the dealer for verification. This extra involvement with the dealer (i.e., the owner of the data) may be undesirable. Indeed, leaders, such as CEOs, heads of states, etc., do not have the time to be involved in protocols that are interactive. So, in our context, they want to start the delegation process and then no longer be involved in any interaction.

   Another motivation is that when initially secret-sharing the data for the cloud, the owner may not consider the future MPC applications, hence choosing some ordinary secret sharing scheme, rather than a VSS.

---

[1] In fact, Q^3 is also necessary for perfect VSS [22].

A dealer who made a backup of the data using ordinary secret sharing, may decease. Some of this data might be so private it should never be reconstructed, while other might be important for the inheritants. The inheritants may want to use MPC to sort out what data (or computed data) should be made public, without reconstructing the complete backup.

2. The dealer uses a mobile device such that connection problems may limit her capability for interaction, while possible implementation faults may hinder her generation of good randomness (see, e.g., [21,28]). Suppose now that the parties who hold the shares are cloud servers, which are powerful in terms of their computation and communication resources. In this case, it would be reasonable to relieve the dealer from the burden of both interacting with the servers and generating a lot of randomness. Note that in the information-theoretic VSS, security depends on the quality of randomness in a crucial manner. In addition, we note that randomness complexity is also of theoretical importance.

3. We observe that in many VSS schemes (e.g., [11,12,16]), a corrupt dealer is effectively given the "second chance" by the honest parties. Specifically, if the dealer originally distributed incorrect shares, she may, upon receiving complaints, broadcast the correct shares and hence get away with her incorrect behavior. This is not a problem in the currently used VSS framework, where the shares are verified immediately after their distribution. However, this observation raises a theoretical question: May be it is unnecessary to give the dealer such an opportunity? We answer this question in the affirmative.

The above points motivate the study of secret sharing schemes that can be *verified without interaction with the dealer*. In our approach, the dealer does not have to be honest either, e.g., she might distribute *most* of the shares correctly in order to ensure reliability, but make only a few of them incorrect to ensure equivocation.

We advocate the use of unconditionally secure protocols in the real-world applications, such as cloud storage. First of all, if the primitives at hands are unconditionally secure, it is easier to construct security proofs, which are an indispensable part of the modern cryptographic standards. Moreover, having perfect security (as in our case) is sometimes better than having statistical security: For instance, Damgård et al. [13, p. 246] used a VSS protocol with perfect security, since "This makes it simpler to analyze its security in the presence of adaptive corruptions". One more advantage of unconditionally secure protocols is that their security is not affected by advances in computation technologies. For instance, the Committee on National Security Systems (linked to NSA) in their "CNSS Advisory Memorandum Information Assurance 02–15," July 2015 stated: "... we anticipate a need to shift to quantum-resistant cryptography in the near future." Unconditionally secure protocols will not be affected by such paradigm shifts.

1.2   Our Contributions

Our work primarily concerns the case of *external* dealer.[2] A typical VSS consists of two protocols: *sharing* and *reconstruction*. In the sharing protocol, the parties interact with the dealer in order to ensure that the honest parties hold consistent shares of some value according to a particular secret sharing scheme. As a result, either the sharing protocol succeeds, or a corrupt dealer is declared dishonest. In the former case, the honest parties are guaranteed to be able to reconstruct a unique value from their shares. In this work, we study the concept of *VSS with non-interactive dealer (VSS-NID)*. Such a scheme consists of the following three protocols: sharing, *verification* and reconstruction. The sharing protocol can be that of any secret sharing scheme (SSS), and it is typically non-interactive for the ordinary SSS. The later two realize the same functionality as an ordinary VSS, except that no interaction with the dealer in the verification protocol is allowed. In an ordinary VSS, the sharing protocol would be immediately followed by the verification, while in VSS-NID, verification can be performed at any point in time after distribution, but before reconstruction or before its use in MPC.

First and foremost, we emphasize that in principle, one must be able to achieve VSS-NID for any LSSS via secure MPC. Indeed, the Q^3 assumption would allow the parties to re-share their shares using VSS and then to use general MPC to check their consistency. In this work, we avoid reliance on general MPC in our first protocol.

First, we show that the Maurer VSS [30] (based on the replicated scheme by Ito et al. [24]) tolerating Q^3 active adversary can be modified to work as VSS-NID. As in the Maurer VSS, the complexity is polynomial in the size of the access structure. Unfortunately, for many access structures, this scheme is very costly on randomness. We address this aspect in our second protocol.

In our second scheme, we observe that in a VSS-NID protocol the dealer does not need to generate any randomness at all. The basic idea is to delegate the generation of randomness to the players.

1.3   Related Works

Assuming Q^4 active adversaries, the VSS-NID schemes can be trivially obtained from some existing ones in the literature, such as, e.g., [36], [12, Sect. 3]. Note that these schemes use $O(k^2)$ randomness, since they are based on [3] and [11], respectively. Moreover, (t, n) threshold *asynchronous VSS (AVSS)* are known [2] to tolerate $t < n/4$ adversaries. Therefore, we may expect perfect AVSS to be easily adaptable as perfect VSS-NID, simply assuming that the dealer in the former never responds after distributing the shares. We emphasize however that the focus of this study are perfect VSS-NID schemes tolerating Q^3 *adversaries*, while no perfect AVSS are known in this setting.

The round complexity of VSS was studied in a line of works originating from the paper by Gennaro et al. [18]. The paper by Patra et al. [34] investigates, in

---

[2] In the current literature on VSS and MPC, it is common to allow the dealer to be one of the parties that later takes part in the protocol.

particular, the roundness complexity of VSS with external dealer, but this work focuses on the setting of statistical security.

Our work is also related to the studies on randomness complexity of cryptographic protocols [7,8,27]. In these works, the randomness complexity is defined as a total number of bits generated by the honest parties. In our work, we seek to optimize *randomness complexity of the dealer*, i.e., the number of random bits generated by her, while not restricting that of the parties. Hereby, in our protocol of Sect. 4, the dealer's randomness complexity is reduced to zero.

1.4 Organization

After presenting relevant notation and definitions in Sect. 2, we introduce VSS-NID based on Maurer's scheme in Sect. 3 and the VSS-NID with no randomness from the dealer in Sect. 4. Concluding remarks and open questions are discussed in Sect. 5.

2 Preliminaries

Let $\mathbb{F}$ be a finite field of appropriate size. We denote by $x \leftarrow_R \mathcal{X}$ a uniformly random sampling of an element x from its domain $\mathcal{X}$. The scalar product of $x, y \in \mathbb{F}^n$ is written as $\langle x, y \rangle$. The cardinality of a set A is denoted as $|A|$. For $M \in \mathbb{F}^{n \times e}$, and $A \subseteq \{1, \ldots, n\}$ we denote by $M_A \in \mathbb{F}^{|A| \times e}$ a restriction of M to rows whose indexes are in A. We set $[n] = \{1, 2, \ldots, n\}$. The expression $\bigvee_{i=0}^{n} x_i$ denotes the OR operation on the bits $x_0, x_1, \ldots, x_n$. For any $n \in \mathbb{N}$, and $\mathbf{x}, \mathbf{y} \in \mathbb{F}^n$, we will write the element-wise summation of these vectors as $\mathbf{x} + \mathbf{y}$ (and replacing "+" with "−" denotes the element-wise subtraction). Running an algorithm A on an input x and obtaining the output y will be written as $y = A(x)$.

2.1 Communication and Adversary Models

We assume that a set of n parties $\mathcal{P} = \{P_1, \ldots, P_n\}$ and an extra party called a dealer D are connected by a synchronous network[3] of pairwise channels, which are private and authenticated. In addition, we assume that all the entities have access to a broadcast channel.

A *computationally unbounded* adversary is allowed to corrupt D and some subset of $\mathcal{P}$ in a *static* manner, meaning that the corrupted entities are decided prior to the protocol execution.

---

[3] In asynchronous network, the global clocking is present so that the protocol execution can be divided into rounds, and hereby, a failure to send a message is easy to detect, for every player. Note that to prevent malleability type of attacks, parties should not be able to see data sent by others before they sent theirs. A strict synchronization enforces this in an obvious way.

Adversary can be *passive* in which case she follows the protocol, or *active* in which case she can deviate from the protocol in an arbitrary manner.

We denote by an *access structure* a non-empty collection Γ of subsets $A \subseteq \mathcal{P}$, if Γ is closed under taking supersets: $\forall A \in \Gamma$, and all $B \subseteq \mathcal{P}$ with $A \subseteq B$ it holds that $B \in \Gamma$. In other words, we require access structures to be *monotone*. The subsets in Γ are called *access* sets. We denote by an *adversary structure* a collection Λ of subsets $A \subseteq \mathcal{P}$, if Λ is closed under taking subsets: $\forall A \in \Lambda$, and $\forall B \subseteq \mathcal{P}$ with $B \subseteq A$ it holds that $B \in \Lambda$. The subsets in Λ are called *forbidden* sets. We call a forbidden set *maximal*, if after adding any new element to it, the resulting set will no longer belong to Λ.

In our work, we assume that Λ satisfies the Q^3 condition [22], meaning that there exists no three sets in Λ whose union covers $\mathcal{P}$. Note that in (t, n)-threshold case, the Q^3 condition is equivalent to $t < n/3$.

Our protocols guarantee *perfect* security (see Definition 1) meaning that they provide perfect privacy, while correctness and commitment are guaranteed with zero error.

Q^3 condition on Λ implies that we can lift an assumption on access to broadcast channel for the price that the parties simulate it using Byzantine agreement.

In the protocols which we consider, if a corrupt party fails to broadcast a prescribed message, she will be declared dishonest. For simplicity of our analysis, we assume that corrupt parties do not take this course of action. If a corrupt party fails to send a prescribed message over a private channel, then the honest party will assume that a default value was sent.

For convenience sake, we will occasionally abuse our notation by associating $\mathcal{P}$ with $[n]$ rather than $\{P_1, \ldots, P_n\}$.

2.2   (Verifiable) Secret Sharing

A secret sharing scheme consists of two protocols. The *sharing* protocol is used by the dealer D to distribute shares of a secret $s \in \mathbb{F}$ to the parties in $\mathcal{P}$ according to an access structure Γ. The *reconstruction* protocol can be used by any set of parties in Γ to compute s from their shares. In this work, we focus on *linear* secret sharing scheme (LSSS) [11,12], where the shares are computed as a linear function of the secret and the randomness. Consequently, the secret is reconstructed as a linear function of the involved shares. An LSSS for a monotone access structure Γ associated with a matrix $G \in \mathbb{F}^{n \times k}$ is constructed as follows:

Sharing Protocol:

(1) On input a secret $s \in \mathbb{F}$, D computes $r_1, \ldots, r_{k-1} \leftarrow_R \mathbb{F}$, and then $(s_1, \ldots, s_n)^T = G(s, r_1, \ldots, r_{k-1})^T$.
(2) D privately sends s_i to P_i.

Reconstruction Protocol: For every set $B \in \Gamma$, the linear span of G_B must contain $(1, 0, \ldots, 0)$. Therefore, there must exist $\alpha_B \in \mathbb{F}^{|B|}$ (called a *reconstruction vector*) such that $\alpha_B M_B = (1, 0, \ldots, 0)$. Let $s_B \in \mathbb{F}^{|B|}$ denote a vector of shares held by the parties in B. Then, they reconstruct the secret by computing $s = \langle \alpha_B, s_B^T \rangle$.

The above presentation is a simplification of the general case, where each party can hold more than one share by "owning" more than one row of G. As pointed out in [11, p. 326]: "... the generalization to many rows per player is straightforward...", but the notation would become more complicated.

A (t, n) threshold Shamir secret sharing scheme [35] works as follows. In the sharing protocol, for fixed and public $x_1, \ldots, x_n \in \mathbb{F}$, D computes $a_1, \ldots, a_t \leftarrow_R \mathbb{F}$, sets $a_0 = s$, hereby defining a polynomial $f(x) = a_0 + a_1 x + \ldots + a_t x^t$ of degree at most t, and then privately sends $s_i = f(x_i)$ to P_i for $i = 1, \ldots, n$. Now, Γ consists of all sets of $\mathcal{P}$ of size at least $t + 1$, and Λ consists of those of size at most t. The reconstruction protocol uses Lagrange interpolation to compute $a_0 = s$. Shamir scheme can easily be shown to be linear by taking in the above general definition: $t = k - 1$, $r_i = a_i$ for $i = 1, \ldots, t$, and G to be the Vandermonde matrix.

In verifiable secret sharing [10] the sharing protocol includes a verification procedure, in which the dealer is involved, such that either the honest parties ensure that they hold consistent shares or a corrupt dealer is disqualified.

In our scenario of verifiable secret sharing with non-interactive dealer (VSS-NID), the dealer performs a non-interactive sharing protocol. Then, the parties execute a *verification* protocol which ensures consistency of shares, while the reconstruction protocol works as in ordinary VSS.

Definition 1. *VSS-NID is called* perfectly Λ-secure *if the following properties hold, even if the adversary corrupts the parties in Λ:*

(1) Privacy: *If D is honest, then the adversary learns no information about s during an execution of both sharing and verification protocols.*
(2) Correctness: *If D is honest, then the honest parties will output s in the reconstruction protocol.*
(3) Commitment: *If D is corrupt, then given that the verification protocol succeeds, there exists a unique value $s^* \in \mathbb{F}$, such that in the reconstruction protocol, the honest parties will output s^* regardless of the behavior of corrupt parties.*

A primitive called *distributed commitment* [11] differs from VSS in that it requires the dealer to submit the secret along with her local randomness in the reconstruction protocol.

We call the shares "almost consistent", if they are consistent everywhere except for a forbidden set of the Q^3 access structure. For example, consider a $(1, 4)$-Shamir scheme where the polynomial of degree 1 (a "line") is used. Then, if all the shares are lying on the line, then they are called *consistent*, and if only one of them is not on the line, then they are called *almost consistent*.

3   VSS-NID for Maurer's Scheme

Let us present a VSS-NID scheme tolerating Q^3 active adversaries which is inspired by Maurer VSS [30]. The latter is based on the replicated secret sharing scheme [24]. In this scheme, D associates a random field element to every for-bidden set $A \in \Lambda$, and then every party *not in A* receives this element as a part of her share. The secret is masked by the sum of the elements in a one-time pad manner.

Let $\Lambda_1, \ldots, \Lambda_k \in \Lambda$ be the list of all maximal forbidden sets of Λ. The sharing protocol is provided in Fig. 1, and the verification and reconstruction protocols are provided respectively in Figs. 2 and 3.

Lemma 1 ([24,30]). *The sharing protocol in Fig. 1 leaks no information on s to any subset of parties in Λ.*

Proof (Sketch). Any (forbidden) set of parties in Λ is jointly missing at least one element r_i that is masking s in the one-time pad manner. □

Maurer observed [30] that as long as the parties holding the same elements check their consistency in a pairwise manner, the replicated scheme can be turned into VSS. If inconsistency is detected, the party complains in public and D broadcasts the share in question.

We modify this step such that if inconsistencies are found, the parties complain and *broadcast the elements in question among themselves*. Then, the local computation stage allows the honest parties to agree on a correct element or to disqualify a corrupt D. We provide the verification and reconstruction protocols in, respectively, Figs. 2 and 3. The reconstruction protocol is the same as in Maurer scheme [30], we provide it for self-containment. Note that here, the broadcast is not required for reconstruction.

Sharing Protocol [24]

1. On input $s \in \mathbb{F}$, D computes $r_1, \ldots, r_{k-1} \leftarrow_R \mathbb{F}$ and $r_k = s - \sum_{i=1}^{k-1} r_i$.
2. For $i = 1, \ldots, k$, D privately sends r_i to every party in $\mathcal{P} \setminus \Lambda_i$.

Fig. 1. VSS-NID based on Maurer's scheme: sharing protocol.

Claim 1. *The verification protocol in Fig. 2 leaks no information on s to the parties in Λ.*

Proof. As in [30], it follows by observing that a complaint is broadcast only when the element r_i is already known to the adversary. Therefore, making r_i public does not affect the privacy of s. □

The following fact concerning the setting of our verification protocol with honest dealer will be useful.

Verification Protocol

Initialization: For $i = 1, \ldots, k$, set $C_i = \emptyset$.

1. For $i = 1, \ldots, k$: Each pair of parties in $\mathcal{P} \setminus \Lambda_i$ privately checks consistency of their respective values of r_i.
2. If an inconsistency is detected, the party P_i complains by broadcasting (i, r_i). Denote by I a set of values i for which a complaint was broadcast.
3. $\forall i \in I$: Each $P_i \in \mathcal{P} \setminus \Lambda_i$ broadcasts (i, r_i), if she did not do so in the previous round.

Local Computation:

a. $\forall i \in I$: If $\exists A \in \Lambda$ such that $\exists$ a unique $r_{i,A}$ such that all the parties in $(\mathcal{P} \setminus \Lambda_i) \setminus A$ broadcast $r_{i,A}$,
    then: Every party in $\mathcal{P} \setminus \Lambda_i$ sets $r_i := r_{i,A}$, and
        each party who broadcast $r_i \neq r_{i,A}$ is added to a subset C_i.
    else: D is declared dishonest.
b. If $\bigcup_{i=1}^{k} C_i \notin \Lambda$, then D is declared dishonest, else the protocol succeeds.

Fig. 2. VSS-NID based on Maurer's scheme: verification protocol.

Claim 2. *If D is honest and a complain was raised related to r_i, then the Q^3 condition implies that there exists a set $A \in \Lambda$ such that for any $i = 1, \ldots, k$, there exists a unique value r_i for which the set of values broadcast by the parties in $\mathcal{P} \setminus \Lambda_i$, that are distinct from r_i, correspond to A. Moreover, this unique value r_i was broadcast by a set of parties that belong to Γ.*

Proof. First, since D was honest, a complain can only be raised due to a dishonest party. Second, we prove that if D was honest and a complain was raised, there exists a set of parties B that belongs to Γ that will broadcast the same value, i.e., r_i, they received from D. Let us call A the set of parties in $\mathcal{P} \setminus \Lambda_i$ that broadcast values different from the one received from the dealer, i.e., dif-

---

Reconstruction Protocol ([30])

Each party privately sends all her shares to all other parties.

Local Computation:

1. For $i = 1, \ldots, k$: Each party reconstructs the share r_i as a (unique) value sent by all parties in $(\mathcal{P} \setminus \Lambda_i) \setminus A$ for some $A \in \Lambda$.
2. Each party computes $s = r_1 + \cdots + r_k$.

Fig. 3. VSS-NID based on Maurer's scheme: reconstruction protocol.

ferent from r_i. We now claim that $B = \mathcal{P} \setminus (\Lambda_i \cup A) \in \Gamma$. Indeed, this follows immediately from the Q^3 property.

Finally, due to our first observation, we know some $A \in \Lambda$ exists and our definition of A used in our proof is the same as the one in our claim. $\square$

Claim 3. *An honest D is never declared dishonest in the verification protocol of Fig. 2.*

Proof. Follows by observing that if D is honest then the unique value r_i in Step (a) of the local computation always exists by Claim 2. Then, the value of r_i which are not equal to r_i can only be broadcast by parties in Λ, therefore D is not declared dishonest in Step (b) of the local computation. $\square$

Lemma 2. *If the verification protocol of Fig. 2 succeeds, then there exists $s^* \in \mathbb{F}$ such that in the reconstruction protocol the honest parties will output s^*.*

Proof. Note that the shares of honest parties consistently define some value $s^* \in \mathbb{F}$ as long as their corresponding values r_i are the same for all $i = 1, \ldots, k$. This point is ensured in Step (a) of the local computation in the verification protocol. Then, these (consistent) values are reconstructed regardless of the values submitted by parties in $A \in \Lambda$. $\square$

Theorem 1. *The scheme presented in Figs. 1, 2 and 3 constitute a VSS-NID tolerating Q^3 active adversaries.*

Proof. We use the results given above. *Correctness:* Follows by Claim 3 and correctness of the replicated scheme. *Privacy:* Follows by Lemma 1 and Claim 1. *Commitment:* Follows by Lemma 2. Using the sets C_i, we arrange an overall check for all the shares r_i and all the sets $\mathcal{P} \setminus \Lambda_i$. $\square$

It is easy to verify that the communication, computation and dealer's randomness complexities of this scheme are polynomial in the size of the access structure Γ.

4   Randomness Versus Interaction

The above results show that secret sharing schemes satisfying the Q^3 condition, even ideal ones, can be turned into a VSS without any additional randomness generated by the dealer.

The next question one may ask could be: Can we further reduce dealer's randomness in VSS, preferably relieving the dealer of the need to generate any randomness at all?

We can answer this question in affirmative using the following simple construction. As before, the dealer D and the players are assumed to be connected by the pairwise secure channels.

Although our idea may be applicable to the schemes supporting the general access structures as well, we focus on the (t, n) Shamir scheme here, for the didactic purposes. In our version of Shamir's scheme, t players each generate a random field element, send it to the dealer, and save it as their respective share. The dealer uses the received values and his secret as the input to the Lagrange interpolation to compute a polynomial of degree at most t, and then the shares of the remaining $n - t$ players, are defined and distributed according to the (t, n) Shamir scheme.

We say that the scheme is *passively* t-*private*, if the passive adversary controlling at most t players has no information about the secret.

Lemma 3. *If the dealer is honest, the above protocol results in a consistent passively t-private (t, n)-Shamir sharing of dealer's secret, assuming that at most $t - 1$ players are corrupted by an active adversary.*

Proof (Sketch). Consistency follows by observing that any $t + 1$ field elements define the polynomial of degree at most t. Privacy follows by the standard argument that any t-subset of corrupt players is jointly missing at least one random share generated by an honest player. Indeed, there must be at least one such player in the above protocol, since at most $t - 1$ players are actively corrupt. $\square$

Note that the resulting scheme remains non-interactive in the sense that the first $t - 1$ players send their shares to the dealer, while she further contacts other players.

If we allow the active adversary to corrupt up to $t < n/3$ players, then the conditions of Lemma 3 are surely satisfied, and then the general MPC, or alternatively the techniques from [14] for the special case of VSS, can be used to verify consistency of the shares, even if the dealer is dishonest.

When extending this construction to general access structures, we may need to allow interaction in the non-ideal case, since the player have to send randomness to the dealer and to obtain some of her shares in response. The extension to the case of general access structures is rather straightforward.

5   Conclusion

We present new verifiable secret sharing schemes, where the dealer does not need to interact with the parties. In particular, our second protocol (in Sect. 4) shows how to relieve the dealer from the necessity to generate randomness in VSS-NID.

Our emphasis is on reducing the round and randomness complexity of the dealer. Obviously, to achieve a truly cloud-friendly VSS, one should also have minimal randomness for the parties (cloud servers). Hence, we wonder whether our techniques can be applied in order to optimize the randomness used by the *parties* or proving that this randomness is minimal (order-wise).

Our work looks at the process of VSS in an asymmetric way, in the sense that we assume the dealer has less power than the other parties. We wonder whether this viewpoint can be generalized.

Our verification protocol focused on the synchronous model. We leave the asynchronous one as an open problem.

Acknowledgments. The authors would like to thank the anonymous reviewers for their helpful comments.

References

1. Asharov, G., Lindell, Y.: A full proof of the BGW protocol for perfectly-secure multiparty computation. Cryptology ePrint Archive: Report 2011/136. https://eprint.iacr.org/2011/136.pdf
2. Ben-Or, M., Canetti, R., Goldreich, O.: Asynchronous secure computation. In: STOC, pp. 52–61 (1993)
3. Ben-Or, M., Goldwasser, S., Wigderson, A.: Completeness theorems for non-cryptographic fault-tolerant distributed computation (extended abstract). In: STOC, pp. 1–10 (1988)
4. Berlekamp, E.R., Welch, L.R.: Error correction of algebraic block codes. U.S. Patent Number 4.633.470 (1986)
5. Blakley, G.: Safeguarding cryptographic keys. In: AFIPS 1979 National Computer Conference, pp. 313–317 (1979)
6. Beerliová-Trubíniová, Z., Hirt, M.: Perfectly-secure MPC with linear communication complexity. In: Canetti, R. (ed.) TCC 2008. LNCS, vol. 4948, pp. 213–230. Springer, Heidelberg (2008). https://doi.org/10.1007/978-3-540-78524-8_13
7. Canetti, R., Kushilevitz, E., Ostrovsky, R., Rosen, A.: Randomness vs. fault-tolerance. J. Cryptol. **13**(1), 107–142 (2000). Conference version in PODC 1997
8. Blundo, C., De Santis, A., Persiano, G., Vaccaro, U.: Randomness complexity of private computation. Comput. Complex. **8**(2), 145–168 (1999)
9. Chaum, D., Crépeau, C., Damgård, I.: Multiparty unconditionally secure protocols. In: STOC, pp. 11–19 (1988)
10. Chor, B., Goldwasser, S., Micali, S., Awerbuch, B.: Verifiable secret sharing and achieving simultaneity in the presence of faults (extended abstract). In: FOCS, pp. 383–395 (1985)
11. Cramer, R., Damgård, I., Maurer, U.: General secure multi-party computation from any linear secret-sharing scheme. In: Preneel, B. (ed.) EUROCRYPT 2000. LNCS, vol. 1807, pp. 316–334. Springer, Heidelberg (2000). https://doi.org/10.1007/3-540-45539-6_22
12. Choudhury, A., Kurosawa, K., Patra, A.: The round complexity of perfectly secure general VSS. In: Fehr, S. (ed.) ICITS 2011. LNCS, vol. 6673, pp. 143–162. Springer, Heidelberg (2011). https://doi.org/10.1007/978-3-642-20728-0_14
13. Damgård, I., Ishai, Y., Krøigaard, M., Nielsen, J.B., Smith, A.: Scalable multiparty computation with nearly optimal work and resilience. In: Wagner, D. (ed.) CRYPTO 2008. LNCS, vol. 5157, pp. 241–261. Springer, Heidelberg (2008). https://doi.org/10.1007/978-3-540-85174-5_14
14. Desmedt, Y., Morozov, K.: Parity Check based redistribution of secret shares. In: ISIT, pp. 959–963 (2015)
15. Schoenmakers, B.: Verifiable secret sharing. In: van Tilborg, H.C.A., Jajodia, S. (eds.) Encyclopedia of Cryptography and Security, vol. 1357. Springer, Boston (2011). https://doi.org/10.1007/978-1-4419-5906-5_14
16. Serge, F., Ueli, M.: Linear VSS and distributed commitments based on secret sharing and pairwise checks. In: Yung, M. (ed.) CRYPTO 2002. LNCS, vol. 2442, pp. 565–580. Springer, Heidelberg (2002). https://doi.org/10.1007/3-540-45708-9_36

17. Fitzi, M., Garay, J., Gollakota, S., Rangan, C.P., Srinathan, K.: Round-optimal and efficient verifiable secret sharing. In: Halevi, S., Rabin, T. (eds.) TCC 2006. LNCS, vol. 3876, pp. 329–342. Springer, Heidelberg (2006). https://doi.org/10.1007/11681878_17

18. Gennaro, R., Ishai, Y., Kushilevitz, E., Rabin, T.: The round complexity of verifiable secret sharing and secure multicast. In: STOC, pp. 580–589 (2001)

19. Gennaro, R., Rabin, M.O., Rabin, T.: Simplified VSS and fact-track multiparty computations with applications to threshold cryptography. In: PODC, pp. 101–111 (1998)

20. Goldreich, O., Micali, S., Wigderson, A.: How to play any mental game or a completeness theorem for protocols with honest majority. In: STOC, pp. 218–229 (1987)

21. Heninger, N., Durumeric, Z., Wustrow, E., Halderman, J.A.: Mining your Ps and Qs: detection of widespread weak keys in network devices. In: 21st USENIX Conference on Security symposium (Security 2012), vol. 35 (2012)

22. Hirt, M., Maurer, U.: Player simulation and general adversary structures in perfect multi-party computation. J. Cryptol. 13(1), 31–60 (2000). (Preliminary version in PODC 1997: 25–34.)

23. Hirt, M., Maurer, U., Przydatek, B.: Efficient secure multi-party computation. In: Okamoto, T. (ed.) ASIACRYPT 2000. LNCS, vol. 1976, pp. 143–161. Springer, Heidelberg (2000). https://doi.org/10.1007/3-540-44448-3_12

24. Ito, M., Saito, A., Nishizeki, T.: Secret sharing scheme realizing general access structure. Electron. Commun. Jpn. (Part III: Fundam. Electron. Sci.) 72(9), 56–64 (1989)

25. Katz, J., Koo, C.-Y., Kumaresan, R.: Improving the round complexity of VSS in point-to-point networks. In: Aceto, L., Damgård, I., Goldberg, L.A., Halldórsson, M.M., Ingólfsdóttir, A., Walukiewicz, I. (eds.) ICALP 2008. LNCS, vol. 5126, pp. 499–510. Springer, Heidelberg (2008). https://doi.org/10.1007/978-3-540-70583-3_41

26. Kushilevitz, E., Mansour, Y.: Randomness in private computations. SIAM J. Discret. Math. 10(4), 647–661 (1997)

27. Kushilevitz, E., Ostrovsky, R., Rosen, A.: Amortizing randomness in private multiparty computations. In: PODC, pp. 81–90 (1998)

28. Lenstra, A.K., Hughes, J.P., Augier, M., Bos, J.W., Kleinjung, T., Wachter, C.: Public keys. In: Safavi-Naini, R., Canetti, R. (eds.) CRYPTO 2012. LNCS, vol. 7417, pp. 626–642. Springer, Heidelberg (2012). https://doi.org/10.1007/978-3-642-32009-5_37

29. Ling, S., Wang, H., Xing, C.: Algebraic Curves in Cryptography. CRC Press, Boca Raton (2013)

30. Maurer, U.M.: Secure multi-party computation made simple. Discret. Appl. Math. 154(2), 370–381 (2006). Journal version of Ueli M. Maurer: Secure Multi-party Computation Made Simple. SCN 2002, 14–28

31. McEliece, R.J., Sarwate, D.V.: On sharing secrets and Reed-Solomon codes. Commun. ACM 24(9), 583–584 (1981)

32. Rabin, T., Ben-Or, M.: Verifiable secret sharing and multiparty protocols with honest majority (extended abstract). In: STOC, pp. 73–85 (1989)

33. Roth, R.: Introduction to Coding Theory. Cambridge University Press, Cambridge (2006)

34. Patra, A., Choudhary, A., Rabin, T., Rangan, C.P.: The round complexity of verifiable secret sharing revisited. In: Halevi, S. (ed.) CRYPTO 2009. LNCS, vol. 5677, pp. 487–504. Springer, Heidelberg (2009). https://doi.org/10.1007/978-3-642-03356-8_29

35. Shamir, A.: How to share a secret. Commun. ACM **22**(11), 612–613 (1979)

36. Stinson, D.R., Wei, R.: Unconditionally secure proactive secret sharing scheme with combinatorial structures. In: Heys, H., Adams, C. (eds.) SAC 1999. LNCS, vol. 1758, pp. 200–214. Springer, Heidelberg (2000). https://doi.org/10.1007/3-540-46513-8_15

Bidirectional Asynchronous Ratcheted Key Agreement with Linear Complexity

F. Betül Durak[1] and Serge Vaudenay[2](✉)

[1] Robert Bosch LLC - Research and Technology Center, Pittsburgh, USA
[2] Ecole Polytechnique Fédérale de Lausanne (EPFL), Lausanne, Switzerland
serge.vaudenay@epfl.ch

Abstract. Following up mass surveillance and privacy issues, modern
secure communication protocols now seek more security such as forward secrecy and post-compromise security. They cannot rely on an
assumption such as synchronization, predictable sender/receiver roles,
or online availability. Ratcheting was introduced to address forward
secrecy and post-compromise security in real-world messaging protocols.
At CSF 2016 and CRYPTO 2017, ratcheting was studied either without zero round-trip time (0-RTT) or without bidirectional communication. At CRYPTO 2018, ratcheting with bidirectional communication
was done using heavy key-update primitives. At EUROCRYPT 2019,
another protocol was proposed. All those protocols use random oracles.
Furthermore, exchanging n messages has complexity $\mathcal{O}(n^2)$ in general.

In this work, we define the bidirectional asynchronous ratcheted key
agreement (BARK) with formal security notions. We provide a simple
security model and design a secure BARK scheme using no key-update
primitives, no random oracle, an with $\mathcal{O}(n)$ complexity. It is based
on a public-key cryptosystem, a signature scheme, one-time symmetric encryption, and a collision-resistant hash function family. We further
show that BARK (even unidirectional) implies public-key cryptography,
meaning that it cannot solely rely on symmetric cryptography.

1 Introduction

In standard communication systems, protocols are designed to provide messaging
services with end-to-end encryption. Essentially, secure communication reduces
to continuously exchanging keys, because each message requires a new key. In
bidirectional two-party secure communication, participants alternate their role
as *senders* and *receivers*. The modern instant messaging protocols are substantially *asynchronous*. In other words, for a two-party communication, the messages should be transmitted (or the key exchange should be done) even though
the counterpart is not online. Moreover, to be able to send the payload data
without requiring online exchanges is a major design goal called *zero round trip
time (0-RTT)*. Finally, the moment when a participant wants to send a message

---

A full version of this paper is available as eprint 2018/889 [8].

© Springer Nature Switzerland AG 2019
N. Attrapadung and T. Yagi (Eds.): IWSEC 2019, LNCS 11689, pp. 343–362, 2019.
https://doi.org/10.1007/978-3-030-26834-3_20

is undefined, meaning that participants use *random roles* (sender or receiver) without any synchronization. They could send messages at the same time.

Even though many systems were designed for the privacy of their users, they rapidly faced security vulnerabilities caused by the *compromises* of the participants' states. In this work, compromising a participant means to obtain some information about its internal state. We will call it *exposure*. The desired security notion is that compromised information should not uncover more than possible by trivial attacks. For instance, the compromised state of participants should not allow decryption of messages exchanged in the past. This is called *forward secrecy*. Typically, forward secrecy is obtained by updating states with a one-way function $x \to H(x) \to H(H(x)) \to \ldots$ and deleting old entries [13,14]. A popular technique in mechanics, that allows forward movement but prevents moving backward is the use of a device called *ratchet*. In the context of secure communication, a ratchet-like action is achieved by using randomness in every state update so that a compromised state is not sufficient for the decryption of any future communication either. This is called *future secrecy* or *backward secrecy* or *post-compromise security* or even *self-healing*. One thesis of the present work is that healing after an active attack involving a forgery is not a nice property. We show that it implies insecurity. After one participant is compromised and impersonated, if communication self-heals, it means that some adversary can make a trivial attack which is not detected. We also show other insecurity cases. Hence, we rather mandate communication to be cut after active attacks.

Previous Work. The security of key exchange was studied by many authors. The prominent models are the CK and eCK models [4,12].

Techniques for ratcheting first appeared in real life protocols. It appeared in the Off-the-Record (OTR) communication system by Borisov et al. [3]. The Signal protocol designed by Open Whisper Systems [16] later gained a lot of interest from message communication companies. Today, the WhatsApp messaging application reached billions of users worldwide [18]. It uses the Signal protocol. A broad survey about various techniques and terminologies was made at S&P 2015 by Unger et al. [17]. At CSF 2016, Cohn-Gordon et al. [6] studied bidirectional ratcheted communication and proposed a protocol. However, their protocol does not offer 0-RTT and requires synchronized roles. At EuroS&P 2017, Cohn-Gordon et al. [5] formally studied Signal.

0-RTT communication with forward secrecy was achieved using puncturable encryption by Günther et al. at EUROCRYPT 2017 [9]. Later on, at EUROCRYPT 2018, Derler et al. made it reasonable practical by using Bloom filters [7].

At CRYPTO 2017, Bellare et al. [2] gave a secure ratcheting key exchange protocol. Their protocol is unidirectional and does not allow receiver exposure.

At CRYPTO 2018, Poettering and Rösler (PR) [15] studied bidirectional asynchronous ratcheted key agreement and presented a protocol which is secure in the random oracle model. Their solution further relies on hierarchical identity-based encryption (HIBE) but offers stronger security than required for practical usage, leaving ample room for improving the protocol. At the same conference, Jaeger and Stepanovs (JS) [10] had similar results but focused on secure communication rather than key agreement. They proposed another protocol relying on HIBE. In both results, HIBE is used to construct encryption/signature schemes with key-update security. This is a rather new notion allowing forward secrecy but is expensive to achieve. In both cases, it was claimed that the depth of HIBE is really small. However, when participants are disconnected and continue sending several messages, the depth increases rapidly. Consequently, HIBE needs unbounded depth.

At EUROCRYPT 2019, Jost, Maurer, and Mularczyk (JMM) [11] designed another ratcheting protocol which has *"near-optimal"* security, and does not use HIBE. Nevertheless, it still has a huge complexity: When messages alternate well (i.e., no participant sends two messages without receiving one in between), processing n messages requires $\mathcal{O}(n)$ operations in total. However, when messages accumulate before alternating (for instance, because the participants are disconnected by the network), the complexity becomes $\mathcal{O}(n^2)$. This is also the case for PR [15] and JS [10].[1] One advantage of the JMM protocol [11] comes with the resilience with random coin leakage as discussed below.

At EUROCRYPT 2019, Alwen, Coretti, and Dodis (ACD) [1] designed two other ratcheting protocols aiming at *instant decryption*, i.e. the ability to decrypt even though some previous messages have not been received yet. This is closer to real-life protocols but this comes with a potential threat: keys to decrypt un-delivered messages are stored until the messages are delivered. Hence, the adversary could choose to hold messages and decrypt them with future state exposure. This prevents forward secrecy. Furthermore, unless the direction of communication changes (or more precisely, if the *epoch* increases), their protocols are not really ratcheting as no random coins are used to update the state. This weakens post-compromise security as well. In Table 1, we call this weaker security *"id-optimal"* (not to say "insecure" in the model we are interested in) because it is the best we can obtain with immediate decryption. The lighter of the two protocols is not competing in the same category because it mostly uses symmetric cryptography. It is more efficient but with lower security. Namely, corrupting the state of a participant A implies impersonating B to A, and also decrypting the messages that A sends. Other protocols do not have this weakness. The second ACD protocol [1] (in the full version) uses asymmetric cryptography.

Some authors address the corruption of random coins in different ways. Bellare et al. [2] and JMM [11] allow leaking the random coins just *after* use. JS [10] allow leaking it just *before* usage only. ACD [1] allow adversarially *chosen* random coins. In most of the protocols, revealing (or choosing) the random coins imply revealing some part of the new state which allows decrypting incoming messages. It is comparable to state exposure. JMM [11] offers better security as revealing the random coins reveals the new state (and allows to decrypt) only when the previous state was already known.

---

[1] For JS, this is only visible in the corrected version of the paper on eprint [10]. Our complexity analysis is based on how those protocols have been implemented (https://github.com/qantik/ratcheted). It was presented at the WSM 2019 workshop.

Table 1. Comparison of protocols: complexity for exchanging n messages in alternating or accumulating mode, with timing (in seconds) for $n = 900$ of comparable implementations and asymptotic; and types of coin-leakage security ($\Rightarrow$ state exposure means coins leakage implies a state exposure).

	Security	Complexity		Coins leakage resilience	Model
		Alternating	Accumulating		
Poettering-Rösler [15]	Optimal	86.3, $O(n)$	5897, $O(n^2)$	No	ROM
Jaeger-Stepanovs [10]	Optimal	58.1, $O(n)$	9087, $O(n^2)$	Pre-send leakage, $\Rightarrow$ state exposure	ROM
Jost-Maurer-Mularczyk [11]	Near-optimal	2.08, $O(n)$	11.4, $O(n^2)$	Post-send leakage	ROM
BARK [this paper]	Sub-optimal	1.46, $O(n)$	1.09, $O(n)$	No	Plain
Alwen-Coretti-Dodis [1]	Id-optimal	1.18, $O(n)$	0.92, $O(n)$	Chosen coins, $\Rightarrow$ state exposure	Plain

Our Contributions. We give a definition for a bidirectional asynchronous key agreement (BARK) along with security properties. We start setting the stage with some definitions (such as *matching status*) then identify all cases leading to trivial attacks. We split them into *direct* and *indirect leakages*. Then, we define security with a KIND game (privacy). We also consider the resistance to forgery (impersonation) and the resistance to attacks which would heal after active attacks (RECOVER security). We use these two notions as building blocks to prove KIND-security. We finally construct a secure protocol. Our design choices are detailed below and compared to other papers.

1. **Simplicity.** Contrary to previous work, we define KIND security in a very comprehensive way by bringing all notions under the umbrella of a *cleanness* predicate which identifies and captures all trivial ways of attacking.
2. **Strong security.** In the same line as previous works, the adversary in our model can see the entire communication between participants and control the delivery. Of course, he can replace messages with anything. Scheduling communications is under the control of the adversary. This means that the time when a participant sends or receives messages is decided by the adversary. Moreover, the adversary is capable of corrupting participants by making exposures of their internal data. We separate two types of exposures: the exposure of the state (that is kept in internal machinery of a participant) and the exposure of the key (which is produced by the key agreement and given to an external protocol). This is because states are (normally) kept secure in our protocol while the generated key is transferred to other applications which may leak for different reasons. We do not consider exposure of the random coins.
3. **Slightly sub-optimal security.** Using the result from exposure allows the adversary to be active, e.g. by impersonating the exposed participant. However, the adversary is not allowed to use exposures to make a *trivial* attack. Identifying such trivial attacks is not easy. As a design goal, we adopt not to forbid more than what the intuitive notion of ratcheting captures. We do forbid a bit more than PR [15] and JS [10] which are considered of having *optimal*

security and than JMM [11] (which has <u>*near-optimal*</u> security)[2], though, allowing lighter building blocks. Namely, we need no key-update primitives and have linear-time complexity in terms of the number of exchanged messages, even when the network is occasionally down. **This translates to an important speedup factor**, as shown on Table 1. We argue that this is a reasonable choice enabling ratchet security as we define it: *unless trivial leakage, a message is private as long as it is acknowledged for reception in a subsequent message from the receiver.*

4. **Sequence integrity.** We believe that duplex communication is reliably enforced by a lower level protocol. This is assumed to solve non-malicious packet loss e.g. by resend requests and also to reconstruct the correct sequence order. What we only have to care of is when an adversary prevents the delivery of a message consistently. We make the choice to make the transmission of the next messages impossible under such an attack. Contrarily, ACD [1] advocates for immediate decryption, even though one message is missing. This lowers the security and we chose not to have it.

In the BARK protocol, the correctness implies that both participants generate the same keys. We define the stages *matching status, direct leakage, indirect leakage*. We aim to separate trivial attacks and trivial forgeries from non-trivial cases with our definitions. Direct and indirect leakages define when the adversary can trivially deduce the key generated due to the exposure of a participant who can either be the same participant (direct) or their counterpart (indirect).

We construct a secure BARK protocol. We build our constructions on top of a public-key cryptosystem and a signature scheme and achieve strong security, without key-update primitives or random oracles. We further show that a weakly secure unidirectional BARK implies public-key encryption.

Notations. We have two characters: Alice (A) and Bob (B). When P designates a participant, $\overline{P}$ refers to P's counterpart. We use the roles send and rec for sender and receiver respectively. We define $\overline{send}$ = rec and $\overline{rec}$ = send. When participants A and B have exclusive roles (like in unidirectional cases), we call them *sender* S and *receiver* R. PPT stands for *probabilistic polynomially bounded*. Negligible in terms of λ means in $\cap_{c>0} \mathcal{O}(\lambda^{-c})$ as $\lambda \to +\infty$.

Structure of the Paper. In Sect. 2, we define our BARK protocol along with correctness definition and KIND security. Section 3 proves that a simple unidirectional scheme implies public-key cryptography. In Sect. 4 we define the security notions unforgeability and unrecoverability. In Sect. 5, we give our BARK construction. Due to space limitation, some material was moved to the full version of this paper [8], including the definition of underlying primitives and the proofs of our results.

---

[2] Those terms are more formally explained on p. 12.

2 Bidirectional Asynchronous Ratcheted Communication

2.1 BARK Definition and Correctness

Definition 1 (BARK). *A bidirectional asynchronous ratcheted key agreement* (BARK) *consists of the following PPT algorithms:*

- Setup$(1^\lambda) \xrightarrow{\$}$ pp: *This defines the common public parameters* pp.
- Gen$(1^\lambda, pp) \xrightarrow{\$}$ (sk, pk): *This generates the secret key* sk *and the public key* pk *of a participant.*
- Init$(1^\lambda, pp, sk_P, pk_{\overline{P}}, P) \to st_P$: *This sets up the initial state* st_P *of P given his secret key and the public key of his counterpart.*
- Send$(st_P) \xrightarrow{\$} (st'_P, upd, k)$: *The algorithm inputs a current state* st_P *for* $P \in \{A, B\}$. *It outputs a tuple* (st'_P, upd, k) *with an updated state* st'_P, *a message* upd, *and a key* k.
- Receive$(st_P, upd) \to (acc, st'_P, k)$: *The algorithm inputs* (st_P, upd) *where* $P \in \{A, B\}$. *It outputs a triple consisting of a flag* acc $\in \{true, false\}$ *to indicate an accept or reject of* upd *information, an updated state* st'_P, *and a key* k *i.e.* (acc, st'_P, k).

For convenience, we define the following initialization procedure for all games. It returns the initial states as well as some publicly available information z.

InitAll$(1^\lambda, pp)$:
1: Gen$(1^\lambda, pp) \to (sk_A, pk_A)$
2: Gen$(1^\lambda, pp) \to (sk_B, pk_B)$
3: $st_A \leftarrow$ Init$(1^\lambda, pp, sk_A, pk_B, A)$
4: $st_B \leftarrow$ Init$(1^\lambda, pp, sk_B, pk_A, B)$
5: $z \leftarrow (pp, pk_A, pk_B)$
6: **return** (st_A, st_B, z)

Initialization is *splittable* in the sense that private keys can be generated by their holders with no need to rely on an authority (except maybe for authentication of pk_A and pk_B). Other protocols from the literature assume a trusted initialization.

We consider bidirectional asynchronous communications. We can see, in Fig. 1, Alice and Bob running some sequences of Send and Receive operations without any prior agreement. Their *time scale* is different. This means that Alice and Bob run algorithms in an asynchronous way. We consider a notion of *time* relative to a participant P. Formally, the time t for P is the number of elementary steps that P executed since the beginning of the game. We assume no common clock. However, events occur in a *game* and we may have to compare the time of two different participants by reference to the scheduling of the game. E.g., we could say that time t_A for A happens *before* time t_B for B. Normally, scheduling is under the control of the adversary except in the CORRECT game in which there is no adversary. There, we define the scheduling by a sequence of actions. Reading the sequence tells who executes a new step of the protocol.

The protocol also uses random roles. Alice and Bob can both send and receive messages. They take their role (sender or receiver) in a sequence, but the sequences of roles of Alice and Bob are not necessarily synchronized. Sending/receiving is refined by the RATCH(P, role, [upd]) call in Fig. 2.

Correctness. We say that a ratcheted communication protocol functions correctly if the receiver accepts the update information upd and generates the same key as its counterpart. Correctness implies that the received keys for participant P have been generated in the same order as sent keys of participant $\overline{P}$. We formally define the CORRECT game in Fig. 2. We define variables. $received^P_{key}$ (respectively $sent^P_{key}$) keeps a list of secret keys that are generated by P when running Receive (respectively, Send). Similarly, $received^P_{msg}$ (respectively $sent^P_{msg}$) keeps a list of upd information that are received (respectively sent) by P and accepted by Receive. The received sequences only keep values for which acc = true.

Each variable v such as $received^P_{msg}$, k_P, or st_P is relative to a participant P. We denote by $v(t)$ the value of v at time t for P. For instance, $received^A_{msg}(t)$ is the sequence of upd which were received and accepted by A at time t for A.

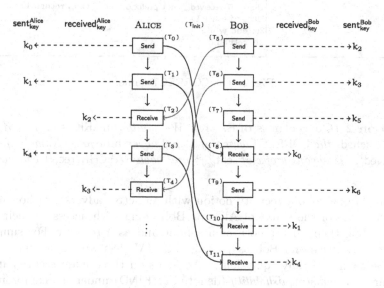

Fig. 1. The message exchange between Alice and Bob.

We initialize the two participants in the CORRECT game in Fig. 2. The scheduling is defined by a sequence sched of tuples of form either (P, send) (saying that P must send) or (P, rec) (saying that P must receive). In this game, communication between the participants uses a waiting queue for messages in each direction. Each participant has a queue of incoming messages and is pulling them in the order they have been pushed in. Sent messages from P are buffered in the queue of $\overline{P}$.

Oracle RATCH(P, rec, upd)	Game CORRECT(1^λ, sched)
1: $(acc, st'_P, k) \leftarrow$ Receive(st_P, upd)	1: set all $sent^*_*$ and $received^*_*$ variables to $\emptyset$
2: **if** acc **then**	2: Setup(1^λ) $\xrightarrow{\$}$ pp
3: $upd_P \leftarrow$ upd	3: Initall(1^λ, pp) $\xrightarrow{\$}$ (st_A, st_B, z)
4: $k_P \leftarrow k$	4: initialize two FIFO lists incoming$_A$ and incoming$_B$ to empty
5: $st_P \leftarrow st'_P$	5: $i \leftarrow 1$
6: append k_P to received$^P_{key}$	6: **while** sched$_i$ exists **do**
7: append upd_P to received$^P_{msg}$	7: (P, role) $\leftarrow$ sched$_i$
8: **end if**	8: **if** role = rec **then**
9: **return** acc	9: **if** incoming$_P$ is empty **then return** 0
	10: pull upd from incoming$_P$
	11: acc $\leftarrow$ RATCH(P, rec, upd)
Oracle RATCH(P, send)	12: **if** acc = false **then return** 1
10: $(st'_P, upd_P, k_P) \leftarrow$ Send(st_P)	13: **else**
11: $st_P \leftarrow st'_P$	14: upd $\leftarrow$ RATCH(P, send)
12: append k_P to sent$^P_{key}$	15: push upd to incoming$_{\overline{P}}$
13: append upd_P to sent$^P_{msg}$	16: **end if**
14: **return** upd_P	17: **if** received$^A_{key}$ not prefix of sent$^B_{key}$ **then return** 1
	18: **if** received$^B_{key}$ not prefix of sent$^A_{key}$ **then return** 1
	19: $i \leftarrow i + 1$
	20: **end while**
	21: **return** 0

Fig. 2. The CORRECT game.

Definition 2 (Correctness of BARK). *We say that* BARK *is correct if for all sequence* sched, *the* CORRECT *game of Fig. 2 never returns 1. Namely, for each* P, received$^P_{key}$ *is always prefix of* sent$^{\overline{P}}_{key}$[3] *and each* RATCH(., rec, .) *call accepts.*

Security. We model our security notion with an active adversary who can have access to some of the states of Alice or Bob along with access to their secret keys enabling them to act both as a sender and as a receiver. For simplicity, we have only Alice and Bob as participants. (Models with more participants would be asymptotically equivalent.) We focus on three main security notions which are *key indistinguishability* (denoted as KIND) under the compromise of states or keys, *unforgeability* of upd information (FORGE) by the adversary which will be accepted, and *recovery from impersonation* (RECOVER) which will make the two participants restore secure communication without noticing a (trivial) impersonation resulting from a state exposure. A challenge in these notions is to eliminate the trivial attacks. FORGE and RECOVER security will be useful to prove KIND security.

2.2   KIND Security

The adversary can access four oracles called RATCH, EXP$_{st}$, EXP$_{key}$, and TEST.

---

[3] By saying that received$^P_{key}$ is prefix of sent$^{\overline{P}}_{key}$, we mean that when n is the number of keys generated by P running Receive, then these keys are the first n keys generated by $\overline{P}$ running Send.

RATCH. This is essentially the message exchange procedure. It is defined in Fig. 2. The adversary can call it with three inputs, a participant P, where $P \in \{A, B\}$; a role of P; and an upd information if the role is rec. The adversary gets upd (for role = send) or acc (for role = rec) in return.

EXP_{st}. The adversary can expose the state of Alice or Bob. It inputs $P \in \{A, B\}$ to the EXP_{st} oracle and it receives the full state st_P of P.

EXP_{key}. The adversary can expose the generated key by calling this oracle. Upon inputting P, it gets the last key k_P generated by P. If no key was generated, $\perp$ is returned.

TEST. This oracle can be called only once to receive a challenge key which is generated either uniformly at random (if the challenge bit is $b = 0$) or given as the last generated key of a participant P specified as input (if the challenge bit is $b = 1$). The oracle cannot be queried if no key was generated yet.

We specifically separate EXP_{key} from EXP_{st} because the key k generated by BARK will be used by an external process which may leak the key. Thus, EXP_{key} can be more frequent than EXP_{st}, however it harms security less.

To define security, we avoid trivial attacks. Capturing the trivial cases in a broad sense requires a new set of definitions. All of them are intuitive.

Intuitively, P is in a matching status at a given time if his state is not dependent on an active attack (i.e. could result from a CORRECT game).

Definition 3 (Matching status). *We say that* P *is in a* matching status *at time* t *for* P *if 1. at any moment of the game before time* t *for* P, $received^P_{msg}$ *is a prefix of* $sent^{\overline{P}}_{msg}$—*this defines the time* $\overline{t}$ *for* $\overline{P}$ *when* $\overline{P}$ *sent the last message in* $received^P_{msg}(t)$; 2. *at any moment of the game before time* $\overline{t}$ *for* $\overline{P}$, $received^{\overline{P}}_{msg}$ *is a prefix of* $sent^P_{msg}$. *We further say that time* t *for* P *originates* from time $\overline{t}$ for $\overline{P}$.

The first condition clearly states that each of the received (and accepted) upd message was sent before by the counterpart of P, in the same order, without any loss in between. The second condition similarly verifies that those messages from $\overline{P}$ only depend on information coming from P. In Fig. 1, Bob is in a matching status with Alice because he receives the upd information in the exact order as they have sent by Alice (i.e. Bob generates k_2 after k_1 and k_4 after k_2 same as it has sent by Alice). In general, as long as no adversary switches the order of messages or creates fake messages successfully for either party, the participants are always in a matching status.

The key exchange literature often defines a notion of partnering which is simpler. Here, asynchronous random roles make it more complicated.

Here is an easy property of the notion of matching status.

Lemma 4. *If* P *is in a matching status at time* t, *then* P *is also in a matching status at any time* $t_0 \leqslant t$. *Similarly, if* P *is in a matching status at time* t *and* t *for* P *originates from* $\overline{t}$ *for* $\overline{P}$, *then* $\overline{P}$ *is in a matching status at time* $\overline{t}$.

Definition 5 (Forgery). *Given a participant* P *in a game, we say that* upd $\in$ received$_{msg}^{P}$ *is a forgery if at the moment of the game just before* P *received* upd, P *was in a matching status, but no longer after receiving* upd.

In a matching status, any upd received by P must correspond to an upd sent by $\overline{P}$ and the sequences must match. This implies the following notion.

Definition 6 (Corresponding RATCH calls). *Let* P *be a participant. We consider the* RATCH(P, rec, .) *calls by* P *returning* true. *We say that the* i^{th} *receiving call corresponds to the* j^{th} RATCH($\overline{P}$, send) *call if* $i = j$ *and* P *is in matching status at the time of this* i^{th} *accepting* RATCH(P, rec, .) *call.*

Lemma 7. *In a correct* BARK *protocol, two corresponding* RATCH(P, rec, upd) *and* RATCH($\overline{P}$, send) *calls generate the same key* $k_P = k_{\overline{P}}$.

Definition 8 (Ratcheting period of P). *A maximal time interval during which there is no* RATCH(P, send) *call is called a* ratcheting period *of* P.

In Fig. 1, the intervals $T_1 - T_3$ and $T_5 - T_6$ are ratcheting periods.

We now define when the adversary can trivially obtain a key generated by P due to an exposure. We distinguish the case when the exposure was done on P (direct leakage) and on $\overline{P}$ (indirect leakage).

Definition 9 (Direct leakage). *Let* t *be a time and* P *be a participant. We say that* $k_P(t)$ *has a* direct leakage *if one of the following conditions is satisfied:*

- *There is an* $EXP_{key}(P)$ *at a time* t_e *such that the last* RATCH *call which is executed by* P *before time* t *and the last* RATCH *call which is executed by* P *before time* t_e *are the same.*
- P *is in a matching status and there exists* $t_0 \leqslant t_e \leqslant t_{RATCH} \leqslant t$ *and* $\overline{t}$ *such that time* t *originates from time* $\overline{t}$; *time* $\overline{t}$ *originates from time* t_0; *there is one* $EXP_{st}(P)$ *at time* t_e; *there is one* RATCH(P, rec, .) *at time* t_{RATCH}; *and there is no* RATCH(P, ., .) *between time* t_{RATCH} *and time* t.

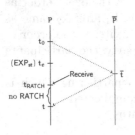

In the first case, it is clear that $EXP_{key}(P)$ gives $k_P(t_e) = k_P(t)$. In the second case (in the figure[4]), the state which leaks from $EXP_{st}(P)$ at time t_e allows to simulate all deterministic Receive (by skipping all Send) and to compute the key $k_P(t_{RATCH}) = k_P(t)$. The reason why we can allow the adversary to skip all Send is that they make messages which are supposed to be delivered to $\overline{P}$ after time $\overline{t}$, so they have no impact on $k_P(t)$.

Consider Fig. 1. Suppose t is in between time T_3 and T_4. According to our definition $P = A$ and the last RATCH call is at time T_3. It is a Send, thus the

---

[4] Origin of dotted arrows indicate when a time originates from.

second case cannot apply. The next RATCH call is at time T_4. In this case, $k_A(t)$ has a direct leakage if there is a key exposure of Alice between T_3 and T_4.

Suppose now that $T_8 < t < T_9$. We have $P = B$, the last RATCH call is a Receive, it is at time $t_{RATCH} = T_8$, and t originates from time $\bar{t} = T_0$ which itself originates from the origin time $t_0 = T_{Init}$ for B. We say that t has a direct leakage if there is a key exposure between $T_8 - T_9$ or a state exposure of Bob before time T_8. Indeed, with this last state exposure, the adversary can ignore all Send and simulate all Receive to derive k_0.

Definition 10 (Indirect leakage). *We consider a time t and a participant P. Let t_{RATCH} be the time of the last successful RATCH call and role be its input role. (We have $k_P(t_{RATCH}) = k_P(t)$.) We say that $k_P(t)$ has an indirect leakage if P is in matching status at time t and one of the following conditions is satisfied*

- *There exists a $RATCH(\overline{P}, \overline{role}, .)$ corresponding to that $RATCH(P, role, .)$ and making a $k_{\overline{P}}$ which has a direct leakage for $\overline{P}$.*
- *There exists $t' \leqslant t_{RATCH} \leqslant t$ and $\bar{t} \leqslant \bar{t}_e$ such that $\overline{P}$ is in a matching status at time $\bar{t}_e$, t originates from $\bar{t}$, $\bar{t}_e$ originates from t', there is one $EXP_{st}(\overline{P})$ at time $\bar{t}_e$, and role = send.*

In the first case, $k_P(t) = k_P(t_{RATCH})$ is also computed by $\overline{P}$ and leaks from there. The second case (in the figure) is more complicated: it corresponds to an adversary who can get the internal state of $\overline{P}$ by $EXP_{st}(\overline{P})$ then simulate all Receive with messages from P until the one sent at time t_{RATCH}, ignoring all Send by $\overline{P}$, to recover $k_P(t)$.

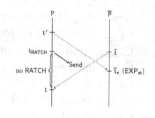

For example, let t be a time between T_1 and T_2 in Fig. 1. We take $P = A$. The last RATCH call is at time $t_{RATCH} = T_1$, it is a Send and corresponds to a Receive at time T_{10}, but t originates from time $\bar{t} = T_{Init}$. We say that t has an indirect leakage for A if there exists a direct leakage for $\overline{P} = B$ at a time between T_{10} and T_{11} (first condition) or there exists a $EXP_{st}(B)$ call at a time $\bar{t}_e$ (after time $\bar{t} = T_{Init}$), originating from a time t' before time T_1, so $\bar{t}_e < T_{10}$ (second condition). In the latter case, the adversary can simulate Receive with the updates sent at time T_0 and T_1 to derive the key k_1.

Exposing the state of a participant gives certain advantages to the attacker and make trivial attacks possible. In our security game, we avoid those attack scenarios. In the following lemma, we show that direct and indirect leakage capture the times when the adversary can trivially win. The proof is straightforward.

Lemma 11 (Trivial attacks). *Assume that BARK is correct. For any t and P, if $k_P(t)$ has a direct or indirect leakage, the adversary can compute $k_P(t)$.*

So far, we mostly focused on matching status cases but there could be situations with forgeries. Some are unavoidable. We call them *trivial* forgeries.

Definition 12 (Trivial forgery). *Let* upd *be a forgery received by* P. *At the time* t *just before the* RATCH(P, rec, upd) *call,* P *was in a matching status. We assume that time* t *for* P *originates from time* $\bar{t}$ *for* $\overline{P}$. *If there is an* $\mathsf{EXP_{st}}(\overline{P})$ *call during the ratcheting period of* $\overline{P}$ *starting at time* $\bar{t}$, *we say that* upd *is a trivial forgery.*

We define the KIND security game in Fig. 3. Essentially, the adversary plays with all oracles. At some point, he does one TEST(P) call which returns either the same result as $\mathsf{EXP_{key}}(P)$ (case $b = 1$) or some random value (case $b = 0$). The goal of the adversary is to guess b. The TEST call can be done only once and it defines the participant $P_{test} = P$ and the time t_{test} at which this call is made. It also defines $\mathsf{upd_{test}}$, the last upd which was used (either sent or received) to carry $k_{P_{test}}(t_{test})$ from the sender to the receiver. It is not allowed to make this call at the beginning, when P did not generate a key yet. It is not allowed to make a trivial attack as defined by a cleanness predicate C_{clean} appearing on Step 6 in the KIND game in Fig. 3. Identifying the appropriate *cleanness predicate* C_{clean} is not easy. It must clearly forbid trivial attacks but also allow efficient protocols. In what follows we use the following predicates:

- C_{leak}: $k_{P_{test}}(t_{test})$ has no direct or indirect leakage.
- $C_{trivial\ forge}^{P}$: P received no trivial forgery until P has seen $\mathsf{upd_{test}}$.
  (This implies that $\mathsf{upd_{test}}$ is not a trivial forgery. It also implies that if P never sees $\mathsf{upd_{test}}$, then P received no trivial forgery at all.)
- C_{forge}^{P}: P received no forgery until P has seen $\mathsf{upd_{test}}$.
- $C_{ratchet}$: $\mathsf{upd_{test}}$ was sent by a participant P, then received and accepted by $\overline{P}$, then some $\mathsf{upd_{ack}}$ was sent by $\overline{P}$, then $\mathsf{upd_{ack}}$ was received and accepted by P. (Here, P could be P_{test} or his counterpart. This accounts for the receipt of $\mathsf{upd_{test}}$ being acknowledged by $\overline{P}$ through $\mathsf{upd_{ack}}$.)
- $C_{noEXP(R)}$: there is no $\mathsf{EXP_{st}}(R)$ and no $\mathsf{EXP_{key}}(R)$ query. (R is the receiver.)

Lemma 11 says that the adopted cleanness predicate C_{clean} must imply C_{leak} in all considered games. Otherwise, no security is possible. It is however not sufficient as it only hardly trivial attacks with forgeries.

$C_{ratchet}$ targets that any acknowledged sent message is secure. Another way to say is that a key generated by one Send starting a round trip must be safe. This is the notion of healing by ratcheting. Intuitively, the security notion from $C_{clean} = C_{leak} \wedge C_{ratchet}$ is fair enough.

Bellare et al. [2] consider unidirectional BARK with $C_{clean} = C_{leak} \wedge C_{trivial\ forge}^{P_{test}} \wedge C_{noEXP(R)}$. Other papers like PR [15] and JS [10] implicitly use $C_{clean} = C_{leak} \wedge C_{trivial\ forge}^{P_{test}}$ as cleanness predicate. They show that this is sufficient to build secure protocols but it is probably not the minimal cleanness predicate. (It is nevertheless called *"optimal"*.) JMM [11] excludes cases where $\overline{P}_{test}$ received a (trivial) forgery then had an $\mathsf{EXP_{st}}(\overline{P}_{test})$ before receiving $\mathsf{upd_{test}}$. Actually, they use a cleanness predicate (*"near-optimal"* security) which is somewhere between $C_{leak} \wedge C_{trivial\ forge}^{P_{test}}$ and $C_{leak} \wedge C_{trivial\ forge}^{A} \wedge C_{trivial\ forge}^{B}$: this cleanness implies the JMM cleanness which itself implies the PR/JS cleanness.

In our construction ("*sub-optimal*"), we use the predicate $C_{clean} = C_{leak} \wedge C_{forge}^A \wedge C_{forge}^B$. However, in Sect. 4.1, we define the FORGE security (unforgeability) which implies that $(C_{leak} \wedge C_{forge}^A \wedge C_{forge}^B)$-KIND security and $(C_{leak} \wedge C_{trivial\ forge}^A \wedge C_{trivial\ forge}^B)$-KIND security are equivalent. (See Theorem 16.) One drawback is that it forbids more than $(C_{leak} \wedge C_{trivial\ forge}^{P_{test}})$-KIND security. The advantage is that we can achieve security without key-update primitives. We will prove in Theorem 19 that this security is enough to achieve security with the predicate $C_{clean} = C_{leak} \wedge C_{ratchet}$, thanks to RECOVER-security which we define in Sect. 4.2. Thus, our cleanness notion is fair enough.

Game $\mathsf{KIND}_{b,C_{clean}}^{\mathcal{A}}(1^\lambda)$	Oracle TEST(P)
1: Setup$(1^\lambda) \xrightarrow{\$} \mathsf{pp}$	1: **if** $t_{test} \neq \perp$ **then return** $\perp$
2: Initall$(1^\lambda, \mathsf{pp}) \xrightarrow{\$} (\mathsf{st}_A, \mathsf{st}_B, z)$	2: **if** $k_P = \perp$ **then return** $\perp$
3: set all sent$_*^*$ and received$_*^*$ variables to $\emptyset$	3: $t_{test} \leftarrow$ time, $P_{test} \leftarrow P$, $\mathsf{upd}_{test} \leftarrow \mathsf{upd}_P$
4: set t_{test}, k_A, k_B to $\perp$	4: **if** $b = 1$ **then**
5: $b' \leftarrow \mathcal{A}^{\mathsf{RATCH},\mathsf{EXP}_{st},\mathsf{EXP}_{key},\mathsf{TEST}}(z)$	5: **return** k_P
6: **if** $\neg C_{clean}$ **then return** $\perp$	6: **else**
7: **return** b'	7: **return** random $\{0,1\}^{|k_P|}$
	8: **end if**
Oracle EXP$_{st}$(P)	
1: **return** st$_P$	Oracle EXP$_{key}$(P)
	1: **return** k_P

Fig. 3. C_{clean}-KIND game. (Oracle RATCH is defined in Fig. 2.)

Definition 13 (C_{clean}-KINDsecurity). *Let C_{clean} be a cleanness predicate. We consider the $\mathsf{KIND}_{b,C_{clean}}^{\mathcal{A}}$ game of Fig. 3. We say that the ratcheted key agreement BARK is C_{clean}-KIND-secure if for any PPT adversary, the advantage*

$$\mathsf{Adv}_{\mathcal{A}}(1^\lambda) = \left| \Pr\left[\mathsf{KIND}_{0,C_{clean}}^{\mathcal{A}}(1^\lambda) \to 1\right] - \Pr\left[\mathsf{KIND}_{1,C_{clean}}^{\mathcal{A}}(1^\lambda) \to 1\right] \right|$$

of $\mathcal{A}$ in $\mathsf{KIND}_{b,C_{clean}}^{\mathcal{A}}(1^\lambda)$ security game is negligible.

3   uniARK Implies KEM

We now prove that a weakly secure uniARK (a unidirectional asynchronous ratcheted key exchange—a straightforward variant of BARK in which messages can only be sent from a participant whom we call S and can only be received by another participant whom we call R) implies public key encryption. Namely, we can construct a key encapsulation mechanism (KEM) out of it. We recall the KEM definition in the full version [8]. We consider a uniARK which is KIND-secure for the following cleanness predicate:

C_{weak}: the adversary makes only three oracle calls which are, in order, $\mathsf{EXP}_{st}(S)$, $\mathsf{RATCH}(S, \mathsf{send})$, and $\mathsf{TEST}(S)$.

(Note that R is never used.) C_{weak} implies cleanness for all other considered predicates. Hence, it is more restrictive. Our result implies that it is unlikely to construct even such weakly secure uniARK from symmetric cryptography.

Theorem 14. *Given a* uniARK *protocol, we can construct a* KEM *with the following properties. The correctness of* uniARK *implies the correctness of* KEM. *The* C_{weak}-KIND-*security of* uniARK *implies the* IND-CPA *security of* KEM.

Proof. Assuming a uniARK protocol, we construct a KEM as follows:

KEM.Gen$(1^\lambda) \xrightarrow{\$}$ (sk, pk): run uniARK.Setup$(1^\lambda) \xrightarrow{\$}$ pp, uniARK.Initall$(1^\lambda, pp) \xrightarrow{\$}$ (st_S, st_R, z), and set pk $= st_S$, sk $= st_R$.
KEM.Enc(pk) $\xrightarrow{\$}$ (k, ct): run uniARK.Send(pk) $\xrightarrow{\$}$ (., upd, k) and set ct $=$ upd.
KEM.Dec(sk, ct) $\rightarrow$ k: run uniARK.Receive(sk, upd) $\rightarrow$ (., ., k).

The IND-CPA security game with adversary $\mathcal{A}$ works as in the left-hand side below. We transform $\mathcal{A}$ into a KIND adversary $\mathcal{B}$ in the right-hand side below.

Game IND-CPA:
1: KEM.Gen $\xrightarrow{\$}$ (sk, pk)
2: KEM.Enc(pk) $\xrightarrow{\$}$ (k, ct)
3: **if** b = 0 **then** set k to random
4: $\mathcal{A}$(pk, ct, k) $\xrightarrow{\$}$ b′
5: **return** b′

Adversary $\mathcal{B}(z)$:
1: call $\mathsf{EXP_{st}}(S) \rightarrow$ pk
2: call RATCH(S, send) $\rightarrow$ ct
3: call TEST(S) $\rightarrow$ k
4: run $\mathcal{A}$(pk, ct, k) $\rightarrow$ b′
5: **return** b′

We can check that C_{weak} is satisfied. The KIND game with $\mathcal{B}$ simulates perfectly the IND-CPA game with $\mathcal{A}$. So, the KIND-security of uniARK implies the IND-CPA security of KEM. □

4 FORGE and RECOVER Security

4.1 Unforgeability

Another security aspect of the key agreement BARK is to have that no upd information is forgeable by any bounded adversary except trivially by state exposure. This security notion is independent from KIND security but is certainly nice to have for explicit authentication in key agreement. Besides, it is easy to achieve. We will also use it as a helper to prove KIND security: to reduce $C^P_{trivial\ forge}$-cleanness to C^P_{forge}-cleanness.

Let the adversary interact with the oracles RATCH, $\mathsf{EXP_{st}}$, $\mathsf{EXP_{key}}$ in any order. For BARK to have unforgeability, we eliminate the trivial forgeries (as defined in Definition 12). The FORGE game is defined in Fig. 4.

Definition 15. (FORGE security). *Consider* FORGE$^{\mathcal{A}}(1^\lambda)$ *game in Fig. 4 associated to the adversary* $\mathcal{A}$. *Let the advantage of* $\mathcal{A}$ *be the probability that the game outputs 1. We say that* BARK *is* FORGE-*secure if, for any PPT adversary, the advantage is negligible.*

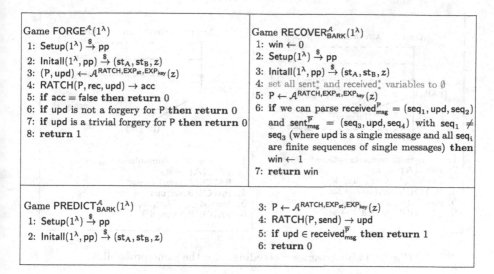

Fig. 4. FORGE, RECOVER, and PREDICT games.

We can now justify why forgeries in the KIND game must be trivial for a BARK with unforgeability.

Theorem 16. *If a BARK is FORGE-secure, then* $(C_{\text{leak}} \wedge C_{\text{forge}}^{P_{\text{test}}})$*-KIND-security implies* $(C_{\text{leak}} \wedge C_{\text{trivial forge}}^{P_{\text{test}}})$*-KIND-security and* $(C_{\text{leak}} \wedge C_{\text{forge}}^{A} \wedge C_{\text{forge}}^{B})$*-KIND-security implies* $(C_{\text{leak}} \wedge C_{\text{trivial forge}}^{A} \wedge C_{\text{trivial forge}}^{B})$*-KIND-security.*

4.2 Recovery from Impersonation

A priori, it seems nice to be able to restore a secure state when a state exposure of a participant takes place. We show here that it is not a good idea.

Let $\mathcal{A}$ be an adversary playing the two games in Fig. 5. On the left strategy, $\mathcal{A}$ exposes A with an EXP_{st} query (Step 2). Then, the adversary $\mathcal{A}$ impersonates A by running the Send algorithm on its own (Step 3). Next, the adversary $\mathcal{A}$ "sends" a message to B which is accepted due to correctness because it is generated with A's state. In Step 5, $\mathcal{A}$ lets the legitimate sender generate upd' by calling RATCH oracle. In this step, *if* security self-restores, then B accepts upd' which is sent by A, hence acc' = 1. It is clear that the strategy shown on the left side in Fig. 5 is equivalent to the strategy shown on the right side of the same figure (which only switches Alice and the adversary who run the same algorithm). Hence, both lead to acc' = 1 with the same probability p. The crucial point is that the forgery in the right-hand strategy becomes non-trivial, which implies that the protocol is not FORGE-secure. In addition to this, if such phenomenon occurs, we can make a KIND adversary passing the $C_{\text{leak}} \wedge C_{\text{trivial forge}}^{P_{\text{test}}}$ condition. Thus, we lose KIND-security. Consequently, security should *not* self-restore.

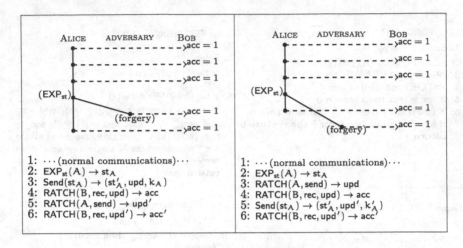

Fig. 5. Two recoveries succeeding with the same probability.

We define the RECOVER security notion with another game in Fig. 4. Essentially, in the game, we require the receiver P to accept some messages upd sent by the sender after the adversary makes successful forgeries in seq_1. We further use it as a second helper to prove KIND security with $C_{ratchet}$-cleanness.

Definition 17 (RECOVER security). *Consider* $RECOVER_{BARK}^{A}(1^{\lambda})$ *game in Fig. 4 associated to the adversary A. Let the advantage of A in succeeding playing the game be* $\Pr(win = 1)$. *We say that the ratcheted communication protocol is* RECOVER-*secure, if for any PPT adversary, the advantage is negligible.*

RECOVER-security iseasy to achieve using a collision-resistant hash function.

To be sure that no message was received before it was sent, we need the following security notion. In the PREDICT game, the adversary tries to make $\overline{P}$ receive a message upd before it was sent by P.

Definition 18 (PREDICT security). *For the* $PREDICT_{BARK}^{A}(1^{\lambda})$ *game in Fig. 4, let A be an adversary. The advantage of A is the probability that 1 is returned. We say that the ratcheted communication protocol is* PREDICT-*secure, if for any adversary limited to a polynomially bounded number of queries, the advantage is negligible.*

Theorem 19. *If a* BARK *is* RECOVER-*secure,* PREDICT-*secure, and* $(C_{leak} \wedge C_{forge}^{A} \wedge C_{forge}^{B})$-KIND *secure, then it is* $(C_{leak} \wedge C_{ratchet})$-KIND *secure.*

5   Our BARK Protocol

We construct a BARK in Fig. 6. We use a public-key cryptosystem PKC, a digital signature scheme DSS, a one-time symmetric encryption Sym, and a collision-resistant hash function H. They are all defined in the full version [8]. First, we construct a naive signcryption SC from PKC and DSS by

$$\text{SC.Enc}(\overbrace{sk_S, pk_R}^{st_S}, ad, pt) = \text{PKC.Enc}(pk_R, (pt, \text{DSS.Sign}(sk_S, (ad, pt))))$$
$$\text{SC.Dec}(\underbrace{sk_R, pk_S}_{st_R}, ad, ct) = (pt, \sigma) \leftarrow \text{PKC.Dec}(sk_R, ct) ;$$
$$\text{DSS.Verify}(pk_S, (ad, pt), \sigma) ? pt : \perp$$

Second, we extend SC to multi-key encryption called onion due to the multiple layers of keys. Third, we transform onion into a unidirectional ratcheting scheme uni. Finally, we design BARK. (See Fig. 6.)

The state of a participant is a tuple $st = (\lambda, hk, \text{List}_S, \text{List}_R, \text{Hsent}, \text{Hreceived})$ where hk is the hashing key, Hsent is the iterated hash of all sent messages, and Hreceived is the iterated hash of all received messages. We also have two lists List_S and List_R. They are lists of states to be used for unidirectional communication: sending and receiving. Both lists are growing but entries are eventually erased. Thus, they can be compressed. (Typically, only the last entry is not erased.)

The idea is that the ith entry of List_S for a participant P is associated to the ith entry of List_R for its counterpart $\overline{P}$. Every time a participant P sends a message, it creates a new pair of states for sending and receiving and sends the sending state to his counterpart $\overline{P}$, to be used in the case $\overline{P}$ wants to respond. If the same participant P keeps sending without receiving anything, he accumulates some receiving states this way. Whenever a participant $\overline{P}$ who received many messages starts sending, he also accumulated many sending states. His message is sent using *all* those states in the uni.Send procedure. After sending, all but the last send state are erased, and the message shall indicate the erasures to the counterpart P, who shall erase corresponding receiving states accordingly. Our onion encryption needs to ensure $\mathcal{O}(n)$ complexity (so we cannot compose SC encryptions as ciphertext overheads would produce $\mathcal{O}(n^2)$ complexity). For that, we use a one-time symmetric encryption Sym using a key k in $\{0,1\}^{\text{Sym.kl}}$. which is split into shares $k_1, \ldots, k_n$. Each share is SC-encrypted in one state. Only the last state is updated (as others are meant to be erased).

The protocol is quite efficient when participants alternate their roles well, because the lists are often flushed to contain only one unerased state. It also becomes more secure due to ratcheting: any exposure has very limited impact. If there are unidirectional sequences, the protocol becomes less and less efficient due to the growth of the lists.

We state the security of our protocol below. Proofs are provided in the full version [8]. In the full version [8], we also show that our protocol does *not* offer $(C_{\text{leak}} \wedge C_{\text{forge}}^{P_{\text{test}}})$-KIND security.

Theorem 20. *We consider the BARK protocol from Fig. 6.*

- BARK *is correct.*
- BARK *is PREDICT-secure.*
- *If* H *is collision-resistant, then* BARK *is RECOVER-secure.*
- *If* DSS *is SEF-OTCMA-secure and* H *is collision-resistant, then* BARK *is FORGE-secure.*
- *If* PKC *is IND-CCA-secure and* Sym *is IND-OTCCA-secure, then* BARK *is* $(C_{\text{leak}} \wedge C_{\text{forge}}^A \wedge C_{\text{forge}}^B)$-KIND-secure.

onion.Enc($hk, st_S^1, \ldots, st_S^n, ad, pt$)	onion.Dec($hk, st_R^1, \ldots, st_R^n, ad, \vec{ct}$)
1: pick $k_1, \ldots, k_n$ in $\{0,1\}^{Sym.kl}$	1: if $|\vec{ct}| \neq n+1$ then return $\perp$
2: $k \leftarrow k_1 \oplus \cdots \oplus k_n$	2: parse $\vec{ct} = (ct_1, \ldots, ct_{n+1})$
3: $ct_{n+1} \leftarrow Sym.Enc(k, pt)$	3: $ad_{n+1} \leftarrow ad$
4: $ad_{n+1} \leftarrow ad$	4: for $i = n$ down to 1 do
5: for $i = n$ down to 1 do	5: $\quad ad_i \leftarrow H.Eval(hk, ad_{i+1}, ct_{i+1})$
6: $\quad ad_i \leftarrow H.Eval(hk, ad_{i+1}, ct_{i+1})$	6: $\quad SC.Dec(st_R^i, ad_i, ct_i) \rightarrow k_i$
7: $\quad ct_i \leftarrow SC.Enc(st_S^i, ad_i, k_i)$	7: $\quad$ if $k_i = \perp$ then return $\perp$
8: end for	8: end for
9: return $(ct_1, \ldots, ct_{n+1})$	9: $k \leftarrow k_1 \oplus \cdots \oplus k_n$
	10: $pt \leftarrow Sym.Dec(k, ct_{n+1})$
	11: return pt

uni.Init(1^λ)	uni.Send($1^\lambda, hk, \vec{st}_S, ad, pt$)	uni.Receive($hk, \vec{st}_R, ad, \vec{ct}$)
1: $SC.Gen_S(1^\lambda) \xrightarrow{\$} (sk_S, pk_S)$	1: $SC.Gen_S(1^\lambda) \xrightarrow{\$} (sk_S', pk_S')$	1: onion.Dec($hk, \vec{st}_R, ad, \vec{ct}) \rightarrow pt'$
2: $SC.Gen_R(1^\lambda) \xrightarrow{\$} (sk_R, pk_R)$	2: $SC.Gen_R(1^\lambda) \xrightarrow{\$} (sk_R', pk_R')$	2: if $pt' = \perp$ then return (false, $\perp, \perp$)
3: $st_S \leftarrow (sk_S, pk_R)$	3: $st_S' \leftarrow (sk_S', pk_R')$	3: parse $pt' = (st_R', pt)$
4: $st_R \leftarrow (sk_R, pk_S)$	4: $st_R' \leftarrow (sk_R', pk_S')$	4: return (true, st_R', pt)
5: return (st_S, st_R)	5: $pt' \leftarrow (st_R', pt)$	
	6: onion.Enc($1^\lambda, hk, \vec{st}_S, ad, pt') \rightarrow \vec{ct}$	
	7: return $(st_S', \vec{ct})$	

BARK.Setup(1^λ)	BARK.Gen($1^\lambda, hk$)	BARK.Init($1^\lambda, hk, sk_P, pk_{\overline{P}}, P$)
1: $H.Gen(1^\lambda) \xrightarrow{\$} hk$	1: $SC.Gen_S(1^\lambda) \xrightarrow{\$} (sk_S, pk_S)$	1: parse $sk_P = (sk_S, sk_R)$
2: return hk	2: $SC.Gen_R(1^\lambda) \xrightarrow{\$} (sk_R, pk_R)$	2: parse $pk_{\overline{P}} = (pk_S, pk_R)$
	3: $sk \leftarrow (sk_S, sk_R)$	3: $st_P^{send} \leftarrow (sk_S, pk_R)$
	4: $pk \leftarrow (pk_S, pk_R)$	4: $st_P^{rec} \leftarrow (sk_R, pk_S)$
	5: return (sk, pk)	5: $st_P \leftarrow (\lambda, hk, (st_P^{send}), (st_P^{rec}), \perp, \perp)$
		6: return st_P

BARK.Send(st_P)
1: pick k at random in $\{0,1\}^{BARK.kl}$
2: parse $st_P = (\lambda, hk, (st_P^{send,1}, \ldots, st_P^{send,u}), (st_P^{rec,1}, \ldots, st_P^{rec,v}), Hsent, Hreceived)$
3: uni.Init($1^\lambda) \xrightarrow{\$} (st_{Snew}, st_P^{rec,v+1})$ $\qquad\qquad$ ▷ append a new receive state to the st_P^{rec} list
4: $pt \leftarrow (st_{Snew}, k)$ $\qquad\qquad$ ▷ st_{Snew} could be deleted immediately to avoid leaking
5: take the smallest i s.t. $st_P^{send,i} \neq \perp$ $\qquad\qquad$ ▷ $i = u - n$ if we had n Receive since the last Send
6: uni.Send($1^\lambda, hk, (st_P^{send,i}, \ldots, st_P^{send,u}), Hsent, pt) \xrightarrow{\$} (st_P^{send,u}, \vec{ct})$ $\qquad$ ▷ update $st_P^{send,u}$
7: $st_P^{send,1}, \ldots, st_P^{send,u-1} \leftarrow \perp$ $\qquad\qquad$ ▷ flush the send state list: only $st_P^{send,u}$ remains
8: $upd \leftarrow (Hsent, \vec{ct})$ $\qquad\qquad$ ▷ $\vec{ct}$ has $u - i + 2(= n+1)$ components
9: $Hsent' \leftarrow H.Eval(hk, upd)$
10: $st_P' \leftarrow (\lambda, hk, (st_P^{send,1}, \ldots, st_P^{send,u}), (st_P^{rec,1}, \ldots, st_P^{rec,v+1}), Hsent', Hreceived)$
11: return (st_P', upd, k)

BARK.Receive(st_P, upd)
12: parse $st_P = (\lambda, hk, (st_P^{send,1}, \ldots, st_P^{send,u}), (st_P^{rec,1}, \ldots, st_P^{rec,v}), Hsent, Hreceived)$
13: parse $upd = (h, \vec{ct})$
14: set $n+1$ to the number of components in $\vec{ct}$ $\qquad\qquad$ ▷ the onion has n layers
15: if $h \neq Hreceived$ then return (false, $st_P, \perp$)
16: set i to the smallest index such that $st_P^{rec,i} \neq \perp$
17: if $i + n - 1 > v$ then return (false, $st_P, \perp$)
18: uni.Receive($hk, (st_P^{rec,i}, \ldots, st_P^{rec,i+n-1}), Hreceived, \vec{ct}) \rightarrow (acc, st_P'^{rec,i+n-1}, pt)$
19: if $acc = false$ then return (false, $st_P, \perp$)
20: parse $pt = (st_P^{send,u+1}, k)$ $\qquad\qquad$ ▷ a new send state is added in the list
21: $st_P^{rec,i}, \ldots, st_P^{rec,i+n-2} \leftarrow \perp$ $\qquad\qquad$ ▷ update st_P^{rec} stage 1: clean up
22: $st_P^{rec,i+n-1} \leftarrow st_P'^{rec,i+n-1}$ $\qquad\qquad$ ▷ update st_P^{rec} stage 2: update $st_P^{rec,i+n-1}$
23: $Hreceived' \leftarrow H.Eval(hk, upd)$
24: $st_P' \leftarrow (\lambda, hk, (st_P^{send,1}, \ldots, st_P^{send,u+1}), (st_P^{rec,1}, \ldots, st_P^{rec,v}), Hsent, Hreceived')$
25: return (acc, st_P', k)

Fig. 6. Our BARK protocol.

Consequently, due to Theorem 16, we deduce $(C_{leak} \wedge C^A_{trivial\ forge} \wedge C^B_{trivial\ forge})$-KIND-security. The advantage of treating $(C_{leak} \wedge C^A_{forge} \wedge C^B_{forge})$-KIND-security specifically is that we clearly separate the required security assumptions for SC. Similarly, due to Theorem 19, we deduce $(C_{leak} \wedge C_{ratchet})$-KIND-security.

6 Conclusion

We studied the BARK protocols and security. For security, we marked three important security objectives: the BARK protocol should be KIND-secure; the BARK protocol should be resistant to forgery attacks (FORGE-security), and the BARK protocol should not self-heal after impersonation (RECOVER-security). By relaxing the cleanness notion in KIND-security, we designed a protocol based on an IND-CCA-secure cryptosystem and a one-time signature scheme. We used neither random oracle nor key-update primitives.

Acknowledgements. We thank Joseph Jaeger for his valuable comments to the first version of this paper. We thank Paul Rösler for insightful discussions and comments. We also owe to Andrea Caforio for his implementation results.

References

1. Alwen, J., Coretti, S., Dodis, Y.: The double ratchet: security notions, proofs, and modularization for the signal protocol. In: Ishai, Y., Rijmen, V. (eds.) EUROCRYPT 2019. LNCS, vol. 11476, pp. 129–158. Springer, Cham (2019). https://doi.org/10.1007/978-3-030-17653-2_5. Full version: https://eprint.iacr.org/2018/1037.pdf
2. Bellare, M., Singh, A.C., Jaeger, J., Nyayapati, M., Stepanovs, I.: Ratcheted encryption and key exchange: the security of messaging. In: Katz, J., Shacham, H. (eds.) CRYPTO 2017. LNCS, vol. 10403, pp. 619–650. Springer, Cham (2017). https://doi.org/10.1007/978-3-319-63697-9_21
3. Borisov, N., Goldberg, I., Brewer, E.: Off-the-record communication, or, why not to use PGP. In: Proceedings of the 2004 ACM Workshop on Privacy in the Electronic Society, WPES 2004, pp. 77–84. ACM, New York (2004)
4. Canetti, R., Krawczyk, H.: Analysis of key-exchange protocols and their use for building secure channels. In: Pfitzmann, B. (ed.) EUROCRYPT 2001. LNCS, vol. 2045, pp. 453–474. Springer, Heidelberg (2001). https://doi.org/10.1007/3-540-44987-6_28
5. Cohn-Gordon, K., Cremers, C., Dowling, B., Garratt, L., Stebila, D.: A formal security analysis of the signal messaging protocol. In: 2017 IEEE European Symposium on Security and Privacy (EuroS&P), pp. 451–466, April 2017
6. Cohn-Gordon, K., Cremers, C., Garratt, L.: On post-compromise security. In: 2016 IEEE 29th Computer Security Foundations Symposium (CSF), pp. 164–178, June 2016
7. Derler, D., Jager, T., Slamanig, D., Striecks, C.: Bloom filter encryption and applications to efficient forward-secret 0-RTT key exchange. In: Nielsen, J.B., Rijmen, V. (eds.) EUROCRYPT 2018. LNCS, vol. 10822, pp. 425–455. Springer, Cham (2018). https://doi.org/10.1007/978-3-319-78372-7_14

8. Betül Durak, F., Vaudenay, S.: Bidirectional asynchronous ratcheted key agreement with linear complexity. https://eprint.iacr.org/2018/889.pdf
9. Günther, F., Hale, B., Jager, T., Lauer, S.: 0-RTT key exchange with full forward secrecy. In: Coron, J.-S., Nielsen, J.B. (eds.) EUROCRYPT 2017. LNCS, vol. 10212, pp. 519–548. Springer, Cham (2017). https://doi.org/10.1007/978-3-319-56617-7_18
10. Jaeger, J., Stepanovs, I.: Optimal channel security against fine-grained state compromise: the safety of messaging. In: Shacham, H., Boldyreva, A. (eds.) CRYPTO 2018. LNCS, vol. 10991, pp. 33–62. Springer, Cham (2018). https://doi.org/10.1007/978-3-319-96884-1_2. Full version: https://eprint.iacr.org/2018/553.pdf
11. Jost, D., Maurer, U., Mularczyk, M.: Efficient ratcheting: almost-optimal guarantees for secure messaging. In: Ishai, Y., Rijmen, V. (eds.) EUROCRYPT 2019. LNCS, vol. 11476, pp. 159–188. Springer, Cham (2019). https://doi.org/10.1007/978-3-030-17653-2_6. Full version: https://eprint.iacr.org/2018/954.pdf
12. LaMacchia, B., Lauter, K., Mityagin, A.: Stronger security of authenticated key exchange. In: Susilo, W., Liu, J.K., Mu, Y. (eds.) ProvSec 2007. LNCS, vol. 4784, pp. 1–16. Springer, Heidelberg (2007). https://doi.org/10.1007/978-3-540-75670-5_1
13. Ohkubo, M., Suzuki, K., Kinoshita, S.: Cryptographic approach to "privacy-friendly" tags. In: RFID Privacy Workshop (2003)
14. Ohkubo, M., Suzuki, K., Kinoshita, S.: Efficient hash-chain based RFID privacy protection scheme. In: International Conference on Ubiquitous Computing (Ubicomp), Workshop Privacy: Current Status and Future Directions (2004)
15. Poettering, B., Rösler, P.: Towards bidirectional ratcheted key exchange. In: Shacham, H., Boldyreva, A. (eds.) CRYPTO 2018. LNCS, vol. 10991, pp. 3–32. Springer, Cham (2018). https://doi.org/10.1007/978-3-319-96884-1_1. Full version: https://eprint.iacr.org/2018/296.pdf
16. Open Whisper Systems. Signal protocol library for Java/Android. GitHub repository (2017). https://github.com/WhisperSystems/libsignal-protocol-java
17. Unger, N., et al.: SoK: secure messaging. In: 2015 IEEE Symposium on Security and Privacy, pp. 232–249, May 2015
18. WhatsApp. Whatsapp encryption overview. Technical white paper (2016). https://www.whatsapp.com/security/WhatsApp-Security-Whitepaper.pdf

A New Approach to Constructing Digital Signature Schemes
(Short Paper)

Ahto Buldas[1], Denis Firsov[1,2], Risto Laanoja[1,2], Henri Lakk[2],
and Ahto Truu[1,2(✉)]

[1] Tallinn University of Technology, Akadeemia tee 15a, 12618 Tallinn, Estonia
[2] Guardtime AS, A. H. Tammsaare tee 60, 11316 Tallinn, Estonia
ahto.truu@guardtime.com

Abstract. A new hash-based, server-supported digital signature scheme
was proposed recently in [7]. We decompose the concept into *forward-resistant tags* and a generic *cryptographic time-stamping* service. Based
on the decomposition, we propose more tag constructions which allow
efficient digital signature schemes with interesting properties to be built.
In particular, the new schemes are more suitable for use in personal signing devices, such as smart cards, which are used infrequently. We define
the forward-resistant tags formally and prove that (1) the discussed constructs are indeed tags and (2) combining such tags with time-stamping
services gives us signature schemes.

1 Introduction

Recently, Buldas, Laanoja, and Truu [7] proposed a new type of digital signature
scheme (which we will refer to as the *BLT scheme* in the following) based on the
idea of combining one-time time-bound keys with a time-stamping service. A
limitation of the BLT scheme is the fact that keys are pre-generated and have to
be used at their designated time-slots only. On practical parameters the number
of keys is rather large, which would make key generation on resource-constrained
platforms prohibitively slow.

BLT scheme prevents other parties from misusing keys by making each key
expire immediately after a legitimate use. First, each key is explicitly bound to a
time slot at the key-generation time, and keys would automatically expire when
their designated time-slots passed. Second, the legitimate use of a key is proven
by time-stamping the message-key pair. Back-dating a new pair (a new message
with an already used key) would allow a signature to be forged. Therefore, the
hash-then-publish time-stamping [12] that avoids key-based cryptography and
trusted third parties is particularly suitable for the scheme.

This research was supported by the European Regional Development Fund through
the Estonian smart specialization program NUTIKAS and by the research measure of
the Estonian IT Academy programme.

N. Attrapadung and T. Yagi (Eds.): IWSEC 2019, LNCS 11689, pp. 363–373, 2019.
https://doi.org/10.1007/978-3-030-26834-3_21

Based on this observation, we generalize and decompose the scheme into two functional components: *forward-resistant tags* and a *cryptographic time-stamping* service. As the forward-resistant tag is a novel construct, we define it formally and prove that the BLT scheme is indeed an instance of forward-resistant tag-based schemes. We then propose other forward-resistant tag systems, prove their security, and observe that the resulting new signature schemes are efficient and have some interesting properties.

2   Related Work and Background

Due to space constraints, we refer the reader to either [7] or the extended e-print [4] for overview of related work on **hash-based signatures, server-assisted signatures**, and **interactive signature protocols**.

Non-Repudiation. An important property of digital signatures (as an alternative to hand-written ones) [10] is non-repudiation, i.e. the possibility to use the signature as evidence against the signer. Solutions where trusted third parties are (technically) able to sign on behalf of their clients are not desirable for non-repudiation, because clients may use that argument to fraudulently call their signatures into question. Therefore, solutions where clients have personal signature devices are preferable to those relying entirely on trusted parties.

Another real-world complexity is key revocation. Without such capability clients may (fraudulently) claim that their private keys were stolen and someone else may have created signatures in their name. With revocation tracking, signatures created before a key revocation event can be treated as valid, whereas signatures created afterwards can be considered invalid. Usually this is implemented using cryptographic time-stamping and certificate status distribution services. No matter the implementation details, this can not be done without online services, which means that most practical deployments of digital signatures are actually server-supported.

Cryptographic Time-Stamping. Cryptographic time-stamps prove that data existed before a particular time. The proof can be a statement that the data hash existed at a given time, cryptographically signed by a trusted third party. Haber and Stornetta [12] made the first steps towards trustless time-stamping by proposing a scheme where each time-stamp would include some information from the immediately preceding one and a reference to the immediately succeeding one. Benaloh and de Mare [1] proposed to increase the efficiency of hash-linked time-stamping by operating in rounds, where messages to be time-stamped within one round would be combined into a hierarchical structure from which a compact proof of participation could be extracted for each message. The aggregation structures would then be linked into a linear chain. The security of linking-based hash-then-publish schemes has been proven in a very strong model where even the time-stamping service provider does not have to be trusted [6,8], making them particularly suitable for our use-case. It is possible to provide such service efficiently and in global scale [5].

3   Forward-Resistant Tags

Definition 1 (Tag system). *By a tag system we mean a triple* (Gen, Tag, Ver) *of algorithms, where:*

- *Gen is a probabilistic key-generation algorithm that, given as input the tag range T, produces a secret key* sk *and a public key* pk.
- *Tag is a tag-generation algorithm that, given as input the secret key* sk *and an integer $t \in \{1, \ldots, T\}$, produces a tag $\tau \leftarrow$ Tag(sk, t).*
- *Ver is a verification algorithm that, given as input a tag τ, an integer t, and the public key* pk, *returns either 0 or 1, such that* Ver(Tag(sk, t), t, pk) = 1 *whenever* (sk, pk) $\leftarrow$ Gen(T) *and $1 \leq t \leq T$.*

The above definition of a tag system is somewhat similar to that of a signature scheme consisting of procedures for key generation, signature generation, and signature verification [11]. The fundamental difference is that a signature binds the use of the secret key to a message, while a tag binds the use of the secret key to a time.

Definition 2 (Forward-resistant tag system). *A tag system* (Gen, Tag, Ver) *is S-forward-resistant if every tag-forging adversary A using computational resources ρ has success probability*

$$\Pr\left[(\mathsf{pk}, \mathsf{sk}) \leftarrow \mathsf{Gen}(T), (\tau, t) \leftarrow A^{\mathsf{Tag}(\mathsf{sk}, \cdot)}(\mathsf{pk}) : \mathsf{Ver}(\tau, t, \mathsf{pk}) = 1\right] < \frac{\rho}{S},$$

where A makes one oracle call Tag(sk, t') *with $1 \leq t' < t$.*

The restriction for A to make just one oracle call stems from the fact that the very purpose of a tag system is to bind the use of the secret key to a specific time. Informally, in order to implement a forward resistant tag system, we have to bind each tag to a time t so that the tag can't be re-bound to a later time. This notion could be seen as dual to time-stamping that prevents back-dating.

The resources represented by ρ are computation time and memory. The total resource budget of the adversary is $\rho = \alpha \cdot \text{time} + \beta \cdot \text{memory}$, where α and β are the costs of a unit of computation time and a unit of memory, respectively.

Security proofs of the proposed tag systems will be based on the following definitions of basic cryptographic properties of functions:

Definition 3 (One-way function). *A function $f : D \rightarrow R$ is S-secure one-way (S-OW in short) if every f-inverting adversary A using computational resources ρ has success probability*

$$\Pr\left[x \leftarrow D, x' \leftarrow A^{f(\cdot)}(f(x)) : f(x') = f(x)\right] < \frac{\rho}{S}.$$

Definition 4 (Collision resistant function). *A function $f : D \rightarrow R$ is S-secure collision resistant (S-CR) if for every collision-finding adversary A using computational resources ρ:*

$$\Pr\left[x_1, x_2 \leftarrow A^{f(\cdot)} : x_1 \neq x_2, \ f(x_1) = f(x_2)\right] < \frac{\rho}{S}.$$

Definition 5 (Undetectable function). *A function $f : D \to D$ is S-secure undetectable (S-UD) if for every detecting adversary A using computational resources ρ:*

$$\left| \Pr\left[x \leftarrow \mathcal{U} : A(x) = 1\right] - \Pr\left[x \leftarrow \mathcal{U} : A(f(x)) = 1\right] \right| < \frac{\rho}{S},$$

where $\mathcal{U}$ generates random values uniformly from D.

Lemma 1. *If $f : D \to D$ is S-UD, then f^n is $\frac{S}{n}$-UD. (Proof in the e-print [4].)*

In the following, we will consider general hash functions $f : \{0,1\}^* \to \{0,1\}^k$ mapping arbitrary-length inputs to fixed-length outputs. We will write $f(x_1, x_2)$ or $f(x_1, x_2, \ldots, x_n)$ to mean the result of applying f to a bit-string encoding the pair (x_1, x_2) or the tuple $(x_1, x_2, \ldots, x_n)$, respectively.

Cryptographic Time-Stamping. We model the ideal time-stamping service as a trusted repository R that works as follows:

- The time t is initialized to 1, and all the cells R_i to $\perp$.
- The query $R.\texttt{time}$ is answered with the current value of t.
- The query $R.\texttt{get}(t)$ is answered with R_t.
- On the request $R.\texttt{put}(x)$, first $R_t \leftarrow x$ is assigned and then the value of t is incremented by 1.

This is done for the sake of simplicity. It turns out that refining the model of the time-stamping service would make the proofs really complex. For example, even for a seemingly trivial change, where R publishes a hash $h(m, \tau)$ instead of just (m, τ), one needs non-standard security assumptions about h such as non-malleability. In this paper, we try to avoid these technical difficulties and focus on the basic logic of the security argument of the tag-based signature scheme.

Definition 6 (Induced signature scheme). *A tag system (Gen, Tag, Ver) and a time-stamping repository R induce a one-time signature scheme as follows:*

The signer $S^R(m)$ queries $t \leftarrow R.\texttt{time}$, then creates $\tau \leftarrow \mathrm{Tag}(\mathsf{sk}, t)$, stores $R.\texttt{put}((m, \tau))$, and returns $\sigma = (\tau, t)$.

The verifier $V^R(m, (\tau, t), \mathsf{pk})$ queries $x \leftarrow R.\texttt{get}(t)$, and checks that $x = (m, \tau)$ and $\mathrm{Ver}(\mathsf{pk}, t, \tau) = 1$.

Definition 7 (Existential unforgeability). *A one-time signature scheme is S-secure existentially unforgeable (S-EUF) if every forging adversary A using computational resources ρ has success probability*

$$\Pr\left[(\mathsf{pk}, \mathsf{sk}) \leftarrow \mathrm{Gen}(T), (m, \sigma) \leftarrow A^{S^R, R}(\mathsf{pk}) : V^R(m, \sigma, \mathsf{pk}) = 1\right] < \frac{\rho}{S},$$

where A makes only one S-query and not with m.

Theorem 1. *If the tag system is S-secure forward-resistant then the induced one-time signature scheme is (almost) S-secure existentially unforgeable.*

Proof. Having a ρ-adversary $A^{S^R,R}$ for the signature scheme, we construct an adversary $B^{\mathrm{Tag}(\mathsf{sk},\cdot)}$ for the tag scheme as follows. The adversary B simulates the adversary A by creating a simulated R of its own. A signing query $S(m)$ is simulated by making an oracle query $\tau \leftarrow \mathrm{Tag}(\mathsf{sk},t)$, where t is the time value in the simulated R, and then assigning $R_t \leftarrow (m,\tau)$.

Every time the simulated A makes (a direct) query $R.\mathrm{put}(x)$, B checks whether x is in the form (m,τ) and $\mathrm{Ver}(\mathsf{pk},\tau,t) = 1$, where t is the current time in the simulated R, and then returns (τ,t) if either: (a) A has never made any S-calls, or (b) A has made an S-call with $m' \neq m$.

It is easy to see that one of these events must occur whenever A is successful. In the first case, B is also successful, because it outputs a correct tag without making any $\mathrm{Tag}(\mathsf{sk},\cdot)$-calls. In the second case, the $S(m')$-query was made at $t' < t$ (as every S-query makes one $R.\mathrm{put}(\cdot)$-query which advances t) and then also the $\mathrm{Tag}(\mathsf{sk},t')$-query was made at $t' < t$ and hence B is successful again.

If the overhead of B in simulating the environment for A is small, the reduction is tight and thus the signature scheme must indeed be almost as secure as the underlying tag scheme. □

3.1 The BLT Scheme as a Tag System (BLT-TB)

Ignoring the aggregation of individual time-bound keys into a hash tree, the essence of the BLT signature scheme proposed in [7] can be modeled as a tag system as follows:

- The secret key sk is a list $(z_1, z_2, \ldots, z_T)$ of T unpredictable values and the public key pk the list $(f(z_1), f(z_2), \ldots, f(z_T))$, where f is a one-way function.
- The tagging algorithm $\mathrm{Tag}(z_1, z_2, \ldots, z_T; t)$ outputs z_t.
- The verification algorithm Ver, given as input a tag τ, an integer t, and the public key $(x_1, x_2, \ldots, x_T)$, checks that $1 \leq t \leq T$ and $f(\tau) = x_t$.

We will refer to this model as the BLT-TB tag system.

Theorem 2. *If f is S-OW, then BLT-TB is an $\frac{S}{T}$-forward-resistant tag system.*

Proof. We assume there's a tag-forging adversary A and construct an f-inverting adversary B based on oracle access to A. Since f is S-OW, irrespective of B's construction, its success probability $\delta' < \frac{\rho}{S}$ (Definition 3). We construct B to process the input $x = f(z)$ as follows:

- generate the secret key components $z_i \leftarrow \{0,1\}^k$ and compute the corresponding public key components $x_i = f(z_i)$ for $1 \leq i \leq T$;
- uniformly randomly pick an index $j \leftarrow \{1, \ldots, T\}$;
- call A on a modified public key to produce a forged tag and its index

$$(\tau, t) \leftarrow A^{\mathrm{Tag}(\mathsf{sk},\cdot)}(x_1, \ldots, x_{j-1}, x, x_{j+1}, \ldots, x_T);$$

- if A succeeded and $t = j$ then return τ, else return $\bot$.

By construction, B's success probability $\delta_j = \Pr[A \text{ succeeded} \wedge t = j]$. Since the distribution of x is identical to the distribution of x_i, the events "A succeeded" and "$t = j$" are independent and thus we have $\delta_j = \Pr[A \text{ succeeded}] \cdot \Pr[t = j]$. Since j was drawn uniformly from $\{1, \dots, T\}$, we further have $\delta_j = \delta \cdot \frac{1}{T}$, where δ is A's success probability (Definition 2).

From f being S-OW, we have $\frac{\delta}{T} = \delta_j \leq \delta' < \frac{\rho}{S}$. Thus, $\delta < \frac{\rho}{S/T}$, and BLT-TB is indeed an $\frac{S}{T}$-forward-resistant tag system. □

3.2   The BLT-OT Tag System

We now define the BLT-OT tag system (inspired by Lamport's one-time signatures [9]) as follows:

- The secret key sk is a list $(z_0, z_1, \dots, z_{\ell-1})$ of $\ell = \lceil \log_2(T+1) \rceil$ unpredictable values and the public key pk the list $(f(z_0), f(z_1), \dots, f(z_{\ell-1}))$, where f is a one-way function.
- The tagging algorithm $\text{Tag}(z_0, \dots, z_{\ell-1}; t)$ outputs an ordered subset $(z_{j_1}, z_{j_2}, \dots, z_{j_m})$ of components of the secret key such that $0 \leq j_1 < j_2 < \dots < j_m \leq \ell - 1$ and $2^{j_1} + 2^{j_2} + \dots + 2^{j_m} = t$.
- The verification algorithm Ver, given as input a sequence $(z_{j_1}, z_{j_2}, \dots, z_{j_m})$, an integer t, and the public key $(x_0, x_1, \dots, x_{\ell-1})$, checks that:
  1. $f(z_{j_1}) = x_{j_1}, \dots, f(z_{j_m}) = x_{j_m}$; and
  2. $0 \leq j_1 < j_2 < \dots < j_m \leq \ell - 1$; and
  3. $2^{j_1} + 2^{j_2} + \dots + 2^{j_m} = t$; and
  4. $1 \leq t \leq T$.

Theorem 3. *If f is S-OW, then BLT-OT is an $\frac{S}{\ell}$-forward-resistant tag system. (Proof is very similar to Theorem 2 and available in the e-print [4].)*

3.3   The BLT-W Tag System

We now define the BLT-W tag system (inspired by Winternitz's idea [14] for optimizing the size of Lamport's one-time signatures) as follows:

- The secret key sk is an unpredictable value z and the public key pk is $f^T(z)$, where f is a one-way function.
- The tagging algorithm $\text{Tag}(z; t)$ outputs the value $f^{T-t}(z)$.
- The verification algorithm Ver, given as input a tag τ, an integer t, and the public key x, checks that $1 \leq t \leq T$ and $f^t(\tau) = x$.

Theorem 4. *If f is S_1-OW and S_2-CR and S_3-UD function, then BLT-W is a $\frac{\min(S_1, S_2, S_3)}{2 \cdot T}$-forward-resistant tag system. (Proof is similar to Theorem 2 and available in the e-print [4].)*

4   BLT-OT One-Time Signature Scheme

The signature scheme induced by the BLT-OT tag system according to Definition 6 would require the signer to know in advance the time when its request reaches the time-stamping service. This is hard to achieve in practice, in particular for devices such as smart cards that lack built-in clocks. To overcome this limitation, we construct the BLT-OT one-time signature scheme as follows.

Key Generation. Let ℓ be the number of bits that can represent any time value t when the signature may be created (e.g. $\ell = 32$ for POSIX time up to year 2106). The private key is generated as $\mathsf{sk} = (z_0, z_1, \ldots, z_{\ell-1})$, where z_i are unpredictable values, and the public key as $\mathsf{pk} = f(X)$, where $X = (x_0, x_1, \ldots, x_{\ell-1})$, $x_i = f(z_i)$, and f is a one-way function.

The **public key certificate** should contain (a) the public key pk, (b) the identity ID_c of the client, and (c) the identity ID_s of the designated time-stamping service. Recording the identity of the designated time-stamping service in certificate enables instant key revocation. Upon receiving a revocation notice, the designated service stops serving the affected client, and thus it is not possible to generate signatures using revoked keys.

Signing. To sign a message m, the client:

- gets a time-stamp S_t on the record (m, X, ID_c) from the time-stamping service designated by ID_s;
- extracts the ℓ-bit time value t from S_t and creates the list $W = (w_0, w_1, \ldots, w_{\ell-1})$, where $w_i = z_i$ if the i-th bit of t is 1, or $w_i = x_i = f(z_i)$ otherwise;
- disposes of the private key $(z_0, z_1, \ldots, z_{\ell-1})$ to prevent its re-use;
- emits (W, S_t) as the signature.

Verification. To verify the signature (W, S_t) on the message m against the certificate $(\mathsf{pk}, ID_c, ID_s)$, the verifier:

- extracts time t from the time-stamp S_t;
- recovers the list $X = (x_0, x_1, \ldots, x_{\ell-1})$ by computing $x_i = f(w_i)$ if the i-th bit of t is 1, or $x_i = w_i$ otherwise;
- checks that the computed X matches the public key: $f(X) = \mathsf{pk}$;
- checks that S_t is a valid time-stamp issued at time t by service ID_s on the record (m, X, ID_c).

Using the reduction techniques from previous sections to formally prove the security of this optimized signature scheme is complicated by both the iterated use of f and the more abstract view of the time-stamping service.

Details of other optimized signature schemes are skipped for brevity. Practical properties are discussed in the following section.

5   Discussion

The BLT-TB scheme proposed in [7] works well for powerful devices that are constantly running and have reliable clocks. These are not reasonable assumptions for personal signing devices such as smart cards, which have very limited capabilities and are not used very often. Generating keys could take hours or even days of non-stop computing on such devices. This is clearly impractical, and also wasteful as most of the keys would go unused.

The BLT-OT scheme proposed in Sect. 4 solves the problems described above at the cost of introducing state on the client side. As the scheme is targeted towards personal signing devices, the statefulness is not a big risk, because these devices are not backed up and also do not support parallel processing. The benefit in addition to improved efficiency is that the device no longer needs to know the current time while preparing a signing request. Instead, it can just use the time from the time-stamp when composing the signature.

Table 1. Efficiency of hash-based one-time signature schemes. We assume 256-bit hash functions, 32-bit time values, and time-stamping hash-tree with 33 levels. Times are in hashing operations and signature sizes in hash values. TS in BLT schemes stands for the time-stamping service call.

Scheme	Key generation	Signing time	Verification time	Signature size
Lamport	1 025	1 024	513	256
Winternitz ($w = 4$)	1 089	1 088	1 021	68
BLT-OT	65	64 + TS	33 + 33	32 + 33
BLT-W ($w = 2$)	65	64 + TS	49 + 33	16 + 33

Efficiency as One-Time Scheme. When implemented as described in Sect. 4, the cost of generating a BLT-OT key pair is ℓ random key generations and $\ell + 1$ hashing operations, the cost of signing ℓ hashing operations and one time-stamping service call, and the cost of signature verification at most $\ell + 1$ hashing operations and one time-stamp verification. In this case the private key would consist of ℓ one-time keys and the public key of one hash value, and the signature would contain ℓ hash values and one time-stamp token. The private storage size can be optimized by generating the one-time keys from one true random seed using a pseudo-random generator. Then the cost of signing increases by ℓ operations, as the one-time keys would have to be re-generated from the seed before signing. This version is listed as BLT-OT in Table 1.

Winternitz's idea [14] for optimizing the size of Lamport's one-time signatures [9] can also be applied to BLT-OT. Instead of using one-step hash chains $z_i \rightarrow h(z_i) = x_i$ to encode single bits of t, we can use longer chains $z_i \rightarrow h(z_i) \rightarrow \ldots \rightarrow h^n(z_i) = x_i$ and publish the value $h^{n-j}(z_i)$ in the signature to encode the value j of a group of bits of t. When encoding groups of w bits of

t in this manner, the chains have to be $n = 2^w$ steps long. This version is listed as BLT-W in Table 1. Note that in contrast to applying this idea to Lamport's signatures, in BLT-W no additional countermeasures are needed to prevent an adversary from stepping the hash chains forward: the time in the time-stamp takes that role.

To compare BLT-OT signature sizes and verification times to other schemes, we also need to estimate the size of hash-trees built by the time-stamping service. Even assuming the whole world (8 billion people) will use the time-stamping service in every aggregation round, an aggregation tree of 33 layers will suffice. We also assume that in all schemes one-time private keys will be generated on-demand from a single random seed and public keys will be aggregated into a single hash value. Therefore, the key sizes will be the same for all schemes and are not listed in Table 1.

Table 2. Efficiency of hash-based many-time signature schemes. We assume key supply for at least 3 650 signatures, 256-bit hash functions, 32-bit time values, and time-stamping hash-tree with 33 levels. Times are in hashing operations and signature sizes in hash values. TS in BLT schemes stands for the time-stamping service call.

Scheme	Key generation	Signing time	Verification time	Signature size
XMSS	897 024	8 574	1 151	79
SPHINCS	ca 16 000	ca 250 000	ca 7 000	ca 1 200
BLT-TB	ca 96 000 000	50 + TS	25 + 33	25 + 33
BLT-OT-N	240 900	64 + TS	45 + 33	44 + 33
BLT-W-N ($w = 2$)	240 900	64 + TS	61 + 33	28 + 33

Efficiency as Many-Time Scheme. A one-time signature scheme is not practical by itself. Merkle [13] proposed aggregating multiple public keys of a one-time scheme using a hash tree to produce so-called N-time schemes. Assuming 10 signing operations per day, a set of 3 650 BLT-OT keys would be sufficient for a year. The key generation costs would obviously grow correspondingly. The change in signing time would depend on how the hash tree would be handled. If sufficient memory is available to keep the tree (which does not contain private key material and thus may be stored in regular memory), the authenticating hash chains for individual one-time public keys could be extracted with no extra hash computations. Signature size and verification time would increase by the 12 additional hashing steps linking the one-time public keys to the root of the aggregation tree. This scheme is listed as BLT-OT-N in Table 2, where we compare it with the following schemes:

- XMSS is a stateful scheme, like the N-time scheme built from BLT-OT; the values in Table 2 are computed by taking $N = 2^{12} = 4\,096$ and leaving other parameters as in [3];

- SPHINCS is a stateless scheme and can produce an indefinite number of signatures; the values in Table 2 are inferred from [2] counting invocations of the ChaCha12 cipher on 64-byte inputs as hash function evaluations;
- the values for BLT-TB in Table 2 are from [7].

As can be seen from the table, the performance of BLT-OT as a component in N-time scheme is very competitive when signing and verification time and signature size are concerned. Only SPHINCS has significantly faster key generation, but much slower signing and verification and much larger signatures.

6   Conclusions and Outlook

We have presented a new approach to constructing digital signature schemes from forward-resistant tags and time-stamping services. We observe that this new framework can be used to model an existing signature scheme, and also to construct new ones. The newly derived signature schemes are practical and it would be interesting to further study their security properties, e.g. present security proofs in the standard model. The novel concept of forward-resistant tags has already proven useful, and thus certainly merits further research.

References

1. Benaloh, J., de Mare, M.: Efficient broadcast time-stamping. Technical report, Clarkson University (1991)
2. Bernstein, D.J., et al.: SPHINCS: practical stateless hash-based signatures. In: Oswald, E., Fischlin, M. (eds.) EUROCRYPT 2015. LNCS, vol. 9056, pp. 368–397. Springer, Heidelberg (2015). https://doi.org/10.1007/978-3-662-46800-5_15
3. Buchmann, J., Dahmen, E., Hülsing, A.: XMSS - a practical forward secure signature scheme based on minimal security assumptions. In: Yang, B.-Y. (ed.) PQCrypto 2011. LNCS, vol. 7071, pp. 117–129. Springer, Heidelberg (2011). https://doi.org/10.1007/978-3-642-25405-5_8
4. Buldas, A., Firsov, D., Laanoja, R., Lakk, H., Truu, A.: A new approach to constructing digital signature schemes (extended paper). Cryptology ePrint Archive, Report 2019/673 (2019). https://eprint.iacr.org/2019/673
5. Buldas, A., Kroonmaa, A., Laanoja, R.: Keyless signatures' infrastructure: how to build global distributed hash-trees. In: Riis Nielson, H., Gollmann, D. (eds.) NordSec 2013. LNCS, vol. 8208, pp. 313–320. Springer, Heidelberg (2013). https://doi.org/10.1007/978-3-642-41488-6_21
6. Buldas, A., Laanoja, R., Laud, P., Truu, A.: Bounded pre-image awareness and the security of hash-tree keyless signatures. In: Chow, S.S.M., Liu, J.K., Hui, L.C.K., Yiu, S.M. (eds.) ProvSec 2014. LNCS, vol. 8782, pp. 130–145. Springer, Cham (2014). https://doi.org/10.1007/978-3-319-12475-9_10
7. Buldas, A., Laanoja, R., Truu, A.: A server-assisted hash-based signature scheme. In: Lipmaa, H., Mitrokotsa, A., Matulevičius, R. (eds.) NordSec 2017. LNCS, vol. 10674, pp. 3–17. Springer, Cham (2017). https://doi.org/10.1007/978-3-319-70290-2_1

8. Buldas, A., Saarepera, M.: On provably secure time-stamping schemes. In: Lee, P.J. (ed.) ASIACRYPT 2004. LNCS, vol. 3329, pp. 500–514. Springer, Heidelberg (2004). https://doi.org/10.1007/978-3-540-30539-2_35
9. Diffie, W., Hellman, M.E.: New directions in cryptography. IEEE Trans. Inf. Theory **22**(6), 644–654 (1976)
10. European Commission: Regulation no 910/2014 of the European Parliament and of the Council of 23 July 2014 on electronic identification and trust services for electronic transactions in the internal market and repealing directive 1999/93/EC (eIDAS regulation). Official Journal of the European Union L 257, 73–114 (2014)
11. Goldwasser, S., Micali, S., Rivest, R.L.: A digital signature scheme secure against adaptive chosen-message attacks. SIAM J. Comput. **17**(2), 281–308 (1988)
12. Haber, S., Stornetta, W.S.: How to time-stamp a digital document. J. Cryptol. **3**(2), 99–111 (1991)
13. Merkle, R.C.: Secrecy, authentication and public key systems. Ph.D. thesis, Stanford University (1979)
14. Merkle, R.C.: A digital signature based on a conventional encryption function. In: Pomerance, C. (ed.) CRYPTO 1987. LNCS, vol. 293, pp. 369–378. Springer, Heidelberg (1988). https://doi.org/10.1007/3-540-48184-2_32

Forensics

GRYPHON: Drone Forensics in Dataflash and Telemetry Logs

Evangelos Mantas and Constantinos Patsakis$^{(\boxtimes)}$

Department of Informatics, University of Piraeus, Piraeus, Greece
emantas000@gmail.com, kpatsak@unipi.gr

Abstract. The continuous decrease in the price of Unmanned Aerial Vehicles (UAVs), more commonly known as drones, has pushed their adoption from military-oriented to a wide range of civilian and business applications. Nevertheless, the many features that they offer have started being maliciously exploited. The latter coupled with the fact that accidents or malicious acts may occur to drones has sparked the interest towards drones forensics.

Trying to fill in the gap of the literature, this work focuses on a particular field of drone forensics that of forensics on the flight data logs. Therefore, we investigate one of the most widely used platforms, `Ardupilot` and the dataflash and telemetry logs. In this work, we discuss a methodology for collecting the necessary information, analysing it, and constructing the corresponding timeline. In this regard, we have developed an open source tool that is freely available and tested it on data provided by VTO Labs.

Keywords: UAV · Drone · Forensics · Ardupilot · Log files

1 Introduction

The rise of technology in the last decade contributed to the development of new concepts that may change the world. Unmanned Aerial Vehicle (UAV) refers to any reusable air vehicle that does not have a pilot on board. These vehicles are already changing the modern day society, from the battlefield to everyday commercial use. UAVs, or simply drones, are currently used for military applications, engaging targets, collecting intelligence or used for surveillance assisting the ground troops. Commercial applications are more challenging since they fall under government regulations and require special operation licensing. Infrastructure inspection, package delivery, crop dusting, first aid, emergency response, and civilian transportation were just concepts in the past which are now becoming a reality.

The use of drones in civilian and business applications is steadily increasing. Globally, drone market volume is forecast to reach 4.7 million[1] units by

---

[1] https://www.businesswire.com/news/home/20160509005554/en/Unmanned-Aerial-Vehicles-UAV-Market-Forecast-2020.

© Springer Nature Switzerland AG 2019
N. Attrapadung and T. Yagi (Eds.): IWSEC 2019, LNCS 11689, pp. 377–390, 2019.
https://doi.org/10.1007/978-3-030-26834-3_22

2020 (other estimates are even more optimistic), with the market for commercial application of UAV technology estimated to soar from \$2bn to \$127bn[2]. This growth projects that over time drones are becoming cheaper and easier to use, as well as regulatory progress. Therefore, more and more drones will be flying in public airspace. The trend is shifting from quadcopters with simple flight boards, to machines with computers that run Operating Systems (OS) and execute complex tasks. As a result, a vulnerability in these systems can be exploited with fatal consequences. Since the flight in densely populated areas implies several risks directly [4, 24] or indirectly [22], public safety must be taken into consideration. Even if an accident happens or a drone "falls to the wrong hands", it must be ensured that the responsible for this action will be identified and held accountable. Thus, a forensic analysis of the drone flight is crucial.

It should be highlighted that regardless of how far-fetched UAV criminality may sound, it has constantly been rising leading us to consider far more scenarios than the typical military-oriented. Unfortunately, the list of crimes committed through the use of drones is increasing, not only in terms of numbers but in terms of sophistication. The recent three-day confusion at Gatwick airport due to an unauthorised flight of drones affected almost 140,000 passengers of 1,000 flights[3] in fear of public safety. While this can be considered as the most significant, as it affected the most people and due to the delays it had a huge cost there was no physical harm. Beyond "traditional" privacy violations, drones have been used to smuggle drugs in prisons[4] and across borders[5], spy on houses for burglary[6], record PINs on ATMs[7]. Finally, Hartmann and Giles [11] discuss how exploitation of UAVs can be used to realise cyber power with effect in the real world.

1.1 Scope of This Work

The continuous growth of the autonomous flying vehicles led to many different flight firmware. One of the first was `Ardupilot`[8], initially developed by amateur hobbyists to control their RC model airplanes. It soon grew to an open source software suite, widely adopted by the airspace industry and used by many enterprises because of its flexibility to support different types of autonomous vehicles making it mainstream in the field. Drone companies like `DJI` may hold the majority of the market share [1] but the fact that their proprietary software

---

[2] https://press.pwc.com/News-releases/global-market-for-commercial-applications-of-drone-technology-valued-at-over--127-bn/s/ac04349e-c40d-4767-9f92-a4d219860cd2.

[3] https://www.nytimes.com/2018/12/23/world/europe/gatwick-airport-drones.html.

[4] https://www.bbc.com/news/uk-england-43413134.

[5] https://www.rt.com/news/225051-drone-meth-crash-tijuana/.

[6] https://www.telegraph.co.uk/news/uknews/crime/11613568/Burglars-use-drone-helicopters-to-identify-targe-homes.html.

[7] https://www.belfasttelegraph.co.uk/news/northern-ireland/drone-filmed-peoples-pin-codes-at-co-antrim-atm-34945847.html.

[8] http://ardupilot.org/.

is not openly available and offers limited flexibility for developers through its SDK, makes it less appealing for enterprises that seek customization, high flexibility and robustness in their flying vehicles autopilot firmware, in contrast to the civilian market where consumers opt for a ready-to-fly quadcopter[9].

This work focuses on drone forensics performed on the ground control station of the UAV under investigation, and the logfiles found on the internal memory. More precisely, the research is focused on the investigation of two specific logs for forensic evidence, the dataflash and telemetry logs.

It is clear, that by capturing a drone one may collect a wide range of forensic evidence, from the serial number of the frame of proprietary drones leading to the person who made the purchase, to fingerprints of the pilot or other ground crew. Indeed, a drone might have other connected devices that store data in an SD card and can be used as forensic evidence. A typical example can be considered a camera. Apparently, a camera and the stored data may be a rich source of forensic evidence since the recorded footage might contain not only visual information but metadata in the form of EXIF data [5]. Nevertheless, the above scenario is considered as out of scope and we only focus on forensic's data from the onboard SD card and the ground control station of a drone with the "minimum" setup. Figure 1 illustrates the different aspects that can be used for drone forensics of Ardupilot compliant UAVs.

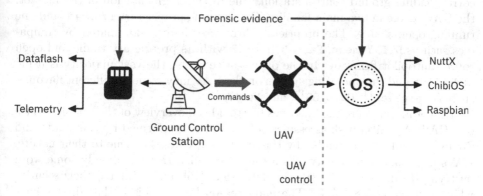

Fig. 1. Sources of forensic evidence of UAVs compliant with Ardupilot.

1.2 Main Contributions

To the best of our knowledge, there is currently no forensics tool for Dataflash log available, nor a detailed methodology on what data need to be collected and how to treat them. To this end, a new tool was created and is available available as an Open Source Project on Github[10]. Existing solutions such as MAVExplorer

---

[9] https://globaluavtech.com/news-media/blog/open-source-ardupilot-software-vs-dji-software/.

[10] http://github.com/emantas/GRYPHON_dft.

mainly focus on displaying data with no flexibility, serving more like diagnostic tools. Since the underlying technology is not stable enough to guarantee that hard changes will not be pushed in the new versions, our forensics tool considers other aspects such as maintainability, flexibility, and sustainability. Therefore, a future update of the MAVlink protocol would have a limited impact in the code compatibility and additions can improve the efficiency and functionality of the forensic research with minimal changes.

1.3 Organisation of This Work

The rest of this work is organised as follows. In the next section, we give a brief overview of the related work in drone forensics. Section 3 describes of the UAV architecture, discussing some specific details regarding the Ardupilot logs. Then, in Sect. 4 we detail our methodology for drone forensics in dataflash and telemetry logs. Finally, the paper concludes, summarising our contributions and discussing open issues and future work.

2 State of the Art

As already discussed, drone forensics can be performed either in the drone or its corresponding ground control station. Due to the fragmentation of the market, the UAVs come in two main families. One running proprietary firmware and one running open-source. The proprietary firmware share is dominated by companies such as DJI, Yuneec, Parrot and 3DR with its proprietary frame and open source autopilot firmware. In the open source share, the vast majority is using Ardupilot and the operating system on the UAV may come in different flavours, such as Raspbian[11], ChibiOS[12], and NuttX[13].

Kim et al. [17] were the first ones to provide an overview of the attack surface of a UAV. An initial risk assessment of UAVs was performed by Hartmann and Steup [12] and later extended by Hartmann and Giles [11]. Due to their nature, UAVs may suffer many networks attacks for which there is already some work on trying to detect them [21], simulate them [16], and reinforce their security while in flight [2,3,8,13,20]. The main reason behind this is that drones have low processing power, so the use of cryptographic primitives implies a significant computational effort. In general, the threats UAVs are exposed to include but are not limited to jamming, interception, and spoofing of the GPS and communications, denial of service, open ports that allow for arbitrary access, injection of forged sensor data [19,23]. For a more detailed overview of these threats for civilian UAVs, the interested reader may refer to [4].

As outlined in [25] IoT forensics imply several new challenges for the forensics investigator as she has to search for evidence in diverse data formats in devices

---

[11] http://ardupilot.org/dev/docs/raspberry-pi-via-mavlink.html.
[12] http://ardupilot.org/copter/docs/common-loading-chibios-firmware-onto-pixhawk.html.
[13] http://ardupilot.org/dev/docs/interfacing-with-pixhawk-using-the-nsh.html.

with different firmware, often proprietary, where physical access to the storage and processing units can be concealed or access-protected. Moreover, digital evidence has a short survival period and many of them reside in the cloud. Bouafif et al. [9] highlight other issues including non-standardization of firmware, hardware, and software, loss of evidence stored in volatile memory due to crash or battery failure, lack of attribution of ownership, and lack of existence of forensics tools or support from mainstream tools.

In the literature, some papers are focusing on data exfiltration from DJI [6, 10, 25] and Parrot [7, 9, 14] drones, but the proposed procedures apply only to specific market models. This paper focuses on a broader spectrum of flying vehicles proposing a forensic methodology applied not only for a civilian hobbyist but also powerful commercial drones. Since the application of drones in everyday life is expected to be expanded, the forensic approach should not be focused on proprietary software, but shifted to open source flight stacks like Ardupilot. This means it is cheaper to acquire or build an open source flying vehicle, making harder to track since there is no financial evidence of a purchase, in contrast to ready-to-fly proprietary drones, or even programming complex flight missions like package deliveries, in the event of an accident or a dreadful scenario.

Other papers focus on technical data, the architecture of components of drones and physical acquisition of the hardware [15]. Although a hardware analysis of the flying vehicles is essential, no hard evidence of malicious behaviour can be extracted, e.g. flying on a no-fly zone. This evidence falls into the scope of software forensics, a scope that this research covers providing a tool to assist the forensic researcher.

There were tries to include the forensic data of open source autopilots, using the telemetry logs [18] provided by the GCS connected to the drone and extracting the flying vehicle's autopilot parameters, but no other data were recovered to perform a thorough forensic examination. However, as it is clearly stated *"GCS and post processing systems, analyzing the sensor data tell 80% of the story"*. This should be the researcher's main focus, exfiltrating the flight data from the log files and if possible acquiring the data from the mobile device's GCS, having the full picture in constructing the forensic's case.

3 Drone Basics

At the very core of a drone is its *flight controller* which is in charge of its avionics, communications, sensor management and other actuators. Due to the complexity of the tasks that have to be performed, the flight controller has changed from simple micro-controllers to small computers, running on a real-time operating system, using a limited processing unit. Depending on the needs, the communication of the drone can be performed over short-range channels including WiFi and Bluetooth, or long-range including radio waves and satellite transmissions.

Before going further, it is essential to distinguish the flight of a UAV from, e.g. a hobbyist's quadcopter. The main difference is the onboard computer, the autopilot. The autopilot manages and orchestrates all the flight components, receives the pilot input from a radio transmitter, and is capable of executing complex commands or taking into action the fail-safe commands automatically, without any manual intervention. For example, a drone can return to the takeoff point, if the autopilot detects that battery level is running low. In this scenario, the drone did not receive any command from a human; the autopilot took control of the flying vehicle. On the contrary, a quadcopter with a flight board receives only the signal from the pilot's radio transmitter. It has limited flight capabilities that depend on the pilot skills. It should be noted that there is a hybrid approach in which the UAV carries out its mission with an operator supervising the progress and intervening when deemed necessary.

Forensic analysis on non-automated vehicles is almost impossible since no events are recorded beyond, e.g. the onboard camera, if one is installed. On the other hand, during the flight of a drone with `Ardupilot` autopilot, two different types of flight logs are generated, the *Dataflash logs* and the *Telemetry logs*. Dataflash logs are generated from the autopilot and are stored on the onboard flash memory, usually an SD card. Telemetry logs are generated from the Ground Control Station (GCS), software to monitor and command the drone, should a connection between the flying vehicle and the GCS be established[14].

When a drone is ready to fly, the pilot should "arm" the system. This command can be given either through a radio transmitter or through a GCS (e.g. Mission Planner, QGroundControl). This command is the "trigger" to generate the Dataflash log. This type of log contains everything that happens during the flight of the drone. More precisely, it contains the values of the RC (Radio Channel) input when the pilot flies manually the drone, the GPS location, values of the onboard sensors, commands sent from the GCS and other data. When the autopilot is connected to a GCS, a Telemetry log is generated and records the flight path, which can be replayed using the Mission Planner GCS.

The autopilot communicates with all the flight components of the drone and transmitters, through the MAVlink (Micro Air Vehicle) Communication Protocol. A MAVlink network is made up of systems (vehicles, GCS, antenna trackers etc.) which are themselves made up of components (Autopilot, camera system, etc.). The protocol defines two IDs that can be specified in messages to control routing of the command to the necessary system and component: the system which will execute the command, called the target system and the component which will execute the command called the target component[15]. MAVLink follows a modern hybrid publish-subscribe and point-to-point design pattern. Data streams are published as topics while configuration sub-protocols such as the mission protocol or parameter protocol are point-to-point with retransmission. These messages are recorded by the autopilot in the Dataflash and Telemetry logs. A proper understanding of this protocol architecture is required to extract

---

[14] http://ardupilot.org/copter/docs/common-diagnosing-problems-using-logs.html.
[15] https://mavlink.io/en/.

the flight data and analyse the recorded events. A MAVLink message is comprised of the following features[16] (Fig. 2):

MAVLink Frame (8 - 263 bytes)

STX	LEN	SEQ	SYS (Sender)	COMP (Sender)	MSG ID	PAYLOAD (0-255 bytes)	CHECKSUM (2 bytes)

MAVLink Frame (11 - 279)

STX	LEN	INC FLAGS	CMP FLAGS	SYS (Sender)	COMP (Sender)	MSG ID (3 bytes)	PAYLOAD (0-255 bytes)	CHECKSUM (2 bytes)	SIGNATURE (13 bytes)

Fig. 2. MAVlink packet architecture. Top: MAVlink v1, Bottom: MAVlink v2. Source: https://mavlink.io/en/guide/serialization.html

- A 24-bit message ID - Allows over 16 million unique message definitions in a dialect (MAVLink 1 was limited to 256).
- Packet signing - Authenticate that messages were sent by trusted systems.
- Message extensions - Add new fields to existing MAVLink message definitions without breaking binary compatibility for receivers that have not updated.

Knowing the structure of each message facilitates the task of a forensic researcher in extracting the necessary data and diagnosing the critical events of the UAV flight.

4 Dataflash and Telemetry Forensics

In what follows we consider that the forensics investigator had access to the ground base station and collected both the telemetry and dataflash logs in a forensics sound manner. Therefore, we discuss how the collected information should be processed and what kind of evidence can be extracted.

4.1 Logfile Acquisition

It is clear that a forensic analysis of a UAV flight requires the generated log files. Although enterprises may come with their own custom logfile genesis solutions for their flying vehicles, the generation of Dataflash and Telemetry logs stays the same.

Telemetry logs, as mentioned before, are automatically generated from the GCS in the computer that is connected to the drone. This type of log file is saved in *.kmz* format and contain the flight path of the vehicle which is replayed, using the GCS built-in functionality.

---

[16] https://mavlink.io/en/guide/mavlink_2.html.

Dataflash logs can be downloaded through a GCS using its built-in functionality or SSH connection to the flying vehicle. The autopilot automatically creates a log file in *.bin* format, after the pilot has armed the drone, saved in the SD card mounted on the autopilot dedicated slot.

It is easily understandable that in the event of a catastrophic failure, e.g. crash-landing, components of the flying vehicle may be damaged or destroyed, dropping the connection between the drone and the GCS. Thus, no log files can be downloaded, and the incidence response will suffice in acquiring the SD card of the autopilot. It is crucial that all the necessary precautions are taken into account in order not to "disturb" the forensic chain of command. This means that an incident response officer should follow all the procedures in ensuring that no key component has been alerted in any way during the acquisition - intentionally or not. For this reason, cloning of the SD card is deemed essential. A further study in the UAV forensic acquisition seems to be decisive in establishing a formal procedure, but this is out of the scope of this research.

4.2 Dataflash Log Analysis Methodology

This research methodology for analysing the Dataflash logs consists of 6 steps. Their scope starts from firmware integrity and goes through trajectory, execution, and error analysis to reach low-level hardware logs and finish with timeline analysis. More precisely, the steps of our methodology are the following:

1. **Check integrity of the UAV:** The goal of this step is to determine whether the firmware running on the drone has been tampered with.
2. **Trajectory analysis:** By visualising the trajectory of the UAV one may determine possible differentiation in the course and decrease the timeline that has to be analysed. For example, one may notice that the trajectory of the UAV is not the expected one after a specific timeframe. Moreover, by detecting anomalies in the trajectories, one may gain further insight on an incident. For instance, a sudden variation in the height of the UAV may imply collision with an object.
3. **Command verification:** The goal of this step is to determine whether all the commands that were submitted by the pilot have been executed.
4. **Error analysis:** In this step, all errors reported by MAVlink are collected to determine whether any of the reported errors resulted in fatal errors or warnings that affected the estimated flight capability.
5. **Analysis of sensors measurements:** The goal of this step is to determine whether all the measurements from the embedded sensors can be considered within the expected range. Anomalies in the sensor measurements may imply a hardware problem in the UAV. Note that such issues may not trigger errors.
6. **Timeline analysis:** A Timeline Analysis is the process of chronologically arranging data of the flight, a crucial part of any digital forensics examination. This part enables the forensic investigator to correlate the found evidence and understand what has happened in the case under investigation (Fig. 3).

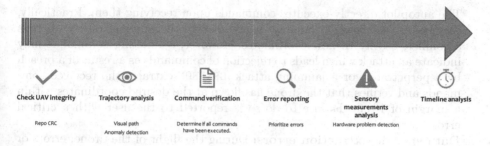

Fig. 3. Brief overview of the proposed methodology.

Based on the above, GRYPHON Drone Forensics Tool provides the following functionality.

– **Extraction of flight data to find anomalies:** The main functionality of GRYPHON is data exfiltration. Since the Dataflash log is in binary format, the recorded flight events must be converted to the corresponding MAVlink format. Multiple independent functions extract and display the data, giving the forensic investigator the ability to monitor the UAV flight behaviour. Each event is displayed with the corresponding timestamp and the value of the MAVlink message recorded. To facilitate reading, we opted for the use of colour coding. Therefore, error information appears in red, whereas warning or medium importance data appear in orange.

– **GPS coordinates mapping:** During the flight, the location of the drone is transmitted using the GPS MAVlink message, which is recorded in the Dataflash logfile. GRYPHON extracts the timestamp, GPS signal strength (e.g. good fix, no signal by correlating numerical value to a readable string output), latitude and longitude as well as the relative altitude (altitude from the ground) and the absolute altitude (altitude from the sea level). These data are displayed along with a coloured output for the GPS signal reception. All data are displayed on a map, using the functionality of mavflightview[17] embedded in the script, revealing the full trajectory of the UAV.

– **Unexpected altitude variation detection:** During the flight, the drone is expected to cruise at a determined altitude. A sudden variation in the altitude within a specific timeframe (from timestamp to timestamp) may imply that the drone is losing altitude from an undetermined factor (e.g. obstacle hit, propeller breakdown). GRYPHON extracts the relative altitude from the GPS and determines if such an unexpected event has occurred.

– **Determine whether a CMD command was executed:** As already discussed, the UAV can execute complex commands given by the pilot through the GCS. A MAVlink CMD message is stored in the Dataflash log, commanding the drone to fly at the coordinations given at a specific altitude.

---

[17] https://github.com/ArduPilot/MAVProxy/blob/master/MAVProxy/tools/mavflightview.py.

The autopilot directly executes commands upon receiving them. Practically, this means that newer commands would discard the previous ones if there is a conflict, e.g. fly to new coordinates. However, conflicting commands may indicate an attack which leads to rejection of commands as a result of a breach by a perpetrator, or a jamming attack. GRYPHON extracts the received commands and verifies that the drone has flown at the desired coordinates within a margin of 10 cm. Failure to do so is reported to the user with a critical error.

- **Data specific extraction errors:** During the flight of the drone, errors or crashes may occur in different flight components (e.g. sensors, GPS, compass). A MAVlink ERR message is stored in the log file and contains the timestamp and the code of the component and the error code. GRYPHON extracts all these error events and performs colour coding, displaying them in red to allow the forensic investigator to distinguish them faster.

- **AC/DC measurements analysis:** A MAVlink CURR message records the battery and flight board voltage and current information. During the flight it is possible that a short circuit or a battery voltage malfunction may occur, resulting in a crash-landing. Extracting the battery voltage and the circuit current consumption gives the forensic researcher the ability to investigate if the values exceeded a 10% acceptable threshold of the median voltage and current value. The latter values are automatically extracted from the PARM messages containing the battery voltage and capacity. These parameter values are given from the pilot of the flying vehicle before the take-off, to ensure that the autopilot can adequately manage the components of the drone.

- **Check CRC from repositories:** The Dataflash log contains the firmware name and its current installed version. A MAVlink MSG message records the firmware info and the vehicle type (e.g. quadrotor, VTOL plane). GRYPHON tries to cross-validate the checksum hash of the firmware of the vehicle with the Ardupilot official Github repository[18]. To achieve this GRYPHON checks whether the collected checksum matches any of the official ones. It should be noted that this indicator can only be considered if a negative result is received. More precisely, if the reported value is aligned with the checksums of the repository, this does not guarantee that the firmware has not been tampered with. Clearly, a tampered firmware can report any value it wants in the log file. However, if the checksum does not match any of the official checksums of the repository, then one can safely assume that the firmware has been tampered with. Unfortunately, vendors do not provide signed hashes of their firmware to facilitate these checks.

- **Timeline Analysis:** As mentioned before the Dataflash log contains all the events recorded during the flight. Only a specific type of messages are useful for forensic analysis. MAVlink messages like GPS, ERR, CURR, MSG, CMD and specific parameters of the flight components (e.g. battery capacity and voltage) have high importance in determining the cause of a failure, or verify that a malicious action took place. After extracting the flight event data,

---

[18] https://github.com/ArduPilot/ardupilot.

GRYPHON sorts the events according to their timestamps, creating a timeline analysis for the forensic investigator. This analysis is generated in a new text file for later use, under the name `logfile_name.bin.analysis`.

4.3 Replaying Data from the Telemetry Log

A useful companion on the forensic research of a flying vehicle is the Telemetry log. When a drone is connected to a GCS on the pilot's device (e.g. a computer, a tablet, a mobile phone), the Telemetry log is generated on the device once the connect button on the GCS is pressed. It contains all the flight data sent to the drone like the Dataflash logfile, but it is a replay log. This means that acquiring and replaying this type of log gives the forensic analyst a better view of the flight. The replay displays all the flight data as if the drone was flying at the moment. Using the built-in functionality of state of the art GCS like the Mission Planner[19], the Telemetry log offers a "real-time" behavioural analysis, from the flight path to the command request and execution. Mission Planner's graphs and other tools like 3D flight path generation for Google Earth, parameters extraction make the visualisation of Telemetry log data easier, multiplying the forensic value of the logs. It must be noted that in the event of a drone crash-landing, the drone should be connected to an associated device GCS to have the Telemetry log in possession. This means that in the dreadful scenario of a drone attack or malicious behaviour (e.g. restricted area flight), the Telemetry log cannot be acquired. Therefore, finding the perpetrator's device connected to the drone lies to the Authorities which have to make a forensic examination to extract the telemetry logs. In any case, the telemetry log is useful for enterprises that maintain fleets of drones to facilitate the forensic examination in case of accidents.

5   Experimental Results

Using the dataset provided from VTO Labs in the Drone Forensics Project[20], we tested the compliance of our tool with the provided binary to determine whether it satisfies the functionalities described in the previous section. More precisely, logs of the `ArduPilot DIY drone` were used since it was the only `Ardupilot` compliant drone available, then we used the tool to another private log file from a drone crash. GRYPHON successfully collected the necessary information from the binaries, extracting the data of various flights. One particular flight serves as an example of the capabilities of the GRYPHON forensic tool. The events of the flight are illustrated in Fig. 4c screenshots of the trajectories of four flights. During the flight of an autonomous flying vehicle a battery failure occurred, resulting in a crash land. The forensic analysis of the events seems to solve the case, see Fig. 4.

---

[19] http://ardupilot.org/planner/.
[20] https://www.droneforensics.com.

(a) Firmware verification and voltage analysis.

(b) Battery failure led to voltage and altitude error detection.

(c) Flight trajectory with colored flight modes to be easily distinguished.

Fig. 4. Screenshots from the trajectory of the crash landing. (Color figure online)

Apart from mapping the trajectories and creating the corresponding timelines, GRYPHON managed to find several events in each flight but no evidence of a malicious act. Each flight mode is displayed in a different colour to facilitate recognition (image flightpath1). GRYPHON reported that during the flight a battery voltage, see Fig. 4, an anomaly caused a crash land. Since the autopilot verified the voltage problem the Return To Land (RTL) mode was automatically triggered. The drone did not manage to return safely to the ground as displayed on and resulted in a crash landing. Additionally, the firmware version of the flying vehicle appears to match the checksum of the Ardupilot Github repository. Therefore, there is no obvious tampering of the firmware.

6   Conclusions

The upcoming rise of the unmanned flying vehicles posses new threats to everyday life. A careful examination of the forensic artifacts should ensure that the perpetrators will face justice or identify the issues that caused e.g. a collision. Since there is no established procedure of drone forensic research to date, this research proposes a detailed plan on how to approach such a challenge from the perspective of the ground control station. We argue that drone forensic examinations should focus on the topics described in this work, despite the wide variety of the underlying autopilot firmware and operating systems. In the future, we plan to extensively test the tool to determine its effectiveness for a proper forensic investigation, leading to a more robust and effective toolkit for a forensic researcher. Nevertheless, we should highlight the lack of available datasets that could be used as baseline for further extension of such work.

Acknowledgements. This work was supported by the European Commission under the Horizon 2020 Programme (H2020), as part of the project YAKSHA (Grant Agreement no. 780498) and is based upon work from COST Action CA17124: *Digital forensics: evidence analysis via intelligent systems and practices* (European Cooperation in Science and Technology).

This paper utilised datasets from droneforensics which is based on research completed by VTO Labs (Colorado, USA); sponsored by the United States Department of Homeland Security (DHS) Science and Technology Directorate, Cyber Security Division (DHS S&T/CSD) via contract number HHSP233201700017C.

References

1. 2018 drone market sector report (2018). http://droneanalyst.com/research
2. Abbaspour, A., Yen, K.K., Forouzannezhad, P., Sargolzaei, A.: A neural adaptive approach for active fault-tolerant control design in UAV. IEEE Trans. Syst. Man Cybern. Syst. **99**, 1–11 (2018)
3. Abbaspour, A., Yen, K.K., Noei, S., Sargolzaei, A.: Detection of fault data injection attack on UAV using adaptive neural network. Proc. Comput. Sci. **95**, 193–200 (2016)
4. Altawy, R., Youssef, A.M.: Security, privacy, and safety aspects of civilian drones: a survey. ACM Trans. Cyber-Phys. Syst. **1**(2), 7 (2017)
5. Alvarez, P.: Using extended file information (EXIF) file headers in digital evidence analysis. Int. J. Digit. Evid. **2**(3), 1–5 (2004)
6. Barton, T.E.A., Azhar, M.A.H.B.: Open source forensics for a multi-platform drone system. In: Matoušek, P., Schmiedecker, M. (eds.) ICDF2C 2017. LNICST, vol. 216, pp. 83–96. Springer, Cham (2018). https://doi.org/10.1007/978-3-319-73697-6_6
7. Barton, T.E.A., Azhar, M.H.B.: Forensic analysis of popular UAV systems. In: 2017 Seventh International Conference on Emerging Security Technologies (EST), pp. 91–96. IEEE (2017)
8. Birnbaum, Z., Dolgikh, A., Skormin, V., O'Brien, E., Muller, D., Stracquodaine, C.: Unmanned aerial vehicle security using recursive parameter estimation. J. Intell. Robot. Syst. **84**(1–4), 107–120 (2016)
9. Bouafif, H., Kamoun, F., Iqbal, F., Marrington, A.: Drone forensics: challenges and new insights. In: 2018 9th IFIP International Conference on New Technologies, Mobility and Security (NTMS), pp. 1–6. IEEE (2018)
10. Clark, D.R., Meffert, C., Baggili, I., Breitinger, F.: DROP (drone open source parser) your drone: forensic analysis of the DJI Phantom III. Digit. Invest. **22**, S3–S14 (2017)

11. Hartmann, K., Giles, K.: UAV exploitation: a new domain for cyber power. In: 2016 8th International Conference on Cyber Conflict (CyCon), pp. 205–221. IEEE (2016)

12. Hartmann, K., Steup, C.: The vulnerability of UAVs to cyber attacks-an approach to the risk assessment. In: 2013 5th International Conference on Cyber Conflict (CyCon), pp. 1–23. IEEE (2013)

13. Hooper, M., et al.: Securing commercial WiFi-based UAVs from common security attacks. In: MILCOM 2016–2016 IEEE Military Communications Conference, pp. 1213–1218. IEEE (2016)

14. Horsman, G.: Unmanned aerial vehicles: a preliminary analysis of forensic challenges. Digit. Invest. **16**, 1–11 (2016)

15. Jain, U., Rogers, M., Matson, E.T.: Drone forensic framework: sensor and data identification and verification. In: 2017 IEEE Sensors Applications Symposium (SAS), pp. 1–6. IEEE (2017)

16. Javaid, A.Y., Sun, W., Alam, M.: UAVSim: a simulation testbed for unmanned aerial vehicle network cyber security analysis. In: 2013 IEEE Globecom Workshops (GC Wkshps), pp. 1432–1436. IEEE (2013)

17. Kim, A., Wampler, B., Goppert, J., Hwang, I., Aldridge, H.: Cyber attack vulnerabilities analysis for unmanned aerial vehicles. In: Infotech@ Aerospace 2012, p. 2438 (2012)

18. Kovar, D., Dominguez, G., Murphy, C.: UAV (aka drone) forensics. Slides of a talk given at SANS DFIR summit in Austin, TX July 7 (2015)

19. Pleban, J.S., Band, R., Creutzburg, R.: Hacking and securing the AR.Drone 2.0 quadcopter: investigations for improving the security of a toy. In: Mobile Devices and Multimedia: Enabling Technologies, Algorithms, and Applications 2014, vol. 9030, p. 90300L. International Society for Optics and Photonics (2014)

20. Schumann, J., Moosbrugger, P., Rozier, K.Y.: R2U2: monitoring and diagnosis of security threats for unmanned aerial systems. In: Bartocci, E., Majumdar, R. (eds.) RV 2015. LNCS, vol. 9333, pp. 233–249. Springer, Cham (2015). https://doi.org/10.1007/978-3-319-23820-3_15

21. Sedjelmaci, H., Senouci, S.M., Messous, M.A.: How to detect cyber-attacks in unmanned aerial vehicles network? In: 2016 IEEE Global Communications Conference (GLOBECOM), pp. 1–6. IEEE (2016)

22. Solodov, A., Williams, A., Al Hanaei, S., Goddard, B.: Analyzing the threat of unmanned aerial vehicles (UAV) to nuclear facilities. Secur. J. **31**(1), 305–324 (2018)

23. Valente, J., Cardenas, A.A.: Understanding security threats in consumer drones through the lens of the discovery quadcopter family. In: Proceedings of the 2017 Workshop on Internet of Things Security and Privacy, pp. 31–36. ACM (2017)

24. Vattapparamban, E., Güvenç, İ., Yurekli, A.İ., Akkaya, K., Uluağaç, S.: Drones for smart cities: Issues in cybersecurity, privacy, and public safety. In: 2016 International Wireless Communications and Mobile computing Conference (IWCMC), pp. 216–221. IEEE (2016)

25. Yaqoob, I., Hashem, I.A.T., Ahmed, A., Kazmi, S.A., Hong, C.S.: Internet of things forensics: recent advances, taxonomy, requirements, and open challenges. Future Gener. Comput. Syst. **92**, 265–275 (2019)

Toward the Analysis of Distributed Code Injection in Post-mortem Forensics

Yuto Otsuki[1]([✉]), Yuhei Kawakoya[1], Makoto Iwamura[1], Jun Miyoshi[1], Jacob Faires[2], and Terrence Lillard[2]

[1] NTT Secure Platform Laboratories,
3-9-11 Midoricho, Musashino-shi, Tokyo 180-8585, Japan
{yuuto.ootsuki.uh,yuuhei.kawakoya.sy,makoto.iwamura.sw,
jun.miyoshi.fu}@hco.ntt.co.jp
[2] NTT Security (US), Inc.,
9420 Underwood Avenue, Omaha, NE 68114, USA
{Jacob.Faires,Terrence.Lillard}@nttsecurity.com

Abstract. Distributed code injection is a new type of malicious code injection technique. It makes existing forensics techniques for injected code detection infeasible by splitting a malicious code into several code snippets, injecting them into multiple running processes, and executing them in each process spaces. In spite of the impact of it on practical forensics fields, there was no discussion on countermeasures against this threat. In this paper, we present a memory forensics method for finding all code snippets distributively injected into multiple processes to defeat distributed code injection attacks. Our method is designed on the following observation for distributed code injection attacks. Even though malicious code is split and distributed in multiple processes, the split code snippets have to synchronize each other at runtime to maintain the order of the execution of the original malicious code. We exploit this characteristic of distributed code injection attacks with our method. The experimental results showed that our method successfully found all distributed code snippets and assisted to reconstruct the original code from them. We believe that we are the first to present a countermeasure against distributed code injection attacks. We also believe that our method is able to improve the efficiency of forensics especially for a host compromised with distributed code injection attacks.

Keywords: Memory forensics · Code injection · Malware analysis

1 Introduction

Protecting premises from malware infections has become harder in each year with the increasing prevalence of more sophisticated attacks and nation-state sponsored attacks [5]. In response to this situation, the cybersecurity industry has been shifting its focus to post-mortem investigations, i.e., forensics. Forensic investigators gather artifacts left behind in a malware-infected host and uncover

© Springer Nature Switzerland AG 2019
N. Attrapadung and T. Yagi (Eds.): IWSEC 2019, LNCS 11689, pp. 391–409, 2019.
https://doi.org/10.1007/978-3-030-26834-3_23

what (malicious) activities malware performed on the host. From that gathered evidence, investigators seek to determine the causes of the infection and provide recommendations to recover from the attack and protect the environment from future similar attacks.

A problem shared among forensics practitioners is the difficulty of finding injected malicious code when analyzing a memory dump acquired from an infected host. This is because there is no evidence to know which process or thread placed the code when you find suspicious code regions. That is, we do not know whether a process or thread created the region by itself or another process or thread injected that. To handle this difficulty, there are several studies for detecting injected code in forensics scenarios [2,6,7,11,17,19,20,24].

We categorize existing detection techniques for code injection into three groups on the basis of their target data: memory contents, memory-management data, and execution states. Among them, pattern-matching on memory contents is one of the most commonly used approaches in practical forensics since it likely has fewer false positives than the other approaches. This is because this approach directly targets injected code, whereas the others indirectly target injected code, i.e., they search for the features often seen around injected code, such as memory regions with the writable and executable attributions or non-file-mapped regions. Thus, forensics practitioners mainly use pattern-matching approaches and use the other approaches complementarily.

In this situation, distributed code injection attacks have emerged as a new type of code injection technique. This technique is composed of code splitting at pre-runtime and; injection and coordination during runtime. It circumvents pattern-matching approaches by breaking a specific detectable byte pattern into multiple non-detectable smaller parts. Theoretically, it can split the malicious code at instruction-level granularity. That is, this technique makes it difficult to generate a pattern for detection with more than one instruction. Thus, we have to rely on non-pattern-matching approaches, even though pattern-matching is the most effective approach for finding injected code in forensics scenarios. This is a challenging problem because, as we mentioned above, the other approaches may generate more false positives than pattern-matching. We need to consider a different technique for reducing false positives so that we make the other approaches practical.

To solve this problem, we present a method to identify all malicious code snippets injected into multiple benign processes. The key idea of our method is to combine a stack-tracking-based technique for code injection detection with a technique for finding threads holding or waiting for synchronization objects. If we only have a stack-tracing-based technique, we have to find code snippets that are not related to distributed code injection attacks, such as just-in-time-compiled (JIT) code. To eliminate those code snippets, we focus on synchronization objects to find the relationship between threads holding the objects and threads waiting for them. This design decision is based on the following observation. The distributed code snippets have to communicate with each other to maintain the order of the execution of the original code, even though they separately reside in multiple processes. We exploit this characteristic by clarifying the mediator for the communication and extracting threads related to that to find the all code snippets executed by the threads.

We implemented our method as a plugin of Rekall [6] and performed an experiment to assess whether our method works as designed. The experimental results show that our method correctly finds all code snippets, which were distributively injected into eight benign processes. In this experiment, we used malWASH[1] as a representation of distributed code injection attack for protecting a simple program, which creates a file, writes data into the file, and sleeps.

We have to acknowledge that, in this paper, we demonstrate only a detection technique for distributed code injection attacks and do not present any technique to reconstruct the entire original code in for analysis. However, we argue that our paper is valuable because distributed code injection attacks will probably be a real intrusion threat in the near future. This is because this attack is easy-to-use for attackers (i.e., they can easily embed this attack into their malware, like a runtime packer) and is the sole solution to defeat several security mechanisms, such as pattern-matching or behavioral detection. Moreover, neither industry nor academia has discussed countermeasures against this attack. As far as we know, we are the first to shed light on a countermeasure against distributed code injection attacks and present an approach to detect them by reasonably extending existing techniques for forensics.

The contributions of this paper are as follows.

- We present our method for finding all distributed code snippets. Our method mainly focuses on *stack traces* and *synchronization objects* to connect the split code snippets residing in different processes via threads holding or waiting for synchronization objects.
- We propose a technique using synchronization objects to reduce false positives that occur when using the stack-tracing-based technique. Specifically, we can eliminate code snippets associated with a just-in-time-complied code.
- We implemented our method into a plugin of Rekall [6] and performed an experiment with malWASH. This experimental results show that our plugin works as we design.
- We explain the details of the implementations of our method in Appendix A so that readers can trace our implementations and the experiment, i.e., for the reproducibility.

2   Background

In this section, we first mention existing detection techniques of code injection attacks by categorizing them into three groups on the basis of the target data for detection: on-memory contents, memory-management data, and execution states. Also, we explain distributed code injection attacks using the modified version of malWASH, as an example of distributed code injection attacks.

---

[1] We modified the code of malWASH, which was downloaded from [9], for fixing bugs.

2.1 Code Injection Detection

We categorized existing techniques for code injection detections into three groups on the basis of the target data (evidence) with which they used to identify injected code: on-memory contents of injected code, system data for memory-management, and the frozen execution state. Then, we consider the applicability of these three approaches for forensics analysis from the viewpoint of false positives.

On-memory Contents. The code and data of malware are likely to have unique byte patterns that have enough characteristics for distinguishing the malware from other malware and benign programs. Injected code and data left in a memory dump are also likely to have such a pattern. We can identify the injected code by finding the associated patterns in the virtual memory space of benign processes. Signature-based scanners like `yarascan` [4, 24] have the capability to detect injected code of known malware on memory. Barabosch et al. [2] proposed a machine-learning-based approach, named Quincy. In their proposal, they define 38 features associated with the injected code, which include features of both on-memory contents and memory-management data. Their experimental results show that many features depending on memory contents contribute relatively more to distinguishing injected code than the other features, such as memory-management data.

Memory-Management Data. Memory regions containing injected code are likely to have several unique characteristic properties dissimilar to other regions. For example, whereas the memory regions containing executable code are likely to reside in an image-mapped section, the ones containing injected code are often in private memory regions. Another example is that whereas the memory regions containing executable code are likely to have only the executable permission, the ones containing injected code often have both the executable and writable permissions. `malfind`, an injected code detector included in The Volatility Framework [24], can check both of the above properties to detect injected code in a memory dump. Membrane [19] also use memory-management data as a feature for machine-learning to detect code-injected processes.

Execution States. A memory dump includes the frozen execution states of processes and threads that were running in the environment when the memory dump was captured. These states are helpful for forensic investigators to find processes and threads executing malicious code. In general, operating systems (OSs) have to save the last execution state of each thread into memory when context switching occurs. Because of this, we can retrieve the stored execution state from a memory dump [18, 21, 23]. Stack-tracing is a technique that allows us to extract the partial execution history of each thread as a call-stack even during post-mortem memory forensics analysis [1, 8, 18, 20, 21, 23]. We can assume that each memory region containing the instructions pointed to by the last execution state or call-stack of each thread should be a candidate of injected code regions [20].

Applicability. Many forensics practitioners prefer to use on-memory content techniques during investigations. This is because this approach tends to have fewer false positives, even though it requires additional effort to create a signature containing patterns for detections. One advantage of the on-memory content approach over the others is that it finds malicious code or data directly, whereas the other approaches find them indirectly. Due to this, the other approaches (memory-management data and execution states) are likely to have more false positives than on-memory contents. This is because, as we already mentioned, these approaches focus on the properties that may appear in a memory region containing malicious code. They do not find the actual injected malicious code itself. One such false positive is JIT compiled code. When JIT code is contained in a memory dump these approaches label the code region as suspicious and generates a false positive. To avoid these false positives, forensics practitioners only use these two approaches to complement on-memory contents approaches and do not use them separately.

2.2 Distributed Code Injection Attacks

Distributed code injection is an evolved version of a code injection attack. This technique first chops an executable (the original code) into small pieces of code (code snippets). Then, at runtime, it injects the code snippets into multiple running processes. The emulator of a code snippet coordinates with other processes to maintain the consistency of the execution of the original code.

The main purpose of distributed code injection attacks is to evade pattern-matching based detection. Theoretically, this technique allows attackers to split the code of malware at instruction-level granularity, i.e., injecting only one machine-language instruction into a single process, for avoiding patterns. Because of this, we cannot make a pattern matching more than one instruction to detect the malicious code. This restriction is probably too severe to create a pattern that can sufficiently distinguish the injected code from any other code.

malWASH [10] is an example of distributed code injection attacks. We can download the code from [9] and try it in our environment. The use of malWASH is as a running example throughout this paper.

Figure 1 explains the details of the behavior of malWASH. malWASH has two phases: pre-runtime and runtime. In the pre-runtime phase, malWASH receives an executable file and splits the file into several code snippets. It generates an injector, which is an executable file responsible for injecting and initializing the code snippets and the emulator. The code snippets are stored as a payload in the injector. When the injector is executed it injects the code snippets and threads into multiple running processes and each thread executes one of the code snippets inside each process. Figure 2 details the state transition of the emulator in a code snippet. The emulator of a code snippet starts its execution with the state waiting for a specific synchronization object. When it successfully acquires the object, it first checks the order of execution. The order of execution is managed by each emulator. That is, each emulator knows which code block is the next to be executed after its code snippet. When the emulator checks the

order of execution, if the next execution is itself, the emulator starts executing
its code snippet. After the execution has been done, the emulator updates the
next executing block, releases the object, and then returns to the waiting state.

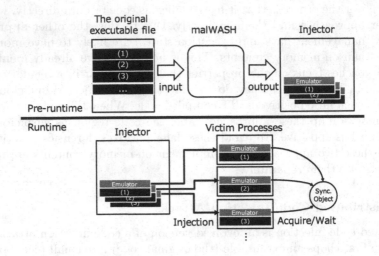

Fig. 1. Overview of malWASH.

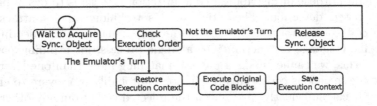

Fig. 2. State transition of the emulator of malWASH.

3 Proposal

In this section, we introduce our specialized memory forensic method for finding
split code snippets for a distributed code injection attack. First, we define the
problem we solve in this paper. Next, we explain the overview of our method.
Then, we dive into its details, i.e., stack traces and synchronization objects.
All implementations presented in this section were targeted for Windows 8.1
x64 environment. We will discuss the platform dependency of our method in
Sect. 5.2.

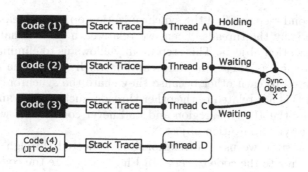

Fig. 3. Linked code snippets via threads sharing a synchronization object.

3.1   Problem Definition

As we explained in Sect. 2.2, distributed code injection attacks make pattern-matching-based approaches infeasible. Thus, we should no longer rely on pattern-matching approaches to fight against distributed code injection attacks. Given that fact, we must rely on memory-management data or execution states to detect them. However, as we also explained, these two approaches are likely to have false positives and negatives, respectively. Therefore, we need a technique to reduce them if we integrate either of these approaches into our method.

In summary, we define the problem to solve in this paper as the following two areas. First, we explore a suitable approach for detecting distributed code injection attacks. Second, we propose a technique, which could be used with the first technique, to reduce false positives. After this subsection, we will explain our method, which is designed to solve the two problem areas.

3.2   Overview

The goal of our method is to find all code snippets that will be coordinating to form the original malicious code, which are distributed to multiple running processes. To achieve the goal, our basic idea is to relate code snippets found in benign processes via threads; we also relate the threads via synchronization objects.

1. Build *Code to Thread* link with stack traces.
2. Build *Thread to Thread* link with synchronization objects.
3. Build *Code to Code* link with the links built in the 1 and 2 steps.

We explain each step of our method by illustrating in Fig. 3. As the first step, we enumerate threads which were running when we acquired a memory dump and then build the stack trace of each of them. Next, we select suspicious code regions from the ones pointed to by the pointers in a stack trace, as a candidate of the code snippets. In Fig. 3, we select the code region (1), (2), (3), and (4) since each of them is pointed to from the stack trace of the thread A, B, C, and D, respectively.

For the second step, we find the synchronization objects which are owned or being waited for by the threads. Then, we relate each thread that handles the same synchronization objects. This step mainly allows us to eliminate unrelated code snippets, such as JIT, from valid candidates. In Fig. 3, the thread A, B, and C are related to each other because they share the synchronization object X. The thread D is not related to the other threads, such as A, B and C, because it was executing the JIT code region and and never coordinates with the other threads via the synchronization object X.

For the last step, we use the relationships collected through the first and second steps to relate the code to code. In Fig. 3, we relate the code regions (1), (2), and (3) via the thread A, B, and C sharing the synchronization object X. Thus, we define the code region (1), (2), and (3) as the code snippets placed for a distributed code injection attack.

After collecting all dependent code snippets of the original code, we have to reconstruct the original code from the code snippets. In this paper, we mainly focus on the collection phase of the distributed code snippets. We define the phase for reconstructing the original code from the collected code snippets as the out-of-scope of this paper.

Our method is implemented as a plugin for Rekall 1.6.0 [6], which is a memory forensics framework forked from The Volatility Framework [24].

3.3   *Code to Thread* Link

The goal of this phase is to establish a relationship between the code and the thread executing the code. As we mentioned above, our method is to relate code via threads. For the first step for realizing our method, we perform stack-tracking for each thread listed from a memory dump. Then, we examine the code pointed to by the pointers in the collected stack trace to check if it is suspicious, in other words, check if the code is part of the original code. If a pointer points to suspicious code, we identify that the thread was executing a code snippet and then establish a relationship between the code and the thread.

Stack Tracing. Stack-tracing is a technique to generate the stack trace of a thread. A stack trace is a set of the return addresses of called functions. These addresses point to the code being executed by the thread. We take advantage of this feature of a stack trace to link a thread with code, which is executed by the thread.

To build the stack traces for each thread from a memory dump, we use the existing stack-tracing method proposed by Otsuki et al. [18]. Their method can extract the last execution state and the stack traces of each thread from a memory dump without depending on Windows x64 or x86 environments. The method is built on a control flow analysis combined with several forensics techniques, which focus on some data structures for exceptional handlings, such as RUNTIME_FUNCTIONs, UNWIND_INFOs, and UNWIND_CODEs.

Table 1. Rules for suspicious code detection.

Memory page type	Detection condition
Type I	$(Rule1 \lor Rule2) \land \neg Rule3$
Type II	$Rule3 \land \neg Rule4$
Type III	$Rule3 \land Rule4 \land \neg Rule5$
Type IV	$(Rule1 \lor Rule2) \land Rule3 \land Rule4$

Suspicious Code Detection. The stack trace of a thread contains the pointers to the code being executed, i.e., called, by the thread at the specific time. It contains both pointers to a benign or malicious code. We need to filter out the pointers to benign code regions and pick out all pointers to malicious code regions so that the malicious code region pointed to from a stack trace becomes a candidate of code snippets.

To do that, we focus on four types of memory pages containing code pointed from the pointers of a stack trace.

- Type I: No file-backed pages with executable, writable, and dirty attributes.
- Type II: Executable and file-backed pages but have no executable image files
- Type III: Invalid executable image file-backed pages
- Type IV: Modified executable image file-backed pages

To find these pages, we define the five rules on the basis of our own heuristics. Each rule is expressed as a predicate, which is a question for which we can answer either true ($\top$) or false ($\bot$). The rules are as follows.

- $Rule1$: Is the page writable?
- $Rule2$: Is the page dirty?
- $Rule3$: Is the page file-backed?
- $Rule4$: Is the page in an image mapped section?
- $Rule5$: Is the page in a region starting with the valid PE header?

To find each type of memory page, we define the conditions by combining some of the rules, as shown in Table 1. For Type I, either $Rule1$ or $Rule2$ should be $\top$ and $Rule3$ should be $\bot$. For Type II, $Rule3$ should be $\top$ and $Rule4$ should be $\bot$. For Type III, both $Rule3$ and $Rule4$ should be $\top$ and $Rule5$ should be $\bot$. For Type IV, either $Rule1$ or $Rule2$ should be $\top$ and both $Rule3$ and $Rule4$ should be $\top$. When we find a memory page satisfying more than one of these conditions, we label the memory region containing the page as a candidate of the code snippets.

3.4   *Thread to Thread* Link

The goal of this phase is to make a relationship between a thread and other threads based on synchronization objects to eliminate code snippets which are not related to a distributed code injection attack. The stack-tracking based technique for detecting suspicious code regions, which was explained in the previous subsection, sometimes generates false positives. This is because, as we explained in Sect. 2.1, this technique does not directly detect malicious contents. This technique detects attributes often seen around injected code and indirectly detects the injected code. Due to this, if a benign program uses a technique leaving artifacts similar with ones of code injections, such as JIT compiled code, we label the region containing JIT code as a suspicious region.

To avoid these cases, we focus on synchronization objects. This is because all code snippets of the distributed code injection attack need to use them for communicating to other threads, and code snippets not related to the attack probably do not have them. For example, in the case of Fig. 3, thread A holds a synchronization object, and other threads B and C wait for the object, we establish a relationship between these four threads A, B, and C via the synchronization object. When a thread does not have any synchronization object, we do not handle the thread as a part of distributed code injection attacks. Thus, we simply ignore it.

3.5   *Code to Code* **Link**

The goal of this phase is to relate a code snippet to another code snippet via threads. We already have the relationships of *Code to Thread* and *Thread to Thread*. We use these relationships to find a new relationship between different code snippets residing benign processes. We define these related two code snippets as a part of the original code was split to perform the distributed code injection attacks. We iterate this relationship traveling and collect all code snippets related to each other. These collected code snippets become the parts for reconstructing the original code.

4   Experiment

In this section, we explain the experiment we had to show the effectiveness of our method. In this experiment, we used a simple program protected with malWASH as the dataset.

4.1   Setup

We explain the dataset prepared for this experiment and the environment where we conducted it.

We first downloaded the original code of malWASH from [9] and then modified it for fixing several bugs and stably performing distributed code injection attacks. Also, we implemented the program for being protected with malWASH by ourselves for this experiment. This program is a 32-bit program that creates a file, writes its thread identifier (TID) into the file, and then sleeps indefinitely. When we protected the program with malWASH, we configured malWASH to

Table 2. The ground truth.

PID	Address	TID
424	0x3a0000	1896
1628	0x3c0000	1776
1860	0xca0000	2464
2240	0x700000	2292
2492	0xe60000	2380
2596	0xb00000	2808
2604	0x7a0000	1164
2800	0x370000	1532

split the executable into code snippets at the basic block granularity and inject the code snippets into eight running processes. Then, we generated the injector of malWASH. Additionally, as a process for being injected a code snippet into by malWASH, we prepared a 32-bit victim program, which simply sleeps.

We conducted the experiment on the Windows 8.1 x64 environment, which was running as a guest OS on VMware. Note that it is as per the instructions in [9] that we prepared both the malWASH-protected program and the victim program as a 32-bit program and executed them on the Windows 8.1 x64 environment.

4.2   Procedure

First, we created the eight processes from the victim program and let them start sleeping. Next, we ran the injector of malWASH on the same environment to let it inject all the code snippets into the victim processes and start the emulators in each process. After the injector finished its jobs, the injector stopped its execution and exited. Then, we suspended the guest OS and generated a memory dump from it.

We read the memory dump with Rekall and ran the plugin in which our method is implemented. The plugin outputted the logs related to *Code to Thread, Thread to Thread,* and *Code to Code* links. To assess if our method correctly works, we modified the malWASH code to generate the ground truth that contains the addresses where the injected code snippets were stored, the process identifiers (PIDs) to identify processes into which the code snippets were injected, and the TIDs[2] that executed the code snippets. Lastly, we compared the outputs of our plugin to the ground truth to assess if our plugin successfully collected all code snippets injected to the victim processes.

---

[2] Note that a TID is *globally* unique in the Windows environment while a thread with the TID is alive. We can use a TID to identify the thread uniquely.

```
* Code to Thread Links
Executor Thread: tid=1896
   - Suspicious Region: pid= 424, address=0x0000003a0000

Executor Thread: tid=1776
   - Suspicious Region: pid=1628, address=0x0000003c0000

Executor Thread: tid=2292
   - Suspicious Region: pid=2240, address=0x000000700000

Executor Thread: tid=2808
   - Suspicious Region: pid=2596, address=0x000000b00000

Executor Thread: tid=2464
   - Suspicious Region: pid=1860, address=0x000000ca0000

Executor Thread: tid=1164
   - Suspicious Region: pid=2604, address=0x0000007a0000

Executor Thread: tid=2380
   - Suspicious Region: pid=2492, address=0x000000e60000

Executor Thread: tid=1532
   - Suspicious Region: pid=2800, address=0x000000370000
```

Fig. 4. The results of *Code to Thread* step. We built a link as a pair of a Suspicious Region and an Executor Thread. tid is the TID of the Executor Thread executing the Suspicious Region placed at the address of the process whose PID is pid.

4.3 Results

Table 2 shows the ground truth of this experiment. For example, the first line tells that a code snippet was placed at the 0x3a0000 address by the injector, the process whose PID is 424 executed the code snippet, and the thread whose TID is 1896 executed the code snippet. We used this result as the ground truth with which to compare the output of our plugin.

Figures 4, 5 and 6 show the output of our plugin, which shows that our method worked correctly. The output includes three types of links: *Code to Thread* (Fig. 4), *Thread to Thread* (Fig. 5), and *Code to Code* (Fig. 6). We explain each link one by one below.

Figure 4 shows that our plugin found eight threads executing suspicious code regions. For example, the thread whose TID is 1896 executed a suspicious code region placed at the address 0x0000003a0000. This is in the memory space of the process whose PID is 424. If we compare the *Code to Thread* links to the ground truth, shown in Table 2, we found that our method precisely established all the relationships between code to thread. Figure 5 shows that our plugin found a semaphore object named "ControlAccess1" that was owned by a thread whose TID is 2808 and being waited for by the other seven threads. When we investigated the source code of malWASH, we found that the name was used for a semaphore for coordination. Thus, we confirmed that our plugin successfully found the semaphore object created by the emulator of a code snippet. Also,

```
* Thread to Thread Links
Synchronization Object: type=SemaphoreObject, name="ControlAccess1", limit=1
        - Running Thread: tid=2808
        - Waiting Thread: tid=2292
        - Waiting Thread: tid=1896
        - Waiting Thread: tid=1164
        - Waiting Thread: tid=2464
        - Waiting Thread: tid=1776
        - Waiting Thread: tid=2380
        - Waiting Thread: tid=1532
```

Fig. 5. The results of *Thread to Thread* step. We can build a link between the running thread and a set of waiting threads. `type` and `name` are the type and name of the `Synchronization Object`, respectively. `limit` is the limit number of the object owner. `Running Thread` is the thread holding the `SemaphoreObject`. `Waiting Thread` is the thread waiting for the `SemaphoreObject`.

```
* Code to Code Links
Code Snippet Group 0:
        - Code Snippets[0]: pid= 424, address=0x0000003a0000
        - Code Snippets[1]: pid=1628, address=0x0000003c0000
        - Code Snippets[2]: pid=1860, address=0x000000ca0000
        - Code Snippets[3]: pid=2240, address=0x0000007e0000
        - Code Snippets[4]: pid=2492, address=0x000000e60000
        - Code Snippets[5]: pid=2596, address=0x000000b00000
        - Code Snippets[6]: pid=2604, address=0x0000007a0000
        - Code Snippets[7]: pid=2800, address=0x0000000370000
```

Fig. 6. The results of *Code to Code* step. We can define a group (`Code Snippets Group`) from the code snippets (`Code Snippets`).

we found that our plugin correctly built the *Thread to Thread* links via the semaphore object. Figure 6 shows that we found the eight code snippets as *Code to Code* links. This output was internally built from the *Code to Thread* and *Thread to Thread* links that we collected in the first and second steps in our method. Comparing this result with the ground truth shows that all injected code snippets were identified by our plugin. Thus, we demonstrated that our plugin successfully worked in this experiment.

5 Discussion

In this section, we discuss validity of experiment, platform dependency, and limitations of our method.

5.1 Validity of Experiment

We have to acknowledge that our experiment that we had in Sect. 4 is not comprehensive. However, we believe that we could show with the experiment that the detection capability of our method for distributed code injection attacks is reasonable. This is because our method is totally independent of original code and not affected by the type of original code. That is, if attackers use distributed code injection to protect their malware, which is more complicated than the simple program, we could detect them with our method. Also, our method is independent of victim processes. That is, if an injector injects its code snippets into other processes, our method is not affected by that at all. Having said that we recognize the necessity to evaluate our method from the different angles, such as false positives or the effects of JIT code to our method, not only for the capability of detections, i.e., true positive point of view. We will leave them as a future work of this paper.

5.2 Platform Dependency

We consider that the design of our method is platform-agnostic, even though we present it targeting Windows platforms in Sect. 3. Specifically, we may be able to implement our method as a tool for other platforms if we can acquire stack traces and synchronization objects from the platforms. Regarding stack traces, we can find several implementations of stack-tracing for other platforms, such as [23]. Additionally, regarding synchronization objects, modern OSs, including Linux platforms, generally provide synchronization mechanisms for user processes and threads. We can extract the threads or processes related to a synchronization object from the mechanisms if we successfully parse specific data structures for that with a forensics technique.

5.3 Limitation

We discuss limitations of our method from the viewpoints of breaking *Code to Thread* and *Thread to Thread* links.

To design our method, we implicitly assume the following two conditions. First is that each thread needs to be the waiting state for synchronization. Second is that each thread needs to synchronize each other with system-supported synchronization objects. Due to these assumptions, we have to have the following cases as a limitation in our method.

- Threads are polling a synchronization object.
- Threads do not depend on system-supported synchronization objects.

When threads are polling a synchronization object without being the waiting state, they do not have any wait dependencies on synchronization objects. Thus, we fail to build *Thread to Thread* links with our method. We consider that we can handle this case with the same approach for extracting threads holding a semaphore object explained in Appendix A.

Malware can use any objects, such as a file or registry objects, for synchronization among threads, instead of system-supported synchronization objects. When code snippets synchronize each other with one of such an object, we fail to build *Thread to Thread* links. We consider that we may be able to handle this case by identifying the objects distributed code snippets use for synchronization and then extracting processes or threads related to the object.

6   Related Work

We explain existing works related to our method. We have already presented the most of basic techniques used for code injection detection in Sect. 2.1. Thus, in this section, we focus on evolved code injection techniques and detections techniques for them.

Code injection techniques have several variations and have been still evolving. For example, Process Hollowing [12], Process Doppelgänging [13], and Gargoyle [14] are techniques that recently appear, as a new type of code injections. Process Hollowing is a technique involving the creation of a process from a benign executable and replacement of the benign code with a malicious code. Process Doppelgänging is similar to Process Hollowing, but it abuses the Transactional NTFS (TxF) mechanism [16] to replace the benign code with a malicious code. Gargoyle is a technique involving injections of a malicious code and a chain for return-oriented programming (ROP) [22] in non-executable memory regions of a process. The malicious code is given the executable permission only when the ROP chain is activated by timer-based callbacks. So, it is difficult to generate a memory dump just when the malicious code is being executed.

It is difficult to detect these sophisticated code injections only with a basic technique, e.g., memory-management data that we explained in Sect. 2.1. To detect them, we need to techniques specially adjusted for them. `hollowfind` [17], `doppelfind` [11], and `gargoyle` [7] are a Volatility plugin that aims to detect Process Hollowing, Process Doppelgänging, and Gargoyle, respectively. These plugins heuristically take advantage of characteristic features of each technique for detections. Distributed code injection is a variety of this line of techniques and we proposed a method to detect them. Thus, we have added a technique specialized for detecting distributed code injection attacks with this paper.

7   Conclusion

Distributed code injection attacks will probably become a threat in forensics fields in the near future. Even though that, we have not thoroughly discussed this problem and its solutions in both academic and industry. This paper is the first to shed light on this problem and we proposed a method to detect code snippets split and injected for distributed code injection attacks. In our experiment, we used malWASH as a representation of distributed code injection attacks and showed that our method correctly detected all code snippets injected by malWASH. Additionally, we provided the details of the implementations of our method in Appendix A for readers of this paper to trace our research. We believe that this paper becomes the first guide for forensic practitioners and researchers to prepare for malware armed with distributed code injection attacks.

A   Implementation Details

In this appendix, we explain how we implemented the component for building *Thread to Thread* links. To build them, we have two steps. First is how we extract the threads waiting for a synchronization object. Second is how we extract the thread holding a synchronization object. To simplify the explanation, we focus our scope into only semaphore from several synchronization objects.

Extraction of Threads Waiting for a Synchronization Object. We first explain the data structure for the extraction, i.e., KWAIT_BLOCK. Then, we explain how to extract threads using the data structure.

All threads waiting for a semaphore object are linked via KWAIT_BLOCKs. KWAIT_BLOCK structure represents a list entry of the wait list for a synchronization object. The wait list is a LIST_ENTRY-based doubly-linked list [15] linking with KWAIT_BLOCKs as many as threads waiting for the same synchronization object. A KWAIT_BLOCK also includes two pointers: Thread and Object. The Thread points to the thread object, i.e. KTHREAD object, corresponding a waiting thread. A KTHREAD object has the WaitBlockList pointing to an array of KWAIT_BLOCKs for synchronization objects waited by the thread [3]. The Object points to the synchronization object waited for by the thread pointed to by the Thread. A synchronization object has the WaitListHead that is the head LIST_ENTRY of the KWAIT_BLOCK list.

By walking each KWAIT_BLOCK list, we can retrieve all waiting threads and the waited semaphore object. After our plugin enumerates thread objects corresponding the threads executing suspicious code regions, it firstly extracts KWAIT_BLOCKs from WaitBlockList of each of the thread objects. Second, our plugin extracts the semaphore object and other waiting threads by traversing the list of each of the KWAIT_BLOCKs. Third, it distinguishes semaphore objects waited for by only threads executing suspicious code regions and defines the semaphore objects as ones for coordinating distributed code snippets. Our plugin finally extracts the threads waiting for the semaphore objects.

Extraction of Threads Holding a Synchronization Object. We first explain the problem on how to identify the thread holding a semaphore object. Then, we explain our approach to solve the problem extracting the thread via the handle for the object opened by a process.

The problem is that there is no explicit evidence to find the owners of a semaphore object in Windows environment. A KWAIT_BLOCK list for a semaphore object is defined to manage only waiting threads and does not include any information regarding the owners of the semaphore object. Semaphore object, i.e. KSEMAPHORE object, also has no direct pointer to the owners. Therefore, we need to find the owner threads of it from other data sources.

To solve this problem, we focus on processes opening the handles of a specific semaphore objects. All processes owning threads holding semaphore objects must hold handles for the semaphore objects. The semaphore objects for coordinating distributed code snippets must be unique and never acquired by threads executing benign code. Therefore, we can use processes as mediators to find out threads holding the semaphore objects.

Figure 7 illustrates how to find out the owner thread in our implementation. The detail of our approach is as follows.

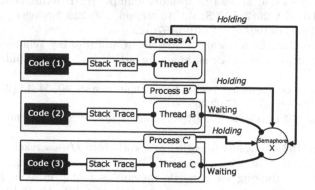

Fig. 7. Linked code snippets via threads sharing a *semaphore* object.

1. Find semaphore objects based on the results of waiting threads extraction.
2. Enumerate processes holding a handle for each of the objects.
3. Extract processes owning threads, which are detected as executing suspicious code and are not waiting for the semaphore object, from the enumerated processes.
4. Define the threads as the owners of the semaphore objects.

We explain each step of our plugin with Fig. 7. Our plugin first detects the thread A, B, and C executing the suspicious code (1), (2), and (3), like in the case of Fig. 3. The thread B and C are waiting for the semaphore object X and our plugin builds a link between the thread B and C from the KWAIT_BLOCK list for the semaphore object X. After that, our plugin starts extracting the owner threads of the semaphore objects. For the first step, it finds the semaphore object X via the thread B and C. For the second step, our plugin enumerates the process A', B', C' as processes holding a handle for the semaphore X. For the third step, it distinguishes the process A' owning the thread A, which is not waiting the semaphore object X, from the others. For the fourth step, our plugin defines the thread A as the current owner of the semaphore object X. Our plugin finally builds a *Thread to Thread* link throughout the thread A, B, and C.

References

1. Arasteh, A.R., Debbabi, M.: Forensic memory analysis: from stack and code to execution history. Digit. Invest. **4**(Suppl.), 114–125 (2007)
2. Barabosch, T., Bergmann, N., Dombeck, A., Padilla, E.: Quincy: detecting host-based code injection attacks in memory dumps. In: Polychronakis, M., Meier, M. (eds.) DIMVA 2017. LNCS, vol. 10327, pp. 209–229. Springer, Cham (2017). https://doi.org/10.1007/978-3-319-60876-1_10
3. CodeMachine Inc.: CodeMachine – Article – Catalog of key Windows kernel data structures. https://www.codemachine.com/article_kernelstruct.html. Accessed 02 Apr 2019
4. Cohen, M.: Scanning memory with Yara. Digit. Invest. **20**, 34–43 (2017). https://doi.org/10.1016/j.diin.2017.02.005
5. FireEye, Inc.: M-trends (2019). https://content.fireeye.com/m-trends. Accessed 02 Apr 2019
6. Google Inc.: Rekall memory forensic framework. http://www.rekall-forensic.com/. Accessed 02 Apr 2019
7. Hammond, A.: Hunting for gargoyle memory scanning evasion. https://www.countercept.com/blog/hunting-for-gargoyle/. Accessed 02 Apr 2019
8. Hejazi, S.M., Talhi, C., Debbabi, M.: Extraction of forensically sensitive information from windows physical memory. Digit. Invest. **6**(Suppl.), S121–S131 (2009)
9. HexHive: Github – hexhive/malwash. https://github.com/HexHive/malWASH. Accessed 02 Apr 2019
10. Ispoglou, K.K., Payer, M.: malWASH: washing malware to evade dynamic analysis. In: 10th USENIX Workshop on Offensive Technologies (WOOT 2016). USENIX Association (2016)
11. KSLGroup: Github – kslgroup/process-doppelganging-doppelfind: a volatility plugin to detect process doppelganging. https://github.com/kslgroup/Process-Doppelganging-Doppelfind. Accessed 02 Apr 2019
12. Leitch, J.: Process hollowing. https://www.autosectools.com/Process-Hollowing.html. Accessed 02 Apr 2019
13. Liberman, T., Kogan, E.: Lost in transaction: process doppelgänging. Black Hat Europe 2017 (2017)
14. Lospinoso, J.: Gargoyle, a memory scanning evasion technique. https://lospi.net/security/assembly/c/cpp/developing/software/2017/03/04/gargoyle-memory-analysis-evasion.html. Accessed 02 Apr 2019
15. Microsoft: Singly and doubly linked lists – Windows drivers—Microsoft docs. https://docs.microsoft.com/en-us/windows-hardware/drivers/kernel/singly-and-doubly-linked-lists. Accessed 02 Apr 2019
16. Microsoft: Transactional NTFS (TxF) – Windows applications—Microsoft docs. https://docs.microsoft.com/ja-jp/windows/desktop/FileIO/transactional-ntfs-portal. Accessed 02 Apr 2019
17. Monnappa, K.A.: Detecting deceptive process hollowing techniques using hollowfind volatility plugin - cysinfo. https://cysinfo.com/detecting-deceptive-hollowing-techniques/. Accessed 02 Apr 2019
18. Otsuki, Y., Kawakoya, Y., Iwamura, M., Miyoshi, J., Ohkubo, K.: Building stack traces from memory dump of windows x64. Digit. Invest. **24**, S101–S110 (2018). https://doi.org/10.1016/j.diin.2018.01.013

19. Pék, G., Lázár, Z., Várnagy, Z., Félegyházi, M., Buttyán, L.: Membrane: a posteriori detection of malicious code loading by memory paging analysis. In: Askoxylakis, I., Ioannidis, S., Katsikas, S., Meadows, C. (eds.) ESORICS 2016. LNCS, vol. 9878, pp. 199–216. Springer, Cham (2016). https://doi.org/10.1007/978-3-319-45744-4_10
20. Pshoul, D.: Community/dimapshoul at master · volatilityfoundation/community · github. https://github.com/volatilityfoundation/community/tree/master/Dima Pshoul. Accessed 02 Apr 2019
21. Pulley, C.: Github – carlpulley/volatility: a collection of volatility framework plugins. https://github.com/carlpulley/volatility. Accessed 02 Apr 2019
22. Roemer, R., Buchanan, E., Shacham, H., Savage, S.: Return-oriented programming: systems, languages, and applications. ACM Trans. Inf. Syst. Secur. **15**(1), 2:1–2:34 (2012)
23. Smulders, E.: Github – dutchy-/volatility-plugins: container for assorted volatility plugins. https://github.com/Dutchy-/volatility-plugins. Accessed 02 Apr 2019
24. The Volatility Foundation: The volatility foundation – open source memory forensics. http://www.volatilityfoundation.org/. Accessed 02 Apr 2019

Author Index

Aikawa, Yusuke   23

Banik, Subhadeep   109
Banin, Sergii   149
Bogdanov, Andrey   129
Buldas, Ahto   363

Cao, Zhenfu   287

Desmedt, Yvo   329
Dumas, Jean-Guillaume   67
Durak, F. Betül   343
Dyrkolbotn, Geir Olav   149

Faires, Jacob   391
Firsov, Denis   363
Funabiki, Yuki   109, 129

Hanaoka, Goichiro   253
Hayata, Junichiro   253
Heinemann, Andreas   221
Hiruta, Shohei   189

Ikeda, Satoshi   189
Imamura, Yuta   241
Isobe, Takanori   109, 129, 306
Ito, Takuma   37
Iwamura, Makoto   391

Kawakoya, Yuhei   391
Kitagawa, Fuyuki   253
Koay, Abigail   207
Kubo, Hiroyasu   129
Kurosawa, Kaoru   3, 53

Laanoja, Risto   363
Lafourcade, Pascal   67
Lakk, Henri   363
Li, Shimin   273
Lillard, Terrence   391

Liu, Fukang   287, 306
Lopez Fenner, Julio   67
Lucas, David   67

Mantas, Evangelos   377
Matsuhashi, Hayato   53
Matsuura, Kanta   253
Mimura, Mamoru   168
Minematsu, Kazuhiko   129
Miyoshi, Jun   391
Morioka, Sumio   129
Morozov, Kirill   329

Nakanishi, Toru   89

Ogata, Wakaha   3
Ohminami, Taro   168
Okishima, Ryo   89
Onuki, Hiroshi   23
Orfila, Jean-Baptiste   67
Orito, Rintaro   241
Otsuki, Yuto   391

Patsakis, Constantinos   377
Pernet, Clément   67
Puys, Maxime   67

Sakagami, Yusuke   53
Sakai, Yusuke   253
Sakamoto, Kosei   129
Sato, Masaya   241
Seah, Winston K. G.   207
Shibata, Nao   129
Shigeri, Maki   129
Shima, Shigeyoshi   189
Shinohara, Naoyuki   37

Takagi, Tsuyoshi   23
Takakura, Hiroki   189

Tomita, Toi   3
Truu, Ahto   363

Uchiyama, Shigenori   37
Ueda, Akinaga   53

Vaudenay, Serge   343

Wang, Gaoli   287
Wang, Xin   273

Welch, Ian   207
Wiesmaier, Alexander   221

Xue, Rui   273

Yamauchi, Toshihiro   241
Yamazaki, Tsutomu   23

Zeier, Alexander   221

Printed in the United States
By Bookmasters